FROM PAUL TO
VALENTINUS

FROM PAUL TO
VALENTINUS
CHRISTIANS AT ROME IN
THE FIRST TWO CENTURIES

PETER LAMPE

TRANSLATED BY
MICHAEL STEINHAUSER

EDITED BY
MARSHALL D. JOHNSON

FORTRESS PRESS   MINNEAPOLIS

FROM PAUL TO VALENTINUS
Christians at Rome in the First Two Centuries

First Fortress Press edition 2003

This edition is published under license from Continuum International Pub-
lishing Group Ltd., London. Translated from the second German edition, *Die
stadtrömischen Christen in den ersten beiden Jahrhunderten: Untersuchungen
zur Sozialgeschichte,* Wissenschaftliche Untersuchungen zum Neuen Testament
2/18 (© J. C. B. Mohr [Paul Siebeck], 1989), with subsequent revisions and
partial updating by the author.

Jacket art © Photodisc, Inc.
Interior design: ediType

ISBN 0-8006-2702-4

The paper used in this publication meets the minimum requirements of American National Standard for Information Sciences — Permanence of Paper for
Printed Library Materials, ANSI Z329.48-1984.

Manufactured in the U.S.A.

07   06   05   04   03   1   2   3   4   5   6   7   8   9   10

ΙΤΧΘΥC

parentibus carissimis:
Karl-Heinrich and Helga

Contents

Foreword

With vivid clarity, I remember the excitement at reading Peter Lampe's book *Die stadtrömischen Christen* on a transantlantic flight in 1987, a few weeks after its initial publication. There had been a remarkable buzz about Lampe's findings at an international meeting of the Society of New Testament Studies, where the book was available for purchase. It digested a massive amount of data from archaeology, epigraphy, ancient historical records, the New Testament, and church history to produce a solid, new perspective on the development of the churches in Rome. For the first time, the profile of these churches, their interrelationships, and even the locations of most of them emerged out of the mist of scholarly surmise. It was as if an entire continent had suddenly been explored and mapped, one whose significance for the history of Christianity had long been known but whose contours had remained impressionistic. Now that a long process of translation and revision has been completed, this important study is finally available to English readers.[1]

Lampe's thesis is that Christianity in Rome flourished in several of the poorest and most densely populated districts of Rome. The earliest as well as subsequent history of Roman house churches through the end of the second century indicates social "fractionation" between many small cells that lacked central coordination. This social pattern matches the profile of the separated synagogues in Rome. "In the pre-Constantine period, the Christians of the city of Rome assembled in premises that were provided by private persons and that were scattered across the city (fractionation)" (364). Not until the latter part of the second century did the monarchical episcopacy emerge to provide a measure of unification. The largest proportion of Christians were Greek-speaking immigrants of low socioeconomic status, though higher-class leaders, including some upper-class women, were active in smaller numbers.

The evidence of early Christian settlement in Rome and Puteoli follows the pattern of Jewish settlement along the main roads that funneled trade from the east into Rome. The Edict of Claudius in the late 40s indicates disquiet regarding Christian agitation in Jewish synagogues, and

---

1. Lampe's work was previously available to English readers only in "The Roman Christians of Romans 16," in *The Romans Debate*, ed. Karl P. Donfried, revised and expanded edition (Peabody, Mass.: Hendrickson, 1991), 216–30.

the case of Prisca and Aquila "suggests that only the key figures of the conflict were expelled" (14). Lampe devises an innovative method to determine which districts in Rome contained these Christian cells. His topographic investigation shows the coincidence among five independent lines of investigation. By comparing the overlapping results of these topographic surveys, the two most likely districts of early Christian settlement emerge: Trastevere and the Appian Way outside of the Porta Capena. Less thorough overlaps include Aventine and Mars Field. No evidence of Christian cells turns up within the old republican boundaries of Rome, where foreign cults were prohibited.

This revolutionary conclusion provides the basis for Lampe's assessment of the social situation of early congregations. Both Trastevere and the area around the Porta Capena were swampy areas where the poorest population of Rome lived. "Trastevere was a harbor quarter, a workers quarter. It accommodated harbor workers...porters...sailors...and also workers from the brickyards on the Vatican slopes...potters... millers," along with tanners and leatherworkers whose workshops "spread a penetrating odor" of urine and refuse (50). Lampe has found ancient statistics that indicate Trastevere was the most densely populated section of the city with the highest percentage of apartment buildings. In an amazing discovery, Lampe investigates the number of bakeries listed for each district and finds that Trastevere has the lowest number per square kilometer of any section of Rome, again indicating very low socioeconomic conditions. This section, which lay across the Tiber from the rest of Rome, was left untouched by the Roman fire, which may account in part for the scapegoating of Christians by Nero.

The second major area of early Christian settlement around the Appian Way outside of the Porta Capena was a damp valley with heavy traffic into the city. The evidence shows that this "quarter was populated by traders, craftsmen, and transport workers.... Hauling with carts was night work in Rome," whose workers had low social standing (56). A third area, the Aventine, featured aristocratic housing as well as poorer residences. "The address list of the Aventine reads like a 'Who's Who in the Empire'" (59). Under the Saint Sabinae church in the Aventine district archaeologists have discovered "residences with magnificent marble floors from the beginning of the imperial period" (59). Under the Saint Prisca church in this district, two large and elegant houses were found, one of them later used by a friend of the emperor, Licinius Sura. In sum, the two regions of Trastevere and Appian Way/Porta Capena were populated by "the lowest social strata" of Rome (65), while Christians living in the two other districts of Aventine and Mars Field probably included some members from higher social levels.

On the basis of their names, Lampe shows that the majority of Christians addressed in Paul's letter were of pagan background, probably drawn from proselytes and sympathizers of Jewish synagogues. The minority of "weak" Christians in Rome "are not to be identified against a Gentile background but rather against the background of Jewish practice of the law" (73). The evidence of persecution after the Roman fire of 64 C.E. indicates that those crucified and executed in other painful ways were not Roman citizens, whereas most Jews at that time enjoyed such citizenship. The evidence of the names in Romans 16, compared with thousands of inscriptions and literary references linked to Rome, shows that of those about which something definite can be concluded, "over two-thirds with a great degree of probability show indications of slave origin" (183). Tracing the evidence down through the end of the second century confirms the picture of a church that remained largely a slave and lower-class institution. While some members of Roman house churches came from high social status, even from senatorial families, the large majority consisted of lower-class immigrants.

The divided nature of Roman Christianity is indicated by the evidence in Romans 16, showing five different "Christian islands," with other Roman Christians mentioned that could not have belonged to fewer than two additional groupings (359). Each of these groups worshiped separately and could be "referred to as a house community" (360). Lampe traces the history through the end of the second century, including the evolution of later heresies, to show the divided nature of these Christian cells, each exhibiting peculiar traits going back to different origins and immigrants from specific parts of the empire. This view is sustained by a detailed exegesis of literary materials written in Rome as well as by a prosopographic analysis of each Christian leader and martyr through the end of the second century.

This study is so masterful in its grasp of a vast array of evidence, so solid and innovative in its methodology, and so audacious in conception that it has already become a classic. With encyclopedic thoroughness and objectivity, every possible detail from history and archaeology is presented and evaluated. The treatments of Hermas, Justin, the Valentinians, and dozens of other leaders comprise virtual monographs within the larger study, developing a variety of methods in assessing social roles and status. Compared with studies by Wilhelm Mangold,[2] Carl Weizsäcker,[3] Karl Schmidt,[4] Henry Donald Maurice Spence-Jones,[5]

---

2. *Der Römerbrief und die Anfänge der römischen Gemeinde: Eine kritische Untersuchung* (Marburg: Elwert, 1866).

3. "Über die älteste Römische Christengemeinde," *Jahrbücher für deutsche Theologie* 21 (1876): 248–310.

4. *Die Anfänge des Christentums in der Stadt Rom* (Heidelberg: Winter's Universität, 1879).

5. *The Early Christians in Rome* (London: Methuen, 1910; New York: John Lane, 1911).

Gladys Mary Bevan,[6] Paul Styger,[7] Arthur Stapylton Barnes,[8] Wolf-
gang Wiefel,[9] Umberto M. Fasola,[10] Fabrizio Mancinelli,[11] Raymond E.
Brown and John P. Meier,[12] James S. Jeffers,[13] Hermann Lichtenberger,[14]
James C. Walters,[15] Mark D. Nanos,[16] Andries B. du Toit,[17] the introductory sections of critical commentaries, and even the recent collection
of essays edited by Karl P. Donfried and Peter Richardson,[18] Lampe's
work represents a quantum leap in specificity and comprehensiveness.
For those interested in interpreting early Christian literature within its
social context, this book opens a new era with ramifications that could
transform our understanding of the Christian movement.

ROBERT JEWETT

6. *Early Christians of Rome: Their Words and Pictures* (London: SPCK; New York:
Macmillan, 1927).

7. *Juden und Christen im alten Rom: Streiflichter aus der ersten Verfolgungszeit*
(Berlin: Kunstwissenschaft, 1934).

8. *Christianity at Rome in the Apostolic Age: An Attempt at Reconstruction of
History* (London: Methuen, 1938; repr. Westport, Conn.: Greenwood, 1971).

9. "The Jewish Community in Ancient Rome and the Origins of Roman Christianity," *Judaica* 26 (1970), repr. in *The Romans Debate*, rev. ed., 85–101.

10. *Peter and Paul in Rome: Traces on Stone* (Rome: Vision, 1980).

11. *Catacombs and Basilicas: The Early Christians in Rome*, trans. C. Wasserman
(Florence/New York: Scala, 1981; distributed by Harper & Row).

12. *Antioch and Rome: New Testament Cradles of Catholic Christianity* (New York:
Paulist, 1982); see also Raymond E. Brown, "Further Reflections on the Origins of the
Church of Rome," in R. T. Fortna and B. R. Gaventa, eds., *The Conversation Continues:
Studies on Paul and John in Honor of J. Louis Martyn* (Nashville: Abingdon, 1990), 98–
115.

13. *Conflict at Rome: Social Order and Hierarchy in Early Christianity* (Minneapolis:
Fortress Press, 1991).

14. "Josephus und Paulus in Rom: Juden und Christen in Rom zur Zeit Neros," in
*Begegnungen zwischen Judentum und Christentum in Antike und Mittelalter: Festschrift
für Heinz Schreckenberg*, ed. D. A. Koch and H. Lichtenberger (Schriften des Institutum
Judaicum Delitzschianum 1; Göttingen: Vandenhoeck & Ruprecht, 1993), 245–61.

15. *Ethnic Issues in Paul's Letter to the Romans: Changing Self-Definitions in Earliest
Roman Christianity* (Valley Forge: Trinity Press International, 1994).

16. *The Mystery of Romans: The Jewish Context of Paul's Letter* (Minneapolis:
Fortress Press, 1996).

17. "The Ecclesiastical Situation in the First Generation Roman Christians," *Hervor-
mde teologiese studies* 53 (1997): 498–512.

18. *Judaism and Christianity in First-Century Rome* (Grand Rapids: Eerdmans, 1998).

Editor's Note

Continuum International and Fortress Press are honored to present the magisterial work of Peter Lampe to the English-speaking world. The German version of this volume has appeared in two editions. While the present work is a translation of the second German edition, it is in fact much more. While maintaining the same shape and overall content, Professor Lampe has gone through the entire translation, revising and updating. We hope that this will continue to generate scholarly debate on these issues as well as advance research methodology.

Introduction

"What's going on in Rome?" When asked this simple question by his friend Minicianus, Pliny found himself bogged down in the sheer abundance of happenings there. Even a long letter, he complained in his reply, could not encompass all the city's many events and affairs (*Ep.* 3.9).

Even now, many centuries later, Rome remains a rich and complex phenomenon for historical observation. Investigating the place of Christians there during the first two centuries, I look first at the beginnings of Christianity in the city down to the separation from the synagogue (Part 1). I next attempt a topographical overview: In which quarters of the city did the Christians live? Who were their neighbors there? What strata of society predominated there (Part 2)? The next parts are diachronic. Part 3 examines the general information provided by the sources. Where are the relevant social-historical materials that give general information about Rome's urban Christianity to be found? To what extent do the sources themselves generalize? Part 4 deals with individuals whose names we know (prosopography). How can the general and the specific in Parts 3 and 4 be related to each other? I shall not take individual cases from the sources for the purpose of generalizing, of "elevating" them to a representative level (there is no method for doing so). Instead I seek to give color, through concrete data, to the generalizations that the sources themselves draw. In Part 5, I offer an overview of urban Roman Christianity as a whole in light of these findings, adding a particular point of view.

Although in the area of Old Testament scholarship social-historical research enjoys a decades-long tradition (Alt, Bertholet, Causse, Pedersen, and Weber, among others), it has long stood in the shadows in the historiography of early Christianity. My book is in line with other historical works focusing on individual cities that have been carried out since 1975 for Syrian Antioch during the first four centuries (Meeks and Wilken, 1975), by Theissen (1974) for first-century Corinth, and by Gülzow (1967/68) for the situation in Rome at the beginning of the third century (Callistus).[1] Fundamental to city-oriented historical study

---

1. Other works of local history, G. Schöllgen, *Ecclesia sordida? Zur Frage der sozialen Schichtung frühchristlicher Gemeinden am Beispiel Karthagos zur Zeit Tertullians,* JAC Erg. 12 (Münster, 1984); idem, "Die Didache: Ein frühes Zeugnis für

is the desire to bring to voice as much of the detailed source material as possible and thus not prematurely to articulate general propositions and theories about the social world of early Christianity.

My interest is twofold. I want to learn about the daily lives of the urban Roman Christians of the first two centuries, the realities of their social lives. To meet these people in their "situation" is a goal of our research *in itself,* independent of the question of how this situation relates to their theology, to their expressions of faith. Second, it must nonetheless be asked where — if at all — interrelations between situation and theology can be discovered. My ultimate goal is to contribute at least one element to a multidimensional interpretation of texts and faith expressions of early Christianity. This is the only way to exclude superficial monocausalisms, such as are produced by a one-sided social-historical interpretation or, occasionally, are suggested by purely inner-theological, history-of-tradition analyses of texts.

We face a tour through a variety of material: literary materials, above all, but also epigraphical and archaeological ones are at hand, which often become illuminating only in combination. What is contested with respect to geographical provenance (e.g., the Pastorals, 1 Peter, Luke-Acts, Mark),[2] is relegated to the "footnote cellar" with the well-known "cf." at relevant points, so that the results will not be burdened a priori by uncertainty. There is an abundance of sufficiently clear urban Roman sources, and for those other text-complexes special studies have already been produced.[3] Even if the Pastorals, 1 Peter, Luke, and Mark

---

Landgemeinden?" *ZNW* 76 (1985): 140–43; A. J. Malherbe, *Paul and the Thessalonians* (Philadelphia, 1987).

On Rome, see now also James S. Jeffers, *Conflict at Rome: Social Order and Hierarchy in Early Christianity* (Minneapolis, 1991); idem, "The Influence of the Roman Family and Social Structures on Early Christianity in Rome," in *SBL 1988 Seminar Papers,* ed. D. J. Lull (Atlanta, 1988), 370–84. Jeffers tries to uncover two different groups behind *1 Clement* and The Shepherd of Hermas that are distinguished from each other by their social standing and by their degree of accommodation to Roman structures of thought. By constructing these two different groups, however, the evidence of fractionation (see below, Part 5) is exaggerated. The author of *1 Clement* writes to Corinth in the name of *all* of the Roman congregations (praescr.), and Hermas wants to make his book accessible to *all* Roman Christians (see below, chap. 41). The observation that Hermas urges less accommodation to Roman "standards" than does *1 Clem.* does not at all mean that there was a "Hermas congregation" apart and opposed to the "established congregations." Finally, by identifying "Clement" as an imperial freedman and connecting the archaeological finds beneath San Clemente with Flavia Domitilla, one returns to the speculative conjectures of the past (see below, chaps. 4, 21, 37).

2. For a provenance of the city of Rome for Mark, see M. Hengel, "Entstehungszeit und Situation des Markusevangeliums," in H. Cancik, *Markus-Philologie,* WUNT 33 (Tübingen, 1984), 1–45.

3. For the Pastorals, see D. C. Verner, *The Household of God: The Social World of the Pastoral Epistles* (Baltimore, 1983). For 1 Peter with localization in Asia Minor, see J. H. Elliott, *A Home for the Homeless: A Sociological Exegesis of 1 Peter* (Philadelphia, 1982). For Mark, e.g., J. Wilde, "A Social Description of the Community Reflected in the Gospel of Mark" (diss.; Ann Arbor, 1977, microfilm).

are related to the "footnote cellar," there is still ample New Testament material left for consideration in the text above. I will attempt to place the New Testament into the context of broader temporal lines and perspectives.

Part 1

INTRODUCTION

*From the Beginnings of
Urban Roman Christianity to
the Separation from the Synagogue*

Chapter 1

The Entrance of Christianity
via the Trade Route

The beginnings of pre-Pauline Christianity in Rome are shrouded in haze. Pre-Pauline Christians are attested for *Rome* (Romans; Acts 28:15) and *Puteoli* (Acts 28:13f.).[1] Concerning the rest of the Italian cities, silence dominates. Luke knows of no Christians for the remaining Italian localities which he names in Acts 28. Tertullian knows that no Christians lived in Pompeii in 79 C.E.: Where were Christians then, "as Vulsinii from heaven, Pompeii was showered with fire by its neighboring mountain" (*Ad Nat.* 1.9.7)?[2] In fact, findings from Pompeii and Herculaneum, from which occasionally it has been concluded that Christians were present, are most ambivalent; there is no persuasive evidence.[3]

---

1. The information "Christians in Puteoli" is pre-Lukan: (a) v. 14 illustrates brilliantly the Lukan key word ἀκωλύτως from the end of the book, but the mention of pre-Pauline Christians in Puteoli is superfluous for the Lukan concept: Luke describes Paul's unhindered presence on Malta (28:1–10) without mentioning Christians there. Also the stops in Myra (27:5–6), Syracuse (28:12), Regium (28:13), the Forum of Appius and Three Taverns (28:15) are narrated without a reception by Christians who resided there. (b) Luke focuses on Paul's missionary activity, with Paul in Rome being the crowning conclusion of world mission (28:22ff., 30–31). That already *before* Paul there were Christians in Italy and without apostolic mediation is not generated out of this Lukan interest.

2. "(Ubi tunc Christiani) cum Vulsinios de caelo (93 B.C.E.), Pompeios de suo monte (79 C.E.) perfudit ignis?" In *Apol.* 40.8, Tertullian alludes back to this notice, but generalizes upon it: not only in the cities of Vulsinii (Etruria) and Pompeii (Campania) were there no Christians, but they were lacking altogether from Etruria and Campania. That this is a hasty rhetorical exaggeration by Tertullian is shown by the tradition of Acts 28:13–14: Puteoli in Campania harbored a Christian congregation. On both passages, see H. Hofmann, "Tertullians Aussage über die Christen in Pompeji," *Wiener Studien* 87 (1974): 160–72.

3. Interpreted as Christian are especially: *CIL* 4:679; 4976; 10477 (bibl.); 10062; 10193; 8123; 8623 (bibl.); 10000; cf. 6175. All told, the epigraphic tradition offers *no* valid indications of Christians: on this, see H. Solin, review of *CIL* 4, Suppl. 3: *Gnomon* 45 (1973): 276f. Additional literature: The research report of J. Decroix and J. Daoust, "Des chrétiens vivaient-ils à Pompéi et à Herculanum?" *Bible et Terre sainte* 126 (1970): 15ff.; A. Varone, *Presenze giudaiche e cristiane a Pompei* (Naples, 1979); idem, "Giudei e cristiani nell'area vesuviana," in *Pompei 79*, Suppl. to no. 15 of *Antiqua* (1979), 131–46 (additional works in press); C. Giordano and J. Kahn, *Gli Ebrei a Pompei, Ercolano, Stabia e nelle città della Campania felix* (Naples, 1979) (there their earlier works on the theme); L. Falanga, *La "croce" di Ercolano: Cronistoria di una scoperta* (Naples, 1981);

7

Examples:

a. In my view, the most interesting example in Pompeii is the graffito *CIL* 4:679, from an atrium wall of the house "Vico del Balcone pensile" No. 22, which has as a constituent part the letters "CHRIS-TIAN."[4] The text obviously speaks of Christians. But the reconstruction of the rest of the text is completely controversial. Are we dealing with a Christian inscription? Or with an insult to the Christians? Whoever made the scribble evidently had once had contact, direct or indirect, with Christians. In Pompeii itself?

Other finds cannot convincingly be connected with Christianity:

b. *CIL* 4:3200 c offers "FIDIILIS IN P": "fidelis in pace," which is possibly, but not provably, Christian. In Rome one meets several pagan "in pace" inscriptions (see *CIL* 6, fasc. 7.4, pp. 4429f.). "Fidelis" too is favored in pagan inscriptions (*CIL* 4:4812; *CIL* 6, fasc. 7.2, p. 2458f.).

c. In the house of Venus in Pompeii, an amphora marked with a Chi-Rho was found in 1952. There are various interpretations: χρήσιμος, χρηστός, or similar attributes which refer to the contents of the container.[5]

d. The well-known "magical square" from Pompeii,

$$R \quad O \quad T \quad A \quad S$$
$$O \quad P \quad E \quad R \quad A$$
$$T \quad E \quad N \quad E \quad T$$
$$A \quad R \quad E \quad P \quad O$$
$$S \quad A \quad T \quad O \quad R,$$

the five words of which read the same way vertically as well as horizontally, forwards as well as backwards, and the letters of which can be grouped as

---

J. Gutmann, "Was There Biblical Art at Pompeii?" *Antike Kunst* 15 (1972): 122–24 (on allegedly biblical motifs in the wall frescoes); A. Baldi, *La Pompei giudaico-cristiana* (Cava dei Tirreni, 1964); idem, *L'anatema e la croce: Ebrei e Cristiani in Pompei Antica* (Cava dei Tirreni, 1983); E. Dinkler, *Signum crucis* (Tübingen, 1967), 134ff.; H. Kähler, "Christliche Kreuze aus Pompeji und Herculaneum," *Bollettino dell' associazione internazionale degli amici di Pompei* 1 (1983): 279–308. The Jewish evidence in Pompeii and Herculaneum, finally, in H. Solin, "Juden und Syrer im westlichen Teil der römischen Welt," *ANRW* 2:29.2 (1983): 587–789, here 725–27 (he regards also *CIJ* 567, "Sodom and Gomora," as Jewish). From 4 *Sibyll.* 130ff. (Vesuvius eruption), it can scarcely be determined that the Jewish author had once lived in Campania; a pagan source lies behind the text: cf. Rzach, "Sibyllinische Orakel," Pauly/Wissowa 2/2:2133.

4. If it is really so to be read; the charcoal scribble has disappeared since 1864, and the extant copies vary. See the versions in Dinkler, *Signum crucis*, 138f.

5. *CIL* 4:10477; cf. 6175. Another amphora marked with Chi-Rho is unequivocally pagan (*CIL* 4:9812: *Serapis dōra*). Also on non-Christian coins and papyri there is evidence of the Chi-Rho abbreviation (for examples see Dinkler, *Signum crucis*, 142).

```
                    P
                  A A O
                    T
                    E
                    R
          PATER N OSTER
                    O
                    S
                    T
                  A E O
                    R
```

can also be interpreted against a Mithraic or Jewish background. Whether or not the possible Christian interpretation was intended by the writers in Pompeii must be left unsolved. That Christians used the square cannot be demonstrated before ca. 500 C.E.[6]

e. A Pompeian scribble reads "Sodom(a) Gomora" (*CIJ* 567; *CIL* 4:4976). A Jewish writer is no less probable than a Christian. Presumably someone traveling through allowed himself to get carried away with this commentary on Pompeian life.

f. In Herculaneum on the Decumanus Maximus in the second story of the Casa del Bicentenario in the living quarters of the domestics there is a modest little room. In the wall plaster the form of a Latin cross is impressed; clearly there was once a cruciform object anchored in the wall plaster here. Below the impression stands a low piece of furniture like a cabinet. The simplest interpretation is still that a secular console hung here on the wall, which was secured in the plaster by a cruciform holder. The anchoring for a similar wall rack was found in a boutique in the Pansa House of Pompeii. The ancient Christians themselves indicate what we ought to think of such "cross" findings: Their pagan fellow men used an abundance of cruciform objects in their daily lives and, yes, even in their cults (Minucius Felix, *Oct.* 29.8; Tertullian, *Apol.* 16.6–8)!

The Christian presence in Puteoli and Rome correlates with a twofold background. (a) Jews had lived in Puteoli since Augustan times (Josephus, *Bell.* 2.104; *Ant.* 17.328). Rome (e.g., Philo, *Leg. ad Gaium* 155), perhaps Aquileia in the north (*CIL* 1²: 3422), and Puteoli accommodated the only pre-Christian Jewish settlements in Italy known to us. This is one more confirmation that earliest Christianity spread along the routes that Judaism had already followed: the synagogues were the setting for the first Christian mission. (b) The Jewish as well as the Christian "axis" Puteoli-Rome has a particular economic-historical

---

6. Cf., e.g., W. O. Moeller, *The Mithraic Origin and Meaning of the ROTAS-SATOR* (Leiden, 1973); E. Dinkler, *Signum crucis*, 160–73; especially H. Hofmann, "Sator-quadrat," Pauly/Wissowa Suppl. 15 (1978): 478–565, esp. 519ff.

background. The stretch Puteoli-Rome was the main trade route between the East and the city of Rome in the first half of the first century.
The road of Judaism and Christianity from the east to Rome followed
in the footsteps of trade. Were there tradespersons and businesspersons
among the first Christians in Italy? Was the tentmaker Aquila from
Pontus (see below) representative of the first urban Roman Christians?

The Puteoli-Rome trade axis: Still in the time of Nero, the harbor of
Puteoli, not that of Ostia, represented the main gateway of Rome to the
East. The Alexandrian grain fleet landed not in Ostia, but in Puteoli —
still under Nero (Seneca, *Ep.* 77.1). Not until the Flavians did Ostia
catch up in importance.

The reason for the pre-Flavian situation was that ships with import
wares for Rome found it easier to get cargo for a return trip in Puteoli /
Campania than in Rome, which was never an industrial center. From
Campania through Puteoli in the first century, however, wine, oil, ce-
ramics, Capuan metal vessels, and many other goods were shipped to
the East.[7] Only in the time of the Flavians did the demand for Cam-
panian export goods soften on the world market; Ostia, expanded by
Claudius (42–54 C.E.), then gained in importance.[8]

That Judaism and Christianity made their way to Rome through
Puteoli, through this *urbs Graeca* (Petron. 81) and Italy's gateway to the
orient, was typical of the entrance of eastern religions into the world's
capital city. There was, for instance, a temple to Serapis in Puteoli already by 105 B.C.E. (*CIL* 1²: 698), while in Rome itself, the cult is
evidenced only from the middle of the first century B.C.E. on Mars
Field.[9] An inscription from the year 79 C.E. informs us that once again
a new god from the East had made its entrance into Puteoli, this time
one from Phoenicia.[10] The Nabatean divinity Dusares had also found its
way there.[11]

---

7. Cf. M. Rostovtzeff, *Gesellschaft und Wirtschaft im römischen Kaiserreich* (Leipzig, 1929), 1:59; idem, *Gesellschafts- und Wirtschaftsgeschichte der hellenistischen Welt*
(Darmstadt, 1955/56), 1425.

8. Puteoli's blooming statio of the Tyrians, for example, was only since the time of the
Flavians put in the shadows of her own daughter, Ostia. On the whole point, Rostovtzeff,
Kaiserreich, 1:135; 306f. (bibl.); R. Calvino, "Cristiani a Puteoli nell'anno 61," *RivArCr*
56 (1980): 323–30, esp. 324f., n. 38 (bibl.).

9. Cf., e.g., H. W. Helck, "Sarapis," *KlPauly* 4:1549.

10. W. Dittenberger, ed., *Orientis Graeci Inscriptiones Selectae* (Leipzig, 1903–5, new
printing 1960 = *OGIS*), no. 594.

11. A. M. Bisi, "Su una base con dedica a Dusares nell'Antiquarium di Pozzuoli,"
Annali Istituto Orientale di Napoli NS 22 (1972): 381–87. Generally on eastern religiosity
in Puteoli: Calvino (1980), 324f. (bibl., n. 9); R. Cagnat, "Le commerce et la propagation
des religions dans le monde romain," *Conférences faites au Musée Guimet* 31 (1909):
131ff. (on Rome and Puteoli); V. Tran Tam Tinh, "Le culte des divinités orientales en
Campania en dehors de Pompei, de Stabies et d'Herculaneum," *EPRO* 27 (1972): 141–58.

Chapter 2

The "Edict of Claudius" and Separation from the Synagogue

With the events surrounding the "edict of Claudius" (Acts 18:2; Suetonius, *Claud.* 25.4; Orosius, *Hist.* 7.6.15f.; cf. Cassius Dio 60.6.6f.),[1] urban Roman Christianity steps for the first time into the light of history. We can derive from the sources four perceptions and propose them as theses: (a) Christianity got its first foothold in one or in several synagogues of Rome; the first pre-Pauline Christians of Rome were Jews or *sebomenoi* (devout people, Godfearers) who were attached to the synagogue. (b) Their witness to Christ led to unrest in one or several synagogues. (c) The authorities expelled the key figures of the conflict. (d) The events are to be dated at the end of the 40s.

There are several points to discuss.

1. Jewish-*Christians* were actually involved in the unrest. The oldest notice of the "edict of Claudius," Acts 18:2, implies that Claudius expelled all Jews (πάντας τοὺς Ἰουδαίους) from Rome, among them also "a Jew named Aquila" (τινα Ἰουδαῖον ὀνόματι Ἀκύλαν). Several observations suggest that Aquila and Priscilla had been expelled from Rome as *Christians* and had emigrated to Corinth.

In Corinth, Paul baptized only Gaius, Crispus, and the household of Stephanas (1 Cor 1:14–16) — not Aquila or Priscilla. The first person converted in Greece by Paul was Stephanas (1 Cor 16:15) — not Aquila or Priscilla. That is startling, because, at the very beginning in Corinth, Paul stayed, lived, and worked not with Stephanas but with Aquila and Priscilla (Acts 18:3).[2] The logical conclusion is that the couple were

---

1. See the bibl. in G. Lüdemann, *Paulus, der Heidenapostel,* I (FRLANT 123; Göttingen, 1980), 183, n. 62 (Engl. trans., *Paul: Apostle to the Gentiles* [Philadelphia, 1984]).

2. This is reliable tradition, because (a) of agreement with 1 Cor 4:12; 9:4, 6–7, 12; 2 Cor 11:7–8; 12:13. (b) 1 Cor 16:19 also fits together with Acts 18:2–3: The married couple apparently knew the Corinthians personally. They were in Ephesus in Paul's entourage, and could easily have gotten acquainted with him in Corinth. (c) The two bits of information "Pontus" and "staying with a fellow craftsman" are without any Lukan parallel or tendency. (d) The crowded sentence in Acts 18:2–3 is best explained if one sees it as the compressing of varying traditions. (e) Even though behind Acts 18:3 no written source is any longer visible, nevertheless oral tradition may be discovered behind ὁμότεχνος

11

already baptized when Paul appeared as the first Christian missionary in Corinth.

That unbaptized Jews had offered work and lodging to a Christian missionary appears less probable than our thesis. The argument can be sharpened even further: Suetonius suggests that Priscilla and Aquila were expelled from Rome because of conflicts over the question of Christ (see below). Had they been expelled as unbaptized Jews, then in Corinth they would as Jewish opponents of Christ have supported a Christian missionary!

There is nowhere any tradition of a conversion and baptism of the couple in Corinth (e.g., by Silas and Timothy who came later), although Luke happily reports other successes of that sort (v. 8).

Ἰουδαῖος in Acts 18:2 does not exclude the meaning "Jewish Christian." Ἰουδαῖος in Acts designates primarily ethnic origin, not confession. That is proved in 13:43; 14:1b; 17:17; 18:4: in the synagogue, in addition to the "Jews," there also sit the "proselytes" (13:43), "Greeks" (14:1b; 18:4), and *sebomenoi* (Godfearers) (17:17). At least the proselytes, confessionally seen, are also Jews, but are excluded from the ethnic term Ἰουδαῖος. Ἰουδαῖος designates Jewish-Christians in Acts 16:1 (mother of Timothy); 16:20 (Paul and Silas); 21:39; 22:3 (Paul); 22:12 (Ananias, according to 9:10, a Christian); cf. Gal 2:13.

Suetonius, in the first third of the second century, wrote, "Iudaeos impulsore Chresto assidue tumultuantes Roma expulit." Do we want to assume that Aquila and Priscilla, who at the latest preached Christ in Corinth, were also involved in a conflict about an urban Roman troublemaker Chrestus?[3] The more probable interpretation of the Suetonius passage is that the proclamation of Christ had caused unrest in one or in several urban Roman synagogues — which is no different from what is attested for the synagogues in Jerusalem (Acts 6:9–15), Antioch in Pisidia (13:45, 50), Iconia (14:2, 5), Lystra (14:19), and Corinth (18:12–17). Followers of the Christ-message were therefore involved in synagogal conflict. They — as members of synagogues — were the first urban Roman Christians.

The displacement of "Chrestus" for "Christus" by Suetonius produces no difficulty: "Chrestians" was a popular designation for the

---

and σκηνοποιός (*hapax legomena*). Ἐργάζομαι is not necessarily a Lukan term either: Paul uses it 12 times; John 8 times; 2 Thessalonians and Matthew each 4 times; Acts 3 times (2 times LXX); Luke once; James twice; seven additional New Testament writings each use it once. Similarly also G. Lüdemann, *Das frühe Christentum nach den Traditionen der Apostelgeschichte* (Göttingen, 1987), 206, 209 (Engl. trans., *Early Christianity according to the Traditions in Acts* [Minneapolis, 1989]).

3. "Chrestos" is nowhere attested as a Jewish name. The feminine "Chreste" is encountered only in *CIJ* 694. *Pace* H. Solin, "Juden und Syrer," 659 (bibl.); 690, who has again argued emphatically but not persuasively for Chrestus as not being Christ.

Christians. Tacitus, *Ann.* 15.44: "Ergo abolendo rumori Nero subdidit reos et quaesitissimis poenis affecit, *quos* per flagitia invisos *vulgus Chrestianos appellabat.* Auctor nominis eius Christus. Tiberio imperitante per procuratorem Pontium Pilatum. . . . " In connection with Nero's persecution of the urban Roman Christians, "Chrestians" appears as the appellation used by the Roman people.[4] Tertullian, *Apol.* 3: " 'Christianus' is, if one wants so to interpret it, derived from 'anointing' (χρίω). Even then when it is wrongly pronounced (*pronuntiatur*) as 'Chrestianus' by you — for you are not even wholly clear regarding the name — it is formed out of the term 'friendliness' . . . (χρηστότης)." According to this, "Chrestianus" was a widespread designation for Christians among the pagans. Further Tertullian, *Ad Nationes* 1.3: "cum corrupti a vobis chrestiani pronuntiatur a vobis."[5]

The explanation for the vowel displacement is quite simple: "Chrestus" was for pagan ears a commonly known personal name; "Christus" was not.[6]

I cannot agree with Lüdemann's thesis (see above, n. 2) that the married couple were first converted to Christianity in Corinth. It is true that Acts 18:2–3 says nothing *expressis verbis* about the Christianity of the couple. But this silence could also be attributed to Lukan redaction. That there were Christians in Corinth already *before* Paul's arrival does not suit Luke's interest in celebrating Paul as the founder of Christianity in that city. In Acts 18:26 — *after* Paul's first preaching activity in Ephesus (vv. 19f.) — Luke cheerfully harks back to the Christian activity of the couple. In vv. 1–3 — prior to Paul's arrival in Corinth — their Christianity is glossed over by him. In other words, if the silence can be interpreted not only as tradition but also as redaction, then, as an argument, it must remain outside the discussion. Only the above arguments remain.

2. The size of the circle of people who were expelled is unclear. In the Suetonius passage, "Iudaeos" is limited by the attributive "impulsore tumultuantes": "*the* Jews, *who* . . . ," but certainly not all of

---

4. E. Koestermann, "Ein folgenschwerer Irrtum des Tacitus (*Ann.* 15.44.2ff.)?" *Historia* 16 (1967): 456–69 alleges that in the source of Tacitus, *Ann.* 15.44.2, Jewish followers of a troublemaker Chrestus were meant, and that 15.44.3, therefore, represents an "error" on the part of Tacitus. In light of both of the following references from Tertullian, this hypothesis appears a superfluous complication.

5. Cf. also Lactantius, *Inst. div.* 4.7 (immutata littera Chrestum solent dicere). Further, F. Blass, "XPHCTIANOI-XPICTIANOI," *Hermes* 30 (1895): 465–70; A. von Harnack, *Die Mission und Ausbreitung des Christentums,* 4th ed. (Leipzig, 1924), 425, n. 3.

6. In the city of Rome, e.g., one encounters "Chrestos/us" ca. 56 times, "Chreste" 80, "Chresti" 16, and "Chresto" 19 epigraphically: *CIL* 6, fasc. 7.5 (index of cognomens), pp. 6324–26.

the Jews. The case of Aquila and Priscilla suggests that only the key figures of the conflict were expelled: Aquila and Priscilla were such leading persons, as may be concluded from their later church involvements (Rom 16:3–5; 1 Cor 16:19). If only the key figures were banned, the silence of Josephus and other historiographers concerning the incident is more easily explained. Luke's formulation that "*all* of the Jews" were expelled (χωρίζεσθαι πάντας τοὺς Ἰουδαίους) appears, by contrast, redactionally exaggerated: πᾶς is a Lukan preferred term.[7] "All" of the Jews were not forced to leave, if only because among the urban Roman Jews there were Roman citizens (see below, Part 3, chap. 3) who could not be excluded summarily, but only after individual trials had been carried out.

3. The dating of the event is disputed. It depends upon when the beginnings of urban Roman Christianity are to be set: before 49 C.E. or already before 41 C.E.

At the time of the writing of the letter to the Romans in the second half of the 50s, urban Roman Christianity had existed already "for a number of years" (ἀπὸ ἱκανῶν ἐτῶν, Rom 15:23). Orosius dates the "edict of Claudius" to the year 49. That suits Acts 18: Between the edict of Claudius and the datable proconsulate of Gallio of the year 51/52 C.E. (v. 12) lay, according to Luke, eighteen months (v. 11) plus προσφάτως (v. 2) minus ἡμέραι ἱκαναί (v. 18). This calculation fits Orosius's dating to 49 strikingly! Where did Orosius get his information? He maintained that he had it from Josephus,[8] but there one finds nothing. Did Orosius infer his date from Luke's note and some sort of date he had available concerning Gallio's proconsulate? That is unlikely. The allusion to "Josephus" as his source speaks against the likelihood of Orosius's using his own reckoning. It points rather to a dependence upon tradition: Orosius still remembers having read the date somewhere. The rest of the question remains then undecidable: where did Orosius's source obtain the date? From a Roman chronographer? However that answer may turn out, the coincidence between the Orosius tradition and the Acts 18 chronology is amazing.

At least two elements of the Acts 18 chronology appear not to be redactional: προσφάτως in v. 2 is a hapax legomenon; the "eighteen months" of v. 11 constitute for Acts an unusually long time for a Pauline stay.

---

7. Frequency scale in the New Testament: Acts 172 instances, Luke 157, Matthew 129; 1 Corinthians 112, then Romans 71, etc. Cf. also the hyperbolic μυριάδες in Acts 21:20.

8. "Anno eiusdem (= Claudius's) nono (= 49 C.E.) expulsos per Claudium Urbe Iudaeos Iosephus refert."

The simplest solution is still that the edict of Claudius occurred in the year 49. G. Lüdemann dates it in the year 41 C.E. He hits upon 41 because he connects Cassius Dio 60.6.6f. to the events around the "Chrestos" conflict. But this is unprovable: Dio writes concerning the year 41: Claudius had instituted a ban on meetings of Jews, but he did not expel them, because they had become so numerous in the city that that would have caused unrest. To what does Dio's notice that Claudius did not expel (οὐκ ἐξήλασε) the Jews refer? For Lüdemann it is clear that it refers to the "Chrestos" events; Dio is here correcting a source which he as well as Suetonius had used (pp. 187f.). But this hypothesis does not bother with Dio's context. Dio is not correcting a source: οὐκ ἐξήλασε, "he did not expel," needs to be completed with "as Tiberius had done." Dio refers here quite clearly back to his own context, to Tiberius's great expulsion of the Jews from Rome (πλεονάσαντας αὖθις: "they had *again* grown in numbers"!), which he had described in 57.18. As a point of comparison, Dio had this passage of his own in view, not some source needing correction that referred to the "Chrestos" conflict. With that, every attempt to demonstrate a bridge between the Dio passage and the "Chrestos" conflict falls away. Why does Lüdemann give Cassius Dio, who edited his chronological information towards the end of the second century at the earliest, more credence than the Acts 18 chronology which is at least 100 years earlier? Even if the latter is burdened with uncertainties, a dating based on Dio's report is even more burdened.

Whatever event Dio envisaged need not interest us further. Even if Dio had had the "Chrestos" events in mind, this would produce nothing essentially new for our concern: That Claudius had expelled not "all," we had already recognized. But that the ringleaders were indeed *expelled* — against Dio — the tradition of Acts 18:2 proves. At best, Dio would contribute the idea that through a prohibition on meetings in one or in several synagogues, those Jewish-Christians who had not been forced to leave the city would have been forced to go underground. They would have had to meet outside of the synagogues, so the edict of Claudius would have abetted urban Roman *Christianity to separate from the synagogue*. But this conclusion can also be reached without the Dio passage, as the following will show.

4. If the separation of Christianity from the synagogue had something to do with disputation and conflict and if we seek for something of that sort in Rome, then we are left with the events surrounding the edict of Claudius, for we know of nothing else. The most plausible solution is that in the wake of these events, urban Roman Christianity separated itself from the synagogue.

The first certain datum is the letter to the Romans. By the time of its composition in the second half of the 50s at the latest, urban

Roman Christianity can be seen as separated from the federation of synagogues.[9] In the year 64 C.E., even the authorities distinguish between Jews and Christians (urban Roman persecution under Nero: Tacitus, *Ann.* 15.44).

---

9. In particular, cf., e.g., Rom 16:5a; 1:5–8; in 15:24 Paul expresses hope for the support of the Romans for a mission to Spain that would be free from the Jewish Law! Differently, W. Schmithals, *Der Römerbrief als historisches Problem*, StNT 9 (Gütersloh, 1975), 87–90: Paul first wants finally to separate the urban Roman Christians from the federation of synagogues with his letter to the Romans; some had not yet finally broken their contact with the synagogue (Rom 14:1—15:6). From Romans 14–15 it is impossible to deduce this (see below); even Schmithals himself in another place (p. 172), based precisely upon 14–15, comes to the conclusion that the majority of the urban Roman Christians already represented Paul's gospel that was free from the Jewish Law.

Part 2

TOPOGRAPHY

Chapter 3

In Which Quarters of the City Did the Christian Population Concentrate?

In which quarters of the world's capital city did urban Roman Christendom of the first two centuries concentrate? To place the topographical investigation, connecting archaeological material with literary sources, at the beginning has the attraction of placing before one's eyes a spatially conceivable framework for everything that follows.

I want to attempt to clarify the question in five steps. Where, if at all, agreements among the results of the five methods appear, I shall be able to claim some certainty for my topographical statements.

1. Local traditions

2. The earliest archaeologically available graves

3. Jewish quarters

4. Concentrations of the Tituli

5. Contemporary literary information concerning businesses of Christians that can be localized

The sequence of the five perspectives is random. None builds upon another. Only because of that can one ask about agreements.

Local Traditions

We begin with the weakest link of the five-membered chain: the urban Roman local tradition. In which quarters of the city was an early Christian presence alleged by the local tradition? Which localities were claimed as early Christian meeting places?

Clearly localizable in the city are the Tituli of late antiquity (see map 1). We only need to know which title-parishes reach back into

19

the first centuries in their roots in order to discover in which parts of the city the early Christians lived. The hagiographical local tradition[1] throws up some "bait": nine title-names are identified by the tradition with persons of the first two centuries. Unfortunately the literary material dates to the fifth century at the earliest, and, because of its legendary form, it does not arouse much confidence. But the individual legends regarding the individual Titulis interest us less than whether the lines of the individual legends yield common points of departure. Possibly the local tradition again and again established its legends about the first and second centuries in the same parts of the city, so that *behind* all of the legendary fantasy there is still hidden a knowledge about the earliest Roman city quarters. I sketch first the founding legends of the nine title-congregations.

1-2. The Roman local tradition has added a complete family story to the *Tituli Praxedis and Pudentis* (or *Pudentianae*). From the legendary tradition:[2]

(a) The Roman senator Pudens hosted in his house the apostles Peter and Paul. (b) From the marriage of Pudens with Sabinella sprang the saints Praxedis and Pudentiana. Both sisters sold their property in order to care for the poor and to bury the martyrs worthily. In Praxedis's house services of worship were frequently held; she founded the Titulus Praxedis in the second century. Also the house of Pudentiana, which she inherited from her father, became a gathering place for worship and became the Titulus Pudentis or Pudentianae, which Pius I (ca. 140–55 C.E.) dedicated. The *Liber Pontificalis* (s.v.) lets the Roman presbyter-bishop Cletus (first century) correspondingly come from "de regione Vico Patricii," in which both Tituli stand.

3. *Titulus Priscae.* The local tradition traces the title-parish Priscae on the Aventine back to the urban Roman house church of the New Testament Prisca (Rom 16). Thus the *Liber Pontificalis* (2.20 Duchesne) offers for the title-church on the Aventine the name "tit. Aquilae et Priscae." A literary tradition available in the sixth century narrates how Pope Eutychian, at the end of the third century, had transported the bones of a saint into the "ecclesia sanctorum martyrum (sic) Aquilae

---

1. Cf., among others, F. Lanzoni, "I titoli presbiteriali di Roma antica nella storia e nelle legenda," *RivArCr* 2 (1925): 195ff.; J. P. Kirsch, *Die römischen Titelkirchen im Altertum* (Paderborn, 1918); F. Halkin, *Légendes grecques de "martyres romaines"* (Brussels, 1973); *Bibliotheca hagiographica latina* (Brussels, 1898–1911); H. Delehaye, *Commentarius perpetuus in Martyrologium Hieronymianum ad recensionem Henrici Quentin* (Brussels, 1931); idem, *Les Légendes hagiographiques* (Brussels, 1905); A. Dufourcq, *Etudes sur les Gesta Martyrum romains* (Paris, 1900), esp. 101ff.

2. "Gesta der Hl. Pudentiana und Praxedis": Mombritius, *Sanctuarium* 2, fol. 194–194^v (Praxedis); fol. 213^v–214 (Pudentiana). *Acta Sanct. Bolland.*, May, 4:299f.; cf. Kirsch, *Titelkirchen*, 52ff., 61ff., 149ff.

et Priscae" on the Aventine.[3] An inscription over the entrance of the Aventine church from the ninth or tenth century runs:[4] Haec domus est Aquilae seu Priscae virginis almae (sic) / Quos, lupe Paule, tuo ore vehis Domino. / Hic Petre divini tribuebas fercula verbi,/ Saepius hoc loco sacrificans Domino.

4. *S. Sabinae.* The local tradition[5] views the Sabina of the Titulus as a Roman martyr under Hadrian. Sabina, an aristocratic matron, was the widow of a high Roman official named Valentinus and through her Syrian-Antiochene slave, Serapia, came to Christianity. According to the tradition, at the place of the Titulus on the Aventine had stood her parental house. From the house-church of Sabina has allegedly grown the title-parish on the Aventine.

5. *S. Balbinae.* Balbina, the alleged founder of the title on the so-called Lesser Aventine, was born under Hadrian as the daughter of the "tribunus," the subsequent martyr Quirinus. While he was still a pagan military tribune, Quirinus had watched the Roman bishop, Alexander, in prison. Alexander had cured Balbina, who was suffering from her thyroid, whereupon the entire household of Quirinus had gone over to the faith.[6]

6. The *Titulus Nicomedis* is named after St. Nicomedes (whose saint's day is 1 June). Nicomedes allegedly was a disciple of the Apostle Peter and became a martyr under Domitian. He also consoled St. Petronilla, daughter of the Apostle Peter, during her fight to the death.[7]

7. The *Titulus Clementis* is bound up in the Roman local tradition, demonstrably since the end of the fourth century, with the "holy Pope" Clement from the end of the first century.[8] G. B. De Rossi[9] accordingly held the opinion that the *Titulus Clementis* goes back to a very ancient Christian "conventiculum" that had witnessed the personal activity of *Clemens Romanus.* But, because at the Roman synod of 499 C.E. the clergy of the title signed with simply "Clementis" (not "sancti Clementis") and a tomb inscription from the first half of the fifth

---

3. *Acta Sanct. Bolland,* January, 2:184–87 (on 18 January). Cf. also the *Sacramentarium Gregorianum* on the 18 of January (ed. Muratori, 521), in Kirsch, *Titelkirchen,* 102f., 162, n. 4.

4. *ICUR* 2:443, no. 165.

5. Text of the legend: *Acta Sanct. Bolland.,* August, 6:500–504. Cf. Kirsch, *Titelkirchen,* 96ff., 163ff. (there the liturgical tradition and the later martyrologies).

6. *Acta Sanct. Bolland.,* May, 1:371ff. Cf. Kirsch, *Titelkirchen,* 172, 94ff.

7. Cf. E. Stadler and J. N. Ginal, *Vollständiges Heiligen-Lexikon* (Augsburg, 1882; Hildesheim and New York, 1975), 4:568.

8. Jerome, *De viris ill.* XV (392 C.E.). *Epistola Zosimi papae* (ed. O. Guenther, *Ep. imper. pontif. coll. Avellana,* 1:99f.). Correspondingly, *Liber Pontificalis* (s.v.) has Pope Clement come, at the end of the first century, from "de regione Celio monte"; the Titulus lies at the foot of the Caelius. Cf. further the monumental inscription from the end of the fourth century in Kirsch, *Titelkirchen,* 37.

9. *Bullet.* (=*Bullettino di Archeologia Cristiana,* Rome) 1863, 29; 1870, 165f.

century likewise omits "sanctus," Kirsch suspects[10] that "Clemens" was an unknown houseowner and donor who was only secondarily identified with the "holy Pope" of the first century. On the archaeological findings, which provide us nothing here, see below, chap. 37.

8. *S. Caeciliae.* Local tradition:[11] Caecilia was born in the second half of the second century in an aristocratic parental house (ingenua, nobilis, clarissima)[12] and was the wife of the rich *nobilissimus vir Valerianus.* She had a higher education, especially a good training in music (patroness of music!). She gave her house in Trastevere to the congregation before her martyr's death. She was buried in the Callistus catacomb by Pope Urban (ca. 222–30) ("inter collegas suos episcopos ubi sunt omnes confessores et martyres collocati"), and her house was dedicated as a house of God by Urban ("domum autem eius in aeternum sanctam ecclesiam suo nomine consecravit").

9. According to local tradition[13] the *Titulus Callisti* in Trastevere also goes back to the Roman Bishop Callistus, who came from Trastevere and gathered Christians there in a house for worship. The domus of the Christian Pontianus stood nearby also.

Result: The local tradition connects nine Tituli with Roman persons whose lives extend into our timespan. I do not maintain[14] that any one of the nine Tituli go back into the first or second centuries; the florid legends which are available beginning with the fifth century scarcely offer reliable information concerning the individual Tituli. But it is indeed interesting that late antiquity's legend-tellers prefer certain quarters of the city when they fabricate Tituli stories about the first and second centuries. The distribution of the nine Tituli over the city's quarters is revealing:

- 2 in Trastevere (Callisti, Caeciliae)

- 3 on the Aventine (Priscae and Sabinae in Augustan Region XIII, Balbinae on the Lesser Aventine in Region XII)

---

10. Kirsch, *Titelkirchen,* 39f., 37.

11. The Acts of the Martyrdom of St. Caecilia (not before the fifth century), in Mombritius, *Sanctuarium,* 1.188–93 (Migne, *PG* 116:163–80). Cf. *Liber Pont.* 1:143. Bibliography: J. P. Kirsch, *Die hl. Cäcilia in der römischen Kirche des Altertums* (Paderborn, 1910); idem, *Titelkirchen,* 113ff.

12. See the material in Kirsch, *Cäcilia,* 39.

13. Passio Callisti, in Mombritius, *Sanctuarium* 1, fol. 150ᵛ–152ᵛ; *Acta Sanct. Bolland.* October, 6:439–41; cf. May, 2:500f. Also the *Liber Pont.* 1:141 (cf. 63) and the Liberian Catalog of Popes (in Duschesne, *Liber Pont.* 1:9) show that in local memory Callistus was connected with Trastevere. Cf. additionally, Duchesne, *Liber Pont.* 1, pp. xciif.; Kirsch, *Titelkirchen,* 104ff., 159f.; Jordan and Huelsen, *Topographie,* 1/3: 647.

14. *Pace* V. Saxer, 204f., whose Italian review of my book unfortunately teems with misunderstandings: *Revista de storia della chiesa in Italia* 42 (1988): 203–9.

- 2 in the area Vicus Patricius/Cispius (Praxedis, Pudentis)

- 2 close to each other at the foot of the Caelius (Clementis in Region III, Nicomedis in Region V).

There are accumulations to be observed for some areas while other quarters of the city go empty. Local tradition sought ancient house-congregations again and again only in certain areas of the city. Obviously there was a conception about which quarters of the city Christians *traditionally* occupied; for those city quarters therefore one could feel it was "allowable" to form legendary stories about the time of the first and second centuries.

That the four results of this perspective can only be adduced — if at all — in combination with corroborating results of the other perspectives for topographical statements concerning the first and second centuries is self-evident.

The Earliest Archaeologically Available Graves

The question in which quarters of the city the pre-Constantinian Christians concentrated can be approached, in my view, from another side. Cemeteries on the radial roads outside of the city can give clues to where their users lived *in* the city. The catacomb was used as a cemetery by the entirety of urban Roman Christians. Rather, as we can demonstrate from the fourth century on,[15] each of the catacombs was assigned to one of the ecclesiastical regions of the city.[16] Beyond that, based on inscriptions, in some cases one is even able clearly to observe how each of the title-congregations in the seven church regions was attached to its own catacomb-cemetery.[17] It is common to the examples (in n. 17) that the

---

15. De facto certainly earlier: cf. Kirsch, *Titelkirchen*, 91, 93, on the proof of the Titulus Fasciolae.

16. See Map 1. See also the unpublished map of Prof. U. M. Fasola, Pontificio Istituto di Archeologia Christiana, Rome, 1976, and *Liber Pont.* 1:250 (ed. Duchesne), 1:112 (ed. Mommsen); in addition, Kirsch, *Titelkirchen,* 215f. On the Ecclesiastical Regions up to the sixth century, C. M. Kaufmann, *Handbuch der altchristlichen Epigraphik* (Freiburg/B., 1917), 258, n. 1; G. v. De Rossi, *La Roma sotterranea Cristiana* (Rome, 1864–77), 3:514ff.; and below, Part 5 (the seven regions have existed since the third century).

17. The Domitilla catacomb was attached to the Titulus Fasciolae (see Kirsch, *Titelkirchen,* 91–93, 207); the Coemeterium S. Sebastiano to the Titulus Byzantis (Kirsch, 207); the Balbina catacomb to the Titulus Balbinae (Kirsch, 95, 207); the Callistus catacomb to the Titulus Sixti (Kirsch, 95, 23); the Coemeterium of St. Pancratius to the Titulus Chrysogoni (Kirsch, 177); the Catacomb of St. Valentino to the Titulus Lucinae (Kirsch, 206); the burial places on the Via Ostiensis to the Tituli Priscae et Sabinae on the Aventine (Kirsch, 207); etc.

In addition to the epigraphical material (summarized by Kirsch, 204–8, and Kaufmann, 258–60), cf. the *Liber Pontificalis* (1:126, 157, ed. Duchesne; 1:36, ed. Mommsen) on

residents of a section of the city naturally maintained their tombs on the
radial streets that lay nearest to their quarter of the city. Whoever lived
in Trastevere in the west ordinarily cared for no tomb in the east on the
Via Tiburtina. This principle is methodologically important, for it can
hardly be denied for earlier times either. In other words, we are able
to draw conclusions from the situation of the earliest Christian burial
places backward to the quarter of the city in which the users of these
grave sites resided. The earliest Christian burial places that fall into the
time span we are involved with, or at least reach back to the beginnings
of the third century, are conserved in at least nine places.[18]

Pope Dionysius: "Hic presbiteris ecclesias dedit et cymiteria et parrocias diocesis constituit!" Similarly *Liber Pont.* (1:222, ed. Duchesne; 1:90, ed. Mommsen): At the beginning
of the fifth century, the catacomb of St. Agnese was allocated to the newly founded
Titulus Vestinae, the youngest title-church in Rome. The connection between Tituli and
Coemeteria lasted until the end of the sixth century; see Kirsch, 217.

18. Contradicting V. Saxer's review of my book in *Rivista di storia della chiesa in
Italia* 42 (1988): 205, it must be emphasized that these nine cannot have been the only
ones. Many early Christian graves remain unrecognized for us (see below, at the end of
Part 3).

As the earliest known Christian graves, I shall list those which go back at least to the
first third of the third century. Most of those named in this chapter existed even already
before the end of the first quarter of the third century. Only the Coemeterium-Bassillae
with its datable inscription *ILCV* 2807 cannot be assigned to Christians before the year
234 c.e. The first Christian frescoes in the Pretestato catacomb, which can be cautiously
dated to the first half of the third century, are placed by Fasola-Testini (op. cit., 1978,
121) "without difficulty" into the first decades of the third century; of course, the datings
of iconologists vary.

The origins of the Catacomb Maius on the Via Nomentana (e.g., Fasola-Testini, 111–
12, 195–96) go back well into the first half of the third century. Two crypts, which in the
early third century were still separate and to each of which a stairway led down, were
soon joined. The southernmost of the two crypts served one family as a private burial
ground. At first, this consisted of a broad walkway at the foot of the steps, but it soon had
added to it a branching off with two decorated cubicula. The suburban villa discovered
above ground may have been occupied by the same family. The second hypogeum, which
is of the same age, was used right from the start by a group with many members. Since the
entrances to the stairs to both crypts above ground lay right next to each other and below
ground the two crypts were quickly joined, it may be accepted that the owners of the
family crypt and that group were socially closely involved with each other. Did a patron
make space on his property so that his freedmen and slaves might have the right to bury
their dead next to his private burial place? Or did a well-to-do Christian family allow their
poorer fellow Christians to lay out a congregational cemetery next to the family crypt on
the property of its own villa? In favor of the latter speaks the fact that the passageways
of the group cemetery were laid out, as with the first Christian nucleus of S. Callisto,
according to the so-called grid-system (see ibid., 112, 195f., with illustration; this grid-
system is, contrary to widespread belief, rare in the Roman catacombs). Also, at least one
of the two cubicula of the family crypt is painted in Christian fashion (Cubiculum no. 3
in Nestori, *Repertorio,* s.v.; among other images, a teaching Christ). These frescoes belong
to the third century, but I hesitate to attribute them already to the first third of the third
century. I do not include the Catacomb Maius in the following topographical investigation
that seeks out the quarters *in* the city that were inhabited by Christians, for the following
reasons. The wall remnants of the above-ground villa, which were found in 1961, may go
back at least to the same time as the beginnings of the catacombs (cf. Fasola-Testini, 111).
If the owners of the family grave site inhabited this suburban villa on the Via Nomentana,

S. Callisto Catacomb

The catacomb complex west of the Via Appia, which today is expanded in size, goes back to two originally independent nuclei, which lie more than 80 m. apart. Archaeologically there is nothing to force a dating earlier than about 200 C.E.[19]

The first nucleus, the region around the so-called Papal Crypt, was used by Christians at the latest in the thirties of the third century when Bishops Anterus (died 236) and Pontianus (died 235) were buried in the crypt.[20] The region, however, was already laid out around 200, since the main galleries (generally designated as "A" and "B") of the region had already been deepened once, before the opening of the Papal Crypt was hewn.

---

then the otherwise normal principle that the users of grave sites outside the city lived in a nearby quarter *in* the city is not valid here. Also for the many-membered group of the second site this principle is not valid: If the group consisted of fellow Christians who were involved with the family in the suburban villa (the same house-church?), that principle did not direct the choice of the group's burial place. Rather, the group's members came out there with their dead because a family friendly to them possessed a suburban parcel of land and opened it up for burials. Where the group members lived *in* the city eludes every grasp. For even if on Sundays they made a pilgrimage out to the suburban villa in order to gather as a house-church, it would be by no means assured that they came from the closest city section to the Via Nomentana. They may have come into contact *somewhere* in the city with the well-to-do family; owners of suburban villas as a rule maintained a city dwelling in Rome (cf., e.g., Martial 6.43; Pliny, *Ep.* 1.9; with 3.21).

All of the other catacombs of Rome originated only around the middle of the third century at the earliest. The oldest in this group are the anonymous catacomb of the *Villa Pamphily* on the Via Aurelia (towards the middle of the third century; e.g., Fasola-Testini, 106f.), the catacomb *Novaziano* on the Via Tiburtina (ibid., 109, 193–94) and the catacomb Giordani on the Via Salaria, in which the martyr Alexander was buried (ibid., 122; both towards the middle of the third century). From the 260s at the latest dates the catacomb *"ad duas lauros"* on the Via Labicana (ibid., 108).

For the social history of the second century, I have not evaluated the Christian inscriptions of the third century found in the catacombs, although those mentioned in the inscriptions may well have been born in the second century: In no case can we know that these persons belonged to Christian congregations already in the second century.

19. On the following, cf., among others, P. Testini, *Le catacombe e gli antichi cimiteri cristiani in Roma* (Bologna, 1966), 61ff.; A. M. Schneider, "Die ältesten Denkmäler der römischen Kirche," *Festschrift zum 200-jähriges Bestehen, Akad. Wiss.* (Göttingen, 1951), 166ff., here 178–82, 190, 193; ILCV (= E. Diehl, *Inscriptiones latinae christianae veteres*, Berlin, 1925f.) nos. 953–61, esp. 954; map of the catacomb, A. Nestori, *Repertorio topografico delle pitture delle catacombe romane* (Vatican, 1975), 107; 99ff. additional literature; P. Styger, *Die römischen Katakomben* I (Berlin, 1933), 38ff. With a somewhat earlier dating again, L. De Bruyne, "La 'capella greca' di Priscilla," *RivArCr* 46 (1970): 291ff., and idem, "L'importanza degli scavi lateranensi per la cronologia delle prime pitture," ibid. 44 (1968f.), 82–113, esp. 102 (oldest painting in the Lucina region: 190s, but the uncertainty remains considerable). P. Styger's stereotypical settings of the catacomb nuclei in the *middle* of the second century have been surpassed. Today (except perhaps for a graffito under S. Sebastiano, see below) scholars can find nothing Christian in Rome's catacombs that can with certainty be dated *before* the time around 200 C.E.

20. Cf. *ILCV* 953f. Brickmakers' stamps that have been found — always only a terminus post quem — go back at the earliest to Severian times; most are attributable to the period of Caracalla's government (211–17 C.E.).

Originally the site looked like this: Two almost parallel stairways, some 20 m. apart, whose entrances faced the Appia, led downward to their respective underground gallery ("A" and "B"). A and B were soon dug deeper and were successively joined together with cross-walks so that a grid system was formed. Only then were cubicula (among others, the Papal Crypt) were added. The grid system suggests that property boundaries above ground were respected, beyond which the diggers did not dare to go. South of B on the surface there was a small remainder of a wall which at only a short distance away runs parallel to B and may well have marked a property boundary.

The first spade cut for the second nucleus, the so-called Lucina Region, appears to have been set towards the end of the second century: the Christian frescoes of the two earliest cubicula x and y (e.g., the baptism of Christ, Daniel in the lions' den, Jonah, shepherd bearing a sheep, fish) are to be dated most probably into the first quarter of the third century.[21] Around 253 C.E. the hypogeum of cubicula x and y was connected with a neighboring vault, which likewise goes back into the first half of the third century.[22]

This archaeological evidence concurs with literary tradition. Hippolytus (*Ref.* 9.12.14) passes on the information that Bishop Zephyrinus (ca. 199–217) had entrusted Callistus, who later succeeded him in the episcopal office, with the administration "of the Coemeterium": εἰς τὸ χοιμητήριον χατέστησεν. Moreover, according to a tradition available in the sixth century, Zephyrinus was buried "in cymiterio suo, iuxta cymiterium Calisti, via Appia,"[23] more specifically, *sursum,* in a surface grave memorial, as the pilgrim of the seventh century could still observe.[24]

Hippolytus's χοιμητήριον is without doubt identical with the "cymiterium Calisti" in the area known yet today as the Callisto catacomb on the Via Appia. What does Hippolytus's note signify? If Zephyrinus entrusted his deacon with the administration of the cemetery, that means two things: (a) Zephyrinus possessed the right of disposition over the property, and (b) he is opening the property for *ecclesiastical* pur-

---

21. Cf. Testini, op. cit. (1966), 64, 288; A. M. Schneider, 181; Brandenburg (1978), 333; Fasola-Testini (1978), 107.

22. Cf. Reekmans, op. cit. (1964), as well as the plan, e.g., in Nestori, *Repertorio,* op. cit. (1975), s.v.; nos. 1 and 2 in Nestori are the cubicula that are otherwise often designated with x and y.

23. *Liber Pont.* 1:139 (ed. Duchesne).

24. Cf. the Itineraries of the seventh century ("sursum": Salzburger Itinerarium/ Notitia ecclesiarum, in Testini, op. cit. (1966), 65, or Duchesne, *Liber Pont.* 1:140, n. 4). This fits with the epigraphical catalogue of Sixtus III (ca. 432–40), which lists the bishops who were buried underground, but does not mention Zephyrinus (in Duchesne, loc. cit. and 234).

poses: fellow Christians can be buried here. Neither is so self-evident as it seems. The church around 200 C.E. cannot be proved to have been a holder of ecclesiastical collective property, which Zephyrinus *as bishop* would have had at his disposal. Every bit of real estate used by Christians was the possession of private individuals.[25] In view of this general state of affairs, I think our special case is to be interpreted as follows: A wealthy Christian makes a piece of property on the Via Appia available so that brothers and sisters in the faith can be buried there. Legally, the "benefactor" remains the owner of the property; de facto the other Christians also use it by constructing subterranean graves under it.

How did Zephyrinus come to have control over the property? The solution is hypothetical, but is easily available: the benefactor was Zephyrinus himself. "In cymiterio *suo*" is to be understood in the most literal sense. This tradition available in the *Liber Pontificalis* meets our insight won from Hippolytus brilliantly. We have before us the property which Zephyrinus *himself* had acquired (or inherited) for his own burial and which he made available to those fellow Christians who did not have the means for their own burial area. The tradition that Zephyrinus was buried above ground in a memorial of his own in contrast to those buried subterraneously fits well if he were the well-to-do owner of the ground and the ones buried in tombs below were poorer fellow Christians. Subterraneous catacomb graves were cheaper[26] than above-ground memoriae; the tuffaceous soil of Rome was easy to dig. That the property owner had himself buried in his private area above ground — "in praediis suis" — is often enough evidenced.[27]

Perhaps we are getting another picture of Zephyrinus than that polemically glossed over by Hippolytus. But also beneath Hippolytus's varnish there is still a piece of recognizable truth: Hippolytus presents Zephyrinus as φιλάργυρος (*Ref.* 9.11.1), avaricious. If we withdraw Hippolytus's taunt, it nevertheless remains true that Zephyrinus did not belong among the poorest; the property on the Via Appia suited Zephyrinus well.

If we conjoin the literary material with the archaeological findings, the nucleus region around the so-called Papal Crypt is to be identified as the original Coemeterium Callisti. The chronology fits. Moreover, in the simple loculi tombs ordinary people found their resting places. The loculi are compartments cut into the wall of a passageway, closed

---

25. On the problem of the legal situation and of the ability of the church to be an owner, see below, chapters 36–37.

26. On this, cf., e.g., F. De Visscher, *Le droit des Tombeaux Romains* (Milan, 1963), 13; or Styger, op. cit. (1933), 3.

27. E.g., *CIL* 14:3482; *ILCV* 3830B ("in sarcofago in hortulis nostris").

with a few cheap tiles. Callistus did *not* have himself buried here, as we shall see.[28]

Hippolytus had spoken of *the* Coemeterium. Archaeology shows, however, that there were also others. How then should Hippolytus be interpreted? In contrast to the other private family tombs — which shall be mentioned shortly — Zephyrinus's property had one peculiarity: it was directly administered by an ecclesiastical deacon. The situation had developed because the property owner and bishop were united in one person.

I see two possibilities for the interpretation of Hippolytus. (a) Either the consciousness had set in very quickly among the Christians that the Coemeterium of Callistus was, in a word, *the* Christian burial place. Or (b) Hippolytus polemically kept silent about the fact that already in his own time the designation "Coemeterium Callisti" had won acceptance. He did not want to record this success of his opponent! In paraphrase, it might run: "He set him as administrator over the Coemeterium — which all of you readers know and of which you know that Callistus had cared for it."[29]

To summarize: During Zephyrinus's time in office (199–217), Christians were buried on the Via Appia, primarily in a piece of property provided for their use by Zephyrinus, but also in the not too distant Lucina region.

S. Sebastiano

We go down the Via Appia a bit farther to the south: to the burial complex under S. Sebastiano.[30] Around the middle of the second century, here under the open sky in a pit of tuff, a small graveyard was laid out, bordered by the façades of three pagan mausoleums. Wealthy pagan contemporaries decorated their interior richly with stucco and paintings. Clodius Hermes, whose Titulus-inscription is preserved over the entrance of the mausoleum on the right (when one stands in front of the façades), called himself a patron of freedmen, to whom the vault was available for their own use also. The whole layout was used until

---

28. I will delve no further into the details, because they go beyond the first two centuries. I am concerned here exclusively with the topographical question: Where are the first Christian monuments to be found? Where are Christians for the first time palpable in Rome? To the social problematic, care of the congregation for the poor, etc., I shall return esp. in chaps. 10 and 11.

29. Cf. similarly, Testini, op. cit. (1966), 66.

30. Cf. from the rich literature, e.g., A. v. Gerkan, "Petrus in Vaticano et in Catacumbas," *JAC* 5 (1962): 23ff.; A. Ferrua, *S. Sebastiano e la sua catacomba*, 3d ed. (Rome, 1968); idem, "Due mausolei da pagani cristiani," *RivArCr* 28 (1952): 13–41; O. Marucchi, "Nota sulle memorie cristiane esplorate nello scavo di S. Sebastiano," *Notizie degli Scavi* 20 (1923): 80–103; Testini (1966), 55.

about the 240s. In the middle hypogeum the three grave inscriptions of the children Gordianus, Pupienus, and Balbinus (*ILCV* 3995A–C), who were named after the emperors of the year 238, were found. Around the middle of the third century, the entire graveyard was given up; the entrances to the mausoleums were blocked up with amphorae, the whole place filled in and, above it, a new site built, the famous "Memoria Apostolorum" of S. Sebastiano, which is datable through a graffito to the year 260 at the latest.

We descend the stairs in the middle mausoleum, the stairway having at first an arched ceiling rich with stucco and going down to the lowest plainer region in which there is scarcely any decoration to be found, and where in rainy times water may be standing. Here below, a Christian took a sharp object and in the still fresh plaster on a pillar scratched the acrostic ΙΧΘΥΣ — with a T-cross engraved between the Ι and the Χ: *Ι*ΗϹΟΥϹ ΧΡΙϹΤΟϹ ΘΕΟΥ ΥΙΟϹ ϹΩΤΗΡ with the cross between ΙΗϹΟΥϹ and ΧΡΙϹΤΟϹ.[31]

When did a Christian have a claim on one of the loculi graves for himself or for a family member? The plaster of the pillar is naturally difficult to date; one hundred years are available within the timeframe mentioned. But one must not date it too late. The plaster would certainly not have been applied shortly before the hypogeum was abandoned. And the new site, which was built above it by 260 C.E. at the latest, was constructed by *Christians* who filled in our little graveyard as this was given up. It appears that there was no continuity between the Christian of the acrostic and the Christian builders of the Memoria Apostolorum. Perhaps around 200, perhaps also earlier, then, the acrostic was put on.

In what way one or several Christians acquired a grave in the mausoleum remains abandoned to fantasy, unfortunately. In its later period, the middle mausoleum was also occupied by members of a club, who called themselves "Innocentiores" on their pagan grave inscriptions.[32] Was a Christian a member here? Had he before his Christian conversion acquired for himself the title to a grave through subscription payments that he did not wish to forfeit?[33] Or did he get here through familial ties? As a slave or as a freedman of the mausoleum's owner? However that may be, two things are interesting: (a) our Christian has left his traces in the plainer, not in the more richly decorated section of the hypogeum. (b) That the proximity of the pagan graves did not disturb him is not surprising. The close coexistence of pagan and Christian graves is encountered again and again. The surface zone above the two

---

31. Cf. on the acrostic, Tertullian, *De bapt.* 1; *Sibyll.* 8.217ff.; and see above, the dedication page.

32. Thus the three Gordianus, Pupienus, Balbinus, mentioned above.

33. Cf. Cyprian, *Ep.* 67.6.

nuclei of the Callistus catacomb was occupied from the Republican period right down into the fourth century C.E. also with pagan graves;[34]
the grave plots were small and were in the hands of many owners —
pagan as well as Christian. The same finding can be observed in the
third century, e.g., in the Vatican necropolis (see below, Part 3). The
graves used by the Christians, like the mausoleum with the Christ-Helios
mosaic, lay tightly crammed in next to pagan burial chambers.[35] We encounter a Christian-pagan symbiosis in the archaeological monuments,
which finds its corresponding reality in the literature: When Hermas (see
chap. 22, below) cloaks Mother Church in the features of the Sibylle of
Cumae, then that is the unconcerned "mixing" which ordinary Christian people practiced more than the ecclesiastical authorities liked. As
is well known, the author of the Muratorian Canon sought to exclude
Hermas's book from public church use.

In the S. Sebastiano catacomb, finally, is to be found a sarcophagus
fragment from the years 200–225 (Bovini and Brandenburg, *Repertorium der christlich-antiken Sarkophage,* no. 248). It shows a bearded
man who holds in his raised right hand a sword or knife (Abraham?); in
the background a fluttering shoulder-cloak and the foliage of a tree are
visible. The motif is not to be found on pagan sarcophagi.

I will leave aside other possibly Christian evidence from under
S. Sebastiano because of its ambivalence. (a) Bovini and Brandenburg
(no. 321) count a fragment of a sarcophagus lid among the Christian
evidence. It comes from the second third of the third century and represents a man (apostle?), who in his left hand bears a scroll. His right hand
is held in a gesture of speaking before the breast, and his gaze is directed
toward the deceased person, presumably represented in the (lost) middle
of the sarcophagus lid. However, I doubt the apostle-interpretation.
No. 1022, a sarcophagus from Ostia from the same time-frame, shows a
woman, the deceased, in the same pose (scroll, speaking gesture); she is
looking over to an Orpheus in the middle of the sarcophagus. (b) On
some loculi-graves, symbols such as an anchor and fish were found.
But even Clement of Alexandria (*Paid.* 3.59.2), who recommended the
use of such symbols, did so in the context of these symbols already being widespread in the pagan realm. He recommended simply that from
among the symbols used by pagans, those be selected that are appropriate for Christian meaning. (c) The mausoleum of Marcus Clodius
Hermes exhibits above its entrance a painting that does not belong to
the most original components of the monument and which *perhaps* has

---

34. Cf. Testini, op. cit. (1966), 69.
35. Cf. Cyprian, *Ep.* 67.6, who was upset by this kind of "mixing" in the cemeteries.
The same state of affairs was also true for the Jews. The Jewish grave inscriptions known
till now in Ostia come from cemeteries in which pagans were also buried (on that, see
Solin, "Juden und Syrer," 731).

a Christian meaning. The state of its preservation, despite recent restoration, is bad and the interpretation most debatable. One wants to see on the right side the swine of Gerasa plunge into the water or next to that the miracle of the multiplication of the loaves. Meal scenes (especially funeral meal scenes), however, and bucolic-pastoral motifs are also frequent in pagan depictions. I am, finally, simply unable to interpret the shepherd on the left in the picture as Christian: Not only *one* "good shepherd" grazes his flock here, but two others who gesticulate in lively fashion.

Pretestato Catacomb

We find early Christian presence on the Via Appia, third, in the area of the Pretestato catacomb,[36] which, like the Callisto catacomb, has come from the growing together of two originally independent ancient nuclei.

The Spelunca Magna, with its beautiful brick façades, was originally a large water reservoir in which graves were laid out since the second century;[37] in this way digging a crypt was not necessary. Various entrances possibly point to the fact that the Spelunca was used by several parties as a burial place.

The second nucleus, at the foot of the so-called Scala maggiore, appears to have been a small private area (ca. 40 x 40 m.) used by only one family group (since the end of the second or the beginning of the third centuries). In the center stands the cubiculum with the fresco of the so-called Coronatio, as well as pictures of the resurrection of Lazarus and of Jesus' encounter with the Samaritan woman.[38]

The earliest Christian traces in the Pretestato catacomb date from the first half of the third century (especially the frescoes on the Coronatio cubiculum).[39] The tradition that Urban, the episcopal successor of Callistus, was buried about 230 in the area of the Pretestato catacomb[40] is uncertain.

---

36. Cf., among others, F. Tolotti, "Influenza delle opere idrauliche sull'origine delle catacombe," *RivArCr* 56 (1980): 7–48, here 32ff.; idem, "Ricerca dei luoghi venerati della spelunca magna di Pretestato," *RivArCr* 53 (1977): 7–102; Testini, op. cit. (1966), 57ff., 153; A. M. Schneider, op. cit., 186ff.

37. Tolotti, op. cit. (1980), 34, 41: since ca. 200 C.E.; differently, idem, op. cit. (1977), 15, 44: second half of the second century. More precise dating of the brickwork is naturally difficult.

38. In Nestori, *Repertorio*, s.v., it is cubiculum no. 3.

39. Close to these frescoes, cf. in the Spelunca Magna the graves of two deacons from the time of the Valerian persecution which are indicated by graffiti.

40. Thus the *Liber Pont.* 1:143 (Duchesne). But the epigraphical list of Sixtus III (ca. 432–40) concerning the bishops buried in Callistus's catacomb also contains Urban's name (see *Liber Pont.* ibid., n. 5).

In the surface zone, as in the Callisto complex, pagans and Christians tolerantly coexisted. Especially in the third century, pagan graves, sometimes quite luxurious, were laid out above the Pretestato catacomb.

Domitilla Catacomb

Still in the area of Via Appia/Via Ardeatina the Domitilla catacomb grew from several original nuclei on the Via delle Sette Chiese.[41]

The so-called Hypogeum of the Flavians — a connection to the Flavians is unprovable — was laid out as a gallery with niches for sarcophagi towards the end of the second century. The pagan visitor reached the interior of the private crypt from the outside via a monumental brick entrance. Inside he was surrounded by Amors, Psyches, and a dolphin pair and other decorative, especially bucolic motifs, which had been painted around 200 C.E. or shortly thereafter. Christian traces (frescoes of Noah in the ark, Daniel in the lion's den, a fisherman) date only from the third century; perhaps only from the time of Gallienus (260–68 C.E.).[42] At that time, Christians were brought into the private hypogeum — possibly as freedmen of the pagan lords who owned the piece of ground. Through inheritances to the liberti the graveyard might have passed into Christian hands sometime in the third century. The other possibility is that noble members of the pagan family themselves had found their way to Christendom.

The second nucleus, the pagan "Ampliatus Hypogeum," did not come into Christian possession before the last quarter of the third century. Christians, however, used the private hypogeum of the "Buon Pastore" in the first decades of the third century already. The so-called Aurelii region, galleries with cubicula, which respected the borders of a small surface, was already laid out at the beginning of the third century by a Christian group with a large membership.[43]

---

41. Cf., among others, Ph. Pergola, "Il Praedium Domitillae sulla via Ardeatina: Anàlisi storico-topografica delle testimonianze pagane fino alla metà del III sec. D.C.," *RivArCr* 55 (1979): 313–35; idem, "La région dite du Bon Pasteur dans le cimetière de Domitilla sur l'Ardeatina: Etude topographique de son origine," *RivArCr* 51 (1975): 65–96; L. Pani Ermini, "L'ipogeo detto dei Flavi in Domitilla, I: Osservazioni sulla sua origine e sul carattere della decorazione," *RivArCr* 45 (1969): 119–73; idem, II: "Gli ambienti esterni," *RivArCr* 48 (1972): 235–69; Tolotti, op. cit. (1980), 36, 41; idem, op. cit. (1966/67), 313; Testini, op. cit. (1966), 52ff.; A. M. Schneider, op. cit., 182ff.

42. So Ermini, op. cit. (1969), 173, and (1972), 268.

43. See the findings in Fasola-Testini, op. cit. (1978), 113f. ("Ampliatus"), 116, 118, 197 ("Buon Pastore"); 118f., 139, 197, 206 ("Aurelii"). Brandenburg, op. cit. (1978), 333, dates the region of the "Buon Pastore" to the second half of the third century in view of the frescoes. The topographical findings (several phases of construction), however, require the beginning of the construction to be laid already in the first decades of the third century (Fasola-Testini, op. cit., 116–18; Christians appear to have administered this region *ab ovo*).

De Rossi's (1:186ff., 266ff.) old and, for the tourists, often repeated hypothesis has not been able to withstand the light of critical archaeological investigation. He had wanted to see in the area of the Domitilla catacomb the grave sites of the Christian Flavians of the first century (see below, Part 4 on Flavia Domitilla). What supported the hypothesis? An inscription from the surface zone of the Domitilla catacomb called "Tor Marancia" proclaimed that here a Flavia Domitilla owned real estate and of that property had placed an area of 35 x 40 feet at the disposal of a man named P. Calvisius Philotas for funeral purposes (*CIL* 6:16246: "ex indulgentia Flaviae Domitillae"). This lady cannot be brought into connection with the Christian nuclei of the Domitilla catacomb, for the following reasons. (a) Her inscription was found *somewhere* on the "Tor Marancia" estate. Should she really once have possessed lands immediately above the first catacomb nuclei, it by no means follows that there was a connection to the Christians. The "Hypogeum of the Flavians" as well as the "Ampliatus hypogeum" (just as the "hypogeum of the sarcophagi" that was destroyed by the building of the basilica) are of pagan origin. (b) There is nothing to prove that the Fl. Domitilla of the inscription had anything to do with the Christian lady of the same name. This is pure conjecture. (c) The inscription, like the other grave inscriptions on the surface, shows no Christian traces.[44]

To summarize: Christian burial places clustered — if not yet in the second century, at least at the beginning of the third century — in a relatively small area of the suburban tract of the Via Appia. In S. Callisto, the subterranean graveyard laid out by Callistus on assignment from Zephyrinus, even hundreds (!) of people appear to have been buried already before the Papal Crypt was built around 235 C.E.[45]

If we seek the users of the graves of the suburban Appia region in the city, we shall find them primarily on both sides of the urban tract of the Via Appia. This result accords well with other information. In the ecclesiastical administration of late antiquity, the four Appian catacombs, indeed, belonged to the first church region stretching to the west of the Appia (= Augustan Regions XI–XIII) or respectively to the second church region stretching east of the Appia (= Augustan Regions I, II, X, VIII, and a part of V).[46]

---

44. The constantly repeated inscriptions *CIL* 6:8942; 948f., like the above epigraph, speak of a Flavia Domitilla ("neptis Divi Vespasiani"), and also mention the giving of a parcel of land for funeral purposes. But with these inscriptions, every connection to the "Tor Marancia" locality is unprovable.

45. Ca. 800 burials. So, e.g., A. M. Schneider, op. cit., 177, in the wake of Styger, op. cit. (1933), 38ff.

46. Cf. Map 1 as well as the map of Fasola, op. cit. (1976). A special affinity between the Domitilla catacomb and the Titulus Fasciolae on the Via Appia can be shown (above, n. 17). The Callistus catacomb Kirsch (*Titelkirchen*, 95, 23) sees especially connected with the Titulus Sixti (= Titulus Crescentianae). The S. Sebastiano cemetery was

What follows? The users of these early Christian burial grounds in the south lived in the city to the left and right of the Via Appia, which led to the Porta Capena on the Aventine, the so-called Lesser Aventine (Region XII), the Caelius, or above all, in the Appian lowland between them, directly on both sides of the great Appian traffic artery.

Via Ostiensis

I proceed in clockwise fashion around the city, to the Via Ostiensis and the "Grave of Paul" beneath S. Paolo fuori le Mura ("St. Paul's outside the Walls").[47] About this grave, unfortunately, not much can be said with certainty, since the opportunity for archaeological excavation after the church burned in 1823 was only poorly realized. Under and next to the church is a pagan cemetery which was used from the first to the third centuries C.E., and in which possibly the apostle was buried. Toward the end of the second century, in any case, Christians honored a "Paul tropaion" (memorial to Paul) here.[48] It may be that at this memorial to Paul — as at the Vatican grave site P, around the "grave of Peter" (see below, chap. 8) — an area of Christian tombs developed.

A Christian grave area from about 200 C.E. on the Via Ostiensis would point to inhabitants of the Aventine.[49] But we must be careful: a famous apostle's grave could also have attracted people from other parts of the city quite naturally.

Vatican and Via Aurelia

The same reservation applies to the Christian graves of the Vatican burial place P that crowd round the "grave of Peter" (see below). The site P otherwise points to the city quarter of Trastevere, for the Vatican belonged to the Augustan Region XIV (= seventh church region), which comprised Trastevere and the Vatican.

On the Via Aurelia, the arterial road leading to the west out of Trastevere, Callistus in around 222 was buried in the Calepodio vault as the first Roman bishop whose resting place was in a catacomb.[50] The original nucleus contained short galleries that branched off from a middle

---

attached especially to the Titulus Byzantis (above, n. 17). On the Pretestato catacomb, cf. *ICUR* 5:14583.

47. On the whole matter, see Testini, op. cit. (1966), 77f.

48. See Gaius, around 200 C.E., in Eusebius, *Hist. Ecc.* 2.25.7.

49. Not merely because of the natural situation (the arterial road leading out of the Aventine region was the Via Ostiensis), but also because of the epigraphical material in Kirsch, *Titelkirchen*, 207.

50. On the excavation, cf. among others A. Nestori, "La Catacomba di Calepodio al III miglio dell'Aurelia vetus e i sepolcri dei papi Callisto I e Giulio I," *RivArCr* 47 (1971): 169–278; idem, ibid. 48 (1972): 193–233; idem, ibid. 51 (1975): 135ff.; as well as Tolotti, op. cit. (1980), 36.

passage. Below the surface, they respected the boundaries of a precisely demarcated rectangular field which is laid out not far from the Via Aurelia Vetus and parallel to it; it is clearly a matter of a precisely bordered (private) property. Callistus found his resting place in the original nucleus at the foot of the entrance steps.

Why Callistus was buried here and not in the cemetery on the Via Appia that he himself had laid out admits of various answers. (a) The galleries under Zephyrinus's property were obviously for the less affluent. Were these galleries not "distinguished" enough for him? (b) Was Callistus the owner of the Calepodius hypogeum? That is possible but not provable. It is more likely that the owner was a Calepodius whose name might be read on an epitaph not far from Callistus's grave. (c) Most probable, it appears to me, is that Callistus simply came from Trastevere, as the local tradition has it.[51] Whoever came from Trastevere and possibly also lived there is most likely to lay claim to a grave site by an arterial road leading out of his section of the city.[52]

Christian presence in the Calepodio catacomb since the first quarter of the third century points to Christian users from Trastevere.

Via Salaria

An early concentration like that on the Via Appia is encountered once again in the north on the Via Salaria:

The Priscilla catacomb on the Via Salaria Nova grew from three nuclei.[53]

1. The so-called Acilii hypogeum shows Christian evidence from the end of the third century *at the earliest* and can thus here be shunted aside.

2. The subterranean Arenar is interesting. It was an abandoned underground sand pit in which simple loculi graves were laid out since ca. 200 C.E.; one saved in this way the work of digging an extra crypt. The brick stampings on the loculus panels — they provide only termini post quem — do not go back beyond the time of Septimius Severus (193–211 C.E.). Simple people were buried here. They wrote their names partly with red coloring, and only here and there does one find a marble panel. Decoration with painting and plaster relief is sparse. Many people found their loculus grave in this intensely occupied zone. Here in the area of

---

51. *Liber Pont.* 1:141f. (ed. Duchesne).

52. Cf. in fact, thus, the epigraphic material in Kirsch, *Titelkirchen*, 208, 204.

53. Cf., among others, Tolotti, op. cit. (1980), esp. 25ff.; idem, *Il cimitero di Priscilla. Studio di topografia e architettura* (Vatican, 1970), 258ff.; idem, "L'area recinta ove ebbe origine il cimitero di Priscilla," *RivArCr* 42/43 (1966/67): 261–314; L. De Bruyne, "La 'Capella greca' di Priscilla," *RivArCr* 46 (1970): 291–330 (literature); A. Grabar, *Le premier art chrétien* (Paris, 1966), 99; Testini, op. cit. (1966), 69ff., 288, 80; A. M. Schneider, op. cit., 188ff.; Styger, op. cit. (1933), esp. 117ff.

the Arenar we come across early Christian traces from the beginning of
the third century: famous among them is the fresco of the prophet with
the Mother and Christchild.

3. The Cryptoporticus, an architecturally refined layout of masonry,
is more distinguished than the Arenar. The painted decorations date
from the first half of the third century and can be — though they need
not be — Christian (not even the depiction of a shepherd carrying a
sheep).[54] According to the topographical investigation of Tolotti, the adjoining Capella Graeca was laid out *after* the Cryptoporticus, so that its
Christian frescoes can scarcely have originated before the second third
of the third century (possibly even later).[55]

From the first half of the third century, finally, comes still other Christian evidence from the Via Salaria: an inscription from the Coemeterium
Bassillae on the Via Salaria Vetus from the year 234 C.E. (*ILCV 2807*) as
well as a sarcophagus from ca. 250 C.E. It is one of the oldest Christian
sarcophagi that we have.[56]

How is this accumulation of data on the Via Salaria to be explained?
In the ecclesiastical administration of late antiquity, the Priscilla catacomb belonged to the fifth church-region, which encompassed the VIIth
(Via Lata) and part of the IXth Augustan regions (Mars Field); it thus
stretched left and right of the Via Lata / Flaminia. Special affinity existed
for the Titulus Marci.[57]

By locating the users of the Salaria graveyards to the left and to the
right of the Via Lata / Flaminia, we find the "exception to the rule."
The Priscilla catacomb lies on the Via Salaria Nova, which feeds into
the Augustan City Region VI (= church region 4). The earliest users of
the cemetery, therefore, would, according to the rule, have lived here.
However, apart from the aforementioned affinity for the Titulus Marci,
for three additional reasons this is less probable: (a) In late antiquity's
church administration (fourth to sixth centuries), the catacombs of the
fourth church region *all* lay on the Via Nomentana (the catacombs

54. See below, chap. 15, before n. 11.

55. Cf., e.g., Tolotti, op. cit. (1970), 368ff.; idem, op. cit. (1980), 28; Testini, op. cit. (1966), 72, 288. The dating battle is huge. The traditional early dating of the Capella Greca is still advocated by L. De Bruyne, op. cit. (1970), 329f., but in moderate form: He dates the decoration of the Capella Greca shortly *before* the paintings of the Lucina Region (cubiculum x-y, see above), which De Bruyne — once again "early" — already assigns to the 190s (see above, n. 19).

56. On the sarcophagus, see A. M. Schneider, op. cit., 195. Pictures of the sarcophagus in Bovini and Brandenburg, *Repertorium*, no. 123 / Table 30 ("second third of the third century"). Also from the Via Salaria, but less precisely datable (third century), is the sarcophagus fragment no. 118. The sarcophagus no. 66 from the Via Salaria originates only from the third quarter of the third century. On the inscriptions *CIL* 6:9057; 8987 from the Via Salaria Vetus, see below, chap. 30.

57. Cf. the inscription of the lector "de Pallacine" in Kirsch, *Titelkirchen*, 206. On the whole, see the map (1976) of U. M. Fasola. The *Liber Pontificalis* (s.v.) has Bishop Sixtus (ca. 115–25 C.E.) come, interestingly, "de regione Via Lata."

Maius, Minus, S. Agnese, Nicomede), while (b) *all* of the catacombs on the Via Salaria were attached to the fifth church region: besides the Priscilla catacomb, the cemeteries Giordani, Trasone, Massimo, Panfilo, and Bassilla. (c) On the Via Flaminia, the arterial road out of the fifth church region, only one single Christian graveyard was actually found: the post-Constantinian catacomb S. Valentino. In view of this clear evidence from late antiquity, it is difficult to maintain anything else for the earlier times. The Via Salaria with its Priscilla cemetery appears to have been used all along as a "burial street" by Christians resident on both the left and the right of the Via Lata.

Why Christians scarcely frequented the Via Flaminia is not easy to account for. Were these Christians who mainly came from the east only slightly interested in this road which led to the *north* (in the direction of Rimini, the coast of the Adriatic, upper Italy and Gaul)? The ancient trade- and salt-road Salaria in the direction of Rieti in the northeast may have been more interesting for them.

Until now, I have had graveyards for Christian groups in view and have looked at individual graves only if they led to the same conclusions as the group burial places. Only group burial places offer significant information for aggregations of Christian population inside the city. For the sake of completeness, the earliest Christian individual finds are added here which come from other city sections. In the topographical evaluation (accumulation of Christian population in certain city quarters), of course, they cannot be given much weight.

a. The sarcophagus of Prosenes from the year 217 C.E. (*ILCV* 3332; *ICUR* 6 [1975]: no. 17246) was found on the surface by the Via Labicana (near Torre Nuova).

b. Two sarcophagi come from the nearer and farther areas, respectively, of the Via Latina: One from the year 238 C.E. was found in the suburb Galetti (*ICUR* 1:8; A. M. Schneider, 194, 168); the other from the year 249 C.E. in the Horti Campani (*ILCV* 3789; A. M. Schneider, 194, 168).[58]

c. I shall refer below to a Valentinian group of the second century on the Via Latina. They, too, can be passed over here. They had, as we

---

58. *ICUR* 1:8 = Bovini and Brandenburg, *Repertorium*, no. 117, where, however, only "e subterraneis coemeteriis" is provided as the origin. As the oldest sarcophagi, cf. in addition to the already named (*Reportorium*, no. 929 Prosenes [Via Labicana], 217 C.E.; no. 248 [S. Sebastiano], 200–225 C.E.; no. 117 [Via Latina?], 238 C.E.; *ILCV* 3789 [Horti Campani], 249 C.E.; *Repertorium*, no. 321 [S. Sebastiano], 123 [Via Salaria], 1022 [Ostia], all from the second third of the third century) also no. 814 (origin unknown) first half of the third century; no. 88 (origin unknown) second third of the third century; no. 976 (Velletri, 30 km. southeast of Rome) mid-third century. From the third century (without any closer determination being possible) are no. 118 (Via Salaria), no. 723 (source unknown), no. 1040f. (Porto). No. 747, found in S. Maria Antiqua at the Forum Romanum, is dated into the third quarter of the third century, by Bovini and Brandenburg, but by Brandenburg, op. cit. (1978), 340, earlier in "approximately" the 240s.

shall see, no representative character for other circles of urban Roman Christendom.[59] Moreover, as they frequented a suburban villa on the Via Latina way outside the city limits, there is no evidence for locating them in any quarter *in* the city.

Summary

Three topographical focal points result: (a) The regions left and right of the inner-city section of the Via Appia, (b) the region left and right of the Via Lata / Flaminia, which includes a section of Mars Field, and (c) Trastevere.

If we compare the results of our second method with the results of the first (local tradition), there are two points of agreement. (a) Trastevere. First method: two house congregations (Callisti, Caeciliae); second method: graveyard P on the Vatican, Catacomb Calepodio. (b) The region of the Aventine. First method: three house churches (Priscae, Sabinae, Balbinae); second method, the graveyards on the Via Ostiensis and on the Via Appia.

Jewish Quarters

Because the urban Roman Christendom developed out of Judaism, there is a third method available to us: Christians of the early period would be found especially in those quarters of the city in which Jews were also domiciled.

The traditional Jewish quarter since the first century B.C.E. was Trastevere.

> Philo, *Leg. ad Gaium* 155, 157: Augustus "knew that the great section of Rome on the other side of the Tiber River was occupied and inhabited by Jews. Most were emancipated Roman citizens. For having been brought to Italy as prisoners of war, they were liberated by their owners.... He neither ejected them from Rome nor deprived them of their Roman citizenship...." (τὴν πέραν τοῦ Τιβέρεως ποταμοῦ μεγάλην τῆς Ῥώμης ἀποτομὴν [ἣν] οὐκ ἠγνόει κατεχομένην καὶ οἰκουμένην πρὸς Ἰουδαίων. Ῥωμαῖοι δὲ ἦσαν οἱ πλείους ἀπελευθερωθέντες· αἰχμάλωτοι γὰρ ἀχθέντες εἰς Ἰταλίαν ὑπὸ τῶν κτησαμένων ἠλευθερώθησαν,...οὔτε ἐξῴκισε τῆς Ῥώμης ἐκείνους οὔτε τὴν Ῥωμαϊκὴν αὐτῶν ἀφείλετο πολιτείαν...).

---

59. The same is true finally for the hypogeum on the Viale Manzoni, which is perhaps from the early part of the third century. A small Christian-heretical group *may* have buried their dead here. But the uncertainty is enormous and the dispute correspondingly so. See the frescoes in J. Stevenson's *Im Schattenreich der Catacomben* (Bergisch Gladbach, 1980), 150ff. Stevenson has tried to identify the group with the Theodotians.

Many of the Jews who had been enslaved by Pompey and deported to Rome were soon emancipated and settled in across the Tiber, where other people from the east also lived. With our third method we find ourselves thus once more in Trastevere![60]

The Trastevere quarter did not remain the sole preferred living area of Jews.

> Juvenal, *Sat.* 3.12–16: "Near the aging and damp Capena,[61] where Numa once ordered his nocturnal girlfriend, the Jews have now leased the temple and the grove with the holy spring. They have among their household effects hay[62] and a carrying basket; for every tree must pay rent to our people, and the forest from which the Camenae were expelled begs."

What Juvenal has in mind is the Nymphaeum of the nymph Egeria, the "nocturnal girlfriend" of Numa, which is situated in the damp Appian lowland southeast of the Porta Capena. Jews had settled as beggars in its neighborhood, so that the muses (Camenae) had fled.

Three Jewish cemeteries on the *Via Appia* (which, however, originated later, not before the third century) also point to Jewish settlement in this quarter. The three cemeteries were in the Vigna Randanini; across from the Vigna Randanini on the Via Appia Pignatelli, and in the Vigna of Count Cimarra.

Such a concentration of three Jewish cemeteries on the Appia is seen nowhere else in Rome; only on the Via Nomentana do we also find two Jewish cemeteries near each other (Villa Torlonia). This finding corresponds thus to the concentration of the earliest Christian cemeteries, which also clustered only on the Via Appia.

Juvenal's notice is strengthened finally through two additional observations: (a) Not far from the zone of which Juvenal spoke, there lived a Jew called Alexander (not, however, before the third century): He lived at the "macellum" (*CIJ* 1:210), by which is meant the meat market macellum magnum. One reaches it easily by foot by one of the cross-streets branching off from the Appia and going up the Caelius slope. (b) Schol. *Juv.* 4.117 knows of Jews of the second century who, expelled from Rome, moved to Aricia in the Alban mountains. The Via Appia leads directly into the Alban mountains! Presumably the expelled Jews came from the Via Appia quarter.

---

60. Trastevere as a Jewish quarter is also evidenced by the Jewish cemetery "Monteverde," to the right of the Tiber outside the Porta Portuensis on the arterial street emerging from Trastevere. It is the oldest Jewish cemetery in Rome and goes back in its origins perhaps into the first century C.E. Cf., e.g., A. M. Schneider, op. cit., 191; R. Penna, "Les Juifs à Rome au temps de l'Apôtre Paul," *NTS* 28 (1982): 332.

61. At the Porta Capena the supporting arch of a branch of the Aqua Marcia ran; cf. W. Krenkel, *Römische Satiren* (Darmstadt, 1976), 563.

62. Hay served to keep food warm on the Sabbath.

Juvenal's notice is amazing. It leads to complete agreement with the results of our second method, which recognized Christian settlements left and right of the inner-city tract of the Via Appia outside the Porta Capena.

The inscriptions *CIL* 6:29756; *CIG* 9905; *CIJ* 1:88, 319, 523 mention the synagoga Campi and the Καμπήσιοι on the Campus Martius (Mars Field). One result of the second method agrees at this point: the users of the Priscilla catacomb lived somewhere to the left and right of the Via Lata / Flaminia.

The pagan inscription *CIJ* 1:531 = *CIL* 6:9821 from the end of the first century C.E. attests a Jewish "proseucha" close to the Republican wall between the Porta Collina and the Porta Esquilina. Here in the northeast part of the city near the Porta Collina the congregation known as the Καλκαρήσιοι, or the Calcarenses (*CIJ* 1:304, 316, 384, 504, 537), are possibly to be sought.[63]

CIG 6447; *CIJ* 1:18, 22, 67, 140, 380[64] finally name the Σιβουρήσιοι: the Jews from the not very reputable business quarter Subura. Also, from a Jewish household of Subura came an amphora stamped with a menorah (*CIL* 15:3552, 1).

One does not find complete confirmation for the preceding two paragraphs from the other methods in this chapter. Only the Tituli Pudentis and Praxedis (see the first method) lie in the immediate vicinity, in the zone *between* both of these areas which were frequented by Jews. The Titulus Pudentis stands on the Vicus Patricius, the Titulus Praxedis on the Clivus Suburanus; both are radial streets from the Subura, which lead to the Portae Viminalis and Esquilina in the Republican wall.

The inscriptionary evidence for synagogue congregations on Mars Field and in the Subura does not come from the first century C.E. Thus, whether there existed already in the first century C.E. Jewish settlements here, out of which Christian circles could have developed, must remain undecided. It is nonetheless certain that in the first century C.E. Jews lived in Trastevere, between the Porta Collina and the Porta Esquilina, as well as before the Porta Capena. Juvenal wrote shortly after 100 C.E., and he does not leave the impression that the Jews had only shortly before that moved into the area of the Egerian Nymphaeum.

---

63. Thus Penna (op. cit. [1982], 332 and n. 90) on the basis of *CIL* 6:9223f. But are lime ovens to be presumed only there? We find right on the shore of the Tiber a region which (still?) in the Middle Ages was called "Calcaria" (cf. *CIJ* 1, p. lxxiv). It lay near the Circus Flaminius, so we may locate the Calcarenses, as the Καμπήσιοι, also on Mars Field.

64. Cf. also the inscription in L. Moretti, *RivArCr* 50 (1974): 219:...ἄρ]χοντος Σιβουρησίων.

Concentrations of the Tituli

Finally, there is a fourth method. Let us examine the topographical distribution of the twenty Tituli of late antiquity given in Map 1. The origins of most of them go back into the third and fourth centuries (see below, chap. 36). At which places in the city do the Titulus congregations accumulate? Could the concentrations of the Tituli of late antiquity indicate where the early Christian settlements lay? Could it be that the city districts which are dense with Tituli were traditional Christian quarters? Let us play it through. Which title churches lay less than 400 meters from each other?

50 m.:

The Tituli Fasciolae and Crescentianae stood before the Porta Capena left and right of the Via Appia immediately across from each other. Nowhere else in Rome do we find two title churches so near to each other. This concentration is intensified by a third Titulus. About 420 m. further along, on the other side of the baths of Caracalla, is the next title church: the Titulus Balbinae. These Tituli stood in the area that commended itself also on the bases of the second and third methods, i.e., they stood in the area of the Via Appia outside the Porta Capena! The Nymphaeum Egeria with the fountain of the Camenae (third method) lies only 300 m. distant from the title-churches Fasciolae and Crescentianae.

100 m.:

The Tituli Gai and Cyriaci in the north of the city in the fourth church region.

120 m.:

The Tituli Clementis and Aemilianae. The Titulus Nicomedis follows at a distance of 450 m., in agreement with method 1, above (Clement, Nicomedes).

150 m.:

The Tituli Praxedis and Equitii. The Titulus Pudentis follows at a distance of 340 m. The Tituli Praxedis and Pudentis surfaced in the first method, above.

230 and 300 m. apart from each other in Trastevere stood the Tituli Caeciliae, Chrysogoni, and Callisti. As in every step thus far, one encounters Trastevere here again!

380 m. on the Aventine separate the Tituli Priscae and Sabinae. The Aventine commended itself also in the first and second methods, above.

The rest of the distances are more than 530 m. The agreements with results of the other methods are nonetheless amazing.[65]

---

65. That the first and the fourth methods are independent of each other is illuminated by the divergences between both series of results. The proximity of the Tituli Gai and

Contemporary Literary Information concerning Localizable Businesses of Christians

Last but not least are two extant sources of reliable information. According to Hippolytus (*Ref.* 9.12), Callistus, in the time of Commodus (probably at the end of the 180s), while he was still a slave and was transacting business for his Dominus, operated a τράπεζα, a bank and exchange business, in which many Christians deposited money. This bank was located in the area of the Piscina Publica (ἐν τῇ λεγομένη πισκινῇ πουπλικῇ). Where would one have opened a bank if hoping for Christian customers? Precisely there where Christians were clustered. The Piscina Publica is Augustan Region XII (with the Lesser Aventine and a portion of the western side of the Appian lowland; see Map 2). Again, we find ourselves close to the tractus urbanus of the Via Appia which leads to the Porta Capena and which is not far, for instance, from Juvenal's Jewish quarter outside the Porta Capena.

Less representative, because tied to a single individual, is Hermas's information that — in the first half of the second century — he possessed a piece of property outside the city on the Via Portuensis (*Vis.* 4.1.2). The Via Portuensis was a radial street out of Trastevere. Once more we stand in Trastevere!

Summary of the Five Methods (with Tables)

Primarily two findings are caught again and again in the outstretched nets (cf. the cross-hatched sections in Map 3). The *agreements* among the five series of results are what count, not so much the individual methods, each of which alone possesses only a limited validity.

Results: a. We are able with great certainty to identify Trastevere, the XIVth Augustan region, as an early Christian residential quarter.

b. The same holds true for the zone inside the city to the left and right of the Via Appia, i.e., the Appian lowland from the Porta Capena to the Almone River.

c. Not so unequivocal (the important third method yielded no result) are the Aventine and the Lesser Aventine (XIIth and XIIIth Augustan Regions, striped on the map) to the left of the Via Appia. They never-

---

Cyriaci and the clustering of Tituli in the Appian lowland are not paralleled by the results of the first method. That means the creators of the local legends (first method) did not get the idea of connecting some Tituli with figures of the first two centuries, because they — like us — observed the clusters of Tituli in the city. They more likely possessed traditions about where the oldest Christian quarters lay, so that they could create legendary stories about the first and second centuries for these quarters.

theless come into question on the basis of the remaining agreements. They connect the two districts mentioned above like a bridge.[66]

d. In addition, at least Mars Field on both sides of the Via Lata/ Flaminia (striped on the map) comes into question on the basis of the second (and third) methods. From Trastevere, this area was easily reached over three bridges, so that here possibly a chronological sequence of expansion can be reconstructed (Trastevere → Mars Field/ Via Lata).

It is interesting how the areas mentioned hitherto produce a coherent semicircle.

Before we illuminate each of the four quarters in question individually (in the following chapter: Trastevere, Appia/Porta Capena, Aventine district, Mars Field/Via Lata), the following observations on the overall findings are worth noting:

a. We are dealing here with perimeter areas which almost without exception are outside the Republican city wall and which were first incorporated into the city by Augustus. This discovery is interesting, because these fringe quarters lay for the most part outside of the Pomerium;[67] the imaginary line of the Pomerium as a rule excluded the worship of foreign gods within its limits. Isis and Osiris (Cassius Dio 40.47.3) and the Egyptian gods in general (ibid. 53.2.4) were banned from the area bounded by the Pomerium. Egyptian and Jewish religious practices, however, were often happily lumped together by the Romans (as in the punitive measures under Tiberius: sacris Aegyptiis Iudaicisque in Rome!),[68] so that probably for Jews too — and as a

---

66. That, at least in the third century, the area of the Aventine/Lesser Aventine was an important Christian region is indicated by the Catalogus Liberianus. Fabian (ca. 236–50 C.E.) established the seven ecclesiastical administrative districts of Rome (Map 1; see Duchesne, *Liber Pontificalis* 1:4–5; 148; 123, n. 6; and see below, chap. 37, end). Like the Augustan enumeration of the fourteen city regions (Map 2), the numbering of the ecclesiastical administrative regions runs counterclockwise around the city center, ending respectively in Trastevere (= Aug. region XIV = eccles. region 7). A deviation between the two numberings is characteristic: The ecclesiastical numbering begins west of the Appia with the area of Aventine/Lesser Aventine/a section of the Appian lowland west of the road: This area gets number 1 in the ecclesiastical numbering. It must have been an important Christian quarter around the middle of the third century.

67. On the inscribed boundary stones of the Pomerium (*CIL* 6:31537ff., cf. Tacitus, *Ann.* 12.24), see von Blumenthal, "Pomerium," Pauly/Wissowa 21/2 (1952): 1867–76, as well as L. Homo, *Rome impériale et l'urbanisme dans l'Antiquité* (Paris, 1951), 94. In specific detail: The region Appia/Porta Capena, until Aurelian, lay completely outside the Pomerium. Only a small part of Trastevere was incorporated into the Pomerium by Vespasian: the Tiber island and an approximately 200-meters-wide piece of land in the bend of the Tiber (boundary stone close to S. Caecilia). The XIIIth Aug. Region (Aventine) was incorporated into the Pomerium, however, by Claudius, and portions of Mars Field by (Claudius and) Vespasian.

68. Tacitus, *Ann.* 2.85.4; Suetonius, *Tib.* 36.1; cf. Josephus, *Ant.* 18.65–84. Also otherwise named together: Ovid, *Ars* 1.76–78.

1. Local tradition	2. The relationships of the burial places to quarters in city	3. Jewish quarter
Trastevere (Caeciliae, Callisti)	Christians lived in: *Trastevere:* later eccles. region 7, XIVth Augustan region (Gravesites: burial place P on the Vatican, Catacomb Calepodio)	*Trastevere:* Main Jewish quarter in first century C.E.
	on both sides of the urban tract of the Via Appia before the Porta Capena, i.e., possibly:	
Aventine (Priscae, Sabinae)	*Aventine,* *Aventine* (Via Ostiensis: perhaps tombs around "Paul's grave")	
Lesser Aventine (Balbinae)	*Lesser Aventine*	
	above all the *Appian lowland* itself	*along the Via Appia* before the Porta Capena
	Caelius	
	(Via Appia Coemeteria: Callisto, Sebastiano, Pretestato, Domitilla)	
North of the Caelius (Clementis, Nicomedis)		
	on both sides of the Via Lata/ Flaminia (Mars Field): later eccl. region 5; VIIth and partly IXth Aug. region (Priscilla and Bassilla catacombs)	Mars Field
		Rep. wall *between the Portae Collina and Esquilina*
Vicus Patricius/Cispius (Pudentis, Praxedis)		
		Subura

4. *Tituli concentrations*	(distances under 400 m) 5. **Contemporary literary notices**	6. *Evaluation*
Trastevere (Caeciliae, Chrysogoni, Callisti)	*Trastevere* (Hermas's piece of property on the Via Portuensis)	Trastevere: 5 positive perspectives
Aventine (Priscae, Sabinae)	In the district of the *Piscina Publica* Callistus's bank with deposits of Christians from *Aventine/*	Aventine: 3 positive perspectives 1 important negative perspective
	_ _ _ _ _ _ _ _ _ _ *Lesser Aventine/*	Lesser Aventine: 4 positive perspectives 1 important negative perspective
on both sides of the Via Appia before the Porta Capena (Fasciolae, Crescentianae)	_ _ _ _ _ _ _ _ _ _ *Appian lowland*	Via Appia before Porta Capena: 4 positive perspectives 1 unimportant negative perspective
		Caelius: 1 positive perspective
Clementis, Aemilianae, cf. Nicomedis		North of Caelius: 2 unimportant positive perspectives
		Mars Field: 2 important positive perspectives
Eccles. region 4; VIth Aug. Region (Gai, Cyriaci)		Eccles. region 4: 1 positive perspective Between Portae Collina and Esquilina: 1 positive perspective
Praxedis, Aequitii, cf. Pudentis		Vicus Patricius/Cispius: 2 unimportant positive perspectives Subura: 1 positive perspective

result for Christians — the Pomerium rule had relevance. The Roman synagogues in any event lay outside the Pomerium.[69]

But I do not wish to overemphasize the Pomerium rule. Vespasian already interpreted the sacral meaning of the Pomerium less narrowly than the old Romans before him. He downgraded the Pomerium to a sort of "customs border" in that he included a portion of the harbor area in the Pomerium limits (see n. 67). Hadrian, on the other hand, obviously had more respect for the sacral tradition; he had the auguries take part in his renewal of the Pomerium (n. 67).

b. The Tiber and the Via Appia, major traffic arteries, led travelers to Rome from the provinces, especially from the east. These arteries flowed into Trastevere and into the Appia/Porta Capena area, i.e., into the quarters most certainly inhabited by Christians in the first two centuries. Those coming from the eastern provinces on the Via Appia or on the Tiber into the world capital were naturally absorbed at first by these city quarters.[70] The location of early Christian living quarters on the fringes of the city, at the reception points of these two traffic arteries, illustrates once more that urban Roman Christians in the first two centuries in large measure were immigrants (cf. as examples in Part 4 Aquila, Hermas, Justin, Marcion, Valentinus, Tatian, Theodotus, Hippolytus, and many others).

c. The residential quarters Trastevere and Appia/Porta Capena are both lowlands between the hills of the city. This represents a further social-historical datum: the unhealthy, moist lowlands of the city were inhabited by the poorer masses of people (Argiletum-Subura, Velabrum, Forum Boarium). The hills like Pincio (= "collis hortulorum"!), Quirinal, Esquiline, and Caelius were favored by the rich in the imperial period. There were villas, and gardens abounded (especially on Pincio and Esquiline).[71] Martial[72] was enthusiastic about the air on the hills: there is where one should live. The thesis of a social descent — in the truest sense of the term — between the hills and the lowlands[73] will be further verified by the examination of our quarters.

---

69. Cf. M. Hengel, "Proseuche und Synagoge," in G. Jeremias et al., ed. *Tradition und Glaube*, Festschrift K. G. Kuhn (Göttingen, 1971), 177, n. 82. Cf. also the Proseuche before the gate of Philippi (Acts 16:13).

70. Cf. further the Via Portuensis, which led into Trastevere, and which came from the Trajanic harbor Porto. The Via Ostiensis from Ostia flowed into the quarters of the Aventine/Lesser Aventine, which above I also suspected of having Christian dwellings.

71. Cf., e.g., the horti of Lucullus on the Pincio, of Maecenas on the Esquiline; see also the enumeration in F. Castagnoli, *Topografia e urbanistica di Roma antica* (Bologna, 1969), 115.

72. E.g., 4.64; cf. 5.22.

73. Cf. Homo's (op. cit., 530–38) separation into "quartiers aristocratiques" and "quartiers populaires." Naturally this thesis does not contend that there were no tenement houses at all on the hill. There were some also there, and Martial lived in one on

d. If the Christians of the first century lived primarily in Trastevere, then Nero's persecution of Christians acquires a new aspect. Nero punished the Christians as arsonists of the conflagration of 64 c.e. (Tacitus, *Ann.* 15.38ff.). How was he able to present specifically them as "scapegoats"? Their "odium humani generis" (15.44) cannot have been the only trigger. What then?

Tacitus, *Ann.* 15.40: "Rome is divided into fourteen regions, among which only four remained intact. Three were burned to the ground, and of the other seven there were only a few houses left, which were severely damaged and half-burnt." Certainly Trastevere — on the *other bank* of the Tiber — was one of the four quarters spared.

Spared also were some perimeter quarters like the VIIth, Vth, and XIIth Regions.[74] That means that if Christians also lived on the Via Lata/Flaminia (VIIth Region), on Mars Field (Nero here erected emergency quarters for those who had been burned out, Tacitus, *Ann.* 15.39!), or somewhere outside the Porta Capena, then they got off relatively lightly!

Those who had saved their own skins and had watched the fiery spectacle from the safety of the other shore became easy targets for suspicion of having set the fire. For demagogic purposes this situation must have appeared ideal. And Nero, himself under suspicion in the rumors of the populace, had every reason to think up a believable diverting maneuver to direct the people's wrath away from himself.[75]

---

the Quirinal, fussing about the steps he had to climb (1.117, 108; cf. 9). The thesis asserts no black-and-white exclusivity, but tendencies. J. Carcopino (*Rom. Leben und Kultur in der Kaiserzeit* [Stuttgart, 1977]) postulates against this position, contending a "brotherly coexistence between upper classes and common people" (49). He concludes: Every attempt to attribute the fourteen districts of the city to particular social classes is impossible (50). A few anachronistic errors have crept into Carcopino's reasoning. According to him, the consul Licinius Sura, e.g., Trajan's trusted friend, was not too proud to live "on the plebian hill of the Aventine" (49). However, in the imperial time, the Aventine had long since changed from the Republican plebian hill into a distinguished neighborhood (see below). Something similar could be said about the allegedly "democratic Caelius" (50), for example.

74. Cf. Castagnoli, op. cit. (1969), 31f., on the extent of the fire in the city.

75. That Nero came upon the idea of maltreating the Christians as arsonists based on hints from the Jews is possible: *1 Clem.* 5:2ff. designates "jealousy and envy" as causing the Neronian persecution; especially the missionaries Peter and Paul were viewed jealously. By whom? In the first place by the Jews who were aware of their competition in the mission field. Two observations hint in this direction: (a) mission activity of urban Roman Jews is attested, e.g., by Cassius Dio 57.18.5a: Tiberius in 19 c.e. expelled the urban Roman Jews because they converted so many Romans. Cf. also Horace, *Sat.* 1.4.142f. (b) Tertullian (*Scorp.* 10) names the synagogues as "fontes persecutionum."

W. Rordorf tried to show that Christian apocalypticists in Nero's time had awaited an end of Rome in fire, and that this had come to the ears of the authorities and thus led them to suspect the Christians of the arson. The texts which are supposed to prove this apocalyptic expectation of the Christians of Rome in the first century come, however, only from the second century and predominantly from Asia Minor ("Die neronische Christenverfolgung im Spiegel der Apokryphen Paulusakten," *NTS* 28 [1981]: 365–74).

Chapter 4

Did Particular Strata of the Population Predominate in the Quarters under Investigation?

Literary sources and, above all, archaeological material are available for a short sketch.[1]

---

1. General literature, among others: G. Carettoni, A. M. Colini, L. Cozza, G. Gatta, *La Pianta marmorea di Roma antica: Forma Urbis Romae*, 2 vols. (Rome, 1960). Castagnoli, op. cit. (1969). Idem, "Roma nei versi di Marziale," *Athenaeum* 28 (1950): 67ff. F. Clementi, *Roma imperiale nelle XIV regioni augustee* (Rome, 1935). F. Coarelli, *Guida Archeologica di Roma* (Milan, 1974); (German edition: Freiburg/B., 1975; citations are according to the pagination of the German edition). Idem, *Roma. I grandi monumenti* (Verona, 1971). G. Cressedi, "I porti fluviali in Roma antica," *Rend. Pont. Acc.*, ser. 3/25–26 (1949–51): 53ff. L. Curtius and A. Nawrath, *Das antike Rom*, 5th ed. (Vienna, 1970). D. R. Dudley, *Urbs Roma: A Source Book of Classical Texts on the City and Its Monuments* (London, 1967). O. Gilbert, *Geschichte und Topographie der Stadt Rom im Altertum*, 3 vols. (Leipzig, 1883–90). P. Grimal, *Les jardins romains à la fin de la République et aux deux premiers siècles de l'Empire*, 2d ed. (Paris, 1969). Homo, op. cit. H. Jordan, *Forma Urbis Romae regionum XIV* (Berlin, 1874). H. Jordan and Chr. Huelsen, *Topographie der Stadt Rom im Altertum*, 1:1–3 and 2 (Berlin, 1871–1907; repr. Rome, 1970). H. Kiepert and Chr. Huelsen, *Formae Urbis Romae Antiquae*, 2d ed. (Berlin, 1912). R. Lanciani, *The Ruins and Excavations of Ancient Rome* (London, 1897) (statistical data). Idem, *Storia degli scavi di Roma* (Rome, 1902–12). Idem, *L'antica Roma* (Rome, repr. 1970). G. La Piana, "Foreign Groups in Rome during the First Centuries," *HTR* 20 (1927): 183ff. G. Lugli, *I monumenti antichi di Roma e suburbio*, 3 vols., Suppl. (Rome, 1930–40). Idem, *Roma antica: Il centro monumentale* (Rome, 1946, repr. 1968). Idem, *Fontes ad topographiam veteris Urbis Romae pertinentes*, 7 vols. (Rome, 1952–69). Idem, "La Roma di Domiziano nei versi di Marziale e di Stazio," *Studi romani* 9 (1961): 1–17. Idem, *Itinerario di Roma antica* (Rome, 1975). Idem, "Il valore topografico e giuridico dell'insula in Roma antica," *Rend. Pont. Acc.* 18 (1941/42), 191ff. Idem, *Nuove osservazioni sul valore topografico e catastale dell'insula in Roma antica, Rivista del Catasto* (1946). G. Marchetti-Longhi, "Il quartiere greco-orientale di Roma nell'Antichità e nel Medioevo," *Atti IV Congr. Naz. St. Romani*, I (Rome, 1938), 169ff. E. Nash, *A Pictorial Dictionary of Ancient Rome*, 2 vols., 2d ed. (London, 1968) (bibl.). A. North, "Libellus de regionibus Urbis," in *Acta Instituti Romani Regni Sueciae*, 3 (1949). S. B. Platner and T. Ashby, *A Topographical Dictionary of Ancient Rome* (Oxford, 1929; repr. Rome, 1965). J. Rykwert, *The Idea of a Town: The Anthropology of Urban Form in Rome, Italy and the Ancient World* (Princeton, 1977). H. Stützer, *Das alte Rom* (Stuttgart, 1971). C. L. Urlichs, *Codex urbis Romae topographicus* (Würzburg, 1871). R. Valentini and G. Zucchetti, *Codice topografico della città di Roma*, 4 vols. (Rome, 1940–53). M. J. Vermaseren, *De Mithrasdienst in Rome* (Nijmegen, 1951). A. Wotschitzky, "Hochhäuser im antiken Rom," *Natalicium C. Jax, 1, Innsbrucker*

48

Trastevere[2]

The XIVth Augustan Region included the Tiber island and the quarters on the right bank of the Tiber: the hills of the Vatican and Gianicolo, as well as the actual Trastevere in the plain. Only this central region in the plain on the bend of the Tiber (ca. 1.3 million m²) was really settled. Vatican, Gianicolo, and the Gardens of Caesar in the south, in total about 2.7 million m², were not incorporated into Region XIV before Septimus Severus.[3]

These expansions were parklike lands decorated with a few villas. On the Ager Vaticanus — the wine that grew there was awful as Martial (1.18) laments — the Horti of Domitia and Agrippina stood out. The remains of the Agrippina Villa, it is believed, were excavated in 1959 under the Hospital S. Spirito. The most ancient building parts date from the beginning of the first century B.C.E. To the magnificent appointments belong the neo-Attic marble basin decorated with marine life in the Thermal Baths Museum as well as the colorful mosaic floors. Also the Circus of Caligula that Nero completed seems to have belonged at first to the Villa Agrippina. In the time of the empire, most of the great villas of the Vatican were in imperial hands.

On the Gianicol there were beautiful gardens. Martial (12.57.18–25; cf. 4.64) enthuses about the quiet and the luxury of the villa of Sparsus on the Gianicolo.

To the south followed the Gardens of Caesar[4] with the Naumachia Augusti (where mock sea battles were presented).

Beitr. z. Kulturwissenschaft, 3 (1955): 151ff. Idem, *Das antike Rom* (Innsbruck, 1950). Maps, among others, A. P. Frutaz, *Le piante di Roma* (Rome, 1962).

2. Literature: S. M. Savage, "The Cults of Ancient Trastevere," *Memoires of the American Academy in Rome* 17 (1940): 26ff. P. Gauckler, *Le sanctuaire syrien du Janicule* (Paris, 1912). B. M. Felletti Maj, "Il santuario della triade eliopolitana e dei misteri al Gianicolo," *Bullettino Comunale* 75 (1953–55): 137ff. V. v. Graeve, "Tempel und Kult der syrischen Götter am Janiculum," *Jb. des Deutsch. Archäol. Inst.* 87 (1972): 314ff. F. Cumont, *Les religions orientales dans le paganisme romain* (Paris, 1929), 98 and 251, n. 11. Homo, op. cit., esp. 537, 107f., 113. F. Castagnoli, *Roma antica: Topografia e Urbanistica di Roma* (Bologna, 1958), 47ff. Platner and Ashby, op. cit., "Transtiberim"; "Regiones Quattuordecim." Jordan and Huelsen, op. cit., 1, third section, 628ff. Coarelli, op. cit. (1975), 309–24, with archaeological map; cf. also the map appendix in Kiepert and Huelsen, op. cit.

Especially on the Vatican: G. Lugli, "Il Vaticano nell'età classica," in G. Fallarini and M. Escobar, *Vaticano* (Florence, 1946), 1ff. C. Buzzetti, "Nota sulla Topografia dell'Ager Vaticanus," *Quaderni dell'Istituto di Topografia Antica* 5 (1968): 105ff.

The Tiber Isle: M. Besnier, *L'île Tibérine dans l'antiquité* (Paris, 1901). J. Le Gall, *Recherches sur le culte du Tibre* (Paris, 1953). M. Guarducci, "L'Isola Tiberina e la sua tradizione ospitaliera," *Rendiconti morali dell'Accademia dei Lincei* 26 (1971): 267ff.

3. Cf. Homo, op. cit., 98, 106–8.

4. Between the Tiber, the first milestone of the Via Portuensis and the Monteverde slopes.

In addition to the suburban villas on the slopes of the hills, there were a few villas directly on the bank of the Tiber (but still outside the densely settled quarter on the bend of the Tiber).

From a "bird's-eye view," the right bank of the Tiber would have looked like a parklike green belt drawn in a semi-circle around a densely populated plain. The plain on the bend of the Tiber, the actual Trastevere, interests us here since there is no trace of any reference to Christians in the villas of the green belt. Correspondingly, all three of the latter trans-Tiber Tituli lie close to each other in the heavily populated quarter of Trastevere.

City Quarter of the Lowest Strata of the Population

A fragment of the Severian marble city plan shows a piece of the Via Campana-Portuensis; it is bordered by large warehouses.[5] Trastevere was a harbor quarter, a workers quarter. It accommodated harbor workers, who unloaded the ships' cargoes, porters of the many warehouses, sailors, and also workers from the brickyards on the Vatican slopes. Many brick-stamps that lie before our feet in the catacombs were pressed in the Vatican brickworks.

Shopkeepers and small craftsmen were drawn by the harbor and its imported goods — ivory carvers, cabinet makers, and potters.[6] Millers from Trastevere ground the imported grains unloaded in the harbor. The mills were along the Tiber[7] and on the east slope of the Gianicolo above the trans-Tiber plain, where they were driven by the water of the Aqua Traiana.[8]

Knacker and tanner operations spread a penetrating odor: The "dog's skin that hangs in Trastevere" stank pervasively (Martial 6.93). The Coraria Septiminiana, a leather factory of the XIVth Region, is thought to have been uncovered beneath S. Caecilia. In the floor of a large room were found seven cylindrically formed, brick-walled basins that seem to have been used for tanning leather. Where the *corarii* (tanners) practiced their industry was the worst living quarter one can imagine. The tanners worked with urine from the public conveniences; the stench hung over the quarter. Martial was disgusted by the Roman tanner who kissed him all over to welcome him back from a trip (12.59).

Trade, industry, transport — the common people of Trastevere lived from them, whether free or slave. Martial (1.41) typifies the inhabi-

---

5. Cf. the map in Coarelli, op. cit. (1975), 309, which reproduces this part of the marble city plan. The warehouses lay across from the Porticus Aemilia.

6. Cf. Coarelli, 1975, 310.

7. Cf. ibid.

8. Cf. the map in Jordan, *Forma Urbis* (1874), as well as Platner and Ashby, "Molinae."

tant of the quarter as a buffoon, exchanging glass sherds for sulphured filaments.

Trastevere was extremely densely populated. In an official inscription of Hadrian from the year 136 C.E. (*CIL* 6:975), there are twenty-two vici listed for Trastevere (Region XIV), while, for other regions (I, X, XII, XIII), only 9, 6, 12, or 17 vici, respectively, are noted.[9] Projected over the surface of the regions,[10] we have these results:

Region
I   1.32 million m², i.e., per vicus there were 146,667 m² available
X   0.24   40,000
XII   0.74   61,667
XIII   1.12   65,882
XIV   1.30   59,091

Region X, the palace quarter Palatine, must be left aside as a special case. We see then that in Trastevere the least space was available for a vicus.

What does that mean? "Vicus," when as here it means "small city district," was an administrative unit directed by four vici magistri and four servi publici. At a crossroads (*compitum*), each vicus had one shrine for Lares, protective deities, at its center (Pliny, *Nat. hist.* 3.66). These administrative units were not defined by a certain surface area they covered,[11] but rather — if their demarcation was not to be wholly arbitrary — by a certain number of inhabitants. The ratio of size of region (in m² to number of vici indicates how densely the inhabitants lived.[12]

---

9. Cf. also Pliny, *Nat. hist.* 3.66, who reports in connection with the Vespasian census of the year 73 that Rome had in toto 265 vici. On average, then, each of the fourteen regions encompassed 18.93 vici. Also, by this comparison, Trastevere had more than the average. "Vicus" here means "city district," not "street."

10. The square-meter counts for the regions provided by Homo (op. cit., 100) serve as a basis here. From the 4 million m² of Trastevere, the 2.7 million m² of the green belt are to be subtracted, which were incorporated into Region XIV first under Septimius Severus.

11. The numbers of the Regionaria of the fourth century (Notitia and Curiosum) exhibit wholly differing counts of vici for the fourteen regions, which in no way correspond to the surface areas of the individual regions. E.g., Region V (2.13 million m²) as well as Region VII (1.45 million m²) each number 15 vici; whereas Region VIII with only 0.26 million m² contains 34 vici. See the statistical data of the Regionaria in Homo (op. cit., 115, table).

12. This methodological principle can be found in the following way. Occasionally "vicus" is defined as a city district which has "a certain number of dwellings" (e.g., *Harper's Dictionary of Classical Literature and Antiquities*, ed. H. T. Peck [New York, 1962], 1659). The Regionaria statistics (see below) refute the notion, however, that those defining the boundaries of a vicus had a certain number of dwellings in mind. Regions I and V, e.g., both show on average 12 *domus* per vicus, but they differed sharply from each other in the numbers of street entrances to *insulae* per vicus, which are indicative of the numbers of dwellings (Region I on average had 325; Region V only 257). If neither a certain number of dwellings nor a certain size of surface area (see above) defined a vicus, then what

The smaller the surface area for the vicus, the more tightly the inhabitants were packed in together, and the more reason there is for regarding
their social status as lower. Trastevere stands, as the Hadrianic statistic
shows, in last place.[13]

The next available statistical data come from the fourth century, from
the Regionaria Notitia and Curiosum (ed. Urlichs).[14] Trastevere has
grown from 22 vici to 78. The region thus exhibits the most vici of the
city. The dimension of the growth reveals itself completely if we compare the remaining regions more closely. In second place lies the IXth
Region with merely 35 vici, which does not even correspond to half of
the Trastevere number. Of course, the green belt has in the meanwhile
been incorporated into the XIVth Region, and the statistic of the fourth
century therefore adds to the Trastevere region the ca. 2.7 mil. m^2 of the
Villa green belt. A part of the increased number of vici may thus simply
result from the surface expansion. But even if we reckon the 78 vici on
ca. 4 mil. m^2, we acquire per vicus only 51,282 m^2. That is about 8000
m^2 *less* than in the Hadrianic period, and that despite the addition of
the thinly settled Villa green belt. The findings yield the conclusion that,
in the quarter on the bend of the Tiber, the inhabitants are even more
tightly crammed together — a development that had set in considerably
after Hadrian in the second century but actually had existed since the
end of the Republic.

A further sociohistorical datum is supplied by the statements of the
Regionaria concerning the number of the *domus* and *insulae*. Trastevere
in the fourth century numbered 150 domus and 4,405 insulae.[15] If we
set the two absolute numbers again in relation to the surface of 4 mil.
m^2, we obtain the result that there was per hectare merely 0.38 domus.
By comparison, the other regions:

---

did? There is something to be said for contending that a certain *number of inhabitants* established the boundaries of a vicus. Each vicus was administered by 4 vici magistri and 4
servi publici (*ILS* 6073; *CIL* 6:35; 445f.). It would be difficult to understand why a vicus
A with more inhabitants than a vicus B would have had the *same* number of vici magistri
and servi publici, especially since these officials were instrumental in the distribution of
grain (on this, see, e.g., H. Volkmann, "Vici magister," *KlPauly* 5:1256)! The vici magistri
in vicus A would have been overworked in comparison to their colleagues in vicus B. The
population of Rome can only be approximated; it is often estimated at about one million
(e.g., Alföldy [2d ed., 1979], 86). If we divide the ca. one million by 265 vici (cf. Pliny,
Nat. hist. 3.66), we get something like 3800–4000 inhabitants per vicus, so that every vici
magister was responsible for almost 1000 people. If the vici each hosted approximately the
same number of people, then it is clear that the less area on average there was available
for a vicus in one region, the more densely the people of this region lived.

13. The count for Region I (146,667 m^2 per vicus, 2 1/2 times as much as in Trastevere) results from the fact that the southern part of the region was half rural: gardens,
villas, graves.

14. C. L. Urlichs, *Codex urbis Romae topographicus* (Würzburg, 1871). The numeri-
cal data are tabulated in Homo, op. cit., 116.

15. Cf. the tables in Homo, op. cit., 541, 638f.

I	1.32 mil. m²	120 domus:	0.90 per hectare
II	0.67	127	1.89
III	0.58	160	2.76
IV	0.70	98	1.40
V	2.13	180	0.85
VI	2.25	146	0.65
VII	1.45	120	0.83
VIII	0.26	130	5.00
IX	2.01	140	0.70
X	0.24	89	3.70
XI	0.36	88	2.44
XII	0.74	113	1.53
XIII	1.12	130	1.16

As was to be expected, Forum Romanum (Region VIII) and Palatine (Region X) lead the scale with 5 and 3.7 domus per hectare, respectively. Trastevere takes last place! The domus inhabited by those who were socially successful were here by far the most thinly sown.

The mass of the *insulae,* the rental dwellings, along with the business buildings, dominate the picture: with 4,405 insulae, Trastevere led the scale of the fourteen regions; the next largest number is offered by Region V with only 3,850 insulae.[16] An example still known to us is the several-storied tenement house Bolani north of S. Caecilia in Trastevere (*CIL* 6:67). Unfortunately, in 1763, upon the discovery of the inscription, only the courtyard with a fountain was excavated.

Let us observe the ratio of the vici to the insulae and domus. Under the presupposition that the vici of Rome each represent more or less the same number of inhabitants (see above), it may be asked how much living space in each case was available to the population unit "vicus." From the statistics of the regions we find that the XIVth Region, Trastevere, numbered per vicus 56.47 insulae and 1.92 domus. Both numbers are once more the tail end of the list of statistics; in all other regions there was more living space available to the people of a vicus.

---

16. Region I: 3,250 insulae; II: 3,600; III: 2,757; IV: 2,757; V: 3,850; VI: 3,403; VII: 3,805; VIII: 3,480; IX: 2,777; X: 2,742 (Not. 2,643); XI: 2,600 (Cur. 2,500); XII: 2,487; XIII: 2,487; XIV: 4,405. On the difficulty of defining "insula," see Homo, op. cit., 643–49. The tenement houses were often not clearly delineated from each other but rather were structurally interlocked into each other. The Regionaria therefore probably did not register the tenement houses themselves, but they enumerated their street entrances (evidence in Homo, op. cit., 649), so that *partes insulae* with their own entrances and stairs went into the statistics as "insulae." A conversion of the absolute numbers into figures per hectare (as with the domus) can be omitted for that reason. The picture would be distorted. Quarters with more fashionable rental houses with their own separate entrances to each of their apartments might well end up with more "insulae" per hectare than poorer quarters, where several families might well have shared the same entrance.

Region	domus	insulae	vivi	domus per vicus	insulae per vicus
I	120	3,250	10	12	325
II	127	3,600	7	18	514
III	160	2,757	12	13.3	230
IV	98	2,757	8	12.3	345
V	180	3,850	15	12	257
VI	146	3,403	17	8.6	200
VII	120	3,805	15	8	254
VIII	130	3,480	34	3.8	102
IX	140	2,777	35	4	79
X	89	2,742 (2,643 Not.)	20	4.5	137 (132)
XI	88	2,600 (2,500 Cur.)	20 (21)	4.4 (4.2)	130 (119)
XII	113	2,487	17	6.7	146
XIII	130	2,487	18 (17 Not.)	7.2 (7.7)	138 (146)
XIV	150	4,405	78	1.9	56

How were the individual city quarters provided with food? This, too, gives information on the social standards of the quarters. The Regionaria provide a statistic concerning the distribution of bakeries in the city. In Trastevere there were 24 bakeries, which is 0.06 bakeries per hectare, by which Trastevere again formed the tail end of the fourteen regions.[17]

Reg. I	1.32 mil. m²	20 bakeries	0.15 per hectare
II	0.67	15	0.22
III	0.58	16	0.28
IV	0.70	15	0.21
V	2.13	15	0.07
VI	2.25	16	0.07
VII	1.45	16 (15)	0.11 (0.1)
VIII	0.26	20	0.77
IX	2.01	20	0.10
X	0.24	20	0.83
XI	0.36	16	0.44
XII	0.74	25 (20)	0.34 (0.27)
XIII	1.12	25 (24)	0.22 (0.21)
XIV	4.00	24	0.06

17. The statistics show that the peripheral regions (V, VI, VII, IX, XIV, I) were least richly supplied with bakeries. Bakeries were most numerous in the central quarters (VII, X, XI). That is partially explainable by the fact that the peripheral regions contained large green areas and so were more thinly settled. But even if one subtracts the green belt in Trastevere and only considers the thinly settled area on the Tiber bend (ca. 1.3 mil. m²), there remains the thin ratio of 0.18 bakery per hectare. This number is undercut only by the most thinly settled green regions, like Esquiline and Pincio, of the Regions I, V, VI, VII, IX, which could not by far match the thick population on the bend of the Tiber.

High Proportion of People from the East:
Eastern Cults

As an area that until Aurelian lay in large measure outside the Pomerium, Trastevere offered itself to foreign cults. In Trastevere we meet in addition to Jews and Christians a plethora of eastern cultic activity: holy places of Dea Syria, of Hadad, of Sol of Palmyra, and, on the Vatican, cultic places of Cybele and of Isis. The temple of Isis was found in the vicinity of the façade of St. Peter's Cathedral.[18]

Let us look more closely at the cultic places of the Syrian deities excavated in 1906 on the south slope of the Gianicolo. A Greek inscription shows that the place was originally dedicated to Zeus Keraunios and the Furrinian nymphs. The old cult was gradually displaced by that of the Syrian deities — already in the first century C.E., as a few inscriptions and the most ancient parts of the building indicate. The temple was renovated in the time of Marcus Aurelius by a Syrian merchant called Marcus Antonius Gaionas. His epitaph and other inscriptions tell about him. The third period of building on the temple dates to the fourth century.

In the basilica of this sanctuary the statue was found of the most important deity honored here; it is that of *Hadad*, the highest of the three deities of Heliopolis, sitting on a throne like Jupiter. At his side *Atargatis* (= Dea Syria) and *Simios* were venerated. In the room across from them on the east side of the sanctuary were found an Egyptian basalt statue (probably Osiris) and a Bacchus with gilded hands and face.[19] In the middle of this east room a triangular altar contained strange findings: some eggs and an Adonis statuette that was wrapped about by a snake. The deity buried in the altar, the eggs (= life), and the seven windings of the snake (= the seven arches of heaven) point to the death and rebirth of the deity. Here obviously in this secluded hall the deity let the cultic initiate take part in his own death-resurrection fate. If a Roman Christian in Trastevere read the passage Romans 6:4f., did he or she associate it with the practices of the Syrian cultic initiate next door?

---

18. The non-eastern sanctuaries are mostly of older, Republican dates, e.g., Dea Dia (on the Via Campana); Fors Fortuna (at the first milestone of the Via Portuensis); Furrina (in the environs of the Villa Sciarra); Fons (on the location of the Ministero della Pubblica Istruzione); in addition cf. between Piazza Nievo and the Trastevere train station on the Viale Trastevere the sanctuary of Hercules Cubans (with portraits of charioteers). On the Tiber isle, cf. the Greek Asclepius; Faunus; Veiovis; Iuppiter Iurarius; the Sabian Semo Sancus; Bellona Insulensis. Bibl.: G. La Piana, "Foreign Groups in Rome during the First Centuries of the Empire," *HTR* 20 (1927): 183–403, here esp. 219f., remains informative.

19. All of the sculptures of the room predate the fourth century, having been taken over from the earlier phases of the temple's history.

The Quarter on the Tractus Urbanus
of the Via Appia[20]

The zone that stretches on both sides of the Via Appia from the Porta
Capena to the River Almone is, like the lowlands of the Subura and
of the Velabrum, a densely populated quarter — in contrast to the
quiet villa hills Caelius and Aventine that border the moist Appian
lowland.

In the Appian valley the stream of traffic pulsates. The local Jews
asked those traveling through for charitable donations, mocks Juvenal (3.12ff.). The typical Roman Jew was one who was pushed by his
mother to go begging (Martial 12.57). The Christians of the quarter
could hardly have lifted themselves much above that social level; the
quarter was populated by traders, craftsmen, and transport workers.
Here lay the Area Carruces,[21] where trading goods were unloaded off
the carts. All around the area those who lived from transportation work
had settled. Hauling with carts was night work in Rome since Caesar,
in the *Lex Julia,* had forbidden vehicular traffic within the city from
sunup to sundown. The poets moan about the nightly rumble (Martial
4.64; Juvenal 3.236ff.). Just how low the social standing of transport
workers, muleteers, and porters was is shown in the fact that almost no
grave inscription in *CIL* 6 mentions their professions.[22] Several crafts
of the region, making glass, working with wool and textiles, are indicated by topographical names such as Vicus Vitrarius, Area Pannaria,
and Campus Lanatarius.[23]

At least in its northern reaches in front of the Porta Capena, this
quarter was densely built up, as a fragment of the Severian marble
city plan shows.[24] The fragment portrays a part of the neighborhood in
which Jews also dwelt (as noted above, they lived near the Fons Camenarum). The dense settlement is further indicated by *four* cross-streets,[25]
which in this area branched off from the Appia and led through the
lowland up onto the Caelius slope, where they first reached the barracks

---

20. Bibliography: A. M. Colini, F. Castagnoli, G. Macchia, *Via Appia* (Rome, 1973);
R. Vielliard, *Recherches sur les origenes de la Rome chrétienne* (Macon, 1941), 40f.;
Coarelli, op. cit. (1975), 325–36, 301–4; Homo et al., op. cit., 116f., 119–21, 124, 562.
On the Porta Capena, cf. Martial 3.47; Juvenal 3.11; Ovid, *Fast.* 6.19.

21. See Platner and Ashby.

22. On the epigraphical findings: Huttunen, *Social Strata,* 120f., 124f., 189.

23. Cf. Vielliard, op. cit. (1941), 40f., and see also the vicus Fabrici in the northern
corner of Region I (map in Jordan, *Forma Urbis*). On the social standing of craftsmen, see
below in detail, Part 4.

24. Depicted in the appendix map in F. Castagnoli, *Topografia e urbanistica di Roma
antica,* Istituto di Studi Romani (Bologna, 1969).

25. Vicus Honoris et Virtutis (named after the temple of the same name there), Vicus
Cyclopis, Vicus Camenarum, Vicus Drusianus.

of the Perigrini and of the Fifth Cohort of the Vigiles, the Neronian slaughterhouse as well as the lupanaria, the brothels. On the Vicus Sulpicius Citerior, the fifth cross-street north of the Appia, lay the Mutatorium Caesaris;[26] there the carriages of the imperial court paused, whereas the private wagons thronged on the Area Carruces, not being permitted to travel inside the city during the day.[27]

We remain in the northern part of the quarter. South of the Via Appia, since the beginning of the third century C.E., stood the gigantic thermal baths of Caracalla, in which 1500 people could bathe simultaneously; numerous additional visitors could use the other features of the facility (Palaistra, Mithraeum, library, etc.) at the same time.[28] Until the construction of Diocletian's thermal baths, it was the largest bathing facility in Rome. Despite its luxury, no one was fooled into thinking that it was anything but a bathing establishment for the masses, in which a common man could rub his back for free[29] on the marble of the caldarium.[30] The ordinary people were bathing and participating in the imperial dedication celebration for the facility (*Hist. Aug. Elag.* 17.9). Aristocratic families stuck up their noses at the idea of visiting the Caracalla thermal baths![31] The luxury of the building in no way contradicts the described sociohistorical character of the Appian lowland.

There were exceptions, however, to this general character. For the construction of the Caracalla thermal baths, several houses had to be torn down. One on the edge of the hill of the Lesser Aventine, which was excavated in 1858 and again in 1970 in the Vigna Guidi, exhibits a rich use of mosaics, paintings, and sculptures; fragments of a magnificent ceiling painting date from the Hadrianic period.

The farther we climb out of the Appian lowland up the hill of the Lesser Aventine (Region XII), the more "elegant" things come into view.[32] Among the residences mentioned in ancient literature, the Domus Cilonis, which was given to the City Prefect and Consul L. Fabius Cilo by Septimius Severus, is archaeologically verified. In the titulus church

---

26. See map in Jordan, *Forma Urbis*. Jordan and Huelsen, 1, Section 3:205, however, maintain that it lay closer to the Porta Capena.

27. That in Jordan and Huelsen, ibid., 200, the Appian valley is designated as "little inhabited" is not convincing (also in view of the numbers of domus and insulae; see above); Huelsen, ibid., 209, himself admits that between Porta Capena and Vicus Sulpicius no graves are found.

28. Cf. E. Brödner, *Untersuchungen an den Caracallathermen* (Berlin, 1951).

29. Cf. Cassius Dio 54.29.4.

30. Cf. the pleasant scene in *Hist. Aug. Hadr.* 17.

31. Cf. Platner and Ashby, "Thermae Antonini"; Coarelli, op. cit. (1975), 296.

32. Why Coarelli, op. cit. (1975), 296, generalizes about Region XII as not only "thickly settled" but also as "simple" is not clear. The statistics of Hadrian from 136 C.E. (*CIL* 6:975) reflect a little larger surface area for the individual vicus than in Trastevere. Region XII had offered on its ca. 740,000 m² twelve vici, i.e., there were 61,667 m² available per vicus. There were fewer in Region XIV (59,091 m²).

S. Balbina, parts of this house are preserved, and in the convent next to it (Ospizio di S. Margherita) wall remnants of Hadrianic opus mistum still exist.[33] Southwest of S. Saba lay the private Domus Hadriani, where Hadrian lived before his accession to office.[34]

We then follow the Appian Way southward. The density of the settlement becomes less. Homo (pp. 116f.) suggests that of the ten vici numbered in the Regionaria for the Augustan Region I, at least eight lay in the northern part (each with about 80,000 m²), and at most two lay in the southern part of the Region (each with about 350,000 m²). Up to the River Almone, the area took on a half-rural character with gardens and graves.[35]

Besides cultic places of Mithras and Bona Dea Subsaxana as well as a small sanctuary to Hercules, which was frequented heavily (Martial 3.47), the presence of disciples of Cybele in our quarter is interesting. They regularly washed their Cybele statue and their sacrificial knife in the Almone River (Martial, ibid.).

The Aventine Hill (Region XIII)[36]

"Hill of Aristocrats"

"You hurry up the hill of Diana (= Aventine: Temple of Diana), at the threshold of the great men your sweaty toga fans you..." (Martial

33. Cf. also in the vicinity the Domus Parthorum Septem (Platner and Ashby, s.v.), which Septimius Severus placed at the disposal of his friends.

34. Cf. Platner and Ashby, "Privata domus Hadriani." In addition cf. here the domus of Cornificia, a close relative of Marcus Aurelius (Platner and Ashby, s.v.); a cohort barracks of the Vigiles (north of S. Saba) as well as northeast from there the temple of the Bona Dea Subsaxana (further see Homo, op cit., 549, 534).

35. This explains that the statistics of Hadrian from 136 C.E. note for Region I an unusually large average surface of 146,667 m² per vicus; nine were spread over the 1.32 mil. m² of Region I. The high average was due to the half-rural character of the south of the region. On the other numbers of Region I, see the tables above. The high quantity of two bakeries per vicus (surpassed only by Region II with 2.14 per vicus) is, in my opinion, to be attributed to the through traffic of the Appia.

36. Literature: A. M. Colini, "La scoperta del santuario di Giove Dolicheno," *Bullettino Com.* 63 (1935): 145ff.; Coarelli, op. cit. (1975), 295–308, map 293; F. M. D. Darsy, *Recherches archéologiques à Sainte-Sabine sur l'Aventin* (Vatican, 1968); Homo, op. cit., esp. 119, 533f., 549, 553, 576f.; G. Gatti, "L'arginatura del Tevere a Marmorata," *Bullettino Com.* 64 (1936): 55ff.; idem, "Saepta Iulia e Porticus Aemilia nella Forma severiana," *Bullettino Com.* 62 (1934): 123ff.; G. Lugli, *I monumenti antichi di Roma e suburbio* (Rome, 1938), 3:548–94; A. Merlin, *L'Aventin dans l'antiquité* (Paris, 1906); Platner and Ashby, op. cit., "Aventinus Mons"; E. Rodriguez Almeida, "Novedades de epigrafia anforaria del Monte Testaccio," in P. Baldacci et al., *Recherches sur les amphores romaines* (Rome, 1972); M. J. Vermaseren and C. C. van Essen, *The Excavations in the Mithraeum of the Church of Santa Prisca in Rome* (Leiden, 1965); Vielliard, op. cit. (1941), 41–43. Cf. also Livy 3.31f.

12.18.3). But the Aventine hill was not always a living area for Roman aristocracy. During the Republican period, the lower classes and foreigners[37] lived here in a densely built-up quarter of residences and businesses. With the advent of the emperors, a radical change took place: the Palatine was reserved for the emperor, so the aristocracy, displaced from there, moved to the Aventine, Quirinal, and Caelius hills. When the city burned in 36 C.E. (Tacitus, *Ann.* 6.45; Suetonius, *Cal.* 16) and 64 C.E. (Tacitus, *Ann.* 15.41), space for luxurious houses was created on the Aventine; the poorer population was displaced to the foot of the hill into the moist plains of Monte Testaccio, of the Velabrum and the Appia, as well as across the Tiber to Trastevere.

The address list of the Aventine reads like a "Who's Who in the Empire." Here lived Trajan before his accession to office; his friend L. Licinius Sura, the three-time consul and famous attorney, who was able from his window "to observe at close quarters the battles in the Circus Maximus" (Martial 6.64); Emperor Vitellius; in the vicinity of the Sabina Titulus the Prefect Sex. Cornelius Repentinus; the Consul M. Valerius Bradua Mauricus (191 C.E.); in the vicinity of the Prisca-Titulus the Legate of the Seventh Legion C. Marius Pudens Cornelianus (about 225); the Consul C. Suetrius Sabinus (under Septimus Severus), etc.[38] Later, the Christian friends of Jerome, Albina and Marcella, lived here, a mother and daughter from the highest nobility, who set up in their house the first convent of the city.

There are beautiful archaeological examples. Whoever views the excavations at the titulus church S. Sabinae will almost want to believe the legend about the founding of the title (see above, chap. 1). Under the church, residences with magnificent marble floors from the beginning of the imperial period were discovered; parts of them can be seen today through gratings in the flooring of the church. Also on the north side of the church, on the Republican wall, private houses with mosaic floors were excavated (the oldest from the second century B.C.E.). Under S. Prisca, two domus were found. In the one, in ca. 110 C.E., a large Nymphaeum with an apse was set up. The other, with a portico, dates from the end of the first century C.E. and was possibly inhabited by Trajan's friend Licinius Sura. Adjacent to this villa, the Surnae thermal baths, named for him, were built in Trajan's time as the first public baths

---

37. On the plebeian Aventine of the Republic, see Homo, op. cit., 586, 533; Coarelli, op. cit. (1975), 295f.; R. Gross, "Aventinus," *KlPauly* 1:786. Still in the time of Seian, at the beginning of the imperial period, one could speak of "improbae comitiae" in respect to the Aventine: *CIL* 6:10213.

38. Cf. further in Homo, op. cit., 534; Coarelli, op. cit. (1975), 296; Platner and Ashby, op. cit., s.v.

of the Aventine.[39] Private structures were probably built onto this public building, *tabernae cum cenaculis,* which offered the common person a residential possibility.[40]

Poorer Population

On the Aventine also poorer strata of population resided. They were, however, less dominant than in the other regions. According to the Hadrianic statistics of 136 c.e. (*CIL* 6:975) there was in Region XIII the relatively large surface of 65,882 m² available per vicus, which signified a less dense population than in the other regions in comparison.[41] The Regionaria of the fourth century still look similarly favorable: they number only 22 insulae per hectare. A lower statistic is to be found only in the garden regions V (18 insulae) and VI (15 insulae) as well as on Mars Field (Region IX; 13.8 insulae), which was equipped with numerous public buildings.[42] The ratio of domus to insulae is, on the Aventine, 1:19.13 (1 domus to 19.13 insulae); only in one single region can a more favorable ratio be found (Region III).[43] That the Aventine had a smaller portion of poorer people by comparison with other regions is finally indicated by the fact that, as far as we can see, it was the sole region that in the time from 136 c.e. to the fourth century did not grow. The Hadrianic inscription numbers 17 vici on the Aventine; the Regionaria catalogue Notitia notes no more.[44]

We are informed about slaves on the Aventine by some neck-collar inscriptions.[45] Some slaves worked at the thermal baths; some, together with other common people of the hill, may have worked in the harbor that lies adjacent to the southwest (Emporium, Porticus Aemilia) and in the granaries and storehouses (Horrea) of the Testaccio plain. Already in the days of the Republic the center of large-scale trade had shifted from the Forum Boarium to the fluvial plain below (southwest) the Aventine

---

39. Cf. Cassius Dio 68.15 and the Severian marble city plan.

40. Other public buildings on the hill, among others: the temples of Diana, of Minerva, of Juno Regina, and of Jupiter Liber.

41. See the numbers in the section on Trastevere, above. Only Region I surpassed the Aventine in this respect. Its higher statistic results from the half-rural southern part of the region.

42. See the statistics above, but also, in n. 16, the limitation.

43. There there were merely 17.23 insulae to one domus (106 domus, 2,757 insulae). Cf. in contrast Region VII: 1 to 31.7 (120 domus, 3,805 insulae).

44. The Curiousum, however, numbers 18 vici. By comparison, only Region I had approximately as little growth; in the year 136 c.e. it numbered 9, in the fourth century 10 vici.

45. Cf. *Dictionnaire d'Archéologie chrétienne et de Liturgie,* ed. Cabrol and Leclercq, 3/2, "Colliers d'esclaves," 2142 and 2146: Slaves of the Aventine "ad mappa aurea" and "ad decianas" (Decius thermal baths).

hill. To Travertine stones of the Emporium, a 500-meter-long quay, ships were moored and the cargo unloaded over steps and ramps. Behind the quay rose the Porticus Aemelia,[46] in which incoming wares were stored. In the imperial period the whole Testaccio plain was gradually built up with storehouses.[47] The large part of the urban Roman Horrea (at the end of the imperial period there were almost 300) were to be found here in this main business quarter. Here stood the grain silos. Here marble was traded, for which reason the area is still today called "Marmorata." In the Porticus Aemilia one met the grocery wholesalers. On the Forum Pistorium bread was sold. The sherds of the broken freight containers, the amphora, were heaped together. Thus arose over the years the unique sherd mount, the Monte Testaccio.

The Eastern Cults on the Aventinus Mons

On the hill that Claudius first included in the Pomerium, the conquered foreign cults had been established in the time of the Republic.[48] In the time of the empire, eastern cults flourished here, but fewer than in the lower class Trastevere. These are the main examples: (a) The cult of Jupiter Dolichenus came from northern Syria. The remains of the Dolocenum (from the second century C.E.) were found in the vicinity of S. Alessio and S. Sabina. The numerous artifacts are today displayed in the hall of the Culti Orientali of the Capitoline Museum. The statues, reliefs, and inscriptions reveal syncretism: Isis, Serapis, Mithras, Sol, Luna — the cult includes them all. (b) North of S. Sabina at the Republican wall, rooms were excavated which in the second century C.E. had been restored and used by a community of Isis; paintings and graffiti demonstrate this. (c) At the end of the second century C.E., in one of the two domus under S. Prisca, a Mithraeum was set up. As terminus ante quem we have the date 21 November 202. An inscription dated to that day was scratched by a Mithras devotee to the left of the large back wall niche. The Mithraeum was magnificently decorated with paintings and stucco figures.[49] Around 400 C.E. Christians apparently destroyed the sanctuary; in the frescoes we see the willful demolition.

---

46. Cf. the Severian marble city plan. Remains are extant between Via Marmorata and Via Franklin.

47. Cf., e.g., the Horrea Galbana (on the marble plan behind the Porticus Aemilia several walls were found), the Horrea Lolliana, Aniciana, Seiana, Fabaria, Sempronia.

48. Cf. Coarelli, op. cit. (1975), 295f., 285.

49. Cf., among others, the stucco head of Serapis in the little museum that is set up in the former Nymphaeum of the domus.

Campus Martius (Mars Field, Regions IX and VII)[50]

The Via Lata / Flaminia divides Mars Field into the western Region IX and the eastern Region VII. The Campus was successively developed and built up from the south to the north, the northern part only from the time of Hadrian.

Public Buildings

The Campus is furnished with monumental state and representational architecture, so that "this place [counts] as the most worthy of all"; artworks are displayed all about it, and the plants remain green all year round (Strabo 5.236). The numerous excavations, the Severian marble city plan, even today's topography[51] reveal the picture of the ancient Campus: abundance of porticos, temples, ustrina (crematoria), sports facilities, thermal baths, four theaters, a circus, a stadium, a gigantic sundial with an obelisk as the indicator, up to the templum Matidiae in which Hadrian had deified his mother-in-law! In the vicinity of the Agrippa thermal baths an artificial lake was dammed up, the stagnum Agrippae, on which Nero used to float with a raft and enjoy wild banquets; the lake shores were bordered with bordellos with noble women (Tacitus, *Ann.* 15.37). In the Saepta, in *the* luxury shopping area of Rome, especially works of art, books, and oriental delicacies were sold (cf. the scene in Martial 9.59). The sculpture known as "Madama Lucrezia" on the corner of today's Piazza S. Marco, a priestess of Isis with a garment knotted in front of her breast, reminds one of the Isis and Serapis temple of Mars Field. Under Augustus and Tiberius, the Isis cult had been strenuously persecuted, the cultic artworks thrown into the Tiber, and the temple destroyed. Caligula and then Domitian (after the devastating fire in the quarter in 80 C.E.), however, rebuilt the temple in magnificent style.

In the Porticus Minucia Frumentaria (in the east of the Largo Argentina) grain was distributed to the common people without cost.

---

50. Literature: F. Castagnoli, "Il Campo Marzio nell'antichità," *Mem. Acc. Lincei* 8/1 (1946): 93ff.; Coarelli, op. cit. (1975), 232–86, map 268; idem, "Navalia, Tarentum e la Topografia del Campo Marzio meridionale," *Quaderni dell'Istituto di Topografia* 5 (1968): 27ff.; idem, "Il complesso pompeiano del Campo Marzio e la sua decorazione scultorea," *Rend. Pont. Acc.* 44 (1971/72): 99ff.; L. Cozza, "Pianta marmorea severiana, nuove ricomposizioni di frammenti," *Quaderni dell'Istituto di Topografia* 5 (1968): 9ff.; G. Gatti, "Caratteristiche edilizie di un quartiere di Roma del II secolo d. C.," *Quaderni dell'Istituto di Storia dell' Architettura* 31–48 (1961): 49ff. (on Via Lata); idem, "Topografia dell'Iseo campense," *Rend. Pont. Acc.* 20 (1943/44): 117ff.; Jordan and Huelsen, op. cit., 1, Section 3, Table VIII, pp. 472ff.; Platner and Ashby, op. cit., "Campus Martius." Literature on the individual structures in Coarelli, op. cit. (1975), 350.

51. Cf. e.g., Piazza Navona = Stadium of Domitian; Piazza Grotta Pinta = Pompeius Theatre. The Via della Scrofa and the Via dei Coronari reflect ancient street layouts.

Ordinary people had the chance of living in public buildings.[52] Beneath the arcades of public buildings shops were often set up, in the back rooms or mezzanines of which the shop lessees lived with their families. On Mars Field there were such boutiques probably at the porticos of the Saepta Iulia, of Pompeius, and of Octavia. Private booths leaned against the theaters of Balbus and of Marcellus.

Private Residences

The question remains whether and where the public buildings left space for residences.[53] The statistics of the Regionaria show that Regions IX and VII, in relation to the other regions, had few domus and insulae.[54] Nevertheless, both archaeologically and literarily, insulae above all can be found.[55] Somewhere in the IXth Region the insula Felicles stood out: the most monstrous tenement house in Rome, which far exceeded the permitted height of 21 m.! Built in the second century under the Antonines, it was still listed in the Regionaria (Notitia) of the fourth century as a curiosity worth seeing. The fame of the "skyscraper" extended across the sea as far as Africa, where Tertullian (*Adv. Val.* 7) mentioned the monstrosity in order to caricature the cosmology of the Valentinians: The Valentinians "present their cosmic system as a sort of monstrous tenement house, at the peak of which, under the roof tiles

52. On this, Homo, op. cit., 576f. Cf. in Ostia the public docks in which common people lived.
53. In the Republican period, Mars Field had public buildings and was scarcely inhabited; it served for worship services, military maneuvers, as well as public meetings. Not until the imperial period did the Pomerium extend partly over Mars Field. Cf. the Pomerium Cippi (in Homo, op. cit., 94) of Claudius and Hadrian in the northwest in the vicinity of the Tiber.
54. Region VII offers 0.83 domus per hectare and thus is in eleventh place in the statistics of the fourteen regions.
In Region IX, 14 insulae are contained in one hectare (fourteenth place). Domus are also rare in Region IX: 0.7 per hectare (twelfth place). Correspondingly thinly represented in Region IX are the bakeries: 0.1 per hectare (eleventh place).
55. Aristocratic villas (*domus*) are to be identified especially *at the periphery* of Mars Field on the slopes of the Quirinal and of the Pincio. On the Pincio slope, the villa of Lucullus rises with terraces and steps; since 46 C.E., it belonged to the imperial possessions. Farther north on the Pincio stood the villas of the Acilii and later of the Anicii and the Pincii. The so-called "Muro Torto" represents the remnants of supporting walls of these villas. In the Mars Field plain proper, we do not know of so many domus. Behind the temples B and C of the Largo Argentina, e.g., were found remains of a domus (atrium and peristyle with colonnades and verandas; cf. Homo, op. cit., 543). In the area of the Campus Agrippae, Agrippa maintained a villa.
From the Regionaria of the fourth century it is clear that in Region VII, 31.7 insulae were present for one domus. With that, Region VII led the statistics for the fourteen regions; i.e., here for the ratio domus/insulae, the insulae come out highest in comparison to the other regions. Left of the Via Lata in Region IX, there appear to have been more domus in relation to insulae. Here there were only 19.84 insulae per domus. Only Regions III (17.2:1) and XIII (19.3:1) exhibit a lower relationship.

(*ad summas tegulas*) they place God. It rises to heaven with just as many stories as the tenement house of the Felicula in Rome"![56]

The insula of the Felicula was an extreme "skyscraper." As a rule, the insulae did not rise above five or six stories. However, considering the lightweight construction, already this height could be frightening.

Juvenal ridiculed Rome's efforts to reach into the sky, with constructions supported only by posts, long and thin, like flutes (3.190ff.); "the third floor is already in flames and you still know nothing about it! ... As the last one, you poor thing, you'll be fried, who are shielded from the rain only by roofing tiles where the love-sick doves lay their eggs" (ibid.). Aelius Aristides[57] reckons that the dwellings of Rome would reach to the Ionian Sea if building permits allowed only one story per building.

In our quarter such insula examples are archaeologically verified: (a) The zone of the Forum Holitorium[58] was an insulae quarter.[59] A tenement house of the second century at the foot of the Capitol (remains under the steps of Ara Coeli) consists of at least five floors. In the ground floor two tabernae are discernible.[60] (b) In the time of Hadrian and Antoninus Pius the quarter along the east side of the Via Lata was urbanized and thickly settled. Eastwards from today's Piazza Colonna between Largo Chigi and Via delle Muratte, the remains of six several-storied brick tenement houses have been excavated. One reveals a ground-floor area of 41 x 61 meters; the ground floors of two others measure 30 x at least 33 and 40 x at least 55 meters. On its frontside one could stroll through porticos along shops.[61] Additional remains of the residential quarter were discovered on the corner of Via di S. Maria in Via/Via dei Crociferi.

In the Via dei Maroniti a several-storied brick insula was found; it even had marble and mosaic floorings. Not every insula inhabitant was eo ipso the poor wretch who lived *ad summas tegulas* between bird droppings and rain spots.

(c) A zone of residential remains was discovered between the Ara Pacis and the Augustus mausoleum on the west side of the Via Lata /

---

56. From Tertullian it may not be concluded that Valentinians lived in this tenement. H. Cancik's ("Gnostiker in Rome," in J. Taubes, ed., *Religionstheorie und politische Theologie,* vol. 2: *Gnosis und Politik* [Munich and Paderborn, 1984], 165–67), could be misunderstood in this way.

57. εἰς Ῥώμην 8 (ed. Klein). Cf. also Pliny, *Nat. hist.* 3.5.67.

58. The vegetable market. Sale of vegetables played an important role, especially in the lives of the poor (Cicero, *Sen.* 16).

59. Cf. Homo, op. cit., 562.

60. Cf. Homo, op. cit., 560f.; Carcopino, op. cit. (1977), 40f., with crosscut; 376, n. 12; picture of a reconstruction in Fasola, op. cit. (1980), 32.

61. Cf. G. Lugli, "Aspetti urbanistici di Roma antica," *Rend. Pont. Acc.* 13 (1937): 73–98; Coarelli, op. cit. (1975), 15; Homo, op. cit., 561; Gatti, op. cit. (1961), 59 (map).

Flaminia.[62] In the neighborhood, ad Ciconias Nixas, ships' cargoes were unloaded;[63] workers for such work probably lived in the near vicinity.

If Christians already in the second century lived on Mars Field, which seems likely, if not entirely certain (see above), then they lived in the insulae left and right of the Via Lata. The basis for accepting this lies not so much in the fact that obviously the majority of the Mars Field inhabitants in the second century lived just along this traffic axis. Two other things point much more to that: (a) The borders of the ecclesiastical regions (since the third century) on Mars Field deviated completely from the Augustan regions, which were usually respected by the ecclesiastical regions. While in the Augustan partition of the city the Via Lata / Flaminia marked the border between Regions IX and VII, in the church administration of late antiquity the Via Lata was the *middle axis* of an ecclesiastical region (ecclesiastical region 5). (b) The Tituli of late antiquity, Lucinae, Marcelli, and Marci, all stand directly on the Via Lata / Flaminia.

Evaluation

I have attempted to sketch a sociographic map that presents a study of the pagan environment of early Christianity in the city of Rome. The question is the extent to which knowledge of the Christian communities of the city can be gained from this.

a. The lowest social strata lived in the two regions, Trastevere and Via Appia / Porta Capena, so that it is not difficult to infer the social status of the Christians who dwelled there.

b. The result in the region of the Aventine is ambivalent: everyone was represented, from consul to slave.

c. The result on Mars Field is not totally clear-cut either. Like most of the inhabitants of this city quarter, Christians there most probably lived in insulae. However, in the insulae of Mars Field, the degree of living comfort could vary significantly, as the archaeological material showed (cf. also Ostia). Thus, the expression "insula inhabitant" is no sufficiently precise sociohistorical information.

d. A presence of Christians in the quarters Aventine and Mars Field proved to be less sure for the first two centuries than in both of the other regions. Interestingly, in those two quarters the sociohistorical result is ambivalent. How can the concurrence of these two observations be interpreted? We have the best chance of meeting Christians from socially

---

62. See Jordan and Huelsen, op. cit., 1, Part 3, 614.
63. See Platner and Ashby, op. cit., "Ciconiae Nixae"; Jordan and Huelsen, op. cit., 601.

higher strata precisely in those two quarters that possibly only *later* than the other two were infiltrated by Christians. Taken together, these two observations could mean that, with the chronological expansion of Christians across the city, social advancement also came hand-in-hand.

On the other hand, if there were Christian dwellings on the Aventine and Mars Field already in the first and second centuries, then already for this time-frame it would be possible to discern the existence of social stratification among the urban Roman Christians. That in fact already in our time-frame not all Christians were "poor" will be shown by other materials below.

e. It is worth noting that at various places there was the proximity of other eastern cults. Moreover, the semi-circular form of our Christian quarters on the fringes of the city illustrates the situation of an immigrant eastern religion — "in Rome, where all of the horrors and abominations of the whole world flow together" (Tacitus, *Ann.* 15.44.3, concerning the Roman Christians!).

Part 3

FIRST DIACHRONIC SECTION
General Information about
Urban Roman Christianity

In Part 2, I was obliged to deal with our two centuries en bloc and without being able to differentiate temporally within this block. Now I will set out a first diachronic section through our period of time: The socio-historically relevant materials concerning urban Roman Christianity in general will be examined.

Chapter 5

Jewish and Gentile Christians

How did the ratio of Jewish Christians to Gentile Christians develop?

1. Gentile Christians may already have belonged to Christianity while it was still thriving *within* the Roman synagogues. Such Gentile Christians would have been recruited from the ranks of the *sebomenoi,* who, on the fringes of the synagogues revered the God of Israel as pagan sympathizers of Jewish monotheism.[1] These folk were the main target of the earliest Gentile Christian mission. Christian teaching was attractive for them because it promised them a full share in salvation without circumcision and thus relativized the second-class status they may have felt within the synagogues. That Aquila and Prisca, immediately after their expulsion from Rome, so unreservedly joined in the work of the Pauline mission to the Gentiles in Corinth (Acts 18; cf. Rom 16:3f.) raises the possibility that they had been accustomed to living together with Gentile Christians already in one or more of the Roman synagogues.[2]

Before Christianity and Judaism separated, Law-abiding Jewish Christians and uncircumcised Gentile Christians might very well have coexisted in the synagogues. Let us consider this: *Sebomenoi* worshiped on the fringes of a synagogue without being circumcised. The first Gentile Christians, i.e., the first *sebomenoi* won over by the Christian gospel of Jewish Christians, would have simply *continued* worshiping at the periphery of their synagogue. Thus, inasmuch as Jews and uncircumcised *sebomenoi* coexisted in a synagogue, also Law-abiding Jewish Christians and uncircumcised Gentile Christians *sebomenoi* coexisted in this synagogue. The fact that everywhere in the Roman Empire uncircumcised pagans — some more, some less observant of the Jewish Law — worshiped the Jewish God in coexistence with Law-abiding synagogues was a situation that probably

---

1. On the use of language: *sebomenos* will be used here in the sense of "a pagan favoring Jewish monotheism, who is not yet a proselyte," even though the term could also be used to designate Jews. Literature on the problem in Solin, "Juden und Syrer," 618, n. 49.

2. That the first Gentile Christians in Rome were won through missionizing followers of Stephen is a possibility. U. Wilckens considers this: Descendants of Roman *liberti* could have belonged to the Jerusalem circle of Stephen (Acts 6:9), who, after their expulsion from Jerusalem, might have gone to Rome to Jewish relatives living there (*Der Brief an die Römer, I: Rom. 1–5,* EKK 6/1 [Zurich and Neukirchen, 1978], p. 38).

encouraged the Law-free Gentile Christian mission significantly. Conflicts first arose, however, when Law-abiding Jewish and uncircumcised Gentile Christians tried to implement the Christian eucharistic tradition by having meals at common tables together. How could this be done? The turmoils in the Roman synagogues in the year 49, caused by the Christian gospel and leading to the "edict of Claudius" as well as to the expulsion of Prisca and Aquila, may well have been kindled by these kinds of issues and not so much by the question of who the true messiah was.

2. After the separation from the synagogues, at the latest at the time of the writing of the letter to the Romans, Gentile Christians (in a large measure probably former *sebomenoi*) predominated. Several times Paul assumes that urban Roman Christians, in general, come from paganism.[3] These univocal expressions must be given methodological priority in the face of the impression elsewhere in the letter's contents of its being written primarily for a Jewish-Christian readership. Since the time of F. C. Baur, this impression has been nurtured by, e.g., Paul's scriptural citations, his proofs from scripture (1:17; 4:6–8, 17; et al.), his use of Jewish-Christian formulae (1:3f.; 3:24f.; 4:25) and of Jewish traditions (Rom 13, with, e.g., its reference to the Creator's will), by his discussion of the significance of the Law and of the problem of "Israel" in chapters 9–11, and also by his direct address to the Jews in 2:17.

These epistolary contents, however, are also conceivable for a largely pagan-born readership, especially if one is dealing with persons who once were *sebomenoi*:

(a) Even the Gentile Christians who are free from the Law may be persuaded through proofs from scripture if they are holding the Old Testament in their hands as their Bible (cf. 7:1 "you who know the Law"). That would hold even more true if they were already acquainted with the scripture as *sebomenoi* in the synagogue — whether it be through scripture readings in synagogue worship or through their own private study. Juvenal (14.96–106) evidences some Roman (!) *sebomenoi* actively studying scripture: "iudaicum *ediscunt...*ius" (14.101), and that indeed *before* any proselyte circumcision (99). Similarly, Luke presupposes among the *sebomenoi* a knowledge of the Old Testament (Acts 13:16ff., also 8:27f.;[4] in addition see also 17:2 and 17:4).

(b) Jewish(-Christian) formulae and traditions, at best, say something

---

3. Rom 1:5f., 13–15; 11:13, 17f., 24, 28, 30f.; 15:15f., 18; 9:3ff.; cf. also 15:9ff.; 6:17–21 in connection with 1:18ff. Cf. also Acts 28:24–31: little mission success among Jews, but more among others. On the abundance of arguments and difficulties (a majority of Gentile Christians? a majority of Jewish Christians?), see, e.g., the history of research in W. Schmithals, 24–52, 57–63, 65ff. Without being able to unroll the entire problematic, I restrict myself to sketching my own view of the situation.

4. In this text, the Ethiopian who is reading privately in Isaiah is neither simply a pagan (προσκυνήσων εἰς Ἰερουσαλήμ, cf. John 12:20) nor clearly a proselyte (εὐνοῦχος). Because of Acts 10, Luke does not designate him unambiguously as a pagan. But he does

about the background of the authors, not of the readers. (c) Romans 2:17 is rhetorical. (d) Chapters 9–11 address themselves specifically also to non-Jews (11:16–32; 9:3–5; 10:1–3). (e) A principal discussion of the Jewish understanding of salvation is integral to the Pauline gospel of justification. That both themes "Law" and "Israel" are so extensively discussed is explicable from the biographical situation of Paul. At that time, Paul was in a conflict in the east with opponents of Jewish origin (Rom 15:30f., συναγωνίσασθαι, ἀπειθοῦντες ἐν τῇ Ἰουδαίᾳ). During his "third missionary journey" he was attacked (Galatians; cf. also 2 Cor 11:22f.; Phil 3:2ff.). It is possible from this polemical situation in the East to explain why he, also in this fundamental theological statement to Rome, chose to deal in depth with the questions "Israel/Law" and responded to the Jewish(-Christian) charges (3:8, that he teaches libertinism, cf. 6:1, 15; 3:31, that he destroys the Law, cf. 7:7; chapters 9–11, that he is an enemy of Israel). That in Rome itself there was no such acute conflict with opponents is indicated by the moderate tone (in comparison to Galatians), but also by his desire to win the Romans as *allies* who pray for him and for resolution of his problems in the east (15:30f.)![5] (f) If the urban Roman readers were chiefly former *sebomenoi*, then the subject "Law / Israel / no privilege of Jew over Gentile" becomes even more comprehensible: Precisely what the *sebomenoi* had experienced in the synagogue, the privilege of the Jews, is contested by Paul. It was a subject that would have been of burning interest to former *sebomenoi* and must even have "pleased" them! And that of course is what Paul wants, too: to "please" his readers, to earn their trust, to render himself agreeable to them, and to win them as allies (1:9–12; 15:24, 30f.; *captationes benevolentiae*, 1:8; 15:14).[6] (g) 7:4–6; 8:15 (πάλιν, cf. Gal 5:1f.) are quite suitable also for former *sebomenoi*.

If many *sebomenoi* belonged to the urban Roman Christians in the beginning, that is then already a sociohistorical clue, although vague in nature. There often was a difference in social status between proselytes

---

not call him a proselyte either, obviously because of the pre-Lukan source of this text. There, the Ethiopian most likely was a *sebomenos*, reading in Isaiah.

5. Cf. the thesis of the "secret" addressees of the letter to the Romans in Jerusalem: J. Jervell, "Der Brief nach Jerusalem: Über Veranlassung und Adresse des Römerbriefs," *StTh* 25 (1971): 61–73. Nevertheless, I would not go so far in making the point: During the formulation of Romans, Paul need not have intended to reach with this writing his eastern opponents also. It suffices that, for himself and for the Romans whom he wants to win for his gospel, he protects his teaching against accusations and thus "seals off" possible weak points. I prefer speaking of a sort of "testament" of Paul, with U. Wilckens (1:47ff.), among others.

6. I do not go as far as Schmithals, 57, who attributes to the Gentile-Christian readers in Rome Judaizing tendencies: Paul wants to heal them from that by contesting any advantage or privilege for the Jews. I agree with Schmithals, 76ff., that the number of *sebomenoi* in the early Gentile-Christian congregations was higher than is usually assumed.

and *sebomenoi*. This is known and has been investigated sufficiently.[7] While proselytes were primarily recruited from among the lower classes of the population,[8] *sebomenoi*, as a rule, were socially better off, even up to the level of the Roman knights. They included fewer slaves than the proselytes did.[9]

The dialogue of Paul with the Jews took place before a public that was predominantly of pagan origin. Those who do not agree with this result have to make shaky assumptions: that Paul uses the term ἔθνη merely to indicate a geographical viewpoint[10] or that Paul merely indicates with ἔθνη that urban Roman Christianity represents the "Gentile church" outside the synagogue and the full observance of the Torah.[11] However, passages like 11:24f., combined with 11:30, 28, 17f., show that ἔθνη is nonetheless used *ethnically* for the urban Roman Christians, thus designating pagan birth.

If the majority of urban Roman Christians are from paganism, that does not exclude the existence of Jewish Christians. (a) In 9:24,[12] Jewish Christians appear to be addressed within the readership. (b) The conflict between "strong" and "weak" in Romans 14f. turns upon questions of the observance of Jewish Law (see below). This implies that Jewish Christians may be involved in the conflict. But it can by no means be deduced that the "weak ones" are derived mostly from Jewish Christians. Characteristic for the "weak" in Romans 14f. are the observance of food regulations (14:2, 15, 20f.) and the keeping of certain "days" (14:5). There is evidence of both also for *sebomenoi*,[13] and the interesting thing is that it is specifically for *sebomenoi* at Rome. Both Juvenal[14] and Horace[15] know of such pagan contemporaries. In view of this evidence and of the generally large influx of *sebomenoi* into the Hellenistic Christian congregations (Acts 17:4, 12; 18:7; 16:14f. et al.), it appears questionable that even in the party of the "weak ones" those Christians

---

7. Cf., on the basis of epigraphic and other materials, K. G. Kuhn and H. Stegemann, "Proselyten," in Pauly/Wissowa Suppl. 9 (1962): 1265–67; H. Gülzow, *Christentum und Sklaverei in den ersten drei Jahrhunderten* (Bonn, 1969), 22f.

8. *CIJ* 256 and 462, e.g., come from the slave/freedperson milieu.

9. E.g., *CIJ* 5. Cf. Josephus, *Ant.* 18.82 (the noble Fulvia); 20.195 (Poppaea).

10. "Every congregation outside of Judea (is just) a congregation 'from the Gentiles,' " even if theoretically Jewish Christians might be in the majority (Ph. Vielhauer, *Geschichte der urchristlichen Literatur* [Berlin, 1975], 180).

11. Wilckens, 1:40.

12. Cf. possibly also 15:7–9. In 7:6 and 4:1 the rhetorical first person plural does not necessarily include the readers.

13. Josephus, *C. Ap.* 2.39: With ζῆλος τῆς ἡμετέρας εὐσεβείας the Jewish food customs are maintained by many Hellenes (πολλὰ τῶν εἰς βρῶσιν ἡμῖν οὐ νενομισμένων) 2.10; cf. also Tertullian, *Ad Nat.* 1.13.

14. *Sat.* 14.96–106: Some Gentiles rigidly observe the Sabbath and the Jewish food prescriptions even *before* any proselyte circumcision.

15. *Sat.* 1.9.68–72: Gentiles observe "tricensima sabbata."

who were born Jewish were the majority and held the upper hand, let alone in the whole community.

That Paul deals with a concrete problem between "weak" and "strong" in the Roman church community and does not just echo 1 Corinthians 8–10[16] seems to me proved by the direct address in the second person (14:1, 10, 13, et al.) and by the different way the "weak ones" are characterized in comparison to 1 Corinthians 8ff. Most key terms are different. There is nothing in Romans of βρῶσις τῶν εἰδωλοθύτων or γνῶσις (1 Cor 8ff.), but instead one finds λάχανα ἐσθίειν, or μηδὲ πιεῖν οἶνον and κρίνειν ἡμέραν παρ᾽ ἡμέραν (Rom 14:2, 21, 5). These characteristics are lacking in the references to the Corinthian "weak ones."

In my judgment, the "weak" are not to be identified against a Gentile background[17] but rather against the background of Jewish practice of the Law. Two things support this opinion.[18] Κοινόν in the sense of "cultically unclean" (14:14) is encountered exclusively in Jewish and then in Christian language.[19] Second, in 15:7–9 Paul places the Roman conflict between "strong" and "weak" into the context of the salvation-historical problem, "Israel — Gentiles." That is, questions about Jewish Torah observance are central to the conflict. But which ones?

The "days" that the "weak" keep may be the Sabbath or other Jewish days of fasting and of celebration. A more precise specification is impossible. Renunciation of meat on principle (14:2) is conceivable, if former *sebomenoi* or Jewish Christians want to keep the Torah's regulations about meat[20] but in Rome cannot easily buy kosher meat slaughtered according to Jewish rites.[21] Moreover, nowhere in the world capital can they be certain that they will not unknowingly carry home from the market meat offered to idols or treated in any other way unacceptable to the Torah. The renunciation of all meat is demonstrable in a Jewish milieu. Some Jewish priests on a trip to Rome in the time of Nero ate only figs and nuts in order to avoid contact with meat offered to idols (Josephus, *Vita* 13–14).[22] They were not far in time and place from the people presupposed in the letter to the Romans! Equally well evidenced

---

16. On the parallels with 1 Cor 8–10, cf. the overview in U. Wilckens, 3:115.

17. Cf. the diverse possibilities in Schmithals, 98ff.

18. Cf. similarly also U. Wilckens, 3:87, 95f., 113f.

19. 1 Macc 1:47, 62; Josephus, *Ant.* 3.181; 11.346; 12.320; 13.4; etc., see further Wilckens, 3:112f. Profane Greek literature is cloaked in silence.

20. See the prohibition of meat sacrificed to idols and of the partaking of blood; cf. among others Acts 15:20, 29; 21:25; Rev 2:14, 20; Lev 17:10ff.; Exod 34:15.

21. Can one really imagine that Jewish butchers in Rome after the mighty conflicts leading to the edict of Claudius still would gladly serve Christian apostates at their stands? (Cf. Wilckens 3:95.)

22. Cf. also Dan 1:5, 8, 10, 12, 16.

is the rejection of wine from Gentile hands:[23] The "weak" could never
be sure of not buying from a wine dealer who also drew abominable libation wine from his amphorae.[24] If the "weak" wanted to exclude such
ἀλίσγημα τῶν εἰδώλων (Acts 15:20), they had to grow their own wine
on the Vatican. But who could do that?

In regard to our question about the ratio of Jewish to Gentile Christians, Romans 14f. does not change the impression that the Jewish
Christians in urban Roman Christianity in the time of Romans are already in the minority. It is not imperative to assume a Jewish-Christian
majority even in the party of the "weak," because the characteristics of
the "weak ones" also suit the former *sebomenoi*.

(c) In Romans 16 Paul designates three urban Roman persons as
συγγενεῖς μου ("my kinspeople"): Andronicus, Junia(s), and Herodion.
With Romans 9–11 (cf. esp. 9:3) in mind, Paul thinks it is important
to emphasize their Jewish origins expressly. Συγγενής does not appear
otherwise in Paul's letters. In the letter to the Romans, however, Paul
had a special interest in emphasizing that Christians are συγγενής of
Jews! We may therefore assume that his highlighting of Jewish origins in
the personal notes of Romans 16 is done in a thorough way. The rest of
the more than twenty people in the list who are not designated as "kinspeople" are consequently Gentile Christians.[25] The Jewish-Christians
appear as a minority. A comparison with the Jewish names attested in
inscriptions in the city of Rome strengthens this. According to Frey's corpus of inscriptions (*CIJ*) only three names from our list were also carried

---

23. Dan 1:5, 8, 10, 12, 16.
24. Cf. Josephus, *Vita* 74: Pious observers of the Torah avoid even oil bought from
Greeks!
25. Only with Aquila (according to Acts 18:2, a Jewish Christian) does the Jewish
background understandably remain unmentioned. Paul had so many other things to report about him and his wife that the ethnic origin is omitted. On Rom 16 as a component
of the original letter to the Romans, see below, chap. 16. That the names of Rom 16 give
no information concerning the pagan or Jewish origins of the names' bearers is correctly
stated by Solin, "Juden und Syrer," 665. On the term συγγενής, V. Fàbrega ("War Junia[s],
der hervorragende Apostel [Röm. 16,7], eine Frau?" in *JAC* 27/28 [1984/85]: 47–64). In
spite of Rom 9:3, he proposed anew (pp. 49f.) to understand συγγενής not as "fellow
countryman" but as "friend." His decision rests upon shaky presuppositions. (1) The συγγενεῖς Jason and Sosipatros (Rom 16:21) were, according to Acts 17:5; 20:4, not Jewish
Christians. But it is uncertain whether the people named in Rom 16 and Acts 17 and 20
were identical. And according to Acts 17:4a, Jason might well have been a Jew! The same
is valid for Sopater, according to Acts 17:10–12. (2) When Paul does not designate the
following persons as συγγενεῖς, it is because they obviously were not Jewish Christians:
Mary most likely bore the Latin name *Maria*, not the Semitic name. Her Latin *nomen
gentile* was widespread in Rome (see below). Fàbrega knows nothing of this alternative!
Rufus and his *mother* need not have belonged to the Jewish-Christian family mentioned in
Mark 15:21. (Why does Paul not mention in Rom 16:13 Rufus's famous father, Simon of
Cyrene?) The context (Rom 9–11, esp. 9:3) remains decisive for the semantic definition of
συγγενής, especially since Paul does not use the term anywhere else.

by urban Roman Jews.[26] In summary, then, in the group of persons of Romans 16 apparently a similar ratio of Jewish to Gentile Christians existed as in urban Roman Christianity as a whole.

If already in Paul's time of the 50s only a minority of the urban Roman Christians were of Jewish origin, then it follows methodologically that sociohistorical discoveries about urban Roman Jews may not simply be transferred to urban Roman Christianity. I will refrain from hasty analogical conclusions.

3. The question of the quantitative ratio between Jewish and Gentile Christians must be methodologically distinguished from the question of the "qualitative" relationship: To what extent did the Jewish Christians exercise a significant theological and pastoral influence? (a) The Jewish Christian Aquila and his wife exercise a leading role within urban Roman Christianity; they lead a house congregation of their own (Rom 16:3–5). And the Jewish Christians Andronicus and Junia(s) are described as "prominent among the apostles" (Rom 16:7). (b) In the urban Roman history of theology of the first century, a broad stream of tradition from the synagogue plays a role. This is obvious in *1 Clement* at the end of the first century. *First Clement* offers a plethora of not just Old Testament[27] but also *post*canonical *Jewish* traditions.

Here is some exemplary material: In *1 Clem.* 23:3f.; 46:2 are found citations from unknown, obviously Jewish apocryphal writings. In *1 Clem.* 17:6 one encounters an unknown apocryphal quotation from Moses. Noah's sermon on penance (*1 Clem.* 7:6) derives from post-testamental tradition, not from Genesis 7. *First Clement* 43:2ff. embroiders Numbers 17 haggadically, as does also Jewish tradition (cf. Josephus, *Ant.* 4.63ff.; Philo, *Vita Mosis* 2[3].21.175–80); similarly also *1 Clem.* 11:2. *First Clement* 31:3 offers the Jewish (not the Old Testament) tradition, that Isaac submitted himself to being sacrificed knowingly and willingly (e.g., Josephus, *Ant.* 1.232ff.) Numerous motifs in *1 Clem.* 24-30 come from Jewish apocalyptic literature.[28] The

---

26. The typically Latin (!) names "Rufus" and "Julia" as well as "Maria." "Maria": *CIJ* 251f., 457, 459, 1, 137, 374f., 511, 96, 12; outside of Rome, Josephus, *Bell.* 6.201; *CPJ* 2:223 (114 C.E.); 227 (116 C.E.). "Julia": *CIJ* 123f., 34f., 352, among others. "Rufus": *CIJ* 145f.; 525; outside of Rome, Josephus, *Bell.* 2.52.74; *Ant.* 17.266.294. For Jews *outside of Rome* one encounters in Josephus and *CPJ* also "Andronicus" (*Ant.* 13.75ff.; *CPJ* 1:18; and 3:470) and "Tryphaina" (*CPJ* 2:421, 183 from the year 73 C.E.; 3:453.20 from the year 132 C.E.). The remaining nineteen names in the Rom 16 listing are not attested there for Jews.

27. More than one hundred Old Testament references. Cf. D. Bonhoeffer, "Das jüdische Element im 1.Clemensbrief," in *Gesammelte Schriften* V, ed. E. Bethge (Munich, 1972), 17–63, 21ff.; W. Wrede, *Untersuchungen zum Ersten Klemensbriefe* (Göttingen, 1891), 62f.

28. See the evidence in L. Sanders, *L'hellénisme de Saint Clément de Rome et le Paulinisme* (Louvain, 1943), 67–69.

long prayer in *1 Clem.* 59:2–61:3 reveals relationship to the synagogal prayer The Eighteen Benedictions,[29] just as other liturgical material
stands close to the synagogue.[30] *First Clement* 28:3 agrees with the Hebrew Old Testament text (καταστρώσω instead of the LXX καταβῶ).
Hebraisms are also present in 12:5; 21:9; 28:3; 34:8; et al.[31]

How is this finding to be interpreted? The author himself probably
did not come from Judaism.[32] As a Gentile Christian, Clement takes up
Jewish traditions that were alive in the urban Roman Christian community. How did those traditions manage to get there? Who imported
them? Were these carriers Jewish Christians?[33] We may also think of
Gentile Christians, who as *sebomenoi* had absorbed the intellectual
richness of the synagogue. One must therefore be cautious in making
conclusions. Neither a quantitative nor a qualitative[34] preponderance of
Jewish Christians can be inferred from the strong synagogal tradition
in Roman church life. We must formulate more generally: *Christians
from the sphere of influence of the synagogues,* Jewish Christians as well
as Gentile Christians, exercised an astonishing influence on the formation of theology in urban Roman Christianity in the first century. These
Christians from the sphere of influence of the synagogues presumably
formed the majority. Most Christians of the first generation, at least before their conversion, would have had contacts with a synagogue. As
sebomenoi or as members of Judaism, they would in varied intensity
have taken in its wealth of ideas.

The strength of the synagogal tradition also could be illustrated by
the letter to the Hebrews from the second half of the first century.[35] Its
urban Roman origin, however, is very uncertain.

---

29. J. B. Lightfoot, *The Apostolic Fathers,* 1: *S. Clement of Rome* 1,2 (London,
1890), 67–69, 394ff.; R. Knopf, *Der erste Clemensbrief,* HNT Ergänzungsband, Die
apostolischen Väter (Tübingen, 1920), 136–48.

30. *1 Clem.* 33:2–6; 34:5–8; 38:3f. Cf., e.g., H. Lietzmann, *Geschichte der alten
Kirche,* I (Berlin, 1932), 209; in addition, W. C. van Unnik, "1 Clement 34 and the
'Sanctus,'" *VC* 5 (1951): 204–48.

31. See further E. Nestle, "War der Verfasser des 1.Clemensbriefes semitischer Abstammung?" *ZNW* 1 (1900): 178–80; Bonhoeffer 26. Additional material on Clement
esp. in A. Jaubert, "Thèmes lévitiques dans la prima Clementis," *VC* 18 (1964): 193–
203; E. Peterson, *Frühkirche, Judentum und Gnosis* (Freiburg and Rome, 1959), 129–57.
On the dependence upon Adam-haggada, see K. Beyschlag, *Clemens Romanus und der
Frühkatholizismus* (Tübingen, 1966), esp. pp. 48ff., 131ff. Additional literature, ibid., 24,
n. 1, and 26, n. 2 (e.g., "Jewish Christian Targumim" in *1 Clem.* 21:1; 42:5?).

32. This can be inferred from his position on the history of Israel: Israel's salvation-
historical uniqueness does not interest him; Israel merely foreshadows Christianity
typologically; cf. *1 Clem.* 29; 30:1; 50:7 (with A. Stuiber, "Clemens," in *RAC* 3:194).
The elements of Hellenistic education in *1 Clem.,* on the other hand, cannot decide the
question of Clement's Gentile- or Jewish-Christian background; see below, chap. 21.

33. On the basis of her material (see above, n. 31), Jaubert thinks of Jewish Christians
who, e.g., go back to priestly circles in Judaism.

34. "Qualitative" = "spiritually and intellectually more influential."

35. Hebrews 2:1–4: second or third Christian generation.

On the origin we may state: The greetings at the end, ἀσπάζονται ὑμᾶς οἱ ἀπὸ τῆς Ἰταλίας (13:24), suggest — if they are not a mere literary device[36] — a writing directed *to* Italy: ἀπό replacing ἐκ (Bl-D-R 209.3) designates the geographical origin of people who for the most part are not presently living where they come from. Matt 21:11; John 12:21; Acts 6:9; but also Sophocles, *El.* 701, et alia.[37] Accordingly, in Hebrews 13:24, some Italian Christians, who are staying at the letter-sending church outside Italy, greeted the addressees at home.

In favor of Roman authorship certain parallels between *1 Clement* and Hebrews might be quoted,[38] if they really point to common liturgical traditions (it is not clear that they do). If Clement had Hebrews lying on his desk, speculations about common liturgical roots are superfluous.[39]

If Hebrews was directed toward Rome, then it at least presupposes that its Jewish traditions would be understood by the Roman Christians.

These are some of the synagogal traditions: Hebrews 11 offers a rhetorical[40] series of paradigms that illustrates a certain leitmotif (v. 1: "faith"). The Old Testament–Jewish content of the series indicates where Hebrews derives the rhetorical method of chap. 11: from Hellenistic-Jewish schools.[41] From there comes also the typological method of Old Testament exegesis. Not only methodologically, however, but also in terms of content, Hebrews often stands close to the Hellenistic synagogue, and especially to Philo.[42]

---

36. This must be suspected for the notices 13:19, 23f.: "...that our brother Timothy is already free again; with him, when he comes, I want to see you"; "...that I may be given back to you all the faster."

37. Matt 21:11; John 12:21; Acts 6:9; but also Sophocles, *El.* 701, et al.; Acts 2:5; Matt 4:25; 3:13; John 3:2.

38. Cf., e.g., Hebrews 2:17f.; 3:1; 4:14f. with *1 Clem.* 36:1; 61:3; 64; esp. Heb 1 with *1 Clem.* 36. On this, see D. Powell, "Clemens Rom.," in *TRE* 8 (1981): 114; G. Theissen, *Untersuchungen zum Hebräerbrief*, StNT 2 (Gütersloh, 1969), 34ff. Already Eusebius, *Hist. Ecc.* 3.38.3, observed language and content parallels between Hebrews and *1 Clement*.

39. Cf. K. Aland, who similarly pleads for an origin of Hebrews outside of Italy: "Methodische Bemerkungen zum Corpus Paulinum bei den Kirchenvätern des 2.Jh.," in A. M. Ritter, ed., *Kerygma und Logos: Festschrift Andresen* (Göttingen, 1979), 29–48, here 42–45, 33ff.

40. See Demosthenes et al. (below), and M. R. Cosby, *The Rhetorical Composition and Function of Hebrews 22: In Light of Example Lists in Antiquity* (Macon, Ga., 1988).

41. See catalogues of paradigms on a mostly ethical theme, e.g., 4 Macc (esp. 16:16–23); Philo, *Praem. et Poen.* 11; idem, *Virtut.* 198ff.; Wisdom 10. Hebrews 11 obviously rests upon a Jewish source: the solely Old Testament–Jewish paradigms end with the time of the Maccabees.

42. Cf. the overview of research in H. Feld, *Der Hebräerbrief*, EdF 228 (Darmstadt, 1985), 38–48. From the multiplicity of common points with Philo, cf., e.g., Heb 1:3 with Philo, *Op.* 146; idem, *Spec. Leg.* 4.123; 1.81 (the spiritual person or the Logos as "reflection"; the same in Wisdom 7:26 of Sophia); 4:12 with Philo, *Quis rer.* 130, 136, 207; the Platonic archetype-reflection terminology in 8:5 (also in 9:23f.) with Philo, *de vit. Mos.* 2.71–76. The midrash 3:7—4:11 on Psalm 95 has its roots in synagogal tradition.

Hebrews shows that learned traditions from the Hellenistic synagogue have made their way into Christianity — by means of educated
Christians who, in the Hellenistic synagogue, had been acquainted with
rhetorical method (chap. 11) and Philo-related contents. That the author of Hebrews himself or herself was a connecting link between the
synagogue and Christianity is unfortunately not provable.

The Jewish Christians and *sebomenoi,* who brought with them cultivated traditions from Jewish teaching[43] and set into motion a process
of passing on the Jewish cultural riches within the Christian circles of
Rome, remain in large measure anonymous for us. *How* these traditions were handed on among Christians often remains opaque in the
sources: through individual teachers, to whom Hermas in *Similitude*
9.16.5; 9.25.2 looks back as phenomena of the past or in any way
analogous to Jewish schools? (See further in Part 4.) What is important here is *the fact that* such a process of passing on Jewish-Christian
knowledge existed in Christian circles of Rome. It shows (a) that at
least some Christians were able to spare time for such activities (socially from a higher class?) and (b) that, independently of the pagan
educational systems, there was among Christians their own educational
and tradition-passing process.[44] (c) Within this independent Christian
process, not only genuinely Jewish but also originally pagan knowledge
could be passed on.[45] After examining additional material I shall return
to this educational process within Christianity (Part 4).

4. Outlook for the second century: Once integrated into the Christian life, the synagogal tradition was carried by people who themselves
were no longer rooted in the synagogue: The Gentile Christian Clement
seems to have been an early example, the Gentile Christian Hermas
a later one.[46] Also the urban Roman gnostic Ptolemy used originally

---

43. Jewish teaching activity in Rome: Inscriptions offer the terms νομοδιδάσκαλος
(*CIJ* 201), διδάσκαλος καὶ νομομαθής (*CIJ* 333), μαθητὴς σοφῶν (*CIJ* 508), γραμματεὺς
ψαλμῳδὸς φιλόνομος (Fasola, *RivArCr* 52 [1976]: 19). According to Philo *Leg.* 156,
πάτριος φιλοσοφία is taught in the Roman synagogues. Todos (Theudas) and Paletion
(Platon) were teaching in Rome before the mid-second century, probably in Greek; they
did not bear the title of Rabbi (cf. *t. Yom Tob* 2.15, 204; *j. Pes.* 7.34a, 47; Str-B 3:23;
Vogelstein and Rieger 1:108–10). Theudas was well-off; he supported Palestinian rabbis
financially (*j. Pes.,* ibid.)! The Palestinian Tanna R. Mattiah ben Heresh led a school in
Rome at the beginning of the second century (*t. Sanh.* 32b; cf. Str-B 3:24). Some rabbis
visited Rome frequently after 70 C.E., e.g., R. Joshua ben Hananiah, R. Aqiba, R. Eleazar
b. Azariah, Rabban Gamaliel (*m. Erub.* 4.1; cf. also *m. Abodah Zarah* 4.7).
44. Cf. outside Rome, e.g., Gal 6:6 or H. Conzelmann's hypothesis of a "school of
Paul" (e.g., in *Der erste Brief an die Korinther,* KEK 5 [Göttingen, 1969], 21, 75f.; Engl.
trans.: *1 Corinthians,* Hermeneia [Philadelphia, 1975]).
45. Cf. above the classical-rhetorical method of using series of paradigms (Heb 11),
which reached the Christians over the detour of Hellenistic-Jewish schooling. Additional
examples of originally pagan learning in *1 Clement* we shall observe in Part 4.
46. On Hermas's originally Jewish materials, see esp. E. Peterson (1959), 281ff. His
attempt to attribute the "Shepherd" to a Palestinian Jewish-Christian sect, however, has

Jewish traditions.[47] Original Jewish tradition took on its own life within circles of Gentile Christians. This process of Jewish tradition becoming independent from the synagogue did not, of course, exclude the possibilities (a) that individual Christians continued to have contacts with Jews,[48] and (b) that for the second century, too, one must still reckon with a direct influx of individuals carrying tradition from the synagogue. The author of the Christian work "De montibus Sina et Sion" from the end of the second century, possibly an urban Roman Christian, speaks Hebrew in addition to Latin: he is a Jewish Christian.[49] *ICUR* 12262 names an "*Aron* Cresteanu(s)"; otherwise the name is found only among Jews.[50] These instances of new converts from Judaism and of contact with Jews do not, however, explain the abundance of Jewish traditions in the Christian literature of the second century.

In general it must be maintained that, wherever one comes across originally Jewish traditions in the second century church, one cannot infer ethnic conclusions: these occurrences do not prove a Jewish origin of the bearer of the tradition, unless other evidence is added (e.g., Hebrew speaking). The broad distribution of originally Jewish traditions in the church of the second century has nothing more to do with the number and influence of Jewish Christians in the second century. Justin reckons with a heavy preponderance of Gentile Christians as self-evident.[51]

---

found no consensus. On Hermas's pagan origin, see below Part 4. Solin's ("Juden und Syrer," 665) categorical contention ("He was certainly a Jewish Christian in any case") goes right by the problems.

47. On this, F. T. Fallon, "The Law in Philo and Ptolemy: A Note on the Letter to Flora," *VC* 30 (1976): 41–45; G. Quispel, *La lettre à Flora par Ptolémée*, 2d ed., Sources chrétiennes 24 (Paris, 1966), 23 et al.

48. Cf. Callistus and his Jewish bank customers (Hipp., *Ref.* 9.12); outside Rome: Justin and Trypho, Aristo of Pella, various Jewish informants of Clement of Alexandria, the Jew mentioned by Celsus, etc.

49. On this, J. Daniélou, *Les origines du christianisme latin* (Paris, 1978), 47, 49, 55f.

50. Cf. additionally *Liber Pontificalis* on Evaristus (ca. 100 C.E.): Jewish origin; and on Pope Zosimus (417–18 C.E.): "Grecus ex patre Abramio," perhaps of Jewish origins.

51. *Apol.* 1.53.3ff.; Gentile Christians: 1.31.7; 49.1, 5; *Dial.* 35.7; 41.3; 30.3; 22.9; 33.2; 34.7; 43.2; 46.7; 52.1f., 4; 64.1; 65.7; 83.4; 91.3; 92.4; 109.1; 110.2; 113.6f.; 119.4f.; 120.3; 121.1f.; 122.3, 5f.; 123.1; 130.2, 4. Jewish Christians: 1.53.6; 54.3; *Dial.* 64.3, 5; 120.2; 136.1.

Chapter 6

Information from Paul's Letter
to the Romans and Acts 28:30f.

1. Social differences, a social stratification, is presupposed in Roman church life, already by Paul, when he calls for the better-off to give alms to the poorer (Rom 12:13, 8). Paul's having selected Rome as a point of departure for his Spanish mission (15:24, 28) shows that he expects possible support from that church community. He hopes that some can afford to go to Spain with him (v. 24 προπέμπεσθαι; cf. 1 Cor 16:6, 11; 2 Cor 1:16). Paul needs traveling companions familiar with Latin. Or, if we press προπέμπεσθαι harder, he hopes to be fitted out by the Romans for the Spanish mission — be it with food, money, or companions.

Finally, Paul assumes in 13:6f. that the Romans have to pay not only taxes but also customs, which implies that they are involved with trade.[1] From the taxes one cannot conclude much sociohistorically because of the various possibilities of interpretation. Peregrini, provincials without Roman citizenship, for example, paid in Rome head- and land-taxes; richer people paid an inheritance tax; slaves' liberation tax was also taken. We do not know which taxes applied to the Roman Christians. At least we know, as we shall see below, that a large portion of the Christians in Rome belonged to the peregrini, the resident aliens.

Summary: Already in Paul's letter to the Romans there is evidence of a certain social stratification: from Christians in need (12:13, 8) to those who are better off, who can engage in trade, who can travel as well as share with and care for the poorer (12:13). However, those who are seeking Christians from the upper classes will, despite all the "stratification," not be able to infer them from the letter to the Romans.

The *integration* of the Christians within the community, including those from different social layers, is promoted in 12:3ff. Christians ought *reciprocally* to deal with each other deferentially and caringly, and thus — if we read the text against the backdrop of the social differences in the community — not only the lower esteem the higher, but

---

1. If Hebrews 10:34 was addressed *to* Rome, some of the urban Roman Christians are, on the basis of *this* passage, to be regarded as somewhat better off: ὑπάρχοντα could point in this direction; cf. Matt 19:21; 24:47; 25:14; Luke 11:21; 12:44; 16:1.

also the higher respect the lower. That little word "reciprocally" appears four times in this passage. According to Paul, the honor of the other is to be placed higher than one's own, even when the other, according to human standards, is less advantaged (cf. v. 10 with 1 Cor 12:23f.; Phil 2:3). One's own social position was relativized by such behavior. Moreover, Christians with a higher social position are not to strive for an even more elevated status; they are not to seek further social advancement but rather they are to be "carried away to humble ways" (v. 16). Sharing in the experience of the other and adapting to the behavior of the other (v. 15!) ought to bring the members of the church closer to one another. How far such parenesis was successful I will investigate in connection with *1 Clement* and the book of Hermas.

2. Acts 28:30f. gives us the tradition that Paul lived two years in Rome ἐν ἰδίῳ μισθώματι, and there he received and taught fellow Christians. May we conclude that no urban Roman Christian possessed a larger house in which Paul as a *guest* might have been able to live and teach? Unfortunately, no: (a) Passages like 1 Cor 9:12, 18, 6, 15; 4:12; 2 Cor 11:7ff.; 12:13 show that Paul as a rule was concerned to live "on his own expense" in the community in which he was working, so that his costs fell on no one as a burden.[2] This would have been especially true for a church in which, at first, he hardly knew anyone. (b) As a state prisoner under accusation of religious crimes, Paul would have compromised a host.

---

2. Cf. the rule of Phil 4:15. Further, W. Pratscher, "Der Verzicht des Paulus auf finanziellen Unterhalt," *NTS* 25 (1979): 284–98. This rule does not exclude that Paul hoped for support from the Romans for his *Spanish* mission (Rom 15:24, 28; cf. 2 Cor 11:8f.).

Chapter 7

Information in Conjunction with the Persecution by Nero

From the literary reports about Nero's persecution in the year 64 C.E. we can pick up several points:

1. The executed Christians represented a "tremendous crowd," a *multitudo ingens* (Tacitus, *Ann.* 15.44.4). *First Clement* 6:1 also refers to the Neronian martyrs as πολὺ πλῆθος, a coincidence that can hardly be explained by imputing rhetorical exaggeration to *both* authors.[1]

2. The condemned Christians were "wrapped in the skins of wild animals and mangled by dogs," or "nailed to crosses (*crucibus affixi*) and burned for nocturnal illumination" (Tacitus, ibid.). These hideous torments are commonly put down to Nero's arbitrariness, with nothing to do with justice.[2] But is that really so? The measures described correspond with Roman penal praxis. Already in the Twelve Tablets (Gaius, *Dig.* 47.9.9), there is the stipulation that arsonists be burned to death.[3] Nero burned the Christians as torches in the night. Wrapping murderers in animal skins, called "sacking,"[4] was still practiced in the imperial time (Seneca, *De clem.* 1.23; Suetonius, *Claud.* 34; cf. Modestinus, *Dig.* 48.9.9).[5] If Nero then in these two modes of execution did not move completely beyond the rules of Roman penal law,[6] then it was probably the same for the crucifixions. If here too Nero did not ignore the rules of penal law completely, those Christians crucified did *not* possess *Roman citizenship.*[7]

---

1. True, one can compare Tacitus to Livy 39.13.14 (description of the Baccanalia scandal). But with that the testimony of *1 Clement* is not explained.

2. E.g., K. Latte, "Todesstrafe," Pauly / Wissowa Suppl. 7 (1940): 1617.

3. "Qui aedes acervumve frumenti iuxta domum positum combusserit, vinctus verberatus igni necari iubetur, si modo sciens prudensque id commisit." Cf. Th. Mommsen, *Römisches Strafrecht* (Leipzig, 1899), 923.

4. Cf. Mommsen, ibid., 921–23.

5. Cf. mangling dogs in this mode of execution also in Modestinus, ibid.; Justinian, *Inst.* 4.18.6; Dositheus, *Hadr. sent.* 16. The "variant" that Nero allowed himself was that he did not, as was usual, cast the victims into the river on top of it.

6. Tacitus, ibid., 4, also hints at hearings before the executions ("fatebantur; deinde indicio eorum ... convicti sunt").

7. As a rule, crucifixion was used for strangers without citizenship, *humiliores,* slaves (*servile* supplicium): e.g., Apuleius, *Met.* 10.12.3; Suetonius, *Galba* 9; Cicero, *In Verrem*

3. That a large number of Christians were without Roman citizen-ship is interesting when compared to Roman Jewry. A high percentage of the urban Roman Jews were Roman citizens (see below). Of course, this comparison does not yet prove that citizenship was found more fre-quently among urban Roman Jews than in the Christianity of the city. But we may take it as another warning against transferring sociohistor-ical discoveries about urban Roman Judaism directly to urban Roman Christianity. We saw that already in the time of Paul's letter to the Ro-mans only a minority of Christians in the city were of Jewish origin (Part 3).

Why were many Jews in Rome Roman citizens? (a) A high percent-age of urban Roman Jews of the first century C.E. were emancipated slaves or their descendants. This is evidenced not only in Philo (*Leg. ad Gaium* 155, above) or in Tacitus (*Ann.* 2.85.4). It is also attested by the epigraphically documented[8] freedperson's synagogues in Rome: the "Au-gustenses," "Agrippenses," and "Volumnenses" synagogues. All three of these belong already to the first century C.E.[9] (b) As freedpersons or as descendants of freed slaves, these urban Roman Jews were for the most part Roman citizens. Where did they get their citizenship? Philo gives evidence that the Jewish slaves taken to Rome by Pompey were set free quite soon, at the latest in the time of Augustus. Also the synagogue of the "Augustenses," i.e., of the Augustus freedpersons, documents the presence of Jewish liberti before the year 14 C.E. Up into the time of Augustus, manumission was as a rule connected with the awarding of Roman citizenship. It was not until around the year 19 C.E. that the *Lex Iunia* reduced the multitudes of freedpersons automatically becoming

---

2.5.12 (punishment for slaves); 5.162–71 (the exclamation, "I am a Roman citizen," suf-ficed to protect one from crucifixion; ibid., 168; "it is a misdemeanor to bind a Roman citizen, a crime to flog him, and nothing else but an assassination to kill him: so what should I call his crucifixion?" ibid., 170); *Pro Milone* 59f.; *Pro Rabiro* 11–17, esp. 16: "All of these things (cross, etc.)...are unworthy for a Roman citizen," the cross is a slave's punishment. If occasionally the crucifixion of a Roman citizen is reported, then this is always expressly commented on as a breaking of the rules (e.g., Suetonius, *Galba* 9.1; Josephus, *Bell.* 2.308; Cicero, *In Verrem* 2.5.12.162–71). Tacitus is scandalized at Nero, but he cannot complain that Nero has violated the rule "no crucifixion for Roman citizens" in his punishments of the Christians. Suetonius describes Nero's punishments of the Christians expressly in that part of the *Vita* of Nero (16.2) in which he reports *not* Nero's illegal infamous actions and crimes but precisely his governmental actions, which from the point of view of the law were correct (see 19.3!).

On punishment by crucifixion: M. Hengel, *Crucifixion,* 2d ed. (Philadelphia, 1978) (pp. 39–45 note the individual cases of crucifixions of Roman citizens, which were, how-ever, never initiated by Nero); J. Schneider, "Stauros," *TWNT* 7:573; Engl. trans.: *TDNT*; V. Schultze, "Kreuz," *RE* 11:90f.; Latte (above, n. 2), 1614ff.; Mommsen (above, n. 3) 918ff.

8. *CIJ* nos. 284, 301, 338, 368, 416, 496; 365, 425, 503; 343, 402, 417, 523.

9. On the dating, R. Penna, "Les Juifs à Rome au temps de l'Apôtre Paul," *NTS* 28 (1982): 321–47, here 328.

full Roman citizens.[10] That means for us that the children and grand-
children of the Pompeius slaves and of the "Augustenses" were Roman
citizens. Philo (ibid. 157) accordingly writes, "(Augustus) did not take
their Roman citizenship away from them (the former Pompeius slaves
or their descendants)" (οὔτε τὴν Ῥωμαϊκὴν αὐτῶν ἀφείλετο πολιτείαν).
They received, like every other free citizen, their grain allotment (Philo,
ibid. 158). When, in the year 19 C.E., under Tiberius, certain penal measures were taken against the Jews (Tacitus, *Ann.* 2.85.4), many Jews
were expelled from the city; 4,000[11] Jewish freedmen or descendants of
freed slaves, however, possessed Roman citizenship (or at least the *La-
tinitas Iunia*) and therefore could not summarily be banished without
individual trials like the others ("ceteri"): They were called up to bear
arms to fight the robber bands in Sardinia. Four thousand men with citizenship of arms-bearing age ("idonea aetas") represented between 7 and
27 percent of the whole urban Roman Jewry.[12] If one subtracts women,
children, and men *un*able to bear arms from the whole of the Jewry of
Rome, then the percentage of Roman citizens rises correspondingly by
much more.

4. The events under Nero presuppose that the Christians already existed in a considerable number, that they were publicly known, and in
general made a bad impression. Therefore they could easily be made into
scapegoats. Tacitus, who was convinced that the Christians were innocent of the burning of Rome, nevertheless believes reports of all sorts
of abominations by the Christians. The allegations peak in the famous
"odium humani generis" ("they hate the human race"), of which Tacitus (*Hist.* 5.5.1) also accuses the Jews. Misunderstanding and hatred[13]
confronted the Christians. The Neronian penal measures heightened the
negative image of the Christians still more. Through these Neronian
measures, the Christians were stamped as outsiders to society. From then
on, they were regarded as potentially dangerous (possible arsonists!),
having to face the possibility of punishment by the authorities.

---

10. Cf. G. Alföldy, "Die Freilassung von Sklaven und die Struktur der Sklaverei in
der römischen Kaiserzeit," in H. Schneider, ed., *Sozial- und Wirtschaftsgeschichte der
römischen Kaiserzeit,* WF 552 (Darmstadt, 1981), 337, 341, 343f.; ibid., 2d ed. (1979),
124f. Also the Lex Aelia Sentia, already from the year 4 C.E., made it more difficult for
younger slaves under 30 to attain citizenship upon their emancipation.

11. From Tacitus, one *could* conclude that the 4,000 were followers of "Egyptian and
Jewish superstition." Suetonius (*Tib.* 36.1), however, after the mention of Egyptians and
Jews, adds the more precise "Iudaeorum iuventus." Josephus also (*Ant.* 18.81–85) speaks
of 4,000 Jews.

12. The sources are disparate. Modern estimates allege between 15,000 and 60,000
Jews in Rome. Bibliography in Solin, "Juden und Syrer," 698, n. 240; 700.

13. Cf. *1 Clem.* 60:3; Justin, *Apol.* I.1.1; 4.4f.; 20.3; 24.1; 57.1; II.8.1f.; *Dial.* 134.6;
Tatian, *Or.* 4.1; 9.4; 25.3; as an early testimony, Mark 13:13. Hengel (1984, 35f.) wants
to connect Mark 13:12f. to the Neronian events.

Chapter 8

Information from
First Clement

1. Sometime in the first century urban Roman Christians sold themselves voluntarily into slavery, giving the proceeds to feed poor fellow Christians: ἐν ἡμῖν...πολλοὶ ἑαυτοὺς παρέδωκαν εἰς δουλείαν καὶ λαβόντες τὰς τιμὰς αὐτῶν ἑτέρους ἐψώμισαν (*1 Clem.* 55:2). This was an example of vicarious suffering. Clement could have interpreted it in a christological fashion, for example, in the sense of a self-humbling imitation of Christ. But he refrains from loading these acts with theological meaning.

Selling oneself into slavery was also practiced in the pagan environs, and not just in isolated cases, as the juristic sources confirm (e.g., *Dig.* 1.5.21; 1.5.5.1; 40.12.7; cf. Dio of Prusa, *Or.* 15.22f.; Philostratus, *Apoll.* 8.7.12). Why would a pagan *homo liber* sell himself? Did she or he do this as pure self-sacrifice, for charitable purposes? Not quite. First, the new master will pay the slave's support and may even train him in a vocation. Second, the *homo liber, qui se vendidit* could as a rule assume that he would later be freed.[1] Third, it was not rare for the period of service as a slave to be agreed upon in advance.[2] And fourth, the temporary sale of oneself could bring social advancement with it later, if a slave by means of his later manumission received his patron's Latin or Roman citizenship. The citizenship also freed him from paying the head-tax.[3] But I do not wish to minimize the severity of the step. Dio of Prusa formulates clearly: "...countless free human beings sell themselves so that through a contract they are slaves, in part

---

1. G. Alföldy worked this out once again decisively (1981, p. 359): On the basis of the legal and epigraphical sources, "it may be maintained that the emancipation of a slave, at the latest when he reached the age of 30 to 40, presumably was almost normal." On slaves selling themselves, cf., e.g., ibid., 365ff.; 2d ed. (1979), 123, 125.

2. *Cod. Iust.* 4.57.1ff.; ibid. 1, a case wherein fifteen years were agreed upon.

3. Cf., e.g., Petronius, 57.4: " 'Why were you a slave?' Because I delivered myself into slavery and wanted to be a Roman citizen rather than someone who pays the head-tax." Also *after* the *Lex Iunia* (see above) it was still possible in principle to obtain citizenship through emancipation. Cf. F. De Visscher, "L'affranchissement des esclaves et son effet acquisitif du droit de cité, *L'Antiquité classique* 14 (1945): 139f.

under by no means acceptable, but rather most difficult conditions" (*Or.* 15.22f.).

That urban Roman Christians grasped at this means[4] of helping their fellow Christians shows us, in my view, at least three things. First, these people who were ready for sacrifice were — again — not Roman citizens, for it runs counter to Roman legal principle that Roman citizens enslaved themselves.[5] Second, apparently the economic need of some Christians in Rome was so large and the possibilities for the other Christians to help them so restricted that this extreme means of making money for the care of the poor (ἐψώμισαν!) was grasped. In other words, it appears that — in spite of rudimentary social stratification — sometime in the first century there were not yet the sorts of wealthy benefactors in the ranks of the Christians who could prevent the need for such acts of self-enslavement. *First Clement* 55:2 even states that these cases were "numerous." Self-enslavement for charitable purposes exemplifies, third, how very successful Christianity was in attaining some solidarity and integration within the lower strata of society. Christians, with nothing to sell but themselves, did that in order to help fellow Christians who were as poor as they themselves. The integration that Christianity succeeded in obtaining within the lower strata was, in the society of those days, certainly not self-evident. Only the upper strata of the empire presented themselves as more firmly integrated groups — above all, the class of the senators. The lower strata in large measure lacked collective consciousness as well as supraregional cohesion. Christianity here provided a socially integrating contribution to society at large, which must not be undervalued.

2. Clement looks back at the incidents of self-enslavement for charitable purposes as events from the past. He himself already knows wealthy people (πλούσιοι) in the church community of the 90s of the first century. Using formulas of traditional speaking,[6] to reflect actual church life, he formulates: "The strong one (ὁ ἰσχυρός) should care for the weak, but the weak (ὁ ἀσθενής) ought to esteem (ἐντρεπέτω) the strong one; the wealthy (ὁ πλούσιος) should aid the poor, but the poor (ὁ πτωχός) should thank God for giving to the rich means through which the poor can be helped in his need. The wise man (ὁ σοφός) ought not show his wisdom in words, but in good works" (*1 Clem.* 38:2). Here

---

4. If 1 Cor 13:3 refers to brand marks of slaves (so H. Gülzow, *Christentum und Sklaverei in den ersten drei Jahrhunderten* [Bonn, 1969], 79f.), then the practice of Christians selling themselves also took place in the east.

5. See Th. Mommsen, "Bürgerlicher und peregrinischer Freiheitsschutz im römischen Staat," in *Ges. Schriften* (Berlin, 1907), 3:1ff.

6. Cf., e.g., Jer 9:22f. = *1 Clem.* 13:1; Luke 16:21f.; James 1:10f.; 3:13; 2 Cor 9:12 11:9; et al.

social stratification becomes visible. How some social balance and material interchange between rich and poor in church life took place in detail we shall discover below in the second century.

3. The fragment of prayer in *1 Clem.* 59:4 obviously stems from the Roman liturgy. The worshipers remember their fellow Christians who are weak (ἀσθενοῦντας) and hungry (πεινῶντας). Christians who lived at the farthest edge of minimal existence thus remained a problem.

Chapter 9

Information from Ignatius's
Letter to the Romans

We move into the second century. At the beginning of the century, in the time of Trajan, Ignatius writes to the Romans:

(1:2—2:1):...I fear your love, that it may damage me. For it is easy (εὐχερές) for you to do what you intend, but it is difficult for me to reach God unless you spare me. For I do not wish you to please humans (ἀνθρωπαρεσκῆσαι)...if you maintain silence you cannot sign your name to a better deed. For if you remain silent concerning me, I shall be a word of God.... (4:1):...I die happily for God, if only you will not hinder it. I implore you not to be a source of inopportune kindness to me (μὴ εὔνοια ἄκαιρος γένησθέ μοι). (4:2): Rather entice (μᾶλλον κολακεύσατε) the wild beasts (i.e., rather cajole the wild beasts that are to eat me instead of the official who can lift my death sentence)... (5:3): Indulge me. I know what is best for me!...May no things seen or unseen (Col 1:16) take pains because of me.... (6:2): Be indulgent with me, brethren! Don't restrain me....Don't give to the world one who wants to be God's, nor lead him astray with material things!... (6:3): Allow me to be an imitator of the Passion of my God... (7:1): The prince of this world wants to abduct (διαρπάσαι) me and to pervert my mind, which is set on God. None of you...should help him.... Do not speak of Jesus Christ and still long for the world! (8:1): I desire no longer to live according to human fashion. And it will happen if you desire it.

Ignatius implores the Roman Christians to undertake nothing that could stand in the way of his martyrdom. He believes they have so much influence that he fears from their side there will be a successful intervention in his trial. "It is easy for you to do what you wish to do" (1:2); "rather entice the wild beasts" (4:2); "for I do not wish you to please humans" (2:1). Ignatius would not have returned to this point again and again throughout the entire letter had he not seriously feared the success of an intercession on his behalf. Obviously, he assumes that at least individual Christians in Rome had "connections," and that through these

88

connections, using cajolery (κολακεύειν / ἀνθρωπαρεσκῆσαι) they could easily (εὐχερές) get Ignatius's death sentence suspended. Εὐχερές is more than a rhetorical compliment for the readers. In the course of his letter, Ignatius so frequently implores the Romans not to interfere that the φοβοῦμαι of 1:2 reflects a genuine fear of the influence of his readers.

Concerning the specific nature of "connections" held by urban Roman Christians, we have information only from the end of the century (below, Part 4). Bishop Victor of Rome had alongside himself a presbyter named Hyacinth. He for his part lived as an imperial slave or freedman at the imperial court, so that through him Victor could contact the concubine of the Emperor Commodus, Marcia. She then put a good word in with Commodus — and lo and behold, the Christian forced laborers in the mines of Sardinia are set free (Hippolytus, *Ref.* 9.12). Unfortunately, Ignatius does not describe his picture of Christian "connections" in Rome in that sort of detail. Perhaps he has in mind the influence of the imperial freedman Claudius Ephebus (see below, chap. 17), who brought 1 *Clement* to Corinth. It must suffice that Ignatius's text again points to a social stratification, particularly to a group of socially more elevated, influential Christians. Pliny testifies for the same period in Asia Minor that Christians already belonged to every social class ("omnis ordinis," *Ep.* 10.97).

The phrase προκαθημένη τῆς ἀγάπης in Ignatius's prescript is unclear. Does he think of exemplary charitable love shown by the Roman Christians, which is evidenced *at the latest* in the middle of the century (see below on Eusebius, *Hist. Ecc.* 4.23.10)? Or does he have in mind the Roman martyrs (under Nero) in the sense of "excellent in love (of Christ)"? In Ignatius's immediately preceding context, the formula πίστις καὶ ἀγάπη Ἰησοῦ Χριστοῦ speaks for the latter interpretation because of the objective genitive in πίστις Ἰησοῦ Χριστοῦ, implying an objective genitive for the term ἀγάπη Ἰησοῦ Χριστοῦ, too.[1]

---

1. On the question, see R. Staats, "Die martyrologische Begründung des Romprimats bei Ignatius von Antiochien," *ZTK* 73 (1976): 461–70.

Chapter 10

The Shepherd of Hermas

Social Stratification in the First Half of the Second Century and the Attendant Conflicts

The Poor

The forceful parenesis to the rich[1] in The Shepherd of Hermas reveals how many hard-pressed poor there were: widows, orphans, destitute (πτωχός, πένης), people who suffered want (ὑστερούμενοι), and those who barely had the minimum for existence, going hungry (πεινῶντες).[2]

"He who is destitute and suffers want of the most necessary things of daily life is in great anguish. . . .Whoever rescues the soul of such a person from necessity (*de necessitate*) gains great joy for himself. . . . For many commit suicide because of such calamities when they cannot bear them."[3]

Vision 3.12.2 points to the social difficulties of the aged who must struggle with poverty (πτωχότης). Hermas formulates the sociomedical insight that, on the one hand, the financial need of the elderly stems from their physical weakness but that, on the other hand, there is a converse possibility, too: The elderly lie feebly on their resting places and await their last hour, but an inheritance (κληρονομία) can also bring them physically to their feet again.[4]

---

1. *Vis.* 3.9.2–6; *Mand.* 2.4–6; 8.10f.; *Sim.* 1.8–11; 2; 10.4.2–4; cf. 9.30.5; 24.2f.; etc.

2. *Sim.* 2; 9.26.2; 27.2; 1.8; 5.3.7; *Mand.* 8.10; *Vis.* 3.9.2–6; 2.4.3. Even if Hermas partly draws on traditional terminology from Jewish and early Christian parenesis regarding the poor (cf., e.g., James 1:27; see St. Giet, *Hermas et les pasteurs* [Paris, 1963], 134ff.), I see no basis to deny that concrete situations of Hermas's Christian community are visible behind the traditional formulations. Hermas did not take up tradition for tradition's sake but to be able to verbalize actual situations. On the basically false alternative, tradition vs. situation, see P. Lampe, "Die Apokalyptiker: Ihre Situation und ihr Handeln," in U. Luz et al., *Eschatologie und Friedenshandeln*, 2d ed. (Stuttgart, 1982), 59–114, here 65ff., esp. 71ff. (tradition as a lens for looking at actual situations).

3. *Sim.* 10.4.2f. The formulation is so general that it is not clear whether also poor Christians chose this last possibility.

4. M. Dibelius, *Der Hirt des Hermas, Die apostolischen Väter*, HNT (Tübingen, 1923), 4:480, wants to see the entire passage as taken over from pagan literature. But only the inheritance motif is actually traditional: e.g., Epictetus, 4.13.22; 2.7.9.

For the needy, especially for widows and orphans (χηρῶν καὶ ὀρφανῶν τὴν ζωήν), the Christian community provides a subsistence through its deacons. Some deacons, however, shamefully enrich themselves instead of faithfully distributing it (*Sim.* 9.26.2). *Similitude* 1.8 points perhaps to slaves who live in pagan houses and who are supposed to have their freedom purchased by the richer members of the community.[5]

The Rich

Hermas also knows many rich (πλούσιοι) in the church community. They have property and monetary means (πλοῦτος, ὑπάρξεις, κτήματα, χρήματα),[6] which they also give out as loans for interest (*Mand.* 8.10). They possess land (ἀγρούς),[7] houses (οἰκίας, οἴκους, οἰκοδομάς, οἰκήσεις),[8] apartments (οἰκήματα, *Sim.* 1) and costly furnishings (παρατάξεις πολυτελεῖς, *Sim.* 1). Interestingly enough, some have attained wealth not as pagans but after they became Christians (*Sim.* 8.9.1). Christianity and business activities are not mutually exclusive for them.

Nor does Hermas conceal the negative side. The wealthy Christians are all too wrapped up in their manifold business concerns and undertakings.[9] Some become nervous already at the slightest incident when it has to do with their business, with their expenditures and their income (ἕνεκεν βιωτικῶν πραγμάτων or περὶ δόσεως ἢ λήμψεως).[10] Involvement in the world colors the morality of Christians who possess property: Deceit (παραχαράσσω, *Sim.* 1.11; cf. *Mand.* 3.3) and greed (*Sim.* 1.11; 6.5.5; *Vis.* 3.9.2, κατάχυμα) sneak into their business practices. The Christianity of these people becomes shallow (περισπώμενοι περὶ τὸν πλοῦτον or περὶ τὰς πραγματείας αὐτῶν).[11] The rich have a "deficiency of piety": the poor must pray for them (*Sim.* 2.5–8).

---

5. "Buy for yourselves afflicted souls" (ἀγοράζειν). Thus also H. Gülzow (1969, 89). On the redactional character of the notice, see ibid. On the possibility of a slave to have his freedom bought by the congregation, cf. Aristides, *Apol.* 15.8; Ignatius, *Ad Pol.* 4; Cyprian, *Ep.* 62; *1 Clem.* 55:2. That the poor Christians envisaged by Hermas represented "no large group" (C. Osiek, *Rich and Poor* [1983], 133), I am unable to say.

6. *Sim.* 1–2; 9.20; *Mand.* 10.4; *Vis.* 1.1.8; 3.6.5; 9.6.

7. ἀγρούς is strongly emphasized by Hermas in *Sim.* 1: he always lists landed property first before all other ownerships, and he notes it seven times altogether, while the other ownerships are mentioned only once or twice.

8. *Sim.* 1; cf. also 8.10.3; 9.27.2.

9. πολλοὶ γὰρ ἀκαταστατοῦντες ταῖς βουλαῖς αὐτῶν ἐπιβάλλονται πολλά, *Sim.* 6.3.5; πραγματείαις πολλαῖς ἐμπεφυρμένοι, *Sim.* 8.8.1; 9.20; *Mand.* 10.4; they are suffocated ὑπὸ τῶν πράξεων αὐτῶν, *Sim.* 9.20; ἀπὸ πολλῶν πράξεων, πολλὰ πράσσοντες, 4.5; ἐπιθυμία πράξεων πολλῶν, *Mand.* 6.2.5.

10. *Mand.* 5.2.2. Interestingly, also women manage businesses.

11. *Sim.* 2.5; 4.9.5; 9.30.4f.; *Mand.* 10.4f.; *Sim.* 6. Cf. Tertullian, *Adv. Marc.* 4.33: "Dominatorem totius saeculi nummum scimus omnes."

Some rich Christians "make their bodies sick from eating too much" (*Vis.* 3.9.3). On their tables stand lavish delicacies; they revel in luxury (πολυτέλειαι ἐδεσμάτων πολλῶν...καὶ ποικίλων τρυφῶν, *Mand.* 6.2.5; πολυτέλεια πλούτου, 8.3; 12.2.1).[12] They participate in the extravagance and splendor of the pagans (πολυτέλεια τῶν ἐθνῶν, *Sim.* 1.10f.), which leads to another problem: They cultivate close contacts to the pagan environment and are involved in friendships with non-Christians (ἐμπεφυρμένοι φιλίαις ἐθνικαῖς, *Mand.* 10.4). Having become rich, they are esteemed in the world (πλουτήσαντες δὲ καὶ γενόμενοι ἐνδοξότεροι παρὰ τοῖς ἔθνεσιν) and show "great pride" in their bearing (ὑπερηφανίαν μεγάλην, *Sim.* 8.9.1; cf. *Vis.* 1.1.8; 3.9.6). The result is that their tie to the Christian community is loosened. They no longer diligently attend to the fellowship (τοῖς ἁγίοις μὴ καλλώμενοι, *Sim.* 8.8.1; οὐκ ἐκολλήθησαν τοῖς δικαίοις ἀλλὰ μετὰ τῶν ἐθνῶν συνέζησαν, 8.3.1).[13] They rather retain their relationship to the community only grudgingly in fear of being solicited for alms (sic: μή τι αἰτιαθῶσιν, *Sim.* 9.20; 8.9.1). They have, to be sure, not turned away from the God of the Christians, but have indeed turned from the works of faith (*Sim.* 8.9.1). Some, however, have also betrayed their faith and, animated by κενοδοξία, have moved entirely over into the pagan camp (*Sim.* 8.9.3). That precisely the wealthy are endangered by apostasy as soon as Christianity is persecuted does not need emphasis (*Vis.* 3.6.5; *Sim.* 8.8.2).

Social Conflict

We do not want simply to observe the static stratification in the Christian community. The Shepherd of Hermas gives us also an insight into the dynamics between the social strata. Where does material interchange take place? As we recognize from the aforementioned passages, two large problems present themselves to the church community: (a) The poor are not well cared for. (b) Many wealthy Christians are secularized and are only marginally integrated into the active life of the church. Both problems are obviously connected with each other. The poor starve, among other reasons, precisely because many wealthy are so shallow in their Christianity and are insufficiently engaged in the life of the church.

---

12. Cf. *Sim.* 9.15.3; 6.2.1f., 4, 6; 6.4.1f., 4; 6.5.1, 3f. Although here, in part, items are taken over from traditional catalogues of vices and virtues, Hermas does not pick up traditional wording without being convinced that it captures his own situation (see n. 2). Hermas finds also some Christian soothsayers, enmeshed in an opulent lifestyle (ἐν τρυφαῖς πολλαῖς), who for pay (μισθούς) "like the pagans" give oracles, not openly before the congregation but privately (*Mand.* 11.12f., 14).

13. Cf. *Vis.* 3.6.2; 3.9.4 (ἀσυγκρασία = lack of communal spirit).

One of Hermas's most important concerns, which he formulates once again at the very end of his book (*Sim.* 10.4.2–4), is that of moving the rich Christians to responsible action toward the poorer ones. The wealthy are to take up their duty.[14] The purpose of wealth (πλοῦτος) is that it be used for the needier people (*Sim.* 2.5, 7f., 10). As such, worldly property is good and given by God (ibid.); indeed, it is necessary. As elm and grapevine need each other — the vine creeps up the unfruitful elm, in order to bring forth fruit — so do the rich and the poor in the Christian community. The rich must support the poor materially; the poor, having strong faith, must pray for the rich (*Sim.* 2).

Similitude 10.4.2–4 appears to want to steer the gaze of the rich even beyond the borders of the Christian community: "Every person[15] must be helped out of his need. For whoever starves and suffers want of the most necessary things of daily life endures great pain. . . . Whoever knows of the need of such a person and does not help him out commits a great sin." All are called upon to give; even those who possess less: they can give to the widows, orphans, and the poor what they save through the religious practice of fasting (*Sim.* 5.3.7). The fear of some of the wealthy of being solicited for alms by the church is a disgrace (*Sim.* 9.20.2). For whoever joyfully shares the profit of his profession (ἐκ τῶν κόπων χορηγέω), to him the Lord will multiply the yield of his hands (ἐπλήθυνεν ἐν τοῖς κόποις τῶν χειρῶν, ἐχαρίτωσεν ἐν πάσῃ πράξει, *Sim.* 9.24.2f.).

The urgency of these appeals to the well-to-do betrays the fact that the wealthy do not sufficiently exercise their responsibility. Some even hide behind the argument that the recipients of alms occasionally feign their need (ἐν ὑποκρίσει λαμβάνοντες, *Mand.* 2.4–6; cf. 2 Thess 3).

The Theological Dimension of the Conflict

The conflict described has a theological dimension. Hermas's book deals not merely with the care of the poor and the social responsibility of the rich for the poor. It strikes up another main theme as well: the prophecy of a postbaptismal, second repentance. At first glance, the two areas — here a social problem, there a theological one — have nothing to do with each other. And yet, in my view, they are closely connected. I propose

14. *Vis.* 3.9.2–6; *Mand.* 2.4–6; 8.10f.; *Sim.* 1.8–11; cf. 9.30.5 and Luke! Although Hermas partially draws on traditional Jewish-Christian exhortations to give alms (see, e.g., Dibelius [1923], 550f., 527), I fail to see also here how Hermas should have propagated tradition for its own sake. An actual situation of burning concern caused him to reach out to such traditions and to use their wordings.
15. Omnem hominem; cf. 4.3: huiusmodi hominis.

the following thesis: Hermas's proclamation of a one and only postbaptismal repentance is directed to all Christians who have committed sin after baptism. When rich Christians repent, this proclamation has the social effect of revitalizing and ensuring the church's assistance to the poor. Or, put otherwise, *one* aim of Hermas's call to repentance is the reintegration of the secularized wealthy into the active church life, so that financial resources for the care of the Christian poor will again flow. The following will explain this thesis.

Penitential Laxity and Penitential Rigorism as Causes of the Deficient Integration of the Rich

Hermas entered the stage at a time when the Roman church was characterized by two conflicting attitudes toward postbaptismal repentance. According to the lax position prevalent in Rome, it was always possible both to defer and to repeat postbaptismal repentance. There was therefore no real deterrent to sinning again after repentance, and sinners often repented half-heartedly and hypocritically.[16]

On the other side, a minority of teachers followed a rigorous course: After the repentance of baptism, the life of the Christian must be holy; a second repentance is not possible (*Mand.* 4.3.1f.).[17]

The secularized, superficial, and nominal Christians, who belong to an already quite sizeable church (e.g., *Mand.* 12.4–7), are very distant from such a "holy life." A life entangled with the world through one's occupation is practically incompatible with rigorism. Hermas ex-

---

16. On the laxity position, see the discussion of the history of research by N. Brox, *Der Hirt des Hermas* (Göttingen, 1991), 476–85.

17. B. Poschmann (*Busse und letzte Ölung*, HDG 4/3 [Freiburg, 1951], 15), disputes that this is the real opinion of the teachers of *Mand.* 4.3: They would only have spoken to catechumens in this fashion — for pedagogical reasons, in order to guard against postbaptismal sins. In sermons to the baptized, these teachers would "perhaps urgently" have called their auditors to repentance. That is speculation. It is important to Poschmann to present the picture of a homogeneous picture of the early church. According to him, long before the time of Hermas, the church had granted comprehensive forgiveness of even serious postbaptismal sins. This is — contrary to the so-called baptismal theory of the older research (e.g., H. Windisch, *Taufe und Sünde im ältesten Christentum bis auf Origenes* [Tübingen, 1908]) — certainly correct (evidence in J. Becker and G. A. Benrath, "Busse," in *TRE* 7 [1981]: 450–52; H. Braun, *An die Hebräer*; HNT 14 [Tübingen, 1984], 171f.). But Poschmann appears to infer from this that in Hermas's time there could not seriously have been rigoristic teachers of the sort described in *Mand.* 4.3. There lies the faulty conclusion. Instead of wanting to present a homogeneous picture, we ought to reckon with the likelihood of finding side by side in early Christianity various theories about repentance after baptism. In fact, we know, alongside of comprehensive forgiveness, *also* rigoristic evidence for the time before as well as after Hermas, e.g., 1 Cor 5; Heb 6:4ff.; 10:26ff.; 12.16f.; 1 John 3:6; Acts 5:1–11; *Barn.* 16:8f. (mentions only the penance of the first conversion); Justin, *Dial.* 44.4 (only those who live sinlessly after baptism earn "the promised good"); Irenaeus, *Haer.* 4.27.2 (knows the thesis that there is no forgiveness after baptism).

perienced this himself: in his former businesses there had been some cheating (ψευδῆ ἐν ταῖς πραγματείαις). He notes that the commandment to be truthful is almost unfulfillable in business life (*Mand.* 3.4f.)! Rigorist ethical theory and real life break apart dramatically in parts of his church. Hermas knows "about human weakness" (*Mand.* 4.3.4), about involvement in businesses and pressures of the world, in which he himself, as he says, had been "kneaded under" (*Vis.* 2.3.1). For all of these Christians, according to the rigorists, there is no further possible repentance. Those who are secularized have lost their chance, especially if they more and more often have stayed away from the gatherings of the community (see above) or live unchastely (*Mand.* 12.2). Already in Hebrews 10:25f.; 12:16f., both were unforgivable.

The conflict that results concerning the care of the poor can be described thus: Rich Christians whose ties to the congregation had loosened were not motivated by either of these two positions to reintegrate seriously into active church life and to feel responsible for the congregation's charity program. The position of laxity left no reason seriously to change one's life-style, because repentance could always be deferred and repeated. And the rigorist position held that no second repentance was possible after baptism (*Mand.* 4.3.1–2). The rigorist theory prevented the sinner's reintegration into active church life. Thus, also in light of this second position, rich sinners felt less than enthusiastic about being active again in the church. In other words, both positions — laxity and rigorism — hampered the reintegration of the secularized wealthy, so that the care of the poor, which depended on the financial resources of the rich, also stagnated. Only when both of the main themes of Hermas's book, repentance and almsgiving parenesis, are coupled with each other in this way (which has not been done in exegesis) can the situation in which Hermas entered the stage be sufficiently illuminated.

Hermas's Proposed Solution: One Postbaptismal Repentance

a. Hermas's call to repentance is a middle stance between the two positions. He liberalizes the rigorist attitude by saying that postbaptismal repentance is indeed possible. And he radicalizes the laxity attitude and shows some rigorist influence (cf. *Mand.* 4.3.2) by saying that postbaptismal repentance is possible, but only once and only within time limits (*Vis.* 2.2.4–5; *Mand.* 4.1.8).[18] In this way, Hermas's call to repentance avoids laxity and becomes urgent, demanding immediate and wholehearted action as well as enduring results. After the repentance to which

---

18. For a balanced discussion of Hermas's teaching about repentance, see Brox, *Der Hirt*, 476–85.

he urges his readers, there will be no return to the old, sinful ways, he warns, unless one wants to lose salvation (e.g., *Mand.* 4.1.11; 4.3.7). Hermas's middle position is new, and whoever comes up with new ideas has to show proof of authority. Hermas therefore describes visions, a heavenly letter, and divine inspiration that support his stance.

One aim of Hermas's call to repentance is to bring secularized Christians back to active church life. Many secularized Christians, however, are rich. This reintegration, therefore, has an effect also on the care of the poor in the congregation, because more financial resources become available. Hermas's proclamation of repentance has a direct social effect, if taken up by its addressees.

b. We would curtail Hermas's speech if we did not mention some specifications. One new possibility of repentance is indeed opened up after baptism — but it is a single one, with a time limit, and only for those who have already sinned after baptism, not for those who are still to be baptized and might be able to find in Hermas's book an excuse for future sins (*Mand.* 4.3.3).

The problem with that is obvious. Hermas's prophecy of only one single additional repentance ensures the care for the poor only for the moment, not for the long haul. If wealthy Christians do not have the right to repent again and again — and that means, again and again to act in "unholy" fashion and to plunge into secular business activities, then, in the long run, their wealth will shrink and there will be less left over for the poor. Hermas knows about the difficulty of bringing ethical rigorism and successful business activities together (cf. *Mand.* 3.3–5). The problem may also be described thus: The fact that Hermas offers only a single opportunity for repenting after baptism would, strictly speaking, call for the moral consequence that after this repentance the rich person would begin to live in "holy" fashion, would renounce his property and give up his business activities. But Hermas is unable to struggle through to this solution — for understandable reasons. If, after this repentance, the Christians were to give up their businesses, the financial means in the church community would shrivel up, and the poor would continue to be badly cared for.

What is to be done? Hermas's solution is a compromise. In order to be able to live in a "holy" fashion after repentance, one who is tangled up in the world must desist from not all but from *many* of his businesses (ἀπὸ πολλῶν πράξεων, οἱ γὰρ τὰ πολλὰ πράσσοντες πολλὰ καὶ ἁμαρτάνουσι). *One* of them he may carry on with (μίαν πρᾶξιν); then he can still serve the Lord without being steered away from the faith (*Sim.* 4.5–7; 1.6). One piece of the world is allowed, only no one is to become too involved in it. The Christian may be a businessperson but, as much as possible, only a small one. True, God desires to "cut off the wealth" from the well-to-do, "but not totally, so that they can do good with that which remains to them" (*Sim.* 9.30.4f.)! Here the reason is clearly expressed *why* Hermas does not want Christians wholly to do without possessing worldly things. The businesses of the rich are needed so that the poor do not starve. Of course, Hermas polemicizes against luxury and wealth.[19] But he does not want to set worldly possessions completely aside either but rather insists that they be rightly used.

Theoretical Remark

Hermas's call to repentance had aimed at ensuring relief for the poor in the church. This thesis needs to be guarded against misunderstandings. (a) The social function of guaranteeing a charity program certainly was not the only function of Hermas's call to repentance. This call was directed to *all* Christians, not only to the rich. (b) To name one of its "functions" does not imply that I "explained" a phenomenon or got hold of its causes. Spring rain has the function of assisting the growth of plants; but we do not therefore know "why" it rains. In other words, my thesis does not explain "why" — on the basis of which reality — Hermas has visions and feels commissioned to proclaim a new, one and only chance for repentance. (c) To talk about "function" does not imply that I took a functionalist approach. True, I looked at the interdependence of a theological concept and a charity program. But this view did not only focus on "social unity" being maintained by this interplay. Massive conflicts have been as prominent in my description as "unity," if not more so.

I propose as a theoretical model for this interplay a cybernetic circle (a *Regelkreis* in which *is* and *should-be values* stand in tension with each other, causing a dynamic process). I am persuaded that in contexts of sociology of religion only more complicated, dynamic models, not static ones (e.g., super-/infra-structure), will help us get further. The cybernetic circle is a dynamic model that could illustrate the reciprocal influence between religious and, e.g., economic factors. How the interplay between Hermas's doctrine of repentance and the practice of charity can be shown in a "Regelkreis" is depicted in Diagrams 4 and 5 in the appendix. The "standard value" (*Regelgrösse*), "disrupting factor" (*Störgrösse*), and "guiding factor" (*Führungsgrösse*) are commonly used designations for components of the cybernetic circle (*Regelkreis*). Hermas's theological teaching about repentance plays in that circle the role of the "guiding factor."

---

19. E.g., *Vis.* 1.1.8; 3.6.5–7; *Sim.* 1; 9.31. Also *Vis.* 3.11.3; *Mand.* 10.1.4f.; *Sim.* 4.5–7; 8.8.1. Further, *Mand.* 6.2.5; 8.3; *Sim.* 1.10.

Integration of Different Social Strata

We do not know how much success Hermas's initiative achieved. It was oriented towards bringing the social strata within Christianity nearer to each other. The wealthy should share from their possessions. Beyond that, they should limit the size of their businesses and, thus, move a bit downwards on the social scale. The hungering poor, on the other hand, should experience some social advancement, because the Christian community defrayed the costs of their subsistence — through the donations of the wealthy. What Hermas intended and the Christians probably also practiced in a limited way (see above on Romans 12 and *1 Clement*) was a modicum of integration of the differing social strata. Christianity here made a contribution to the life of the society at large that is worth notice, even if it was not unique. Also in the pagan funereal *collegia* of the city of Rome, for instance, some social integration took place. In their *columbaria* we discover inscriptions of freeborn citizens and slaves, of superiors and subordinates, side by side.[20] The difference lies in the fact, however, that such pagan groupings did not develop ethics for everyday life to the extent that the Christians did. The drawing closer of the strata in these groups did not have many repercussions in everyday life. The Christians, at least in their caring for the poor, interacted with each other on a daily basis.[21]

Where in both the Christian and the pagan worlds did the different social strata come close to each other, even to the extent that emotional bonds developed between masters and slaves? This place was the *oikos*

---

20. On these inscriptions, see Huttunen, *Social Strata Rome,* 121.
21. A parallel is also offered by the integration achieved by the Dionysus cult. (a) *SIG* 985 is often cited: Dionysus "gives free access to his house for men and women, free and slaves" (first century B.C.E.; again in K. Berger and C. Colpe, *Religionsgeschichtliches Textbuch zum Neuen Testament*; NTD Textreihe 1 [Göttingen, 1987], 274–76: an "equalizing cult"; cf. also the evidence in J. Leipoldt, *Dionysos*; Angelos-Beiheft 3 [Leipzig, 1931], 53–57). (b) We should not ignore the *integration* fostered by this cult. The alleged *equal status* of the Dionysus cult participants, however, has often been overemphasized (e.g., by Wiefel [1972], 47f.). The inscription of the Dionysus mystery of Pompeia Agrippinilla of Tusculum with ca. 500 initiates (second century C.E.; see below), e.g., shows that the many cultic offices are hierarchically structured — and the cultic hierarchy reflects the hierarchical stratification in Agrippinilla's gigantic household. The cult united Agrippinilla's household slaves, servants, clients, relatives, and children, and thus undoubtedly contributed to the integration of this *familia,* but did not break up its hierarchical structure. (c) The integration within this cultic community had repercussions in the everyday life of the cult participants. But this was not a typical characteristic of a Dionysus cultic group. These repercussions resulted from the special identity of cultic group and household. Where this identity was absent, the Dionysus *thiasoi* organized festival parades, festive meals and rites, and occasionally the burial of members. (Cf. the inscription of Cumae, fifth century B.C.E.; illustration in Cumont [1975], plate 8.1: "No one has the right to be buried here except for the initiate of the Bacchus mysteries." The group maintained a cemetery.) But rarely do we hear that the initiates associated with each other in everyday life on a regular basis and that the integration experienced in the cult thus resulted in an ethic for everyday life.

(the household). No wonder that the Christian community called itself "household of God" (1 Tim 3:15; cf. Heb 3:6; Tit 1:7; Eph 2:19; 1 Cor 4:1). In this "house" some integration took place, as the book of Hermas shows. Tatian emphasizes that at Christian gatherings all take part equally without regard to status — from the old woman to the young boy who has no beard yet (*Or.* 32.3, 1; 33.1).

Chapter 11

The Writings of Justin

The Social Structure of Christianity at the Middle of the Second Century

Social stratification is again noticeable around the middle of the second century, especially in the writings of Justin.

1. We begin at the bottom of the social ladder. *Apology* 1.60.11: Among the Christians there is a group of illiterate (τῶν οὐδὲ τοὺς χαρακτῆρας τῶν στοιχείων ἐπισταμένων),[1] of people simple and of unrefined language (ἰδιωτῶν καὶ βαρβάρων τὸ φθέγμα…). There are cripples, blind (ibid.), and needy (1.13.1; 1.14.2; 1.15.10; 1.67.1). *Apology* 1.67.6: For these needy,[2] for orphans, for widows, for imprisoned Christians, and for the strangers in the Christian community who are staying in Rome as guests for a time, there is — in every house church in Rome[3] — a cash box set up. *Apology* 1.13.1 evidences providing food for these poor (δεομένοις). This cash fund is administered by a "presiding person" (προεστώς) who, in addition to this social assignment as "caregiver" (κηδεμών), has also the duty of leading the worship liturgy (1.67).

Apology 1.67.6: This fund was filled up every Sunday at the worship service. All gave according to their own discretion and possibilities (οἱ εὐποροῦντες δὲ καὶ βουλόμενοι κατὰ προαίρεσιν ἕκαστος τὴν ἑαυτοῦ ὃ βούλεται διδωσι…). This formulation alone already sufficiently indicates social differences within the Christian community. Thus there were also the εὐποροῦντες, who possessed sufficient means to give to the needier ones (1.67.6; 1.67.1; 1.14.2; 1.15.10). 1.14.2: There were also those Christians who before their conversion loved their fortunes and possessions (χρημάτων and κτημάτων) above all, but who now contribute from their goods to every needy fellow Christian (νῦν ἃ ἔχομεν εἰς κοινὸν φέροντες καὶ παντὶ δεομένῳ κοινωνοῦντες). The cash amount

---

1. Conjectures about the extent of illiteracy in the city of Rome in J. P. V. D. Balsdon, *Life and Leisure in Ancient Rome* (London, 1969), 105f.

2. Justin, ibid., shows that social decline is because of sickness.

3. On the plurality of worshiping congregations of Christians in Rome, see Part 5. There exegetical details on Justin, *Apol.* 1.67, will be given.

in the funds appears already to have grown quite respectably. About ten years before Justin wrote, Marcion had given the urban Roman Christians 200,000 sesterces (see Part 4). And when a few years later (144 C.E.) Marcion was excommunicated from the fellowship of the "Great Church," he could be given back this large sum very promptly![4]

Somewhat later than Justin, around 170 C.E., Dionysius of Corinth wrote in his letter to the Romans about the charitable monies in Rome (in Eusebius, *Hist. Ecc.* 4.23.10): "From the beginning you had the custom of helping all of the brethren in many sorts of ways and of sending support to many congregations in all cities. Through the gifts which you have been sending all along, ... you have eased the poverty of the needy. ... Your bishop, Soter [ca. 166–75 C.E.], has richly distributed gifts to the saints."[5] Eusebius adds to that (ibid., 9) that the Roman Christians had continued this readiness to help up to the Diocletian persecution. And in another place (7.5.2) he cites a letter of Dionysius of Alexandria from the middle of the third century: "... all of Syria and Arabia, where you (Romans) have always been sending and have just now sent support."[6] Eusebius can report no other Christian community with a similar economic engagement not only for "their own needy" but for many other Mediterranean cities as well. This allows a cautious social-historical comparison between the individual Christian communities of the Mediterranean world. In the second century, Rome apparently had the largest budget and the most members able to donate.

What did these well-off believers look like? Let us look again at Justin and further examine the stratification. *Apology* 1.16.4: There are Christians who travel and who carry on business and trade. 1.17.1: They pay appropriate customs and taxes (φόρους and εἰσφοράς). 2.12.4: There are Christians who own slaves (οἰκέται τῶν ἡμετέρων). Justin notes a case that has "just" (v. 3) happened in Rome: male and female slaves have been dragged away from Christian masters to be tortured in order to extract incriminating evidence from them about their Christian masters' conduct. Whether these slaves were themselves Christians is unclear.

Apology 2.10.8 attests, in addition to the economically strong, an intellectual elite, "philosophers" and "scholars" standing in contrast to the illiterate. At the same time, the passage illustrates the stratification: among the Christians are "not only φιλόσοφοι and φιλόλογοι, but also

4. Tertullian, *De praescr.* 30; cf. *Adv. Marc.* 4.4.

5. That the Romans not only in the second century but "right from the beginning" had sent help to foreign congregations appears questionable in view of the urban Roman self-enslavements for charitable purposes. These self-enslavements reveal that the Roman Christians sometime in the second and third quarters of the first century scarcely had sufficient money available for the care of their *own* poor. Dionysius's eulogy ("right from the beginning," etc.) was enthused by Soter's generous sending of help and therefore exaggerated rhetorically.

6. Cf. in addition Basil, *Ep.* 70 *ad Damas.*

craftspersons (χειροτέχναι)[7] and completely ordinary people (παντελῶς ἰδιῶται)." *Dialogue* 139.5 (cf. 140.1) evidences the coexistence of slaves and freepersons in the Christian community.

2. The social mix corresponds to an ethnic mixture. *Apology* 1.15.6: Many elderly in the church community[8] belong to every "sort of humans" (γένος ἀνθρώπων); γένος means for Justin less the social stratum than the ethnic "race or tribe."[9] 1.14.3: In the Christian community people gather at one table (ὁμοδίαιτοι γινόμενοι) who, before their baptism, because of their differing ethnic customs, would not have had fellowship around the hearth together (ἑστίας κοινάς). The integration achieved by Christianity is here nicely expressed. Justin never tires of praising the ethnic multiplicity of the Christians.[10]

3. Correspondingly manifold are the religious origins. "Many" have been Christian from their youth on (ἐκ παίδων, 1.15.6). Others in a "countless crowd" (ἀναρίθμητον πλῆθος) only during the course of their lives reached Christianity from paganism (1.15.7; 1.16.4). In the Christian community are former adherents of Dionysus, of Apollo and Asclepius, of the μυστήρια (mysteries) of Persephone, Aphrodite, and others (1.25). Some Christians previously practiced magic (1.14.2).

4. Finally there are Christians who are such in name only, without corresponding conduct in their lives (βιοῦντες, 1.16.8, 14). This observation points to an already considerable number of urban Roman Christians.

5. How growth took place, how pagans were won for Christianity,[11] is illustrated in 1.16.4. Some are won through the moral example

---

7. On Christians working with their hands, cf. also Athenagoras, *Suppl.* 11.3; 2 Thess 3:10; perhaps Hermas *Mand.* 2.4.

8. Sixty- to seventy-year-old women and men, which is interesting for the average life expectancy.

9. 1.31.7: εἰς πᾶν γένος ἀνθρώπων = τοὺς ἐξ ἐθνῶν ἀνθρώπους; clearly 1.32.4: ἐκ πάντων ἐθνῶν = ἐκ πάντων γενῶν ἀνθρώπων. In 1.25.1, on the other hand, ἐκ παντὸς γένους ἀνθρώπων designates the multiplicity of the *religious* provenances of the Christians. On this see the following.

10. They are not ὁμόφυλοι (1.14.3) but ἀπὸ παντὸς ἔθνους ἀνθρώπων, 1.53.3; the same in 1.31.7; 1.32.4; 1.39.3; 1.42.4; ἐκ παντὸς γένους ἀνθρώπων, 1.1; 1.40.7; 1.50.12; 1.56.1; cf. also *Dial.* 139.5; 117.5; 121.3. Of course, when emphasizing ethnic multiplicity, Justin does not only have Christianity in Rome in mind. He rather speaks more generally about the missionary success of Christianity in all lands. This fact, however, does not exclude the possibility that information about Roman Christians is contained in these passages. Justin writes his *Dialogue*, e.g., after he has already spent *years* stationary in Rome; i.e., he reports situations of Christians that are immediately before his eyes. From that it is reasonable to assume that his general statements concerning Christianity are also realized in urban Roman Christianity.

11. Cf. on the missionary perspective towards the pagan environs *Apology* (first part) 1.44.13; 28.2; 39.3; 40.7; 53.11; 55.8; 57.1f.; 67.7; 68.1f.; (second part) 14f. (esp. 15.4); *Dial.* 35.8; 96.2. A general missionary perspective in *Apology* (first part) 6.2; 10.5; 12.11; 14.3; 16.3f.; 18.2; 23.2.

of Christian businesspersons, who on trips and in business transactions (συμπραγματεύειν) show infinite patience (ὑπομονὴ ξένη), even if someone tries to cheat them (πλεονεκτεῖν). The Christians could also use other social relationships of Christians for mission purposes. By means of their conduct, they could convince the pagan neighbors in their houses (γείτων: 1.16.4; 2.1.2); the situation of a tenement house is implied here.

Pagans and Christians not only coexisted door to door within one and the same tenement building[12] but also within the same family dwelling. They even got along together in friendship. 2.1.2: Many Christians may have a pagan friend, a pagan brother, even a pagan child,[13] an unbelieving husband, or a pagan wife. The problems concurrent with a mixed marriage are illustrated with an example in 2.2 (see Part 4).

When Christians in a mission effort try to bring pagan neighbors "to their senses" (σωφρονίζειν), they do not, of course, always meet open ears but even run the danger of being denounced as Christians to the authorities (2.1.2).[14] Limits restrict the success of Christian mission: vile suspicions and insults about Christianity circulated in the environs.[15] Upon accusation, legal measures were initiated against individual Christians, which often enough ended in martyrdom.[16] And last but not least, the Jews were also active in missions, and they even attempt to entice Christians away:[17] *Dialogue* 47.4 knows of persons who as Gentile Christians "at first confessed that Jesus is the Christ, but then — going over to the life of the Law — denied that Jesus is the Messiah."[18]

---

12. Cf. *Dial.* 10.3: in contrast to the Jews, Christians do not separate from the pagan world; cf. also *Apol.* 2.1.1.

13. This is possible if, e.g., the parents converted after the child was already grown up.

14. How suspiciously the mission activity of Christian slaves in pagan households was viewed is exemplified by Celsus (Origen, *Contra Cel.* 3.55: enslaved cobblers, fullers, and uneducated people talk above all the women and children into their gospel nonsense).

15. Christians allegedly adhere to immoral practices: *Dial.* 10.1f.; *Apol.* (first part) 26.7; 2–4; 10.6; 23.2f.; 26.7; 27.5; 29.2; (second part) 12.1ff.; 13.1; 14.1f. Reproach of atheism: (first part) 4.7; 5.1.3f.; 6.1; 13; 46.3. Suspicion of political insurgence: 11. The Christians are ridiculed and denigrated: cf. *Dial.* 9.1; 17.1, 3; 101.2; 110.5; 117.3; 119.4; 120.4; 134.6; *Apol.* (first part) 1; 3; 13.4; 14.3; 20.3; 24.1; 49.6. Whoever is at risk of entering the sphere of influence of the Christians is advised by his pagan fellows to "hold fast to the old ways" (49.6). Οἱ πολλοί in Rome had an anti-Christian prejudice (*Apol.* (second part) 3.[8].2; 13.1).

16. *Apol.* (first part) 2–5; 7f.; 11; 17.4; 24.1; 31.5; 39.3f.; 45.5f.; 48.4; 57.1–3; (second part) 1f.; 4f.; 7(6).3; 8(7).3; 3(8).1; 11.1,8; 12.1ff.; 14.2; *Dial.* 18.3; 19.1; 30.2; 34.7; 35.7f.; 39.6; 44.1; 46.7; 82.2; 110.4f.; 114.4; 121.2; 131.2.

17. Cf. *Dial.* 8.4; in addition 17.1; 108.2; also 19.3; 117.3; 120.4.

18. Cf. Eusebius, *Hist. Ecc.* 6.12. Cf. also how the genuine Christian name "Petrus" spread into Jewish circles (in P. Lampe, "Das Spiel mit dem Petrusnamen," *NTS 25* [1978/79]: 229): this can be explained easily if one assumes conversions from Christianity to Judaism.

Chapter 12

The Excavation Complex
at the Vatican

After this crosscut from the middle of the second century, we go some-what deeper into the second half of the century, over to the slopes of the Vatican, where interesting things were still happening in Justin's lifetime (d. ca. 165 C.E.). The archaeological complex surrounding the supposed grave of Peter gives some social historical information about, while not the whole, at least a larger part of urban Roman Christianity.

The Roman Christian Gaius wrote about 200 C.E.: "I can point to the victory signs (τὰ τρόπαια) of the apostles. You may go to the Vat-ican or to the road to Ostia..." (in Eusebius, *Hist. Ecc.* 2.25.7). No one any longer seriously doubts that the Vatican Tropaion mentioned by Gaius has been archaeologically excavated. The Vatican edicula (Fig. 6),[1] which has been found, is located directly under the apse of the Constantinian Church of Peter. Constantine had to undertake large-scale movement of earth to be able to erect a basilica at the place of the Tropaion on an unfavorable incline (he had to remove one portion of the slope and fill in the other with the help of mighty subconstruc-tions to make it level, Fig. 7). All of this means that the builders of the basilica about 325 C.E. were convinced that the (now excavated) edic-ula was a monument to Peter. But if the Christians of about 325 C.E. know of a monument to Peter on the Vatican, and Gaius about 200 C.E. likewise knows a memorial to Peter there, then the identity of the two monuments is as good as certain.

Otherwise there would have been two different monuments on the Vatican which during the third century vied for the status of being a memorial to Peter. Of such a competition we hear nothing.

If the excavated edicula is identical with the Tropaion of Gaius, then the constructors of the small monument were *Christians*. If they had not been Christians, we would have to assume that between the construc-tion of the monument by pagans (about 160 C.E.; on the date, see below)

---

1. Report of the excavation team: B. M. Apollonij Ghetti, A. Ferrua, E. Josi, E. Kirschbaum, L. Kaas, *Esplorazioni sotto la confessione di S. Pietro in Vaticano. eseguite negli anni 1940–1949* (Vatican, 1951); cited as *Esplorazioni*.

and the year 200 the Roman Christians sought out a recent pagan monument on the Vatican and arbitrarily "converted" it into a memorial to Peter. Tertium non datur.

The builders of the edicula were Christians, who were convinced that they were constructing not only a memorial but rather a sepulchral monument over (what was at least formerly) a grave. In the flooring of the edicula they inserted a covering slab which is not oriented in the same way as the edicula but rather lies at an angle to it.[2] Transposing the excavation results into history, we arrive at the following: Sometime around the middle of the second century, *before* the construction of the little edicula was begun, Christians stood on the Vatican at a place they identified as a grave. They diagnosed the orientation of the grave as running from WSW to ENE.[3] In about the year 160 C.E., the "red wall," which today runs behind the edicula, was built in a N-S direction. Thus, it was not situated at a right angle to the grave that was visited by Christians but rather at angles of 101 and 79 degrees, respectively (Figs. 8 and 6). But the constructors of the edicula had to build according to the orientation of the wall! Thus arose the awkward situation in which the Peter memorial came to stand obliquely above the venerated grave. Why could the Christians not prevent this? With this question we approach our first socialhistorically relevant datum!

But first let us look at the further excavation findings insofar as they are relevant for us (Fig. 9 and esp. Fig. 10). The edicula leans against the so-called red wall and faces a small courtyard, "P," which is adjacent to two pagan mausoleums (Fig. 8). This area P is approachable only from the N and NE, that is, only from above, for the terrain falls as a slope predominantly from N to S (Fig. 7). The red wall was not erected by Christians (see the angled position of the covering slab in the floor of the edicula!) but by pagans who used the burial places Q and R'. As an entrance way to these two rooms, they built the *clivus* with its stairs (Fig. 11), and, in the same construction phase, they shut off this entrance way to the outside world: in the south with a door,[4] in the east by means of the red wall.

---

2. Cf. Fig. 6. The deviating angle is 11 degrees; cf. the photo in E. Kirschbaum, *Die Gräber der Apostelfürsten*, 3d ed. (Frankfurt, 1974), plate 21a, as well as p. 144. The orientation of the covering slab is indicated by a preserved groove.

3. This is the orientation of the covering slab; cf. Figs. 6 and 8. In addition to this slab, a second small monument indicates how one saw the orientation of the grave before the construction of the edicula. In the same direction as the covering slab a small wall (called m^1) runs a little south of the revered grave site, which during the latter part of the first half of the second century was erected as a flanking protective wall for this grave. (Photo of m^1 in Kirschbaum, plate 19. Cf. *Esplorazioni*, 119ff., 135ff.) The dating can be inferred from the level: m^1 lies higher than γ and θ (see below), so that m^1 is younger than they.

4. Cf. *Esplorazioni*, 102.

The clivus and the red wall are datable. During the construction of
the clivus, a drainage channel was laid out underneath it. The five tiles
covering this channel all bear identical stamps, which come from the
period after ca. 146 C.E. and before 161 C.E.[5] Clivus and red wall,
accordingly, are to be dated to this period, cautiously even to its end
around 160 C.E. About this there is a broad consensus. Somewhat more
difficult is the dating of the edicula, which was attached to the outside
of this self-contained pagan burial complex. The terminus ante quem
non is the red wall (RW). But did the edicula originate simultaneously
with the RW, as the excavators claim?[6] In fact, this dating has withstood
heated questioning: the tropaion was erected around 160.[7]

The following points are important for us:

a. Because of the course of the red wall, the Christians were unable
to place their edicula squarely over the venerated grave site. They were
forced to comply with the building measures of their pagan neighbors.

b. Moreover, the RW cuts across the revered grave; the "cut off"
portion was built over by the clivus and the RW.[8] The Christians were
unable to hinder that. Almost the only concession the builders of the
RW made was this: At the edicula they did not build the foundation of
the RW to its normal depth but rather they lifted the foundation a bit
here — in a sort of triangular style — so that the RW foundation climbs
up over the venerated grave site.[9]

---

5. Cf. *Esplorazioni*, 102; Fig. 75. The matching of all stamp dates makes it improbable that these tiles — as otherwise is often the case — were gathered together from
abandoned buildings and here were reused, so that the clivus would have been younger
than the stamps.

6. Cf. *Esplorazioni*, 119–31.

7. The critique was based on drawings of the excavation report, which were open
to misunderstanding: the niche in the masonry between the little columns (cf. Fig. 6) had
been irregularly drawn, so that it appeared to be secondary and broken into the wall. The
actual finding is this: The upper niche as well as the niche between the two little columns
represent a regular curve in the wall, giving every appearance of having been made *during*
the construction of the RW (cf. Kirschbaum's correction of the partially erroneous drawings: 114f.; cf. also 80). Only *later* marble incrustation from the third century endowed the
niche between the little columns with the irregularity, which went into the incorrect drawings and caused the critics to assume the edicula niche came later than the wall (thus, e.g.,
Th. Klauser, *Die römische Petrustradition im Lichte der neuen Ausgrabungen unter der
Peterskirche*; A.G.f.Forsch. des Landes Nordrhein-Westfalen 24 [Cologne and Opladen,
1956], 48; or A. v. Gerkan, "Petrus in Vaticano et in Catacumbas," *JAC* 5 [1962]: 23ff.).
As additional findings we ought to add (a) that no seams are visible in the masonry and
(b) that the remainder of the red wall's plaster extends "over a corner brick of the niche's
edge" (Kirschbaum, 80, 115) so that any building-in of the niche is excluded.

8. Cf. Fig. 8 and see *Esplorazioni*, 136. Simultaneously the small protective wall m¹
was partially destroyed by the RW.

9. "Sorpassandola": *Esplorazioni*, 120f., 139, and cf. in Kirschbaum, 113, the correction of the unclear drawings of the excavation report, which had caused vehement doubts
(e.g., Klauser [1956], 52). The photograph in Kirschbaum, plate 23, with the triangular
elevation is clear.

The second concession consists in the fact that the wall's builders in the outside of their wall agreed to plan two niches (see above, n. 7), which the Christians could use for their edicula. This "agreement" between neighbors also had advantages for the pagan wall-builders. In the upper niche they were able to install a small window (Fig. 6), which lit for them the steps in the roofed clivus. The Christians had to live with this profane element in the center of their monument.

c. Before the construction of the RW it was possible for Christians to visit the venerated grave site also from the south, from the lane of the necropolis. A fish graffito[10] on the eastern outside wall of R may be a trace left by Christians using this access. After the construction of the clivus and the wall, this approach was blocked to them.

d. The edicula is a simple monument. The lower niche, which lies under the travertine shelf held up by the small columns, measures merely 1.34 m. high (cf. Fig. 6). The upper niche ends at ca. 2.35 m. What the monument above the travertine shelf looked like we do not know. Only the niche with its little window was found. The small columns are made of white marble,[11] but the sill on which they stand[12] and the shelf which they support[13] are merely of travertine, common limestone from the not too distant stone quarry at Tivoli. That sort of small monument,

---

10. Illustration of the graffito in Kirschbaum, 143; cf. 135. Close by, a certain L. Paccius Eutychus wrote on the wall:

ΕΜΝΗΣΘΗ Λ ΠΑΚΚΙΟΣ
ΕΥΤΥΧΟΣ
ΓΛΥΚΩΝΟΣ

"L. Paccius Eutychus remembered
Glykon (as he
visited this place)."

The writing style fits into the second century C.E. The fish and the inscription *could* come from the same hand, given their close proximity to each other, so that there is a chance that both Eutychus and Glykon were Christians. Of course, the fish in itself is no strong indication (see above). But Kirschbaum (ibid.) points out that such inscriptions, tituli memoriales, were used at places of particular natural beauty (which is excluded here) or of cultic reverence (e.g., CIG 2872). The latter would only work if Eutychus had come here to honor an apostle's grave! I do not exclude this possibility, but I remain more skeptical than Kirschbaum. Such tituli memoriales are found also at graves of ordinary people. I think of the little gravestone from Didyma, for example, which Ammias set up for Anteros: "Anteros...Ammias remembered you" (no. 539 in Th. Wiegand and A. Rehm, *Didyma*, II: *Die Inschriften* [Berlin, 1958]. Our Paccius Eutychus may therefore just as well have visited the pagan mausoleum R as the final resting place of Glykon; he scribbled his inscription next to the entrance of this mausoleum!

"Paccius" was a known latinized *nomen gentile* (clan name) both in the first (*CIL* 10:8260; Tacitus, *Hist.* 4.41.3) and in the second centuries C.E. (*ILS* 440). Since Paccius Eutychus spoke Greek, he was probably not a freeborn member of the Roman gens Paccia but one of their slaves, who, at his emancipation, had acquired the *nomen gentile*.

11. Cf., e.g., Kirschbaum, 64; photo, plate 17.

12. Cf. Kirschbaum, 72; photo, plate 20d.

13. Cf., e.g., Kirschbaum, Fig. 11.

plain and without inscription, was no rarity. On the "Isola Sacra," the necropolis alongside the arterial road from Porto, not far from Ostia, we find a well-preserved, similar monument: the small grave edicula of Sabinus Taurus. Standing — again — in an unobtrusive location, it leans against the back of a larger mausoleum. The Roman traveler going by on the arterial road did not see it. He would have had to go around the mausoleum that lay at the roadside in order to be able to discover it. The grave edicula stands, in the truest sense of the word, "in the second rank."[14]

Only in the third century was the revered site on the Vatican partially clad in marble by the Christians and the flooring of area P decorated with mosaics.[15]

e. Not until the third century do we find Christian burials in the magnificent mausoleums of the necropolis close by.[16] In the second century everything here was still pagan. Only in area "P," already in the second century, a memorial to Peter was honored by Christians and, at the same time, as we shall shortly see, Christians sought to place their graves near to his.

From these findings we can, in my view, infer something like a social-historical terminus ad quem for the devotees of the Peter memorial. In the second century they did not yet belong to the social stratum of the owners of mausoleums. Who did own the Vatican mausoleums? The richness of the mausoleums (they originated since the first half of the second century) is striking. The owners invested in valuable stucco works, frescoes, mosaics, and marble sarcophagi, sometimes even of artistic excellence. The inscriptions name almost exclusively freedpersons and their families. The wealth of many freedpersons in the first half of the second century was proverbial (Martial 5.13.6).[17] The devotees of the Peter memorial did not yet belong to this stratum.

---

14. A photo of the Isola sacra edicula — but without the described topographical context — in Th. Klauser (1956), plate 10; on his plate 11 see a similar monument from Monselice, and in Kirschbaum, plate 27, the edicula for an urn on the Via Ostiense. In the "third rank" then there are only simple graves laid into the ground with tile coverings. Such grave are also found on the Isola Sacra: in the third row, scarcely visible from the street, behind the back of the mausoleums and beyond that grave edicula. Photographs in, e.g., Kirschbaum, plates 25b and 22.

15. Cf., e.g., the photograph in Kirschbaum, plate 20c; pp. 144f.; *Esplorazioni*, 111, 141; Klauser (1956), 59; U. Fasola, *Peter und Paul in Rom* (Rome, 1980), 134 (see the caption for the illustration); M. Guarducci, "Die Ausgrabung unter St. Peter," in R. Klein, ed., *Das frühe Christentum im römischen Staat* (Darmstadt, 1971), 364ff., here p. 380.

16. Cf. Fig. 9. Christians were buried primarily in mausoleum M. It is interesting that also in the third century only few Christian burials took place here and that, in comparison to the others in the necropolis, they were relatively modest (see the evidence, e.g., in Fasola [1980], 137–41; on the necropolis, also Klauser [1956], 38ff.).

17. Cf., e.g., also 5.70 (Syriscus is supposed to have squandered "ten millions") as well as the freedman buried under marble on the Via Flaminia (6.28). Further see *ILS* 7196; 7812.

Our little graveyard "P" under the open sky contrasts sharply with the rich mausoleums. It is one of the typical, small funeral fields for poorer people that are frequently found in the Roman necropolises.[18] It lay "in a corner" squeezed in among more stately family mausoleums. Those buried here were without sufficient means to create a somewhat planed burial terrain,[19] much less to erect a mausoleum.

f. The picture is completed when we examine the individual graves that cluster around the venerated grave site in "P." We are dealing with grave sites β, γ, η, θ, ι, κ, λ.[20]

The findings are a bit complicated. The terrain of "P" ascends predominantly from the south towards the north, and in the course of time its level rose more and more, whether from soil washing down the slope in rain storms or from the earth and rubble removed during the construction of the surrounding mausoleums. For the relative chronology of those graves we can use two criteria (on the following, cf. Figs. 12 and 13).

First criterion: If a grave lies deeper than another and if it is at the same time partially overlapped by it (e.g., η over θ), then it is certainly older. Second criterion: If it lies deeper but is not overlapped by it, then it is only probably older.[21]

The data that can be unequivocally recorded with the first criterion can be expressed, in my view, very simply in five formulae:

(" > " = "older"; "RW" = red wall; "T" = tropaion, which was erected simultaneously with the RW)

- $F1 =: \iota > \kappa > \lambda$

- $F2 =: \gamma > \beta$

- $F3 =: \gamma > RW$

- $F4 =: \gamma > \eta > T/RW$

- $F5 =: \theta > \eta > T/RW$

Equally certain in terms of relative chronologies are the following:

---

18. On this, e.g., Fasola (1980), 131.

19. A leveling of courtyard P is not discernible before the laying out of the mosaic floor in the third century; see above, n. 15; and cf. Klauser (1956), 44.

20. Cf. Figs. 12 and 13 as well as Klauser (1956), plate 18a. μ lies already above the third-century mosaic flooring and therefore is of no interest here. α, δ, ε were dug out from the floor of the Constantinian basilica (cf. Kirschbaum, 83). ζ comes from the third century and is a poor grave. A couple of brick tiles leaned against the wall of the mausoleum — nothing more (cf. the description in Kirschbaum, 148).

21. Uncertainty is created by two facts. (a) The original terrain ascended, and (b) it may have been uneven. The difference in levels *alone* does not permit absolutely compelling chronological conclusions.

- F6 =: RW > β. (β is oriented at a right angle according to the course of RW. In addition, above β on the RW a relief decorated β; cf. the findings in Kirschbaum, 83.)

- F7 =: RW > κ > λ. (Both clay coffins, κ and λ, lie over each other and are oriented *along* the RW.)

The second criterion, the difference in levels produces one certain result:

- F8 =: ι > η (Although the slope ascends to the north, ι lies deeper than η. That means, unequivocally, ι lies in an older stratum.)

  If F8 is correct, then in my view the highly contested[22] relationship of ι to the RW can be convincingly solved. From the logical combination of F8, F4, and F5 results:

- F9 =: ι > RW/T. It is surprising that this simple logical combination has played no role in the controversy concerning the archaeological findings at the NW corner of ι (n. 22).

  While F1–9 are certain, the following two formulae are probable:

- F10 =: γ ≈ θ. When θ was first built, its upper ridge lay either close under or right at the original surface.[23] Now it is located 1.70 m. below the Constantinian flooring. The foot of the brick altar of γ (cf. Figs. 13 and 14) lies 40 cm. deeper, at 2.10 m. below this flooring. Originally this brick altar was above ground with its foot marking the level of the original terrain. Since the slope here originally ascended from south to north, the difference of 40 cm. is to be attributed to this incline. One cannot infer that γ and θ belong to temporally different strata (θ would otherwise be younger than γ). The original incline of the slope is still clearly to be seen immediately adjacent to the clivus. In its last, northern 420 cm. the clivus climbs 2 m.,[24] so that a stairway was built. Two m. result on average in the considerable ascent of 48 percent. If we compare the 40 cm. difference between γ and θ, which lie 80 cm. apart from each other horizontally, there results likewise an ascent of the terrain of 50 percent between the two graves. Even Kirschbaum

---

22. The dispute was kindled by an uncertainty in the excavation findings. Does the RW run a little bit over the NW corner of ι? Or does ι exactly *parallel* the course of the wall? The differing drawings in the diverse publications show the uncertainty (cf. e.g., *Esplorazioni*, 115f.; Kirschbaum, 109, plate 25; pp. 89f.; 260, n. 46; Klauser [1956], 46 and plate 18; A. v. Gerkan [1962], 30, n. 21). The dispute can be discarded, because it does not have to be decided on the basis of the ambivalent findings at the "NW corner of ι." In my view, it can be decided on the basis of compelling logical deductions from the overall findings in P.

23. Cf. Similar graves on the Isola Sacra; photograph in Kirschbaum, plate 25b.

24. Cf. the measurements in Kirschbaum, plates 15 and 22 and p. 100.

with his detailed investigation of levels (100ff.) did not notice this coincidence, which indicates that θ and γ come from the same time.[25]

- F11 = : $\iota \gtrsim \theta$. Often ι and θ are dated in approximately the same time period, because they lie on the same level.[26] This dating, however, does not take the general ascent of the slope from south to north into account. This ascent could indicate a temporal priority for ι. First ι, with its covering tiles only a bit beneath the surface, was constructed. Then the surface rose about 30 cm., and θ, again just below the surface, was constructed (cf. Fig. 13).

The formulae can then be logically put together and so provide chronological information:

$$\iota \gtrsim \theta \approx \gamma > \eta > \text{RW/T} > \beta$$
$$> \kappa > \lambda$$

From there we proceed forward to an absolute chronology. A tile stamp of γ (*CIL* 15:1120a) falls into the years between 115 and 123 C.E. γ consequently did not originate before 115. The same is true for θ,[27] and approximately so for ι.[28]

None of the graves constructed in the area "P" in the immediate vicinity of Peter's grave, therefore, comes from the first century. Most date from the first half or the middle of the second century (ι, γ, θ, η).

The evidence for calling graves β, γ, η, θ, ι, κ, λ Christian is as follows (see Figs. 12 and 15):

1. The graves crowd around the grave site that was venerated by Christians around the middle of the second century. These graves overlap and superimpose on one another.

---

25. The 80 cm. are horizontally measured from the *north* side of the γ-brick altar to the ridge of θ (cf. Fig. 13). Kirschbaum erroneously assumes that the slope connected with the north side of the brick altar a half meter above its foot (cf. Kirschbaum's plate 23). But the little ledge found at a half meter from the foot on the north side is in all probability insignificant secondary damage (cf., e.g., A. v. Gerkan [1962], 29, n. 20). Not that little ledge but the clearly marked edge at the *foot* of the brick altar, which is also discernible on its north side, shows where the original earth level was.

26. E.g., Kirschbaum, 108. Both graves overlap at one corner. Unfortunately we can no longer decide which grave pushed the other.

27. θ's tile stamp from the time of Vespasian (*CIL* 15:1237a) says nothing in view of the relative chronology (F10!). The brick tile appears to have been reused from somewhere else, which is not surprising with a poor person's grave. Photograph of the stamp in Kirschbaum, plate 20b.

28. If ι was older than θ, which cannot be excluded (see above), this would certainly not be by much. Between $\gamma \approx \theta$ and the RW/T lie at maximum 45 years; during this time, the surface rose by more than 1 meter. Correspondingly, there would be at least 14 years difference between ι and θ, because the surface appears to have risen by 30 cm. between the constructions of ι and θ. This indicates a date for ι at ca. 100 C.E. at the earliest. ι, presumably the oldest grave in the chronology, is simultaneously the poorest one of the group (on this see below).

2. However, these graves exclude as well as possible from this over-lapping cluster the very space that was later covered by the tropaion. Efforts were made for them to be close to it but not to extend over it.[29]

3. γ and θ, the oldest, are oriented according to Peter's supposed grave site, lying in the same direction. The axis of the covering slab in the floor of the tropaion as well as the axes of γ and θ run parallel (ι lies almost at a right angle to that).

4. Area "P" shows no trace of any cremations. Interments became fashionable again only from Hadrian's time on, so that one always finds in comparable graveyards of the first half of the second century both sorts of burials (e.g., on the Isola Sacra).[30] "P" is an exception! Next to it, the interior of mausoleum O from the 30s of the second century, for instance, was planned only for urns of ashes.

5. Neither the libation pipe which goes through it nor its similar-ity to an altar speaks against the Christian character of γ.[31] We have no contemporary comparative materials that would "prescribe" what a Christian grave of this early time would have to look like. Any *petitio principii* — "that cannot have been so" — thus does not help. In the time of Augustine, Christians at the grave sites still held meals to the memory of the deceased, meals that looked "exactly like pagan su-perstition." The Christians brought wine with them. If, during a trip to the cemetery, several memorials were honored, each with a drink, the whole affair could degenerate into a tipsy procession (*Conf.* 6.2). In the fourth century Christian graves with libation openings are evidenced.[32]

---

29. Only the *younger* η — in a higher level — with its SW corner appears to extend somewhat over Peter's supposed grave. The reason is obvious. The level had further risen (between θ and η by nearly 1 m.!). Therefore, at about the middle of the second century the eastern boundary of "Peter's grave" was either no longer completely clear or, because of the higher level, it seemed permissible at one corner to get even closer to the apostle's grave.

Also westward, on the other side of the RW, at least one grave existed before the clivus with its drainage channel and its steps was built. It lay in the immediate vicinity of the ven-erated grave site and came from the first half or the middle of the second century. Under this grave lay another older one (cf. M. Guarducci, "Documenti del primo secolo nella necropoli vaticana," *Rend. Pont. Acc. Rom. di Archeol.* 29 [1956f.]: 121ff.; A. Prandi, *La zona archeologica della confessione vaticana,* I monumenti del II.sec. [Vatican, 1957]; Kirschbaum, 89, 108, 129, 267f., nn. 16f.).

30. Cf. the Isola Sacra photograph in Kirschbaum, plate 22. Further on this, e.g., Fasola (1980), 131; Kirschbaum, 83.

31. Vs. Klauser (1956) 46 et al.

32. Cf. in Klauser himself, ibid. Christian meals to the memory of the dead in the third century are evidenced, e.g., in *ICUR* 1:17; NS 5:13886; Snyder (1985), 141f.: C, D, E, K. Paulinus of Nola (353–431 C.E.; Poem 27 concerning St. Felix, Carmen 9) emphasizes the ignorance (*rutes*) of the Christians who pour wine over graves (*perfusis mero sepulcris*). Libations were also performed by Christians in the fourth century at the apostle's memo-rial under S. Sebastiano (see the graffiti in O. Marucchi [1923], 91–94). Other catacombs also yield up evidence. *Domitilla:* representation of a woman praying, of a dove, and of a man who at the grave of his daughter with one hand puts a chalice to his mouth and with the other pours [wine] from a cask on the floor (illustration.: *Nuovo Bullettino di Archeol.*

This is reminiscent of the mixture of Christian and pagan in the funeral realm that we saw (Part 2, chapter 4, end). This mixing was done with as much ease as when Hermas painted his figure of the Mother Church with the features of the Sibyl of Cumae.

The seven graves clustering around the venerated grave site on the Vatican belonged to poor people. The poorest grave is ι. The corpse was laid in a naked hole in the ground, without flooring or sidings for protection. On top there were merely three brick tiles laid out flatly. That was all.[33]

The same held for the poor person's grave θ, except that someone had given θ the "luxury" of using six rather than three brick tiles and had placed these against each other like a small roof. These tiles are in part really tiles brought here from somewhere else.[34]

With its libation pipe and its altarlike top, γ is somewhat more elaborate. In its terra-cotta coffin, surrounded by the masonry work, lay a child.[35] But even here the masonry is poor.[36]

Further on in the second century, there is evidence of a somewhat higher social level. The chronology corresponds to a small "social advancement." With η — although still simple — a marble lid is used around the middle of the second century. The corpse was likewise simply placed in a hole in the ground. Only on the sides and above was it protected by simple brick tiles. Above that a stone-mortar mixture was laid out, and on it the marble slab was placed, which was visible on the surface.[37]

Cr. [1922] plate II). *Priscilla:* Graffito from the year 375: "ad calicem venimus" (illustration: *Bullet.* [1888], plates VI–VII.). *S. Ermete / Bassilla:* Christian fresco with a woman offering a chalice (the fresco in Nestori [1975], 3: Cubiculum 6).

33. Cf. the finding in, e.g., Kirschbaum, 89, 108. On bricks as the cheapest material, see Kirschbaum, 88.

34. Cf. the photograph in Kirschbaum, plates 21c; 20b, and pp. 87f. On similar graves on the Isola Sacra, see above, n. 14. The appearance of the venerated grave has to be visualized in analogy to ι or to θ. Material traces — they were after all only three bricks and a few skeletal remains — have not remained from "Peter's grave." All that remains for us is its location — and the certainty that Christians around the middle of the second century honored this place as the grave of the apostle and believed it possible even to discern the orientation of this grave.

Who took away the three bricks and the bones — of whoever they were — and deposited them somewhere else (*translatio ad catacumbas* during the persecution under Valerian? immurement of the bones in the graffiti wall in Constantine's time?)? This is not important for our purposes, nor is the question whether or not this venerated grave already in the first century was a "grave of Peter." The latter is in my view still the best explanation for the findings of the second century.

35. 1.26 m. coffin length. Photograph in Kirschbaum, plate 21b; cf. the findings on p. 86.

36. On the poor masonry, see in detail Kirschbaum, 263, n. 31.

37. Photograph, e.g., in Kirschbaum, plate 14d; findings, e.g., in *Esplorazioni*, 114; Kirschbaum, 72, 85f., 134, 264, n. 51.

With β, κ, and λ we are very probably in the third century already.[38] The marble slabs of β form a case, which is roofed with brick tiles leaning against each other at an angle. A relief decoration for the grave is attached to the RW. Inside there glitter a couple of gold threads from the shroud.[39] κ and λ are two simple clay coffins.[40]

g. Finally, it is interesting to note that the Christians of area "P" first put up a monument — however modest — at "Peter's grave" only when the building activities of the owners of Q, R', and of the clivus came precariously near to this grave and finally cut across a portion of it. Then the Christians were forced to save what they could and to compensate for what was lost (see the decisive points a–c above) by decorating this grave with a small monument. In other words, before all this happened, there had not been any wealthy church members who on their *own initiative* had come forward to donate money for any kind of monument to Peter. Only external forces compelled the Christians to act.

All seven points converge at the conclusion that the users of the little area "P" with their Petrine memorial belonged to the *humiliores,* to the common people.

From this result I return to the first three points (a–c), which indicate to what extent the Christians helplessly had to give way to the activities of the pagan constructors of the red wall and of the clivus. The three points emerge persuasively from the material. But how should they be interpreted? Why were the Christians unable to hinder these proceedings? Two observations help to explain (cf. Fig. 9): (a) The Vatican necropolis of mausoleums originated in relatively quick stages in the years ca. 120–55 C.E.[41] (b) On the map the mausoleums are seen as a well-ordered chain. Both observations indicate that around 120 C.E. the land was systematically divided up and sold.[42] The rapid construction of one mausoleum after the other as well as the ordered layout point in this direction. For our question this means that Christians failed around 120 C.E. to buy the parcel upon which very quickly R, R', Q, and the clivus were to be built. Did they not have enough money? Did they not have enough foresight to realize what results the ownership claims of near neighbors could have for their grave site? Whichever way one decides, they were apparently *humiliores.*[43]

---

38. So also Kirschbaum, 148, 85.

39. Cf. the findings in *Esplorazioni,* 111; Kirschbaum, 83, 148.

40. Cf. the findings in, e.g., Kirschbaum, 85, 148.

41. Cf. on this and on the following, Klauser (1956), 39; Kirschbaum, 129.

42. Similarly, Fasola (1980), 134.

43. The legal uncertainty in which the Christians lived presents, in addition to the *humiliores* thesis, only one other very limited possible explanation for our findings: (a) A Christian group had no legal status and must have feared denunciations. This could indeed explain why the Christians did not defend themselves against the unpleasant constructions of their neighbors. However, this does not explain why no Christian bought the parcel

How does the result of this chapter fit in with the clear descriptions, e.g., of Hermas and Justin, that in the first half and the middle of the second century there were already many rich among the urban Roman Christians, indeed, that at Sunday worship services considerable sums were gathered into the cash funds? The following conclusion seems to me certain when we compare the preceding chapters with the result of this one. The idea that urban Roman Christianity as a unified whole (with one bishop at its head) around 160 C.E. set up on the Vatican a monument to Peter,[44] is untenable (details on this in Part 5). What sort of circle of Christians was it, then? We remember that the Christians of the various city quarters each cared for their own burial sites. If we compare the sociology of the grave area "P" with the sociology of the city region attached to the Vatican, Trastevere (Part 2, above), both parts fit together seamlessly. The Christians of Trastevere, most likely cared for the grave area "P."

There still remains the question why richer Christians from other parts of the city did not jump in and contribute finances for a more monumental decoration of the apostle's grave. There are several possible answers. (a) For Christians a grave was inviolable and worthy of honor.[45] But we only find real veneration for martyrs from the middle of the third century onwards.[46] It appears that interest in "holy graves" was not yet so strongly developed in the second century that the wealthy felt financial responsibility there. The collections for the cash funds were used for the socially weak fellow Christians, obviously not for prominent graves. Of course, some lower-class people sought the proximity of

---

on which others constructed the red wall and the clivus over a part of the grave honored by Christians. (b) Their legal uncertainty explains why the edicula was not marked as Christian. The builders did not want to be conspicuous as Christians. However, it does not explain the simplicity of the little construction. That the marble and mosaic with which it was decorated in the third century were not put on earlier can scarcely be explained by the desire to be conspicuous; a more richly decorated monument would not have been conspicuously Christian. And the Christians' precarious legal situation also continued in the third century! (c) Would it have been an affront to decorate the grave of an executed "criminal"? Would that explain the simplicity of the monument? Surely not. For who, besides the Christian devotees of this grave, after 100 years still knew anything of the "criminal" in this grave? It was not recognizable from the outside as Christian or Petrine. That *humiliores* in the second century honored that grave on the Vatican, sought to bury their dead in the closest possible proximity to it, and decorated it with a modest edicula is still the most plausible explanation of the archaeological findings.

44. Thus, e.g., Kirschbaum, 136, 120.

45. In that, they would not have been different from pagans and Jews. Jewish grave-stones were common since the Hasmonean period (1 Macc 13:27–29; Josephus, *Ant.* 16.182; t.*Ohaloth* 17.4; p.*Erubin* 5.22a). A Jewish urban Roman grave inscription apparently from the second century (in Solin, "Juden und Syrer," 655f., no. 7) threatens possible molesters of the grave with a curse. Jews also decorated graves annually (*CIJ* 777 for Hierapolis/Phrygia).

46. On that see, e.g., Kirschbaum, 68; Dinkler, *Signum Crucis*, 156. The oldest certain evidence in Rome is the triclia under S. Sebastiano (see above), where Peter and Paul were venerated (260 C.E.).

"Peter's grave" with their own graves, but Callistus and Zephyrinus, for example, had no interest in that and were buried elsewhere. (b) Hermas shows us that there were indeed many wealthy among the urban Roman Christians, but that these often displayed little interest in the Christian community's affairs. Some even feared being solicited by fellow Christians (*Sim.* 9.20; 8.9.1). At least from this group, no great donation was to be expected. (c) May we visualize already for the period around 160 a closed, monolithic urban Roman church (with a single bishop at its head)? I can here only ask this question. The reader must be patient until Part 5. We may, however, say that the result of this Vatican chapter tends against such a "monolith."

Chapter 13

Social Stratification
at the Time of Commodus

1. For the period of Commodus's reign (180–92 C.E.), Irenaeus attests imperial slaves or freedpersons at the imperial court ("qui in regali aula sunt fideles").[1] Their support was drawn from the emperor's purse ("ex eis quae Caesaris sunt"). They had a good livelihood. Each of them gave as much as he could to those in want ("his qui non habent unusquisque eorum secundum suam virtutem praestat"). As is to be expected, also in the subsequent period of Septimius Severus (193–211 C.E.) there were Christians on the Palatine Hill, where the emperor had his house (Tertullian, *Apol.* 37.4).

2. Eusebius writes (*Hist. Ecc.* 5.21.1) that under Commodus several of those in Rome who enjoyed highest esteem as a result of wealth and birth (οἱ ἐπὶ Ῥώμης εὖ μάλα πλούτῳ καὶ γένει διαφανεῖς) converted to Christianity with their entire household and family. Eusebius does not reveal the source of his information. In the subsequent context he names only a single example, the distinguished Apollonius, about whom he possessed source material (see below, chap. 29). The question arises whether Eusebius has, on his own, generalized the single example of Apollonius without any evidence of further cases. The question cannot be decided from Eusebius's text. We ourselves must look for further evidence that will confirm Eusebius's general statement.

3. At least for the period of Septimius Severus (193–211 C.E.) Tertullian attests Christians of every social stratum,[2] including some among

---

1. Irenaeus, *Haer.* 4.30.1. Regarding imperial slaves and freedpersons in the east, see already Phil 4:22: οἱ ἐκ τῆς Καίσαρος οἰκίας. There existed many opportunities to station them on imperial lands in the provinces, in administrative positions or in garrisons.

2. "Omnis dignitatis": *Ad nat.* 1.1f.; *Apol.* 1; 37; *Ad Scap.* 4f.; cf. Origen, *Contra Cel.* 3.9; 7.54. For the time of Trajan, Pliny the Younger writes (*Ep.* 10.96.9): "multi omnis ordinis" (as highest social ranks Pliny, at best, envisions members of the decurion class, i.e., patricians of a municipality or colony, and of the equestrian class. For the period of Trajan and Hadrian only two senators are known from Pontus-Bithynia: Flavius Arrianus from Nicomedia and probably Cassius Agrippa from Nicea. Christians would hardly be found in their families. Cf. Eck, "Eindringen," 384, n. 10). In the late 170s, Celsus denigrated the Christians as scum from the lower classes (e.g., Origen, *Contra Cel.* 1.27; 3.44), but he refutes himself somewhat in that he appeals to educated readers of upper social

the senatorial nobility ("clarissimas feminas et clarissimos viros"; cf. *Ad Scap.* 4.7).[3] Parallel to this observation stands the fact that under Septimius Severus the number of eastern senators increased notably. Almost one-third were now from the eastern territories of the empire.[4] The interpretation of these two phenomena may be obvious. The Christian members of the senatorial class at the time of Septimius Severus were probably predominantly eastern.[5] In other words, that several Christians in the senatorial class are attested from the time of Septimius Severus is connected most readily with the fact that, since his reign, eastern membership in this class increased appreciably.

Unfortunately, it is not directly clear whether these Christians of the senatorial class belong to the Christian community of the city of Rome or to the Christian communities of the provinces.[6] Nevertheless, one may say that even the senators of the second century who were not born in Italy maintained a residence in Italy. Indeed, they were legally *required*[7] to invest their wealth in Italian property. From the time of Trajan one-third of their fortune was to be invested, and from the period of Marcus Aurelius, one-fourth. This testifies to the presence

---

strata who obviously sympathize with Christianity. He also challenges (cf. 8.75) Christians to apply for official positions in their native cities. That means that there were Christians, particularly in the decurion class, who could fill such official positions. Celsus confirms that there was a multiplicity of social classes within Christian circles, even though he does not give evidence of the existence of Christian equestrians in higher imperial service, as T. Klauser believes. In regard to Origen, *Contra Cel.* 8.73, 75, see W. Eck, "Christen im höheren Reichsdienst," 449–64. For a different opinion, see T. Klauser, "Christen seit Mark Aurel," 60–66.

3. Cf. *Apol.* 1; 37.4 ("implevimus senatum"; written c. 197 C.E.); *Ad nat.* 1.1; *Ad Scap.* 4.7 (Severus was aware of their adherence to Christianity but did not bother them); 5.2f. (possibly Christian senators from Carthage). At a later date (c. 258 C.E.), one finds senators and equestrians in greater number: they cause concern to the state (Cyprian, *Ep.* 80.1; cf. also 8.2.3).

4. Vespasian, and above all Trajan, had already opened the doors of the senate to citizens of the eastern provinces. The number of eastern senators was small throughout the second century until Septimus Severus. See further, G. Barbieri, *L'Albo Senatorio*, 441f., 458ff., 473: at the time of Septimus Severus and Caracalla c. 32.6 percent were from the east, c. 15 percent were from Africa, c. 8.8 percent were western, and c. 43 percent were Italian. Cf. H. Halfmann, *Die Senatoren*, esp. 71ff. Finally on this topic see Solin, "Juden und Syrer," 666, with further literature.

5. Among the senatorial Christians of the third century known by name were indeed men and women from the provinces: Astyrius from Syria Palestine at the time of Gallienus (cf. Eusebius, *Hist. Ecc.* 7.15–17); Aurelia Tatia from Phrygia (cf. W. Eck, "Das Eindringen," 394); C. Iulius Nestorianus and his sister show an affinity for Lycaonia (Eck, "Das Eindringen," 394); Crispina comes from Africa proconsularis (Eck, "Das Eindringen," 388); M. A. I. Severianus and his wife from Mauretania (Eck, "Das Eindringen," 390); Hydria Tertulla from Arles (Eck, "Das Eindringen," 389).

6. So, for example, the senator Astyrius from the period 260–68 C.E.: Eusebius, *Hist. Ecc.* 7.16f. The eastern senators, who rose to their senatorial rank through wealth and ability, were particularly useful in the provincial administration.

7. Marcus Aurelius renewed Trajan's obligation. Cf. Pliny, *Ep.* 6.19; *Hist. Aug. Vita Marci* 11.8; also *Dig.* 1.9.11; A. Chastagnol, *Le problème*, 43–54.

and participation of senatorial Christians at Roman worship services. According to *Dig.* 1.9.11, senators from the provinces maintained a residence in Rome.

The number of Christians in the senatorial class at the turn of the second century to the third cannot, of course, have been great: Christians despise "honors and scarlet robes" (Minucius Felix, *Oct.* 31.6; cf. 8.4; 37.7ff.). Also in the area of prosopography, we can name,[8] before Constantine, not even forty individual persons of the senatorial class as Christian; two-thirds of these are women.

4. Tertullian presents Christian noblewomen *before* their masculine counterparts (*Ad Scap.* 4), and it is crystal clear in Hippolytus (*Ref.* 9.12.24) that from aristocratic circles more women than men found their way to Christianity. The disproportion was a social problem that Callistus during his term as Roman bishop (c. 217–22) attempted to solve. The problem undoubtedly had existed since the end of the second century, if not longer.

> When women from the noble class (αἱ ἐν ἀξίᾳ) were unmarried and in the heat of their youthful passion desired to marry and yet were unwilling to give up their class (ἑαυτῶν ἀξίαν) through a legal marriage (διὰ τοῦ νομίμως γαμηθῆναι), he [Callistus] allowed them to choose a partner, whether slave or free (οἰκέτην εἴτε ἐλεύθερον), and to consider him to be their husband without a legal marriage. From that time on the alleged believing women began to resort to contraceptive methods and to corset themselves in order to cause abortions, because, on account of their lineage and their enormous wealth (διὰ τὴν συγγένειαν καὶ ὑπέρογκον οὐσίαν), they did not wish to have a child from a slave or from a commoner.

a. Young Christian girls who belonged to the upper class and possessed great wealth had difficulty finding partners from their own social class in the Christian community. There was a quantitative predominance of noblewomen over noblemen in the Christianity of Rome.[9]

---

8. For a more extensive treatment of this topic see Part 3. The statistics presented there for the third century can serve as a framework for our period. For the first and second centuries see in Part 4: the wives of two governors whose husbands are pagan (c. 200 C.E.); Flavia Domitilla under Domitian; Apollonius under Commodus; not very probable but possible, Pomponia Graecina; improbable, Acilius Glabrio.

9. Tertullian (*Ad uxor.* 2.8.3ff.) is aware of the same problem in Africa ("Christianam fidelem fideli re minori nubere piget, locupletiorem futuram in viro paupere"). The inscriptions of the third century offer four examples of Christian women of the senatorial class in unions with men of lower class: (1) A third-century inscription (cf. E. Josi, *Il Cimitero*, 104; *ILCV* 158; Barbieri [*L'Albo*, no. 2169] considers it prior to 285 C.E.; Eck ["Das Eindringen," 389] considers it to date from the beginning of the fourth century) from the catacomb of Callistus reports: "the 'coniux' (spouse) of a nonsenatorial man, Aelius Saturninus, was named Cassia Faretria and she was a 'clarissima femina.'" (2) Hydria

The ladies helped themselves by joining to men of lower rank without marrying.[10]

b. We must seek to clarify the legal background in these marriages. Hippolytus's intimation concerning the legal situation can be misunderstood. A legally valid marriage ("matrimonium iustum"; Hippolytus: νομίμως γαμηθῆναι) between a slave and a Roman woman or between a freedman and a Roman lady, whose father, paternal grandfather, or great-grandfather was a senator, was impossible[11] and could, therefore, not lead to the social decline of the woman. Women suffered from the loss of the noble rank of "clarissima" when they married a freeborn man of inferior status ("inferioris dignitatis"). Ulpianus (*Dig.* 1.9.8) writes: "clarissimarum feminarum nomine senatorum filiae, nisi quae viros clarissimos sortitae sunt, non habentur: feminis enim dignitatem clarissimam mariti tribuunt, parentes vero, donec plebeii nuptiis fuerint copulatae...."[12] (Daughters of senators are not entitled to the name of

---

Tertulla's (third century; Barbieri, *L'Albo*, no. 2183) father was a senator. Her husband, Terentius Mus(a)eus, was not a senator. Likewise, her daughter, Axia Aeliana, did not belong to the senatorial class. (3) In the last quarter of the third century, Varia Octabina, a "clarissima femina," buried her nonsenatorial husband in a sarcophagus (*ILCV* 224; Bovini and Brandenburg, Repertorium no. 918, there is also the correct form of the name ["Octabina"] as well as the picture of the sarcophagus; cf. further, W. Eck, "Eindringen," 391). (4) Luria Ianuaria, a "clarissima femina," was the wife of a distinguished man ("vir egregius") from the equestrian class (*CIL* 6:31731 = *ILCV* 157; dated perhaps third century). It is not clear whether these woman, after their marriage, retained the title "clarissima" unlawfully or by special dispensation.

10. An example of Christian concubinage during the time of Callistus can be found in the Christian funeral inscription *ILCV* 2807 (234 C.E.): About two years after the death of Callistus (c. 222 C.E.), a man by the name of Titus Claudius Marcianus and a woman named Cornelia Hilaritas became parents of a daughter who took, not the name of the father (Claudia), which would be expected in the case of a married couple, but the name of the mother, Cornelia Paula. The daughter died in 234 when she was ten years old. While Titus Claudius might have been the descendant of a freedman belonging to the imperial Claudian household, Cornelia Hilaritas *could* have belonged to the senatorial Cornelian family. Members of the Cornelian family were appointed consuls in the years 199 (*CIL* 6:1352) and 216 (*CIL* 14:137). A somewhat younger contemporary, Iulia Cornelia Salonia, became the wife of the emperor Gallienus (born c. 218, emperor from 260 to 268). After the persecutions of the Christians under Decius and Valerian, Gallienus handled them more mildly. The Christians praised him for this (cf. Dionysius in Eusebius, *Hist. Ecc.* 7.22.12; 7.23). A Cornelius was also bishop of Rome c. 251–53. A connection between these Cornelian data can only be surmised.

11. (a) Legally valid marriages with slaves were impossible: Ulpianus, *Dig.* 5.5; Paulus, *Sententiae receptae* 2.19.6; cf. Ulpianus, *Dig.* 33.7.12.7; 23.3.39 pr.; 21.1.35; 50.17.32. (b) Legally valid marriages were impossible between freed persons and senators or their descendants, explicitly also between freedmen and women who, on their paternal side, had a senator as father, grandfather, or great-grandfather: Paulus, *Dig.* 23.2.44 pr.; Celsus, *Dig.* 23.2.23; Mod., *Dig.* 23.2.42.1; Ulpianus, 13.1; *Cod. Iust.* 5.4.28 pr.; esp. also for the period since Marcus Aurelius and Commodus: Paulus, *Dig.* 23.2.16 pr.; Ulpianus, *Dig.* 23.1.16; 24.1.3.1; cf. Cassius Dio, 54.16.2; 56.7.2. This type of union was considered concubinage (cf. Ulpianus, *Dig.* 24.1.3). For literature see A. Chastagnol, "Les femmes," 3–28, esp. 10ff.

12. The regulation originates probably from the year 211/212: cf. A. Chastagnol, "Les femmes," 15–17, 19. Nevertheless, see M.-T. Raepsaet-Charlier, "Tertullien et la

noblewomen, except those who married noblemen: for husbands give noble dignity to the women, but parents only until a wedding with a commoner takes place.) A Christian woman who wished to retain the title "clarissima" had two options. She could marry a pagan of the same social status and forgo marriage with a socially inferior Christian.[13] Or she could live in concubinage with a socially inferior Christian without being legally married. This second option received the blessings of Callistus in Rome. In this way he prevented two things: mixed marriages with pagans and the social decline of Christian women. Both were in the interests of the community.

c. Callistus explicitly also tolerated sexual unions with slaves. In these cases the slaves were of the same household. Unions with slaves from other masters could result in legally unpleasant consequences for the women. Since the time of the Senatusconsultum Claudianum in 52 C.E. it was usually the law that, if Roman women entered into unions with slaves of other masters, they themselves would be reduced to the status of freedwomen. If they entered such unions without the knowledge or agreement of the slave's master, free Roman women would even be degraded to slaves.[14] Callistus, however, wished to prevent just such social declines. He sanctioned the union of Christian women with their own Christian slaves and in this way provided a clear conscience for the Christian women of his community.

d. That with Callistus's decision Christianity declared itself for the first time unequivocally in favor of "equal rights for slaves outside the liturgy and the arena"[15] is the unquestionable consequence of the decision. It cannot be proved, however, that this was the primary motivation for Callistus's action. Callistus wished to avoid mixed marriages and to prevent the social decline of aristocratic women from his community. His decision was motivated less by a desire to "emancipate the slaves" than we would today like to infer. Incidentally, relationships with slaves could silently be tolerated even in a pagan milieu (Paulus, *Dig.* 16.3.27).

Législation," 263, n. 44: since Marcus Aurelius. After such a marriage, a "consularis femina" retained her title of nobility only on the grounds of a special imperial favor, which was granted foremost to relatives of the imperial house. *Hist. Aug. Heliog.* 4.3: "In earlier times, on the Quirinal Hill the respectable women gathered... when a woman received the rank of a consul's wife, which earlier Caesars (before Elagabal) granted to relatives, especially to such women who did not have noble husbands but should not remain without noble status." See Ulpianus, *Dig.* 1.9.12, for such a case.

13. Cf. Tertullian, *Ad uxor.* 2.1ff.; *De monog.* Canon 15 of the Synod of Elvira spoke out against "Christian virgins entering into marriage with pagans because of the great number of marriageable girls" in the Christian community. Such cases clearly occurred.

14. Tacitus, *Ann.* 12.53.1; Gaius, *Inst.* 1.84; cf. 1.91; 1.160; Paulus, *Sententiae receptae* 2.21a.1. See also Tertullian, *Ad uxor.* 2.8 (Raepsaet-Charlier ["Législation," 253–63] also considers this passage). The Senatusconsultum was not always strictly applied, however: Paulus, *Dig.* 16.3.27, cites a case where the degrading of the woman did not occur.

15. This is emphasized by H. Gülzow, *Christentum und Sklaverei,* 172.

One could make the point that the "virtue" of Callistus's decision was born of necessity. It was born of the dearth of aristocratic men in the community. It was not so much Callistus as the Christian noblewomen of Rome before him who created out of this necessity the virtue of the emancipation of slaves by living with men of lower social status. Callistus only gave his blessing to this state of affairs, which undoubtedly existed already in the second century.

5. An additional document will make it clear that Eusebius did not fabricate from fantasy his general statement about the conversion of distinguished and wealthy Romans (see above 2). Between 180 and 190 C.E., that is, still during the reign of Commodus, the fictitious *Acta Petri* was written in Rome or, more probably, in Asia Minor.[16] This document narrates the apostle's activity in Rome before his death. One cannot, of course, consider the Acts of Peter as a historical source for the events of the first century, although it might incorporate oral traditions.[17] In two respects the Acts of Peter contain historical information: (a) The document illustrates what people from the end of the second century without any problem considered easily believable for the Roman community of the first century. Allegedly there were in Rome three senators, several equestrian noblemen, and aristocratic women who, as Christians, flocked together about the person of the apostle Peter. It is true that edifying folk literature, such as the Acts of Peter, has a predilection for aristocratic figures. They are, indeed, a characteristic of the genre (cf. n. 27 below). But the author could hardly have made his work believable in the second century if it did not in some remote way reflect real community circumstances in Rome at the end of the *second* century. We can clarify our method of argument in the following way: If, at the end of the second century, there had not been, for example, one or two equestrians among the Christians of Rome, then the story's

---

16. The content of the book, which takes place principally in Rome, speaks for Rome as the place of origin. (But, of course, Shakespeare did write his play about Julius Caesar in England!) Pointing to Asia Minor as the place of origin is the fact that there is a similarity between this work and the Acts of Paul, which, according to Tertullian, originated in Asia Minor. Cf. E. Hennecke and W. Schneemelcher, *Ntl. Apokryphen*, vol. 2, 4th ed. (Tübingen, 1971), 188. In my opinion the memorial tomb of Peter in the Vatican gives indirect evidence against Rome because of the following: With reference to Matt 27:60, *Act. Verc.* 40 narrates unabashedly that the senator Marcellus took Peter's body down from the cross and "buried him in his own tomb." This story could hardly have been told to Roman readers at the end of the second century, since any child could see that Peter's tomb was certainly not that of a senator. Finally, the occurrence of mostly Greek names also for aristocratic people belies Rome as the place of origin.

17. The opinion of A. Harnack [*Geschichte der altchristlichen Literatur*, 2/1:505] is still valid: "The assumption suffices without exception that the author did not freely invent everything but rather, more likely, founded his material upon an oral tradition that was continually embellished through one century and also preserved some small original characteristics." Where, however, the historical "crumbs" are preserved cannot be determined.

presentation of three senators in the first century would have been "embarrassing" and impossible. Therefore, a thesis can be formulated: It is not the details in the Acts of Peter but the total impression this book conveys of a Christian community with believers on all social levels from slaves to senators that appears to offer to the reader reliable information concerning Roman Christianity at the end of the *second* century.

Let us look at the fictitious material in the Acts of Peter in detail. First, in regard to slaves: In the first century the slaves of the senator Marcellus (*Act. Verc.* 14) allegedly were Roman Christians. Likewise, "Kleobius, Iphitus, Lysimachus, and Aristeus of Caesar's [Nero's] household" were members of the Roman Christian community (*Act. Verc.* 3), since Peter, while in Rome, "made some of his [Nero's] servants disciples" (*Act. Verc.* 41). These citations show how it was considered self-evident at the time of the composition of the Acts of Peter that slaves, especially imperial slaves, belonged to the Roman community.[18] In this way the Acts of Peter gives us information concerning the period of its author.

Another passage makes this particularly clear. In *Act. Verc.* 28, the senator Nicostratus has died and his mother pleads with Peter to resurrect him. Peter lets the body be brought to him. Peter's rival, Simon Magus, is unable to bring the dead man back to life, but Peter accomplishes the miraculous feat. Immediately before Peter raises Nicostratus from the dead, a short dialogue, which interrupts the action, is interwoven into the plot. If one removed the dialogue, its absence from the context would be unnoticeable. Since the author insisted upon presenting the passage, he and his readers are not indifferent to its content. The themes of the dialogue are slavery and manumisson.

> ...before he [Peter] awoke him [the senator] from the dead, he spoke to the nobleman's mother, "Should these youths, whom you have freed in honor of your son, continue to serve their master as freedmen once he will be alive again? I know, namely, that some of them will feel hurt if they see your son rise to life and they should again be his slaves. But they should all remain free and be fed as they were previously. For your son will rise and they should be together with him." Then Peter observed her for a long time, wondering what she thought. Finally, the mother of the young man said, "What else can I do? Therefore, I will declare in front of the prefect that everything I was willing to spend for the burial of my son shall be theirs."

---

18. Cf. similarly *Acta Pauli* 11.1: "A great number of believers" came "from Caesar's household"; one of them "was a certain Patroklus, a cupbearer of the emperor."

The mother of the young senatorial lord had released her son's slaves
upon his death. Three concessions are important for the text. (1) Those
who were freed should not return to slavery after the resurrection of
the senator. (The event that occasioned the release of the slaves, the
death of the master, comes to nothing because of the miraculous resurrection.) (2) The freed slaves should not lose their jobs but may
remain in the service of their patron. (They should "be fed as they were
previously...they should be together with him.") (3) Along with their
freedom, they should be provided with sufficient financial means. The
mother gives them as seed money "everything I was willing to spend for
the burial of my son." All three concessions are confirmed. The readers
of the story breathe a sigh of relief and we would not be wrong in seeking these readers predominantly among the ranks of slaves and lower
class freedmen from whose perspective this dialogue was composed. The
modern reader catches a glimpse not only of the desire for manumission
but also of the social problems that can accompany those set free. A
continual economic dependency between freed slaves and their patron
indeed was often the foundation of their existence. Many former slaves
continued to work in the patron's industry and thus were economically
secure after their emancipation.[19]

Besides the slaves, poor widows,[20] a soldier and his wife[21] and a
house owner named Narcissus,[22] the following honorable figures appear as Christian: a senator Demetrius;[23] the above-mentioned senator
Nicostratus and his mother, who donated 6,000 gold pieces[24] for the
widows of the congregation; a senator Marcellus, of aristocratic lineage (22) who possessed a magnificent house with colonnades (19),
dining rooms (14; 19), and a vestibule decorated with a marble statue
of Caesar (11). "His house became know as a hostel for pilgrims and
the poor" (8), because the widows and the orphans of the community

19. In regard to this problem see, for example, *Dig.* 38.1.1ff.; *Cod. Iust.* 6.3.1ff.;
for further literature see G. Fabre, *Libertus*, esp. 331ff.; Huttunen, *Social Strata*, 124,
189; M. Rouland, *Pouvoir politique et dépendance personnelle dans l'antiquité romaine:
Genèse et rôle des rapports de clientèle*, Coll. Latomus 166 (Brussels, 1979); M. Kaser,
"Die Geschichte der Patronatsgewalt," 88ff.; A. M. Duff, *Freedmen*, esp. 36ff.; J. Lambert,
Les operae liberti: Contribution à l'histoire des droits de patronat (Paris, 1934).

20. *Act.Verc.*, 19f.; 29; 25; 27. The social problem of widows can be seen clearly. They
are uncared for as soon as their sons die, because only their sons "provided a living for
them by the work of their hands" (c. 25). Cf. c. 27: "the grey-haired widow who cannot
help herself without her son."

21. *Act.Verc.*, 1: Candida and Quartus, who allegedly belonged to Paul's guard.

22. Narcissus assembled the Christian community in his multistoried house (*Act.Verc.*,
13–15) and hosted the apostle along with his companions (3f.; 6f.; 14). One may suspect
that the Narcissus mentioned in Rom 16 was the model for this literary figure.

23. *Act.Verc.*, 3.

24. *Act.Verc.*, 28f.

sought "rest" (25) under his roof (22, 25, 27, 29, 19f.). Roman equestrians appear behind the three senators: "Dionysius and Balbus from Asia, Roman equestrians and distinguished men" (3).[25] "Many senators, several equestrians, wealthy women and matrons were strengthened in their faith" (30); likewise, "two matrons, Berenike and Philostrate" (3). A "very wealthy woman" with the nickname "Chryse" or "Goldie" (from chrysos / χρυσός = gold), "because all the vessels in her house were of gold," donated 10,000 gold denarii for the "oppressed" of the Christian community (30). The four concubines of Agrippa, the prefect of the city, and the spouse of Albinus, a friend of Caesar, converted to Christianity (33f.), also Gemellus, who had previously financed the ventures of Simon Magus (32).

The Acts of Peter portrays clearly an aristocratic element in the Christian community living side by side with those who are in need; "the former travel in carriages, the latter on foot" (3). There are "rich and poor, orphans and widows, lowly and mighty" (36). The social responsibility of the rich members for the poor of the community is described especially through the example of the senator Marcellus.

The list of material increases when we add to it the *Acta Pauli,* composed shortly before 200 C.E. in Asia Minor. In Rome, "Barsabas Justus, the flatfoot, and Orion from Capadoccia and Festus from Galatia, the great men of Nero" (οἱ πρῶτοι τοῖ Νέρωνος) declared themselves Christian.[26] The same is true of the prefect Longus and the centurion Cestus, both in Rome.[27]

b. If the *Acta Petri* was composed in Rome and primarily for the readers of that city, for which the material, however, offers little certainty (cf. n. 16), then the *Acta* would also be valuable for us from a

---

25. See also the legendary tradition in Clement of Alexandria that Peter preached before some of Caesar's equestrians in Rome (Clement of Alexandria, *Adumbr. ad 1. Petr.* 5:13).

26. *Acta Pauli* 11.2, 6 (Lipsius, *Aa,* 1:109f., 116).

27. *Acta Pauli* 11.3–7 (Lipsius, *Aa,* 1:112–17). Needless to say, the *later* acts of the apostles are not considered here, even though they pretend to give social-historical information about the first two centuries. For example, they assert that the spouse of the emperor Nero, together with high officers, was converted by Paul and Peter (*Acta Petri et Pauli* 31). The fictitious Pseudo-Clementines, which could only, at the earliest, have been fixed in written form in Syria during the first half of the third century, must also remain unconsidered. According to them, the Roman bishop Clement, a Roman citizen (H 1.1.1; H 12.20.1), was allegedly very highly versed in philosophy and Greek culture (H 1.3.1; H 4.7.2; *Epit.* 2.146, 147). He owned a house in Rome (R 1.10.2) and, at least before his conversion, possessed an imposing fortune (R 1.11.6; 1.12.1). His mother, Mattidia, was related to Emperor Tiberius, and his father, Faustus, grew up with the emperor. "Many important men of the emperor's family" (H 12.8.2f.; H 4.7.2; H 14.6.2; R 7.8) were related to him. A great number of slaves belonged to his father's household (H 12.9.1; H 14.7.4). In Rome, Peter converted "many . . . important and unimportant people and finally also the social leaders among the aristocratic women" (*Epit.* 2.144)!

second point of view. As popular entertainment literature, it would reflect the tastes of a broad Christian reading public in Rome, who had a
penchant for fictitious literature, enjoyed all kinds of action and mystery,
and were not interested in long theological discussions. We have before
us folk literature, written for the masses.[28] Philip Vielhauer[29] raised the
objection that the various acts of the apostles also had literary ambitions
and were intended to reach a reading public "of a considerable sociological breadth," thus also "the so-called educated." However, the fact that
the authors of the acts of the apostles cherish "literary ambitions" does
not prove that they aim at socially elite readers. It only proves how very
popular the demand for literary art forms, even in the literature for the
lower classes, had become. Plümacher[30] demonstrates "literarily ambitious" classicisms in the romantic novel of Chariton of Aphrodisias and
in the novel of Achilles Tatius. Because of the vulgar language in the
rest of their books, both authors along with their readers are, nevertheless, to be numbered, at the very most, among the "half educated"
middle class. The same can be said, for example, of the Ninos novel and
of the Ephesian Tale of Anthia and Habrocomes by Xenophon of Ephesus (cf. Plümacher, *Lukas*, 61) as well as of our fictitious acts of the
apostles.[31] The ancient novel was *not* read in educated circles.[32] It is a
"valuable index...to the soul of the middle and lower class people of
the Greco-Roman world."[33]

---

28. On this topic see, e.g., R. Söder, *Die apokryphen Apostelgeschichten und die
romanhafte Literatur der Antike* (Stuttgart, 1932, repr. 1969); B. E. Perry, *The Ancient Romances: A Literary-Historical Account of Their Origins* (Berkeley, 1967); Perry,
"Chariton and His Romance," 93–134; R. Helm, *Der antike Roman*, 2d ed. (Göttingen,
1956).

29. *Geschichte*, 715, 718.

30. *Lukas*, 58–61.

31. In regard to the language of the acts of the apostles, see Dobschütz, "Der Roman,"
61.

32. Cf. Plümacher, *Lukas*, n. 137, and Zimmermann, "Aus der Welt," 294.

33. Perry, "Cariton and His Romance," 98; idem, *The Ancient Romances*, 5. Petronius
and Apuleius are exceptions. Both writers offer profound irony and literary artistry.

Chapter 14

Traditio Apostolica

On the pedestal of the headless statue of Hippolytus in the Vatican museums the Ἀποστολικὴ παράδοσις is noted among Hippolytus's writings. With laborious attention to detail, it is possible to reconstruct this text, written in Rome c. 215 C.E.[1] Since it explicitly wishes to preserve *tradition* for the Roman reader, it reflects Roman conditions from at least the period around 200.

Social stratification is also visible here.

1. With the income from charitable donations the deacons care for those at the lowest level of the social ladder, who stand partly on the edge of the minimal level of existence (cf. chaps. 8; 24). The social task of the deacons appears to be so extensive that subdeacons were assigned to assist them (cf. 13: "ut sequatur diaconum").

First, the sick were cared for (*infirmis:* 8; 24; 34). *Infirmus* is not only a medical term but also a social concept. We saw above in Justin that sickness often leads to a decline in social status, at least for those who do not live on the income from their property but who gain their livelihood from handwork.[2]

Second, the widows make up a large group, having the particular duty of prayer (chap. 10). A specific passage is dedicated to them in chapter 10. Other passages (chaps. 20; 24; 30) also refer to them, which indicates how great a problem they posed for the Christian community. Chapter 24 indicates that aid was distributed by the church to the homes of the widows, as it was to the sick. It is specifically prescribed that the bearer of the aid should bring the donation to the widow on the same day. If he fails to do this, he must donate something in addition from his own food, "quia mansit apud eum panis pauperum" (because the bread for the poor remained with him). This was to prevent carelessness in the process of distribution, which must have occurred often. When

---

1. Today this writing is, for the most part, acknowledged as original. Our textual critical basis is B. Botte, *La Tradition apostolique de Saint Hippolyte: Essai de reconstitution,* 4th ed., LWQF 39 (Münster, 1972).

2. Cf. similarly, Galen, *Protrept.* 14.38f.: Whoever chooses the vocation of a craftsman ("χειρωνακτικάς --- διὰ τῶν τοῦ σώματος πόνων") sees himself left in need in old age (τὸ...γένος αὐτῶν ἀπολείπειν εἴωθε γηρῶντας τοὺς τεχνίτας).

this type of delay was possible, it indicates, in my opinion, how great an administrative effort was expended and how numerous the recipients of aid must have been. Unfortunately, the number of recipients is known only for the middle of the third century. This is in a letter of the Roman bishop Cornelius (cf. Eusebius, *Hist. Ecc.* 6.43.11f.). The statistics serve as terminus ad quem to illustrate the material. In the middle of the third century, seven deacons and seven subdeacons took care of 1500 widows and other people in need.

The problem of the widows who were uncared for is also reflected in chap. 30 of the *Traditio Apostolica*. Not only the administrators of the church's treasury but also private individuals are encouraged to alleviate the material need of the widows. Private support can occur when people invite widows into their homes and serve them food and drink. They may take home with them the leftover food. Of course the *Traditio* imposes on (male) benefactors the condition that they invite only widows of "more mature age" and send them home before dark..."! Chapter 20 also shows how important a role the group of widows played in the Christian life of Rome:[3] Catechumens were explicitly judged according to how they conducted themselves in regard to widows ("an honoraverint").

Chapters 9 and 15–16 deal with Christians among the *slaves.*

a. Slaves with *pagan masters* were often punished by them because of their Christian faith (chap. 9: "castigatus est"; "castigatione domestica").[4] One can suspect the reasons for the punishment: Were the Christian slaves disobedient in carrying out orders that were not compatible with their faith? For example, did they refuse to participate in pagan sacrifices and rituals or immoral debauchery? Chapter 15 appears to answer these questions. Any activities that are associated with pagan cult, superstition, circus games, or sexual intemperance are unacceptable for Christians. Significant passages in this regard are also found in Tertullian, *De idol.* 15 and 17: Immorality and idolatry are beyond the limits of obedience for slaves. A slave who hands a cup of wine to his master at a pagan sacrifice is already ensnared in idolatry.

Chapter 15 of the *Traditio* rules that a Christian slave should, as far as possible, appease (*placere*) his pagan master,[5] so that no blasphemy — evidently on the part of the master — occurs (*ne blasphemia fiat*). Chapter 16 deals with cases of female slaves living in concubinage with their pagan masters and bringing up their children (*concubina/*παλλακή).

---

3. In regard to the east of the empire, see, e.g., 1 Tim 5:3ff.
4. In regard to the disciplining of slaves by their master, cf. Th. Mommsen, *Römisches Strafrecht,* 16ff.; in regard to corporal punishment see pp. 983ff. Disciplining of Christian slaves can already be seen in 1 Pet 2:18–20.
5. See also, e.g., 1 Tim 6:1.

Such a concubine may be admitted to the Christian catechumenate as long as she remains faithful to this one man.[6]

b. Noteworthy is that there are many slaves among the *new converts* to Christianity. In chaps. 15f., which deal with all possible cases of those entering the catechumenate, the case of slaves is spoken of first and in great detail. One may conclude from this that a great many slaves are registering for the catechumenate. One of the first questions asked of a candidate is whether he or she is married or is a slave.

c. Chapter 15 divides slaves into two groups: those with pagan masters and those with *Christian masters*. A Christian master must give his permission when a slave wishes to become a Christian! ("Et si quis est servus alicuius fidelis, et dominus eius ei permittit / ἐπιτρέπειν, audiat verbum.") Were there Christian masters who did not show any particular interest in having domestic servants by their sides as Christian sisters or brothers?[7] One should of course not read too much into the text. In the next line we read: "Si dominus non dat testimonium de eo *quia bonus est,* reiciatur." This testimony corresponds to the custom of checking up on *all* candidates concerning the reasons they wish to become Christians ("de causa / αἰτία propter quam accedunt," chap. 15). A recommendation was sought from the Christians who recruited a convert and brought him along with them: "dent testimonium super eos illi qui adduxerunt eos an sit eis *virtus ad audiendum verbum*" (chap. 20). Evidently there were curiosity seekers, people with ignoble motives and perhaps informers who lacked true sincerity and had to be filtered out from those entering the catechumenate. The testimony of the Christian master concerning his slave is to be interpreted in this sense: In case the master was of the opinion that his slave was *bonus,* that he possessed "virtus ad audiendum verbum," then the slave was allowed to be taken into the catechumenate. The requirement of a recommendation from the master could indicate that slaves were not always sincere about becoming Christian, simply wishing to be Christian because of the accompanying benefits, such as receiving better treatment from their Christian masters and living in easier circumstances. The complete passage regarding the master's testimony is:

Qui autem adducuntur noviter ad audiendum verbum, ... interrogentur de causa (αἰτία) propter quam accedunt ad fidem. Et dent

---

6. If a Christian man is living in concubinage, he should marry: "sumat uxorem secundum legem." Unfortunately, the two cases are not explicitly brought into relation with one another, in this sense, that a *Christian* master living with a Christian slave in concubinage should marry her. Such a marriage would constitute the manumission of the concubine, who, as a slave, is legally unable to marry (cf. chap. 13, n. 11, above).

7. See the parenesis in 1 Tim 6:2, which evidently presupposes that Christian slaves occasionally do not show sufficient respect to their Christian masters because they are "brothers." Similarly, Ignatius, *Polyc.* 4:3: Christian slaves should not be "puffed up."

testimonium super eos illi qui adduxerunt eos an sit eis virtus ad audiendum verbum. Interrogentur autem de vita eorum qualis sit: an sit ei mulier vel an sit servus. Et si quis est servus alicuius fidelis, et dominus eius ei permittit, audiat verbum. Si dominus non dat testimonium de eo quia bonus est, reiciatur.

The socially inferior among the brothers and sisters play a role in three additional passages. As already in the time of Justin (see above), there were *illiterates* among the Christians of Rome. The proviso in chap. 41, "si potest legere," clearly indicates this.

Chapter 40: The church's treasury assists the poor, when they must bury one of their own ("ne gravetur homo ad sepeliendum hominem in coemeteriis: res enim est omnis pauperis"). This treasury helps to pay for the gravedigger and for the bricks or tiling that seal the grave (pretium laterum / κέραμος). We have archaeological material from the Vatican and the Isola Sacra (see Part 3, chap. 12) that illustrates what paupers' graves, sealed with bricks, look like. It is also worth remembering the catacomb cemetery on the Via Appia, constructed by Callistus under the supervision of Zephyrinus, in which up until 235 C.E. about eight hundred Christians of little means were buried. Actually the *Traditio Apostolica* (40) appears to presuppose such a communal area for Christian burial when it specifies that grave diggers and other cemetery workers should be fed out of the church's treasury so that "no one will be burdened" ("qui sunt in loco illo [i.e., the cemetery] et qui curam habent, episcopus nutriat eos ut nemo gravetur ex eis qui veniunt ad haec loca").[8] The passage reflects a regulation that was evidently valid for the Via Appia cemetery administered by the deacon Callistus. During the time period in question, this cemetery was the only one directly supervised by an ecclesiastical official (see above, chap. 3).

Similar to the dinner invitations to the widows, other poor brothers and sisters were invited into homes for food and drink (chaps. 27–29, esp. 28). Occasionally there appear to have been very hungry guests among those invited. Chapter 28 admonishes that each should eat one's fill, but still leave some leftovers ("ut quod supererit vobis," or "gustate ut et superet"). Several brethren also drained their glasses too often and are admonished concerning sobriety ("non ad ebrietatem"). It is explicitly stated that these invitations are not to eucharistic meals (26: "non eucharistia"), but to agapes in the homes of well-to-do hosts. As at pagan feasts, guests may take home with them gifts (ἀποφορητόν, 28; cf. Athenaeus, 6:229c). Petronius 56 describes such *apophoreta*: a side of bacon, salt pretzels, a whip, a knife, raisins in Attic honey, a rabbit, an eel....

---

8. Christians taking care of the burial of their poor sisters and brothers can be seen also in Aristides, *Apol.* 15.7f.; Tertullian, *Apol.* 39.

2. We have already encountered Christians of a *higher social level* in the Christian slave masters (*Traditio* 15) and in the donors of food for the widows and the poor (*Traditio* 30; 28; also 23). Appeals for donations, as in chaps. 31f., also presuppose well-to-do people as addressees.[9] According to chap. 21, a number of Christian women wore golden jewelry (*ornamenta*/κόσμησις, *auri et argenti*) which they were told to set aside when entering the baptismal bath.

3. Chapter 33 also mentions Christians who sometimes when at sea forget the time of Easter. ("Si quis in navigio ignoravit diem paschae...". Unfortunately, it is not clear from the text whether these people are on business trips, ordinary sailors, tourists, or even merchants and shipowners like Marcion.

4. The occupations mentioned in chap. 16 must be treated separately.

First, we consider occupations which are not (or should not be) found among Christians, because they are connected with a pagan cult or with intolerable immorality. The list in chap. 16 serves the purpose of excluding these people from the catechumenate if they refuse to give up their occupation. It is worth looking at this list briefly, because it may reflect[10] the occupations of individual Christians, at least *before* their conversion.

(a) All who were engaged in the pagan games in the amphitheaters or circus were excluded from the catechumenate. These could include officials (publicus/δημόσιος) of the gladiatorial games, fencing teachers, or the gladiators themselves, whether they be chariot drivers or hunters in the arena.[11] A sociological classification of these functions is difficult. Basically, they are socially unspecific. Among the participants in the arena all classes are represented — from slaves (Tacitus, *Ann.* 15.46), artisans, and laborers[12] to equestrians.[13] Occasionally a few gladiators became very wealthy.[14] Naturally, the majority are predominantly from the lower classes of society, slaves and free persons on the lower social scale who for the duration of a contract live as gladiators, taking on a

---

9. In chaps. 31f., it is not astonishing that city dwellers donate agrarian produce. While living in Rome, Hermas cultivated a field outside the city (*Vis.* 3.1.2; 4.1.2).

10. In spite of imperatives such as those listed in chap. 16 of the *Traditio Apostolica*, there were, however, at least in other places, Christians who manufactured pagan idols (Tertullian, *De idol.* 7; 5), a Christian astrologer (ibid., 9), Christian race drivers, Christians who owned a racing stable (Jerome, *Vita Hilarionis* 20), and a Christian who taught acting (Cyprian, *Ep.* 2). The list in *Traditio Apostolica* 16 might therefore reflect not only the reality *before* but also *after* an individual's conversion to Christianity. Someone who had not learned another occupation could not give up his old one from one day to the next. He still had to support himself financially, since the church treasuries were not in the position to provide for him continuously. This is indicated in the section concerning teachers in *Traditio* 16 and by Cyprian in *Ep.* 2.

11. The tradition of Christian opposition to the games was later legally codified. Cf. *Cod. Theod.* 9.40.8.11. See also W. Weismann, *Kirche und Schauspiele* (Würzburg, 1972).

12. K. Schneider, "Gladiatores," Pauly/Wissowa Suppl. 3:766.

13. Ibid., 764–66 for references; 771 mentions Commodus himself.

14. Ibid., 784, for references.

position similar to that of slaves. Their fate often ends in suicide.[15] The social position of the official engaged in gladiatorial matters ("publicus qui est in re gladiatoria") is not concretely ascertainable either. In Rome, predominantly quaestors are entrusted with the games.[16] However, the formulation is so broad that it does not exclude the subordinate "servus publicus," who sells entrance tickets on behalf of the quaestor.

b. Likewise, it is difficult to categorize sociologically those engaged in drama or theater (*scenicus* / θεατρικός, "vel qui facit demonstrationem in theatro"). The range extends from miming slaves[17] to the actor who moves in the highest imperial circles, knowing the right people and pulling strings in legal affairs (Josephus [*Vita* 16] describing a certain Aliturus, an actor, who is a favorite of Nero and of Jewish origin).[18] Generally it is valid to say that "the performing artist, in particular the actor, never again assumed such a respected position in the cultural world as in the Hellenistic-Roman period."[19] On stage he would be enthusiastically idolized. But this does not mean that he would be equally revered in everyday life. His social esteem should not be overestimated. Legally valid marriages between freeborn citizens and actresses (Ulpianus, *Dig.* 13.2) or between descendants of a senator and performers (Ulpianus, *Dig.* 13.1; Paulus, *Dig.* 23.2.44 pr.; Mod., *Dig.* 23.2.42.1) were impossible. Not even the sons or daughters of performers could marry descendants of senators (Paulus, *Dig.* 23.2.44 pr.).[20] Theatrical arts are rarely mentioned on grave inscriptions in Rome, which indicates that, as a civic vocation, they enjoyed little prestige.[21] The majority of performers were not free, made do with a miserable salary, and had hardly enough clothing (Seneca, *Ep.* 80.7f.).

c. Finally, there is a list of moral defects that are socially unspecific (forgery, intemperance, prostitution and pimping / πορνοβοσκός). Also listed are activities connected with pagan cult and superstition: magicians, astrologers, fortunetellers, dream interpreters, the charlatan "who confuses the people" ("qui turbat populum"), and, lastly, priests or custodians of idols ("sacerdos vel custos idolorum"). I will name only three examples illustrating the sociologically unspecific character: Apuleius's

15. Ibid., 773–75, 784.
16. Ibid., 765f.
17. For example, *Dig.* 21.4.4. For an example of freedmen as actors see Pliny, *Ep.* 5.19, 7.24, 9.34. Further material is found in J. Marquardt, *Das Privatleben der Römer,* 162, esp. n. 4, and 163, esp. n. 1; G. Fabre, *Libertus,* 354f.: in regard to slaves and freedmen.
18. Overlooked by H. G. Marek, "Die soziale Stellung," 105; he names other examples of well-paid and respected actors.
19. F. Poland, "*Technitai,*" Pauly/Wissowa 5/2:2474–2558, esp. 2555–58; our quote, 2558.
20. For other legal disadvantages see Marek, "Die soziale Stellung," 108–10.
21. For the inscriptions see Huttunen, *Social Strata,* 122.

magician, Meroe, is a sloppy innkeeper (*Met.* 1.7f.); on the other hand the magician Pamphile is a distinguished lady (ibid., 3.19ff.). Among the charlatans confusing the people, the *Sententiae Pauli* (5.21, cf. 5.22) identifies both aristocrats who are only to be banished and common folk who are to be punished by death. Pagan cultic functions are performed by the mistress of an enormous household as well as by her slaves. This is impressively exemplified by the inscription[22] witnessing the Dionysian rites of Pompeia Agrippinilla from Tusculum. Sociologically ambiguous are also those who manufacture amulets. They can be either entrepreneurs on a larger scale[23] or enslaved artisans employed by the former.

d. Social status is first unequivocal in regard to the "state official who is clothed in purple" ("magistratus civitatis qui induitur purpura"). Only high-ranking officials, those above the office of quaestor such as consuls, praetors, and the *curule aediles,* wear a toga with a purple border called "toga praetexta" and beneath this a tunic also adorned with a purple strip. The office of quaestor already means entrance into the senate.[24] One wonders why these men had to give up their office before they could become catechumens. It was required when the office encompassed the "power of the sword." ("Qui habet potestatem gladii, vel magistratus civitatis qui induitur purpura, vel cesset vel reiciatur.") Governors of senatorial rank had the "power of the sword" or the power of execution ("ius gladii").[25] The question arises whether the *Traditio Apostolica* reflects actual cases that occurred among candidates for the catechumenate or whether it lists a catalogue of theoretically possible cases to be turned away. A final remark in the text, "If we left unmentioned another thing ... " ("si omisimus aliam rem") speaks for the latter possibility. However, the source gives no other clue that would enable us to answer the question definitively. Nevertheless, even if we were presented only with theoretical cases, we still see what the author of the *Traditio* considered possible. For him it is thinkable that a senatorial official would seek to become a Christian. This conclusion is in agreement with material cited above, which, for the same period, testifies to the existence of Christians from senatorial nobility.

The three following cases differ from the others in that the convert must not give up (immediately) his occupation but is merely subjected to

---

22. Cf. A. Vogliano, "La Grande Iscrizione," 215ff.

23. For example, Demetrius in Acts 19:24f.: παρείχετο τοῖς τεχνίταις οὐκ ὀλίγην ἐργασίαν/εὐπορία.

24. Cf. Kübler, "Magistratus," Pauly/Wissowa 14/1, esp. 418, 433.

25. For example, Ulpianus, *Dig.* 1.18.6.8. The expression "gladii potestas" is found in *Dig.* 50.17.70. Further see Th. Mommsen, *Römisches Strafrecht,* 243–45. In the fourth century, Bishop Paulinus of Nola (*Carm.* 21.395f.) is happy that during his tenure as governor he did not carry out any executions.

special conditions. Christians were permitted at least temporally to exercise these occupations. Once again the question remains open whether these instances are actual or potential cases.

a. On a lower level the subordinate[26] soldier is almost as problematic as the person of senatorial rank who possesses the "potestas gladii." Soldiers are permitted into the catechumenate but then they may not kill anyone or swear an oath. However, the military oath of allegiance (*sacramentum*) to the flag and to the emperor is a compulsory oath[27] that is sworn not only upon entrance into service but also repeated every year.[28] The above regulation in the *Traditio* therefore basically amounts to a ban from the military profession, because catechumens from the military must quit their job before they have to repeat their oath of allegiance. Also all catechumens who wish to become soldiers ("qui volunt fieri milites") should be excluded.[29]

In the city of Rome there were many areas of activity for a member of the military who was joining Christianity. He could perhaps belong to the praetorian cohorts,[30] perhaps also to the "castra peregina" (the foreign garrison), whose barracks have been discovered by archaeologists south of S. Stefano Rotondo. Soldiers of the provincial armies lived there when they were in Rome on special missions, being assigned to the police or the palace unit or acting as messengers. The aspiring Christian could also be a member of one of the seven regiments of the *vigiles*.

---

26. "He is ordered" (*iubetur*).

27. Cf. Klingmüller, "Sacramentum," in Pauly / Wissowa 1/2:1668. Klingmüller reports the discussion about Livy, 22.38 and Frontinus (*Strat.* 4.1.4). These two texts are the only ones that offer (very uncertain!) evidence for a freely sworn oath. For information concerning the content of the soldier's oath see Gellius, 16.4.

28. On every third of January and on every anniversary of the emperor's proclamation.

29. It is uncertain whether the regulation reflects the general practice of the Roman Christian community or whether it is to be ascribed to the rigorous Hippolytus. Tertullian (e.g., *De idol.* 19; *De corona*) and Origen (*Contra Cel.* 8.73; 5.33) also considered military service and being a Christian to be incompatible. However, the early church was not of one opinion on this subject, as the existence of numerous Christian soldiers attests. (Cf. the references in the next note; Tertullian, *De corona* 1.1 as well as the literature cited by J. Helgeland, "Christians and the Roman Army," *ANRW* 2.23.1 (1979): 724–834; L. J. Swift, "War and the Christian Conscience I," ibid., 835–68; W. Schäfke, "Frühchristlicher Widerstand," ibid., 460–723, here 542–47.

30. Cf. Tertullian, *De Corona* 12; the passage presupposes Christians in the imperial guard. There are several inscriptions, not prior to the third century, however, that testify to Christian praetorian guards in Rome: *CIL* 6:32654, 32691, 32980. Further references can be found in A. Ferrua, "L'epigrafia cristiana prima di Costantino," 589, n. 25, 591, 596. The local Roman tradition concerning the martyrs Nereus and Achilleus who are designated as soldiers of Domitian gives nothing more than a colorful legend. (The two saints are tangible for the first time in an inscription of Pope Damasus, which can be found in M. Durry, *Les cohortes prétoriennes*, 353; see also the acts of the two martyrs edited by H. Achelis, *Acta SS. Nerei et Achillei*.) For references to Christian soldiers outside of Rome during the reign of Marcus Aurelius and Septimius Severus see, e.g., Eusebius, *Hist. Ecc.* 5.5.6; also Tertullian, *Apol.* 37.4 ("in garrisons and fortresses"); 42.3 (*militarus*); *Ad Scap.* 4. It is not explicitly stated that the people ἐν τῷ πραιτωρίῳ in Phil 1:13 are Christian (*pretorium* usually denotes the central building of a military camp).

These were the city's fire brigades, which also functioned as police. The *vigiles* consisted mostly of freedmen.[31] In the second century, members of the praetorian cohorts were no longer exclusively Italian.[32] Under Septimus Severus (193–211 C.E.) the praetorian guard was completely restructured. The old guard was dismissed and replaced with soldiers from the provincial armies, so that in Rome "a motley swarm of soldiers appeared: barbaric, wild in appearance and raw in speech."[33]

b. If he had learned a craft, the *teacher* ("qui docet pueros") should better give up his occupation. If he had not, he may continue teaching ("bonum est ut cesset; si non habet artem / τέχνη, permittatur ei"). It is not clear whether this refers to the elementary teacher, the *grammatikos* (the equivalent of today's high school teacher), or (probably) both. Since these teachers must use pagan texts in their classes, mostly myths concerning the gods, Christians had some reservation regarding the occupation (cf., e.g., Tertullian, *De idol.* 10).

The elementary teacher ("ludi magister") enjoys only low social esteem.[34] Each morning some place near the Forum behind a canvas tarpaulin, under the porch of a store and in the midst of street noises, he teaches writing and arithmetic. His methods of caning students amuse adults (e.g., Tertullian, *Adv. Marc.* 1.8) but hardly raise his esteem. Some of the privileges guaranteed to philosophers, orators, physicians, and also to *grammatikoi* elude this teacher.[35] His work does not belong to the intellectual occupations.

The occupation of the *grammatikos* is different. In the imperial era, he participates in the generally increased appreciation of intellectual occupations. During the imperial age (unlike that of the republic), an intellectual occupation ranks higher on the social scale than all physical labor. Education became a social factor.[36] Within the intellectual occupations, however, the *grammatikos* only holds a lower position.[37] He is

---

31. See M. Rostovtzeff, *Kaiserreich*, 1:37, 43.

32. Cf. ibid., 1:92, 109; 2, chap. 9, n. 12.

33. Cassius Dio 74.1f.; cf. *Historia Augusta*, Sept. Sev. 7.2f., 6 (in regard to undisciplined conduct, see *Dig.* 1.18.6.2). On this entire topic, see Rostovtzeff, *Kaiserreich*, 1:111; 2:114.

34. Cf. e.g., W. H. Gross, "Schulen," *KlPauly* 5:39.

35. For example, the privilege of immunity (*immunitas*); the exemption from civil duties ("vacatio civilium munerum"); cf. E. Ziebarth, "Schulen," Pauly / Wissowa 2/1: 764f.

36. Cf., e.g., Galen, *Protrept.* 14.38f: ἔνιαι...λογικαί τ' εἰσὶ καὶ σεμναί, τινὲς δ' εὐκαταφρόνητοι καὶ διὰ τῶν τοῦ σώματος πόνων, ἃς δὴ βαναυσούσους τε καὶ χειρωνακτικὰς ὀνομάζουσιν. In Lucian's Ἐνύπνιον the παιδεία (10ff.) is praised as a means to social advancement, also for those who come from poverty (18); high esteem is attributed to the educated person, even by those who are the upper class through wealth and birth. Official positions are offered to the educated intellectuals. Cf. further, J. Christes, *Bildung und Gesellschaft*, 234–36, and see also below, Part 4.

37. Cf. J. Christes, *Bildung und Gesellschaft*, 239ff.

simply a prepartory "supplier" for the more respected rhetoric instruction and jurisprudence.[38] *Grammatikoi* come from among the slaves, freedmen, or the free inhabitants of the provinces; in any case they are generally from the fourth class.[39]

c. The third case is the painter and sculptor (*sculptor, pictor* / ζωγράφος). He may continue to work as long as he does not manufacture any idols (*idola* / εἴδωλον). These two artistic professions are again difficult to classify sociologically. Even a contemporary, Galenus (*Protrept.* 14.38f.), is uncertain whether sculpturing and painting (γραφική, πλαστική) belong to the venerable educational occupations (σεμναὶ λογικαὶ τέχναι) or simply to the crafts of which he speaks contemptuously (εὐκαταφρόνητοι). Lucian's uncle (Ἐνύπνιον 2–9) is a sculptor and his occupation is described as a skill worthy of a free man and from which he earns a living. According to Lucian, the sculptor can have honor and esteem, even as great as that of Polyclitus and Phidias, in his native country, which he need not leave because of his substantial income. On the other hand — and here in Lucian we encounter the same uncertainty in the evaluation of this occupation that we saw in Galenus — the profession is connected with τῷ σώματι πόνοι and as such subordinate to the intellectual occupations of the Παιδεία.[40] The young Lucian as offspring of an artisan's family fled very early from his sculpturing class (of course one reason was also that he was beaten because of his clumsiness; 3f.). In the end Lucian advises his young readers to be like him and to flee into the arms of Paideia, whom he attractively personifies and pictures as clothed in fine garments.

Famous artists are well paid for their works as well as for their instruction, while the little-known ones remain correspondingly poor and are contemptuously renounced as handworkers.[41] Although painting was originally an occupation of a free person who was forbidden

---

38. Only isolated *grammatikoi* who held the position of directors of libraries or tutors for princes enjoyed highest imperial esteem: Suetonius, *Gramm.* 17; 20f. Three others in Verona, Como, and Benevent were promoted to decurions (*CIL* 5:3433; 5278; 9:1654). Julius Caesar, however, had already granted citizenship not only to philosophy and rhetoric teachers but also to *grammatikoi*: Suetonius, *Caes.* 42. See above n. 35 for other privileges.

39. Cf. the material in L. Friedländer, *Sittengeschichte Roms*, 1:173ff.

40. Cf. also appraisals such as ταπεινὸς τὴν γνώμην; ἀφανής; βάναυσος καὶ χειρῶναξ καὶ ἀποχειροβίωτος; the income is ὀλίγα καὶ ἀγεννῆ. From the perspective of the upper classes manual labor is judged contemptuously. Cf. similarly Cicero, *Off.* 1.42. 150f. ("opifices omnes in sordida arte versantur"); Cassius Dio, 46.4.2; Seneca, *Ep.* 90.24–26. The ideal of the upper class is to be economically independent, to live off the returns from their properties, and to dedicate oneself to politics or culture. Also the Christian Justin holds little esteem for manual work: *Dial.* 2.1 indicates that for Justin the manual laborer is on the same level as the common folk. In *Dial.* 88.8 he sees Jesus' occupation of carpenter as an expression of his coming "without glory." Among the common folk themselves, however, manual work is more respected; 2 Thess 3:10 is a reference for this.

41. Cf. Lippold, "Malerei," Pauly / Wissowa 14:1, 896f.

to initiate slaves into the art (Pliny, *Nat. hist.* 35.77), nevertheless in the imperial age also slaves exercised the occupation (Juvenal, 9.146; cf. *CIL* 6:9786). The occupation forfeited esteem during imperial times "after the shameless Alexandrians discovered a quick method for this great art..." (Petronius, 2.9; 88.10.1f.).

Similar to our own day, the artistic occupations, viewed in their entirety, evade decisive sociological grasp. From the point of view of social history, only the individual artist might be classifiable (according to his origin, income, his status as a dependent, half-independent, or independent artisan, on the basis of his reputation, etc.); his branch of occupation is not in itself classifiable.

Chapter 15

Summary and Conclusion

1. From the beginning to the end of the diachronic section the broad stream of believers who stand at the lower level of the social scale is obvious. Minucius Felix again emphatically confirms their existence in Rome at the beginning of the third century. The quantitative predominance lies with the lower classes: "the majority of us are poor" (*plerique pauperes*), admits Octavius (36.3; cf. 36.5–7; 16.5; 37.7). He concedes that "the pomp of magnificent phrases and of pleasing expressions" is wanting for the Christians (16.6).

The pagan environment's opinion about the Christians, as it is reported by Minucius Felix, corresponds to these observations: "uneducated, rude, ill-bred, boorish heads";[1] "the most ('pars maior') suffer want and cold, hardship and hunger."[2] Further, 8.3f. states: "from the lowest dregs of folk assemble the uneducated and the gullible women who fall for everything, ... " "an obscure group, shunning the light, dumb in public, garrulous in private," "pitiable ... half naked, they despise office and rank."[3]

We need only recall the social history of the Christian area Trastevere in order to understand the "plerique pauperes." The expression "plerique pauperes," however, describes not only a characteristic of the Christian community but also a phenomenon of all Roman society. The poor made up a great majority of the *entire* population (cf. Seneca, *Helv.* 12.1) so that the Christian community simply participated in this state.

---

1. 12.7; similarly 5.4; 16.5f. ("inliteratos pauperes inperitos").

2. 12.2. Cf. also 12.4: Christians are threatened by crucifixion (*cruces*), which indicates that they do not have Roman citizenship. See above, chap. 10.

3. In regard to the latter cf. 31.6: "honores vestros et purpuras recusamus" (the passage confirms the corresponding previous passage in the *Traditio Apostolica* 16: Persons of senatorial rank occupying the highest government positions with the power to inflict capital punishment are not admitted to the catechumenate). Similarly see, for example, Celsus in Origen, *Contra Cel.* 1.9f., 27, 28, 62; 2.46; 3.44, 55; 6.13f.; also Lucian, *Peregr.* 13, and Aristides the rhetorician, *Or.* 46. The pagan polemic is not created out of thin air. It became a caricature, however, because it ascribed the Christians *exclusively* to the "lowest sediment" of the people without taking into account the social stratification within Christianity. Further see J. Vogt, "Der Vorwurf der sozialen Niedrigkeit des frühen Christentums," *Gymnasium* 82 (1975): 401–11.

2. The "plerique pauperes" is valid, but Minucius Felix's *Octavius* is cautious about wholesale estimation: Christianity does not *only* belong to the lowest level of folk ("nec de ultima plebe," 31.6). We saw how, at least throughout the entire second century, the socially elevated Christians raised a considerable amount for charity in order to support the poorer members of the Christian community. At the threshold to the third century, not only were widows and those in need paid from this collective fund, but even ecclesiastical functionaries (*Trad. Apost.* 24: "qui operam dat ecclesiae" or "negotiis ecclesiasticis vacat et officiis").[4] Therefore, above that mass who stand socially at a low level and who partly live on the edges of minimal existence, there is a stratum of socially elevated Christians. In the first century this circle of people appears to be still small. Even though already in Paul's letter to the Romans a slight distinction in different social positions is indicated, on the whole, the stream of low class and poor people is dominant. (Recall the selling of oneself as a common means of income for Christian social welfare work [*1 Clem.* 55:2]; apparently there were no other lucrative sources available.) Really "rich people" (πλούσιοι) become discernible for the first time in the 90s of the first century. In the second century the group of socially elevated increases constantly. By the time of Hermas this group is already polymorphic and, in the last fifth of the second century, it stretches into the upper classes, even into senatorial circles.

This "social ascent" of Roman Christianity takes place within a larger context. In general, during the second century the upper strata of all Roman society sharply increased and the number of slaves decreased.[5] Therefore, also in this case, Roman Christianity participates in the development of the whole society. Since the portion of people in the upper strata increased in the society, the probability arose that the number of socially elevated Christians also increased. It would be alluring to compare the percentage of increase in the whole society to that within the Christian community, but we would be groping in the dark.

Nevertheless, we recognize at least two points (*plerique pauperes;* increase in the number of socially elevated people in the second century) in which Christianity reflects the social development of the entire society.[6]

---

4. Cf. also the stipend that Bishop Victor paid to Callistus during his stay in Anzio: Hippolytus, *Ref.* 9.12. What Callistus did during his sojourn remains unfortunately completely in the dark.

5. Cf., e.g., M. Rostovtzeff, *Kaiserreich*, 1:106; G. Alföldy, *Die Freilassung*, 367.

6. Especially E. A. Judge (*Christliche Gruppen in nichtchristlicher Gesellschaft* [Wuppertal, 1964]) and W. A. Meeks (*The First Urban Christians* [New Haven, 1983]) were interested in this type of correspondence between Christianity and society as a whole. G. Schöllgen ("Was wissen wir über die Sozialstruktur der paulinischen Gemeinden?" *NTS* 34 (1988): 71–82), however, criticizes Meeks's thesis concerning congruent structures (cf. W. A. Meeks, *Urban Christians,* 73) according to which the social structure of Pauline

Of course we may not stop with this insight. The next step suggested itself especially in light of the Shepherd of Hermas and of *1 Clem.* 55:2. It is not sufficient simply to examine the social statuses of the Christians and then to observe that the social stratification in Christianity corresponds (at least partially) to that in the entire society. The *inherent dynamic* that is developed by the Christian community as a social system is of interest, too. We saw that in Christianity representatives of the different social strata come closer together than in many other areas of society. Not only is the integration within the lower strata encouraged (see the above reference to *1 Clem.* 55:2), but also the representatives of the higher social positions are brought into an intensive exchange with the representatives of the lower strata (see, for example, Shepherd of Hermas, above, chap. 10). In this regard Christianity undoubtedly contributes to a social integration of the entire society. Apart from that, to a considerable extent the social positions of those who become Christians change. The position of some is *raised* slightly, namely, those who were starving on the edge of the minimal level of existence and who as converts now receive material support for their existence from the Christian community. In addition, the Shepherd of Hermas wished to *lower* the social position of the wealthy Christians by recommending that they decrease their various business activities, curtail themselves, and distance themselves from luxury. It is of course questionable whether he succeeded to any great extent. From his forceful imperatives we see how much opposition he encountered. His imperatives presuppose actual oppositional conditions. That means the socially downward movement occurred much less than Hermas wished it to occur. Nevertheless, the wealthy Christians raised a considerable amount of money for their poorer brothers and sisters and this contributed to a limited material equalization between the social levels. One may conclude that Christianity, from the point of view of the entire society, had a socially integrating impact. Beyond this, Christianity also changed, of course in a very modest way, the social position of those who embraced it.

3. If we take seriously the result that most Roman Chirstians were poor, summarized in the formula "plerique pauperes," we are in the position to give *one* interpretation of the archaeological silence mentioned in Part 2. There it was said that, with very few exceptions, no Christian inscriptions, sculptures, mosaics, or sarcophagi are found in the first two centuries.[7] The reason for this is that many Christians apparently

---

communities reflected essentially that of the surrounding urban society. The source material is much too meager to support such far-reaching theses. At most, as in Rome, one can discern individual points of correspondence.

7. An exception are the Valentinian inscriptions (see below, chap. 27). The three inscriptions, dated from the years 71, 107, and 111, by G. B. De Rossi (nos. 1–3 in *ICUR* 1, cf. p. cxvii; 1–32; 573f.) are untenable as Christian witnesses for this period (cf. e.g., A. M.

had little means to afford them. Actually, innumerable poor and slaves in Rome were buried without epitaphs in public cemeteries (puticuli).[8] There is no doubt that lower social strata are underrepresented in the inscriptions because of their poverty.

It is always problematic to interpret a silence. It is possible that other, different circumstances lie at the basis of this negative evidence as well:

a. The commandment forbidding images operated in the ancient church.[9]

b. We saw that the Christians of Rome first began to bury their dead in underground cemeteries about 200 C.E. Such catacombs easily preserved archaeological material. Surface monuments, by contrast, suffered much more damage during the centuries, so that therefore the silence of the first two centuries is understandable.

If one combines the "plerique pauperes" with this point, one no longer wonders concerning the silence of the evidence. Collective cemeteries for the poor above the earth did not enjoy a long life, as we know from an example on the Esquiline: "Once the slave carried here the dead slave in a cheap coffin... here was a common sepulcher for the poor folk (miserae plebi)" (Horace, *Serm.* 1.8.9ff.). But soon afterwards Maecenas planted on the same spot his beautiful gardens, "where only recently a gruesome field of bleached bones offered a sad sight."

c. Many monuments, particularly graves, in the first and second centuries were not distinguished as Christian by their builders because of the legal uncertainty. Therefore, it is possible that we could possess Christian monuments of which we are unaware. We saw that the graves on the Vatican site "P" were probably to be considered Christian only because of "external criteria" (choice of location, their arrangement, etc.) and not because they exhibit in themselves any Christian symbols. Two examples illustrate that it was not desirable, at least in the first two centuries, for the average Christian to advertise his or her Christianity openly, let alone engrave it on stone. In Tertullian's *De cultu feminarum* 2.11, Christian women defend wearing finery and jewelry with the argument that without them they would be noticeable as Christians! There is a second example. Until the middle of the third century Christians usually had pagan names. Especially Christian or biblical cognomina were seldom found.[10] The pagan reproach that the Christians were an

---

Schneider, *Die ältesten Denkmäler* 168, n. 11. The earliest Christian witnesses are mainly graffiti, which cost nothing; see above on the fish graffito at the Vatican (mid-second century) and the acrostic beneath S. Sebastiano (ca. 150–250), chaps. 4 and 12.

8. See P. Huttunen, *Social Strata*, 43–45; also, e.g., Frontinus, n. 21.15L.

9. See, for example, Th. Klauser, "Erwägungen zur Entstehung der altchristlichen Kunst," *ZKG* 76 (1965): 1–11.

10. Material can be found in Harnack, *Mission und Ausbreitung*, 436ff. See also *SICV*: Among the 330 inscriptions, one finds at the most 25 specifically Christian names. Also in the Talmud one reads, "the majority of the Jews in the diaspora has the same names as

obscure group, shunning the light ("latebrosa et lucifugax natio, in publicum muta"), which the pagans in Min. Fel. 8 raised above all against the Christians of Rome, appears to contain a kernel of truth. Seen in this manner, the silence of the evidence attests not only to the "plerique pauperes." It also indicates how Christians wisely did not reveal their identity to every potential denunciator.

This was still the case even in the third century. It is true that Christian pictures of the third century do portray biblical figures. One finds the picture of the Good Shepherd carrying a sheep, Jonah resting, and Daniel among the lions. But these figures are placed within the traditional idyllic pagan scenes of bucolic or maritime life and are often subordinated to these scenes. The idyllic motifs are certainly more dominant than the biblical. (See the inventory in Brandenburg, *Ursprung der frühchristlichen Bildkunst*, 338–49.) A Christian interpretation of these frescoes and reliefs on sarcophagi is evident only to those who already know the Bible. A pagan observer would take joy in the idyllic landscapes without becoming suspicious. A youth among lions, resting or carrying a sheep are nice bucolic themes for a non-Christian viewer. The Good Shepherd is used as a pagan motif, for example, on oil lamps manufactured in Ostia. The shepherd carrying a sheep represents for the pagans the bucolic life, the idyllic quiet of peace and blissful security. Although the Christian character of these third-century pictures is certain (also from inscriptions), it remains "hidden" and only visible to the initiated. The legal uncertainty in the pre-Constantine period partly explains this evidence; Brandenburg does not consider it when speaking of explanations exclusively relating to art history.[11]

4. One can only speculate about the *number* of Roman Christians. It is hardly possible to say more than that their number constantly increased (Minucius Felix, 31.7: "quod in dies nostri numerus augetur... "), that already at the time of Nero an "ingens multitudo" existed (see above, chap. 7), that Roman Christianity represented the largest (μεγίστης / maximae) Christian unit in the world (Irenaeus, 3.3.2) and that already by the time of Hermas it was possible to divide Christians into twelve (!) different categories — a multiformity that suggests a great number (cf. Hermas, *Vis.* 3; *Sim.* 9). In spite of occasional optimism,

---

the pagans" (*Gittin* 1b). Among the Roman Jews the ratio of Latin and Greek names to Jewish-Aramaic names is six to one (cf. already Solin, "Juden und Syrer," 711).

11. Two further explanations for the silence in inscriptions, mosaics, and statues of the first and second centuries are the expectation of a near end of the world and the early Christian rejection of luxury. Both of these were of course not shared by all Christians (cf. the waning of the expectation of a near end already in the second Christian generation as well as Hermas's polemic against the de facto presence of luxury among Christians). Both factors taken alone offer again only a very limited explanation.

we do not even know the total number of inhabitants of Rome.[12] The previously mentioned statistics of Cornelius from the middle of the third century (Eusebius, *Hist. Ecc.* 6.43.11f.) lists 1,500 widows and people in need, supported by the church, as well as 46 presbyters, 7 deacons, 7 subdeacons, 42 acolytes, 52 exorcists, lectors, and doorkeepers. How do these numbers relate to the total number of Roman Chirstians? How many believers were served by one presbyter? What was the quantitative relation of the 1500 who received charity to the remaining members of the church, who for the most part apparently also belonged to the lower level of society? How does one evaluate the 800 burials in the cata-comb of Callistus? The factors with which we must multiply remain unknown, and speculative estimations have little value. (In the past, scholars estimated the Roman Christians to number between ten and thirty thousand in the middle of the third century.)[13] Bishop Cornelius himself did not know the exact total population of Roman Christianity, because he adds to his statistic: "... in addition to the very large and incalculable folk."

5. During the period of time we are considering, the *language* of Roman Christianity was chiefly Greek.[14] This indicates that the ma-jority of Roman Christians were nonindigenous residents. Immigrants speaking Greek were, however, not a special characteristic of Roman Christianity; they were typical of the entire city. Juvenal writes, "Greek is the city... for a long time the Syrian flood of the Orontes has been flowing into the Tiber and it has brought with it customs and language as well as the flute, the diagonal strings of the harp and the tambourine, native to the East" (Juvenal, 3.60ff.). The "major part" of the city's population were not born in Rome (Seneca, *Helv.* 6).[15]

In the middle of the third century a change to the predominance of Latin occurred within Roman Christianity. The inscriptions in the

---

12. For a critical evaluation of the state of the research, one may still profitably consult F. G. Maier, "Römische Bevölkerungsgeschichte und Inschriftenstatistik," *Histo-ria* 2 (1954): 318–51. Pleasingly guarded is P. Salmon, *Population et dépopulation dans l'Empire romain,* Coll. Latomus 137 (Brussels, 1974), 11–22; P. Huttunen, *Social Strata* 29. We may estimate the population of Rome in the first and second centuries to be about 1.1 million. Under the Antonians the population reached its highest, probably at most 1.2 million.

13. A bibliography can be found in G. Lüdemann, "Zur Geschichte des ältesten Christentums in Rom," *ZNW* 70 (1979): 102, n. 44. Modern estimations of the Jewish population of the city of Rome are between 30,000 and 60,000. (Literature in H. Solin, "Juden und Syrer," 698, n. 240.) Solin (700) estimates the Roman Jewish population in the first century C.E. between 15,000 and 40,000.

14. See above all the study of C. Mohrmann, "Les origines de la latinité chrétienne à Rome," *VC* 3 (1949): 67–106, 163–83 (lit.); G. Bardy, *La question des langues dans l'église ancienne I* (Paris, 1948), 81ff.; J. Daniélou, *Les origines du christianisme latin,* Histoire des doctrines chrétiennes avant Nicée 3 (Paris, 1978) 11ff. (lit.).

15. Cf. also, e.g., T. Frank, "Race Mixture in the Roman Empire," *AHR* 21 (1915/16), 689ff.

catacombs from the beginning of the third century testify to the use of Latin on a par with Greek.[16] With Novatian the first Latin author of influence appeared upon the literary scene in Roman Christianity. Nevertheless, the inscriptions on the tombs of the Roman bishops still remained in Greek in the third century. Also Hippolytus and Gaius still composed their works in Greek. Only in the fourth century was Greek as a liturgical language compulsorily abolished.[17] That Bishop Victor wrote in Latin at the end of the second century is only stated in an uncertain note by Jerome (*Vir. ill. 53*).[18]

Traces of Latin in second-century Roman Christianity are in many ways uncertain. They indicate, nevertheless, that a Christian Latin element was already present in second-century Rome. This element, to judge according to the language, was primarily recruited from common folk:[19]

a. The Latin version of *1 Clement* most likely originated in second-century Roman circles.[20] It reveals a very vulgar language.[21] To give an example, one may cite the inconsistencies in the translation of prepositions,[22] which betray the translator's lack of education. Since the translation was entrusted to him, one may presume that he belonged educationally "to the top" of the Latin-speaking group. He was, nevertheless, bilingual. And he at least *desired* occasionally to present a polished literary style, although he was not successful. His effort remains on the level of naive ornamentation (e.g., an embellishment, in 5:3; alliterations in 23:1; 3:2; 6:2).[23]

b. Already in the second century (probably at the end) there existed the demand for a Latin translation of the Shepherd of Hermas. Rome is its possible place of origin. The text resembles that of the Latin text of *1 Clement*. Written in awkward language, it adheres literally as much as possible to the Greek original.[24]

---

16. Cf. H. Solin, "Juden und Syrer," 704, 708, n. 264c.

17. Cf., e.g., Th. Klauser, *Der Übergang der römischen Kirche von der griechischen zur lateinischen Liturgiesprache*, Miscellanea G. Mercati 1 (Vatican, 1946), 467–82.

18. As far as the Roman Jews are concerned, Solin ("Juden und Syrer," 701, 705) notes that in the third century Greek is still the main language, but Latin is represented.

19. On this point Roman Jewry evidently distinguishes itself from the Christians. Latin was used more by the socially elevated Jews, while Greek was found more in the lower classes. Latin inscriptions are mostly written correctly and are on a higher level than the Greek (cf. H. Solin, "Juden und Syrer," 706f.).

20. See the argument for this in C. Mohrmann, "Les origines," 78–87, 103f.

21. Cf. the references in C. Mohrmann, "Les origines," 94–97; J. Daniélou, *Les origines*, 24f.; F. Tailliez, "Un vulgarisme du Clemens latinus (inpinguis = pinguis!) et la langue vulgaire de Rome," *Neophilologus* 35 (1951): 45–50.

22. Cf. C. Mohrmann, "Les origines," 96f.

23. Cf. C. Mohrmann, "Les origines," 97.

24. Cf. C. Mohrmann, "Les origines," 67ff.; J. Daniélou, *Les origines*, 25, 88.

c. About 200 C.E. or later, someone in Rome or elsewhere undertook to translate into quite barbaric Latin[25] the *Canon Muratori*, which had been written in Greek in Rome before 200 C.E. Because of the lack of clarity of the translation, the reader is occasionally subjected to dizzying bewilderment.

d. One can presume that a Latin translation of the Old Testament was already in use in Rome by the second century. Old Testament quotations in *1 Clement* differ from the remaining Latin text of *1 Clement*. The differences, however, are not significant enough to distinguish different quality levels of language that could be evaluated from the point of view of social history.[26]

e. Hermas uses in *Sim.* 5.1.1f. as a *terminus technicus* for the practice of fasting the term "statio" (of soldiers "post," "have watch," "guard" = "to keep the fast"). The formation of such technical terms and their usage by Greek-speaking Chirstians such as Hermas indicate a Latin-speaking group of considerable size within Roman Christianity.

f. It appears that Tatian's *Diatessaron* was very early translated into Latin (probably in Rome?). Unfortunately the translation is lost and only the order of its material has found an echo in *Codex Fuldensis* (sixth century).[27]

g. In summary, the Latin-speaking Christians of second-century Rome did not reach up to the intellectual level of the Greek Christian writers known to us from this time and place. This Latin-speaking group preferred to translate texts rather than to create works on their own.[28] If all this is true, then we must be cautious in making quantitative statements. There *could* have already existed a great number of Latin-speaking Christians,

---

25. Cf., for example, E. Hennecke and W. Schneemelcher, *Ntl. Apokryphen,* 1:18.

26. See the evidence in C. Mohrmann, "Les origines," 89ff. On the vulgar character of Old Testament Latin translations, see J. Daniélou, *Les origines,* 22. The disputed Latin Marcionite prologues to the Gospels come at the very earliest from the end of the second century. Therefore, it is not necessary to consider them here. On possible Latin translations of the Bible in the Marcionite church, see A. Harnack, *Marcion,* 151ff., 242ff.; G. La Piana, "The Roman Church," 223. Perhaps the *Canon Muratori* indicates a Latin translation of the New Testament in Rome before 200 C.E.; see J. Daniélou, *Les origines,* 22, 27.

27. Cf., for example, B. Altaner and A. Stuiber, *Patrologie,* 72; J. Daniélou, *Les origines,* 23.

28. A writing originally composed in Latin is the pseudo-Cyprian text *De montibus Sina et Sion,* which was *perhaps* produced in Rome at the end of the second century. It is written in terribly barbaric Latin and uses a limited vocabulary (see J. Daniélou, *Les origines,* 55f., 47, 49). It is interesting that the author also knows Hebrew and might be a Latin-speaking Jewish Christian. It is only with great uncertainty that other original Latin-language works may be attributed to Rome at the end of the second century: the pseudo-Cyprian tractate *De Aleatoribus,* also written in vulgar Latin (cf. J. Daniélou, *Les origines,* 87–91; B. Altaner, *Patrologie,* 177); the Latin text *Adversus Iudaeos* (cf. J. Daniélou, *Les origines,* 46; B. Altaner, *Patrologie,* 177); also 5 Ezra (cf. J. Daniélou, *Les origines,* 31–41; whether the original text was written in Latin or whether it is a Latin translation is disputed).

not only in North Africa but also in Rome. But they would have been primarily common people who therefore left to prosperity no great literary works and are underrepresented in our sources.

6. In regard to the role of *women* in Roman Christianity up to now, only a few observations are possible.

a. The number of Christian women in relation to men apparently increases in proportion as one ascends the social scale. The high-ranking women who live with socially lower-class men illustrate this situation. Hippolytus (*Comm. in Dan.* 1.22) correspondingly composed his scholarly work with an eye toward female readers who would be able to understand it.[29]

Roman women of the upper classes were attracted not only to Christianity but also to Judaism. Ovid in *Ars amat.* 1.76 recommends to his reader boldly to wait for the Jewish Sabbath if he is interested in a relationship with a lady. At that time many beautiful Roman women would have their day of rest. Josephus gives examples of aristocratic Roman women sympathetic to the Mosaic law, for example, the noblewoman Fulvia (*Ant.* 18.82) and allegedly the empress Poppea (*Ant.* 20.195; cf. *Vita* 16; Tacitus, *Ann.* 16.6).

b. Hermas is aware not only of Christian businessmen but also Christian businesswomen who are active in economic matters and even become nervous when the "daily business," "debits and credits," do not go well (*Mand.* 5.2.2).

c. That Christianity found a hearing predominantly among women, in Rome (Minucius Felix, 8.4; cf. Tatian, *Or.* 32f.) and elsewhere,[30] is sufficiently known and testified. All the more interesting is the passage in *Trad. Apost.* 41 (concerning prayer) that deals with the case of mixed marriage. The example cited represents not what we would expect, namely, a Christian woman married to a pagan man (so, for example 1 Pet 3:1), but the opposite: A Christian man, if his wife is still not a member of the faithful, should leave their common bed for midnight prayer. He should leave their bedroom and pray alone by himself in a neighboring room ("si autem coniunx tua"; "mulier . . . necdum est

---

29. See also the fictitious *Acta Petri*, which does not describe events at the end of the first century, as it purports, but rather reflects the situation from the end of the second century (see above, chap. 13). *Act. Verc.* 30: Many rich women and matrons in Rome were strengthened in their faith by Peter; the "extremely wealthy woman" Chryse donated 10,000 gold pieces to the Christian community. *Act. Verc.* 33f.: Peter won over to Christianity the four concubines of the prefect of the city, also the wife of Albinus, a friend of the emperor Nero. *Act. Verc.* 28: The mother of the senator Nicostratus can prove her faith. See also *Ps. Clem., Epit.* 2.144: Peter converted "the authoritative among the high-ranking women" of Rome.

30. See the examples in Luke-Acts as well as Clement of Alexandria, *Strom.* 3.6.53; Origen, *Contra Cel.* 3.44; further material in A. Harnack, *Mission*, 589ff.

fidelis, in alio cubiculo secedens ora"). Is the marriage between a Christian man and a pagan woman a typical example of a mixed marriage? One should be cautious with conclusions. This passage from the *Traditio Apostolica* was probably formulated the way it is simply because it was written by a man.

d. The willingness of Roman women to suffer martyrdom is praised as much as that of Roman men (*1 Clem.* 6:1f.; cf. 55:3).

e. Although women sit separately from men during the Roman worship services (*Trad. Apost.* 18), the same as in the synagogues, their religious equality is explicitly formulated: "In the same way God has also given to a woman the possibility to do everything that is just and virtuous. We know that men and women are not just or unjust because of their bodily constitution, which is visibly different, but that piety and justice decide" (Justin, *Dial.* 23; cf. also Tatian, *Or.* 32f.).[31]

f. We cannot, however, in the *general* information presented for debate in Part 3, identify active leading roles of women in Roman church life.[32] For this we must wait for the individual examples of Part 4, when we shall meet the names of such outstanding women. We may conclude that women in individual cases, but not generally, contributed to the leadership of Roman church life. In any case, they did not have much influence on the sources that convey this picture to us. Only in individual heretical circles (see below) did the influence of women take on a more general character.[33]

Explicitly restrictive are passages in *1 Clement. First Clement* 21:7 makes the influence of women upon community life impossible. They should "reveal the gentleness of their tongues by *silence* (σιγῆς)." This section, from the traditionally formed[34] community code, is similar to the prohibition in 1 Tim 2:11f. In addition, *1 Clem.* 1:3 emphasizes the subordination of women and defines their area of influence within the limits of household activity. It is true that most of the time such parenesis presupposes the opposite cases in practice. But in *1 Clement* the

---

31. The same Justin had of course earlier in his *Apology* (1.64.5) announced that he found it "most ridiculous to present a female [θηλειῶν μορφήν, he means Athena] as an image of thinking and reflection (ἐννοίας)." This is not a friendly remark. Was Justin of another opinion than Hippolytus (see paragraph a, above), less convinced of the intellectual ability of women? Was he, unlike Hippolytus, not surrounded yet by educated women? One must guard against placing too much weight on such quotations. Justin names at least one woman, Charito, as a member of his Christian philosophical school (see below *Acta Iust.* 4).

32. Above we saw that widows were commissioned with the particular task of prayer, but otherwise they appear only as receptive, particularly as receivers of charity offerings.

33. E.g., Tertullian, *De praescr.* 41: ipsae mulieres haereticae, quam procaces! — quae audeant docere, contendere, exorcismos agere, curationes repromittere, forsitan et tingere.

34. Cf., e.g., 1 Tim 2:8ff.; 3:11; 1 Pet 3:1ff. For the background of *1 Clem.* 1:3, cf., e.g., Prv 31:10ff.; Tit 2:4ff.; 1 Tim 2:11ff.

moralizing is directed toward Corinth and not Rome. Therefore, it cannot be proved that a considerable number of women among the Roman Christians did not nurture "gentle silence." On the contrary, *1 Clement* is understood as a writing by the whole community, including women. For the "community" to be able to formulate *1 Clement* 1:3; 21:7 in a restrictive manner means that women at the end of the first century in Rome were actually silenced.

A. Harnack (*Mission,* 597f.) came to a similar conclusion on the basis of Hermas: "In the Shepherd of Hermas women are not mentioned (with the exception of the unpleasant wife of the author). Therefore, one may assume that they were more in the background in the Roman community than in other places." Harnack overlooked those Christian women who ran their own businesses (see above, *Mand.* 5.2.2) as well as Grapte, who instructed widows and orphans (*Vis.* 2.4.3). Nevertheless, that does not change the overall findings.

In summary: in spite of women forming the majority, there is a diminishing of their influence.

7. At the end of Part 3 and before we proceed to the prosopography of Part 4, we may shine a spotlight on the third and fourth centuries. It reveals again that most Christian aristocrats were women and that the great majority of Christians belong to the lower classes — or, one could say that there was only a slow penetration of Christianity into the aristocratic circles of Rome.

For the third century[35] one can identify *at most* 32 individuals of senatorial rank as Christians; 22 of them are female and only 10 male. That means that more than two-thirds of the Christian members of the senatorial class of the third century were probably women.[36] The total number of fewer than 40 identifiable Christian members of the senatorial class in the first three centuries (at most 32 in the third century and at most six in the first and second; cf. above, chap. 13, n. 9) is a negligible amount in view of the at least 15,000 people[37] who belonged to the senatorial class during this period of time. It is true that there would have been de facto more senatorial Christians than the 40 gleaned from our sources. A living senatorial noble would rather hide his Christianity from the outside world than put himself in danger. Also the inscriptions before 200 C.E. are hardly recognizable as Christian. In view of the uncertain legal situation, not only senatorial Christians but Christians in general hesitated as a rule to carve their religious belief in stone (see above, no. 3). Thus there was without a doubt a considerable

---

35. Cf. the material in W. Eck, "Das Eindringen," 388–91, 393–95 (including nn. 40 and 53).

36. Cf. also the predominance of aristocratic women in the Acts of Paul, Acts of Andrew, and Acts of Thomas; summary in W. Eck, "Das Eindringen," 400.

37. For the statistics see W. Eck, "Das Eindringen," 396.

number of senatorial Christians unknown to us. But even if we multiply the number 40 by 15 (= 600), the total number of senatorial Christians in the first three centuries would only amount to four percent of the senatorial class.

A cursory glance into the fourth century reveals the opposition that faced Christianity in aristocratic circles. Roman aristocratic families were still in the post-Constantine period the last bastion of paganism. Symmachus and his senatorial circle serve as examples of this. Only in the fifth century can one begin to speak of an extensive Christianization of Roman aristocracy. In the time of Augustine, *"tota fere* Romana nobilitas" still depended obstinately upon the gods (*Conf.* 8.2.3). The circumstances of the fourth century offer some framework for our consideration of the first two centuries. They show clearly how difficult, even more so in the earlier centuries, it was for Christianity to gain a foothold in Roman aristocracy.[38] Two examples: (a) We are relatively well informed concerning the old noble Roman family of the Ceionii at the end of the fourth century.[39] Two brothers, Ceionius Rufius Albinus, who was prefect of Rome during the years 389–91, and Publilius Ceionius Caecina Albinus, who was governor of Numidia about 365, married Christian women but remained committed pagans.[40] The daughters and the granddaughters of both marriages (Albina, Laeta, Melania Jr., and Paula) were raised as devout Christians and married Christians.[41] With the sons, however, it was different. The son of Rufius Albinus, Rufius Antonius Agrypnius Volusianus, remained pagan until his deathbed in 437 C.E. The same was true of his cousin Ceionius Contucius Gregorius, the son of Caecina Albinus.[42] The Christian mothers, sisters, and nieces

---

38. The pagan spirit held its ground so tenaciously in the Italian aristocracy that the secular traditions of Rome continued to live in the aristocratic class under a Christian surface well into the sixth century. See, e.g., P. R. L. Brown, "Roman Aristocracy," 1–11 (it deals with the fourth and fifth centuries). Further literature in W. Eck, "Der Einfluss," 571, n. 39. In regard to the meager Christianization of the leading class before Constantine see W. Eck, "Das Eindringen," 381–406; reasons for this on pp. 401ff. Even among the Roman bishops of the fourth century and the first half of the fifth century, one does not find any who came from among the leading class of the empire (cf. W. Eck, "Der Einfluss," 585). In regard to Christian members of noble families who lived in the distinguished Caelius area of Rome and whose names can be seen after c. 400 in the Praetextus catacomb (Via Appia) see E. Josi, "Cimitero di Pretestato," 18–24. They were members of the *gentes* (extended families) Postumia, Insteia, Carvilia, Laterani, Annii, and Anicii, among others.

39. A. Chastagnol, "Le sénateur Volusien," *REA* 58 (1956): 241–53.

40. In regard to the first see Macrobius, *Saturnalia* 3.4.12; 6.1.1. In regard to the latter as "Pontifex" see Jerome, *Ep.* 107.1; Symmachus, *Ep.* 8.25.

41. See Jerome, ibid., and the Life of Melania, edited by M. Rampolla (*Santa Melania Giuniore* [Rome, 1905]).

42. In regard to the former, who, like his father, identified with the pagan reaction of Rutilius Namatianus, see Rutilius Namatianus, *De Reditu* 1.168, 415ff.; M. Rampolla, ed., *Vita Melaniae Jr.* 72 (he was converted by his niece Melania on his deathbed); also Augustinus, *Ep.* 123, 136; his letter to Augustine, *Ep.* 135 (CSEL 44, 89ff.). In regard to

could not change the pagan spirit of the family, which held the male members of the family together. The men of the family preserved the pagan family tradition even after the official suppression of paganism, while the women gave the family the necessary Christian appearance. This example also shows that, still in the fourth century, the road to Christianization led through the female members of the family.[43]

(b) The existence of paganism next to Christianity in distinguished families during the fourth century is seen in the beautiful paintings of the so-called anonymous catacomb on the Via Latina. It was a private family tomb and can be reached today through a small trapdoor on the sidewalk. Christian frescoes are in immediate proximity to pagan mythological scenes. While in room 11 soldiers play for the tunics of Jesus, and Jonah falls into the sea, in the next, room 12, Hercules steals the apples of Hesperides, kills a Hydra, and gives his hand to Athena.[44] The pagan element of this family was well represented throughout the fourth century.

---

the latter, cf. *CIL* 6:1706: "veteris sanctitatis exemplar"; on his brother Ceionius Caecina Decius Albinus cf. Symmachus, *Ep.* 7.35ff.

43. See also the Christian woman who was married to a pagan Roman prefect and was driven to suicide by Maxentius; Eusebius, *Hist. Ecc.* 8.14.16f.

44. For a full description of the iconography of the catacomb see A. Nestori, *Repertorio Topografico,* 71–80.

Part 4

SECOND DIACHRONIC SECTION
Prosopographic Investigation

Will the individual examples of the second diachronic section confirm and color the results of the first section?

Chapter 16

The Roman Christians
of Romans 16

Excursus: Romans 16 as a Text
Addressed to the Romans

First, evidence must be presented that we have a glimpse of *Roman* Christians in Romans 16:1–16. The problem of the relationship of Romans 16 with the rest of the letter to the Romans is connected with the question of the chapter's addressees. Was Romans 16 originally addressed to Rome or to Ephesus? This question can be discussed on different levels.

There are, first, arguments speaking directly *against* the Ephesus hypothesis. The Ephesus hypothesis is problematical on the following points: (a) How would the literary character of this "letter to the Ephesians" be determined? Of course, letters consisting primarily of greetings did exist.[1] But can one credit *Paul* with such a letter? (b) Why was this "letter to the Ephesians" connected with the letter to the Romans? Indeed, parallels demonstrate that a number of Pauline letters could be combined into one (2 Corinthians), but none of these was originally directed to a *different* community. (c) Why do we encounter only the names of Paul's coworkers Urbanus, Aquila, and Prisca (Rom 16:3, 9) in the list of greetings to "Ephesus"? Where are all the others who were in Ephesus at least shortly before?[2] Did they all leave? Did Paul fail to send them greetings?[3]

On the one hand, I want to list the reasons that speak *for* the original connection of this chapter to the letter to the Romans; on the other hand, the evidence that led to the Ephesian hypothesis should be

---

1. Cf. J. I. H. McDonald, "Was Romans XVI a Separate Letter?" *NTS* 16 (1969/70): 369–72.

2. Phlm 23f. (cf. Col 4:7–14): Epaphras, Mark, Aristarchus, Demas, Luke; 1 Cor 1:1: Sosthenes; 1 Cor 16:12, 17: Apollos, Stephanas, Fortunatus, Achaicus; Col 4:7–14: Jesus Justus, among others. Cf. W.-H. Ollrog, "Die Abfassungsverhältnisse von Röm 16," 240.

3. Cf. Ollrog, op. cit. (lit.).

discussed. It can be proved that this evidence, with Roman addressees, is equally meaningful — if not more meaningful — than in a letter to the Ephesians. In this way the foundation for the Ephesian hypothesis will be undermined.

1. The first argument comes from textual criticism, which, try as we may, finds no seam between Romans 16 and 1–15. Of the fourteen different textual forms[4] of the Romans manuscript, none ends with chapter 15.

a. Generally (with two significant exceptions) it is valid to say: When 16:1–23 is missing from a manuscript, chapter 15 is also missing. In the text tradition chapter 15 and 16:1–23 form a unity. Either they are both missing en bloc[5] or they both appear en bloc.[6] One of the two sections is explicitly addressed to the Romans (15:22ff.), so that, from the point of view of the history of the text, no other addressee may be postulated for the other section.

b. The two exceptions are Minuscule 1506 (= text form no. 15) and P46 (=no. 14).

Minuscule 1506 from the year 1320 offers the text Rom 1–14; 15; 16:25–27. It is only here that one encounters chapter 15 without 16:1–23. Clearly, this curious form of the text is partially dependent upon Marcion's short version (Rom 1–14) and therefore cannot represent the original text. Futhermore, both Aland's and my own stemma[7] indicate a dependence of this form of the text upon forms in which chapter 15 and 16:1–23 clearly belonged together as a block. Therefore, the alleged exception of no. 15 actually confirms the rule. Only at a later stage of the development (no. 15) were chapter 15 and 16:1–23 separated from each other, with 16:1–23 being deleted. It is interesting that the minuscule actually has a half-empty page at the place of the deletion and only on the next page does one find the continuation of 16:25–27.

The old papyrus 46 (c. 200 C.E.) is to be taken more seriously. It contains Rom 1–14; 15; 16:25–27; 16:1–23. We do indeed find chapter 15 and 16:1–23 together but this time (and only in this single instance) they are not en bloc. Did the letter to the Romans once contain only 1–14; 15; 16:25–27? Did P46 develop from:

    1–14; 15;
    1–14; 15; 16:25–27
  → 1–14; 15; 16:25–27; 16:1–23 (= Papyrus 46)?

---

4. An overview can be found in K. Aland, "Der Schluss des Römerbriefs," 284ff. I am using here Aland's numbering system.

5. In text-forms nos. 2 and 3.

6. In nos. 4–14.

7. P. Lampe. "Zur Textgeschichte des Römerbriefes," 273–77.

It is methodologically necessary to reconstruct a meaningful stemma from *all* fourteen forms of the text. As much as one tries, it is not possible to construct a complete stemma in which the above-mentioned hypothetical ancestor of P46 (Rom 1–14; 15) could assume the status of the original form, from which all the other forms of the text could be deduced. Such a stemma would include a number of "missing links"[8] and thus prove to be methodologically deficient. In Aland's and in my stemma Papyrus 46 is dependent upon a text form (1:1 — 16:23, 25–27) in which chapter 15 and 16:1–23 stood together en bloc.

Conclusion: The two exceptions with their previous histories *confirm* the unity of chapter 15 and 16:1–23.

2. Also, from the point of view of source criticism, one cannot discover a seam between chapter 15 and 16:1–23. (a) δέ in 16:1 indicates a *preceding* text. (b) The wish for peace in 15:33 requires a *subsequent* text (see below), similar to that of 16:1–23, which contains final greetings.

Both facts are related to one another. One can best explain the facts if 15 and 16:1–23 belonged together from the beginning. Otherwise, a lost text would have broken off after 15:33 and another lost text fallen away before 16:1 and both broken edges joined together because they fit so well with each other! Looked at individually, 15:33 is inconceivable as the end of a letter. Neither the wish for peace nor the formula "God be with you" is found anywhere as a conclusion.[9] All parallels to Romans 15:33 (Phil 4:9; 2 Cor 13:11; 1 Thess 5:23; 2 Thess 3:16; Heb 13:20; 3 John 15) are first followed by greetings, as in Romans 16:1–23, before the letter ends.[10]

3. On the one hand, Romans 16 contains peculiarities and singularities in comparison to the rest of the Pauline corpus. On the other hand, Romans 1–15 represents the singular phenomenon that Paul is writing to a community unknown to him and outside of his missionary territory. He wishes to establish a foothold in this community as a base for missionary activity in the west. If we piece both phenomena together, the unique characteristics of Romans 16 can be explained in an instant: Precisely *because* Romans 1–15 is singular, so also is Romans 16!

The singularities of Romans 16:

a. The ecumenical greeting in verse 16 is singular: "All the churches of Christ greet you." Why this global perspective? It is understandable if

---

8. See the evidence presented in Aland, 296.

9. There is one non-Pauline exception in 1 Pet 5:14.

10. Also the more distant parallels to Rom 15:33 (Gal 6:16; Eph 6:23) are not final verses. Cf. also the good wishes in Rom 15:5f., 13; 1 Thess 3:11–13; Col 3:15; Phil 4:9: these would be "endings of the letter" in the *middle* of the text. Finally, ἀμήν is also found in the *middle* of the text: Rom 1:25; 9:5; 11:36; Gal 1:5; 1 Thess 3:13; 1 Tim 1:17; 6:16; Eph 3:21; 1 Pet 4:11; etc.

Paul, standing on the threshold between east and west, is turning to the Romans. First, on the threshold between east and west, Paul looks back upon his missionary work in the east. Considering his work there ended, he summarizes it (vv. 15, 19, 23) and, in so doing, sees passing before his eyes "all the churches of Christ" in the east. Second, Paul looks to the future. He wishes to gain a foothold in Rome and to create there a base of trust.[11] When "all the churches" of the east now send their greetings through Paul, this is a glowing recommendation for Paul himself, an element that "builds trust." It is valid to observe that Romans 16 is, above all, a "recommendation" for Paul himself and only incidentally also a letter of recommendation for Phoebe.

b. If Paul is seeking to recommend himself in Romans 16, then both the following unique elements can be explained: (1) the unusually *long* list of greetings as well as (2) the greetings sent to *individual* persons, which is usually not encountered in Paul. Precisely because Paul does not know the Roman Christian community as a whole, he asks this community to greet all his acquaintances in Rome. In this way they serve as references for him. He shows the community that he is already personally bound to them through many common friends. This builds trust.

If the quantity of the common acquaintances is one side of the picture, the other side is their quality. Paul's friends in Rome are to some extent very creditable and commendable (e.g., vv. 4, 6). They possess authority (v. 7) and therefore shed light upon Paul himself. With such friends Paul is intimately (ἀγαπητός) connected; he cannot possibly be bad.

Conclusion: "Common acquaintances" more easily convert strangers to confidants. They span a first bridge of trust between two foreign shores. The bridge is more easily built the greater the number (length of the list) and the laudability of the "common acquaintances."

The parallel in the deutero-Pauline letter to the Colossians is interesting. Here we find the same constellation. In a letter to an unknown community "Paul" uses again personal contacts (4:7ff.) and commissions greetings to individual persons (v. 15; cf. v. 17).[12]

If this is the function of the commissions to greet certain persons, then it is also understandable why Paul does not directly address or greet individuals but rather lets his greetings be communicated through the

---

11. Cf., e.g., Rom 15:22–32; 1:11, 13–15; see also the "captationes benevolentiae" (e.g., Rom 1:8) as well as the assertions that, for a long time, he has been feeling close to the Romans (Rom 1:9f., 13, 15). Rome is to be won over as companion and comrade in arms (Rom 15:24, 30).

12. It remains undecided whether this procedure of Paul in Colossians is a literary invention — in imitation of Romans — or historical. It is always conceivable that Colossians was written by a companion of Paul during the imprisonment in Ephesus.

community: The real addressee is indeed not each individual person but the community itself, who receives a signal through the commission to convey greetings.

c. There is another unique element. Timothy is never otherwise introduced as "my fellow worker" (Rom 16:21). The eastern communities know his identity, while an introduction of this kind is significant for the unfamiliar Romans.

4. Since inscriptions from Ephesus are accessible for investigation, it is possible to compare our list of names with those found at Ephesus. The result is that the names in Romans 16 correspond better with Rome than with Ephesus.[13]

The following discussion in paragraphs 5 to 8 attempts to neutralize those facts that speak neither for Rome nor for Ephesus, although they are constantly brought into the scholarly debate as arguments. It deals with facts that are conceivable with both places, with illusory arguments that should be kept out of the discussion of "Rome — Ephesus."

5. The knowledge of twenty-six individual persons in the community that Paul addresses is not less conceivable for Rome than for Ephesus.

Paul need not know *personally* all those named. The ten persons listed at the end (vv. 14f.) need only be known by Paul through the report of a third party. The greetings to these people are pallid; only the names of each are mentioned. Paul has "for many years" cherished an interest in the Roman Christians (15:22f.; 1:13) and has had a conduit of information through his fellow workers experienced in Roman church life (Aquila and Prisca).

It is possible that Paul is personally acquainted with the other sixteen people, because he inserts for each one a short or lengthier note. This means that sixteen people, or less, have been at some time during the past years in the east and have met Paul there. There are three conceivable possibilities as to how this could have happened. It might be that certain people such as Aquila and Prisca were forced out of Rome in the wake of Claudius's edict and have now returned there. It might be that some as easterners have emigrated to Rome. It might be that some as Romans traveled in the east.

Are sixteen persons "unthinkable," are they a "mass migration," as is time and again cited? Those who have position and name in early Roman church history do not come from Rome (see below): Aquila, Hermas, Marcion, Valentinus, Justin, most of his students, Tatian, Hippolytus, the presbyter Evaristus, and Anicet.[14] The long survival of the

---

13. See the unpublished manuscript of H. Solin.

14. *Liber Pontificalis* s.v.: Evaristus c. 100 C.E., "natione Grecus Antiochenus"; Anicet c. 160 C.E., "natione Syrus."

Greek language in the community — throughout the entire second century — signals a high proportion of non-autochthons. How great ancient mobility was is illustrated in *CIG* 3920: The craftsman (ἐργαστής) Flavius Zeuxis sailed seventy-two times (ἑβδομήκοντα δύο) from the east to Italy, passing the Peloponnesian Cape Malia. Naturally, the normal extent of travel was less, otherwise Zeixis would not have recorded his travels on his gravestone. Nevertheless, the inscription indicates the extremes of travel possible.

Sixteen Roman Christians with an experience of the east represent a ridiculous number when compared to the more than 8,000 members of the Jewish community in Rome (Josephus, *Ant.* 17.300f.). Many Jews traveled extensively between Rome and the east.[15]

6. The presence of Aquila and Prisca among the addressees is not less conceivable for Rome than for Ephesus.

a. The couple worked in Ephesus as Paul's missionary *vanguard* (Acts 18:18–21, 24–26; 19:1). The same is conceivable for Rome, where Paul wished to gain a foothold with his gospel. Paul allows them to be greeted first, and he praises them as his "fellow workers" (Rom 16:3f.). They have again diligently assembled a community in their home (v. 5). The return of the couple to Rome could be conceivable as a "strategic" move previously agreed upon with Paul.

b. The couple would have returned to Rome between the composition of 1 Cor 16:19 and Rom 16:3, i.e., about the year 55/56. The date corresponds well with the death of Claudius in the fall of 54, under whose reign the couple were exiled from Rome. His death would be a sufficient reason to overcome any reluctance to return. The edict of Claudius had once sought only to control isolated incidents of disorder; it had no lasting validity.

c. Aquila, a businessman, had moved at least three times during his life, Pontus — Rome — Corinth — Ephesus. Why not a fourth move? He was the apostle's fellow worker (v. 3). Other Christians had undertaken even longer trips in their lifetime. For example, the exploits of the seventy-two-year-old Aberkios are recorded in the famous Aberkios inscription.[16] In the second century he lived in Phrygia, in Rome, in Syria, and traveled across the Euphrates to live with the Christians in Nisibis.

d. The Pastoral letters presuppose Aquila and Prisca still to be in Ephesus (2 Tim 4:19) while Paul is already in Rome. This is one of the historical inconsistencies found in the Pastorals.

For example, when Paul moved from Ephesus to Macedonia, by no means did Timothy remain behind in Ephesus, as 1 Tim 1:3 supposes:

---

15. For example, Acts 2:10. Rabbis visited Rome after 70 C.E.: Joshua ben Hananiah, Aqiba, Eleazar b. Azariah, Rabban Gamaliel (*m.ʿErubin* 4:1; cf. *m.ʿAbod. Zar.* 4:7 and P. Schäfer, "Rabbi Aqiba and Bar Kokhba," 113–30).

16. Second century. See literature in B. Altaner and A. Stuiber, *Patrologie*, 98.

Acts 19:22; 20:1–4; 2 Cor 1:1; Rom 16:21. In 2 Tim 1:16–18; 4:13, 16ff., 20, the author attempts to place himself in the situation of Acts 28:16–31 and in the previous journey, whose purpose was the collection (Acts 20:2f., 5ff., 15ff.). But at least during the sojourn at Corinth, Timothy is present (Acts 20:4; Rom 16:21), so that for Timothy, who is the recipient of the letter, the information "Erastus remained in Corinth" in 2 Timothy 4:20 is superfluous. In no way did Trophimus remain "ill at Miletus" (2 Tim 4:20); rather, he accompanied Paul heartily to Jerusalem (Acts 21:29; 20:4).

How did the author come to the mistake regarding Aquila and Prisca? If we look into Christian tradition for names of persons upon whom one could build literary fiction based in Ephesus, we discover four who lived in Ephesus for a longer period of time. Not surprisingly, the four appear also in 2 Timothy:

Trophimus from Ephesus (Acts 20:4; 21:29) — whom "I left ill at Miletus" (2 Tim 4:20).

Tychicus from Ephesus (Acts 20:4; Col 4:7; Eph 6:21) — according to the Pastoral letters he is promptly sent to Ephesus (2 Tim 4:12).

Aquila and Prisca (Acts 18:26; 1 Cor 16:19) — they are greeted as Ephesians in 2 Tim 4:19.

Even Mark, who spent some time with Paul in Ephesus and then traveled further (Col 4:10; Phlm 24), is according to 2 Tim 4:11 temporarily residing in Ephesus.[17]

Conclusion: In a search for appropriate names to create a literary fiction based in Ephesus, the prominent names of Aquila and Prisca could not miss falling into the hands of the deutero-Pauline author. That means, however, that one cannot argue from 2 Tim 4:19 against the presence of the couple in Rome.

7. This is also true of Epaenetus, "who was the first converted in Asia" (Rom 16:5). He is named immediately after Aquila and Prisca and thus may have moved together with them from Ephesus to Rome.

8. Whoever wishes to allow the polemic against false teaching in verses 17–20a to originate from Paul cannot use this in favor of the "Ephesus" hypothesis.

---

17. Other names which the New Testament associates with Ephesus belong to missionaries who only temporarily stayed in Ephesus. The deutero-Pauline author had no cause to address them in 2 Timothy as living in Ephesus. Apollos from Alexandria (Acts 18:24, 27); Gaius and Aristarchus from Macedonia (Acts 19:29; 20:4; Col 4:10; Phlm 24); Erastus, Stephanas, Fortunatus, and Achaicus from Corinth (1 Cor 16:17; Acts 19:22); Onesimus and Epaphras, who are from Asia but not from Ephesus (Col 4:9, 12; Phlm 12, 23); perhaps also Epaphroditus from Philippi (Phil 2:25; 4:18). Luke and Demas (Col 4:14; Phlm 24) were not continuous residents of Ephesus (cf. 2 Tim 4:10f.). Also Jesus Justus (Col 4:11) and Sosthenes (1 Cor 1:1) sojourned in Ephesus, but it is unclear if it was permanently or only in the company of Paul. It is uncertain whether Chloe (1 Cor 1:11) was from Ephesus. Tyrannus (Acts 19:9) was not a Christian.

a. The sharp tone of verses 17–20a by no means speaks against their inclusion in Romans. The blunt tenor is directed not towards the community but towards a third party: toward possible false teachings, which have not (yet) found root in the community. The community itself is praised ("your obedience is known to all, so that I rejoice over you," 16:19), and this corresponds to the rest of the body of the letter (1:8; 15:14).[18]

b. The potential false teachers are perceived as an external threat and as a common enemy. The threat and "common enemies" are likely to bring the author of the letter and the addressees closer together in solidarity and this is exactly Paul's intention (15:24, 30; 1:11, 13–15).

Two points allow us to show that Romans 16 is written in the same historical situation as the body of the letter to the Romans.

9. On the basis of Romans 15:19–29 we have no other choice but to date the composition of Romans at the end of the so-called third missionary journey to Greece (Acts 20:1–5). If this is correct, then the following observations are interesting. Just as the main portion of the letter, Romans 16 was also written in Greece. Paul dispatches Phoebe from the Corinthian harbor of Cenchreae (Rom 16:1). Moreover, the persons whom, on the basis of Acts 20, we expect to be in the proximity of Paul during the composition of Romans appear in Romans 16:21–23 as those who send greetings. The agreement between Romans 16:21–23 and Acts 20:4 is startling. In both lists we encounter Timothy, So(si)patros,[19] and Gaius.[20] Literary dependence between the two lists is excluded.[21]

10. There is a linguistic affinity between Romans 16 and Romans 1–15. It suggests that Romans 16 was dictated "in the same breath" as the rest of the letter.

The methodological starting point is the consideration that an author's preferred vocabulary can be diagnosed not only in comparison to other authors but that one and the same author at different times can have a different preference of vocabulary and of characteristics of style.

---

18. The only pointed word directed to the community is παρακαλῶ. It is also found in Rom 12:1 and 15:30. In light of 16:17–20, E. Käsemann (*Römer*, 399f.) is surprised at the lack of any sharp tone in the body of the letter. But if the false teachers are outsiders, whose influence upon Rome is to be feared, and not elements within the community itself, then Paul had no reason to speak harshly already in the body of the letter.

19. Both forms are linguistically identical; cf. W. Bauer, *Wörterbuch*, s.v. This is also demonstrated by the later history of the text of Acts 20:4.

20. If Gaius (Rom 16:23) should be, on the other hand, the Corinthian of 1 Cor 1:14, then that corresponds even more splendidly to the situation of the composition of the body of Romans, namely, in Greece and at Corinth.

21. Both lists have names that are missing from one another. Moreover, the name So(si)pater is written differently in both lists.

A famous, and perhaps extreme, example are the discrepancies between Goethe's language in his younger and "more mature" years.[22]

Each person can observe for himself how his style and his favorite words change. After snatching up a relatively unusual word, one incorporates it into one's vocabulary by using it frequently for some time. Already our everyday experience teaches us that the active language of an individual can undergo great changes.

I will attempt to show that at the time of the composition of Romans 1–15 the language of Romans 16 (choice of words and other grammatical phenomena) was more than otherwise on the lips of Paul.[23] A great number of grammatical phenomena in Romans 16 are statistically overrepresented in Romans 1–15 in comparison to the rest of Paul.

a. ἔθνος (16:4) appears twenty-seven times in Romans 1–15 as against only sixteen times in all the rest of Paul. It is interesting that in Romans 15 alone ἔθνος appears ten times. The word is still on Paul's lips in 16:4.

b. συγγενής (16:7, 11, 21) is found elsewhere in Paul only in Romans 9:3. Here also Paul's use of the word in 9:3 occasions its use again in chap. 16.

It is interesting that the body of the letter circles conceptually around the theme Israel / Gentile and also around the relation of ἔθνος and συγγενής. The structure of thought that Paul has in his mind produces the use of both concepts, ἔθνος and συγγενής, again immediately in Rom 16. This has, I think, its more significant meaning in chap. 16 when Paul explicitly emphasizes the kinship (συγγενής) of six persons (cf. Romans 9:3 and chaps. 9–11).

c. Similarly, we observe that ἐκλεκτός (16:13) is still on the lips of Paul. We encounter the word only in Romans 8:33.

d. παρίστημι (16:2) appears in Romans 1–15 seven times and in all the rest of the Pauline writings only three times.

It is interesting that the chronological sequence, 1 Corinthians — 2 Corinthians — Romans corresponds to a continuous increase in the use of παρίστημι: 1 Cor = 1x; 2 Cor = 2x; Rom 1–15 = 7x.

Also the grammatical phenomena in Romans 16 are overrepresented in Romans 1–15 compared to the rest of Paul.

e. Emphatic ἐμοῦ in connection with another genitive[24] (αὐτοῦ καί ἐμοῦ, Rom 16:13) is encountered again only in Rom 1:12 (ὑμῶν τε καί ἐμοῦ).

---

22. Grillparzer mused over the elder councillor and later development of his language: "And whether he occasionally speaks officialese, as to fade ink and color . . . a housecoat looks good only on one who has first worn the suit of armor."

23. By "otherwise" I mean the rest of the Pauline letters, 1 and 2 Cor, Gal, Phil, 1 Thess, Phlm, which may be considered as a unity because, I believe, they were written *before* Romans, and that is presupposed.

24. Cf. Bl-D-R §284.2.

f. In Romans 1–15 one finds a genitive of origin with the verbal adjective ἀγαπητός used as a substantive: ἀγαπητός with a genitive of origin is found in Romans 1:7, i.e., one out of three examples in Romans 1–15. In the rest of Paul the statistics appear less favorable: ἀγαπητός with a genitive of origin is found only in two out of twelve examples (1 Cor 10:14; Phil 2:12).[25]

In relation to the high incident of ἀγαπητός with the genitive of origin in Romans 1–15, the phenomenon appears immediately three times in Romans 16 (16:5, 8, 9).

g. How the unconscious use of "small words" can be a measure of an author's language profile, I have attempted to show in other places.[26] With ἵνα a Koine author has the choice between the classical (final) use and other unclassical usages. If Romans 1–15 uses the conjunction exclusively in the literally classic sense (twenty-nine of the examples are classical and there are no nonclassical examples), then the relation to the rest of Paul does not appear to be good (one finds 115 classical usages as against twenty-six nonclassical examples).[27] In other words, if the author avails himself of the classical usage in Romans 16:2, that corresponds to the high incidence of the classical usage of ἵνα in Romans 1–15. There is an exception, namely, that in the comparable chapter where Paul conveys greeting, 1 Corinthians 16, he has a penchant to use the unclassical ἵνα.[28]

h. ἄν (Rom 1:2) has an above average usage. It is encountered in Romans 1–15 (= 7,130 words) some seven times (7/7,130) and in the rest of Paul (17,013 words) only fourteen times (14/17,013). In order not to be forced into laborious decimals, we multiply the quotients by 104. We obtain as comparable frequency value:

Romans 1–16: 10
the rest of Paul: 8

Romans 1–15 uses ἄν more often than the rest of the Pauline texts.

i. A relative sentence with ἄν (16:2) is found in Paul three times in Romans 1–15 (Rom 9:15 twice; 10:13); in all the remaining Pauline

25. Also with comparable verbal adjectives used as substantives, κλητός, ἐκλεκτός, one finds in Rom 1–15 the genitive of origin more often than in the rest of Pauline writings: ἐκλεκτός, Rom 8:33; i.e., one out of one example in Rom 1–15; in the rest of Paul, nil out of nil. κλητός, Rom 1:6; i.e., one out of four examples in Rom 1–15; in the rest of Paul nil out of three. Cf. further Bl-D-R § 183.

26. P. Lampe, "ἵνα," *EWNT* 2 (1981): 460–66; "μή," *EWNT* 2 (1981): 1038–40; "μήποτε," *EWNT* 2 (1981): 1044–45. With ἵνα one can observe, for example, a significant difference between Paul and the deutero-Pauline letters. Paul uses the conjunction classically 83 percent of the time and unclassically 17 percent, while in Col and 2 Thess the classic usage is found 46 percent or 43 percent (ibid., 465).

27. Cf. P. Lampe, ibid., 465.

28. Ibid., 465.

material, only twice (1 Cor 11:27; 2 Cor 11:21). Once again we have a high incidence of usage.

The phenomena cited above are related, I believe, to the fact that Paul is writing to a unknown community and involuntarily uses a better style than if he were writing to his own communities.

j. Not only the relative sentence with ἄν but also relative sentences in general (ὅς, ἥ, ὅ) are more frequent in Romans 1–15. The same is true of the articles.

	Absolute Number			Frequency value[29]		
	Rom 1–15	Rest of Paul	Rom 16	Rom 1–15	Rest of Paul	Rom 16
Relative ὅς, ἥ, ὅ	83	147	4	116	86	161
ὁ, ἡ, τό	1,039	2,122	44	1,457	1,247	1,767

The table shows that Romans 16 shares with Romans 1–15 the "delight for articles" (1,767 stands closer to the frequency value of Romans 1–15 than to the rest of Paul). Likewise, the inclination to build relative sentences (ὅς, ἥ, ὅ) is shared (161 stands closer to the frequency value of Romans 1–15 than to the rest of Paul).

k. Preference for the same "small words" is also shared between Romans 16 and Romans 1–15.

	Absolute Number			Frequency value		
	Rom 1–15	Rest of Paul	Rom 16	Rom 1–15	Rest of Paul	Rom 16
ἐκ	58	115	2	81	68	80
αὐτός	148	231	9	208	136	361
the participles ὤν, οὖσα	16	25	2	22	15	80
ἀλλήλων	13	18	1	18	11	40
μόνος	12	25	1	17	15	40
the construction οὐ μόνος/ν–ἀλλά	10	10	1	14	6	40
ἐμοῦ	4	9	3	6	5	120

The table shows: (a) the corresponding small word of Romans 16 and Romans 1–15 has a higher incidence in comparison to the rest of the

---

29. The frequency value of Rom 16 is calculated from the number of examples in Rom 16:1–16, 20b–23 divided by 249, the number of words in Rom 16:1–16, 20b–23. The names of persons and places are not counted in the 249. Also Rom 16:17–20a is not considered in calculating the frequency value. The question whether it is a deutero-Pauline text is, in my opinion, completely open.

Pauline material (judged from the comparison between the frequency value of Romans 1–15 and the rest of Paul). At the time of the composition of Romans 16, Paul had a special affinity for the respective word. (b) In addition, the frequency value of Romans 16 is closer to that of Romans 1–15 than that of the rest of Paul.[30]

1. In 16:2 Paul commends Phoebe, who is about to depart, to his readers. Paul uses a Latinism, προστάτις (= *patrona,* Bl-D-R §516) which otherwise never occurs. I am able to interpret this in no other way than to say that Paul, who was a Jew for the Jews and a Greek for the Greeks, now becomes a Roman for the Romans.

Romans 16: Evaluation

Romans 16:3–16 introduces twenty-eight individual persons. Twenty six are named; Nereus's sister and Rufus's mother are not named. Since Lietzmann's[31] brief comments, the twenty-eight persons have not attracted particularly great interest. Nevertheless, after the 1974 publication of computer-generated concordance *CIL* 4 containing the Roman inscriptions of the imperial period[32] and the appearance of H. Solin's, *Die griechischen Personennamen in Rom* (Berlin, 1982), I will attempt once again to approach the names. I see a number of ways to evaluate the list of persons:

- Relation between men and women

- Relation between autochthon and immigrant

- Do the names belong to specific strata; do they show at least an affinity to certain strata of the population?[33]

1. To begin with, two social-historical facts from verses 10b and 11b are immediately clear. Two persons, Aristobulus and Narcissus, are exceptions in the list; they are non-Christian. (a) They themselves are not greeted, but people in their family are. If the heads of the two house-

---

30. See also H. H. Schade, *Apokalyptische Christologie bei Paulus,* GTA 18 (Göttingen, 1981), 184–89. Schade attempts to show with a limited choice of vocabulary that the Pauline use of this vocabulary shifts slightly. All the Pauline letters considered, "Christos" constantly gains the upper hand over "Kyrios." I am pleased with the comparable formulation of the question (although the reasons for chronologically placing Philemon after Romans do not appear to be sufficient).

31. *Die Briefe des Apostels Paulus,* HNT 3 (Tübingen, 1913; 5th ed., 1971), 125f. Also, H. Solin, "Juden und Syrer, 662–65 (with further literature).

32. *CIL* 4:7, fasc. 1ff. (Berlin, 1977ff.): Indices vocabulorum nominibus propriis inclusis. Cf. also the indices *CIL* 6:6.

33. The relation between Jewish Christian and Gentile Christian has already been considered above, chap. 3.

holds were fellow Christians, Paul would have sent his greeting to them (as in vv. 3–5, 14, 15). (b) A further indication that both *"patroni"* are not Christian is that not all but only a part of their household are Christian:

οἱ ἐκ τῶν Ἀριστοβούλου (not: οἱ Ἀριστοβούλου)
οἱ ἐκ τῶν Ναρκίσσου (not: οἱ Ναρκίσσου)

c. The attribute οἱ ὄντες ἐν κυρίῳ aims in the same direction: "those from Narcissus's people who are in the Lord," as opposed to the others. The Christians are clearly either slaves or freedmen of these two masters[34]

The master Narcissus himself could have been a freedman. The name is found as a slave's name about 50 times in Rome.[35] A very powerful freedman of Claudius was called Narcissus,[36] another Nero.[37] Also the freedman named Narcissus in *CIL* 6:9035 has his own slaves.

The master Aristobulus was hardly an autochthonous Roman. The masculine form of his name appears only twice in *CIL* 6 (17577; 29104); the feminine form, "Aristobula,"[38] once. Aristobulus, who may have been a member of King Herod's household, emigrated to Rome. If he brought his Christian slave with him from the East, then *we have come upon one of the channels through which Christianity infiltrated the capital.*

The Relation of Women and Men

Aside from these two households, there are 26 people indicated as Christians, 8 women and 18 men. That relationship changes when one observes which persons Paul singles out as active in the community:

Junia[39] v. 7 συναιχμάλωτός μου, ἐπίσημη ἐν ἀποστόλοις
Prisca v. 3f. συνεργός etc.
Mary v. 6 πολλὰ ἐκοπίασεν εἰς ὑμᾶς

---

34. Not only slaves but also freedmen who live in the house of the master; see Pliny, *Ep.* 2.17.9.

35. See the dissertation from J. Baumgart, *Die römischen Sklavennamen* (Breslau, 1936), 40. (It is based upon Roman inscriptions.) One inscription contains the *cognomen* Narcissus for both master and slave: *CIL* 6:22874.

36. Cf. Suetonius, *Claudius* 28; and see H. Chantraine, *Freigelassene und Sklaven*, 325.

37. Cassius Dio, 63.3.4.1.

38. The name belonged to a female slave (cf. J. Baumgart, *Sklavennamen*, 20, and *CIL* 6:18908).

39. The following points speak for the feminine form "Junia" in Romans 16:7: (1) In the majuscules Ἰουνιᾶν (the accusative of the masculine "Junias"; so also in many minuscules of the Middle Ages) cannot be distinguished from Ἰουνίαν (the accusative of "Junia).

Tryphaena and
Tryphosa v. 12 κοπιώσας ἐν κυρίῳ
Persis v. 12 πολλὰ ἐκοπίασεν ἐν κυρίῳ
   possibly also Rufus's mother v. 13 μήτηρ καὶ ἐμοῦ
Aquila vv. 3f. συνεργός etc.
Andronicus v. 7 and
Urbanus v. 9 συνεργὸς ἡμῶν
   possibly also Apelles v. 10 δόκιμος ἐν Χριστῷ
   possibly also Rufus v. 13 ἐκλεκτὸς ἐν κυρίῳ.[40]

The list indicates a proportion of 7 to 5 (perhaps even 6 to 3) of women to men. *The active participation of women in the community life* can be ascertained through three other observations. (a) κοπιάω[41] is used four times exclusively of woman and never of a man. (b) The activity attested of Andronicus and Urbanus appears to refer more to their past work in the east than to a present role in the Roman community (συναιχμάλωτοι μου, ἡμῶν); whereas Mary's service to the Roman community is explicitly mentioned (εἰς ὑμᾶς). (c) With Prisca and Aquila the wife is mentioned *before* the husband (v. 3). This also occurs in 2 Tim 4:19; Acts 18:18, 26. The opposite sequence is found only in 1 Cor 16:19 (cf. Acts 18:2).

But, as I am now convinced (Paris, Bib. Nation., Grec 14, p. 100 verso, l. 1), Minuscule 33 from the ninth century places an acute accent and writes the feminine ἰουνίαν, so that, contrary to Aland's text-critical apparatus, we have a witness for the feminine variant. Aland's apparatus would have to be correspondingly changed. (2) In antiquity the name "Junia" was widespread, while "Junias" (a possible short form of "Junianus," cf. Bl-D-R §125⁶) is attested nowhere. (3) The church fathers of late antiquity correctly perceived that Andronicus's companion was not a man. This changed only with Aegidius of Rome (1245–1316 C.E.). For the history of the interpretation of Romans 16:7 see B. Brooten, "Junia... Outstanding among the Apostles (Romans 16:7)," *Woman Priests,* ed. L. Swidler and A. Swidler (New York, 1977), 141–44. One may take exception with Fàbrega's history of interpretation (1985). He relies on the variant "Junias" in Migne, *PG* 14:1281B and 1289A (Commentary on Origen), although the other text tradition, including the quotation in Hraban of Fulda (*PL* 111:1608D), reads "Junia." (4) For a scribe of the Middle Ages copying minuscules it is easier to imagine a man in an active missionary role than a woman. From the perspective of the scribe, "Junia" would be the "lectio difficilior." Andronicus and Junia could have traveled as a married couple proselytizing in the countries they visited. This is attested for the "other apostles" in 1 Cor 9:5. Whether ἐπίσημος κτλ. means that Andronicus and Junia belonged to the circle of apostles or only enjoyed the admiration of that group, need not be considered here. It is sufficient that both actively worked for the gospel (συναιχμάλωτοι μου). Those who, in spite of the evidence presented, wish to decide in favor of "Junias," an embarrassing solution fabricated by men, should consider in their evaluation of the evidence not only "Junia" but also "Junia(nu)s."

40. Epaenetus is called ἀγαπητός and ἀπαρχὴ τῆς Ἀσίας but this does not presuppose that he is active in the Roman community. The same may be said for Ampliatus and Stachys, who are called ἀγαπητοί μου. Verse 12b speaks of "the beloved (ἀγαπητός) Persis, who has worked hard in the Lord." The addition of the relative clause shows that ἀγαπητός is not an indication of activity.

41. This is a technical term in missionary language. In Gal 4:11; 1 Cor 15:10 the word is predicated of Paul himself.

Apparently, Prisca was more prominent in community activity than her husband.[42]

The active role of certain women in the community as we encounter it in Romans 16 stands in contrast to the previous observation of the diminishing influence of women on the formation of community life (above, chap. 15). There are two conceivable explanations for this decision, although the paucity of material does not admit a decision. (a) Was an active role in community life for women more possible in the early period of Roman Christianity, in the 50s of the first century, than later at the end of the first century (since *1 Clement*)? Could voices such as *1 Clem.* 21:7 (see above) have increasingly prevailed since the second and third Christian generations and repressed the influence of women?[43] (b) Or does Romans 16 offer only a random selection of individual cases that are not representative of the early period of Roman Christianity, so that we cannot venture a more general comment on women's active role in the community during the that time?

The Relation of Autochthons and Immigrants

The text characterizes twelve persons as coming from the east:

- *Prisca* and
- *Aquila* συνεργοί μου, ὑπὲρ τῆς ψυχῆς μου τράχηλον ὑπέθηκαν; cf. Acts 18:2: Aquila was born in Pontus.
- *Epaenetos* ἀπαρχὴ Ἀσίας, ἀγαπητός μου[44]
- *Andronicus* and

---

42. W. A. Meeks (*Urban Christians*, 59) attributes the sequence of Prisca before Aquila to the woman's higher social position. Our source (Rom 16) is not, however, secular, but early Christian. It stands in the broader context of Gal 3:28 and does not show how a person was revered in the society at large but indicates the significance of this person *in the community* (cf. Rom 16:3b, 4, 5a). Also 16:21–23 does not list first the socially respected (Erastus with his civil office and Gaius with his grand house) but five other Christians are listed first, among them a fellow missionary and Paul's secretary. If Luke had known of Prisca's higher social position, he would certainly not have left it unmentioned in view of his partiality to prominent women (for example, Luke 8:3; Acts 17:4,12; cf. 17:34; 16:14).

43. One is lead to believe that there was in other respects throughout the world a strong repression of the influence of women (for example, 1 Tim 2:11f.). I can here refer to the pertinent material in A. Harnack, *Mission und Ausbreitung*, 589–611, for example, 595f., 609f. It is possible to conclude in view of all the admonitions in 1 Tim 2:11f. that they, on the basis of their imperative structure, presuppose in practice the contrary activity. Therefore, there were perhaps at a later date still influential women in the community. This consideration raises considerable uncertainty in judging the actual relationship. On this question see P. Lampe and U. Luz, "Nachpaulinisches Christentum und pagane Gesellschaft," *Die Anfänge des Christentums*, ed. J. Becker et al. (Stuttgart, 1987), 185ff.

44. Cf. *CIL* 6:17171 speaks of the pagan Epaenetus of Ephesus, whose family also immigrated to Rome.

- *Junia* συναιχμάλωτοι μου, πρὸ ἐμοῦ γέγοναν ἐν Χριστῷ[45]
- *Urbanus* συνεργὸς ἡμῶν
- *Rufus* and
- his *mother* are personally known to Paul: μήτηρ καὶ ἐμοῦ. Paul also knows of Rufus's faith: ἐκλεκτὸς ἐν κυρίῳ.

As "my beloved," who are also personally known by Paul, are:
- *Ampliatus,*
- *Stachys,*
- *Persis.*
- *Apelles,* to whose distinguished faith and personal acquaintance Paul attests.

The other fourteen persons are not convincingly portrayed as personal acquaintances of Paul. One cannot exclude the possibility that Paul has learned of them through secondhand reports. For example, when Paul characterizes Mary as one ἥτις πολλὰ ἐκοπίασεν εἰς ὑμᾶς, he is not speaking from personal experience. The relative clause presupposes that he has heard stories of her activity. Romans is Paul's letter of recommendation for himself, with which he wishes to win the trust of the community. Therefore, one may conclude that he sends greetings to everyone in Rome who is known to him, directly or indirectly, by name as Christian. (Paul's style is similar to ours when we say, "Although I have never met John, please give him my regards.")

Conclusion: At least twelve out of twenty-six persons are known personally by Paul, have lived at some time in the east and have traveled between the east and Rome. Those born with some certainty in the East are: Aquila (Pontus), Epaenetus (Asia), Andronicus, and Junia (the latter two πρὸ ἐμοῦ γέγοναν ἐν Χριστῷ and are closer to the original Palestinian apostles). On the basis of the edict of Claudius it would be "inappropriate" to exclude the possibility that autochthonous Roman Christians fled to the east (Acts 18:2) and at a later date returned to the city.

A second approach to the question may be attempted through the computer-generated list (*CIL* 6:7) and H. Solin's book of names.[46] The following names are very often or only seldom represented in Rome.

The figures in parentheses give the highest number of persons who come in question as contemporaries. That is, it allows one to subtract from the total figure in the first column the clearly earlier and later persons, so that the result is the figure in parenthesis.

---

45. ἐπίσημοι ἐν τοῖς ἀποστόλοις presupposes, minimally, that they were personally acquainted with the Palestinian apostles; see above, n. 39.

46. *Die griechischen Personennamen in Rom* (Berlin, 1982). It should be noted that we depart from numbers in Solin's data on Romans 16 listed by Solin.

Julia	over 1,400	
Hermes	841	(640)
Rufus	c. 374	
Junia	over 250	
Prisca/Priscilla	over 200	
Maria	c. 108	
Urbanus	c. 95	
Ampliatus	c. 80	
Tryphaena	60	(47)
Nereus	36	(28)
Tryphosa	32	(29)
Andronicus	29	(19)
Aquila	c. 28	
Apelles	c. 27	(15)
Philologus	23	(18)
Stachys	13	(11)
Phlegon	9	(7)
Persis	6	(3)
Hermas	6	(3)
Epaenetus	4	(3; one of whom is clearly foreign, cf. *CIL* 6:17171)
Asyncritus	2	(1)
Olympas	2	(0)
Patrobas	0, it is, however, derived from	
Patrobius	8	(4)

Herodion: this short form is otherwise not attested in Rome. One does eventually find the Greek equivalent (cf. below, no. 8) of Herodian 6 times, cf. *CIL* 6:9005; 32624; 13126; H. Solin, *Personennamen* 1362; 214.

[*Junias* is attested neither in the east nor in the west. It could be a short form of Junianus. Junianus is attested 21 times in Rome.][47]

Agreements with the first section above are apparent: (a) We find the name Epaenetus, which is ranked low on the Roman frequency scale, is in the first list the name of a person from the east. (b) In the lower part of the frequency scale (< 30) are the names Persis, Stachys, Apelles, Aquila, and Andronicus. Persons of these names also appear in the first list, where it is more or less certain[48] that Andronicus and Aquila are from the east. There are only indications for the eastern origin of Persis, Stachys, and Apelles. These agreements are able to show that the frequency statistics are not an inefficient instrument for determining eastern origins. If this is so, then we come one step further. We have the well-grounded suspicion that the remaining names in the lower section of the frequency scale belong to non-autochthon Christians.

---

47. At least one of them was not autochthon: *CIL* 6:16247: "ex Hispania citeriore."

48. That "Aquila" (cf. also "Junia") are of Latin origin, plays no role. In the second century one finds the name Justinus in the east. During the imperial period the etymological language of origin of a name does not say anything about the geographical origin of a person. Already in the period before Nero, slaves born in the West, for example in Germany or Spain, can have *Greek cognomens.* (See M. L. Gordon, "The Nationality of Slaves," 93ff. 103.; H. Chantraine, *Freigelassen und Sklaven,* 134f.) On the question of how much or how little the language of origin of *cognominens* can tell us about the geographical origin of a person, see H. Solin, "Probleme der römischen Namenforschung," 297–300; H. Solin, *Personennamen,* 146ff.; H. Chantraine, *Freigelassen und Sklaven,* 132ff. (the history of the research since T. Frank).

Both lists together suggest an eastern origin for fourteen persons. This is more or less certain for Junia, Epaenetus, Aquila, Andronicus. It is probable for Herodion, Patrobas, Olympas, Asyncritus, Hermas, Persis, Phlegon, Stachys, Philologus, Apelles. For those remaining, eastern origin is not excluded, but there is no indication for it. In regard to Aquila's wife, Prisca, we do not have any hint, since we do not know whether Aquila met his wife earlier in Pontus or only later in Rome.

Names Belonging to Specific Classes?[49]

It makes a difference whether a list of names to be investigated comes from the middle of the first century or from the later imperial period. The deterioration of the nature of names, the leveling of names,[50] was not so advanced in our period as later. The difference between aristocratic and nonaristocratic names was not fully faded. In the middle of the first century, one can ask whether a name, even when it cannot belong clearly to a definite class, possesses at least some affinity to a certain class of the population, so that it indicates a socially specific tendency. In regard to the social-historical identification of the individual names in Romans 16, this would yield a degree of probability.

---

49. Selected bibliography: For the names of slaves based upon Roman inscriptions, see J. Baumgart, *Sklavennamen.* H. Chantraine, *Freigelassen und Sklaven,* especially chapter 7, "Das Cognomen der kaiserlichen Freigelassen und Sklaven," pp. 128ff.; further literature regarding slave names on p. 128, n. 1. G. Fabre, *Libertus,* 104ff. for literature. E. Fraenkel, "Namenwesen," Pauly/Wissowa 16²: 1611–70; especially §7 col. 1647f, division of the social strata; further §6 no. 5 col. 1643; col. 1660 as well as 1662–66 for slave names. H. Raffeiner, *Sklaven und Freigelassene.* W. Schulze, *Geschichte,* 512f., 524, for the social aspects. C. M. Kaufmann, *Handbuch,* 97f., chapter 4, deals with selected epigraphs of secular and social life, classes of people, occupations, and information about homeland; especially pp. 98f., which lists for Rome sixteen names. Further, T. Frank, "Race Mixture," 689–708. T. Frank, *Economic History,* 207ff. S. Copalle, *De servorum graecorum nominibus.* M. Lambertz, *Sklavennamen.* F. F. Bruce, "Roman Slave-names," 44–60. B. Doer, *Namengebung.* F. Bechtel, *Frauennamen,* especially pp. 63–68, which deals with women's names as an indication of place in society. L. Ross-Taylor, "Freedmen and Freeborn," 113–32, containing a history of the research. H. Solin, *Namenforschung,* 276–300, for literature and pp. 276–81, for an overview of the research. H. Solin, *Personennamen.* I. Kajanto, *Cognomina,* 132–34, containing socially specific names. P. R. C. Weaver, "Nomina ingenua," 311–26; P. R. C. Weaver, "Irregular Nomina," 323–26. B. Rawson, "Family Life," 71–83, for socially specific names.

50. J. Baumgart, *Sklavennamen,* 82f.; B. Doer, *Namengebung,* 201. There are reasons for this phenomenon: Freed slaves climbed socially to posses great property and influence, so that slave names bubbled to the top. On the other hand aristocratic names trickled "downward" (a) because old Roman aristocracy became impoverished and sank to the proletariat and (b) because the lower levels of society sought after the names of the nobility, etc. The permanent fluctuation of the rise and decline of families that took place within the society, without actually touching the class structure, led to a leveling of names that had previously been clearly socially specific.

1. A first rule of thumb says that bearers of Greek names in first century Rome were mostly descendants of slaves.[51] If we look at our list, we discover that two-thirds of the twenty-four names are Greek. Only eight names, Ampliatus, Julia, Junia(nus), Mary (see below), Aquila, Prisca, Rufus, and Urbanus are Latin. At first sight one concludes that the group of people named in Romans 16 has a high affinity to circles whose ancestors were slaves. This conclusion corresponds well to the understanding of the first century presented in Part 3. Nevertheless, one must be cautious. This rule is only a rough approximation for us, since twelve of the sixteen Greek names in our list belong to immigrants from the east (see above, certainly Epaenetus and Andronicus; probably Herodion, Patrobas, Olympas, Asyncritus, Hermas, Persis, Phlegon, Stachys, Philologus, Apelles). These could, however, be freeborn persons with Greek names. Foreigners in the east had no inhibitions about giving their freeborn children Greek names. The above rule is valid for Hermes, Nereus, Tryphosa, and Tryphaena, concerning whom we have no information of eastern origin.

Besides the first rule there are four further criteria:

2. There are names that were originally created for slaves. They have not lost the flavor of slave names, but rather throughout the first century C.E. held a certain affinity to the lower classes (cf. examples nos. 1–4).

3. In the groups of names an imposing majority of the freeborn (and descendants of freeborn) bear *gentilica* or noble names, so that for the social-historical identification of the individuals named there is a degree of probability that such person's ancestors were slaves (see examples nos. 5–7).

4. Particular forms of names indicate descendants of slaves (see following nos. 7 and 8).

5. The most uncertain criterion is: What is the relationship on the basis of inscription statistics (computer concordance in *CIL* 6 and the statistics in Solin, *Personennamen*) between the total number of Romans who bear a name and the number of Romans who bear names that originate from slaves? On the basis of more than fifty percent of the total number of times that a slave/freeborn name appears, can one conclude that there is an affinity of the name to people who are descendants of slaves?

There are uncertain factors: (a) Freed slaves commissioned inscriptions more frequently than freeborn people of the lower and middle

---

51. For evidence of this see the material in H. Solin, *Personennamen*, 121ff., 43, 133ff., 159 and "Namenforschung," 289, 293–96. In first century Rome Greek cognomens were as a rule given to slaves. Free Roman citizens avoided using Greek names for their freeborn children. After the first century this became less and less the rule. See the critical remarks of P. Huttunen, *Social Strata*, 195f.

classes. The inscriptional material is therefore only conditionally representative of all the bearers of a name.[52] (b) There is a second reason
why the great number of persons bearing names indicating slave ancestry does not mean that the name was a specific slave name. In the total
population of Rome a great proportion of people were of slave ancestry
(cf. Seneca, *Clem.* 1.24.1; Tacitus, *Ann.* 4.27; Dionysius of Halicarnassus, 4.24.4ff.). How high the portion was, we do not know. In Italy
alone, one could estimate that about 40 percent of the total population
were living in slavery.[53] For this reason the portion of slave/freed persons within the group bearing a name attested by inscriptions may have
been very high without the names possessing a socially specific affinity.
The sociology of the group bearing a name reflected simply the sociology of the total society, so that the name itself had no influence on
the group. I would begin to speak of a socially specific affinity or tendency when the group bearing a name exhibits other proportions than
the total society.

If there are the two uncertain factors, then two counter-weights
remain which could again balance the "negative points" of the uncertainties so that criterion 5 would still possess some validity: (c) The
inscription statistics of the names of persons from slave ancestry represent only minimal values: Many slaves and above all those set free
would have kept a "genteel" silence concerning their past in the inscriptions (cf. Martial, 6.17, who mentions the freedman who changed his
previous cognomen in order to eradicate his past). Therefore, the actual unknown portion of slaves/freed persons within the name group
attested by inscriptions is higher. I would attribute a socially specific tendency to a name which is recognizably used by over 50 percent slaves/
freed persons. (d) A second consideration points in the same direction.
Since in many cases an inscription can be dated only approximately to
the first to third centuries, the statistical figures contain unrecognized
inscriptions of the later imperial period, in which the leveling of names
continued to occur. These later inscriptions, which witness the use of
previously pure slave names for socially prominent individuals, "falsify"
the picture of the percentage of slaves in the first century name lists, as in
the case of the original slave name "Hermes." In the middle of the first

---

52. Cf. G. Alföldy, *Freilassung*, 340, n. 18; P. Huttunen, *Social Strata*, 191, 194.
H. Solin, *Personennamen*, 135–37: At least 70 percent of the residents of Rome attested in epigraphs were born slaves. Nevertheless, this does not correspond to the actual
proportion of slaves to freedmen in the Roman population (cf. p. 136 for reasons).

53. Cf. G. Alfödy, *Freilassung*, 337ff., and *Sozialgeschichte*, 121f. Specific information
is available only for Pergamon, where about one-third of the total population were slaves
(Galen, 5.49). Huttunen gives a lower estimation (*Social Strata*, 183f., 187, 193, 195)
of about 20 percent slaves and an equal percentage of freeborn over against 60 percent
freeborn in Rome.

century the percentages of slaves must have been higher than inscription statistics indicate, so that statistics again figure as minimal values. Among the people in Rome who are called "Hermes" only about 41 percent can be shown to be from slave ancestry and yet undoubtedly in the middle of the first century C.E. the name is used principally for slaves (see below). We can see with this example how the 41 percent represents a minimal value.[54]

It will be important to observe at which places the results of the above rules of thumb coincide.

Rule 2:

No. 1. "Ampliatus" was in the period of Augustus created for slaves. The name continually remained in the lowest class, since it too clearly revealed its origin to be adapted in noble circles.[55]

From about eighty Roman epigraphs of the imperial period listed in CIC 6, thirty *at least*[56] are those of slaves (37.5 percent). To this may be added fourteen female slaves represented by the feminine form of the name.[57]

Examples for illustration: Among those freed,[58] the name Claudius is particularly prominent, for example in CIL 6:14918; 115509. Persons freed by the emperor Claudius or Nero are called "Ti. Claudius Ampliatus" (CIL 24 857; 15 552).[59] Some of those freed accumulated so much wealth that they themselves rose to "Patron" and had their own slaves or freedmen (CIL 6:5154; 37 775; 23 339). One other Ampliatus was a soldier (3589).

No. 2. "Hermes" was a god's name that occurred mostly in Italy. As with all names of gods, it was in the beginning given only to slaves and people of the lowest class. Therefore, it did not persist into the higher circles. Along with "Eros," "Hermes" was *the* Roman name for slaves.[60]

From the total of 841 examples in Rome (the HERMA-inscriptions are included) 640 are contemporary (= first century). Of these 640, 240 indicate for certain a slave ancestry (slaves / freed persons) and forty-two

---

54. Immediately one concludes that a value of less than 50 percent by no means indicates that the name is favored by freeborn.

55. See J. Baumgart, *Sklavennamen*, 30f.

56. (a) "At least" denotes that the most certain examples are counted. One can presuppose that many slaves concealed their past on their inscriptions (cf. above). The term "at least" is valid for all the following statistics concerning slaves. (b) Included in these statistics and those that follow are naturally all the inscriptions of freed persons insofar as they had the cognomen as their first name during the period of their slavery.

57. See the concordance in CIL 6:7, 1 p. 245, and J. Baumgart, *Sklavennamen*, 30, where he strives for completeness (p. 1). Cf. for example the slaves CIL 6:22856; 16615.

58. Cf. for example CIL 6:21 101; 28 028; 8528.

59. For nomenclature see H. Chantraine, *Freigelassene und Sklaven*, 62.

60. On the whole topic see J. Baumgart, *Sklavennamen*, 44, 47, 49; H. Solin, *Beiträge zur Kenntnis*, 137.

probably a status of freed person,[61] that is, thirty-eight or forty-four percent (a minimal value, as we saw above). The rest of the examples are
uncertain: only one freeborn person, three freed sons and one knight are
recognizable.

Examples for illustration: Of slave ancestry were a cook (*CIL* 6:
9267), a mule drover (9646), a temple custodian (675), and an ironware
dealer (9664). In 60 C.E. a slave named Hermes worked as "Nummularius" taking care of his master's financial affairs.[62] The baby boy of
a slave named Hermes was called with the diminutive "Hermadion"
(*CIL* 6:5115). The daughter of another slave named Hermes was called
"Hermocratia" (*CIL* 6:28 209). In the same household two slaves were
called at the same time Hermes: so were both "colliberti" (freedmen) in
CIL 6:34 832. Two others (*CIL* 6:27 303) were distinguished by "senior" and "junior." Imperial slaves were those of *CIL* 6:19 407; 23 09;
33 204; 19 387; 25 997. Imperial freedmen were those from *CIL* 658;
25 085; 18 546; 9073; 19 385f.; 19 720; etc. Claudius's freedmen with
the cognomen Hermes, whom our Christian Hermes could have met on
the street (when he himself didn't belong to them), were exceedingly numerous in Rome.[63] In *CIL* 6:15 102 we read that a freed slave named
Claudius Hermes possesses his own slaves and *liberti* (freedmen). Masters of slaves and freedmen are found also in 26 889; 5423; 28 320; 29
653; 14 543; 15 965; 12 903; 20 054; 21 071; 25 349.

No. 3. "Nereus" as a god's name exhibits, just as "Hermes," special affinity to slaves or freed slaves. The name of the sea god was used
by thirty-six persons in Rome.[64] Of the thirty-six, twenty-eight are possibly contemporary. Out of the twenty-eight, fifteen are certainly and
one probably of slave ancestry (= 54 or 57%). That means that, besides
criterion 1, criteria 2 and 5 are also fulfilled.

Examples for illustration: *CIL* 6:5248 mentions is a former slave of
the emperor Tiberius; 4344: a *corpus custos* — a bodyguard from among
the servants of Claudius; 8714: another imperial slave; 8117–19; 26
771; 11 147; 12 740; 20 914: *liberti*; 9019: a person freed in the Flavian
period; 8121: a patron named Nereus with his own freedmen.

No. 4. "Persis" is found four times in Rome. Of these, three are possibly contemporary. One of the three examples indicates a female slave;
one is probably a freed person (= 33 or .67%) and one is undetermined

Ethnic names — "Perserin" — were typical first names of slaves.[65]
That they inform us about the geographical origin of the individual is

61. Cf. *CIL–Concordance*, s.v., and H. Solin, *Personennamen*, 342ff., 1361.
62. Cf. R. Herzog, *Geschichte des Bankwesens*, 38–39.
63. See for example *CIL* 6:15 097–15 110; 12 642; 15 557.
64. Cf. H. Solin, *Personennamen*, s.v.
65. Cf. E. Fraenkel, "Namenwesen," 1643; J. Baumgart, *Sklavennamen*, 60–63. For
examples of slaves named "Persis" outside of Rome, see Bauer, *Wörterbuch*, s.v.

not in all cases certain. The origin of this type of name lies in the cus-tom of calling slaves, who were merchandise, according to their country of export. Slaves from neighboring lands of Campania and Etruria (Tus-cany) were often named after their native *city* (for example, the Roman slaves "Herculanius," "Neapolitanus," "Florentinus..."). The names of cities were used less, when the land of exportation was farther away from Rome. Then national or tribal names moved to the fore: There were Roman slaves named "Bretanicus," "Dacus," "Parthus," "Hellas" (nine times), "Ponticus" (seven times), "Persicus" (twice), etc.[66] Familiar ethnic names can also be attributed to indigenous Romans.

Criterion 3:

No. 5. "Julia," found in *CIL* 6 more than 1400 times, is not a cognomen but a *gentilicium* (a family or "gentile" name, particularly in-dicating descent from a patrician family). It was enough to name women only by the paternal gentile name (in feminine form).[67] Therefore, as an example, the daughters of Germanicus — Julia Agrippina, Julia Drisilla, Julia Livilla — can be called only Julia in the inscriptions or in litera-ture.[68] If we do not wish to accept that our Roman Christian woman of the 50s was a noble lady of the Julian house, there remains as the most probable alternative that she was one of the many freed persons or a descendant of a freed person of the Julian family. To categorize her as a *liberta* of one of the Julian emperors is only one of many possibilities. (She could also be numbered among those persons from the province who were granted citizenship by Caesar or Augustus. Nevertheless, this group of people was less extensive than that of the Julian freedmen and suggests very little for the identification of our Julia.)

In Rome one encounters freedwomen named Julia very frequently.[69] Some of them have slaves and freed persons at their disposal who carry on the Gentile name. For example, *CIL* 6:20 356: "Iulia Galatia Iulias Agathes libertae"; 20685: "Iuliae Soteridis Iulius Clarus et Iulia Nice patroni alumnae."[70]

No. 6. "Mary." The Jewish-Christian name Mary or Maria can nat-urally not be eliminated for our Christian woman. Nevertheless, the quantitative relationship of pagan to Jewish examples in Rome opens

---

66. Examples in J. Baumgart, *Sklavennamen*, nn. 62f. Other country-names used by Roman slaves on p. 60. The inscriptions show, for example, with the names of relatives, that they are, in many case, genuine indications of the place of origin. One must, of course, exercise caution with ethnic names not to draw conclusions concerning geographical origin; cf. H. Solin, *Beiträge zur Kenntnis*, 152f.

67. Cf. B. Doer, *Namengebung*, 210, and J. Reichmuth, *Gentilicia*, 99.

68. Cf. *CIL* 6:10 563; Suetonius, *Claud.* 29 with *Cal.* 7.

69. Cf. for example *CIL* 6:13670; 20222; 19919; 20282; 20378; 35609 v; 14843 d; 20092; 20538; 20038; 20439; 19060; 20714; 4258; 35579; 5322; etc. In Ostia 500 freed persons named Julia: A. Licordari, "Considerazioni sull' Onomastica Ostiense," 242.

70. Cf. also 30485; 19979; 24689; 35597; 17569; 20275.

up the possibility that we have before us the feminine form of the pagan Latin name Marius. The Roman Jewish examples are few[71] in comparison with the pagan Latin form of "Maria," which appears in *CIL* 6 about 108 times.[72] If the Mary in Romans 16 is a Gentile Christian, which is more probable,[73] then with certainty her name is Latin. Biblical names were only much later — from the middle of the third century — used by Gentile Christians.[74]

If we have before us a Latin name, then "Marius / Maria" is a *gentilicium*, as was "Julia" above, by which a woman was adequately identified without having to use a cognomen. In our period the following prominent bearers of Gentile names appear: The rich Spaniard Sex. Marius, who was a friend of Tiberius and later thrown to his death by him (Tacitus, *Ann.* 4.36.1; 6.19.1; Cassius Dio 58.22.2). Tiberius paid debts to the senator Marius Nepos (Seneca, *Benef.* 2.7.2; Tacitus, *Ann.* 2.48.3). In 45 C.E. a Marius Cordus attainted the office of *consul suffectus* (the consul appointed to succeed those who held office during the early months of the year) and before 58 C.E. became proconsul of Asia.[75]

Since, in principle, the majority of those bearing *gentilicia* were not noble patrons but the freed persons of a Gentile family (and their children), there is a probability value for the Christian Maria. There are examples of freed persons with the Latin name: *CIL* 6:22223; 22211; 22191; 22244; cf. 22194; 22200; 4402.

No. 7. "Iunia(s)" is either the feminine form ("Iunia" in *CIL* 6 more than 250 times) or a short form, for which there are no examples, of "Iunianus," which appears in *CIL* twenty-one times. A distinguished Roman family (Brutus!) was called "Iunius." If it is the feminine form, which is most probable in the light of the previous discussion, then there are analogies to "Iulia." Iunia belonged to the freed persons or the children of a freedman or woman of the Iunia family.[76]

Also in the "-anus" ending of the masculine form "Iunianus" there hangs a social-historical tale. With this form we proceed to criterion 4.

---

71. *CIJ* 1:251f.; 457; 459; 511; 374f.; 137; 96; 12; 1. Cf. the Semitic name also in *CIL* 6:14025; 27948 (first century); 12907; the bearer of the names are two freedwomen and one female slave. The Semitic name is probably also found in 11175; 19039; 123717; 10881. A Jewish Mary is perhaps also mentioned on the inscription in H. Solin, "Juden und Syrer," 657, no. 68.

72. For example, *CIL* 22229; 22240; 22212; 22204; 22239; 22191; 22244, etc. The Gentile name "Marius" stands parallel, for example, in 22191; 22198; 22244; 22192; 22223; 22179; 22232; 22215; 1457; 22200; 9447; cf. *ICUR* 13584 (Christian).

73. See above, chap. 5. Only Aquila, Andronicus, Iunia(s), and Herodion can be shown in the list to be Jewish Christian.

74. See above, chap. 15, especially n. 10.

75. Coins, Brit. Museum: Phrygia 94 nos. 143–45.

76. It is to be identified with the senatorial lady Iunia Lepida, the daughter of the consul M. Silanus in the year 19.

The freedman Parvenu Trimalchio — one could call him a southern Italian contemporary of those named in Romans 16 — had adopted the splendid name "C. Pompeius Trimalchio Maecenati *anus*" (Petronius, 71). He had four names, just as a freeborn person. The author Petronius adds an "-anus" to his proud *agnomen* (the surname or the name given to a man for some service, for example Africanus) and exposes the ostentatious front of his hero, revealing his slave ancestry. This type of *gentilicum agnomen,* constructed with "-anus," was used mostly by former slaves of senatorial or equestrian masters. The names were constructed from the Gentile name of the previous masters.[77] To illustrate: The slave "Diadumenus Aug. Ser. Aemilianus praegustator" (*praegustator* = foretaster) (*CIL* 6:5355) at one time belonged to the aristocrat Aemiliu. He passed over into the possession of the emperor and now, as an imperial slave, carried the second name Aemilianus.[78] Mainly with imperial or community slaves we find *agnomen* that recall the previous owner.[79] A Christian Iunia(nu)s would be sought primarily among the slaves of the imperial household or the public fund. After the emancipation the *agnomen* would be retained (for example, *CIL* 10:2857).

No. 8. "Herodion." This short form of the cognomen is not attested otherwise in Rome.[80] "Herodianus" is found in Rome only six times (H. Solin, *Personennamen,* 214; 1362). One of these is contemporary, the Roman "Herodian" who was the "foretaster of the divine Augustus" (*CIL* 6:9005): "Genio Coeti Herodian Praegustator Divii Augusti...." The epigram is to be interpreted that Coetus was the previous slave of Herod and then became the possession of the emperor.[81] One learns from the rest of the inscription that Coetus was later set free and became a patron of one called Iulia Prima. As a freedman he worked as a steward (*vilicus*) in the gardens of Sallust.

Probably the Roman Jewish-Christian "Herodion" had a similar history behind him as the freed park custodian. Since "Herodion," a Greek

---

77. Cf. H. Chantraine, *Freigelassene und Sklaven,* 351f.; 375; Th. Mommsen, "Grabschrift aus Rom," 156ff. The construction of republican cognomens of adoption with "-anus" hardly comes into question here.

78. Cf. on this inscription H. Chantraine, *Freigelassene und Sklaven,* 296, 299f., analogous to "Amyntianus." Martial, 1.81 names a former slave "Septimianus." *CIL* 6:1884: Phaedimianus Augustus liber (*liber* = freedman) is a former slave of Phaedimus.

79. Cf. J. Baumgart, *Sklavennamen,* 77–80. Often the example "Aemiliani" is found among the public servants ("servi publici"): *CIL* 6:2372; 4462; 4463; 4466.

80. Cf. elsewhere in the area there is only the grave inscription of Kom-el-Gadi, in Bauer, *Wörterbuch,* 689 (sixth / seventh century), as well as the Alexandrian veterinarian Herodion from the fourth century C.E. (Oder and Hoppe, eds., *Hippiatrica,* 82).

81. Cf. H. Chantraine, *Freigelassene und Sklaven,* 354, 317, for the inscription (with literature), as well as an explanation of "Iunianus" above.

name constructed with "-on," is almost singular in the world (cf. n. 80), it is readily possible that it has the same meaning as the Latin ending "-anus," indicating slave ancestry.[82] Our Jewish-Christian would then be a former Herodian slave who was most likely sold to the imperial household or to the public fund (analogous to "Iunianus"). Actually a synagogue of the Herodians in Rome (συναγωγὴ Ἡροδίων, *CIJ* 1:173) indicates that not only *one* former Herodian slave had been brought to Rome.

Criterion 5.a: 50 percent or more of the examples can be traced back to people who were of slave ancestry:

No. 9. "Asyncritus": from the two examples one is contemporary, an imperial freedman in *CIL* 6:12565 (second half of the first century).

No. 10. "Patrobas": In Rome the name is used only by Martial (2.32) for a (fictitious) imperial freedman. Patrobas is a short form of "Patrobius."[83] (Found in Rome eight times; of these four are possibly contemporaneous and from these four [= 53%] have slave ancestry).

CIL 6:11 095 witnesses a M. Aemilius libertus (first century C.E.). Suetonius (*Galba*, 20) knows a Patrobius freed by Nero, upon whom, in the sixty-ninth year, some freedmen are dependent.[84]

"Nereus" (54 or 57%) see above, no. 3.

No. 11. "Andronicus": Of the twenty-nine Roman examples, nineteen or twenty are possibly contemporaneous. Out of the nineteen or twenty, 10 (53%) betray a slave ancestry. To this we may add a female slave, with the name appearing in the feminine form.[85]

Examples for illustration: *CIL* 6:626: a slave; 5326: a freedman, C. Iulius Andronicus, who is perhaps identical with the patron in 5325 (5325 is passed over in H. Solin, *Personennamen*); 138: a *vicarius*, an under-slave, who is subordinate to another slave. 9689; 14675; 19076; 27249: *liberti*. Finally, there is in H. Solin ("Juden und Syrer," 675) a Roman freedman, born in Syria, M. Pompilius Andronicus.

No. 12. "Philologus": found in total twenty-three times; of these, eighteen are possibly contemporaneous and of the eighteen, nine (50%) are slaves or freedmen.[86]

---

82. The Latin form "Herodianus," meaning "a former slave of Herod," would not therefore be translated into Greek as Ἡρῳδιανός, because that form already possessed another meaning, as in Mark 3:6; Matt 22:16; and other passages. The Greek ending "-on" offered itself as a suitable form because it was known from slaves' names (cf. "Parmenon" and other examples in J. Baumgart, *Sklavennamen*, 72.)

83. Cf. Bl-D-R §125.

84. Outside of Rome see *CIL* 10:8043,72.

85. Cf. *CIL* 6–*Concordance*, 278f., with J. Baumgart, *Sklavennamen*, 20; also H. Solin, *Personennamen*, 17.

86. Cf. J. Baumgart, *Sklavennamen*, 19; H. Solin, *Personennamen*, 1025. Besides these, in Italy *CIL* 5:7462; 9:5120.

CIL 6:8601: a freedman of the emperor Claudius, *"ab epistulis"* (from epistles); 2215: an *"aedituus"* (keeper of a temple) of slave origin who belonged to the lowest class of officials; 6250: a house-steward of slave ancestry; H. Solin, *Personennamen,* 1025: a *medicus* (physician) of slave ancestry; Plutarch, *Cic.* 48.2; 49.2: a freedman; CIL 6:4981: a Philologus sold two *ollas* (urns); 28073: a patron. Although in the first century B.C.E. the Greek slave L. Ateius Praetextatus, who was a war slave and rose to distinction in Rome as a famous grammarian (Suetonius, *Gramm.* 10), especially valued the surname "Philologicus," this is not evidence against the thesis that the name carried connotations of a slave name in Rome. This blemish did not disturb Ateius Praetextatus, because he had other interests in the name. As did his predecessor, the Alexandrian grammarian Eratosthenes (Suetonius, ibid.), he wished to indicate his occupation with the "Philologus."

"Persis" (33 or rather 67%) see above, no. 4.

No. 13. "Olympas" — the masculine short form of Ὀλυμπ-names,[87] is witnessed only twice applied to imperial freedmen. Both examples are from the first half of the second century.

The different examples of Ὀλυμπ-names in Rome indicate likewise slaves or freedmen.[88]

Criterion 5.b: Less than 50 percent:

No. 14. "Apelles": of the twenty-seven examples, there are fifteen that are possibly contemporary. Of these fifteen, there are 4 certain and 2 probable from slave ancestry (27 or 47%).

These slaves were named after the great painter Apelles (Pliny, *Nat. hist.* 35.79). The Roman slaves Praxiteles, Zeuxis, Phidias, and Themison[89] were also named after artists. CIL 6:38012 a servant; 9183 an imperial freedman.

No. 15. "Tryphosa": appears in total thirty-two times; twenty-nine of these are possibly contemporaneous. Of the twenty-nine, eight certainly and five probably have slave origins (28 or 45%).[90]

---

87. Cf. Bl-D-R §125.

88. "Olympas" outside of Rome, in the district of Latium in CIL 14:1286. In Rome cf. *"Iulia Olympias"* (fem.) in the milieu of the imperial slaves: CIL 6:13609; 11288; further 13018; 5431. In total it appears as a Roman slave name twenty times (J. Baumgart, *Sklavennamen,* 64). "Olympus": In Rome it occurs a total of seventy-five times, of which fifty are possibly contemporaneous. From the fifty, there are twenty-four that are certainly of slave ancestry, in addition to three possible freedmen. "Olymphia" appears twice as a slave name in Rome (J. Baumgart, *Sklavennamen,* 52). "Olympheius," "Olympius" and *"Olympiodorus"* appear as slave names in Rome (J. Baumgart, *Sklavennamen,* 51f., 62.) Olympianus appears once, possibly a contemporary example of a female slave. "Olympicus" appears nineteen times, of which eighteen are possibly contemporaneous. Of these eighteen, two are of slave ancestry and one probably a freedman. (cf. H. Solin, *Personennamen,* 634f.).

89. In J. Baumgart, *Sklavennamen,* 59.

90. Cf. J. Baumgart, *Sklavennamen,* 29; H. Solin, *Personennamen,* 787f.

Examples: *CIL* 6:17862 a female slave; 26281 a freedman; 15280 (cf. 15241) a freedman of Claudius;[91] 4866 and 25090 each mention a "patrona" with this name.[92]

No. 16. "Tryphaena" appears a total of sixty times. Of these 47 are possibly contemporaneous. Of the forty-seven, 115 certainly and five probably indicate slave origins (32 or 43%).[93]

Examples: *CIL* 6:15624 presents a freedwoman of the house of Claudius;[94] 38003 the *conturbenalis* (live-in companion) of an imperial slave; 33771 a Tryphaena with a patron; 16794; 28080 and 18103 all mention a *liberta* (freedwoman); 27678 a *conserva* (fellow-servant); 36460 an *alumna* (foster child); 20042 also a female slave; 8163: but also a *Domina* (mistress of a house) can be called "Tryphaena."

No. 17. "Phlegon" in total appears nine times. Of these, seven are possibly contemporaneous. In ancient Greece, it was a dog's name (Xenophon, *Cyneg.* 7.5) In Rome it was used three times (43%) by possible contemporaries (= first century) of slave origin.

Examples: *CIL* 6:8965: a slave Phlegon *ex paedagogio Caesaris* (from the Caesar's slaves who accompany children to and from school) from the institute for young noble boys (cf. Pliny, *Ep.* 7.27.13); also an imperial page; 26146: a *conservus* (fellow-servant); 15202: a freedman.[95]

No. 18. "Hermas" is derived through the suffix from the above mentioned god's name "Hermes." It is mentioned, in total, six times, three of which are possible contemporaries, one (33%) with slave origin: *CIL* 15:6476 mentions a slave of the first century (The "Herma" illustrations are counted with the "Hermes" examples; so also H. Solin, *Personennamen*, s.v.).

No. 19. "Epaenetus": there are four Roman examples. Three are possible contemporaries and one of these (33%) indicates a freedman.[96]

No. 20. "Stachys": found in total thirteen times, of which eleven are possibly contemporary. Of the eleven, three (27%) are witnesses of slave origin. Examples: *CIL* 6:26732: a slave of the imperial household; 4452: a physician of slave origin.

---

91. Cf. the freedmen in the district of Latinum in *CIL* 14:1728. Further *CIL* 10:2523; *CIG* 2:2819; 2839; 3348.

92. Cf. also *CIG* 14:2246.

93. Cf. J. Baumgart, *Sklavennamen*, 18; H. Solin, *Personennamen*, 783f.; Baumgart (*Sklavennamen*, 18) also mentions once "Tryphana" for a woman slave.

94. Cf. in the district of Latinum the freedmen of *CIL* 14:415; 734. Further, the freedmen in *CIL* 12:3398 and the courtesan in Lucian (*Het. dial.* 11). Finally, the Tryphaena in *Acta Pauli* 27ff.

95. Cf. beyond this the slave of the district of Latinum in *CIL* 14:2008a; further, the historian Phlegon of Tralleis who was a freedman of Hadrian.

96. *Ineditum* (not known) from the *Antiquarium Comunale*; H. Solin, *Personennamen*, 898. J. Baumgart, *Sklavennamen*, 34, 43, 78; Also "Epaenus," "Epaenis" are found in Rome as slave names.

No. 21. "Urbanus": in *CIL* 6 it is found in total about ninety-five times. Of these, about twenty-five times as the name of (former) slaves (26%); further, there are sixty woman slaves named "Urbana."[97] The name expresses a wish. One wishes the person thus named to be *urbanus* (refined in manner), cultivated, ingenious.[98]

Examples: *CIL* 6:29576: a *verna* (slave born in the house) Urbanus who was named after his mistress Urbana; 27810: an Urbanus with eleven other *colliberti* (fellow freedmen), whose Latin names are formed from adjectives. This was, so to speak, a predilection of their patron (Felix, Rufa, Clara, Donatus, etc.); 29573: an imperial slave; 1968: a slave with the office of *nomenclator censorius* (a slave who told his master, the censor, the names of his clients at his reception);[99] 33764 and 4237: imperial freedmen; 8438: a slave freed by Flavius who has his own freedmen; 44, 1945, and 26195: freedmen; 25314: owner of a parcel of land; 17916 and 37408: patrons with their own freedmen; 1704f.: a noble.

No. 22. "Prisca, Priscilla" ("Ancient," "Severe"): in *CIL* over two hundred times. There are thirty-one (freed) female slaves of this name (16%). There are thirty male slave with the name "Priscus."[100]

Examples: *CIL* 6:15752: this former woman slave served along with a Priscus — which indicates the master's predilection to call his slaves by the same name.[101] Other women of this name, dependent upon a patron, are also freed persons (26467a; 28418; 20999; 22635; 5155; 9913; 14190; also 18215). Several are wives of imperial slaves[102] or imperial freedmen.[103] Several have their own slaves and freedmen at their disposal.[104]

No. 23. "Aquila": a animal name which appears in *CIL* 6 a total of about twenty-eight times. Four[105] (14%) were certainly names of slaves.

No. 24. *"Rufus"* ("red head") is found in *CIL* 6 about 374 times in total; only thirty can be shown to be (former) slaves (8%); 50 are woman slaves.[106]

---

97. Cf. J. Baumgart, *Sklavennamen*, 21, 79.

98. There are similar Roman "wish-names" which apparently expressed what a master hoped from his slave. Cf. J. Baumgart, *Sklavennamen*, 21f.: Epaphroditus ("lovingly attractive"), Pulcher ("beautiful"), Laetus ("proud"), Genialis ("pleasant"), Lasciva ("playful"), Ridicula ("funny"), etc. In general, as with Urbanus/a, the feminine form predominates in this group.

99. See Th. Mommsen, *Staatsrecht*, 1:282, n. 6.

100. Cf. J. Baumgart, *Sklavennamen*, 16, 66.

101. Other examples in Rome: Primus–Prima (*CIL* 6:11100; 17754); Tertius–Tertia (14342); Chilo–Chila (16488).

102. *CIL* 6:25997; 16595.

103. *CIL* 6:18407f.; 35306; 33131; 26670; 7010; 9018; 33782.

104. *CIL* 6:28015; 22732; 13848; 20635; 28460; 10689; 11130; 15566.

105. J. Baumgart, *Sklavennamen*, 41. Cf. also p. 24, "Aquilina," a freedwoman of a soldier.

106. Cf. J. Baumgart, *Sklavennamen*, 23, 12; the name is found already in the republican period in the masculine and feminine form: J. Baumgart, *Sklavennamen*, 26f.

Examples: *CIL* 6:13208 an imperial freedman; 3441 an *evocatus Caesaris* (a veteran who served his time but was liable to be called up in an emergency). Also a senator under Domitian could have this cognomen (Philostratus, *Vita Apoll.* 7.8). There are patrons in *CIL* 6:21590; 16744; 16087; 35702; 25585; 23702; 18321; 23484; 11220. A soldier (Urbanicianus) from Syria, presently in Rome in *CIL* 6:2910 (first century). Other freed persons in *CIL* 1²:1256; 1336; 1862; 1263; 1405; 1418; 2688. At the time of Cicero, Rufus was still often used as a slave name (*Pro Mil.* 60) but that was a century earlier than Romans 16. Even consuls of the first century had this name: *CIL* 6:8639b; 2051; 541; 397.

We can now summarize the results of the investigation. The chart represents the indications for slave origins:

Criteria:	1	2	3	4	5
Nereus	x	x			x
Hermes	x	x		x	
Persis	(x)	x			x
Herodion	(x)			x	
Tryphosa	x				
Tryphaena	x				
[Iuna(nu)s				x	
Iunia			x		
Iulia			x		
Ampliatus		x			
Asyncritus	(x)				x
Patrobas	(x)				x
Philologus	(x)				x
Andronicus	((x))				x
Olympas	(x)				(x)
Apelles	(x)				
Phlegon	(x)				
Hermas	(x)				
Stachys	(x)				
Epaenetus	((x))				
Maria			(x)		
Urbanus					
Prisca					
Aquila					
Rufus					

(In regard to criterion 1 — Greek cognomen — a double parentheses is used when it is most certain that the name is that of an immigrant from the east, a single parentheses when it is probable. Immigrants with Greek names could also be freeborn; see above).

First, the four Latin names (Urbanus, Prisca, Aquila, Rufus) at the end of the chart deserve special attention where one observes on the whole no affinity to circles of slave origin.

a. That we know more precisely about the bearers of the names "Aquila" and "Prisca" (see chap. 6), is hardly due to chance.

b. Another coincidence is surprising: In Romans 16, it is precisely only Aquila, Prisca, and Urbanus who are given prominence as συνεργός of Paul, no one else. Is their being a "συνεργός" connected with their origin as free persons?

c. It suits Rufus's freeborn origins that his mother was once a mother for Paul when he was in the east (Rom 16:13). This characterization lets one picture a matron who is head of a household. Exercising this function, she was in a position to show hospitality to Paul and to "mother" him.

d. In contrast to these four names, the others reveal at first glance an affinity to slave origins. The names of Nereus, Hermes, and Persis stand out in particular, where two or more criteria point in this direction. It is also most probable that Herodion, Tryphosa, Tryphaena, Iunia [Iunianus], Iulia, and Ampliatus, nine in all, have a slavery background.

The four names "Asyncritus," "Patrobas," "Philologus," and "Andronicus" possess in Rome, on the basis of criterion 5, an affinity to people of slave ancestry. Nevertheless, certainly Andronicus and probably the other three are immigrant Christians. We must investigate more exactly how high a proposition of slaves in the *east* bore a name of a wealthy person. (But from which part do the Christians originate? From Greece, Asia Minor, Syria, or Palestine?) Only then will one know whether one is dealing with slave names in the east. To continue this investigation, we must have at our disposal a representative computer concordance, as we do for Rome. For the remaining names, Olympas, Apelles, Phlegon, Hermas, Stachys, and Epaenetus, no statement is presently possible, for the same reason (immigration from the east). With the name Maria, there is also the uncertainty whether it is a *gentilicium,* "Maria" of a freedwoman, or a Semitic name.

In conclusion, we can say that most probably four persons are freeborn and at least nine are of slave origin. That means, of the thirteen persons, about whom it was possible to make a statement, over two-thirds with a great degree of probability show indications of slave origin. It would remain to be shown how far this relationship (2:1) is representative of early Roman Christianity. Nevertheless, the family of Aristobulus and Narcissus (see above, 1), also named in Romans 16, do not stand alone in regard to their slave lineage.

Chapter 17

Claudius Ephebus
and Valerius Biton
(*1 Clem.* 63:3; 65:1)

First Clement 63:3; 65:1: Two of the Roman Christians who in the 90s brought the first letter of Clement to Corinth were Claudius Ephebus and Valerius Biton.

From their youth both men belonged to Roman Christianity (ἐν ἡμῖν). At the time of the composition of *1 Clement* in the 90s, they were both aged men (ἀπὸ νεότητος . . . ἕως γήρους). That means that they would have experienced the beginnings of Roman Christianity.

Their Greek cognomens betray a slave background (see above, criterion 1), which is made precise through the Latin *gentilicia*, indicating that they were freedmen of the Claudian and Valerian families. The infamous Messalina (c. 25–48 C.E.), the wife of Claudius, belonged to the Valerian clan. Claudius Ephebus comes most likely from the imperial Claudian slaves.[1] As an imperial freedman, he is named in *1 Clement* before the freedman of the Valerian clan.

That Judaism and Christianity of the first century had success with more than one member of the domestic staff of the Valerian clan is revealed, in my opinion, by *CIL* 6:27948 (first century). Along with other freedpersons of the Valerian clan, the inscription names a freedwoman, Valeria Maria. "Maria" is clearly the cognomen, since the *gentilicium* is "Valeria" (the cognomen Maria is found only seven times in all of *CIL* 6; see above, chap. 16, n. 71). Therefore, "Maria" represents in this case the Semitic name. Apparently, Jewish members of the Valerian clan gave this name to the slave girl at her birth. This opens up the possible background of Valerius Biton's Christian faith, who experienced the beginnings of Roman Christianity in the synagogues. We discover an interesting scenario: Valerian Jews, presumably her slave parents, named a little slave girl Maria. This Maria grew up to be a Jewish (or Jewish Christian) freedwoman. Valerius Biton became a Christian when Roman

---

1. Cf. in the east at the same time "those of Caesar's house," in Phil 4:22.

Christianity was still located in one or several synagogues. He thus was a Jewish Christian. Was Valeria Maria even his mother — or an aunt? We will never know.

The Roman Christians chose with deliberation (63:3f.) their representatives to deliver *1 Clement,* because the imperial freedman Claudius Ephebus and Valerius Biton were to function not only as simple "postmen." Above all, in Corinth itself, they should (as the immediate context of 63:4, 2 reveals) lend personal emphasis to the appeal for peace in the letter. As μάρτυρες μεταξὺ ὑμῶν καὶ ἡμῶν (63:3), they should appear as representatives of Roman Christianity.

How are the both suited for representatives? In the eyes of the Roman Christians, Claudius and Valerius embodied authority, because of their irreproachable Christian behavior (63:3), perhaps also because of their admitted age. In addition, they undoubtedly enjoyed respect and authority because of their social status. Verse 65:1 proudly presents both men with the *gentilicium* next to the cognomen, while the third ambassador, Fortunatus, is simply mentioned by his individual name and labeled with σὺν καί as an appendage.

No word need be lost on the prominent social position of imperial freedmen. "Often my neighbor, Patrobas, disregards our field boundaries. But he is an imperial freedman! Therefore I don't have any chance" (Martial, 2.32). That a freedman of the emperor's household should own an estate outside the gates of the city is not unusual (Suetonius, *Nero* 48.1). How wealthy an imperial freedman can become is illustrated by *ILS* 7196: a freedman of Hadrian donates 200,000 sesterces to his native city in Asia Minor, emphasizing the "modesty" of his wealth. Imperial freedmen of the first century *could*[2] climb to the highest administrative positions or assume an influential position at court, so that people held them in reverence (*reverentia;* e.g., Pliny, *Ep.* 6.31.8f.). The imperial freedmen were a special case in society. In regard to their financial situation and their political power, many could be counted among the upper class.[3] Nevertheless, because of the blemish of slave origin[4] they were not seen as equal by the members of the three upper classes, decurions, equestrians, and senators, and therefore, as a rule, were not taken into their orders. The senatorial order remained completely closed to them.[5] Of course, this did not hinder the population,

---

2. Besides them, there are, of course, also imperial *liberti,* who are satisfied with hand work: see below on *CIL* 6:9053; 9053a.

3. Cf., for example, G. Alföldy, *Sozialgeschichte,* 116f., 130f.

4. In regard to this see G. Alföldy, ibid., 116f., 99, 94.; Pliny, *Nat. hist.* 33.32; Suetonius, *Claudius* 24.1 and *Nero* 15.2; Horace, *Serm.* 1.6.6.

5. In regard to this see, e.g., G. Alföldy, ibid., 116f.; Pliny, *Ep.* 8.6 (only praetorian insignia for Pallas, not formal acceptance into the senatorial class); *liberti* in the equestrian order: Martial, 2.29; 3.29.

aside from the three noble classes that constituted less than one percent of the total population of the empire,[6] from "looking up" to the
imperial freedmen.

What position did our Claudius Ephebus hold *within* the stratification of the imperial household? It is conceivable that he, as the
majority of imperial freedmen in Rome, belonged to the lowest ranks
of officials, as a kind of office manager, for example ("praepositus tabu-
lariorum"; *CIL* 6:8445; 8505) or to an even lower level, as an archivist,
bookkeeper (*tabularius*; *CIL* 6:8410; 8485; 8515; 8580; 9055; 10090;
33725), scribe, cashier, or an assistant to one of these ("adiutor tabu-
larii"; *CIL* 6:8420; 8430; 8510; 8530; 8615; 8635; 33730; 33770). Also
one cannot, of course, exclude the possibility that Claudius Ephebus belonged to the middle management. To this level belongs, for example,
a freedman in charge of the imperial wardrobe (8550, 37745), an assistant to the praefect in charge of the procurement and supply of food
for the capital ("adiutor praefecti annonae": 8400), a sub-administrator
of the imperial household ("subprocurator domus Augustianae": 8640),
also a manager who procures building material for imperial constructions; he was well to do and in charge of his own freedmen (8480; cf.
P. Huttunen, *Social Strata*, 87f.).

That the Roman Christians saw Claudius and Valerius as persons of
authority, that they selected them as their representatives to the Corinthians, and that they emphasized their *gentilicia*, contrary to the usual
usage in early Christian letters, indicates, in my opinion, their position
at the sociological "apex" of Roman Christianity in the first century.
Most of the other Christians in Rome "looked up" to them.[7]

6. Cf., e.g., G. Alföldy, ibid., 130.
7. It is possible that Ignatius (see above) was afraid of their influence when he asked
that nothing be undertaken that could hinder his sentencing.

Chapter 18

Aquila and Prisca

1. Aquila from Pontus and Prisca, the tentmakers (Acts 18:3), were not dependent laborers but independent craftspersons. At their own discretion they employed Paul in their Corinthian workshop (Acts 18:3). We have already seen that they were freeborn persons and had traveled (chap. 16).

We want to look into their milieu. In Rome, there are three inscriptions that mention tentmakers (*tabernacularii*). *CIL* 6:5183b records the inscription on a grave shrine, an *edicula*, of one C. Iulius Chrysantus, who was a member in a tentmakers' guild ("collegium tabernaclariorium" [sic]). Also in *CIL* 6:9053 and 9053a, we hear of the Roman "collegium tabernaculariorum" to which freedmen and slave laborers from the imperial household ("ex domo Caesarum") belong. It was not unusual that slaves and freedmen of the imperial household in lower positions, as here an artisan occupation, established guilds.[1] Often a guild possessed its own building, called a *schola* or *templum*. The above-mentioned C. Iulius Chrysantus, who according to his name was a freedman of Augustus or Caligula,[2] functioned as guardian (*aedituus*) of the Roman tentmakers' house. As Aquila, he would have died in the second half of the first century.

It is interesting that the burial place of Iulius Chrysantus later fell into the possession of a second imperial freedman, P. Aelius Aug. Lib. Eutychus. According to his name, he was freedman of Hadrian and held the office of overseer of awnings ("praepositus velaris castrensibus," *CIL* 6:5183a). In this post, he saw to it that the place designated for competitive and theatrical games for soldiers and court personnel ("ludi castrensibus") would be covered from the sun's rays by awnings

---

1. See, for example, P. Huttunen, *Social Strata*, 104, 107.
2. Cf. H. Chantraine, *Freigelassene und Sklaven*, 61. Less probable as patrons are C. Caesar, the adopted son of Augustus, and Livia, who had been adopted by Augustus through a testament. The text of the inscription is grammatically clumsy. In the arch of the edicula we read (*CIL* 6:5183a): C.IULIO CHRYSANTO; added later: ET P.AELIUS AUG.LIB. EUTYCHUS PRAEPOSITUS VELARIS CASTRENSIBUS FECIT ET SIBI ET SUIS POSTERISQUE EORUM; on the edicula itself (5183b): C.IULIO CHRYSANTO AEDITUO COLLEGI TABERNACLARIORIORUM DONATUM SIBI LOCUM QUEM PETIT AR TROPHIMO INMUNE QUEM IUSSIT SA PECUNIA FACERE SIBI ET FIEIS SUIS ET CONIUGI.

(*velaria*).[3] The short history of the burial place, where an imperial tentmaker and an official responsible for sun awnings were reposed, illustrates a piece of economic history: The awnings used for protection from the sun during competitive games were manufactured in the workshops of the imperial tentmakers (*tabernacularii*). Suetonius (*Caes.* 39) calls the sun awnings that Caesar erected over streets and plazas *tabernacula!*[4] Pliny (*Nat. hist.* 19.23) designated the same constructions as *vela.* Caesar had the whole Forum, including the Via Saca, covered with them as protection from the sun.[5] Nero, a contemporary of Chrysantus and Aquila, erected sun awnings over his wooden amphitheater on Mars Field (cf. Tacitus, *Ann.* 13.31.1). They were held in place by strong ropes, called *rudentes,* and painted blue with stars (Pliny, *Nat. hist.* 19.24). The whole thing was nothing other than a tent covering as was usually used in other theaters (ibid., 23f.). The material of all these tent coverings was linen.[6]

The material produced by the imperial tentmakers was determined by imperial demand. Thus, besides sun awnings, they would also have cut widths of leather for military tents. *Tabernacula* of leather[7] were primarily taken by the military.[8]

What business did Aquila, who did not belong to Caesar's household, carry on? That he, as a small[9] independent craftsman, supplied the military is improbable. As manufacturers of tents for the army, there came in question (1) the larger entrepreneurs of private business (if at all), (2) the imperial tentmakers, and (3) above all, skilled workmen from the legions themselves.[10] Aquila would more likely have sewn together sun awnings of linen for private customers seeking protection from the

---

3. Chrysantus and Eutychus would hardly have known each other personally. Chrysantus designated one named Trophimus as administrator of his estate after his death (*CIL* 6:5183 b). It is most probable that Trophimus was a younger friend and colleague from the tentmakers' guild in which Chrysantus was active. The overseer Eutychus had then acquired the shrine from the tentmaker Trophimus.

4. "Ad quae omnia spectacula tantum undique confluxit hominum, ut plerique advenae aut inter vicos aut inter vias tabernaculis positis manerent...."

5. "Caesar dictator totum forum Romanum intexit viamque sacram ab domo sua et clivum usque in Capitolium, quod munere ipso gladiatorio mirabilius visum tradunt." Whoever has lived in Rome in August knows why.

6. *Carbasina.* Pliny, *Nat. hist.* 19.23 or the whole chapter 6. Cf. Cicero, *Verr.* 2.5.30, 80; Lucretius, 4.75–84; 6.108–13; Propertius, 3.18.13; 4.1.15; Valerius Maximus, 2.4.6; Cassius Dio, 43.24.2 (even silk); Josephus, *Ant.* 11.187 (linen and purple fabric).

7. E.g., *Hist. Aug. Claud.* 14; Livy, 13.18.5.

8. For example, Josephus, *Bell.* 3.79–83; Caesar, *Bell. Gall.* 3.29.2; Vegetius, *De re. mil.* 2.10. Cf. further, J. Marquardt, *Privatleben,* 2:739; or Lammert, "tabernaculum," Pauly/Wissowa 4/2: 1872f.; R. F. Hock, *Social Context,* 20–25, who, however, has in mind only the old thesis of leather work and military tents for Paul and Aquila.

9. See 2 below.

10. On the latter, see Vegetius, *De re. mil.* 2.11. Further, A. Burford, *Künstler und Handwerker,* 76: The legions were "best equipped to supply their own needs for perishable goods, as boots, pots, undergarments, harnesses for horses and armaments." Burford

hot Roman sun. According to Pliny (*Nat. hist.* 19.24), this type of linen sun roofs covered the atrium of private houses. They were colored red and held the water in the cisterns cool.[11] Also Cicero (*Verr.* 2.5.29–31, 80–82) knows of *linen* tents ("tabernacula carbaseis intenta velis") for private use. During the summer heat, they were set up on the shore and provided shade for banquets. The same type of structures can be still seen today in Turkey. Even in winter, Aquila could count on private customers. The shopkeepers needed market stands out of linen ("casas de linteis") in order to offer for sale gifts for Saturnalia (the feast beginning with December 17 at which there were public festivals and presents were exchanged; *Schol. Juv.* 6.153). In my opinion, it is less likely that the tentmaker Paul produced leather military tents and more likely that he constructed linen awnings such as these. Paul came from Tarsus, where linen was manufactured (Dio Chrysostom, *Or.* 34.21ff.). Since he sewed linen awnings, he belonged to a further manufacturing branch of the industry of his native city.

2. How does one sketch the "social status" of an independent craftsman of Aquila's type? His colleagues from the imperial household do not help us to answer this question.

The normal case in the social surrounding is the small craftsman who belongs to the lower and poorer folk. The linen weavers of Tarsus (Dio Chrysostom, *Or.* 34.21ff.) are free but too poor to have the 500 drachma fee to buy for themselves access to political rights. As small handworkers, they work alone or with only a few people. A rich shoemaker, who sponsors games and therefore, "as king of the patch," "gambles away his leather," is characterized as a dimwit exception. He is an upstart whose money does not aid him in attaining social recognition (Martial, 3.16; 3.59). The normal shoemaker and leather worker braiding whips were located in the notorious Subura section of Rome. Prostitutes lived next to them (Martial, 2.17; cf. 6.66.2; *ILS* 7547) and garbage collected on the streets (Martial, 5.22).[12] The words of Juvenal's poem are appropriate, "Honest skills are valued in Rome no more and labor yields profit nevermore ... " (3.21f.).

The inscriptions indicate that Juvenal does not simply exaggerate. In the Roman epitaphs, relatively few handworkers are mentioned who are in the private sector, that is, those who exercise their trade apart

---

refers to the many inscriptions on Hadrian's wall alone that testify to the skilled workmen within the ranks of the army.

11. "Rubent in cavis aedium et muscum ab sole defendunt."

12. There are shoemakers whose only possession is their knife! Libanius, *Or.* 46.22). Concerning the generally low income of craftsmen, see also Dio Chrysostom, *Or.* 7.105. The carpenter in Apuleius, *Met.* 9.5–7 who, however, is not independent but dependent on an entrepreneur, lives "on scanty pay in indigent poverty." His wife spins wool at home to supplement their income. In regard to income, see, for example, A. Burford, *Craftsmen,* 135–44.

from the "familia Caesaris" or the state. Among the 10,892 persons mentioned in the inscriptions, only 72 are recognizable as some kind of craftsman of the private sector. That is less than one percent. In comparison to their actual proportion in the population (presumably considerably more than only double as many), handworkers of Aquila's kind are under-represented in the inscriptions.[13] That means: (a) Most of the craftsmen of the private economic sector, free or enslaved, belong to the lowest levels of the population. They were buried without name or epitaph or interred in the *columbarium* of a burial association, in urns that carry names but no occupations. The occupations of those interred here did not enjoy so much prestige that they were considered worthy of being named. (b) The persons who are *mentioned* on the inscriptions as craftsmen of the private sector represent, as a rule, the highest level among the privately working craftsmen. They are well-to-do entrepreneurs who are proud of their business and therefore are willing to name it on their grave inscription. They buy their own burial places for themselves, their family, and their freedmen. (c) Most of these upwardly mobile craftsmen named in the epitaphs work as goldsmiths, jewelers, or manufacturers of luxury articles.[14] Six Roman "purpurarii" (manufacturers of purple cloth) in *CIL* 6:9843–48, for example, and the Christian Lydia of Thyatira, who deals in purple wool (Acts 16:14), are to be counted in this social level.[15] For Aquila the circumstances appear otherwise. Points (a) and (c) — most craftsmen do not belong to the upwardly mobile entrepreneurial class and those that do manufacture generally luxury items — make it improbable that Aquila with his tentmaking business belongs to this class.

John Chrysostom[16] correspondingly labels Aquila's occupation as ἀγοραῖος. Paul evaluated this work in a similar manner: It had something to do with ταπεινοῦν, when Paul took up this occupation in order to be able to preach the gospel without pay (2 Cor 11:7; cf. 1 Cor 9:18f.). Tentmaking, at least in Paul's case, is not bound to great wealth; it is not accompanied by reputation or prestige (1 Cor 4:11–13) but by μόχθος (1 Thess 2:9).[17]

---

13. In regard to the inscription findings, see P. Huttenen, *Social Strata*, 122f., 71. There is a second interesting ratio: Of the 290 persons whose occupation in the private sector is attested in the inscriptions, only 72 are craftsmen. That is not even one-fourth. Also in this respect, we probably have an under-representation.

14. P. Huttunen, *Social Strata*, 122, n. 319 for references. It deals with 57 of the 72 persons named.

15. Lydia had probably manufactured the product that she sold (cf. J. Marquardt, *Privatleben*, 512). In the eyes of the upper classes such *negotiatores* (wholesale dealers) were not very respected: Quintilian, 1.12.17 (although they could be wealthier and even better educated than a rhetor (teacher of rhetoric); Cicero, *Off.* 1.42.494.

16. *De laud. S. Pauli*, 4, 494 (Migne, *PG* 50:491).

17. See R. Hock, "Tentmaking," 555–64, who interprets this Pauline passage in this sense.

That Aquila, born in the east, works as a craftsman in Rome is typical for the western cities. Generally, the merchants and business people there were composed of freed people, of lower class people, and *immigrants*.[18] The immigrant who moved from the east to the capital city "is doing everything:...surveyor, painter, masseuse, doctor...he understands everything...the hungry Greek aspires to the heaven..., the sailor's wind blows him to Rome together with plums and figs (the latter were imported especially from Syria)..."[19]

In the newer exegetical literature, Aquila and his wife are often assigned a higher social status than I have portrayed here. In Rome Aquila allegedly owned a business that, during his absence after the edict of Claudius, might have been managed by one of his slaves![20] He may have owned a house not only in Rome but also in Ephesus.[21] Aquila may be the master of a business undertaking with branch establishments in which not only Paul would have worked.[22] The house church of the couple in Romans 16:5a was allegedly composed above all from Aquila's domestic servants, since it would be improbable (really?) that Paul had already received new information concerning the founding of yet another house church in Aquila and Prisca's home in Rome. Epaenetus (16:5b) may be one of Aquila's domestic servants.[23] What of such conjectures? Are they probable? No; if we look closely into the New Testament sources, we come across some evidence that corresponds to the picture of an average craftsman of lower social status that I sketched above from the pagan sources.

a. In 2 Cor 11:9, Paul writes that in Corinth he suffered want (ὑστερηθείς), which only the brothers from Macedonia alleviated with their gift of money. That means that the employment in Aquila's Corinthian workshop, in which Paul at that time worked for his livelihood (Acts 18:3), appears to have yielded little profit.[24]

b. Neither in Corinth nor in Ephesus did Aquila and Prisca's home come into question as the location for Paul's preaching, although, at least in Corinth, he did live with Aquila.[25] This finding most readily

---

18. Cf. A. H. M. Jones, "Wirtschaftsleben," 71, in the example of Lyon.

19. Juvenal, 3.61ff.; cf. Seneca, *Helv.* 6.

20. See, for example, W.-H. Ollrog, *Paulus und seine Mitarbeiter*, 26f., n. 105.

21. U. Wilckens, *Römerbrief*, 3:134.

22. M. Hehel, *Eigentum und Reichtum*, 46.

23. W.-H. Ollrog, in *Kirche*, FS Bornkamm, ed. D. Lührmann and G. Strecker (Tübingen, 1980), 239.

24. Was this the reason why the couple stayed only a little more than 18 months in Corinth (Acts 18:11, 2)? This is a conjecture of G. Theissen, "Soziale Schichtung," 252f.

25. Acts 18:3, 6f.; 19:9. The information apparently contains pre-Lukan tradition: συνομορέω and σχολή are hapax legomena; μεταβαίνω is found in Acts and in Luke only once each; in Matthew, e.g., it appears 6 times. σχολή must by no means stand in the service of the Lukan tendency to lend Christianity a shade of cultivation (e.g., in Acts 17). We

means that, at that time, the living quarters of the couple did not offer sufficient room for so many listeners.

Of course, in Corinth Paul had chosen the house of Titius Justus as the teaching location also because it was next to (συνομοροῦσα) the synagogue and thus well situated for the mission to the Godfearers. But this was not the only reason. It is interesting that it is expressly said of Titius Justus and not of Aquila that he owned a house. Second, the coincidence that, in Corinth as well as in Ephesus, Aquila's home did not come into question as the place for a great gathering of listeners also supports our evidence. For it cannot be established at all that the auditorium of Tyrannus in Ephesus was more conveniently located than the lodgings of Aquila.

c. Although the lodgings of the couple did not come into question as the assembly place for Pauline preaching, nevertheless a house church is attested in the home of the couple both in Ephesus and in Rome (1 Cor 16:19; Rom 16:5: ἡ κατ᾽ οἶκον αὐτῶν ἐκκλησία). Of how many persons did a house church consist? Undoubtedly, the number is determined by the size of the house, so that the question leads us in circles. Can one say 15 or 20 persons or more?[26]

The closest analogy to Aquila's lodgings in the pagan environment are the many small workshops, identified by archaeologists, that a craftsman could rent. In the shop the artisan would ply his craft; in a back portion of the shop or in the mezzanine above he would sleep. Apuleius vividly describes the *taberna* (shop) of a fuller. Where the fuller eats with his guests (sic), the tools and equipment of his trade are scattered about. The cloth is bleached on a wicker stand with sulfuric steam, so that the steam tickles the nose during the meal (*Met.* 9.24f.). Some of Aquila's guests would have correspondingly sat on piles of tent panels when the group assembled for worship services. In Corinth *tabernae* in the form of long rows of shops have been excavated.[27] The small row of boutiques north of the southern colonnade presents 14 shops along a front of about 44 meters, which allows a width of only a little over 3 meters for each boutique; their length measures somewhat under 4 meters. The shop front west of the Forum sets "larger" stores next to each other. They are about 4.5 meters in width and about 6 meters in length. In

---

saw above that the quarters used by a guild of craftsmen were called "schola." (Further examples can be found in J.-P. Waltzing, *Etude historique*, 1.215ff.).

26. As unsuccessful I consider M. Gielen, "Zur Interpretation," 109–25: She presumes that the formula ἡ κατ᾽ οἶκον ἐκκλησία denotes the assembly of all Christians of one town. (a) As she herself concedes (n. 70), the thesis stands or falls on the untenable (see above) assumption that Romans 16:1–16 represents an originally independent letter. (b) A plenary assembly of all Christians of one town is verifiable only for Corinth (Rom 16:23). But the formula is never attested for Corinth.

27. Cf., for example, M. I. Finley, *Atlas,* 154ff.

a shop area of 27 square meters about 20 members of a house church could assemble.

d. Aquila and Prisca, already after about 18 months, moved away from Corinth (Acts 18:11, 2). This appears to indicate that they did not possess real estate in Corinth that would have held them back.

That ἡ κατ᾽ οἶκον αὐτῶν ἐκκλησία indicates neither real estate property nor slave property is clear: κατ᾽ οἶκον, as a prepositional expression placed in attributive *hyperbaton,* means simply "at home": "the community at their home"! As in 1 Cor 11:34; 14:35, οἶκος means "home." From this one cannot conclude the possession of real estate.[28]

Still less does the expression indicate slave property. A. Strobel[29] and G. Theissen[30] have disagreed with each other whether "oikos/oikia" can indicate slave property. For Phlm 2 and Phil 4:22 that is true, but for the other nine Pauline passages there is nothing to show this to be the case. It is interesting that in the greetings only the Christian community with Aquila and Prisca consistently appears but never an expression like "the house of Aquila and Prisca." Especially in 2 Tim 4:19, such an expression could have easily been used. It is the passage where, next to Aquila and Prisca, greetings are conveyed to the *house* of Onesiphorus. In summary, one cannot be speaking about "domestic servants" of the couple. Paul remains the only verifiable employee of Aquila's workshop. That means that we have no evidence for a middle-sized industry employing up to a dozen slaves.[31]

e. One cannot evaluate the fact that Aquila and Prisca returned to Rome from Ephesus. By no means must economic ties have determined their return (cf. the hypothesis quoted above that Aquila's workshop in Rome could have been managed by one of his slaves during his absence). Just as conceivable are human ties or "strategic missionary" purposes ("vanguard" for Paul) — or simply an economically unprofitable enterprise in Ephesus that necessitated the couple changing their venue.

f. Aquila's verifiable trips (Pontus — Rome — Corinth — Ephesus — Rome) do not yield much information. On the one hand, travel expenses were lamented (Apuleius, *Met.* 11.28.1), to such an extent that once a friend even had to subsidize the cost of a trip (cf. Pliny, *Ep.* 3.21).

---

28. Cf. only as an example also τὰ κατὰ τὸν οἶκον = the domestic work of a woman (*1 Clem.* 1:3) or ἐν οἴκῳ = at home (Strabo, 1.3.2); further see below, chap. 22.

29. "Der Begriff des Hauses," 91–100.

30. *Studien zur Soziologie,* 246–50.

31. In regard to typology (businesses without slaves, small businesses with a few slaves and freedmen as employees, middle-sized businesses with about a dozen slave laborers), see I. Hahn, "Freie Arbeit und Sklavenarbeit," 141. For an example of a small to middle-sized business, see Apuleius, *Met.* 9.26–31: a freeborn miller owns his own mill with a number of slaves and a few beasts of burden; he even reveals a tinge of legal education (27.4f.).

Nevertheless, on the other hand, also an orphaned minor can work his way from Miletus to Olympia (Apuleius, *Met.* 2.21.2). The less wealthy traveled distances over land by foot (e.g., ibid., 1.17.6). How much were the traveling expenses of our couple? *CIL* 9:2689 charges the sum of 13 1/3 *asses* to the account of a farmer who was transporting products to the city market with his mule and who stayed overnight in a city pension. This included: wine (1 sicilicus = 1/3 as), bread (1 as), something to eat with the bread (2 asses), fodder for the mule (2 asses) and a girl (8 asses!). For Aquila and Prisca together, one can subtract the cost of the girl, and they would spend not quite 11 asses for each night's lodging. That is close to 3 sestertii.[32]

For verification: In the first century C.E. flour for a pound of bread costs a little over 2 asses = 0.5 sestertius (Pliny, *Nat. hist.* 18.89); the loaf of bread for a slave in Pompeii who lives off of it for about one and a half days costs 2 asses (the graffiti of Pompeii in Duncan-Jones, *Economy,* 244).

The price of wheat *pro modius* (= ca. 8.74 liters = 1/3 amphora = 16 sextarii) amounts to 30 asses (7.5 sestertii) in Pompey (*CIL* 4:4811). Another graffito of Pompeii (in Duncan-Jones, ibid., 146) has the amount of 3 sestertii. The normal price in Italy of the first century C.E. amounted to hardly more than 4 sestertii (ibid., 345).

The wine price in Pompeii (*CIL* 4:1679) amounts to 1 *as* for a measure (= one sextarius = a little more than a half a liter) of ordinary wine, 2 asses for a measure of good wine, 4 asses (= 1 sestertius) for a measure of Falerian wine (from "Ager Falernus" in the Campania region). A bar in Herculaneum charges similarly for different types of wines, 2, 3, 4, and 4.5 asses pro sextarius (wall drawing first published in Duncan-Jones, *Economy,* 46, n. 3). The author Columella (3.3.8) mentions 1.25 as for a measure of wine. Martial (12.76) has a sum similar to the above inscription concerning the farmer's overnight lodging, 0.4 as for a measure of wine (20 asses for an amphora). Wine prices for a measure thus range between 0.4 and 4.5 asses.

According to these figures, it would cost Aquila and Prisca between 4.8 and 13 asses a day for two loaves of bread (= 4 asses) and two measures of wine. That amounts to 1.2 to 3.25 sestertii.

The author Petronius's (45; 71) per-person price of 8 sestertii for a festive dinner marks the outer limit for the daily expenditure of our couple. A half-century later the price for a festive meal would be between 8 and 20 sestertii (Martial, 12.26; 9.100; 2.57; 4.68).

---

32. Since the second century B.C.E., 1 as = 1/16 denarius = 1/4 sestertius. Cf., for example, H. Chantraine, "Kleingeldrechnung," *Kleine Pauly* 3:231f.; "Denarius," ibid., 1:1488; "As," ibid., 1:633; "Sestertius," ibid., 5:148.

The price for a ship passage in the first century should not be estimated too high. Aquila's contemporary, Seneca (*De ben.* 6.15.6–16.1), writes, "certo tamen et *levi pretio* fultura conducitur."

Transport fares by sea are available in Diocletian's price edict. However, after the inflation, the price level now lies considerably higher than in the first century (for wheat 25 to 50 times higher!). Transport of goods between Africa and Gaul now costs 16 sestertii per *castrensis modius* (= ca. 13 liters), between Alexandria and Rome, 64 sestertii (cf. Duncan-Jones, *Economy* 367f.).

On the whole, Aquila and Prisca would have paid for all four trips mentioned above a total sum of far less than 1,000 sestertii, that is, on the average, less than 250 sestertii for each trip. This fits well when we remember that 500 drachmae (= 1,500 sestertii; possibly also 2,000 sestertii)[33] already lie beyond the budget of the individual small linen weaver in Tarsus. The four trips of the couple give no basis to place the tentmaker Aquila higher on the social-historical scale than we have done above. The "great entrepreneur," as which he often was presented, he was not.

For those to whom 1000 sestertii appears to be too small a sum, they may be satisfied with a sum bordering on the highest limit for the cost of Aquila's travels. The city of Byzantium paid the yearly salary of an ambassador who traveled from Byzantium to Rome and back in order to make a formal visit in the name of the city to the emperor in Rome. The ambassador received for travel expenses, food and board in Rome, including his commission, the sum of 12,000 sestertii, which Pliny estimated as extravagantly high (*Ep.* 10.43).

Were Aquila an overpaid diplomat, Byzantium would have paid him a sum of about 18,000 sesterii for his trip between Pontus–Rome–Corinth / Ephesus–Rome. An attorney earns this amount with two or three cases (Pliny, *Ep.* 5.9; 5.4). For this amount he can buy a piece of land 200 meters by 225 meters.[34] Once again, the sum of 18,000 would have been a dream amount on the outer limits of expenses for Aquila's travels. The Christian entrepreneur Marcion dealt with ten times that amount when he donated 200,000 sestertii to the Roman Christians (see below, chap. 24).

---

33. Most of the time, one drachma was 3/4 denarius = 3 sestertii; also 1 attic drachma = 1 of Nero's denarii = 16 asses = 4 sestertii; also occasionally: 1 denarius = 18 asses. Cf. H. Chantraine, "Drachme," *Kleine Pauly* 2:156; "Uncia," ibid., 5:1052; "Assarion," ibid., 1:652.

34. According to Th. Mommsen's calculations, 2,500 square meters of land costs on the average 1,000 sestertii during the time of Pliny ("Bodentheilung," 393–416). Cf. R. Martin, *Plinius, d.J.* 203; Duncan-Jones, *Economy*, 48–52.

Chapter 19

Pomponia Graecina

In the highest social circles, the first possibility to discover Roman Christians is the case of Pomponia Graecina. It is a very uncertain possibility. Pomponia Graecina, the daughter of the *consul suffectus* of the year 16 C.E., P. P. Graecinus, was married to the consul Aulus Plautius, who held the office of *consul suffectus* in the year 29 C.E. and led Claudius's British expedition in the year 43 C.E.

Tacitus (*Ann.* 13.32) reports: "The legal proceedings against Pomponia Graecina, a noblewoman, who was married to Plautius — he had, as reported,[1] celebrated a small triumph over the Britons — and who was charged with practicing a foreign religion ("superstitionis externae rea") were transferred to her husband as the appropriate judge in this matter. And, according to the old custom in the presence of the family relatives, he passed judgment on the conduct and the reputation of his wife and declared her innocent." Pomponia Graecina was accused of "superstitio externa," which was considered conjugal misconduct. The charge therefore was transferred to the husband's tribunal. The family tribunal found her not guilty. The proceedings took place in the year 57 C.E., according to the context of the *Annals*. Tacitus immediately continues: "The life of this Pomponia was accompanied by long and continuous suffering. Because, since Iulia, the daughter of Drusus lost her life through the malice of Messalina (ca. 43 C.E.), she spent forty years in mourning clothes and sorrow (i.e., till ca. 83 C.E.) ("per quadraginta annos non cultu nisi lugubri, non animo nisi maesto egit"). She was not reproached for this demeanor during the reign of Claudius. Later it redounded to her honor." Why she mourned for Iulia[2] for such a long time is not mentioned.

It has been suspected for a long time that Pomponia's "superstitio externa" might have been the Christian faith.[3] Is there anything that points in this direction?

---

1. In the lost sections of *Ann.* 11; cf. Tacitus, *Agricola* 14; Cassius Dio, 60.19–21 and 30; Suetonius, *Claudius* 24.3.

2. Cf. *Ann.* 6.27; 3.29; Cassius Dio, 58.3.9; 60.18.4; Suetonius, *Claudius* 29.1.

3. For example, W. Sontheimer, *Tacitus*, 266, n. 97; further, G. B. De Rossi, *Roma*, 1:319; 2:64; Friedländer, *Sittengeschichte Roms*, 1:490f.; 3:534; A. Harnack, "Christianity and Christians," 262ff.; A. St. Barnes, *Christianity at Rome*, 129–31. A. Hasenclever

In Tacitus, *Ann.* 15.44, Christianity is actually classified as a "superstitio." This is likewise seen, for example, in Suetonius, *Nero* 16 and Pliny, *Ep.* 10.96.8. Moreover, the suggestion has been made to interpret the 40 years (!) in "mourning clothes" and "sorrow" not as the result of Iulia's death but as a characteristic of this "superstitio externa." Actually, the praxis of the Christian faith would appear to outsiders as mourning. When someone as a Christian no longer partakes in the amusements and invitations of upper society (cf., for example, Minucius Felix, *Oct.* 8: Christians are a "latebrosa et lucifugax natio" (a people with a secluded life, afraid of the light), this behavior resembles mourning. The gossip of "society" explains Pomponia's behavior by the death of Iulia. But could it last 40 years? Iulia was not even her sister.[4]

If the "mourning for Iulia" and the "superstitio externa" are to be related to each other, that means that, all her life, Pomponia understood how to hide the "superstitio" from the aristocratic milieu in which she lived, concealing it under the label of "mourning for Iulia."[5] If neither a mystery religion nor Judaism was hidden beneath the "superstitio," the result would be that, in the first century, a member of the highest social circle of Rome kept strictly secret from her peers her Christian faith.

["Christliche Proselyten," 34–78, 230–71], in his extensive study, wishes first to assign her to Judaism, from which she allegedly converted to Christianity. M. Stern [*Authors*, 2:383] refers to a relative of Pomponia Graecina who was married to the "legatus pro praetore" in Syria (Publius Petronius, 39–42 c.e.) and therefore could have been sympathetic to Judaism.

4. Whenever unusual mourning is mentioned, then it is for such family members as a husband or a son: Tacitus, *Ann.* 16.10 (but not 40 years, only 4); Seneca, *Dial.* 6.2 ("only" 12 years!).

5. Even the family tribunal of her husband in 57 c.e. — 14 years after the death of Iulia — evidently believed her label, since it declared her innocent of the charge.

Chapter 20

T. Flavius Clemens
and Flavia Domitilla

T. Flavius Clemens,[1] consul of the year 95, and a senatorial woman, Flavia Domitilla, both close relations of the emperor Domitian, were condemned[2] in the year 96 C.E. The consul was executed; Flavia Domitilla was exiled to an island. The sources name different reasons for the condemnation: "Godlessness, because of which also many others, who deviated to the practices of the Jews, had been condemned" (Cassius Dio), Christian faith (Bruttius/Eusebius), and groundless suspicions of Domitian (Suetonius).

a. Cassius Dio 67.14.1f.: Κἀν τῷ αὐτῷ ἔτει ἄλλους τε πολλοὺς καὶ τὸν Φλάουιον (τὸν) Κλήμεντα ὑπατεύοντα, καίπερ ἀνεψιὸν ὄντα καὶ γυναῖκα καὶ αὐτὴν συγγενῆ ἑαυτοῦ Φλαουίαν Δομιτίλλαν ἔχοντα, κατέσφαξεν ὁ Δομιτιανός. (2) ἐπηνέχθη δὲ ἀμφοῖν ἔγκλημα ἀθεότητος, ὑφ' ἧς καὶ ἄλλοι ἐς τὰ τῶν Ἰουδαίων ἤθη ἐξοκέλλοντες πολλοὶ κατεδικάσθησαν, καὶ οἱ μὲν ἀπέθανον, οἱ δὲ τῶν γοῦν οὐσίων ἐστερήθησαν· ἡ δὲ Δομιτίλλα ὑπερωρίσθη μόνον ἐς Πανδατερίαν: "In the same year Domitian executed among many others, also consul Flavius Clemens, although he was a cousin and his wife was Flavia Domitilla, a relative of Domitian. Both were accused of godlessness, a crime on account of which also many others, who were inclined to Jewish practices, were condemned. Some lost their lives, others at least their fortunes. Domitilla was only exiled to Pandateria."

b. Suetonius, *Domit.* 15.1: "Flavium Clementem, patruelem suum, contemptissimae inertiae... repente ex tenuissima suspicione tantum non in ipso eius consulatu interemit": (Domitian) unexpectedly killed his own cousin Flavius Clemens, (a man) of most contemptible laziness, on a very feeble suspicion, shortly after the end of his consulship." For Suetonius, the baseness of Domitian's action expresses itself in different

---

1. Cf. Tacitus, *Hist.* 3.69.3; Cassius Dio, 65.17.2; Suetonius, *Domitian* 15.1; *CIL* 6:8942; Eutropius, 7.23.3.

2. Cassius Dio, 67.14.1f.; Suetonius, *Domitian* 15.1; Eusebius, *Chron. Dom.* 16; *Ecc. Hist.* 3.18.4; cf. Philostratus, *Vita Apoll.* 8.25. Literature in, e.g., W. Eck, *Eindringen*, 392, n. 59; E. M. Smallwood, *The Jews*, 378ff.; M. Stern, *Authors*, 2:381f.; P. Keresztes, "The Jews," 7ff.

ways: Domitian liquidates a close relative; the latter just finished a term as consul; the punishment comes out of the blue sky ("repente"); the suspicion was unfounded, because Clemens was so lazy ("inertia") that he could hardly be a political threat for Domitian. Nothing is said of the fate of Flavia Domitilla.

c. Eusebius, *Ecc. Hist.* 3.18.4, offers a third version: In the year 96 "Flavia Domitilla, a daughter of the sister of Flavius Clemens, a Roman consul at that time, was exiled to the island of Pontia because of her Christian faith. Many others were exiled too in that year." (ἐν ἔτει πεντεκαιδεκάτῳ Δομετιανοῦ μετὰ πλείστων ἑτέρων καὶ Φλαυίαν Δομέτιλλαν ἱστορήσαντες, ἐξ ἀδελφῆς γεγονυῖαν Φλαυίου Κλήμεντος, ἑνὸς τῶν τηνικάδε ἐπὶ Ῥώμης ὑπάτων, τῆς εἰς Χριστὸν μαρτυρίας ἕνεκεν εἰς νῆσον Ποντίαν κατὰ τιμωρίαν δεδόσθαι).

The passage differs on three points from Cassius Dio's text. Nothing is said about the execution of the consul and his religious confession. Flavia Domitilla is not his wife but the niece of the consul. She is not exiled to Pandateria but to Pontia.

Eusebius expressly emphasizes that he has taken his information from sources: from pagan historiographers (οἱ ἄποθεν τοῦ καθ᾽ ἡμᾶς λόγου συγγραφεῖς). With this comment he cannot have meant Dio, who contradicts him. It is more likely that Eusebius is referring to a no longer extant work of the Roman author Bruttius who wrote in the second or third century. In the *Chronicle* (*Chron. Domitian* 16, ed. R. Helm, 192), Eusebius writes how Bruttius reports that Flavia Domitilla, the niece of consul Flavius Clemens, was exiled to the island of Pontia because of her Christian belief. ("Scribit Bruttius plurimos Christianorum sub Domitiano fecisse martyrium. Inter quos et Flaviam Domitillam, Flavii Clementis consulis ex sorore neptem, in insulam Pontiam relegatam, quia se Christianam esse testata sit.")

We have to consider Bruttius's testimony (second or third century) as of equal value next to that of Dio and Suetonius. Because Eusebius, both in his *Ecclesiastical History* as well as in his *Chronicle,* renders the circumstances almost identically verbatim, we must conclude that in each case he is accurately reporting from Bruttius.

That all three sources are literarily independent of each other is obvious. On which points are the three witnesses in agreement?

- Because of her religious belief, one (or two) Flavia Domitilla(s) have provoked suspicion and therefore is or are condemned (Dio, Bruttius; Suetonius does not contradict them, because he does not say anything about Flavia Domitilla).

- The consul Flavius Clemens is not a Christian believer (Bruttius, Cassius Dio, Suetonius).

We cannot deny the second point; it is closest to the source. At least Suetonius, our oldest witness, and Bruttius know nothing about the Christianity of the consul. This silence is especially eloquent in Bruttius's case. Bruttius mentions the Christianity of the close relative Domitilla as the reason for the condemnation: It is improbable that he would not have also brought this reason into play and named it with Flavius Clemens, whom he mentions by name, if this reason had actually existed. Why Bruttius should have been silent about the Christianity of one and mentioned it with the other would be inexplicable. For his part, Eusebius would have loved to take up a report of the Christianity of the consul if it had been mentioned by Bruttius.[3] The Christian faith of the consul was first asserted by Syncellus in the ninth century (ed. Dindorf, 1:650). Syncellus repeats the information from Eusebius's *Chronicle* and adds: Κλήμης ὑπὲρ Χριστοῦ ἀναιρεῖται.

With Flavia Domitilla we must solve the contradictions between Dio and Bruttius. There are two possible way of doing this.

1. We are dealing with two persons named Domitilla. One of them, the wife of a consul, was sympathetic towards Judaism. The other was a Christian, the niece of the same consul and belonged as senatorial lady to the Flavian house as well. Both women were exiled to two different islands, Pandateria and Pontia, which lie off the Neapolitan coast.

2. We are dealing with the same woman. One of the two authors, Dio or Bruttius, has confused the name of the island, which is understandable in view of the geographical proximity of both islands and the alliteration of their names.[4] Beyond this, Bruttius appears to have confused Domitilla's relationship to consul Clemens with her relationship to Domitian. She was not the niece of the consul, but his wife; she probably was, however, the niece of Domitian. These two contradictions would be easy to solve. There remains the third. What was Domitilla's religion? Is it more probable that she was Christian or that she was sympathetic towards Judaism?

First, we must clarify what is behind the accusation of "godlessness" (ἀθεότης) in Dio. The accusation of atheism rests apparently upon the fact that Domitilla, as a Christian or a Jewish sympathizer, did not participate actively in the cult of the emperor and therefore, brought suspicion upon herself as unloyal. Under Domitian, many were condemned because of lèse-majesté (Seutonius, *Dom.* 11f.). "Every action

---

3. In the immediately preceding context, Bruttius most likely reported the condemnation of the pagan consul Clemens. This is apparent from the following observation: Bruttius introduces Flavia Domitilla into his story by presenting her to the reader as a relative *of this consul*, not as a relative of Domitian.

4. The usual place of banishment was Pandateria: Suetonius, *Tib. 53;* Cassius Dio, 55.10; Tacitus, *Ann.* 14.63; 1.53. That means that the "lectio difficilior" speaks in favor of Eusebius's and Bruttius's version.

or speech against the majesty" endangered your life. "Pietas" was defined essentially as loyalty and love of *Caesar.* "Impietas" was seen as lèse-majesté, as "impietas in principem" (the last two words could be omitted; during the reign of Domitian they are self-explanatory; for example, Pliny, *Ep.* 7.33.7; 1.5.5f., 13; cf. further Pliny the Younger, *Paneg.* 33.3f.). All this points to interpreting ἀθεότης in Dio as the refusal to worship Domitian as god. Also the immediate context (67.13) speaks in favor of this interpretation: The agitator Celsus saved his skin by greeting Domitian as θεός, "as it already was done by the others." A refusal of the cult of the emperor is conceivable for a Christian woman or a Jewish sympathizer. Which solution can be suggested in the present case?

For a number of reasons, I believe it is more probable that Dio found information identifying Flavia Domitilla as a "Christian" and changed this to a woman "inclined towards Jewish practices." This is more likely than that Bruttius, who also was a non-Christian author (Eusebius, *Ecc. Hist.* 3.18.4), changed "sympathizers with Judaism" to "Christian."

The reasons are as follows: First, Dio continuously avoids mentioning the Christians,[5] although he might know of their existence. Second, to designate Christians as Jews is possible into the time of Dio, even though the pagans, at least since the persecution by Nero, know to distinguish Christianity as an independent entity from Judaism. Not only Suetonius in *Claudius* 25 ("edict of Claudius") and Lucian[6] but also Christian texts show that pagans often did not hesitate to categorize Christians as "Jewish" (for example, Acts 16:20f.; the *Acts of Peter* chap. 22, from the second half of the second century; still even in *Ps. Clem.* H 4.7.2). The formulation of the last text represents a parallel to the "Jewish customs" of Cassius Dio. A pagan reproaches the hero of the novel that "he thinks and acts according to *Jewish* customs" since his conversion to Christianity!

A third finding also possesses some weight as evidence: If Domitilla, accused of ἀθεότης (godlessness) was a *Christian,* we will be able to find parallel cases. If she sympathized with Judaism, no such parallels would occur.

Parallels:

a. Domitilla as *a Christian* would correspond to Christians of Asia Minor in the Apocalypse of John who, at the same time, near the end

---

5. In *72.9.3ff.* (Loeb edition) the Byzantine Xiphilin formulates the passage himself (cf., for example, Eusebius, *Ecc. Hist.* 5.5) Also in 70.3.1ff., Dio is not speaking. The section presupposes, among others, Eusebius, *Ecc. Hist.* 4.9. The text 73.4.7 is dependent upon Hippolytus *Ref.* 9.12 (compare, for example, εὐηργετηκέναι with Hippolytus's wording, Μαρκία ἄργον τι ἀγαθὸν ἐργάσασθαι).

6. *Peregr.* 11; see H. D. Betz, *Lucian* 8.

of the reign of Domitian, refuse to acknowledge Domitian's divinity and are prepared to suffer persecution for this.[7]

b. Christians were repeated, accused of atheism, particularly Roman Christians. Justin's *Apology* gives abundant evidence that Roman Christians were charged with "godlessness": "ἄθεοι κεκλήμεθα, we are called godless." Actually, "we concede, in regard to these types of false gods, that we are deniers of the gods" (1.6.1; ibid., 1.5.4; also 1.13; 1.46.3: ἄθεοι). Christians are accused of ἀσέβεια (1.4.7; cf. also *Apol.* 2.10.4 ἀσεβεῖς) and τὰ ἄθεα δοξάζειν (1.5.1). *Apol.* 1.5.3: As the Athenians condemned Socrates as ἄθενον and ἀσεβῆ, "in the same way they (the pagans) proceed against us," the Christians in Rome (cf. also 2.10.5). In Rome the cynic Creszens reviles the Christians as ἄθεοι and ἀσεβεῖς (2.3[8].2). A few years later, what Justin wrote in his *Apology* was confirmed in the proceedings against him. In the authentic (see below) *Acts of Justin*, chap. 4, the codefendant Liberianus is asked by the prefect: Χριστιανὸς εἶ; οὐδὲ οὐ εὐσεβεῖς? As a Christian, he is accused of lacking the fear of God because he refuses to offer sacrifices to the gods: chaps. 5 and 1! According to the *Acts of Peter* (*Act. Verc.* c. 36; *Aa* 1, p. 90), already Peter was crucified in Rome "because of godlessness." The accusation is encountered continuously: Tatian, *Or.* 27.3; Minucius Felix, *Oct.* 8.1–4; *Martyr. Polyc.* 9 (because Polycarp did not swear by the fate of the emperor; cf. Eusebius, *Ecc. Hist.* 4.15.6,26); Athenagoras, *Suppl.* 3; 4; cf. 30; Tertullian, *Apol.* 10f. (together with the charge of lèse-majesté); Celsus in Origen, *Contra Cel.* 7.62; cf. 25; also Porphyry begins his work against the Christians with this reproach (in regard to Celsus and Porphyry see Eusebius, *Praep. ev.* 1.2.1ff.); Lucian, *Alex.* 25 and 38. Also Roman Christians were accused of superstition (Tacitus, *Ann.* 15.44; Suetonius, *Claud.* 25.3; *Nero* 16.2; cf. Pliny, *Ep.* 10.96.8): *superstitio* can be defined as *asebeia* (Plutarch, *De superstitione* 169–170a; 168ab; 171b–f). The δυσσέβεια of those "in Palestine" (Aelius Aristides, *Or. XLVI De Quattuorviris* 309) can refer to Jews as well as Christians.

c. Such parallel material cannot be found for those sympathizing with Judaism. It is attested that Jews were accused of atheism.[8] By contrast, there is no known case in which the charge of atheism had been leveled against a *Godfearer* because of his inclination to "Jewish customs." Tacitus, *Hist.* 5.5.2, points out only the already circumcised proselytes, who are taught to show disrespect for the gods. At best, a very distant parallel in Juvenal, 14.96ff., would come into question: uncircumcised sympathizers "pray to nothing but the clouds alone and the divinity ('numen') of the heaven."

---

7. Cf. in regard to Revelation and its situation, e.g., P. Lampe, *Apokalyptiker*, 94ff.
8. The references in E. M. Smallwood, *The Jews*, 379, n. 82.

All three reasons attest that Dio changed the Christianity of Domitilla to an "inclination to Jewish customs" and not that Bruttius might have changed Domitilla's sympathy towards Judaism into "Christianam esse."

However we decide on the next step — two different Flavia Domitillas (1) or one and the same (2) — we can in each case discover a Christian woman of senatorial rank from the Flavian house at the end of the first century. If we decide in favor of the second solution, we must once again turn back to the consul Clemens. According to Dio, "atheism" and "Jewish customs," which in the second solution both have the same meaning as "Christianity," also were charged against the consul. He, however, can not have been a Christian, because of the constellation of three sources, as we saw. In view of Dio's text that means: Dio's redaction attached the reason for condemnation, namely ἀθεότης / "Jewish customs," which he found in his sources in relation to the consul's wife, Domitilla, to her husband as well. How could he so easily do this? "Impietas in principem"[9] had actually been the historical reason for the condemnation not only of Domitilla but also of Clemens, as well as of many other pagan contemporaries, who for their alleged disloyalty to the ruler had neither a Jewish nor a Christian background.[10] Domitian's suspicion against the consul was fed probably by the following facts. Suetonius, who stands chronologically closest to the events, gives an important indication (*Dom.* 15.1): Flavius Clemens was the father of the young boys Vespasian and Domitian, chosen to succeed him ("cuius filios etiam tum parvulos successores palam destinaverat et, abolito priore nomine, alterum Vespasianum appellari iusserat, alterum Domitianum"). This suggest that Domitian did not trust the consul, because he was the father of these designated successors. The father could have worked toward the goal that his sons prematurely obtained power or he himself attained it. This must have been Domitian's "highly flimsy suspicion" (Suetonius).[11]

Conclusion: Two solutions are available, to which, in my opinion, the same degree of probability is due. (1) The Domitilla named in the sources is always the same: she is a Christian, does not participate in the cult of Caesar, and is, therefore, exiled. Her husband, the consul T. Flavius Clemens, is a pagan and is, likewise, suspected by Domitian (apparently in respect to his sons). (2) A Flavia Domitilla, niece of the

---

9. Lèse-majesté; cf. for example, Pliny, *Ep.* 7.33.7; 1.5.5f., 13; in Cassius Dio, 68.1.2 synonymous with ἀσέβεια; in our passage of Dio synonymous with ἀθεότης.

10. For example, Mettius Modestus in Pliny, ibid.; cf. Suetonius, *Dom.* 11f.

11. That the consul and his wife were both charged with "impietas in principem," but each for different motives, is perhaps also apparent from their different punishments: death was appropriate punishment for the possible political usurper but exile for the less dangerous wife.

consul T. Flavius Clemens and close relative of Domitian, is a Christian. She does not participate in the cult of Caesar and is, therefore, exiled to an island. The consul himself and his wife sympathize with Judaism. Therefore, they cannot likewise religiously worship the emperor, and their loyalty is suspected.

Thus, there is a 50 percent chance for the possibility that two members of the Flavian family were inclined toward Judaism. In both cases, however, the consul was not a Christian. And in both cases, a woman of the Flavian family of the senatorial rank named Flavia Domitilla was a Christian.

Under Nerva (96–98 C.E.), our Christian Flavia Domitilla must have returned from a less than one-year exile to the Roman Christians. According to Cassius Dio (68.1.2; cf. Eusebius, *Ecc. Hist.* 3.20.8f.), Nerva issued an amnesty for those who were charged with *asebeia*. Nerva, furthermore, disapproved of charges of "Jewish way of life" and brought back people living in exile, "giving them back their wealth, as Eusebius's pagan sources report."[12]

Only with the greatest uncertainty does it come into question that *M. Acilius Glabrio,* the senator and consul for the year 91, was a Christian. He was executed by Domitian in 95 C.E. (Suetonius, *Dom.* 10; Cassius Dio, 67.14.3; Juvenal, 4.94f.). According to Cassius Dio he was accused as the many others (καὶ οἶα οἱ πολλοί), that is, according to the context, of ἀθεότης and the inclination to "Jewish customs." Suetonius, however, knows only of alleged subversive plans as the charge ("quasi molitor rerum novarum").

G. B. De Rossi (*Bullettino* 1865, 21; *Roma* 1:219) attempted to make the Christianity of the consul probable with the help of the allegedly Christian inscriptions of the Acilii in the so-called burial crypt of the Acilii in the catacomb of Priscilla. The inscriptions attest to persons named Acilius of senatorial rank: "Acilius Glabrio," "Acilius Valerius," "M. Acilius V(erus) c(larissimus) v(ir)," "Priscilla c(larissima femina)" (*CIL* 6:31679–81 and others). In view of these inscriptions the Christianity of Acilius Glabrio, the consul for the year 91, was certain for De Rossi. However, the first certain Christian finds from this catacomb region date from the third and fourth centuries. They are two inscriptions from the end of the third and from the fourth centuries, respectively

---

12. We already observed that the above-mentioned (chap. 3) inscriptions concerning Flavia Domitilla contribute little information about our Christian woman. The name appears in at least three generations of the imperial family (Suetonius, *Vesp.* 3; *Dom.* 17; *CIL* 6:8942; 948). Also the late Acts of Nereus and Achilleus must remain aside. These Acts, which narrate the martyrdom of Domitilla (the consul's niece), originate, at the earliest, from the fifth century when the fantasy of the faithful had already been occupied with the fate of this martyr. At the time of Jerome, tourists to the island of Pontia were shown the cells in which the Christian Domitilla was alleged to have spent her exile (Jerome, *Ep.* 108.7.1).

(in P. Testini, *Le catacombe*, 70f.) One of the two actually concerns an Acilius, an Acilius Rufinus whom the inscription wishes ζήσης ἐν θεῷ (illustration in C. M. Kaufmann, *Handbuch*, 102). Earlier epigraphical evidence of persons named Acilius cannot be taken as Christian. Furthermore, their inscriptions were not found *in situ* but come from either the burial region above the earth or from galleries bordering this subterranean chamber.

Cassius Dio's text remains the only and very weak evidence of a Christian faith of the consul for the year 91. Against his being Christian speaks that he fought as a gladiator (Dio, ibid.)!

Chapter 21

The Author of *First Clement*

First Clement, from the end of the first century, presents itself as a letter from the community written in the first person plural. Its style and language, however, point to one author, who, in second-century tradition, is called "Clement."[1]

Social-Historical Hypotheses regarding the Person of Clement

From a social-historical point of view, the person of the author cannot be more closely defined, and hypotheses that claim otherwise are mistaken.

Often we read the hypothesis, for example, in D. W. F. Wong's "Natural and Divine Order in 1 Clem,"[2] that Clement of Rome was a freedman from the house of the consul Titus Flavius Clemens. It is a well-known fact that the *gentilicium* of the patron, that is, "Flavius," was carried over onto the freed slaves of that household, but not the *cognomen*. The cognomen Clemens does not indicate anything.

There is no basis at all to think of identifying Clement with the above-named consul[3] or to connect Clement with the "Titulus Clementis," the title of Clement.[4] In both cases we have nothing to base this upon but the similarity of the name "Clement." In identifying our author we also

---

1. Dionysius of Corinth in Eusebius, *Ecc. Hist.* 4.23.11; Hegesippus in Eusebius, *Ecc. Hist.* 4.22.1; Irenaeus, *Haer.* 3.3.3; Clement of Alexandria, *Strom.* 1.38.5; 4.105; 4.111.1; 6.65.3. It is tempting to identify him with the Clement in Hermas, *Vis.* 2.4.3, although this clashes somewhat with the probable dating of the book of Hermas (toward the middle of the second century). The Clement in Hermas was a contemporary of Hermas and entrusted with the in- and outgoing mail of the Roman Christians. To understand the book of Hermas as fictitiously predated leads to insurmountable difficulties; see R. Joly, *Hermas le Pasteur,* 14. We are dealing either with two different men named Clement or with the same person who at the time of Hermas was an old man.

2. VC 31 (1977): 81–87.

3. This was often done in the older research, e.g., by A. Hasenclever, "Christliche Proselyten," 251ff.

4. In the older research see, for example, the article by de Waal in Kraus's *Real-Encyklopädie der christlichen Alterthümer* (Freiburg/B., 1882–86), 301.

must exclude the fictional "Clement" from the Pseudo-Clementines, who was not created before the third century.

M. S. Lösch[5] wished to discover an imperial chancery style in the entire letter and concluded that the author had once been one of the correspondence secretaries ("ab epistulis") of the imperial chancery. What Lösch, however, indicates to be "chancery style" is supported by much too small a text-base.[6] In addition, Sanders demonstrates with his extensive Hellenistic parallel material that a "chancery style" is not to be diagnosed in *First Clement* with certainty. The numerous nonofficial language parallels to Clement's alleged "official style" show that the spirit of the imperial office did not especially inspire Clement. What can actually be attested as chancery style[7] does not allow us to draw any sociological conclusions concerning the author. It remains on the level of general knowledge.

From *1 Clem.* 37:2f. ("observe the soldiers who serve our commanders, how ordered,...not all are chief officers, commanders of thousands, or commanders of hundreds, or commanders of fifty...") one can at least conclude that Clement was not a soldier. Clement had no idea of the organization of the Roman army or its ranks of command. In the Roman army, there is no πεντηκόνταρχος (*1 Clem.* 37:3). However, one finds the term in Exod 18:21, 25 and Deut 1:15.[8]

The Education of Clement

It remains for us to pay attention to the elements of education, particularly to the Stoic elements in *1 Clement*. What is the author's level of education? Had he enjoyed a pagan higher education?

L. Sanders places Clement close to the "diatribe stoïcienne; pratiquée dans la ville éternelle au siècle de Clément par des maîtres de morale, tels Epictète, Dion Chrysostome, Sénèque..." (159). "La rédaction personnelle de Clément révèle sa connaissance approfondie de l'hellénisme. Loin d'emprunter à la Bible grecque la matière ou le style de ses

---

5. *Epistula Claudiana* (Rottenburg, 1930), 42ff.; 38f., for example. See also M. S. Lösch, "Der Brief des Clemens Romanus," *Festschrift for P. Ubaldi*, Pubblicazioni della Università cattolica del Sacro Cuore, Series 5/16 (Milan, 1937), 177ff.

6. Claudius's letter to the Alexandrians. Cf. for the refutation of Lösch's thesis L. Sanders, *L'hellénisme*, 139, n. 1.

7. For the individual passage *1 Clem.* 5:5–7 see R. Knopf, *Der erste Clemensbrief*, 53: the long series of praising participles is comparable to the encomium in Hellenistic decrees of honor, for example, *OGIS* 2:529. In *1 Clem.* 44:3, Knopf (p. 119) calls attention to the official style that was cultivated at the installation and honoring of Hellenistic officials. Speculation on the author of Luke's Gospel offers a good comparison. A few juridical and medical expressions do not establish Luke as a doctor or a jurist.

8. There one also finds the other "ranks" enumerated by Clement. Further see 1 Sam 8:12; 2 Kgs 1:9–14; Isa 3:3; 1 Macc 3:55; CD 13.1f.; 1 Enoch 69:3; 75:1; 82:11f.

développements originaux, il les trouve dans la rhétorique stoïcienne, plus ou moins assaisonnée de platonisme et de pythagorisme, que pratiquaient *les milieux lettrés* de la Rome du Iᵉʳ siècle... L'épître de Clément témoigne donc de la pénétration du christianisme, dès la fin du Iᵉʳ siècle de l'ère chrétienne, *dans les cercles les plus cultivés de la ville éternelle*" (162). Indeed?

One must first state that the general philosophical education of the first two centuries C.E. was based not upon Stoicism but upon a Platonic-peripatetic combination. Indidividual Stoic teachings found their way into Platonism, but the genuine Stoic teaching with its strict materialism had been relegated to an outside role by the lively interest in the hereafter and in the immortality of the soul. This situation in intellectual history makes it in principle difficult to speak of a special Stoic education for the author of *1 Clement* that might have been only "spiced" with Platonism ("assaisonnée de platonisme").

The Example of 1 Clement *20*

The main example for a Stoic background of Clement was always *1 Clem.* 20. At the same time, the passage allows one to grasp the problem: (a) Have the Stoic motifs reached Clement only indirectly through the tradition of Hellenistic Judaism? Is Clement not directly dependent upon Stoic sources, so that conclusions about his pagan literary schooling are impossible? (b) Beyond this, are the alleged Stoic motifs nothing other than popular commonplaces and therefore give no indication of a literary education?

The principal idea in *1 Clem.* 20 is that the *cosmos,* the ordering of nature, makes moral *imperatives* possible (21:1). The social virtues of ὁμόνοια and εἰρήνη (20:3, 10f.; 21:1), embodied in nature, should be realized in human community life. Nature serves as an ethical model. The same configuration of argument, which is based on the Stoic close connection of physics and ethics, is found also, for example, in Dio Chrysostom, *Or.* 40.35 (also with ὁμόνοια); Cicero, *De nat. deor.* 2.14.37; *De off.* 1.43.153; Euripides, *Phoen.* 541–48; Plato, *Gorg.* 483cff.; cf. 508a; Poseidonios (Clement of Alexandria, *Strom.* 2.21).

For the individual motifs in chap. 20, one can easily cite numerous pagan parallels:

For ὁμόνοια and εἰρήνη (20:3, 10f.; 21:1), compare Epictetus, *Diss.* 4.5.35; Dio Chrysostom, *Or.* 40.35; 36.30f.; Stobaios, *Ecl.* 2.7.11 B and M (*Stoic. vet. fr.* 3 no. 625 and 630); Zeno (*Stoic. vet. fr.* 1 no. 263); cf. Pseudo-Aristotle, *De mundo* 5. For the cosmic τάξις and for the great number of ταγ-stems in Clement, cf. for example, Sextus Empiricus, *Adv. mathem.* 9.111; Pseudo-Aristotle, *De mundo* 6; *Corp. Herm.* 5.3. For the other individual motifs of *1 Clem.* 20 cf., for example,

Sextus Empiricus, *Adv. mathem.* 9.26ff.; Dio Chrysostom, *Or.* 12.28f.
34; 40.35ff.; Pseudo-Aristotle, *De mundo* 1ff.; 5f.; Cicero, *De nat.
deor.* 2 (especially 38.97–53.133); Seneca, for example, *Ad Marciam*
18; *De benef.* 4.25; *Nat. quaest.* 5.13ff.; *Ad Helviam* 8.6; Euripides,
Phoen. 535ff.; Cleanthes in Arius Didymus, *fr.* 29; Cleomedes, *De motu
circ.* 2.1.84–86; Aetius 1.6; *Corp. Herm.* 5.3ff., 9; 12.20B–21; Plato,
Menexenos 238A.

W. C. v. Unnik[9] relativized these parallels, which had been collected mainly by L. Sanders and G. Bardy.[10] Van Unnik referred to
1 Enoch 2–5 and other Jewish, sometimes even Jewish-Palestinian
texts,[11] which praise the cosmic order in the universe and in nature
and likewise draw an ethical conclusion: Nature realizes, in a well disci-
plined manner, God's order, thus it is also possible for man . . . ! If even
Jewish-Palestinian texts resound in this way, how little specifically Stoic,
how very commonplace is then the topos? Also the glorification of the
cosmic beauty in the magical papyri, which can be compared to *1 Clem.*
20, shows that the theme treated in *1 Clem.* 20 is a popularized topos.[12]
In 20:5, Clement moves completely from Stoic cosmology into popular
mythology of Hades, as it was also cultivated in Jewish-Christian tradition.[13] In other words, concerning a "cultivated" "literary" education of
Clement, chap. 20 yields precious little.

Nevertheless, we can attempt another approach. Chapter 20 offers
some linguistic and stylistic high points.[14] The poetic flavor catches
one's eye, particularly the bold pictures of the "pregnant earth" (γῆ κυο-
φοροῦσα, 20:4) and of the "eternally flowing springs" which offer their
"life-giving breasts" (20:10). *First Clement* 20:10 chooses for "breasts"
the poetic expression μαζοί from Homeric language, not the normal prosaic μαστοί. For the "pregnant earth" Plato's *Menexenos* (238A) offers a
parallel (οὐ γὰρ γῆ γυναῖκα μιμεῖται κυήσει . . .). Philo (*De opif. mundi*
131ff.) cites the Plato passage. In the same passage in Philo, one encounters the comparison "springs/breasts," but with the prosaic word
μαστοί. Philo (*De aeternitate mundi* 66) reports that the Stoic opponents

9. "Is 1 Clement 20 Purely Stoic?" 181–89; then, among others, H. Helfritz, "1 Clem.
20,1," 1–7 (emphasizes the LXX concepts).

10. "Expressions stoïciennes dans la Iª Clementis," 73–85.

11. Cf. also 1 Enoch 41:5–8; T. Napht. 3:1–5; As. Mos. 12:9f.; Ps. Sol. 18:12–14;
further, 1QH 1:1–20; Sib. Or. 3.7–43; Philo, De opif. mundi 53ff.; 69ff.; 77; 131–33; De
congr. erud. gr. 51; De spec. leg. 1.32ff.; 1.210; 3.187ff.

12. Th. Schermann, *Griechische Zauberpapyri*, 2.

13. Regarding this, see R. Knopf, *Clemensbrief*, 79. Among other points, the technical
term of the Greek cosmology reads βυθός, not ἄβυσσος (so LXX). In 20:6 there follows
the un-Stoic, half mythical nature-image of the sea, that God has confined in its place with
bars. Cf. Gen 1:9; Job 38:10f.

14. Cf. W. Jaeger, "Echo," esp. 333, 335.

of the peripatetic Critolaus (second century B.C.E.) spoke of the pregnancy of the earth and of the springs of the earth as breasts (μαζός!). All in all, we have before us an old Stoic topos[15] which, however, as the passages from Philo testify, could have moved through Hellenistic Jewish tradition to Clement.[16]

The situation remains puzzling; the basis is too small to gain information concerning a pagan literary education of Clement. Certainly the motif of the "worlds on the other side of the ocean" (20:8) is pagan-Hellenistic[17] and without parallel in the Jewish tradition. Certainly the motif of the animals as moral models (20:10) is a "locus communis" in Platonism (Plutarch, Porphyry) and in the Cynic-Stoic philosophy.[18] It is without parallel in 1 Enoch 2–5. But there is actually nowhere in *1 Clem.* a quotation or at least a literary dependency. There are only content parallels and common motifs. The channels by which these motifs arrived in *1 Clem.* (these channels would be relevant from the point of view of social history) remain unknown.

The Remaining Material Referring to Education in 1 Clement

This problem, illustrated by the example of *1 Clem.* 20, may be traced through the rest of the material in *1 Clem.* The pagan philosophical topoi *could* have reached Clement (and here lies the ambivalence) (a) through Jewish-Hellenistic tradition or (b) through early Christian tradition, in which cases no conclusions can possibly be drawn concerning Clement's pagan literary and philosophical education. A further possibility is (c) that we are dealing with popular and commonplace topoi, which likewise do not testify to a pagan literary education.

I will list briefly the most important material, because it is hardly anywhere in the literature accessible in a concise overview.

a. *Topoi encountered in both pagan philosophical tradition and in Jewish-Hellenistic tradition.* On the basis of the example of εἰρήνη βαθεῖα (*1 Clem.* 2:2), W. C. v. Unnik and K. Beyschlag have presented the problem in a learned dispute. Van Unnik[19] saw in the motif

---

15. W. Jaeger ("Echo," 339f.) goes a step further and suspects that a lost poetic verse of tragedy lies at the basis of this topos.

16. Of another opinion is W. Jaeger ("Echo," 334f.) who thinks that one can conclude a Stoic literary source behind chap. 20.

17. Cf. Poseidonius's writing about the ocean; Cicero, *De rep.* 6.20 (21); Eratosthenes in Strabo 1.4.6 and other places. Clement's note corresponds to the contemporary taste for exotic and ethnological themes in literature. Cf. also Acts 8:27 and E. Plümacher, *Lukas,* 13 (literature in n. 35).

18. Seneca, *De ira* 2.8; Dio Chrysostom, *Or.* 40.32ff. Further references in J. J. Thierry, "Note," 235–44.

19. W. C. v. Unnik's argument can be found in the two articles, " 'Tiefer Friede' (1.Klemens 2,2)," *VC* 24 (1970): 261–79 and "Noch einmal 'Tiefer Friede,' " *VC* 26 (1972): 24–28.

of "deep peace" an established expression (pagan references beginning with Dionysius of Halicarnassus), which Clement directly took over from secular Greek political thought. Beyschlag,[20] on the other hand, saw the motif transmitted through Hellenistic Judaism. Clement has drawn it from Jewish-Christian tradition. This learned fight concerning "peace" illustrates that every attempt to show Clement's direct dependence upon pagan educational sources is untenable. The elements of education *could* indeed be "secondhand" from Jewish-Christian tradition. Beyschlag's book *Clemens Romanus und der Frühkatholizismus* conclusively demonstrates this.

First Clement 5–7 portrays the Christian martyrs Peter and Paul analogously to the philosophical presentation of the virtuous athletes (ἀθλητής, ἀθλεῖν) as the Cynic-Stoic diatribe celebrates them in the form of the virtuous heroes Heracles and Diogenes. (For example: Dio Chrysostom, *Or.* 8.26–30; Epictetus, *Diss.* 4.10.10; Apuleius, *Florida* 22; Cornutus, *Theol. gr.* 31). *First Clement* 5ff. presents the motif of the moral *agon* or athletic contest, as, for example, Seneca, *Ep.* 13.2f.; *De prov.* 2.3f.; Dio Chrysostom, *Or.* 8.11–15; Epictetus, *Diss.* 3.22.58–60; Stobaios, *Ecl.* 3.4.111. According to *1 Clem.* 5:7, Paul taught the world the δικαιοσύνη — as Heracles (Epictetus, *Diss.* 3.26.31f.; 2.16.44).The Christian martyr overcomes many kinds of πόνοι (*1 Clem.* 5:4) as Heracles (Epictetus, *Diss.* 3.26.31; Dio Chrysostom, *Or.* 8.27) and Diogenes (for example, Dio Chrysostom, *Or.* 8.11–13). He endures imprisonment and exile (φυγαδευθείς, *1 Clem.* 5:6) as the virtuous heroes of the diatribe (for example, Dio Chrysostom, *Or.* 8.16; Epictetus, *Diss.* 1.11.33; 2.1.10; 19.18; 3.24.113), etc.[21]

We are standing on the ground of the popular philosophical diatribe. But did Clement pick up the motifs directly from there? The topos of the moral battle is found also in the Jewish tradition.[22] Beyschlag (*Clemens Romanus,* 314; 330ff.) demonstrates the *possibility* that behind *1 Clem.* 5f. stands an older writing, rooted in the tradition of the Jewish apologetic, concerning the Roman martyrs during the time of Nero's persecution. "The Letter of Clement is not a fabricated literary work of a stoicized Paulinist who simply speaks in the idiom of his intellectual milieu. On the contrary, he has behind him the entire previous tradition of Jewish-Christian apologetic which had long ago assimilated Hellenism" (334). Thus Clement did not take over the model of Heracles directly from pagan popular philosophy (287). Who had been educated in popular philosophy and assimilated Hellenism? Apparently,

20. "Zur ΕΙΡΗΝΗ ΒΑΘΕΙΑ (*1 Clem.* 2:2)," VC 26 (1972): 18–23.

21. See further L. Sanders, *L'hellénisme,* 8ff.

22. For example, 4 Ezra 7:91f., 127f.; Syr Baruch 15:8; T. Job 4; 4 Macc 6 and 17, cf. also 9:23; 16:16; Wis. Sol. 8:7 (πόνοι motif); Philo, *De agric.* 119; *De congr. erud. gr.* 162; *De migr. Abr.* 200; *Quod omnis probus liber* 88.

Jews and those sympathetic to Judaism who allowed their Hellenistic knowledge to enter into the tradition of the synagogue community, so that from there Jewish Christians and "Godfearers" (σεβόμενοι τὸν θεόν) could carry over the Hellenistic motifs into Christianity. That means there remains no room to conclude anything about the pagan course of education of Roman Christians.

For *1 Clem.* 6:4 ("Jealousy and envy destroy great cities and uproot great nations"), one finds parallels in Horace, *Carm.* 1.16.17–21; Plutarch, *Moral.* 825AD; Catullus, *Carm.* 51; Euripides, *Phoen.* 533. For W. Jaeger[23] it was certain that Clement had taken over directly the topos from the rhetorical schools. In Jewish tradition, however, the topos can also be found, namely, in Sir 28:14.

ζῆλος, ἔρις, φθόνος (*1 Clem.* 3–6) are often found together in Hellenistic literature (cf., for example, Democritus, *fr.* 191; Plato, *Phileb.* 47E; *Leg.* 3.679C; Lysias, *Or.* 2.48; Herodian., *exc. d. Marci* 3.2.7; Apuleius, *Florida* 22). But one can also compare 1QS 4.10; Sir 40:4, as well as the New Testament catalogues of vices in Gal 5:20f.; Rom 13:13; 2 Cor 12:20; James 3:14, 16; 4:2; 1 Cor 3:3; 13:4.

The saga of the Phoenix in *1 Clem.* 25 (since Herodotus 2.73; cf. Ovid, *Metam.* 15.392ff.; Seneca, *Ep.* 42.1; Martial, 5.7; and others) is used similarly in Pliny, *Nat. hist.* 10.2; Pomponius Mela, *Chorogr.* 3.8. The motif is, however, not foreign to the Jewish tradition either (Gr. Bar. 6–8; Sl. 2 Enoch 12:1ff.; 15:1; 19:6; other references can be found in R. Knopf, *Clemensbrief,* 89). Tacitus's *Annals* (6.28) reports how well-known the bird named Phoenix had become after its appearance in 34 C.E., so that it offered "material for a multitude of discussions."

The motif of God's εὐεργεσίαι (*1 Clem.* 19:2 and other places) can be found not only in Hellenistic philosophy (for references see R. Knopf, *Clemensbrief,* 75), but also in Wis 16:2; Pss 12:6; 56:3; and often in Philo (for example, *De spec. leg.* 1.209, p. 242).

A Stoic expression, πνεῦμα ἡγεμονικόν, in *1 Clem.* 18:12 was transmitted through the LXX (Ps 50:14) (cf. R. Knopf, *Clemensbrief,* 73, and J. Schneider, "Πνεῦμα ἡγεμονικόν," *ZNW* 23 [1935]: 62–69).

For the term διακοσμέω, *1 Clem.* 33:3, one may compare the LXX (2 Macc 3:25), Philo (*Opif. mundi* 53), and the Stoic technical term (for example, Sextus Empiricus, *Adv. mathem.* 9.27; 9.75; Stobaios, *Ecl.* 1.21.5: *Stoic. vet. fr.* II no. 527).

The idea of God's διοίκησις (*1 Clem.* 20:1) is found not only in pagan Hellenistic parallels (for example, Chrysippus in Plutarch, *De repugn. stoic.* 9.5; *Stoic. vet. fr.* I.98; 102f.; 107; 499; II.528), but also in the LXX (Wis 12:18; 15:1). See in particular, *Letter of Aristeas* 234 and

---

23. *Das frühe Christentum,* 87; also in "Echo," 331.

254, which, as *1 Clem.* 19:3, also speaks of God's lack of anger (cf. Epictetus, *Diss.* 3.20.9; Seneca, *De. ira* 2.27.1).

For the Platonic-Stoic color of *1 Clem.* 60:1 (references in R. Knopf, *Clemensbrief,* 143) see also Wis 7:17. In regard to *1 Clem.* 19:3 see not only Seneca, *Nat. quaest.* 7.30.3, but also Philo, *De mon.* 2.214.

In regard to the Stoic elements listed by Bardy, the author himself includes Jewish-Hellenistic parallels, for the most part Philo. In other words, these elements are not specifically Stoic; a direct connection between Clement and Stoicism is not verifiable.

b. *Pagan philosophical topoi which could have reached Clement via early Christian tradition,* so that no conclusions are possible concerning a pagan philosophical or literary course of education for Clement.

A nice example of the ambivalence is the κῆρυξ title used for the apostle (*1 Clem.* 5:6). Cynic philosophers were designated in the same way (Epictetus, *Diss.* 3.22.69). But the title is also present in the Christian tradition (2 Tim 1:11; 1 Tim 2:7; 2 Pet 2:5).

In regard to the Clementine hymn of love (49f.) see Simplicius, *In Ench. Epict.,* p. 208, ed. F. Duebner (but he has φιλία instead of ἀγάπη) as well as 1 Cor 13. For "bond of love" (*1 Clem.* 49:2) see Col 3:14; Simplicius, ibid.

The picture of the body and its members (*1 Clem.* 37:5; e.g., Marcus Aurelius, 2.1; Dionysius of Halicarnassus, *Ant. Rom.* 6.86.1–5; Seneca, *De ira* 2.31.7; Plutarch, *Coriol.* 6) may be compared to 1 Cor 12; Rom 12:4f. Paul in 1 Cor 12:7 offers the Stoic idea of utility (*1 Clem.* 37:5; for example, Sextus Empiricus, *Adv. Mathem.* 11.22). When L. Sanders (*L'hellénisme,* 85–93) emphasizes that Clement, in this passage, stands closer to the philosophical tradition than to 1 Cor 12, that is correct for the concept of the σῴζειν of the body through the harmony of the members (*1 Clem.* 37:5; 38:1; Dionysius of Halicarnassus, *Any. Rom.* 6.86.1–5; Seneca, *De ira* 2.31.7; Maximus of Tyrus, *Diss.* 15.4FG; in Paul, one finds only a correspondence in regards to content: 1 Cor 12:25). Also the conception of the σύμπνοια (*1 Clem.* 37:5) is a genuine Greek idea that has found its way from medicine (Hippocrates, Περὶ τροφῆς 23) into philosophy, particularly Stoicism (W. Jaeger, *Das frühe Christentum,* 16, 89; cf. also Josephus, *Ant.* 7.105; Philo, *Conf. ling.* 69). But does that speak for Clement's philosophical schooling? Paul and also the above-mentioned Maximus of Tyrus betray that the topos of the body and its members — *with* σῴζεται — is a commonplace philosophical motif. Maximus did not receive a profound philosophical education.[24]

---

24. See H. Dörrie, "Maximus von Tyros," *KlPauly* 3:1115.

God as ἀπροσδεής (*1 Clem.* 52:1; Greek and particularly Stoic references in R. Knopf, *Clemensbrief,* 129) is found in Acts 17:25 as well as in Hellenistic Judaism, for example, Philo, *Leg. alleg.* 2.1.2.

Military imagery and formulations (*1 Clem.* 37 and other places) can be found in the popular philosophical diatribe (for example, Epictetus, *Diss.* 3.24.31–35; 3.26.29f.; 1.14.15ff.; Seneca, *Ep.* 107.9; Pseudo-Aristotle, *De mundo* 6), in the Mithras cult (Apuleius, *Metam.* 11.14f. and 24; Tertullian, *De corona* 15; *De praescr. haer.* 40) as well as in the Hellenistic-Jewish[25] and Christian tradition (for example, Eph 6; 2 Cor 10:3f.; 1 Tim 1:18; 2 Tim 2:3f.). Also the previous context (*1 Clem.* 36:4–6) deals with the *biblical* theme of God's battle against his enemies (Pss 2:7ff.; 110:1; cf. Heb 1:13; 1QM; Wis 5:17–23).

c. *The purely pagan Hellenistic elements of education* (without the indicated ambivalence) are commonplace elements from oral tradition which do not reveal any tangible literary dependency, quotations, or, therefore, a literary education in regard to Clement.

The proverb concerning great and small (*1 Clem.* 37:4) is found in this sense in Sophocles (*Ajax* 158–61) and Plato (*Lex.* 10.902DE), without Clement having any literary contact with them. The same can be said of the parallel tragic Greek fragment of Euripides, *Aeolus* no. 21 (ed. A. Nauck), where the theme of the "small" and the "great" is connected with the topos of σύγκρασις,[26] as in Clement. The entire topos originates from the tradition of popular philosophical wisdom of proverbs.

First Clement 24:3 sees in the change from day and night a natural proof for the nondefinitiveness of death. The theme is reminiscent of Stoicism, e.g., Seneca, *Ep.* 36.10f. But does it not have the flavor of a commonplace element?

The humble acceptance of exile (*1 Clem.* 54:2f.) is a topos of Stoic ethics (for example, Epictetus, *Diss.* 2.19.23f.; 1.4.23f.; Seneca, *Ep.* 24.3f.; 82.10; Cicero, *Pro Milone* 93; Musonius, fr. 9; Plutarch, *De ex.* 17; cf. Stoic cosmopolitanism). Clement in 55:1 refers to examples from the pagan sphere — nevertheless only in a general way without naming any names. He could have referred, for example, to Athen's Solon or to Sparta's King Lycurgus or in the Roman sphere to P. Rutilius Rufus or Metellus (Seneca, *Ep.* 24.4ff.) Seneca (*Ep.* 24.6) betrays the source of the knowledge of such historical tidbits: "These are fairy tales which one recites aloud in every school" ("decantatae in omnibus scholis fabulae istae sunt"). The entire topos is commonplace. At best, this lets one

---

25. See A. Jaubert, "Les sources," 74–84: Test. Job 37; 4 Macc. 9:24; cf. 16:14.

26. In regard to the Stoic topos of κρᾶσις, cf., e.g., Chrysippus in Stobaios, *Ecl.* 1.17.4 (*Stoic. vet. fr.* 2 no. 471).

conclude that Clement did attend a grammar school (usually until 17 years of age).

An analogous situation exists for examples of famous pagans who freely offer themselves to death (*1 Clem.* 55:1). Here also there is only a general reference without any mention of names. As examples, Clement could have cited Menoiceus, Leonidas, father and son P. Decius Mus, M. Curtius, et al. Cicero notes that the topos was widely circulated (*Tusc.* 1.116; cf. 89). If Clement had experienced a first-hand rhetorical education, he would not have blundered with this topos by referring only to βασιλεῖς and ἡγούμενοι. He would also have cited the famous pagan women who with their sacrificial death, of course, belonged to the list exemplifying this topos. They are, for example, the daughters of King Erechtheus of Athens (Cicero, *Tusc.* 1.116; Euripides, fr. no. 362, ed. A. Nauck III; Aelius Aristides, *Panathen.* 1, etal.), Iphigenia of Aulis (Cicero, *Tusc.* 1.116; Euripides, *Iphig. Aul.* 1553ff.), the daughters of Orion of Thebes (Antoninus Liberalis, *Metamorphoseon synagoge* 25), and King Leo's daughters from Athens (Demosthenes, *Or.* 60.29; Pausanias, *Graec. descr.* 1.5.2; Aelius Aristides, *Panathen.* 1, et al.).

Danaids and Dirce in *1 Clem.* 6:2 belong to the sphere of popular proverbs.[27]

A commonplace element with roots in Orphism (see Sanders, *L'hellénisme,* 104ff.) is the "place of the pious" (χῶρος εὐσεβῶν) in *1 Clem.* 50:3.

Individual concepts originally of philosophical provenance, as παλιγγενεσία (*1 Clem.* 9:4; for example, Marcus Aurelius, 11.1) or καθῆκον (*1 Clem.* 1:3; 3:4; 41:3; in Stoicism since Zeno; Menander, fr. 532.2, ed. Körte and Thierfelder) or the classical virtue of (ἀ)φιλοξενία (*1 Clem.* 1:2; 10:7; 11:1; 12:1; 35:5; for example, Epictetus, *Diss.* 3.11.4; since Homer, *Od.* 14.56ff.) may likewise have been picked up in the grammar school.

The Rhetorical Methods

The thesis that Clement's educational level at best represents that of a grammar school graduate is also sufficient when we examine the rhetorical fashion of *1 Clem.* Rhetorical methods were "moderately"[28] employed, in comparison to contemporary literature.

Examples: As in the diatribe, Clement uses rows of paradigms in order to support his moral instruction. One encounters Old Testament and Christian paradigms in *1 Clem.* 4–7; 9–12; 17f.; 31:2–4; 45:4–8; 51:3–5; 52:2—53:5; 55:2ff.; 55:1. In the diatribe one may compare, for example, the cynic Teles in Stobaios, *Ecl.* (ed. Wachsmuth and Hense)

---

27. See M. Dibelius, "Rom und die Christen," 198, n. 43.
28. A. Stuiber, "Clemens Romanus," RAC III, 195.

4.32(1).21; 33.31; 3.40.8; Musonius, fr. 9. As in the diatribe (cf., for example, the last-named passage of Teles; Epictetus, *Diss.* 1.29.56f.; Seneca, *Ep.* 24.11; *De const. sap.* 2.2; Demosthenes, *Contra Androt.* 14), Clement offers not only paradigms from history but also from the present (*1 Clem.* 5:1; 6:1).[29]

But did Clement take over this style of argumentation directly from the pagan diatribe? (a) His paradigms contain essentially Old Testament material. In those places where he refers to pagan paradigms (55:1), they remain general without any specific names. (b) The Christian tradition before Clement (for example, Heb 11) knew of series of Old Testament paradigms. (c) Clement speaks of ὑποδείγματα (5:1; 6:1), while the Atticistic technical term is παράδειγμα. All three observations speak for the fact that Clement learned this mode of argumentation only through the Jewish-Christian tradition, in the end through the tradition of the Hellenistic synagogue.[30]

Isolated incidents of elevated literary expressions (for poetic elements, see above) can be found in the following: *1 Clem.* 20:10 the literary πρός with genitive (for example, Thucydides, 3.59.1). *First Clement* 48:6 the more choice κοινωφελές (for references see R. Knopf, *Clemensbrief*, 125). *First Clement* 63:1 the choice θεμιτόν; 65:1 the elevated ὅπως θᾶττον and εὐκταῖος (R. Knopf, *Clemensbrief*, 149f.). *First Clement* 63:1 (τὸν τῆς ὑπακοῆς τόπον ἀναπληρῶσαι), on the other hand, seems affected.

One should further observe: *rhetorical questions*, 50:2; 49:2f. *Pictures*, for example, 46:7; 57:1; 2:8; 19:3; 36:2; 59:3. Urgent *didactic repetitions* and *anaphora* 49f., particularly 49:5 (ἀγάπη); 46:9; 32; 36; 4:7—6:4 (ζῆλος, and ἔρις and φθόνος); cf. Musonius, fr. 8; Seneca, *De prov.* 3.5–10; but also Heb 11. *Antitheses*, for example, 49:5 βάναυσον — ὑπερήφανον, σχίσμα — ὁμόνοια; 55:3, γυναῖκες — ἀνδρεῖα. *Rhyme*, 7:3; 10:2; 30:1; 48:5. *Benevolent logomachy* (*captationes benevolentiae*), 1:2f.; 2; 53:1. *Play on words*, 56:1 ἐπιείκεια–εἶξαι; 5:1 γενεᾶεμς–γενναῖα. *Short parallel structures*, 45:4; 48:5. *Parallelisms*, for example, 49. 9:1: four *colons* of almost equal length, three ending in αὐτοῦ. 46:5–7: *questions with the same beginning* (cf. similarly, 48:5); multiplication of εἷς; *synonyms* in ascending series; in v. 9 *anaphora* and *climax*. 37:2: *exclamatory sequence* of πῶς...πῶς...πῶς; cf. 53:5, exclamations. But there is in 65 chapters no incident of μέν — δέ! Like the evangelist Luke, Clement *imitates a*

---

29. Because of the rows of paradigms, W. Jaeger (*Das frühe Christentum*, 9, 14, 87) celebrates Clement as the "second Demosthenes," who argues completely in the style of the contemporary rhetorical schools and who had allegedly studied the handbooks of rhetorical τέχνη.

30. Cf. H. Thyen, *Der Stil*, 12: Clement is seen as strongly dependent upon the Jewish-Hellenistic homily.

biblical style with reminiscences and echoes of the Old Testament.[31] But I do not venture to believe that one can see here a conscious application of the classicistic technique of mimesis.[32]

The task of individual studies would be to investigate to what degree Clement had control of the literary Atticistic language, which, since the first century C.E., sometimes was even communicated in elementary school instruction.

Stuiber calls Clement's use of rhetorical means moderate. Such could be assumed of a grammar school graduate. In the grammar school the pupil would be instilled, by means of the classics, with a sensitivity to style. There, through a pedantic sentence-by-sentence explanation of classical works, the rhetorical figures would be discussed. There, one read the classical texts, particularly Homer, Euripides, and Demosthenes.[33] And it was Demosthenes who understood the use of both historical and contemporary paradigms as Clement employed it (5:1; 6:1).

All in all, the individual author of *1 Clem.* remains remarkably in darkness, in spite of the abundance of material. What above all is of importance for us is the collective process of education that is visible behind *1 Clem.*: the transmitting of educational elements that came from the Hellenistic synagogues and were passed on in Roman Christianity of the first century (see above, chap. 5). *First Clement* reveals itself as a product of this collective educational process and, although written by one individual, as a genuinely communal work.

---

31. See the collection of passages in W. Wrede, *Untersuchungen,* 62f.
32. Contrary to E. Plümacher, *Lukas,* 63, n. 142.
33. In this regard see, e.g., S. Oppermann, "Schulen," *KlPauly* 5:38f. Similarly, J. Carcopino, *La vie quotidienne à Rome,* 164f.

Chapter 22

The Person of Hermas

The Shepherd of Hermas Offers Biographical Information Whose Authenticity Is Disputed

Vision 1.1

Vis. 1.1.1: "My θρέψας sold me to Rome to one Rhoda. Many years later I met her again.... "

Someplace outside of Rome[1] Hermas was born as a slave: As *verna*, a slave born in a master's (ὁ θρέψας) house.[2] This master sold Hermas to a Roman lady by the name of Rhoda who, in turn, sold him again or set him free. Actually, Hermas appears to have presented himself in later life as a freedman. In the rest of the book he does not speak again of his servile origin. Hermas managed businesses (see below) on his own responsibility and at his own risk. This corresponds more with a freedman than a slave. The general evidence from the milieu also points in this direction: A slave in Rome could normally reckon with being set free when he reached the age of 30.[3]

There follows in *Vis.* 1.1.1f. the bath scene: "...I met her again (ἀνεγνωρισάμην) and was attracted to her as a sister. Some time after, I saw her bathe in the Tiber. I reached out my hand and helped her out of the river. When I beheld her beauty, the thought arose in my heart: 'How happy (μακάριος) I would be, if I had a wife such as her, so handsome and so noble in character (τῷ τρόπῳ)." The bath scene incited suspicion among scholars.[4] Doubt concerning its autobiographical character is justified:

---

1. The *Liber Pontificalis* (ed. Mommsen, I, p. 14, names the Italian "Aquilegia" as his home town, which, however, cannot be verified. Even if εἰς means "in," as often in Hermas (Hilhorst, 32), the sense would remain the same because of the word order: "...sold me to one Rhoda in Rome" (contrary to C. Osiek, 11).
2. Hermas thus was θρεπτός, δοῦλος οἰκογενής. Cf. Sophocles, *Oedipus* 1123, Plato, *Menon* 85E. For θρέψας see further references in H. Gülzow, *Christentum und Sklaverei,* 85f., n. 3; 86, n. 1.
3. On the basis of juridical and epigraphical testimony, see G. Alföldy, *Freilassung,* 336ff., 359, 369.
4. Particularly, M. Dibelius, *Hermas,* 425ff., 419ff., 445f., 449; R. Joly, *Hermas,* 17ff.

a. From a history-of-traditions point of view, the scene is based upon a piece of pagan erotica,[5] a love story, in which first acquaintance grows into attraction, and seeing the beautiful woman bathing arouses the desires of the lover. The scene is devoid of any religious tone. Also in the terms μακάριος and τρόπος (in the sense of "conduct, character") no shade of Christian connotation is recognizable[6] — deviating from the usual use in early Christian literature. The motif of ἀναγνωρίζειν is a much-loved theme in the romances of the New Comedy.[7] The pagan influence continues in the subsequent context, where the beloved, now a messenger of God, appears to Hermas in a vision. It becomes apparent in 1.7 that Hermas adores his beauty like a *goddess* (ὡς θεὰν ἡγησάμην), which is strange to the Christian point of view but not to the pagan.[8] In 1.8 the adored woman breaks out in laughter (γελάσασα), which corresponds poorly to the sacred situation of a vision. Also inappropriate for the situation of a vision is the earthy Ἑρμᾶ χαῖρε (1.4), with which the visionary messenger of God addresses Hermas. Equally inappropriate is Hermas's answer to the one who has appeared before him, "What are you doing here?" (τί σὺ ὧδε ποιεῖς;). The vision threatens to degenerate into caricature. Hermas is not completely successful in hiding profane elements under the cloak of his Christian redaction. All things considered, Hermas interweaves motifs from pagan light fiction, material from novels, into the text.[9] That means that the bath scene appears to be more a literary fiction than an autobiographical account. Other observations lead in the same direction:

b. In itself the scene is hardly realistic. A Roman lady whose morality is beyond question (2.3; 1.2) does not bathe in the Tiber at a place open to the public. She also does not allow a man, who happens to pass by, to help her out of the water.

c. It is strange that, in the subsequent book, Hermas's sinful thoughts which occurred in the bath scene ("the evil desire arose in your heart," 1.8) remain unmentioned (especially in *Mand.* 4, for example, 4.1.1). Hermas's purity and πολλὴ ἐγκράτεια are unhesitatingly extolled (*Vis.* 2.3.2).

---

5. Cf., e.g., (Ps.) Plutarch, *Amatoriae narrationes* 1.2; Ps. Aeschines, *Ep.* 10 (Hercher, *Epistolographi Graeci*, 38f.). The pagan elements mentioned below teach us that Jewish sources come less in question (cf. Bathsheba in 2 Sam 11:2; Bilhah in T. Reuben 3:11).

6. Cf., on the other hand, Heb 13:5; Did. 11:8, where τρόπος means a specific Christian way of life. μακάριος without religious color is used of persons only in Acts 26:2; 1 Cor 7:40; cf. Luke 23:29, while an abundance of references is religiously colored, also in Hermas *Vis.* 2.2.7; 3.8.4; *Sim.* 9.29.3; 5.3.9; 6.1.1, etc.

7. In Menander as then in Plautus and Terence; cf. W. J. Wilson, "The Career," 23, n. 2.

8. Cf. G. Lieberg, *Puella divina.* Also Apuleius, *Met.* 4.28ff., and other places.

9. Cf. M. Dibelius, *Hermas*, 429. We must later return to this finding.

Prematurely, scholars deduced from the findings that the *entire* passage, including the introductory sentence concerning Hermas's servile origins, is a literary fiction (see n. 3). I wish to show that this is not the case. Between the fictive romantic bath scene and the introductory sentence referring to slavery there exists a tension. The tension testifies to the historicity of the introductory sentence, especially since no motive can be found for its fabrication.

The tension consists of the following:

a. The bath scene neglects fully that Rhoda was Hermas's previous mistress (*domina*). One hears nothing more of the mistress-slave relation.[10] Moreover, Hermas's origin in slavery stands in contradiction to the bath scene. Masculine slaves, even though they may be freedmen, do not serve a bathing woman. That is indecent (Clement of Alexandria, *Paid.* 3.32.3; Juvenal, 6.422) and does not correspond to the moral purity of Rhoda (2.3). In other words, the credibility of the fictitious bath scene *suffers* from the fact of Hermas's servile origin.

b. Hermas, as a slave, was once sold to Rhoda in Rome (1.1). That "after many years" Rhoda, as a flowering beauty, still awakes erotic feelings sounds hardly plausible.

In summary, one would maintain the autobiographical character of the first sentence (ὁ θρέψας με πέπρακέν με Ῥόδῃ τινὶ εἰς Ῥώμην), precisely because the sentence runs counter to the following fictitious context (μετὰ πολλὰ ἔτη κτλ.). In addition, the first sentence is verifiable for the Roman reader, which is not the case for an individual experience such as the bath scene. In regard to the contested question, whether Hermas's autobiographical data is authentic or fictitious, one cannot generally answer with a simple yes or no, but one must investigate each case individually. Hermas combines literary fiction with authentic autobiographical material.

Hermas's Household

Owner of a house?

Often Hermas speaks of his *oikos,* by which he means sometimes a building and at other times the persons of the "household," the *familia.* Did Hermas own a house? A look at the passages in which οἶκός μου refers to a building raises some doubt.

a. *Mand.* 4.4.3; *Sim.* 7.1; 9.1.3; 10.3.1, 3, 5; 4.5 speak stereotypically of a heavenly being taking up residence with Hermas (or the opposite: εἰς τὸν οἶκόν σου κατοικῆσαι / "in domo mea habitare"; ἐκ τοῦ οἴκου

---

10. Also not in 1:5 (the κυρία-address), because generally αἱ γυναῖκες εὐθὺς ἀπὸ τεσσαρεσκαίδεκα ἐτῶν ὑπό τῶν ἀνδρῶν κυρίαι καλοῦνται (for example, Epictetus, *Enchirid.* 40).

μου ἐξελθεῖν / "a domo tua discedere"). The expressions do not go beyond what a tenant of a domicile can say: it is "his home" (cf. Mark 8:3; also one cannot read Mark 5:19 as "house owner").

b. In *Vis.* 5.1, προσευξαμένου μου ἐν τῷ οἴκῳ means "as I prayed at home...," from which one cannot conclude that he possesses a house. The question then is whether in *Sim.* 6.1.1, καθήμενος ἐν τῷ οἴκῳ μου καὶ δοξάζων τὸν κύριον, which reflects the same situation as in *Vis.* 5.1, something other than "at home" is meant. The same obtains for *Vis.* 2.4.2, ὅρασιν εἶδον ἐν τῷ οἴκῳ μου. In all three passages, ἐν τῷ οἴκῳ (μου) illustrates in a stereotypical way the external frame for the encounter with a celestial being: Hermas sits "at home," when the vision visits him. It comes in the night,[11] when he is "at home," a traditional motif (cf., e.g., Dan 7:1).

c. The text in *Sim.* 10.1.1, unfortunately no longer extant in the original, describes the same situation of revelation with the words, "in domum in qua eram," not "in domum meam."

Therefore, one cannot conclude that possession of a house is indicated.

Master of slaves?

The passages in which οἶκος signifies the "household," the "*familia*," of Hermas offer little information (*Mand.* 12.3.6; *Sim.* 5.3.9; 7.3.6; cf. *Vis.* 1.3.1; 2.3.1 et al.). Formulations such as σὺ μετὰ τῶν τέκνων σου καὶ ὅλου τοῦ οἴκου σου, or οὔτε τὰ τέκνα σου οὔτε ὁ οἶκός σου, suggest that not only his own children but also servants / slaves belong to Hermas's *familia*. But, above all, M. Dibelius[12] has gathered references that Hermas stylized his "family" as a literary figure[13] in order to illustrate models of Christian transgression and penance. *Vis.* 1.1.9 states, τὰ ἁμαρτήματά σου καὶ ὅλου τοῦ οἴκου σου καὶ πάντων τῶν ἁγίων: the model of Hermas's family with the different transgressions of the children (apostasy, denunciation of Christians to the pagans) is transparent for "all the saints" of the Christian community.[14]

Did Hermas create a totally fictional family? Or does he stylize a historically existing family as a model? I tend to believe the latter. The existence of his family was for the Roman reader verifiable. Thus, with some reservations, can one conclude that slaves / freedmen belonged to Hermas's family.

---

11. *Vis.* 5.1: καθίσαντος εἰς τὴν κλίνην. Cf. also *Vis.* 3.1.2; 3.10.6f.

12. *Hermas*, 419f., 445f., 449, et passim; cf. R. Joly, *Hermas*, 19, 55 et passim. Cf. also already J. Réville in his 1900 book, *La valeur du témoignage historique du Pasteur d'Hermas*.

13. Does *Sim.* 7.3 show the true reaction of a father? Why does Hermas not think of "his own children" in *Sim.* 6.4.2? Cf. the same in *Vis.* 4.1.3; 4.2.5f.; 4.3.6; *Sim.* 6.2–4.

14. Cf. also the writing from heaven: The model of the "children" obtains meaning for the universal church; the supposedly special proves to be typical for "all the saints" (*Vis.* 2.2.2—5.4.3).

The Landed Property

Hermas possesses a field (ἀγρός) on the Via Campana, situated ten stadia (c. 1,850 m.) from the Via Campana but easily (ῥᾳδίως) reached from there (*Vis.* 4.1.2; cf. 3.1.2f.). The Via Campana runs as a state highway from one of the city gates, the Porta Portuensis, along the right bank of the Tiber, to the Campus Salinarum by the sea (*CIL* 6:2107.3, 14; 6:29772; 6:10250; Suetonius, *Aug.* 94.7). The specific location is verifiable for any Roman reader. There seems little possibility that this is a literary fiction.[15]

Hermas's ἀγρός is of considerable size. This is seen in *Vis.* 3.1.3: Hermas asks where on the property he should situate himself and is directed to "a nice remote place" of the property (τόπον καλὸν ἀνακεχωρηκότα).[16]

Hermas cultivated the area with χονδρίζειν:[17] with barley or spelt. The Latins would call it "far" or "alica." The spelt porridge had once been for the old Romans the meager main course of all social groups,[18] which, by the time of Hermas, had long been replaced by bread and, on the tables of the rich, by gourmet delights. Whoever bought this produce in Hermas's time belonged to the less well off.[19] Why did Hermas utilize his land in this way? He continually waged a polemic against the luxury found at the tables of rich Christians:[20] It is possible that with his cultivation he symbolically pointed back to the old Roman idea of moderation, thus propagating the virtue of modest living. In another context, in *Sim.* 1.6, he vehemently advocates *autarkeia* or self-sufficiency. His agricultural efforts correspond to what he preaches.

Hermas's Business, His Depleted Wealth

Hermas as a landowner looks back to a time in which he was wealthy (ὅτε ἐπλούτεις). He had acquired the property through worldly business transactions (ταῖς πραγματείαις ταῖς πονηραῖς; ἀπὸ πολλῶν πράξεων; ἀπὸ τῶν βιωτικῶν πραγμάτων), in which he was "kneaded under" (συνανεφύρης). Through θλίψεις ἰδιωτικαὶ he lost his wealth.[21]

---

15. The situation is different in regard to the geographical references of "Arcadia" and "Cumae," which originate from bucolic and Sibylline tradition and possess symbolic character: *Sim.* 9.1.4; *Vis.* 1.1.3).

16. In *Sim.* 5.2.2 ἀγρός even signifies an estate with "many slaves" and diversified crops; in one part of the ἀγρός wine is cultivated. Although nothing more concrete is known of the extent of Hermas's *agros*, we should not estimate it to be small.

17. *Vis.* 3.1.2; hapax legomenon, no doubt = χονδρεύειν.

18. For example, Pliny, *Nat. hist.* 18.62.

19. Cf., for example, G. Maddoli, "Speisen und Getränke," 45ff., 47. L. A. Moritz, "Far," *KlPauly* 2:514f.

20. For example, *Mand.* 6.2.5; see above, chap. 10.

21. *Vis.* 3.6.7; 2.3.1; 1.3.1, κατεφθάρης ἀπὸ τῶν βιωτικῶν πράξεων ("you became unfit for the business of daily life"); *Mand.* 3.5; *Sim.* 7.2; 4.5; cf. *Vis.* 3.11.3.

The type of business and the circumstances of his financial decline
are only vaguely identifiable. If we are trying to trace Hermas's previous
fields of business, our best bet is to examine the milieu from which he
took his literary examples. *Vis.* 1.3.2 looks at a smith hammering out his
work; *Sim.* 9.32.3 pictures a fuller who is harassed by a customer whose
garment he tore. *Mand.* 11.15 and 12.5.3 (the same twice) observe a
man who stores oil and wine and especially takes precautions for the
half-full wine jars because their contents sour more quickly. Did Hermas
deal at one time in oil and wine?

According to *Sim.* 4.5–7 (cf. *Mand.* 6.2.5), Hermas indulged sometime in "*many* businesses" (ἀπὸ πολλῶν πράξεων; τὰ πολλὰ πράσσειν;
περισπώμενος περὶ τὰς πραγματείας),[22] while he now only engages in
one activity (μίαν πρᾶξιν), the farm.

The reason for his economical decline is intimated: For some length
of time Hermas endured suffering (σε χρόνον τινὰ θλιβῆναι) and was
torn from his normal milieu (πάλιν ἀποκατασταθήσῃ εἰς τὸν τόπον σου,
Sim. 7.2, 6; cf. 7.3, 5). How are we to interpret this? Was Hermas in
prison? Was his property confiscated in a persecution? Did the property waste away because of Hermas's imprisonment and the subsequent
stagnation of the business? Several observations point in this direction:
(a) In other passages of the book there is mention of persecution. There
is persecution by judicial hearings (*Sim.* 9.28.4); pressure to deny "the
name of the Lord" and to participate in pagan sacrifices;[23] persecution
by martyrdom;[24] and betrayal from Christians. Explicitly it is noted that
Hermas too was denounced.[25] (b) In *Sim.* 9.21.3; *Vis.* 3.6.5; 3.2.1; 2.3.4;
Sim. 8.3.7, θλῖψις actually denotes persecution of Christians by pagan
authorities. In *Sim.* 7.2, it is even used in regard to Hermas in this way.
(c) *Vis.* 3.2.1 calls φυλακάς a component of persecution. (d) *Vis.* 3.1.9
(cf. *Sim.* 7.6) represents "a prophecy after the fact" of Hermas's suffering under persecution.[26] In regard to the persecution mentioned by
Hermas, one thinks most readily of the measures taken against Christians during the time of Trajan.[27] The denunciations of Christians under

---

22. For a "libertus" a multitude of possibilities stood open: epigraphical evidence indicates over 160 activities in production and commerce in which freedmen engaged. See the
list of references in G. Vitucci, "Libertus," *Dizionario epigrafico,* ed. E. de Ruggiero and
A. Ferrabino (Rome, 1958), 4:930–33.

23. *Sim.* 9.21.3; *Vis.* 3.6.5; 3.2.1; 3.5.2; 3.1.9; *Vis.* 2.3.2, 4; *Sim.* 6.2.3; 8.8.2; 8.10.3;
9.19.3; 9.26.3, 6; 9.28.3–5.

24. *Vis.* 3.1.9; 3.2.1; 3.5.2; *Sim.* 8.3.6f.; 9.19.3; 9.28.

25. *Vis.* 2.2.2; cf. *Sim.* 8.6.4; 9.19.1.

26. καθίσεις μετ᾽ αὐτῶν (= who "have already suffered for the sake of the Name") καὶ
ὅσοι ἐὰν . . . ὑπενέγκωσιν ἃ καὶ ἐκεῖνοι (= αὐτῶν) ὑπήνεγκαν. . . .

27. With M. Dibelius, *Hermas,* 422. On the basis of internal criteria, the book was
written most likely in the 120s, 130s, or 140s (M. Dibelius, ibid.; Altaner and Stuiber,
Patrologie, 55). The value of the external witness of the Muratorian fragment is often
overestimated (e.g., by R. Joly, *Hermas,* 14). Canon Muratori, 73ff.: Hermas wrote "not

Trajan in Ignatius's Antioch and in Bithynia offer parallels (Pliny, *Ep.* 10.96f.).

We can summarize the picture we have gleaned of Hermas. Born outside of Rome as a *verna*, he was sold to a lady by the name of Rhoda in Rome. Sometime later he was set free and gained for himself some fortune by engaging in different business ventures (dealing in oil and wine?). He was denounced as a Christian and imprisoned. Separated from his economic endeavors,[28] his property and businesses sustained considerable losses (ὅτε ἐπλούτεις, *Vis.* 3.6.7). After the crisis, he (still) possessed an ἀγρός on the Via Campana, where he cultivated spelt, and refrained from engaging in his many earlier ventures. It is interesting to observe the upward, as well as the downward, social mobility reflected in his life. Hermas shared with innumerable contemporaries at least the upward mobility of slaves into economically successful freedmen.

Correspondences between Hermas's Life and His Ethical and Theological Thought

It is interesting to observe how Hermas theologically masters his biography, its upward and especially its downward movement. Which theologumena and ethical elements correspond to this life?

We saw (chap. 10) that the Shepherd of Hermas preached a new, one-time repentance and recommended to industrious Christian businessmen to abandon their *many* businesses and be satisfied with "*one* praxis" after this repentance. In the prosopographical investigation we now observe how much Hermas's preaching corresponded to what he himself had experienced in his own life. (a) Hermas personally had experienced how difficult it was for a businessman who wished to be successful to practice the ethical rigorism of some theologians. Frauds had crept into his former numerous businesses (*Mand.* 3.4f.). Hermas, the preacher of repentance, had himself been a businessman ensnared in the world, having been himself desperately in need of a new repentance.[29] (b) Hermas

---

long ago in our time in the city of Rome" ("nuperrime temporibus nostris in urbe Roma"), when his brother Pius sat upon the bishop's chair of the church of Rome. (a) In order to discredit the canonicity of the "Shepherd," the Muratorian Canon attributes a late date to Hermas's book. (b) The alleged monarchical episcopacy at the time of Hermas is refuted by the book of Hermas itself (see below, Part 5). His brother was probably a presbyter Pius. E. Peterson's attempt to dispute the Roman origin of Hermas's book has not found a following (E. Peterson, *Frühkirche*, 281ff.). Later Peterson himself decided in favor of Rome ("Giudaismo e Cristianesimo," *RSLR* 1 [1965]: 381).

28. *Vis.* 1.3.1 (above n. 20).

29. Without a doubt, this was *one* reason for Hermas's proclaiming of a new repentance. We must, however, avoid explanations based on only one cause. Not only the biographical reason but also certain conditions in the community motivated him to stand up as a prophet who announced a new and one-time possibility for repentance (see

had also accomplished the change from numerous enterprises to a single one. He who demanded from his fellow Christians the reduction of their worldly businesses had practiced this himself, at first only out of necessity because of persecution but then with assent. He did not immerse himself again into "numerous businesses" but was satisfied with the cultivation of his field. The "is" value of individual existence figures as a "should" value of the ethic because it had been found beneficial (*Vis.* 3.6.7) by Hermas. I do not see why this prototypical character of Hermas's existence should speak against the authenticity of the autobiographical notes.[30] Ἀπὸ σεαυτοῦ πρῶτον γνῶθι (*Vis.* 3.6.7): Hermas had done exactly that for his ethical preaching.

Let us observe the passages which are universally formulated by Hermas but still at the same time are descriptions of his own situation, therefore echoes of his personal experience of "reduction" and of social decline. "Some are punished by losses, others by want (ζημίαις, ὑστερήσεσιν)...for many are restless in making plans (ἀκαταστατοῦντες ταῖς βουλαῖς αὐτῶν) and undertake many things (ἐπιβάλλονται πολλά)....When they suffer all kinds of afflictions (ὅταν θλιβῶσι πάσῃ θλίψει)...they become strong in the faith of the Lord" (*Sim.* 6.3.4–6). *Sim.* 9.30.4f.: "Their wealth has made them somewhat blind and dumb to truth, although they never departed from God, nor did any evil word come from their mouth....When the Lord recognized their attitude, that they loved the truth and could live good lives, he allowed their riches to be cut down, although not completely, in order that they might be able to do some good with what remained." "But this world, together with its vain treasures, must be distanced from them; then will they be fit for the kingdom of God."[31] The negative experience of social decline is elevated to the positive by Hermas. Through the decline "faith in the Lord becomes strong," and the believer "becomes fit for the kingdom of God." The wish to ascend socially, on the other hand, is criticized as lustful desire. *Mand.* 6.2.5 lists "desires for numerous businesses" and "greed," that is, the motivation to climb socially, among the evil temptations that arise in the heart and are to be fought.[32]

---

above in detail, chap. 10). Not only he in his past, but also many others had become worldly, wealthy Christians whose bond to the community had become increasingly tenuous, so that the care for the poor was no longer sufficiently secure. In this situation of the *community*, Hermas's prophecy of a new repentance, as we saw, represents a helpful innovation.

30. Contrary to, for example, M. Dibelius, *Hermas,* passim, especially 419ff.

31. *Sim.* 9.31.2. The same in *Vis.* 3.6, where the correspondence between the general (6.6) and the personal formulation (6.7) is particularly clear.

32. *Vis.* 1.1 could also be possibly interpreted in this way (I thank Prof. G. Theissen for this comment): Hermas helps his former mistress out of the bath in the Tiber and thinks to himself, "How happy would I be if I had such a wife, so beautiful and noble in character." This desire, classified as "evil" (1.1.8), need not be sexual only — Hermas praises in the rest of the book his *enkrateia* (*Vis.* 2.3.2) — but it also has a second aspect.

Hermas makes all these remarks in a general way, although they also reflect personal experience. With the statements concerning socially ascending and descending mobility, Hermas treats not only a personal but also a more widespread phenomenon. (a) *Sim.* 8.9.1 presupposes the upward mobility of other Christians ("they have become rich and have made a name for themselves...").[33] (b) Other Christians have experienced decline (see above, *Sim.* 9.30.4f.). These are aided to overcome their loss. (c) Hermas wishes to motivate fellow Christians who have the "desire" for social advancement to free themselves from it. (d) He would like to motivate those who already live luxuriously to limit themselves and to take upon themselves voluntarily a lower social status. All these remarks presuppose social mobility as a phenomenon common to the whole of society. The person of Hermas who experienced firsthand this mobility, upwards as well as downwards, proves himself to be representative of wider circles of Christianity, if not of the contemporary society.

Other ethical elements correspond to Hermas's biographical data: *Mand.* 8.10, as 1 Tim 2:2, formulates the ideal of a quiet and peaceable life. This is appropriate for a freedman, modest in his demands, who cultivates a piece of land before the gates of Trastevere and turns his back upon the "manifold" business activities.

Hermas's catalogue of sins includes sins of the flesh, desire for riches, culinary delights, and a lavish lifestyle (*Mand.* 12.2.1 and others). These are things that appear as temptations on the horizon of an average man. Fame and power, as Philo describes[34] them as objects of desire, lie outside this horizon.

The freedman Hermas is no theologian in the proper sense. Flights of speculative thought are foreign to him. Only in *Sim.* 5 did he venture a Christological-theological discussion — which is not free of contradiction. His Christology corresponds to that of the popular, unsophisticated *Acta Pauli*. It amalgamates angelology in other parts of the book, and his teaching on the spirit is not free from animism.[35] A learned Logos Christology is foreign to him. He is closer to the popular pragmatic thought which makes the individual businessman's success directly dependent upon the degree of his piety (for example, *Sim.* 6.3.4–6; 9.24.2f.; cf. 10.1.2f.).

The wish of the former slave to marry his mistress is the desire to climb socially. At the end of the section (1.1.8), the boasting about one's wealth is criticized as the worst sin, worse than sexual desire.

33. C. Osiek (*Rich and Poor,* 127f.) supposes correctly that the wealthy people involved in business in Hermas are above all freedmen — as is Hermas himself.

34. *De Decalogo* 151–53; *De spec. leg.* 4.87–91; cf. M. Dibelius, *Hermas,* 544.

35. L. Vouaux, *Les Actes de Paul,* 72f.

What Level of Education Does Hermas Represent?

Material and Sources

We saw at the beginning (the section about *Vis.* 1) that Hermas reworked motifs from pagan erotic light fiction. The same evidence is found in another passage. Behind *Sim.* 9.10.6–11.8 there likewise stands fictitious erotic material. A number of young women hold a man captive overnight. At the beginning he defends himself and, being chaste, he raises objections, but without success. They cuddle with him, amuse themselves and finally also him with song, dance, and play. The Christian veneer that Hermas puts on the scene is too weak and foreign (prayer, alleged sisterly intimacy) in order not to betray the pagan origin of the tradition.[36]

Behind the pastoral elements, above all in *Sim.* (particularly the shepherds with the different pastoral symbols) stands the tradition of the pagan *bucolic,* as it is represented in Vergil's *Bucolica* but also in the novels of the second century (Longos's Ποιμενικὰ κατὰ Δάφνιν καὶ Χλόην). Vergil had become famous overnight with his *Bucolica;* the celebrated Cytheris[37] danced them in the theater, which indicates the popularity of these pastoral poems. At the time of Nero, the bucolics experienced a new blossoming.[38] J. Schwartz[39] lists parallels between Hermas and Vergil's *Bucolica* without, however, being able to prove literary dependence.[40] Hermas has adopted the motifs from the ordinary bucolic tradition. Also the motif "Arcadia" (*Sim.* 9.1.4) derives from there. Already Theocritus wrote of "Arcadia, rich in sheep." Since Vergil, "Arcadia" was known as the dreamy, imaginary landscape of bucolic poetry which the god Pan inhabited.[41] As Vergil made Arcadia a land of symbols, Hermas makes it a land of apocalyptic allegory. Also

---

36. Regarding this whole topic, see M. Dibelius, *Hermas,* 618f.; R. Joly, *Hermas,* 48. Whether Hermas desires here actually to defend the "virgines subintroductae" or not does not influence our decision about the tradition-critical origin of the material.

37. The elegist Gallus praised her in a song as his beloved Lycoris. Cf., e.g., M. Fuhrmann, "Gallus," *KlPauly* 2:687; W. H. Gross, "Vergilius," *KlPauly* 5:1194.

38. Cf. the "Hermit Poems" and T. Calpurnius Siculus; see G. Schmidt, "Bukolik," *KlPauly* 1:964ff. and "Einsiedler Gedichte," *KlPauly* 2:214; M. Fuhrmann, "Calpurnius," *KlPauly* 1:1025f. In my opinion, Luke's story of the announcement to the shepherds (Luke 2) is to be seen against the background of bucolic literature. With this motif, Luke appeals to the literary taste of his readers.

39. "Survivances littéraires païennes dans le 'Pasteur' d'Hermas," *RB* 72 (1965): 240–47, especially 244f.; cf. H. Schulz, *Spuren heidnischer Vorlagen im Hirten des Hermas,* Diss. Rostock, 1913.

40. *Sim.* 6.5.5 — cf. *Buc.* 2.65 (passion). *Sim.* 2 — cf. *Buc.* 2.70 (vine and elm). *Sim.* 8 (willow) and *Sim.* 2.5 (vine) — cf., for example, *Buc.* 10.40. *Sim.* 1.4. — cf. *Buc.* 1.3 (banishment from one's own land).

41. Theocritus, *Idyll.* 22.157; cf. 7.106. Vergil, *Ecl.* 4.58–59; 10.26; *Georg.* 3.392. Cf. B. Snell, "Arkadien, die Entdeckung einer geistigen Landschaft," *AuA* 1 (1945): 26–41. Dibelius, *Hermas,* 603, 494–96, proposed as alternative: "Arcadia" was picked up

the "Sibyl at Cumae" (*Vis.* 1f.) is encountered in the bucolic tradition.[42] However, she was a well-known figure, not necessarily adopted from the bucolic tradition, since even street urchins knew of her (Petronius 48).[43]

It is interesting how timidly Hermas reveals that his literary figures are dependent upon pagan prototypes. (a) *Vis.* 2.4.1: " 'Who do you think the old woman is...?' 'The Sibyl,' I said. 'You are mistaken,' he answered, 'she is not!' 'Who is she then?' I asked. He said, 'The church.' " Naturally, the pagan Sibyl sits for the portrait of the aged church. Already the occurrence of "Cumae" twice, in *Vis.* 2.1.1 and 1.1.3 betrays this. Hermas's dialogue scene tries to prevent any possible criticism of his pagan tendencies: Whoever should come upon the idea of discovering in the aged church characteristics of the Sibyl is mistaken. The church is not the Sibyl. One senses the reluctance of transferring characteristics of pagan figures into a Christian context; and yet there is a certain delight in doing so. (b) The presentation of the "shepherd" for the first time in *Vis.* 5 is similar: "As I was at home sitting on my bed praying, a distinguished looking man entered. He was like a shepherd, clothed with white goat's skin carrying a knapsack upon his back and a rod in his hand.... Since I thought he had come to tempt me (ἐκπειράζων), I spoke to him, 'Who are you?' And I added, 'I know to whom I have been entrusted (as guardian angel).' " At first sight of the "shepherd," Hermas's countenance reflects alarm and resistance. Again the literary dialogue anticipates the possible reaction of the reader. It anticipates the alarm about pagan motifs being used in a Christian context. Is this "shepherd" an ambassador of evil? No, he is not (4ff.)! The text calms the disturbed reader and apparently the author himself when he integrates pagan elements into his Christianity.

---

by Hermas because it was the homeland of the god Hermes. This assumption, however, presupposes the uncertain hypothesis that the god Hermes in shepherd attire served as a model for Hermas's shepherd figure. For a survey of several hypotheses about the origin of the Arcadia motif, see N. Brox, *Der Hirt des Hermas* (Göttingen, 1991), 384–85; G. Snyder, *The Shepherd of Hermas* (Camden, N.J., 1968), 128–30. R. Reitzenstein (*Poimandres,* 11ff., 32ff.) goes too far in attempting to find the origin of the shepherd figure of Hermas in Hermetic literature, especially in *Poimandres* (particularly is *Vis.* 5 compared with the beginning of *Poimandres*). The dependence of Hermas upon the Hermetic literature has remained a vague hypothesis; at best one may be able to consider a common source (for example, W. Kroll, "Hermes Trismegistus," Pauly/Wissowa 8:822; G. Bardy, "Le Pasteur d'Hermas et les livres hermétiques," *RB* 8 (1911): 391–407; R. Joly, *Hermas,* 12; M. Dibelius, "Der Offenbarungsträger," 105–18.

42. Vergil, *Buc.* 4.4.

43. In regard to the Sibyl of Cumae cf. further, for example, Juvenal 3.1ff.; Ovid, *Met.* 14.101ff.; Vergil, *Aeneid* 6.9ff., 42ff. That she transmits her message in written form (*Vis.* 1.4.1; 2), finds a parallel, for example, in Dionysius Halicarn. *Antiqu.* 4.62 (she brings nine books of sayings to Rome). That the Sibyl/church appears in Hermas in three figures of different ages could be influenced by three statues in the Roman Forum which were associated with three Sibyls (Pliny, *Nat. hist.* 36.5.22; cf. E. Peterson, *Frühkirche,* 267).

A multitude of further popular pagan representations can be found in Hermas. These are some examples:

Behind *Vis.* 5.3f. (cf. *Sim.* 9.1.3; 10.4.5) stands the concept of the personal protective god who resembles the person being protected (cf. Aelius Aristides 6.57). Hermas amalgamates it with the Jewish belief in the guardian angel (cf. also Matt 18:10). In regard to the two angels assigned to each individual (*Mand.* 6.2), similarly both Jewish[44] and pagan[45] parallels can be found. *Sim.* 9.1.8 takes up the popular fairy tale motif about the plants which always grow more strongly the more they are eaten by cattle and birds. Behind *Sim.* 8 (particularly 2.7) stands the popular pagan belief in the eternal germinating power of the willow.[46] *Mand.* 6 shows a knowledge of the two-ways schema, which, since the time of Hesiod, was widely circulated also in Jewish circles. The motif of the heavenly letter originates from popular literature (*Vis.* 2). The old four-color tradition is commonplace (*Vis.* 4.1.10; Apuleius, *Metam.* 11.3; Rev 6; Zech 6; 1:8), as is also that of the "four elements" (*Vis.* 3.13; also in Jewish literature, *Wis.* 19:17ff.). Behind *Vis.* 5.1 (ἔνδοξος τῇ ὄψει) stands the widely disseminated belief that gods appear in the form of beautiful persons. For the revelation or epiphany scenes in Hermas, E. Peterson has worked out the pagan models: Hermas relies upon the popular topic of Hellenistic revelation literature, particularly that of revelation magic as it is typified in the magical papyri.[47] Also Jewish revelation literature lies beneath Hermas's book, as Hermas himself narrates: for example, the lost apocalypse of the prophets "Eldad and Modat" (*Vis.* 2.3.4; cf. Num 11:26ff.!). Parallel material is also found in 4 Ezra.[48]

---

44. T. Jud. 20:1; T. Asher 1:3f.

45. P. Boyancé, "Les deux démons personnels," 189ff.

46. Cf. H. Rahner, *Griechische Mythen*, 361–413, esp. 382, 390.

47. E. Peterson (*Frühkirche*, 254ff.) looks, for example, in *Vis.* 1 and 3 at the motifs of the salutations and of the appearances and departures of the revealing figure. For the technique of the supplementary vision or the supplementary explanation of a previous vision (*Vis.* 2.4), M. Dibelius (*Hermas*, 450f.) cites Aelius Aristides (*Sacr. Serm.* 4.57) as a parallel (literary dependence is excluded). *Vis.* 5 is comparable to the beginning of *Poimandres*, without exhibiting literary dependency (see above n. 40). What *Vis.* 5 presents is "vulgar apocalyptic" (M. Dibelius, *Hermas*, 491).

48. For example, 4 Ezra 5:16 — *Vis.* 3.10.7; 4 Ezra 4:3 — *Vis.* 5.5; 4 Ezra 12:10 — *Sim.* 5.6.8; 4 Ezra 4:10f. — *Vis.* 3.2.3. For a more complete list of Jewish traditions in Hermas, see, e.g., M. Dibelius, *Hermas*, 424, 432–34, 436f., 440, 448, 488, 494 (the angel of repentance), 497, 499ff., 515, 520, 546, 548f., 556, 581, 588f., 605. R. Joly, *Hermas*, 47, 146, n. 1 (the demonology), 248, n. 1f., 340, n. 1, 343, n. 2. L. W. Barnard, "Hermas and Judaism," *SPB* 8 (1966): 3–9; St. Giet, "Un courant judéo-chrétien à Rome au milieu du IIe siècle," *Aspects du judéo-christianisme, Colloque de Strasbourg* (Paris, 1965), 95–112. The numerous Semitisms are transmitted through the Jewish-Christian tradition, particularly the LXX (for example, *Vis.* 1.1.2, διαλογίζομαι ἐν τῇ καρδίᾳ μου λέγων — cf. Mark 2:6, 8; Luke 3:15; Matt 9:4; LXX often) without necessarily ascribing Jewish origins to Hermas. Contrarily to Th. Zahn, *Hermas*, 487ff., who also considered numerous widely circulated Koine expressions as genuinely Jewish. The many pagan elements call

In summary, we encounter in Hermas popular pagan material, from novels and other sources; the novel certainly counts among the forms of "Volksliteratur."[49] A philosophical education, on the other hand, is absent, although a few motifs do find parallels in philosophical tradition:

a. The Christian spending his time on earth as a foreigner (ἐπὶ ξένης, *Sim.* 1.1) has parallels in Christian apocalyptic literature but also in Stoic and Hellenistic-Jewish tradition (cf. Philo, *De conf. ling.* 76; *De agric.* 65; *De cherub.* 120; regarding this theme see M. Dibelius, *Hermas,* 550f.). The idea is in vogue and indicates no literary education.

b. Only in one place does there appear to be a literary dependency, in *Sim.* 6.5.5: τρυφή is defined completely along the lines of the Stoic teaching on emotions (everything that a person ἡδέως does, is τρυφή: violent temper, adultery, avarice, slander, lying, drinking, etc.). Untypical for Hermas are the words πάθος (only here and in *Mand.* 4.1.6) and νόσος. Dibelius (584) calls the passage "a Stoic patch." Its origin is, in my opinion, Jewish-Hellenistic, since νόσος in the sense of "vice" is found frequently only in Philo (Bauer, *Wörterbuch* 1076).

c. Behind *Mand.* 12 (concerning evil desires) is Stoic tradition (*Stoic. vet. fr.* 1, no. 211; 3, no. 378; see M. Dibelius, *Hermas,* 544). However, that does not necessarily mean that Hermas directly borrowed here, because the motifs are also found in Hellenistic Judaism (cf. Philo, *De decalogo* 142–53; 173; *De spec. leg.* 4.79ff.).

d. The personification of virtues and vices (*Vis.* 3; *Sim.* 9) is found in popular philosophy, but it is also a well-known practice in Hellenistic Judaism (on Ps. Kebes' *Tabula* 20.3 see below; cf. also *Corp. Herm.* 13.8ff.; Philo, *De cherub.* 43ff.).

e. The chain of vices, ἀφροσύνη → πικρία → θυμός → ὀργή → μῆνις in *Mand.* 5.2.4 is Stoic: the false teaching, the ἀφροσύνη, is the originating point of human failure. Conversely, γνῶσις gives birth to virtues: see the chain in 2 Pet 1:5–7! 2 Peter indicates the popularity not only of this content but also of the form of a chain of virtues and vices. Regarding the originally Stoic definition of the relationship between θυμός–ὀργή–μῆνις cf. Diogenes Laertius 7.114; Andronicus, περὶ παθῶν 4 (*Stoic. vet. fr.* 3, nos. 397, 395); Ps. Phocylid. 64; but also Pss. Sol. 2:23.

f. When Hermas calls upon his reader to share with the poorer people (*Vis.* 3.9.2, 4f.; *Sim.* 10.4 et al.), the same appears in the Stoic

into question that Hermas had a Jewish origin. Hermas could have learned the Jewish elements from the Christian tradition (see above, chap. 8, in regard to *1 Clement*).

49. The ancient novel was a voice of the people (vox populi), a "valuable index...to the soul of the middle and lower class people of the Greco-Roman world," according to B. E. Perry ("Chariton and His Romance," 98). See also B. E. Perry, *The Ancient Romances,* 5. The popularity of novels is also shown through the close relationship between novel and mime (cf. R. Helm, *Der antike Roman,* 7). The exceptions are of course Petronius and Apuleius, who offer background irony and literary artistry to the educated.

tradition, for example, Musonius, p. 101 [ed. Hense]; Epictetus fr. 24
in Stobaios, p. 468 (ed. Schenkl), but also indeed in, e.g., Paul (2 Cor
8:14). The same is true of the condemnation of gluttony (*Vis.* 3.9.3;
Stoic parenesis: Seneca, *Ep.* 18.5; 108.18; Musonius pp. 97, 99, 101,
104 (ed. Hense); further references in Dibelius, *Hermas*, 475. In the
New Testament: Matt 24:49; Luke 12:19, 45; 1 Cor 15:32; already in
Isa 22:13). Likewise *commonplace* are individual concepts encountered
also in popular philosophical tradition. Among others: περισπᾶσθαι as
"being drawn away" by the superficialities of life (*Sim.* 2.5; 4.5; cf.
Epictetus 4.1.159; further Marcus Aurelius 2.7.1; 4.3.7; 6.22; 8.1.4);
προτίθημι: *Mand.* 12.3.5 and, for example, Epictetus 2.8.29; 4.6.26;
αὐτάρκεια (*Mand.* 6.2.3) as a beloved Stoic virtue that is also encountered in 1 Tim 6:6; "much business": *Sim.* 4.5 and, for example, Marcus
Aurelius 3.5.1; τὰ ἀκόλουθα: *Mand.* 8.4 and, for example, Epictetus
4.8.12. λύπη as vice: *Mand.* 10; *Sim.* 9.15.3 and, for example, *Corp.
Herm.* 13.7; 6.1.

Parallels are often cited between Hermas and the *Tabula* of Pseudo
Kebes,[50] the Κέβητος Φηβαίου Πίναξ, a popular moral work, in which
a picture is allegorically interpreted and Cynic-Stoic elements come to
bear without the author diagnosing them as such. He is of the opinion that they represent Pythagorean wisdom. The parallels indicate no
literary dependency on the part of Hermas. Nevertheless, the common
elements lead to the conclusion that especially behind *Vis.* 3 and *Sim.* 6
stands an allegorical literature which is to be sought in the close vicinity
of Ps. Kebes Tabula. It is similarly popular and originates from the popular philosophical milieu. With this, Hermas's level of education reaches
its upper limits.

Literary Ability

Let us consider Hermas's *literary ability*. Verdicts such as "awkwardness
in writing," "not in control of the material," "clumsy," "disorderly,"
"contradictory," "childish inexperience," "crudities," and "oddities"[51]
are numerous. On the other hand, rays of light occasionally illuminate
the scene.

Examples of the former are: (a) *Vis.* 5 describes a traditional epiphany
scene (see above), but the motif of disguise is not mastered: it remains

50. Particularly *Vis.* 3 and *Sim.* 6. *Sim.* 6.3.3–6 is to be compared to the scenery of
the *Tabula* and *Vis.* 3.8 to the allegorical system of the *Tabula.* In regard to individual
passages one can compare Ps. Kebes 27.3 with *Vis.* 3.7.1; 20.3 with *Vis.* 3.8 (*Sim.* 9.2);
15f. with *Mand.* 6.1.3f. and *Sim.* 6.2.6; 20.3 and 23.2 with *Mand.* 8; 10.2 with *Sim.*
6.2.5. Further details in R. Joly, *Hermas*, 51–53; *Le Tableau de Cébès*, 81–83, 46, 49, 60;
J. Schwartz, "Survivances," 243–46.
51. M. Dibelius, *Hermas*, 423, 425; R. Joly, *Hermas*, 53, Altaner-Stuiber, *Patrologie*,
55; W. J. Wilson, "The Career," 34, 28.

unclear in which way the shepherd changes and how Hermas recognizes him. (b) Many things in the scenes are carelessly presupposed without previously being mentioned (for example, *Sim.* 7). *Vis.* 1.1.9 refers back to the sin of Hermas's family, although it has never before been mentioned. *Vis.* 3.10ff. wishes to interpret previous things, but what is interpreted was to a great extent never told; 3.10.3–5 makes up for the absence. Contradictions with what was previously said come to light (e.g., *Vis.* 3.11.2: 2.4.1). (c) *Vis.* 2.3.2 ignores Hermas's sin of thought in *Vis.* 1.1. *Vis.* 1.3.1 ("not because of this...") nullifies the rhetorically effective introduction in *Vis.* 1 (a drastic example of a Christian sin is given: already small sins of thought are sins of Christians! The reader is shocked and motivated! 1.1.6ff.; 1.2.1, 4). (d) *Sim.* 5.2 narrates in a popular manner a parable of a vineyard in which traditional elements are so ineptly combined that absurdities arise (for details, see M. Dibelius, *Hermas,* 562ff., 576). Traditional elements are so developed that inconsistencies arise (*Sim.* 5.2) and, for example, *Vis.* 3; cf. Dibelius's comment in regard to this section). Amalgamation of different images and motifs leads to diffusion (for example, *Sim.* 9.13 and 9.26; *Vis.* 3.3.3; the heavenly interpreter belongs to what is to be interpreted; the image of the shepherd is an iridescent composite of an interpreter of revelation, an angel of repentance and a personal guardian angel). (e) In *Mand.* 5.1.6 the words καὶ ἐν αὐτῇ κατοικεῖ disrupt the picture. Moreover, the verse grates against 5.1.3 (there the Holy Spirit is contaminated, here patience). (f) At the end of the book (*Sim.* 10) there appears the holy angel, the Son of God: a climax is expected, but the reader experiences in truth nothing new. The applied energy is dissipated.

"Rays of hope": (a) Occasionally, plays on words illuminate the scene (*Mand.* 12.4.3: κύριος — κατακυριεύω; *Sim.* 9.27: ἐπίσκοποι... ἐσκέπασαν, the latter word takes up the picture of the δένδρα σκεπάζοντα; *Mand.* 3.3: πάντοτε — πανούργως — μετὰ πάντων; *Mand.* 7 plays with different meanings of φόβος; *Mand.* 11.3.13 plays with κενός). (b) Hermas's *Mandata* betray at least the author's *desire* to give his presentation a literary form: *Vis.* 5 is an introduction; *Mand.* 12.3.2ff. a conclusion; in between there are the roughly symmetrically laid out *Mandata,* most of which end with a refrain (ζῆν τῷ θεῷ; cf. further W. J. Wilson, "The Career," 36f.).[52] (c) Hermas is familiar with the dialogue form (for example, *Mand.* 12.3ff.; see also the dialogue scenes cited above) and knows how to employ it as a literary means. In *Mand.* 12.4.1 the author brings the dialogue into a fictional crisis in order to emphasize a specific idea. In all the dialogues, Hermas plays the role of the unknowing person who, with his penetrating questions, exacts more

---

52. In *Mand.* 8.3 observe the artistic structure of the catalogue of vices; it originates from the tradition. For details see M. Dibelius, *Hermas,* 526.

clarity from the interpreter of the revelation. *Sim.* 9.33.2 offers a nice change in the otherwise stereotyped dialogues: Hermas, who normally bothers the shepherd with a continuous line of questions, has this time "forgotten" to ask about a specific point, and the shepherd himself must press Hermas to the question. (d) *Sim.* 9.11, with its originally pagan-erotic material (see above), happily distracts the reader for a time, a delightful intermezzo.

Summary: No one would dispute that Hermas possessed a rudimentary literary ability. Also the sheer volume of the book is astonishing.[53] In spite of its colorful absurdities, it sticks to its theme: the new repentance.

Language

Already the Codex Atheniensis felt obliged to correct the language of Hermas. His language is folksy;[54] the style is often clumsy.[55]

Examples: Instead of the Greek accusative of relation, the dative appears (*Vis.* 1.1.2; 3.10.5; 5.1; *Sim.* 9.9.5, 7, etc.). εἰς and ἐν are used interchangeably (*Vis.* 1.2.2; 1.1.2; 2.4.3; 3.7.5; etc.). As in folksy speech, the comparative appears in place of the superlative (*Vis.* 3.4.3). *Sim.* 5.4.2 offers the casual form ἠκουκώς (cf. P. Ox. 237, col. 7.1, 23). The subject of the main sentence and the subject of the genitive absolute can be identical (*Vis.* 1.1.3; 1.2.2; 2.1.1; 3.1.5, etc.; however, this was possible also in classical Greek: Kühner-Gerth, *Grammatik* II, 2d ed. §494); likewise, the subject of the main sentence and the subject of an accusative with infinitive introduced by μετά can be identical (*Sim.* 9.18.3). The tenses are carelessly changed (e.g., *Vis.* 1.1.3). The optative does not appear. In return, one encounters endless parataxis. If an authentic Greek participle construction is begun, the writer eventually stumbles out of it (*Vis.* 1.1f.; 2.1; 3.1; cf. Th. Zahn, *Hermas*, 495).

---

53. It is possible that the book originated and was introduced to the public in successive stages. For the investigation of this problem, see, e.g., R. Joly, *Hermas*, 15. W. J. Wilson ("The Career," 21–62) postulates several publications between 94 and 100 C.E. Harnack assumed six different parts, which occasions Joly's deep sigh, "C'est là une de ces acrobaties gratuites dont est si friande l'érudition allemande!" The often-repeated hypothesis of multiple authorship (e.g., C. Osiek, *Rich and Poor*, 6f.) is not convincing. The language points to a single author (A. Hilhorst, *Sémitismes*, 19–31). In regard to content and language, Osiek herself notes linkages between the alleged three different parts (49; 61, n. 10; 84, n. 23; 125; 127).

54. Cf. Altaner-Stuiber, *Patrologie*, 55; R. Joly, *Hermas*, 56; E. Norden, *Kunstprosa*, 513: "sensible naiveté"; Th. Zahn, *Hermas*, 486ff.: "just as Hermas writes, many people must have spoken"; "the unelaborate language of a man from the folk"; "not only uneducated but a writer who does not form his speech from the spirit of the Greek language"; "uniform and monotonous," "the same expressions occur through the entire book," "with a multitude of words, a deficiency in vocabulary."

55. Cf. R. Joly, *Hermas*, 56; M. Dibelius, *Hermas*, 425.

The Roman milieu leads to Latinisms, e.g., *Vis.* 2.3.4: ἐάν σοι φανῇ —
si tibi videtur; 3.1.4, etc.: συμψέλιον — subsellium, λέντιον — linteum,
κερβικάριον — cervical; 4.1.1: ὁδὸς καμπανή — Via Campana; possibly
2.2.6 ἐκ πλήρους — in pleno; *Sim.* 6.5.5 τὸ ἱκανὸν ποιεῖν — satis-
facere (cf. Mark 15:15); possibly 1.1.2: ἑτοιμάζειν — comparare. For
στατίων — statio in *Sim.* 5.1.1 see above, chap. 10.[56]

Conclusion: Hermas as a Typical Representative of Roman Christianity

In Hermas we encounter a man from the common folk. A higher literary
education is missing; his geographical origin is not Roman; he was born
into slavery; as a freedman and rather wealthy, he was involved in many
worldly businesses.[57] Therefore, as Callistus, the representative of the
Roman Christian community, later does with his edict, he points out the
necessity for theological compromise and musters the courage to present
in Rome a new practicable teaching on repentance. That Hermas's milieu is representative of wider circles of Roman Christianity is clear from
our observations concerning his social mobility (above, chap. 3). It is
also indicated in that his brother, also a house-born slave (*verna*),[58] functioned as a presbyter in Rome (cf. above, n. 27). It is unlikely that the
other presbyters were of a higher class. It is not even known if any of
them were literarily productive, as was Hermas.[59]

---

56. Other possible Latinisms in Th. Zahn, *Hermas,* 487, n. 2; Ch. Mohrmann, "Les
origines," 75–78; A. Hilhorst, *Sémitismes.*

57. The connection between little education and lucrative business ability is also characteristic of the freedman Trimalchio, the type of upstart with whom Petronius amuses
his educated readers, particularly in the vulgar speeches of the *Cena Trimalchionis.* E.g.,
58.7f.: "I have not learned such stuff as geometry, literature and the nonsense in the style
of 'Sing of wrath' [beginning of the *Iliad*] but...I say percentages of small change, the
pound, the dollar...." Cf. also the connection between deficit in education and origins
from slavery which R. P. Duncan-Jones has statistically established ("Abrundung von Altersangaben, Analphabetentum und soziale Differenzierung im Imperium Romanum," in
H. Schneider, *Sozial- und Wirtschaftsgeschichte,* 396ff.).

58. If Hermas was a house-born slave (*verna*), his brother possibly was too. Since the
master who brought up Hermas did not live in Rome and both brothers later lived there,
it is possible that not only Hermas but also his brother was sold to Rhoda in Rome.

59. Of the Roman presbyters or "bishops," as they are catalogued in the Roman
bishop list of the latter quarter of the second century (see below, Part 5 on Irenaeus 3.3.3),
we know hardly anything other than the names. (The information contained in the *Liber
Pontificalis,* compiled in the sixth century, must be set aside or is relevant only if there is
agreement with other sources.) L. Hertling (*Namen*) wished to conclude from the names
that almost all the Roman "bishops" of the second century were of slave origin (e.g.,
Alexander, among others). From the point of view of methodology, I have serious reservations about his approach. A social-historical evaluation of names, as we attempted above
in regard to Rom 16, is still possible for the middle of the first century C.E. After that point,
the decline of the nature of names is so advanced that one can no longer speak of names

W. J. Wilson is of another opinion.[60] He interprets *Vis.* 3 in the sense that the official representatives of Roman Christianity at the time of Hermas were aware of his intellectual insufficiencies and denied him full acknowledgment, while they themselves stood on a higher intellectual level. 3.1.9: "When I wanted to sit down on her right, she [the church] did not permit me, but with her hand beckoned to me to sit down on the left. While I was thinking about this, and feeling sorry that she did not let me sit on the right, she said, 'Are you sad, Hermas?' ... '" According to Wilson, out of sympathy the official church was kind toward the poor man and consoled him because he was sad and disappointed that his prophetic gifts were not fully recognized. 3.2.1: "To the others belongs the left side. Both, however [and now comes the consolation, according to Wilson], those on the right and those on the left, have the same gifts and the same promises, only those who sit on the right have a type of place of honor. You are very eager to sit on the right with them, but your shortcomings are too many." Actually, Wilson distorts the text. The discussion regarding the seating plan is by no means concerned with the acknowledgment of Hermas as a prophet but with the place of honor of the martyrs. 1.9–2.1: "The place at the right is reserved for others who have suffered for his name's sake ... but continue abiding in your honorable way of thinking, as you now do in your simplicity, and you will sit with them and with all who ... bear what they have suffered ... (namely) scourges, prisons, great tribulations, crosses, wild beasts, for God's name's sake. Therefore the right side of the sanctuary is assigned to them and to everyone who will suffer for God's name's sake." Hermas's self-confidence in regard to the presbyters is astonishing. He severely criticizes them (*Vis.* 3.9.7–10; *Sim.* 9.31.6; et al.) and threatens to compare them to drug-mixers if they do not put aside their dissension (*Vis.* 3.9.7). It is not necessary for Hermas to whisper his message in secret (*Mand.* 11.8). He desires to speak publicly before the presbyters (*Vis.* 2.2.6; 2.4.2f.; 3.8.11; 3.9.7). When *Vis.* 3.1.8 allows him to take his place before the presbyters, it is possible that this reflects a situation of rivalry between him and the presbyters — but hardly in the sense described by Wilson.

Wilson's idea to interpret *Vis.* 3.1.4f. psychologically is also original.[61] 1.4f.: "I see an ivory seat. On the seat lay a linen cushion and above it was spread a covering of fine linen. When I saw this and yet no one was there, I began to fear. Trembling seized me, my hair stood on end, and shuddering horror came upon me." The feeling of anxiety

---

as belonging to specific social strata. I have the same reservation regarding C. Osiek, *Rich and Poor*, 104–11.

60. "Career," 34f.
61. Ibid.

at the sight of an empty seat is a classic example of stage fright. According to Wilson, Hermas reproduces here the feeling that he harbored
when he presented for the first time one of his visions to the community.
However this may be, 1.4f. with its charming "stage fright" also does
not allow us to draw conclusions concerning any problems of recognition, at least not in the sense that the presbyters considered his work as
of an unacceptable niveau.

That Hermas is representative of wider circles of Christianity can be
illustrated by the history of the effects of his writings. Some decades
later, the *Canon Muratori* witnesses the popularity of the book of Hermas in that its authors felt moved to turn down attempts to treat this
work as a canonical book. According to the *Canon Muratori,* the book
does not fit into the accepted lists of prophets or apostles for liturgical reading. When council after council must exclude the book from the
canon,[62] that testifies to its popularity. According to Eusebius (*Ecc. Hist.*
3.3.6) Hermas's book was declared by some to be "indispensable, especially for elementary teaching. Therefore, as far as we know, it was
already publicly read in some churches and, as I have established, used
by some of the oldest authors." The first Christian catacomb pictures
found in Naples are inspired by material from Hermas.[63] Hermas clearly
represented in his ideas a broad section of Christianity not only in Rome
but in other Christian communities as well.

---

62. For details, see Wilson, ibid., 61.
63. See, for example, U. Fasola, *Peter and Paul in Rome,* 11; H. Achelis,
"Altchristliche Kunst," 346ff.; J. Daniélou, *Les origines,* 25.

Chapter 23

The Woman from
Justin's *Apology* 2.2

An encounter with a lady is found in Justin's *Apology* (2.2). Her name is not known, at least not from Justin. It is possible, nevertheless, to discover it in some other way. But first we look at Justin's text.

1. We are in Rome during the time of the praefect (Praefectus Urbi) Quintus Lollius Urbicus (c. 144–60 C.E.; Justin, *Apol.* 2.1.1, 3). A formerly pagan woman, now a Chrsitian, lives together with her pagan husband in a mixed marriage. Formerly, she participated in the licentious life-style of her husband (2.2.1, 7: ἀκολασταίνειν). After her conversion, however, she attempts to bring her husband to his senses (σωφρονεῖν), but without success. They are estranged from each other; she refuses to have sexual intercourse with him (συγκατακλίνεσθαι) and wishes to divorce him (τῆς συζυγίας χωρισθῆναι ἐβουλήθη; 2.4). "Her people" (οἱ αὐτῆς, evidently Christians) counsel her to remain with him with the hope of eventually reforming him (2.5).[1] Initially, she follows their counsel but after renewed excesses by her husband, she gives him according to Roman law a letter of divorce (2.6). Her husband takes revenge and denounces her as a Christian. Legal action is initiated against her and her Christian teacher, who is subsequently martyred.

What identifies this Christian woman as "a lady of society"? Let us work through the social-historically relevant material. (a) Both ὑπηρέται and μισθοφόροι, servants and people being paid, slaves and clients (2.7), belong to the household of the couple. (b) The husband travels temporally to Alexandria (2.6). From this reference we can conclude that he does not belong to the senatorial rank, since senators were denied access to Egypt, which was the personal possession of the emperor.[2] (c) 2.9: The woman receives her Christian education from a certain (τις) Ptolemaeus (διδάσκαλος ἐκείνης τῶν Χριστιανῶν μαθημάτων

---

1. Were these people influenced by 1 Cor 7:13–16?
2. Cf., e.g., H. Volkmann, "Senatus," *KlPauly* 5:107.

γενόμενος). He is her private teacher.[3] (d) 2.10ff.: The husband has a centurion (ἑκατόνταρχος) among his friends (φίλος).[4] (e) 2.8: In response to the charge brought against her by her husband, the wife petitions the emperor.[5] Her letter of appeal (*libellus*) contains the request that the trial against her be postponed, because her household affairs (τὰ πράγματα αὐτῆς / τὰ ἑαυτῆς) must be put in order and administered to (διοικήσασθαι / διοίκησις)! A poor person does not know of such considerations. (f) The letter met with success. The reasons given by the wife were accepted by the authorities and the trial was postponed!

As a result, the husband vents his anger against Ptolemaeus, the wife's Christian teacher, and presses charges against him. Ptolemaeus is condemned to die (2.9ff.). Two other Christians, concerning whom we only know that they were among the spectators at the trial against Ptolemaeus and that one is named Lucius, are also condemned to death. They were condemned because they loudly voiced protest against Ptolemaeus's death sentence and confessed themselves as Christians (2.15–19). Justin mentions these three victims. His description in *Apol.* 2.2 is one of the oldest authentic reports of martyrdom that we possess from Rome.[6]

What happened to our Christian woman? Justin does not list her among those killed, although that would correspond to the tendency of 2.1f. This text serves to emphasize the disgraceful situation of the Roman legal practice regarding Christians. Another truly distinguished woman martyr would have raised the rhetorical power. But we hear nothing about what happened regarding the postponed trial.[7] Is the silence eloquent? (a) If the woman is not dead, she is still alive when Justin writes *Apol.* 2. Actually, 2.1.3 confirms that her story was only the cause, ἡ αἰτία, for those three death sentences. (b) Justin is silent concerning her name, although he is otherwise willing to reveal the names of Ptolemaeus and Lucius. Would the Romans know the woman, if Justin mentioned her name? Is she a well-known aristocrat of the city? Is her anonymity considered a protection? (c) Is the trial still pending at

---

3. Cf. L. Friedländer, *Sittengeschichte Roms*, 296ff., about distinguished Roman ladies who surround themselves with educated persons.

4. In 2.10ff. it becomes clear how the husband uses this connection. Through the centurion, he subjects the imprisoned Christian teacher to chicanery.

5. For this *libellus* procedure as a legal means see H. H. Holfelder, "EUSEBEIA KAI PHILOSOPHIA," 249, esp. n. 124.

6. Justin also shows how such reports of martyrdom (Acts of the Martyrs) could orginate: (a) The proceeding before the praefect is public so that Christians can listen from among the spectators (2.15ff.) and later report what took place. (b) Justin is chronologically close to the event that he records: χθὲς δὲ καὶ πρῴην, 2.1.1. The case took place during the term of the praefect Urbicus (144–60 C.E.).

7. 2.2.9 is the last one hears of the woman. The accusing husband was πρὸς ἐκείνην μὴ δυνάμενος τανῦν ἔτι ("momentarily no longer") λέγειν, and consequently he turned against the wife's teacher.

the time of the composition of *Apol.* 2?[8] The events described in 2.2 occurred recently (χθὲς καὶ πρῴην). By means of *Apol.* 2, does Justin wish
to influence not only the trials of Christians in general but particularly
the trial against the woman so that what happened to Ptolemaeus and
Lucius is not repeated?

The story of the woman is breathtaking. As a result of her marital dis-
cord, three Christian brothers were drawn (ἡ αἰτία) to their death, while
she is still alive. She submits a letter of appeal and her trial is officially
delayed. But in the meantime the teacher is executed. The student, who
was charged first, remains spared for the time being. She is not arrested
and remains under official dispensation. Meanwhile, the teacher, before
he is able to defend himself in front of the praefect, is tormented in
prison and subjected to the chicanery of the centurion, who is incited by
the husband of the accused woman.[9] Ptolemaeus must wait a long time
until his trial (τελευταῖον, 2.12). One can do all this to him. And all this
only because his student has to tend to her private financial affairs first.
The differences between the student and the teacher are impressive. The
discrepancy is undoubtedly based upon social differences.[10]

2. Who is the woman who is estranged from her pagan husband and
whose name Justin discreetly does not mention? Is she Flora, to whom
a Valentinian Roman teacher wrote a letter: the letter of Ptolemaeus,
which Epiphanius preserved in his "medicine chest" against heretics
(*Panarion Haer.* 33.3–7)?

There is evidence that the two teachers named Ptolemaeus are the
same person. (a) The Valentinian διδάσκαλος Ptolemaeus lived in second-
century Rome,[11] where the name is not often found.[12] Name, teaching
function, time, place, and a private teaching relationship to a distinguished
lady — all these characteristics correspond. (b) There is also a further
element. The Valentinian Ptolemaeus, who treats in the Flora letter the
essence of the Old Testament laws, puts the question of divorce at the
beginning of the presentation (33.4.4–10); its treatment is lengthy and
broad and the first example, even before the theoretical discussion in 33.5.
The letter and the situation found in Justin 2.2 (namely, the wife is for a
long time undecided whether to divorce her husband or not) correspond
very well.

---

8. Does μὴ τανῦν ἔτι (see previous note) mean "momentarily no longer, but again in
the future"?

9. 2.9ff.: ἐν δεσμοῖς . . . ἐπὶ πολὺν χρόνον ἐν τῷ δεσμωτηρίῳ ἐκολάσατο κτλ. (2.11f.).

10. Cf. Josephus, *Ant.* 18.79f.: The principal accused, a member of the equestrian
class, is only exiled, while the *peregrini* and the freedmen are sentenced to death.

11. The terminus ad quem is the composition of Irenaeus's *Haer.* H. Langerbeck
("Aufsätze," 174) reckons with the possibility that Ptolemaeus traveled with Valentinus
to Rome already during the 130s.

12. In *CIL* 6 it appears 13 times. In regard to the thesis of identity see G. Lüdemann,
"Zur Geschichte," 101f., n. 41, which contains the literature since Harnack.

Ptolemaeus treats the question of divorce in the following manner: Certainly divine law opposes divorcing one's husband, but "out of necessity because of the weakness" of humans (33.4.6) Moses allowed divorce: "Moses wished to do away with this unfortunate relationship, in which they [the estranged couple] lived and through which they ran the risk of being corrupted. On his own, he gave them a second commandment about divorce in order to exchange, out of necessity, a greater evil for a lesser" (7f.). A divorce appeared to Moses to be more advantageous than to be forced through a torturous marriage into injustice and badness, "from which might result complete corruption" (33.4.9).

In this theoretical treatment of the biblical divorce laws, no direct conclusion for the behavior of the Christians is drawn. Ptolemaeus in his letter to the "beautiful Flora" (33.3.1) is too cautious in drawing any conclusions. But, as we know, the woman mentioned in Justin 2.2 did actually decide to seek a divorce after exercising patience for an extended period of time. If the identity of the woman is the same, it is clear what role Ptolemaeus played in the case. Also the rage which the husband unleashed on Ptolemaeus is understandable.

If the identity is the same,[13] one can arrive at yet another social-historical fact in regard to the woman in Justin, *Apol.* 2.2. With his artful and theoretical exposition concerning the Old Testament laws,[14] presented in clear philosophical logic, Ptolemaeus presupposes a high level of reflection on the part of Flora. Explicitly, he notes that she herself has already discovered the different Christian views about the Old Testament and the God of the Old Testament. She has also noted the contradictoriness of these teachings (33.3.1ff.). She is an interested and educated woman.

If the identity is not the same (which I consider unlikely), then in Flora, the addressee of the Valentinian Ptolemaeus letter, we encounter an additional Roman lady of considerable status.

---

13. That Justin acknowledges Ptolemaeus in 2.2 as a Christian teacher does not speak against the Valentinian identification. In *Apol.* 1 and 2 (especially 1.26) Justin does not yet describe the Valentinians as heretics. Only about ten years later in *Dial.* 35.5f. has he "seen through them" and fights them. More on this topic is found below in chap. 40. That the Valentinian Ptolemaeus was still alive at the time of Irenaeus's *Haer.* 1 can hardly be deduced from Praef. 2 (νῦν...οἱ περὶ Πτολεμαῖον). Irenaeus is fighting contemporary followers of Ptolemaeus and not Ptolemaeus himself.

14. See below, chap. 27, regarding the Valentinian Ptolemaeus.

Chapter 24

Marcion

At the sane time as the aforementioned lady, there lived in Rome a wealthy Christian entrepreneur. "Sub Aniceto invaluit," under the Roman presbyter Anicet (ca. 155–66 C.E.), he strengthened with his teaching (Irenaeus 3.4.3). According to Tertullian, he lived during the reign of Emperor Antonius Pius (138–61 C.E.).[1] From Clement of Alexandria, we learn that he already appeared during the reign of Hadrian (117–38).[2] Clement further notes that he was no longer alive during the reign of Marcus Aurelius (from 161 C.E.) and that, although he was a contemporary of Basilides and Valentinus, he was considerably older than they (... ὡς πρεσβύτης νεωτέροις συνεγένετο).[3] Justin, his contemporary, notes he is "still now" teaching in the 150s (καὶ νῦν ἔτι ἐστὶ διδάσκων; Apol. 1.26 and 1.58). A specific date is given with July 144 (Tertullian, Adv. Marc. 1.19). Probably in this month the break between this man and Roman Christianity took place.[4] Before this break, he had lived for some time in communion with Roman Christians.[5] His activity in Rome is thus to be in the 140s and 150s.

References to the entrepreneur Marcion are scattered in the various sources.

1. Marcion's occupation is shipowner, *naukleros*. So writes Tertullian, *De praescr.* 30; *Ad. Marc.* 5.1; 4.9; et al. Tertullian uses the Greek term ναύκληρος and not the Latin term *navicularius*. We see here a credible tradition of the Greek-speaking Roman Christian community. Also Marcion himself spoke Greek and gave his occupation in Greek. When the student of Tatian, Rhodon, a Roman, calls Marcion a "seaman" (ναύτης, cited in Eusebius, *Ecc. Hist.* 5.13.3), this does not contradict

---

1. *De praescr.* 30; *Adv. Marc.* 1.19; 5.19 et al.
2. *Strom.* 7.17.106f. The statement is credible. In this passage Clement is concerned to place the heretics chronologically as far away as possible from the apostolic period.
3. Ibid. Cf. the interpretation of A. Harnack, *Marcion,* 14*f. Harnack estimates that he was born about 20 years earlier, around 85 C.E.
4. Harnack's interpretation of this date is, in my estimation, still the most plausible (ibid., 18*–20*). For the Edessa Chronicle and Fihrist cf. ibid., 29*f.
5. Cf., e.g., Tertullian, *De praescr.* 30; *Adv. Marc.* 4.4; Hippolytus, *Syntagma* (for the latter see blow, n. 27).

Tertullian's tradition, since ναύτης is a comprehensive term and not a technical term (e.g., "ordinary seaman").[6]

Tertullian alludes to "merchandise" and "freight," which Marcion transports. He mentions ships (plural!) of Marcion's.[7]

A *naukleros* is a shipowner or a captain of his own or a rented ship with which he conducts business in his own name.[8] The extreme risk of overseas trade not only presupposes capital but also yields profit. Numerous bequests and donations of considerable size made by *naukleroi* testify that their occupation is lucrative. At the time of Marcion, under the emperor Hadrian and his successors, their material situation was best.[9] Their social position was elevated and respected.[10] In Egypt the shipowners were the wealthiest men among the population.[11] Here and there they were even assigned special seats in the theater, just as senators and other dignitaries.[12] Already according to Cicero (*Off.* 1.42.150f.) shipowners were greatly respected, as opposed to small merchants and other trades people. They can invest the money gained by sea trade in property. The status of the *naukleros* is coveted. In the second century C.E., many who are not shipowners nevertheless attempt to sneak into the membership of a *naukleroi* guild.[13]

Particularly attractive are the privileges attached to the *naukleros* status. Claudius had already granted special rights to the shipowners and grain merchants in Rome.[14] Nero dispensed those engaged in the transportation of overseas foodstuffs from paying taxes on their ships.[15] Since Hadrian the *naukleroi* of the second century are, above all, free from paying municipal taxes.[16]

The *naukleros* enjoys these privileges as long as he places his transport capacity at the service of the *annona,* the imperial agency for importing

---

6. Cf. also the lexical research of H. Conzelmann, "Miszelle zu Apk 18,17," 288–90.

7. Tertullian, *Adv. Marc.* 5.1: "Pontice nauclere, si nusquam furtivas merces vel inlicitas in acatos tuos (in your pirate ships) recipisti, si nusquam onus avertisti vel adulterasti.... " This is not a very friendly remark.

8. Cf., e.g., E. Berneker, "Naukleros," *KlPauly* 4:8; Stoeckle, "Navicularii," Pauly/Wissowa 16/2:1900ff.; M. Rostovtzeff, *Kaiserreich,* 1:132f., 140f., 146f. (see also chap. 5, n. 22, for literature); 2:99, 338 (and chap. 8, nn. 37 and 46). The κυβερνῆται stand *under* the ναύκληροι (Stoeckle, op. cit., 1907).

9. Stoeckle, ibid., 1911; M. Rostovtzeff, *Kaiserreich,* 1:126f.

10. Cf. Stoeckle. In Lugdunum their corpus was called splendidissimum; they issued decrees of their own (cf. A. de Boissieu, *Inscriptions antiques,* 265, 391f).

11. M. Rostovtzeff, 2:18. Cf. also Petronius, 101.4ff.: A shipping magnate from Tarent possesses considerable property and trading personnel.

12. *CIL* 12:3316–18; see Stoeckle, 1911f. Also cf. A. de Boissieu, *Inscriptions antiques,* 396.

13. Stoeckle, 1912 and 1915 with a reference to *Dig.* 50.6.6.6 and 9 (Antoninus Pius and Marcus Aurelius).

14. Suetonius, *Claud.* 18f.; *Gaius,* Inst. 1.32c; Ulp. fragm. 3.6; cf. Stoeckle, 1914.

15. Tacitus, *Ann.* 13.51.

16. *Dig.* 50.6.6.5 §4f.; 6 (Marcus Aurelius and Lucius Verus); 8 (Hadrian); 9 (Pius); cf. also 50.6.6.3; Stoeckle, 1914f., 1928.

grain and other foodstuffs into the capital city.[17] The imperial *annona* provided the population of Rome and the army with, above all, grain, meat, oil, and wine. It needed shipping for huge amounts of goods. Since the commercial life lay in the hands of individual entrepreneurs — there were no business combines, big companies, cooperatives, etc. — the partners of the *annona* were the individual shipowners and merchants such as Marcion, who become increasingly important and indispensable as the provisioning with produce from overseas develops into one of the most urgent duties of the state. The state enters into a contractual relationship with the shipowners for a certain period of time.[18] At least during Marcion's time, the state shows its thanks to shipowners not only through privileges but also by paying transport fees (*vecturae*).[19] Consequently, it could have been not only the missionary perspective that drew Marcion together with his teaching into the capital,[20] but contracts with the imperial *annona* could have equally well led him to Rome.

In the second century, the *naukleros* still enjoys a considerable freedom in regard to the state. It was up to him to travel the seas on the state's behalf or not. He was free to distance himself completely from public service (and its privileges), or he could develop to his heart's content private enterprises alongside the official contacts. (This freedom was limited in the second century only during war; see below.) Only in the third century did the dependence upon the state become stronger, and public services grew into a heavy burden.[21]

A peculiar phenomenon is the guilds of merchants and shipowners. The state welcomes the associations of merchants dealing in overseas trade. An organized corporate body issues useful lists of entrepreneurs available. In this way, negotiations with the individual shipowners are made easier. The corporations limit the individual activity of their members only minimally; each member is responsible for his own business dealings.[22]

The privileges of the *naukleros* in the second century are not yet bound to membership in a guild but are only connected to the possession of a ship. Membership is not yet obligatory,[23] which might be important for a Christian shipowner.

---

17. Cf. *Dig.* 50.5.3; 50.6.6.3; Stoeckle, 1902f., 1913, 1928.
18. Stoeckle, 1913f.
19. *CIL* 2:1180, middle of the second century.
20. So Harnack, *Marcion*, 24f.
21. Stoeckle, 1911–14; cf., e.g., *Cod. Theod.* 14.15.2; 13.5.33; *Cod. Iust.* 11.23.1; 11.2.5.
22. Only in time of crisis does it appear that the state deals directly with a guild — when taxes and compulsory services are demanded of all the members (cf., e.g., *CIL* 3:14165.8; M. Rostovtzeff, *Kaiserreich*, 2:326). The guilds were originally cultic communities. Their actual function remains uncertain.
23. *Dig.* 50.5.3: "his . . . muneris publici vacatio praestatur *ob navem*"; cf. *Dig.* 50.6.1; 50.6.6.9; Stoeckle, 1915; M. Rostovtzeff, *Kaiserreich*, 2:338.

During Marcion's time, we find guilds of merchants and of ship-
owners everywhere.[24] We find them in Rome, Ostia, Puteoli, and
Aquileia. Already at Marcion's time, the arcade behind the theater in
Ostia housed the offices of corporations, which had beautiful mosaics
of ships in the floors. (The present form is from the time of Septimius
Severus.)

It is interesting in regard to Marcion that a *naukleros* must not necessarily himself travel on his ships — not even in the later imperial times,
when public obligations burden the shipowners.[25] In my opinion, this
explains why Marcion precisely in *July* 144, when the sea is "open,"
has time to spare for decisive theological discussions in Rome. He himself provokes that Roman "synod" of presbyters and teachers in July
144 (see below). Could he have not waited for the "mare clausum"
(the closed seas) between 11 November and 10 March? Where did he
find time for all his theological, exegetical, and text-critical work? Marcion appears to have a relatively large shipping business, delegating
responsibilities to other people.

2. *Traveling* corresponds to the occupation of *naukleros*. Traces of
some of Marcion's journeys are still preserved in the sources. Coming
from Pontus,[26] from the commercial city of Sinope,[27] Marcion traveled
into Asia.[28] Finally, we find him in Rome,[29] where he has established his
permanent residence since about 140. Marcion not only travels but he
also sends other people on missions. Before he immigrated to Rome, he
sent ahead of him a woman follower to prepare for his arrival.[30]

---

24. Gaius, *Dig.* 3.4.1.; cf. Stoeckle, 1903. For guilds of *naukleroi* sailing the Black Sea,
see Stoeckle, 1901f.; Marcion came from Sinope in Pontus (see below).

25. Stoeckle, 1921. It was possible to rent one's ships to another businessman (ibid.,
1902). A *naukleros* with personnel is cited by Petronius 101.4. If a *naukleros* entrusted
with a public contract does not personally travel with his ship, he of course cannot lay
claim to the privileges for himself; cf. *Dig.* 50.5.3; 50.6.6.3; Stoeckle, 1928.

26. E.g., Justin, *Apol.* 1.26 and 58; Rhodon in Eusebius, *Ecc. Hist.* 5.13.3; Irenaeus
1.27.2; 3.4.3; Tertullian, *De praescr.* 30; *Adv. Marc.* 1.1, 19; 5.1; et al. Clement of
Alexandria, *Strom.* 3.4.25.

27. Son of the bishop of Sinope, so Hippolytus, *Syntagma against 32 haereses*. The
original *Syntagma* is lost, but it was presumably used by Ps. Tertullian, Epiphanius, and
Filastrius (the last also read Epiphanius). A reconstruction of the *Syntagma's* statements
concerning Marcion on the basis of these three sources was attempted by Harnack (*Marcion*, 24ˣ–28ˣ). "Hippol. *Synt.*" will refer in the following to this list of statements of the
Syntagma put together by Harnack.

28. Cf. Filastrius, *Haer.* 45 (the text is easily accessible in Harnack, 13ˣ) as well as
Papias's Prologus to the Gospel of John (although it is questionable). (Text of the three
codices in Harnack, *Marcion* 11ˣ.)

29. E.g., Justin, *Apol.* 1.26; 1.58; Hippol. *Synt.*; Filastrius, *Haer.* 45. Tertullian knows
Marcion only since his arrival in Rome; of Marcion's previous life he knows no more than
"Ponticus" (cf. n. 26 above).

30. A scattered note from an unknown source recorded by Jerome, *Ep.* 133.4:
"Romam praemisit mulierem, quae decipiendos sibi animos praepararet."

3. When Marcion entered the Roman church, he generously donated 200,000 sesterces to its members, which was returned to him when he separated from them later.[31] In order to get an idea of the amount, we can compare it to the amount of capital that people had to own if they wanted to be accepted into the ranks of nobility; this amount was called in Latin a *census*. The *census* for the equestrian class was 400,000 sesterces,[32] for senators since Augustus one million.[33] Pliny writes to a friend, "From your status as municipal councillor (*decurio*) in our town, we may conclude that you have a *census* of 100,000" (*Ep.* 1.19.2). What Marcion generously donated is double the minimal fortune of a municipal *decurio* and half the minimum fortune of a Roman equestrian. It corresponds to minimum fortune of a *iudex ducenarius*,[34] and to the yearly income of a *ducenarius*, one of the highest imperial officials of the equestrian order (*procurator*).[35]

There are other comparisons to this amount: In Martial (3.52) a house in the city of Rome costs 200,000 sesterces. "With 200,000 one can get a manor near Patrai" (Martial, 5.35). A "little manor" (*agellus*) that Pliny gave to his wet nurse is worth 100,000 sesterces (Pliny, *Ep.* 6.3) According to the land prices mentioned above (chap. 18, n. 34), Marcion could have obtained a 50 hectare piece of land (0.5 km x 1 km) for 200,000 sesterces, which corresponds to the cultivatable area of an independent middle-sized farm.[36]

Did Marcion belong to the equestrian order, which in imperial times controlled trading and banking? The equestrian rank would be quite conceivable for a second-century provincial from Asia Minor (Juvenal, 7.14f.). The possession of merchant ships was forbidden for senators

---

31. Tertullian, *De praescr.* 30: "Marcion cum ducentis sestertiis, quae ecclesiae intulerat...in perpetuum discidium relegatus." Cf. also Tertullian, *Adv. Marc.* 4.4. The alternative translation of "ducentis sestertiis" is of course "two hundred sesterces," but this translation is not applicable here. The memory of such a relatively paltry sum of money would not have survived into the time of Tertullian. The frequent use of the genitive form "sestertium" with numbers over a thousand had the result that "sestertium" was treated as a neuter nominative (from which the plural "sestertia" was derived); therefore "sestertium," without mention of "mille," means "thousand sesterces." "Sescenta sestertia" are, e.g., 600,000 sesterces (cf., e.g., K. E. and H. Georges, *Handwörterbuch*, 2:2639f.). An element of uncertainty comes from another quarter: "ducenti, ae, a" can also denote *indefinite* large sum (examples in Georges, *Handwörterbuch*, 2:2302). In any case, a great sum is intended, so that the following considerations will not be superfluous.

32. For the time of Marcion, cf. Pliny, *Ep.* 1.19! Cf. further, Livy, 5.7.1; 34.31.17; Nepos Cornelius, *Att.* 1.1; Ovid, *Trist.* 4.10.8; *Ex Ponto* 4.8.17; Polybius, 6.20.9; Cicero, *Planc.* 32.

33. Cf., e.g., H. Volkmann, "Senatus," *KlPauly* 5:107.

34. Suetonius, *Aug.* 32.3. This judge presided over small-claims court.

35. Apuleius, *Met.* 7.6.1. Claudius had given to the *ducenarii* the consular signs of honor (Suetonius, *Claud.* 24.1). Among the provincial procurators, who in most cases earned 100,000 sesterces (centenarii), these ducenarii were the highest ranking.

36. See R. Martin, *Plinius d. J.*, 220.

since the time of the "Lex Claudia."[37] Therefore, the members of the equestrian class moved all the more readily into this lucrative area.[38] Although Marcion possessed the financial means, however, he hardly would have tried to rise into the nobility of the equestrian order. He cultivated an ascetic life-style, defying the creator of the world and insisting on strictly observing the beatitudes (Luke 6:20!) as the *proprietas* of Christ's teaching.[39] With contempt for the world, he addressed his followers as "miserable" and "hated" by the world.[40] While the creator God promises happiness to the rich, Christ promises it to the poor.[41] This theological background allows one to understand why Marcion easily parted with so great a sum of money, 200,000 sesterces, in order to prepare the groundwork for his teaching in Rome. Marcion's convictions of faith influence his social history. Faith defines his handling of money and allows no room for higher social aspirations. Whoever rigorously invests in Christianity does not save 400,000 sesterces in order to place his name on the list of those aspiring to nobility.[42] At least from this point of view, Hermas may have enjoyed Marcion (see above, chap. 22).

4. Only one side of the relationship between theology and social background is thus described. It is also valid to make an attempt in the opposite direction. At first glance, one is surprised that a financially prosperous man is angry with the creator of the world and practices contempt for the world. Why? I will first make two observations. (a) Let us examine more closely the portrait of the Marcionite demiurge. The "ruler of the world" desires wars; he is the "instigator of wars, inconstant in his decision, and he contradicts himself."[43] (b) We reliably learn from Clement that Marcion appeared with his teaching already during the time of Hadrian (*Strom.* 7.17.106f.; see n. 2). Thus the embryonic stage of Marcion's teaching reaches back to the time of Trajan.

---

37. Cf. Livy, 21.63.4; *Dig.* 50.3.3.

38. For equestrian and municipal officials listed among shipowners see, e.g., Boissieu, *Inscriptions antiques,* 207, 209, 197, 390. Under Constantine all *navicularii* were to be members of the equestrian order (*Cod. Theod.* 13.5.16).

39. Tertullian, *Adv. Marc.* 4.14. Cf. also Marcion's comment on Luke 12:22ff.: "Christus deprecator creatoris non vult de eiusmodi frivolis (clothing, food, etc.) cogitari" (text in Harnack, *Marcion,* 127 n. 2).

40. συνταλαίπωροι / συμμισούμενοι; cited by Tertullian, *Adv. Marc.* 4.9, 36. (The Greek vocabulary in Tertullian's text, which he translates for his readers, betrays that he is quoting Marcion at this point.) The comment cannot be evaluated from a social-historical point of view in the sense that Marcion's followers came from the lowest social classes. The comment reflects much more Marcion's ethical rigorism. The faithful free themselves from all earthly things in order to escape from the creator God and his order.

41. Cf. the report of this Marcionite teaching by Esnik von Kolb, *Wider die Sekten,* ed. Schmid, p. 193. Although it is a late reference, it is nevertheless written before the Council of Chalcedon. (Text in Harnack, *Marcion,* 378ˣ.)

42. Examples of the latter in Martial, 4.67; 5.38; 5.19.

43. In Irenaeus, 1.27.2. Cf. from Marcion's "Antitheses" also Harnack, *Marcion,* 85.

I will first state my thesis: The two characteristics of the demiurge just cited (warlike, inconstant/contradictory) are transparent for the experiences of a *naukleros* during the reign of Trajan. This horizon of experience makes it possible to explain why Marcion in describing the picture of the demiurge chose specifically these two characteristics from the tradition and considered them of value.

What experiences did a *naukleros* have under Trajan? During Trajan's time a nearly permanent state of war existed that obliged the private transport industry to render taxing compulsory service to the government. Constant movement of troops to the theaters of war, particularly in Dacia and Mesopotamia, had to be executed; large quantities of food had to be assembled at strategic points. Regular provisions of weapons, clothing, and shoes had to be secured, and this over a period of years. If transport in such a great capacity was needed by the state, it was unavoidable that the shipowners were obliged to offer compulsory service.[44] The reliefs on Trajan's column depict sailing ships transporting troops; ships transport fresh supplies for the army from the Greek cities along the estuary of the Danube and from southern Russia as well as down the Danube from northern Italy and Aquileia. The burden placed upon shipowners during Trajan's wars becomes evident from the subsequent politics of Hadrian: In view of the alarming deterioration of the economic situation within the empire, Hadrian hastened to free Italy from the customary change-of-throne tax and to reduce it for the provinces. He removed the debts owed to the treasury in Italy and generously subsidized the cities of the empire. And he took measures specifically for the benefit of the shipowners *(navicularii)* who were in the service of the state. The principal privilege that he granted them was to free them from the municipal liturgies.[45] How brutally undisciplined soldiers in everyday life could commandeer compulsory services for the state is indicated in an edict of M. Petronius Mamertinus.[46] Marcion, as a shipowner from Pontus, certainly did not escape the compulsory services of Trajan's wars. That is apparent from the geographic situation:

44. See M. Rostovtzeff, *Kaiserreich,* 2:99 and on p. 326 the inscription CIL 3:14165.8. Cf. also Pliny's description of Domitian's journey after the war with the Suebes and Sarmates (*Paneg.* 20.4). For compulsory transport for the state cf. finally Simon of Cyrene (ἀγγαρεύω! Matt 27:32). Parallel to this is the gardener from Apuleius's *Met.* 9.39, whose ass was recruited by a legionnaire "for the luggage of our governor." Also see Epictetus, 4.1.79.

45. For the privileges granted by Hadrian and his successors, see the references above in n. 16 and M. Rostovtzeff, *Kaiserreich,* 2:326, n. 37.

46. See M. Rostovtzeff, *Kaisereich,* 2:325, n. 34, with additional literature. A further example of rough handling of "the sea lords" *(domini navium)* is that they were denied their claim to the "excusatio tutelae" (exemption from guardianship) by Trajan's administration (*Dig.* 27.1.17.6; cf. Pauly/Wissowa 16/2:1929). For the privilege of exemption from the civil obligation of *tutela,* the taking over of guardianship, cf. A. Schulten, "*Tutela,*" Pauly/Wissowa 7/2:1497ff.

Pontus lies in the middle between the two main theaters of war, Dacia and Mesopotamia.[47] It is thus by no means astonishing that Marcion groans under a warlike demiurge. For him, behind the Roman imperial administration stands the demiurge. In one passage in his *Antitheses*, Marcion himself characterizes the Roman bureaucracy explicitly as a representative of the demiurge.[48]

It is also plausible that Marcion accuses the demiurge of being "inconstant in his decision and self-contradictory." From the perspective of the *naukleros*, imperial politics run hot and cold. Trajan demands compulsory service; Hadrian grants privileges. Each of these two emperors considered by himself can also appear contradictory to the *naukleros*. That Trajan enlists the shipowners for compulsory service is dictated by superordinate political exigency and does not correspond to his own original intention. A relief on the arch of Trajan in Benevento (ca. 107–14 C.E.) indicates that the emperor desires to be on good terms with the representatives of the merchants and shipowners. He greets them in a friendly manner, wearing civil dress and not his military uniform. On the other hand, Hadrian is likewise from the point of view of the *naukleros* "erratic." He grants privileges and puts an end to offensive politics. But, on the other hand, he also cannot completely forgo military action (e.g., fights with the Sarmates). What from the imperial perspective appears as rational politics must appear contradictory to the shipowners.

There is still a second, more remote possibility to find a background situation for the motif of the warlike demiurge in Marcion. As a God lusting for war, the Jewish God, the creator of the world, revealed himself also in the Zealot movement of the Jewish war of 115 to 117 C.E. (cf. also 66–73 and 132–35 C.E.). Cassius Dio (68.32.1–3) and Appian (*Arabicus Liber*, fr. 19) emphasize the military zeal of the Jewish rebels in North Africa at the time of Trajan (cf. also Orosius, 7.12.7; Eusebius, *Ecc. Hist.* 4.2.2). Corresponding to this, the gnostic Basilides, writing in Alexandria, characterizes the demiurge, ruler of the world and God of the Jews, as the one who "wished to subject the remaining people of the world to the Jews" (in Irenaeus, *Haer.* 1.24.4). Basilides undoubtedly

---

47. From the foregoing chronology (particularly, Clement of Alexandria, *Strom.* 7.17.106f.) one may conclude that Marcion at least participated in the Parthian war (114–17 C.E.) as a *naukleros*.

48. According to Marcion, in the official persecutions of Christians by the state the demiurge himself acts, since he has the hearts of the kings in his hand (text in Harnack, *Marcion*, 296x). Already apocalyptic literature (e.g., 1 Enoch 85–90) lets mythical persons, tormenting angels, become transparent figures for real political authorities. It is all the more understandable that for Marcion the demiurge, the God of the Jews and rulers of the world, stands behind the emperor when we observe the analogies between the emperor / state, on the one hand, and Judaism, on the other: (a) Laws and confidence in law play an equally prominent role for emperor and state as for the Jews. (b) The glorification of war in the Greek tradition since the time of Homer corresponds to the tradition of the holy war in Judaism.

here refers to the Jewish revolt originating in Egypt and Cyrene. Marcion did not live in Egypt, as did his contemporary Basilides. Things looked different from his perspective. Events such as the Jewish revolt hardly touched the existence of the shipowner from Pontus as closely as Trajan's military machine in Dacia and Mesopotamia did (together with its compulsory measures against the shipping magnates). Therefore, the latter has precedence methodologically as the situational background for the interpretation of Marcion. The Jewish uprising at the time of Trajan could have been a further background of Marcion's theological thinking; it was, however, hardly the primary one.

I have attempted to correlate specific situations to individual characteristics in Marcion's doctrine of the demiurge, not, however, to the general idea of a lesser world creator. It is clear that this attempt is not meant as a lineal derivation. It by no means excludes traditional internal theological and exegetical derivations of Marcion's demiurge doctrine: Whoever, as Marcion, reads the Old Testament as literal and true and does not engage in allegorical interpretation is not obliged to but *can* naturally push toward the thesis that the demiurge is zealous for war (holy war!) and inconstant, subject to emotions.[49] The post-Old Testament tradition is also cognizant of a warlike god (e.g., 1QM). This topos is without doubt in the tradition. My question is, however, *why* Marcion used this element of the tradition for his demiurge theology. Was it the experience of the *situation* that inspired Marcion to emphasize some traditional elements and to ignore others? Did the situation direct him in his relation to the tradition? Jewish scribes also cultivated literal exegesis of the Old Testament but arrived at a completely different picture of the creator of the world than did Marcion.

A tradition-historical derivation and a deduction from the social-historically describable situation are just as little excluded as the height and breadth of a room. I have called this type of understanding "three-dimensional interpretation" in other places;[50] references to situation and tradition complement each other.

I am open to every internal theological and tradition-historical derivation. But in this way a complete "explanation" has hardly been already given. On the other hand, a social-historical explanation is also in the same way insufficient when it is offered as the only pattern for understanding. A social-historical explanation should not be in competition with an inner theological interpretation on a two-dimensional level but should be seen as a further additional dimension.

---

49. Cf., e.g., Tertullian, *Adv. Marc.* 1.2: The Marcionites base the evil character of the demiurge on an exegesis of Isa 45:7 ("I am the one who establishes evil" ["ego sum qui condo mala"]).

50. Cf. P. Lampe, "Die Apokalyptiker," 71f., 88, 92f.

5. In July of 144 Marcion left the community of the orthodox churches in Rome and founded his own church. The 200,000 sesterces were returned to him. One can conclude that he immediately "invested" them in the expansion of his own movement. In other words, *at least* 200,000 sesterces were available to Marcion's community as seed money, a circumstance that is interesting enough when one observes the rapid development of Marcion's church.

Justin testifies that Marcion's heresy had already in the 150s gained a foothold in all the provinces (πᾶν γένος ἀνθρώπων; πολλοί: *Apol.* 1.26 and 58). One can imagine the extent traveled by Marcion's followers. In this period Marcion represented the principal danger for the established church. In the *Apology* (1.25 and 58) Justin names Marcion along with the traditional archheretics Simon and Menander, while other heresies are treated summarily without name. A few years later, in *Dial.* 35.6, other names of heretics are added, but the name of Marcion remains in first place: Marcionites, Valentinians, Basilidians, Satornilians.[51] Irenaeus mentions (4.6.2) that Justin wrote a specific work against Marcion.[52] The existence of such a writing indicates how dangerous Justin considered Marcion's doctrine. Justin's statement that Marcion's poison infiltrated into all the provinces is easy to illustrate. Already in the second century Marcion's doctrine was contested throughout the empire, which indicates how great the Marcionite "danger" was considered. A presbyter[53] in Asia Minor and Hegesippus[54] fought against Marcion's work, along with Dionysius of Corinth in a letter to Nicodemia.[55] One also finds evidence of the battle against Marcion's work in Theophilus of Antioch,[56] Philip of Gortyna in Crete,[57] a certain Modestus, whose place of origin is unknown,[58] Irenaeus of Lyon,[59] and, perhaps, Melito of Sardis.[60] In Rome in the second century Rhodon writes against the Marcionites,[61] and in Alexandria, Clement.[62]

---

51. Cf. similarly, Hegesippus in Eusebius, *Ecc. Hist.* 4.22.5.

52. Even if this work were Justin's lost *Syntagma* against all heresies (*Apol.* 1.26; cf. Tertullian, *Adv. Val.* 5), it would not change matters. Irenaeus would then be a witness that the *Syntagma* was directed primarily against Marcion. The previously mentioned evidence from the *Apology* speaks for the latter, because when in the 150s only Marcion plays a major role next to Simon and Menander as heretics, this situation holds true all the more for the *Syntagma*, which was composed before the *Apology*.

53. Cf. Irenaeus, 4.27–32.

54. Cf. Eusebius, *Ecc. Hist.* 4.22.4ff.

55. Eusebius, *Ecc. Hist.* 4.23.4.

56. Eusebius, *Ecc. Hist.* 4.24, and Theophilus, *Autol.* 2.25.

57. Eusebius, *Ecc. Hist.* 4.25.

58. Ibid.

59. Cf., e.g., Irenaeus, 1.27.2f.; 3.12.12.

60. Cf. as source Anastasius Sinaita in A. Harnack, *Marcion*, 318[x] n. 2.

61. Eusebius, *Ecc. Hist.* 5.13.

62. E.g., *Strom.* 7.17.106f.

Celsus is also aware of the Marcionite church.[63] There are also "several others" (Eusebius, *Ecc. Hist.* 4.25) who fight against Marcion.[64] At the turn of the century Tertullian (*Adv. Marc.* 5.19) correctly observes: "Marcion's heretical tradition filled the *whole world*" (Marcionis traditio haeretica *totum* implevit *mundum*).[65]

Besides the rapid external increase in the second century that provoked the opposition of the established church throughout the empire, there stands a securely established internal organization of the Marcionites' movement (contrary to gnostic circles — according to all that we know). The opponents themselves begrudgingly admitted that what developed was not an unorganized school community but rather a proper church with tightly organized communities. "As the wasps also build honeycombs, so do the Marcionites also build churches,"[66] with baptisms and other rites[67] and with ecclesiastical distinction between baptized and catechumens, clerics and laypersons.[68] After the death of Marcion, several theological schools found a place *within* the Marcionite church.[69]

One can conclude that Marcion in his lifetime undoubtedly surpassed all other heretics in effectiveness.

Only after the death of Marcion, the Gnostics, the Valentinians and others, became likewise a threat to the church. In Irenaeus and Hippolytus the Marcionites no longer stand first in the list of heretics, as they do in Justin (cf., e.g., Irenaeus, 1.1–22, 23–26, 27, 28–31). At

---

63. Origen, *Contra Cel.* 2.27; 5.62; 6.51ff., 74; 7.25, 74; cf. A. Harnack, *Marcion* 154: Celsus "speaks sometimes as though there are only two churches, the 'established' church and the Marcionite church, and next to these only a gnostic thicket."

64. Cf. also Ptolemaeus in Rome, who possibly wrote against Marcion in his letter to Flora (in Epiphanius, 33.3.2, 6f.); in Asia Minor the unknown anti-Montanist whom Eusebius cites (*Ecc. Hist.* 5.16.21); cf. possibly also the lost polemical writings against heresies written by Miltiades and Proclus in Asia Minor (Tertullian, *Adv. Val.* 5; cf. Eusebius, *Ecc. Hist.* 5.28.4).

65. Cf. also Tertullian, *De praescr.* 30: Among all the heretics, Marcion and Valentinus had the most followers. Accordingly, Epiphanius later marked out the areas to which the Marcionites had spread: Rome, Italy, Egypt, Palestine, Arabia, Syria, Cyprus, Thebais, Persia, and elsewhere (42.1).

66. "Faciunt favos et vespae, faciunt ecclesias et Marcionitae." (Tertullian, *Adv. Marc.* 4.5).

67. Cf., e.g., Tertullian, *Adv. Marc.* 1.14; 1.23; 3.22; Cyprian, *Ep.* 73.4; 74.7; Augustine, *De bapt. c. Donat.* 3.15.

68. Bishops and presbyters (Eusebius, *De mart. Palaest.* 10.3; *Adamant. de recta in deum fide* 1.8). Cf. further A. Harnack, *Marcion,* 146; Harnack (*Marcion,* 154, n. 1) assembles a list of the Marcionite bishops and priests. According to Harnack (*Marcion,* 146) Marcion himself had already introduced this organization — although there is no direct evidence for this. Nevertheless, documentation begins very early.

69. Cf. perhaps Tertullian, *De praescr.* 42; especially Rhodon in Eusebius, *Ecc. Hist.* 5.13. Rhodon writes that in spite of different schools of thought, all Marcionites were basically of one opinion. The only visible split that occurred within the Marcionite movement is that of Apelles (Tertullian, *Praescr.* 30).

the latest after 250 C.E., the Marcionite church begins to shrink in the West, although in Rome Novatian still fights against it.[70] Cyprian (*Ep.* 73.4; 74.7) and Dionysius of Rome still testify to it there.[71] In Rome, Hippolytus still considers it necessary to write a special work against it.[72]

The rapid growth of the Marcionite movement and its early consolidation in the mold of a proper church, in my opinion, are also explained by the initial financial basis mentioned above. In addition the vocation of a shipowner was directly predestined to encourage geographical expansion. Both social-historical motives should be considered if Marcion's missionary success is to be evaluated.

Marcion's Education

The literary works. (a) Marcion worked text-critically. He purified the "genuine" text of the Gospel and the Pauline letters from Judaizing "interpolations." To venture upon such a text-critical endeavor presupposes education. One who completed the school of the grammarian had sufficient education for this. When the teacher in the grammar school analyzed the classical texts, the copies which the students held in their hands had first of all to be brought into agreement with each other. "Corrections" of the text were made before any commentary and exegesis. The text was purged of mistakes.[73] Formally, Marcion's text restoration consists primarily of deletions; additions are rare. Changes occasionally betray linguistic skill: one word is replaced by another in which the letters are similar (e.g., ἀγοράσαντος — ἀγαπήσαντος Gal 2:20). Active and passive pronouns and particles are interchanged in order to purge the text of alleged "Judaizing adulterations."[74] Marcion presumably gained the knowledge for such finesse in the grammarian's school. However, that he at some time corrected the text on stylistic

---

70. References are collected in A. Harnack, *Marcion*, 335[x]f., n.5.

71. Text in A. Harnack, *Marcion*, 336[x], n. 1.

72. Eusebius, *Ecc. Hist.* 6.22. Is it identical with the writing περὶ τἀγαθοῦ καὶ πόθεν τὸ κακόν, which is noted on the statue of Hippolytus?

73. Cf., e.g., J. Carcopino, *Rom. Leben und Kultur*, 164f.; decisions were often made from the point of view of aesthetics. Pliny (*Ep.* 4.26) illustrates how often one had to reckon with text corruptions: Nepos had procured writings by Pliny and asked Pliny to let these copies be corrected (*emendandos*). The same can be found in Martial (7.11 and 17). (E.g., "the seven books sent by me which the reed of the author himself corrected . . . the correction must indeed increase the value" of the books). On the διόρθωσις and ἔκδοσις of the grammarians, cf. H. Erbse, "Iliasausgaben," 275–303; especially 296, 299–301; R. Pfeiffer, *Geschichte*, 97f., 122, 141ff., 152f., 177ff., 264f., 267, 335; especially with reference to the text criticism of Homer since Zenodot.

74. Cf. the examples in A. Harnack, *Marcion*, 62f.

or aesthetic grounds, as occasionally occurred[75] in the grammarians' schools, is not demonstrable.[76] Marcion's changes were motivated by dogma and as such original. They deviated from the ethos of grammar.

This ethos is revealed in the ancient critique of Zenodotus, which accused the old master of text criticism from Alexandria of arbitrary changes on false internal grounds and according to subjective opinion.[77] If a decision according to aesthetics and individual stylistic taste was despised by conscientious grammarians,[78] although it was often practiced, even more despised was the conscious effort to purify texts according to an "ideological" and dogmatic point of view. Such was Marcion's unabashed method. And he even was not consistent in how he himself applied it.[79]

We can conclude that Marcion's education originates from the time he was a seventeen-year-old student in the school of a grammarian. His procedure, however, is "ungrammatical."

(b) Marcion composed the critical work *Antitheses,* which came out in addition to his text of the Gospel and the Apostle. Its literary character is not completely clear. Next to short antitheses which, with the help of biblical passages, contrast[80] the words and work of the creator of the world with those of the good God, extensive "argumentations" appear concerning the correct interpretation of biblical passages, as well as exegetical,[81] historical, and dogmatic critical explanations.[82] There is total unclarity concerning the arrangement of the work. Is it a continuous commentary on Marcion's New Testament text, just as classical texts were commented on in the schools of the grammarians? The extent of the work was considerable[83] and consumed whatever time remained to the author from his usual job.

Marcion did not develop a philosophical-theological "system." He was a biblicist who, in contrast to most gnostics, barricaded himself with a canon of scripture and a biblical theology from mythological

---

75. Zenodot was occasionally motivated in text-critical decisions by his predilection for clear syntactical structure and the greatest conciseness in texts (cf. R. Pfeiffer, *Geschichte,* 143).

76. This negative finding is in A. Harnack, *Marcion,* 44, 64f.

77. Cf. R. Pfeiffer, *Geschichte,* 146; H. Erbse, "Iliasausgaben," 302.

78. H. Erbse, "Iliasausgaben," 300.

79. In comparing what Marcion changed and what he left remaining, there are often inconsistencies. Cf. A. Harnack, *Marcion,* 66, 44ff.

80. E.g., Tertullian, *Adv. Marc.* 1.19; 2.29; 4.1; 4.4; 4.6. The form of the antithesis might have been suggested by the Pauline antitheses in Galatians and Romans or by Jesus's parables of the good and bad tree and of the new garment and old patch which Marcion placed at the beginning of his presentation. Cf. A. Harnack, *Marcion,* 89.

81. E.g., Tertullian, *Adv. Marc.* 4f.

82. Like that concerning the apostolic period and Gal 1f. (cf. Tertullian, *Adv. Marc.* 4.1ff.) or that concerning the "Judaistic Christians." Cf. further A. Harnack, *Marcion,* 78–83.

83. Cf. A. Harnack, *Marcion,* 80, 83.

and cosmological speculations as well as from philosophical influences. Philosophical studies are not to be found anywhere in Marcion, and the Hellenistic spirit does not flutter from his work. When he interspersed individual philosophical motifs, these betray at best a popular philosophical knowledge and not a special philosophical education. Only J. G. Gager[84] has wished to show a special Epicurean influence. According to him, Marcion's argumentation for a higher god is partly Epicurean. Gager relies above all upon Tertullian's *Adv. Marc.* 2.5.1f. (Marcion) and compares Lactantius's *De ira dei* 13.20f. (Epicurus).[85]

Marcion: "If God is good (*bonus*) and knows (*praescius*) the future and is able (*potest*) to prevent evil, why did he allow mankind to be encircled by the devil? If he were *bonus . . . , praescius . . .* and *potens,* this would not have happened. . . . Because it now happens," God, the ruler of the world, cannot be *bonus, praescius, potens.*" "Just as such would not happen, if God were *bonus . . . , praescius . . .* and *potens,* so it did happen because he is not such a God."

Epicurus: "God desires (*vult*) either to eliminate evil and is not able to (*potest*) or he can do it and does not wish to. Or he neither wishes nor can do it. Or he desires and is able to do it. If he desires it and is unable to do it, he is a weakling . . . ; if he is able to do it and does not desire to do so, he is begrudging. If he neither can nor desires, he is begrudging as well as a weakling. If he desires and is able . . . , from whence comes evil and why does he not eliminate it?"

Both texts observe that the evil that is in the world and God's attributes (*bonus, potens,* etc.) contradict each other. From the contradiction it follows that *this* god cannot be responsible for the things in the world. Gager claims that Marcion might have been familiar with Epicurean philosophy. He concedes to him "some degree of philosophical sophistication" and extols the "complexity of the argument."[86] But does not any thoughtful high-school senior or undergraduate climb to the same heights of argumentation without Epicurus's footstool? The parallel to Epicurean philosophy does not need special philosophical education. It betrays at most that Marcion paged through one of the ordinary philosophical compendiums. The elements used in the argumentation of both texts were nothing more than commonplace in the popular philosophy of the Hellenistic Roman period, a platitude that circulated under the label Epicurean.[87]

---

84. "Marcion and Philosophy," *VC* 26 (1972): 53–59.

85. As a third text, Sextus Empiricus's *Pyrr.* 3.9–11 could be compared where the same structures of argument appear.

86. J. G. Gager, "Marcion and Philosophy," 57.

87. Besides Lactantius cf., e.g., Cicero, *Div.* 2.50.104, *Nat. Deor.* 3.31.76ff. Sextus Empiricus (n. 85) quoted this thought as a compromise without attributing it to a particular philosophical school.

Let us examine the texts more closely. Lactantius clothes his thoughts in strict logic. All four possibilities of the combination of *"vult"* and *"potest"* are orchestrated: If he does not will, although he can, then...; if he does will, but cannot, then..."; etc. (similarly Sextus Empiricus). This academic "unraveling" of ideas is absent from Marcion.[88] The thought is flat, insofar as the three if-clauses more or less remain the same in a somewhat boring, repetitious style ("if *bonus, praescius, potens,* then...").

Finally, J. G. Gager[89] suggested that Marcion's rejection of allegorical interpretation of the Old Testament[90] is the result of a philosophical education. As known, Plato, Eratosthenes, Aristarchus, and Epicurus came out against allegory.[91] Nevertheless, Harnack has shown that Marcion's rejection of allegory can be attributed to "internal" influences.[92] If we compare a philosophically educated person such as Clement of Alexandria, who uses allegorical interpretation, or any of the Greek philosophers, who use allegorical exegesis to interpret myths and poetry, above all Homer, we could even find Marcion's renunciation of allegory "uncultured." Marcion's nonallegorical exegesis reveals no evidence of a pagan education.[93]

A similar situation prevails with the other individual philosophical motifs. When Marcion finds it unacceptable that God might be subject to emotions, he is dependent on a general popular philosophical knowledge, which is at best supplied from ordinary philosophical compendiums.[94] Marcion appears to know the Stoic idea of apathy,[95] as well as the Stoic definition of remorse.[96] The idea of the indolence of God

---

88. Cf., by way of contrast, the strict logical train of thought of his student Apelles in the fragments preserved by Origen (the texts are assembled in A. Harnack, *Marcion,* 412xff.).

89. "Marcion and Philosophy," 58.

90. Cf. reference material in A. Harnack, *Marcion,* 259xf.; cf. Tertullian, *Adv. Marc.* 5.18.

91. Cf. J. G. Gager, "Marcion and Philosophy," 58.

92. Cf. A. Harnack, *Marcion,* 87.

93. A. Harnack (*Marcion,* 22, cf. 67, 30ˣ) suspected that Marcion might have grown up in a family of Jewish origin. He based his supposition on the similarities with the exegesis of orthodox Judaism. These exegetical similarities are: exegesis is based upon the literal wording of the Old Testament without allegory or typology; the Old Testament text is in its totality creditable and not interpolated; the Old Testament prophesies do not refer to Christ. Tertullian can correspondingly bring some of the same arguments against the Jews as against Marcion (cf., e.g., *Adv. Marc.* 3.6; 3.8; 3.16). Harnack (*Marcion,* 86), however, admits that a deeper understanding of the Old Testament is wanting in Marcion.

94. Marcion: If God is angry and jealous, he is also mortal (Tertullian, *Adv. Marc.* 2.16; cf. further, M. Pohlenz, *Stoa* 1.410f.). Carneades and Panaetius conclude: "quod dolorem accipit, id accipiat etiam interitum necesse est" / "dolere..., ergo etiam interire" (Cicero, *Nat. Deor.* 3.32; Cicero, *Tu.* 1.79f.; "dolere" = generally the emotions). Marcion's conclusion corresponds to this; literal echoes are absent.

95. Tertullian, *De praescr.* 7.3 (*tranquillitas*).

96. Cf. Tertullian, *Adv. Marc.* 2.24 with Stobaeus's *Anthologium* 2.102.25ff. (ed. Wachsmuth).

might come from Epicurus.[97] A few philosophical motifs say nothing concerning a philosophical education.

When the church fathers portray Marcion as wandering through all kinds of philosophies, that testifies little to his actual education. Their portrait corresponds to the usual polemic against heretics, which discredits opponents as "philosophers" of pagan origin and to be especially dependent on the despicable denier of God, Epicurus. Tertullian believed Marcion to be influenced by Epicurus.[98] According to him, Marcion's higher God was a "deus philosophorum" (*Adv. Marc.* 2.27.6). In other places, Tertullian calls Marcion "*Stoicae* studiosus" (*De Praescr.* 30.1 and 7.3; cf. *Adv. Marc.* 5.19). Hippolytus believed Marcion was dependent upon Empedocles and the Cynics (*Ref.* 7.29–31; 10.19). Clement of Alexandria calls him a confused Platonist.[99] These contradictory voices refute themselves.

Summary: Nothing can be ascertained about a higher education that Marcion might have had with orators or philosophers. Although Marcion's disciples were called *discipuli*,[100] his movement did not take the form of a philosophical school but rather that of a church. Marcion himself was no philosopher, and in this he distinguished himself from his opponent, Justin.

As was the custom, until the age of seventeen, Marcion attended a grammarian's school; otherwise he would hardly have achieved his text-critical and exegetical proficiency. Also knowledge of mathematics, geometry, and astronomy, which were disciplines learned in a grammarian's school, can be presupposed for a shipowner. Here it is interesting to note Tertullian's polemic (*Adv. Marc.* 1.18): "The Marcionites are for the most part mathematicians. Also they do not blush when they (as alleged astrologists) make their living from the stars of the demiurge."

On the sparse references to relevant social-historical elements concerning Marcion's disciples, see Appendix 1. The evidence lets one suspect that Apelles was better educated in pagan philosophy than his teacher, Marcion.

---

97. Cf. Tertullian, *Adv. Marc.* 5.19.7, with Cicero, *Div.* 2.50.103.

98. Tertullian, *Adv. Marc.* 5.19.7; 2.16; 1.25.3; cf. similarly Jerome, *Comm. in Isa.* 7, on Isa 18:1–3.

99. *Strom.* 3.3.21. Cf. also Origen, who characterizes him as "doctissimus" (in Jerome, *Comm. in Ose.* 2 to Hos. 10:1).

100. E.g., Irenaeus, 1.27; Tertullian, *Adv. Marc.* 1.1.

Chapter 25

Justin

In regard to Justin, direct and indirect social-historical information complement each other. The sources available to us are Justin's *Apology* 1 and 2, his *Dialogue with the Jew Trypho,* and the *Acts* of Justin's martyrdom.[1]

Introduction

First I will list the direct information and then, in the second section, deal with it critically. Justin, the philosopher,[2] lived in Rome as an immigrant. Born of a pagan family in Flavia Neapolis in Samaria, which is today Nablus in the West Bank (*Apol.* 1.1; *Dial.* 120.6), he had the benefit of a pagan philosophical education in the east. For a considerable time, he was first a student of a Stoic (*Dial.* 2.3) and then of a Peripatetic who demanded payment from his new student already after the first days of class. Justin turned his back on him (*Dial.* 2.3).[3] He turned to "a very famous Pythagorean," but did not pass the teacher's entrance examination. Justin lacked the necessary propaedeutic knowledge in music, astronomy, and geometry. So the teacher "sent him on his way because I admitted to him that I knew nothing about these

---

1. Besides Justin's *Apology* 2.2 (cf. chap. 23) and the *Acts of Apollonius* (cf. chap. 29) they are the only authentic Acts of martyrs from Rome for our period. The *Acts of Justin and His Companions* is available in several recensions of the text (see below). On the whole they are reliable — also because of their brevity. Text edition: H. Musurillo, *The Acts of the Christian Martyrs* (Oxford, 1972); literature in Altaner and Stuiber, *Patrologie* 65f., 90, 554, 559.

2. This self-portrayal (φιλόσοφος/φιλοσοφία), e.g., in *Dial.* 1.1, 6; 2.1; 3.2–4; 8.2. *Apol.* 1.14.4: As a philosopher he taught (διδάσκειν) the Christian διδάγματα. Besides these self-portrayals, Tertullian is the first to refer to Justin as a philosopher (*Adv. Val.* 5.11).

3. The avarice of the Peripatetics was a constant motif in the polemics against philosophers (Lucian, *Vitarum auctio* 26; *Men.* 5; *Dial. mort.* 10.11; *Nigrinus* 25; *Piscator* 14f., 36; Aelios Aristides, *Or.* 45. For δριμύτης as a topos cf. Attikos in Eusebius, *Pr. Ev.* 15.13.1 about Aristotle). Therefore, the color of this autobiographical note pales somewhat. Conclusions concerning Justin's financial means are unfortunately not permitted.

subjects" (*Dial.* 2.4f.).[4] This not-exactly "splendid career," which, if it does not betray a slender purse (n. 3) but does indeed reveal deficits in propaedeutic education, ended with a "prominent" Platonist "in our city" (in Neapolis?). Here, finally, "I made progress and improved myself as much as possible from day to day. The spirituality of the incorporeal interested me very much; the contemplation of ideas inspired my thinking,...I cherished the hope of contemplating God directly, for this is the aim of Plato's philosophy" (*Dial.* 2.6; cf. *Apol.* 2.12.1; 13.2). At the end of his life, during the trial before the Roman municipal praefect, Justin states that he endeavored to get to know all philosophical systems (*Acta Iustini* 2.3; recensions A and B).

Sometime before 135, while in the east, the Platonist converted to Christianity. If the *Dialogue with the Jew Trypho* is supposed to have a historical background, as Eusebius believed, then that type of disputations between the Christian Justin and the "Jew Trypho" took place in the east during the Bar Kochba insurrection (135 c.e.).[5] Perhaps Justin also personally experienced Bar Kochba's persecutions of Christians in Palestine (*Apol.* 1.31.6; cf. Eusebius, *Chron. Hadrian* 17 [ed. Helm, 201] and saw the Jewish countryside devastated by Hadrian (*Apol.*

---

4. In the reference to "deficiency of knowledge in propaedeutic disciplines," I see a genuine autobiographical note. Not only for the Pythagoreans (cf. Lucian, *Vitarum auctio* 2; Tertullian, *De anima* 31.4) but also for Middle Platonism, which still influenced Justin after his conversion to Christianity (see below), propaedeutic sciences were considered of great importance. For example, in the second century, Theon of Smyrna wrote his work Τὰ κατὰ τὸ μαθηματικὸν χρήσιμα εἰς τὴν Πλάτωνος ἀνάγνωσιν (What mathematical knowledge one needs for the reading of Plato) (ed. H. Dupuis [Paris, 1892]). Besides arithmetic, the theory of music and astronomy, were, among other subjects, set forth in this book. There is mention of a treatise on geometry, but it is not extant in the manuscripts we possess. A similar value was placed upon propaedeutic by the Platonist Albinos (*Didask.* 7); further in Plato, *Rep.* 7:522CD; Xenokrates, *Frag.* 2 = Diogenes Laertius 4.10; Clement of Alexandria, *Strom.* 6.84.1f.; Origen in Eusebius, *Ecc. Hist.* 6.18.3. In other words, *although* Justin, during the period he was writing *Dialogue* 2, is influenced by presuppositions of the Platonic school (see below), he deviates from this school at this particular point; real life shines through. If Justin's *Dialogue* 2.4f. were totally structured according to traditional patterns, which obscure authentic biographical elements, then he would have to emphasize the opposite, that he did indeed learn music, astronomy, and geometry and thereafter had also finally studied Plato....

N. Hyldahl's (*Philosophie und Christentum*, 154–58) general denial of genuine autobiographical elements in *Dial.* 2.3ff. is, I believe, erroneous. The stated "lack of congruence between the reported things and the function which these things have in Justin's context" (p. 154) could actually speak in favor of historical authenticity. The remaining "reasons" appear to me to be far-fetched (e.g., the alleged contradiction between *Dial.* 2.5 and 3.6, which I simply don't understand). Hyldahl's hypothesis of a rounded-off literary source in *Dial.* 2.3–3.1 refutes itself. Justin would have changed this source on "decisive points (in 2.6 and 3.1)" (p. 159). How, then, does one still strictly prove there is a source? In regard to linguistic-stylistic details, we look in vain for proof of non-Justinian language.

5. *Dial.* 1.1, 3 and 9.2: the dialogue took place during the Bar Kochba insurrection in the "stadium of Xystus." According to 1.3, it was in any case in the east; according to Eusebius, *Ecc. Hist.* 4.18.6, in Ephesus; according to N. Hyldahl, *Philosophie und Christentum*, 97, in Corinth.

1.53.9: "Whoever wishes can see their land lying bare, barren, and burnt").

Before his final immigration to Rome, Justin had already visited the capital once (*Acta Iust.* 3; recensions A and B). He returned to Rome sometime after 135 C.E. and remained living there until his martyrdom without interruption (παρὰ πάντα τὸν χρόνον, ibid.) or change of lodging. He lived "above Myrtinus's baths."[6] Justin there held meetings of his students. Before the judge, he even asserts that he had not learned of any other Christian place of assembly in Rome than this one (*Acta Iust.* 3; recensions A and B).

As a Christian, Justin retains the mantle of the philosopher (*Dial.* 1.2; 9.2) — a costume that not only Origen's fellow student Herakles[7] but also Tertullian (to the astonishment of his fellow citizens) will wear, and concerning which the latter will compose an exquisite little work entitled, "Concerning the Pallium or the Mantle of the Philosopher."[8] On the street, the garb of the philosopher is unmistakable, so that it is even caricatured: the pallium, light sandals, a staff, and the beard of a goat (Apuleius, *Met.* 11.8.2; cf. Martial, 4.53). Also Trypho immediately recognizes Justin's dress as the costume of an educated man (*Dial. 1*).

Although Eusebius, from the literary works of the Roman philosopher Justin, knew about eight[9] "most useful benchmarks of his educated spirit" and had heard[10] of the existence of "numerous others," only

---

6. ἐγὼ ἐπάνω μένω τοῦ Μυρτίνου βαλανείου, *Acta Iust.* 3, ibid., rec. A. A topographical identification is impossible. Nevertheless, the note indicates a rented apartment. Recension B reads, Μαρτίνου τοῦ Τιμιοτίνου: a secondary reading, which attempts an identification; nobody knew the correct place anymore.

7. Origen in a letter in Eusebius, *Ecc. Hist.* 6.19.14.

8. The mantle of the philosopher in Justin's text is by no means only a literary topos, as it is not in Tertullian. Tertullian's little work "De pallio" would have been unintelligible to his readers if the author had not actually worn the pallium. Likewise, the first readers of *Dial.* 1.2 would have shaken their heads if Justin had not actually gone about in the pallium. (Contra N. Hyldahl, *Philosophie und Christentum*, 88–112. I do not see how the literary topic in *Dial.* 1.1f. — in the introduction to a dialogue, the philosopher's σχῆμα is usually commented on — could exclude the historicity of Justin's wearing the philosopher's mantle.)

9. *Ecc. Hist.* 4.18.1–8. Especially the two works against the Hellenes, as their title indicates, had philosophical content (ibid., 3f.). The work "Concerning the Sole Sovereignty of God" used pagan "Greek writings" in a learned manner. In the "scholastic manual concerning the soul" Justin discussed "the views of Greek philosophers" (ibid., 4f.). Photius (*Bib. cod.* 125.95) names two further works not listed by Eusebius, concerning nature and a refutation of anti-Christian arguments.

10. Ibid., 8f.; cf. also 1 ("very many"). Eusebius passes on the themes of two of them: One writing was directed against Marcion (ibid., 9, with reference to Irenaeus, 4.6; cf. also Eusebius, *Ecc. Hist.* 4.11.8). Another work, "Against the Heresies," is cited by Justin himself (*Apol.* 1.26); Eusebius *(Ecc. Hist.* 4.11.10) apparently only knows of it from this quotation. On the possible identity of both works see above, chap. 24, n. 52.

Apology 1 and 2 and the *Dialogue with the Jew Trypho* have come down to us.[11]

Apology 1 and 2 are dedicated to the emperor Antoninus Pius and to his co-regents Marcus Aurelius and Lucius Verus (1.1; 2.15.5).[12] Other data correspond well to this. *Acta Iust.* 1: Justin suffered martyrdom under the municipal Roman praefect Iunius Rusticus (163–68 C.E.). *Apol.* 2.2 narrates an event that took place under the municipal Roman praefect Quintus Lollius Urbicus (144–60 C.E.). *Apol.* 1.29 mentions a previous petition to the Alexandrian governor Felix (148–54 C.E.). And *Apol.* 1.46.1 maintains that Christ was born 150 years ago.

Therefore, *Apology* 1 and 2 fall within the 150s. The *Dialogue* is the latest of the three writings.[13] The repeated address to the pagan Romans[14] makes it probable that *Apology* 1 and 2 were already composed in Rome. One can also ascertain this from Justin's knowledge of Roman topology as he describes it in *Apol.* 1.26.2f.

Indirect Social-Historical Information: Components of Education

The direct information of the previous section, particularly the autobiographical listing of educational experiences in *Dial.* 2, can be cross-checked by means of the components of education in Justin's writings. Was the enumeration of philosophical teachers of different provenance simply literary convention, by which authors narrated experiences in different philosophical schools in order to be able to criticize them?[15]

When discovering such similar texts (as in the previous footnote), we need to keep in mind that their literary parallelism in itself says nothing about the historicity or nonhistoricity of what is reported — just as

---

11. The authenticity of the fragments of *De resurrectione* is disputed (for the authenticity, e.g., E. S. Osborn, *Justin-Martyr,* 13; contra, L. W. Barnard, *Justin Martyr,* 172).

12. Also *Apol.* 2 has the same dedication: 2.15.5 concludes *Apol.* 2 by taking up the play on words in which Justin in 1.2.1f.; 3.2f.; 4.1; 12.5 had played upon the names and titles of the persons addressed ("Pius" and "Philosophus"). For the literary unity of *Apology* 1 and 2 see the detailed presentation of H. H. Holfelder, "EUSEBEIA KAI PHILOSOPHIA."

13. *Dial.* 120.6 quotes *Apol.* 1.26. Furthermore, the *Dialogue* already knows more divergent heretics than *Apol.* 1 and 2 (cf. above, chap. 23, n. 13; chap. 24, n. 51).

14. E.g., 1.56.3f.; 44.13: Justin has in mind as readers not only the emperor and his co-regents but also the "senatus" and "populus romanus." In *Apol.* 1.63.16; 32.3, "you" refers simply to the Romans in general, not only to the imperial regents. Cf. also *Apol.* 2.1.1: ὦ Ῥωμαῖοι.

15. Cf. Lucian, *Menippus* 4–6; the introduction of Thessalus's letter to the emperor Claudius (ed. P. Boudreaux, *Catalogus Codicum Astrologorum Graecorum* 8, 3 [Brussels, 1912], 134ff.); Josephus, *Vita* 2.9–12; Ps.-Clem. H. 1.3.1ff.; further Ps.-Justin, *Coh. ad Graec.* 2–7.

little as the stereotypical *Vitae* of the lives of today's doctoral candidates permit the conclusion that the candidate simply exercised "literary convention" and had described nothing that might be autobiographical or historical. What is stereotypical in this "literature" follows primarily from the stereotypical experiences in real life (all go through the same system of education). Only secondarily can literary stylizing, conformity to "convention" and to the requisites of the genre "Vitae" be made responsible for the impression of stereotypes.

Eclectic education was part of stereotypical "real life" in Justin's period. In his youth, Galen, the doctor, went through a philosophical education with Stoics, Platonists, Peripatetics, and Epicureans. It was customary to attend the lectures of several teachers of different schools.[16]

We saw (n. 4) that at least one passage in *Dial.* 2 reflects Justin's real life. Beyond this it is interesting that Justin does not claim that he had *several* philosophical teachers, as one would expect if he simply were dependent on literary convention; rather he mentions only two, the Stoic and the Platonist. He remained with the Peripatetic for only a few days, and he did not pass the entrance examination of the Pythagorean. These deviations from the norm are interesting. They reflect something that is authentic and personal.

Justin's Philosophical-Literary Education

Justin not only refers to pagan "poets," "philosophers," and "writers" in general[17] but also to several authors by name: to Plato[18] and Socrates,[19] Homer,[20] Pythagoras,[21] Heraclitus,[22] Empedocles,[23] and Xenophon.[24] He also refers to Epicurus and his writings;[25] references are

16. Cf. Mewaldt, "Galenos," Pauly/Wissowa 7:578.

17. *Apol.* 1.4.8f.; 18.5; 20.4f.; 21.2; 22.1; 23.3; 33.3; 36.2; 44.9; 53.1; 54.1f.; 59.1, 5f.; 2.5(4).5; 8(7).1; 10.2, 6; 11.8; 12.5; 13.2, 5; etc.

18. *Apol.* 1.8.4; 18.5; 20.4; 44.8; 59.5, 1; 60.5, 1; 2.12.1; 13.2; *Dial.* 2.6; 3.7; 4.1; 5.4, 6; 6.1; 7.1; 8.3. *Dial.* 5.4 and *Apol.* 1.60.1 mention the Timaios dialogue by name.

19. *Apol.* 1.5.3f.; 18.5; 46.3; 2.3(8).6; 7(6).3; 10.5f., 8.

20. *Apol.* 1.18.5; 2.10.6.

21. *Apol.* 1.18.5, *Dial.* 2.4; 5.6; 6.1; 7.1.

22. *Apol.* 1.46.3; 2.8(7).1.

23. *Apol.* 1.18.5.

24. *Apol.* 2.11.2, 3f.: Xenophon, *Mem.* 2.1.21f. stands behind the text.

25. *Apol.* 2.12.5; 15.3. In 2.7(6).3 there is a polemical reference to Epicurus's fame and abundance (ἀφθονία). Does Justin here allude to Epicurus's house and garden (κῆπος), in which he pandered to a spiritual hedonism among a private circle of friends (cf. Diogenes Laertius, 10.10ff.)? Justin is not alone in his polemic against Epicurus. Criticism of the godless Epicurus belonged to the repertoire of the Middle Platonists, e.g., Attikos, in Eusebius, *Pr. Ev.* 15; Plutarch, *De comm. notit.* 32; *De Stoic. repugn.* 38. Cf. Origen, *Contra Cel.* 1.21; 8.45.

found to Sotades, Philainis, Archestratos,[26] Hystaspes,[27] and the Sibyl.[28] Justin mentions "the comic poet Menander,"[29] the Stoic Musonius Rufus,[30] and the second century contemporary "Corinthus the Socratic" in Argos.[31]

It is evident from *quotations, summaries, or literary allusions* that Justin knows authors such as these not simply by name. It is worth assembling a table of the most important material that goes beyond the usual index of word-for-word quotations.[32] An attempt to assemble such a summary table is found in Appendix 2.

Evaluation of the Summary Table

a. Let us first consider Justin's use of references to Plato from a quantitative point of view. Reference is made to at least 11 of Plato's 36 works. This lies clearly *above* the level of a generally educated person in imperial times. The generally educated person has a knowledge of the core of the *Timaeus* (ca. 27A–45A) as well as a few other sentences of Plato that are repeatedly cited.[33]

The finding speaks against Hyldahl's opinion (*Philosophie und Christentum*, 273, for example): Justin might have been a Platonist before his conversion but had received no philosophical education and would hardly be acquainted with the school philosophy of Middle Platonism.[34] The findings show that Justin's philosophical knowledge was above that of generally educated or self-educated persons.

In spite of Justin's above average knowledge, on the other hand, we also encounter Platonic passages that are known by the generally educated:

- Of the nine passages that remind us of *Timaeus*, seven originate from the core of *Timaeus*. One of the passages is *Tim.* 41A, one

---

26. *Apol.* 2.15.3.

27. *Apol.* 1.20.1; 44.12. For a book of oracles under his name, cf. Clement of Alexandria, *Strom.* 6.43; Lactantius, *Inst. div.* 7.15ff.

28. *Apol.* 1.20.1; 44.12. Cf. Plato, *Phaedr.* 244B, *Theag.* 124D, where there is likewise mention of only *one* Sibyl.

29. *Apol.* 1.20.5.

30. *Apol.* 2.8(7).1.

31. *Dial.* 1.2. Cf., finally, the reference by name to different philosophical schools: to the Stoics (*Apol.* 1.20.2, 4; 2.13.2; 8(7).1; 7(6).3f., 8; *Dial.* 2.1, 3), to the Platonists (*Dial.* 2.1, 6; 5.1), the Peripatetics (*Dial.* 2.1, 3), the Pythagoreans (*Dial.* 2.1), and the Epicureans (*Apol.* 2.15.3).

32. E.g., in E. J. Goodspeed, *Die ältesten Apologeten*, 379f.

33. Cf. further, H. Dörrie, "Rez. A.-J. Festugière," 230ff., here 240f., 237f.

34. Cf. also N. Hyldahl's (*Philosophie und Christentum*, 288) paradoxical assertion that "Justin had received no instruction in Platonic School philosophy, and yet one cannot catch him in misunderstandings or misinterpretations of Platonic philosophy of that time."

of the most frequently cited passages of Plato during the imperial period. It marks the high point in the myth of the *Timaeus*
dialogue.[35]

• Another example is the doctrine of *Phaedrus* 245Cff. (immortality,
the eternal motion of the soul), which is also known[36] to Justin.
This is one of the few teachings that belong to the knowledge
of the generally educated and trickle down into the circles of the
philosophically half-educated.[37]

b. The table in Appendix 2 indicates two points of emphasis. The
most frequently encountered educational elements are Platonic, first,
and Stoic, second. This quantitative finding confirms impressively the
previously mentioned direct information from *Dial.* 2, that Justin studied philosophy for an extended period of time, only with a Stoic and
then, above all, with a Platonist.[38]

c. Not only quantitatively but also substantively considered, the list
of material places Justin in the Platonic camp. Even the Stoic elements
are presented to the reader from the Platonic point of view. Justin has, so
to speak, "worked through"[39] his Stoic past in his subsequent Platonic
education.

C. Andresen therefore is probably correct in assigning Justin to the
religiously influenced Middle Platonism, in spite of all the difficulties
that originate[40] from this classification and that are connected with the
fact that Middle Platonism itself was not a uniform phenomenon. (*Dial.*
3.1f. does *not* appear to be a caricature.)

---

35. On this passage cf. H. Dörrie, "Rez. A.-J. Festugière," 239.

36. Cf. in Appendix 2, *Phaedr.* 246ABE; 247C; 248AB; 249ACDE.

37. E.g., in Hermetic circles; in regard to this see H. Dörrie, *"Rez. A.-J. Festugière,"*
240, 236; cf. *Corp. Her.* 3.72.

38. The same biographical background becomes also evident in individual assessments:
(a) In *Apol.* 2.13.2, only the Platonists and the Stoics are mentioned by name, for their
teachings are not totally foreign to Christianity (sic). The Platonists are named before the
Stoics. (b) As a Christian, Justin still agrees with Plato *expressis verbis* in respect to philosophy (2.12.1; 13.2), if only on individual points. (Justin confirms agreements between
Christianity and Platonism; nevertheless, he does not strive for a complete reconciliation
between the two. Platonism represents for him an obsolete stage of the history of philosophy. The Christians rediscovered the original philosophy of humankind, from which
Platonism and the other philosophies had been derived only secondarily. See below.)

39. One could object that Justin had first gained knowledge of the Stoic elements of
education during his schooling in Platonism (that is, eclectically). What speaks against
this opinion is the quantitative finding that he refers much more often to Stoic elements
than to, e.g., Aristotelian, Epicurean, or Pythagorean elements, which also were treated
eclectically by school Platonism. Particularly behind *Dial.* 5.2–6; 6.1f., and 3.6f. stands
material obviously gleaned directly from Stoic sources: in regard to this, see, e.g., N. Hyldahl, *Philosophie und Christentum,* 226f. Similarly, also behind *Dial.* 4.7 (concerning the
natural knowledge of God and morality) appears to stand a more Stoic than Platonic train
of thought (cf. N. Hyldahl, *Philosophie und Christentum,* 285).

40. Cf. H. Dörrie's review of Andresen in *Gnomon* 29 (1957): 185–96. The skepticism
is taken up, e.g., by E. S. Osborn, *Justin-Martyr,* 200, et passim.

At least, it is clear that Justin does not refer in many places to the original Plato but to the Plato seen through the "glasses" of contemporary Platonists. This is true not only of the wording of quotations from Plato (cf. the table for Plato's *Timaeus* 28C) but also true of the interpretation of quotations from Plato (cf. in the table, e.g., Plato's *Phaedrus* 247C; *Timaeus* 41AB; 34AB/36BC).

Altogether one may maintain "that Justin's understanding of Plato is as qualified as that of many pagan 'Platonists' of his time."[41] Let us compare Albinos: As professional philosopher and teacher, he writes in his *Didaskalikos* an εἰσαγωγὴ εἰς τὴν Πλάτωνος δογματοποιΐαν (26), but also with him it is questionable whether he is using the original Plato or is only reading compendia.[42] In its schools Middle Platonism is customarily based on a selection from Plato. Besides *Timaeus*, material is presented from the same texts in *Phaedrus, Phaedo, Symposium,* and the *Republic* (especially 6.509f.) as well as from *Theaetetus* 176B; *Ep* 2.312DE; 6.323D; 7.341C.[43] This selection is actually reflected by Justin in the table. He certainly is on the same level as those contemporaries who presented themselves in the robes of Middle Platonism philosophers.

d. If Justin is not so much dependent upon the genuine Plato but more upon the Platonic tradition of the schools, this suggests that he gained the elements of his education principally through listening to lectures by teachers and less from his own reading. *Apol.* 2.15.3 states explicitly that one can be informed about philosophical teaching not only through books but also through lectures. Lectures are mentioned *before* books. In *Apol.* 1.3.3, we observe how Justin cites Plato's *Republic* 5.473DE from memory, without at the moment being aware that the quotation comes from Plato: "one of the ancients had somewhere said." Justin cites here something that he learned in Platonic school instruction, retained by memory, and that he now does not reproduce literally. The contemporary Platonists Albinos *(Didask.* 34) and Apuleius (*De Plat.* 2.24) confirm that Plato's *Republic* 473DE indeed played a role in Platonic instruction.

Timaeus 28C is also cited freely and without knowledge of Plato's context. The words are mistakenly placed in the mouth of Socrates, although in Plato's original text they are spoken by the Pythagorean Timaeus. Justin did not consult Plato himself (*Apol.* 2.10.6; cf. also *Tim.* 41AB/Justin, *Dial.* 5.4).

Some passages, such as *Dial.* 4.4 can, I believe, be best explained as reminiscences of oral Platonic lectures (cf. the Platonic parallels in the

---

41. W. Schmid, "Frühe Apologetik," 178.
42. Cf. in this regard, e.g., N. Hyldahl, *Philosophie und Christentum,* 291, n. 83.
43. Cf. N. Hyldahl, *Philosophie und Christentum,* 289f.

table). Here is reproduced not a verbatim quotation from Plato but a whole conceptual complex from Platonic tradition.

Furthermore, reminiscences of individual literary expressions of Plato can also be explained in this way. For example, *Dial.* 3.3 — *Phaedo* 85CD; *Crito* 43D/*Apol.* 19A (for the protreptic language in *Dial.* 3.3f. cf. *Euthyd.* 281B; 282C; 306AB; Aristotle's *Protr.* fr. 51 = 56.24f. Rose; Iamblichus, *Protr.* 10 = 55.6f Pistelli). As a further example: *Dial.* 4.2 the "regal mind" — Plato, *Phileb.* 30D.

e. If some of Justin's literary and philosophical elements of knowledge were based directly on something written, then we would have to think most likely of presentations in a handbook (such as those in the monographs by Albinus or Apuleius) or a florilegium that contains τόποι and δόξαι. In *Apol.* 1.18.5, we appear to be on the trail of such a dependency upon a florilegium when, like clockwork, philosophical authorities for the topos "immortality of the soul" are enumerated: Empedocles, Pythagoras, Plato, Socrates, and others.[44] In other words, when Justin refers to many literary personalities by name (cf. above), he knows these either from lectures or from such collections. A substantive discussion with these authors seldom takes place; discussion is reserved for Stoic and Platonic teaching.

General Pagan Education

Besides his philosophical education Justin reveals a good general pagan education. He makes mistakes only occasionally.

Pagan mythology appears often. One may mention:

- the Mithra saga, *Dial.* 70.1; *Apol.* 1.66.4

- the Dionysus legend, *Dial.* 69.2; *Apol.* 1.54.2, 6; 21.2; 22.3f.; 25.1

- the Heracles saga, *Dial.* 69.3; *Apol.* 1.21.2; 54.9; 2.11

- the Asclepius saga, *Dial.* 69.3; *Apol.* 1.54.10; 21.2; 22.3f., 6; 25.1

- the circumstances of Perseus's birth, *Dial.* 67.2; 70.5; *Apol.* 1.21.2; 54.8 (1.22.5: Christ was born of a virgin, like Perseus, whom Zeus fathered of Danae by means of a shower of gold.)

- Zeus's daughters, Core and Athene, *Apol.* 1.64

- Zeus and his sons (*Apol.* 4.9; 21.1ff.; 33.3; 54.2, 6; 55.1; 56.1; 2.5.5; 12.5) who suffered as Christ had suffered (*Apol.* 1.22.3f.): Asclepius was struck by lightening, Dionysus eaten by the Titans.

---

44. Justin is dependent upon excerpts and florilegia not only in his use of Greek literature but also of the Old Testament. Justin draws his Old Testament quotations most probably from a list of testimonies; cf. in regard to this E. S. Osborn, *Justin-Martyr*, 115–19 (the history of research).

- Hermes, *Apol.* 1.21.2; 22.2

- Bellerophon on the winged horse Pegasus, 1.21.2; 54.7

- the Dioscuri, *Apol.* 1.21.2

- the Sons of Leda, *Apol.* 1.21.2

- Poseidon and Pluto, *Apol.* 2.5.5

- Ariadne, *Apol.* 1.21.3

- Ganymede, *Apol.* 1.21.5; 25.2

- Cronus and Zeus as murderers of their father, *Apol.* 1.21.5, cf. 2.12.5

- Semele, Latona and Apollo, Persephone, Aphrodite and Adonis, Antiope, Thetis, and Achilles, the concubine Briseis, *Apol.* 1.25

- *Apol.* 2.7 (6).2 names the hero of the deluge, Deucalion

- *Apol.* 2.7 (6).3, the luxurious life of the legendary Sardanapal: a literary topos since Herodotus 2.150. Statues of Sardanapal were placed in villas, as shown by the sample excavated in the villa of the emperor Lucius Verus in Monte Porzio Catone near Frascati. (Today it is in the Vatican Museums.) That the statue was found in the house of Lucius Verus, to whom our text of Justin was addressed, is an interesting coincidence.

Justin betrays from whence he knows all this colorful material: from the reading of "poets" and "the writings of historians" (*Apol.* 1.33.3; 21.2, et al.); more clearly: "such things are written for growing youth" (*Apol.* 1.21.4). "Those who pass on the myths devised by poets offer to the youth (νέοις) who learn them ... " (*Apol.* 1.54.1). Justin reaches back into his school education, to the material learned in the school of the grammarians and taught from Greek texts to the youth up to the age of seventeen.

The knowledge of pagan myths corresponds to the knowledge of pagan cults, which are argued against not only in general (*Apol.* 1.24.1, 3; 25; 2.5.4; 14.2) but with more accurate knowledge:

The mysteries of Dionysus and Mithra are characterized as aping Christianity (*Apol.* 1.25; 54.6; 66.4; *Dial.* 69.2; 70.1; 78.6). Justin knows that in the Mithra cult bread and a cup of water are placed before those who are about to be initiated (*Dial.* 70.4; *Apol.* 1.66.4). *Apol.* 1.54.6 knows of the role of the ass in the Dionysus cult (cf. Pliny, *Nat. hist.* 24.1). Further things are mentioned:

- the mysteries of Cybele with allegedly shameful practices, *Apol.* 1.27.4

- the Saturn mysteries (μυστήρια Κρόνου) with their sacrifices, *Apol.* 2.12.5; cf. Tertullian, *Apol.* 9; Minucius Felix, *Oct.* 30; Diodorus Siculus, 13.86

- the μυστήρια of Apollo, Persephone, Aphrodite, and Asclepius, *Apol.* 1.25

- the oracles of Amphilochus, Dodona, and Pytho, *Apol.* 1.18.4

- *Apol.* 1.27.4f. knows of the serpent as a cultic symbol in many pagan cults (cf. Vestals, Aesculapius, the above-mentioned [chap. 4]) archaeological example in Trastevere, etc.).

- *Apol.* 1.62 argues against the purification and bathing rites in pagan religions.

- *Apol.* 1.64.1 knows the custom of erecting the statue of Demeter's daughter, Persephone, by springs (otherwise obviously not literarily mentioned).

- *Apol.* 2.12.5 knows the cult of Jupiter Latiaris, to whom was offered annually the blood of an executed person. It took place near Rome in the Alban mountains.

- *Apol.* 1.29.4 polemicizes against the cult of the youth Antinous, which was staged by Hadrian (cf. Ammianus Marcellinus 22.16.2 and the commemorative inscriptions such as that of the city of Rome, *CIL* 6:1851). Antinous's tomb was located in Rome outside the Porta Maggiore, as the inscription on the obelisk standing on the Pincio reveals. Rome preserved for us an abundance of portraits of Antinous (in the Vatican, in the villa Albani, the palace of the *Conservatori*). As at least the last two examples reveal, Justin draws from everyday experience in the city of Rome.

Legal Elements of Education

- *Apol.* 2.2.6 knows that according to Roman law the wife can also give a letter of divorce. Even the Latin technical term, *repudium,* is mentioned.

- *Apol.* 1.15.5 shows knowledge of civil legislation according to which, after a ratified divorce, a second marriage is possible while the first wife is still alive.

- *Apol.* 1.7.5 is aware of the legal principle that the punishment that was intended for the accused catches up to the libelous plaintiff: *Cod. Theod.* 9.2.3; 3.6.

- *Apol.* 1.44.12 recalls the prohibition of Tiberius of consulting oracles concerning the life of the emperor or political matters (cf. Paulus, *Sent.* 5.21.3; further Suetonius, *Domit.* 15). Books such as those of Hystaspes and the Sibyl were forbidden (Suetonius, *Aug.* 31).

- *Apol.* 1.47.6 knows of Hadrian's prohibition for any Jew to set foot in Judaea.

- Concerning Hadrian's rescript in *Apol.* 1.68, cf. A. Wlosok, "Christliche Apologetik," 148f.

- *Apol.* 1.27.2 knows of Caligula's morality tax (Suetonius, *Cal.* 40), which was valid until Justinian (*Cod. Ius.* 11.41.6)

The legal terms in *Apol.* 2.14.1; 15.1 (βιβλίδιον, ὑπο — and προγράφειν, προθεῖναι) are taken from the official process of petition (*a libellis*).[45] Justin's *Apology* has a definite *Sitz im Leben* in which to interpret these legal terms: it is the presentation by a private citizen of a letter of petition to the imperial office *a libellis*. Justin chooses the direct way of petition provided for by Roman private law (cf. also *Apol.* 1.1 ἔντευξις / *petitio*) in order to reach the top of the government bureaucracy. His aim is to decriminalize the Christian name (*nomen christianum*). The authorities should not in the future condemn a person simply on the basis of being a Christian but only punish according to actual penal offenses. Justin asks the imperial regents to meet his request by making a legally binding imperial decision (προθεῖναι, *subscriptio;* 2.14.1). What we have before us is the attempt to directly influence the religious politics of the Antonini. By following the legal path open to a private citizen, he offers evidence of a certain degree of judicial knowledge. Not everyone is knowledgeable in the ways of administrative authority and official procedure. But this did not affect the unsuccessful outcome of Justin's legal and political attempt. Justin's own trial that led to martyrdom shows that condemnation continued to be pronounced simply on the basis of being Christian. Justin did not live to see the imperial legal decision that he hoped to bring about by means of private law.

Geographical, Ethnological, and Linguistic Knowledge

- In view of his origin, knowledge of local geography in Samaria is not surprising: *Apol.* 1.26.2, 4 mentions the villages Gittae and Capparetaea.

---

45. Cf. in regard to this H. H. Holfelder, "EUSEBEIA KAI PHILOSOPHIA," 248f., especially n. 124, which refers to U. Wilcken's research of the terminology in imperial rescripts. Accordingly, the imperial address of the *Apology* is not literary fiction; cf. convincingly, H. H. Holfelder, ibid., 57; 248f.; 50, n. 11 for literature.

- Knowledge concerning Judea: *Apol.* 1.34.2; 53.9; 32.6

- Arabia: *Dial.* 78.8, 10

- the animal of India in *Dial.* 3.6 as a literary topos; cf. Pliny, *Nat. hist.* 7.2.21

- Justin reads the LXX, but it is possible that he possesses knowledge of a Semitic language: *Dial.* 103.5; 125.3; *Apol.* 1.33.7; 65.4

- Justin, a Roman by choice, appears not to have felt at home with Latin. He characterizes the word "repudium" (*Apol.* 2.2.6) as a foreign word ("so say you Romans"). If Justin had read Horace, Vergil, Propertius, or Lucanus, he would not have blundered in *Apol.* 1.31 by making King Ptolemaeus Philadelphos (died 247 B.C.E.) a contemporary of Herod the Great. He could have read there that in the first century B.C.E. a charming woman named Cleopatra sat as the last descendant upon the Ptolemaic throne.

- Justin's deficiency in western Latin education becomes clear through another mistake: In *Apol.* 1.26.2f.; 56.1–4 we accompany Justin on a walk through the city of Rome. "In the middle of the Tiber River" on the island "between the two bridges," he came upon an inscription. He read upon it that Simon Magus had been worshiped as god in Rome. He mildly disgraced himself by requesting the senate to pull down the statue. Actually, archaeology has brought to light such inscriptions on the Tiber island and in other places, but they were dedicated to "Semo Sancus Dius Fidius,"[46] the old Sabine god of swearing. How could an oriental easterner have known this?[47]

The elements listed bear witness to Justin's eastern origins. They call again to mind his itinerant life (cf. section 1.) Before he finally settled in Rome, he had once visited there from the east. Besides Palestine, he traveled the Aegean; the Dialogue with Trypho may have taken place in Ephesus or Corinth.[48]

Justin's Literary Ability

At first sight, Justin does not appear to possess exceptional literary skill. He deviates and cannot follow the organization of material that he

46. Full cult name in *CIL* 6:30994: Semoni Sanco Sancto deo Fidio.
47. Another example of a mistake is found in *Apol.* 1.34. Justin believes Quirinius to have been the first Roman "*Epitropos* in Judea." Quirinius was governor in Syria, to which Palestine belonged, but he was not the first.
48. Did he visit Egypt? *Apol.* 1.29 reports incidents from the Christian community in Alexandria; cf. also 1.24.1.

proposed in his table of contents, *Apol.* 1.23. At times, he becomes confused in long-winded syntax. It is endearing that Justin is aware of this,
"I do not strive for a completely artful presentation, because I do not
have the talent for this" (*Dial.* 58.1). Following this confession there is
the charming scene in which he lets Trypho object, " 'When you claim
to possess no talent for artful presentation, you appear to feign ignorance.' I replied, 'Since you think so, be it so. I am, however, convinced
that I have spoken the truth' " (58.2). It strikes Justin himself that he
continuously repeats himself, particularly in the *Dialogue.* He even end-
lessly repeats this laudable self-criticism (*Dial.* 85.4f.; 87.6; 88.6; 92.5;
113.1; 118.4f.; 123.7f.; 128.2; 137.4). The *Dialogue with Trypho* fades
near the end into a monologue.[49] Near the end, Trypho only enters the
conversation to apologize for the repetitions, e.g., 118.5.[50]

Scholars have sometimes been confused concerning Justin's arrangement of material in his writings.[51] Since J. Geffcken,[52] critical voices
have not been silent. Today's literary tastes are overwhelmed by the unsystematic arrangement of the material, in the *Dialogue* even more than
in the *Apology.* That this modern point of view is not completely appropriate[53] is evident from the studies[54] of Seneca and Horace. Both
ancient authors create problems for us in the loose arrangement of
their material. One can also show digressions by Aristotle, Tacitus,
and Cassius Dio. Dio of Prusa was good at extremely unstructured
chattering (λαλιά), without being considered uneducated. Pliny found
a long, excessive digression ("longissimus excessus") by Demosthenes
to be extremely beautiful (*pulcherrimus; Ep.* 9.26.9). The digression
(παρέκβασις, *egressio*) was considered a rhetorical medium. Digressions
were allowed to flourish, provided they stood in logical connection
with the main theme ("ad utilitatem causae," Quintilian, 4.3.14). They
offered an entertaining change (cf. Quintilian, 4.3.1f.). "Most of the
extant philosophical writings [of Seneca] do not have as their primary

---

49. Suddenly, in 114.1, for example, it is no longer Trypho but the reader who is
directly addressed. For many pages Trypho has not been mentioned. He appeared for the
last time in 110.1.

50. "Trypho replied, 'You do well (to repeat this). You should know that, although
you repeat the same thing often, I and my companions take pleasure in hearing you....' "

51. Cf. concerning the structure of the *Apology,* W. Bousset, *Jüdisch-christlicher Schul-
betrieb,* 300–303; concerning the structure of the *Dialogue,* P. Prigent, *Justin et l'Ancient
Testament;* E. S. Osborn, *Justin-Martyr,* 12. Literature in H. H. Holfelder, "EUSEBEIA
KAI PHILOSOPHIA," 51f., n. 15.

52. *Zwei griechische Apologeten,* 97ff.

53. Cf. H. H. Holfelder, "EUSEBEIA KAI PHILOSOPHIA, 53, and in other places;
before him, without finding many advocates, e.g., Th. M. Wehofer (*Die Apologie Justins*),
K. Hubik (*Die Apologien des Hl. Justinus*), U. Hüntemann ("Zur Kompositionstechnik
Justins," 410ff.); cf. also E. Norden (*Antike Kunstprosa,* 90, n. 2).

54. I. Hadot, *Seneca;* U. Knoche, "Betrachtungen über Horazens Kunst."

purpose the demonstration of a philosophical doctrine but its application. The structure of the writings aims at directing the soul. Above all they are constructed according to rhetorical and not according to philosophical and systematic rules. This lies at the basis of the apparent lack of systematic composition... with the sudden introduction of new topics, apparent diversions, dead ends, and repetitions."[55] A digressive arrangement of material that lets the argument develop in various ways was considered a conscious philosophical technique of presentation. B. Keil[56] already surmised that this "technique" of ancient literature arose out of the same motive as our present-day practice of footnotes. The ancients did not know of notes. Instead of this, they led the reader and listener digressively over a many-colored "tapestry." Clement of Alexandria compares one of his works already in its title with patchwork (*"stromateis"*) Thus, Justin's arrangement of material cannot be criticized for extraordinary aesthetic blunders. Unsystematic presentation was in itself not considered offensive. The problem lies rather in his immoderate use of the digressive technique in a work which belongs to the "apologetic" genre. In the composition of an apology one could expect more according to the requisites of the genre (cf., e.g., Quintilian, 4.5). Therein lies the actual aesthetic mistake. All in all, Justin was not a good writer — but not as bad as has been presumed since the time of Geffcken.

The *Apology*, directed to the emperor and co-regents, is, nevertheless, a little more strictly arranged than the *Dialogue*. Here we also find the wordplays that Justin makes with the names and titles of his imperial addressees. The *Apology* is dedicated to Antoninus *Pius* (εὐσεβεῖ), to his son Verissimus (Marcus Aurelius), the *philosopher*, and Lucius Verus, the son of a *philosopher*.[57] In *Apol.* 1.1; 2.1f.; 3.2f.; 4.1; 12.5; 2.2.16; 15.5, Justin plays with both these attributes of the rulers, εὐσέβεια and φιλοσοφία: the rulers may show not force and caprice but "piety" and "love of wisdom" and judge the Christians without prejudice. "A name is neither a good nor a bad criterion, apart from the actions implied by the name" (1.4.1), i.e., "whether you are (pious and wise) will reveal itself" (1.2.2). Justin brings forward the rhetorical argument from the name ("argumentum ex nomine").[58] That Justin has a sense of humor is seen in the exchange of blows with the cynic Crescens (2.3.1ff.). Justin insults this philosopher using biting plays on words, such as philo*p*sopher (φιλόψοφος: someone who loves noise and empty talk) and

55. I. Hadot, *Seneca*, 37f.
56. *Die solonische Verfassung*, 179.
57. *Apol.* 1.1. Lucius's father was an educated man (cf. *Hist. Aug. Aelius Verus* 5); Justin's manuscript mistakenly calls Lucius himself a philosopher.
58. Cf., e.g., Quintilian, 6.3.55. Another "argumentum ex nomine" is in Justin's *Apol.* 1.4.5 in regard to the "nomen christianum."

φιλοκόμπος (admirer of clatter and boasting; v. 6 plays with the words φιλόσοφος and φιλόδοξος).

Of course, the limits of his literary ability again become evident. Justin lacks the literary language of classicism, in contrast to his younger contemporary Tatian.[59] This deficit may partly be due to the fact that Justin grew up at a time when extreme classicism (optatives, dual, etc., cf. Clement of Alexandria born in around 150 C.E.) did not yet control the entire higher education system. On the other hand, this deficit was also due to the fact that Justin's higher education consisted only of philosophical lectures but *not* of rhetorical exercises.

Justin's Role as Philosopher

The Claim to Be a Philosopher

Justin's philosophical education corresponds to his claim to be understood and seriously accepted as a philosopher even after becoming Christian. This claim is signaled to the people on the street through the philosopher's mantle and is indicated by the choice of the literary genres. The *Apology* is a speech which, as a petition, seeks to influence the educated pagan reader. The *Dialogue with the Jew Trypho* seeks to imitate the dialogue form that suits a former Platonist.[60] Justin represents his authorities, the Old Testament prophets, as philosophers (*Dial.* 7.1ff.; cf. *Apol.* 2.10.8); according to him, the Old Testament had already made use of the philosophical dialogue (1.36.1f.).[61]

Justin presents to the philosophically interested reader a discussion concerning *heimarmēnē*, ethical responsibility and free will (1.43f.)[62] and thus responds to the primarily ethical questions posed by those

---

59. Cf. C. Fabricius, "Der sprachliche Klassizismus," 187ff.; R. M. Grant, "Aristotle," 79ff.; 246ff. It would be the task of a monograph to investigate in detail the extent of Justin's command of Attic Greek.

60. That Justin did not completely satisfy the demands of the genre concerned us above. Here we are concerned with his claim. In Christianity before Justin, only the Christian writer Aristo of Pella had borrowed the dialogue form from literature (*Discussion between Jason and Papiscus concerning Christ*). For a definition of a Platonic dialogue, cf. Diogenes Laertius, 3.48. For the form "dialogue" in Middle Platonism, cf. C. Andresen, "Justin," 183. That the *Dialogue with the Jew Trypho* strives to be a learned philosophical work is clear from *Dial.* 1.2; cf., further, e.g., 64.2. The philosophical conversation with the stranger in *Dial.* 3ff. is strongly reminiscent in places of the Platonic-Socratic dialogue (especially in the use of formal linguistic characteristics: e.g., ἦν appears instead of ἔφην, as in Plato; further details in N. Hyldhal, *Philosophie und Christentum*, 176; cf. also below, Appendix 2, for the dependence of Justin's *Dialogue* on Plato's *Protagoras*).

61. "... as is also seen in your (pagan) authors, one writes a complete work in which he introduces persons who converse with each other." Justin himself draws the parallel to the dialogue of Greek literature.

62. Cf. 1.28.3f.; 2.7(6).3ff., 8f.

interested in philosophy at that time. Christianity elicits, as does philosophy, piety, and justice (*Dial.* 110.3; cf. Seneca, *Ep.* 90.3). It leads to a happy life, as does philosophy (*Dial.* 8.2; cf. Seneca, *Ep.* 6.1; 90.28). It is "certain and profitable," as is philosophy (*Dial.* 8.1.; cf. Lucian, *Menipp.* 4). "To get to know the Christian God" and "to understand philosophical truth" is one and the same process (cf. *Dial.* 8.1f; 4.1). Christianity even is the crown (ὑπέρτερος) of philosophy; it comprises all those teachings of earlier philosophies that had some value. It is the rediscovered original philosophy, in face of which the contemporary philosophies of the schools, including Platonism, are only derivatives (2.13; 15.3, 5; cf. further 8(7); 1.2.1–3; 12.5; 21.1; *Dial.* 2.1; 8).

Accordingly, parallels are drawn between philosophers and Christians (2.10.4; 1.7.3; 4.8f.; 20.3f.; 24.1; 26.6; 59.5f.; 60.10; *Acta Iust.* 2.3). The fate of the persecuted Christians can be compared with that of Socrates, condemned by the Athenians (1.5.3; 46.3; 2.10.4ff.; 7[6].3), or with that of Heraclitus (1.46.3; 2.8[7].1) or of the Stoic Musonius Rufus (2.8[7].1) who was banished by Nero (Tacitus, *Ann.* 15.71). The Christian evangelists did not write "Gospels" about Jesus but ἀπομνημονεύματα, "memorials," as Xenophon did about Socrates (1.66.3 and other places). The Christians worship God with their intellect (1.6.2; 12.8, 11; 13.2; 46.3f.; 2.1). They are σοφοί (1.7.3), a people *sui generis,* to be acknowledged as equals in the cultured world and who are to be distinguished from the contemptible barbarians (*Dial.* 119.4).

How Prepared Was the Environment to Accept the Claim That Justin's Christianity Was Philosophy?

Justin's claim was something new; it must have appeared bold to the pagan Romans as well as to the Christians. In previous Christian literature, the term "philosophy" had only denoted pagan systems of learning, in a negative sense.[63] And pagans had simply dismissed Christianity as superstition.[64] A younger Roman contemporary of Justin was the first among the pagans to compare Christians and philosophers. He conceded that Christianity, on the basis of its high ethical standards, was a "philosophical" school. This was the judgment of the renowned medical doctor Galen.[65]

---

63. See the article by G. Bardy, " 'Philosophie' et 'philosophe' dans le vocabulaire chrétien des premiers siècles."

64. Cf. Pliny, *Ep.* 10.96.8; Suetonius, *Claudius* 25.3; *Nero* 16.2; Tacitus, *Ann.* 15.44.

65. (1) An extant fragment in Arabic, composed by Galen circa 180 C.E. in Rome (edited by R. Walzer, *Galen on Jews and Christians* [London, 1949], 16): In ethics, the Christian is not inferior to the ἀληθῶς φιλοσοφοῦντες. (2) Galen's *De pulsuum differentiis* 2.4 (composed in Rome between 176 and 192 C.E.): They are a διατριβή, a school. (3) In the same work (3.3), Galen compares the Christians to contemporary dogmatic schools

In contrast to Galen, the philosopher Celsus took care not to designate the Christians as potential philosophers, but his verbose essay
against the Christians shows that philosophy found itself to be increasingly in competition with Christianity. Lucian (*Pereg.*
13 and 11) could
label Jesus as σοφιστής and the Christian doctrine as σοφία, although
it may be "without exact proof." Tatian (*Or.* 40.3) appears to verify
that people proficient in Greek occupied themselves with Christianity
(οἱ παρὰ τοῖς Ἕλλησι λόγιοι). And as prominent an orator as Fronto of
Cirta condescended to compose a speech against the Christians (Minucius Felix, 9.6; 31.2). Tertullian (*Apol.* 46.2f.) will finally confirm that
the philosopher's mantle not only embodied a claim of the apologists,
but that parts of the pagan world actually considered Christianity to be
a type of philosophy ("philosophiae genus"). "One says, 'the philosophers also demand the same virtues and embrace them.'...According
to doctrine we are compared to them." The pagan philosophers may be
"pares nostri" in the eyes of the surrounding world. Tertullian reports
here in chapter 46 explicitly the opinion of the social surroundings,
not simply a Christian claim. In 46.8ff., the placing of Christianity
on the same level with the philosophers is even too much for him, so
that he starts to distance himself from this position. The recognition
of Christianity as a "philosophy" was not astonishing in the intellectual situation of that time. Eclecticism, religious undertones, oriental
traditions — all this had become quite acceptable for philosophy.

How much Justin would have been seen by his contemporary world
as a philosopher has of course not yet been sufficiently answered. A
further investigation is necessary.

In Which Social Relations Did Justin Live?

Contact with Pagan Philosophers

a. In *Dial.* 5.4[66] Justin speaks up for one of the positions that were in
competition in the Platonic school disputations by maintaining that the
world came into existence.[67] Justin consciously takes up this position in
the internal Platonic disputes; he shows in *Dial.* 5.1f. that he is aware

---

of philosophers and medical doctors. According to him, the Christians, however, are exactly as dogmatically obstinate, uncritically believing and incapable of μεταδιδάσκεσθαι,
as these schools. (4) Also in 2.4 and in the Arabic fragment (p. 15), Galen criticizes Christians for their faith in authority and tradition and for their neglect of proofs and evidence
(ἀναποδείκτων). Galen sees in this a parallel to the dogmatic incrustation of the philosophical schools of the second century (cf., e.g., Lucian, *Hermotimus* 7). He himself does not
want to be associated with any of these schools. (5) For contact between Galen and the
Christian Theodotians see below, chap. 33.
   66. Cf., further, *Apol.* 1.10.2; 2.4f.; 2.4.2; *Dial.* 41.1.
   67. Cf., e.g., Atticus, in Eusebius, *Pr. Ev.* 15.6.8; Plutarch, *De animae procreatione*
4.1013EF.

of the opposing opinion (see above). In other words, Justin, the philosopher, takes a position in a current Platonic school discussion, and he does this as a Christian.

This philosophical positioning takes place not only on the literary level.[68] As a philosopher in Rome, Justin also enters into oral discussions with pagan philosophers. We no longer know these philosophers by name; only one example of such a disputation is extant,[69] the dispute that Justin waged with the Roman Cynic Crescens (2.3.[8].1ff.; 11.2; Tatian, *Or.* 19). Crescens had publicly criticized Christianity in order to amuse,[70] so Justin believed, the rabble in Rome. Thereupon, at least one dispute erupted between Justin and Crescens. Apparently, Justin took the initiative, because 2.3.4ff. speaks of the questions that he directed to Crescens and of the answers given by Crescens. Both philosophers had so violently argued against each other in public that Justin himself seriously reckoned that the imperial authorities could have heard of these "conversations" (κοινωνίαι τῶν λόγων; 2.3[8].4–6).

We get a glimpse of the content of this dispute in 2.9:[71] The dispute dealt, at least partially, with ethics and the question of the motivation for actions. Also 2.11, where Crescens is named as the opponent (11.2), concerns ethical questions. Tatian (*Or.* 19.3f.) finally confirms that the theme of Justin's dispute with Crescens was the philosophers' way of life. Ethics indeed dominated the contemporary philosophical enterprise.[72] The dispute between Justin and Crescens turned out to be typical for the philosophical scene of that time. That means that Justin

68. For the literary level see further the appendix table: Justin polemically discussed Stoic positions from the Middle Platonic point of view. Cf. also the frequent polemic against pagan philosophers (as in *Apol.* 1.14.5; 19.5; 20.2; 43f.; 2.13.2; 15.3; 7[6].3f., 8f.; *Dial.* 1.4f.; 2.2–6; 4.7; 5.1; 7.1).

69. Not only 2.9.1; 11.2 but also Tatian, *Or.* 19.4, indicates that the case of Crescens was not the only example of disputes with philosophers. Justin argued against philosophers (in the plural).

70. πρὸς ἡδονὴν τῶν πολλῶν 2.3.2f. Cf. 9.1: also other philosophers argued against Christianity.

71. 2.9.1 argues only in a general way against the "alleged philosophers" (plural). Nevertheless, with regard to content, 2.9 also attacks Crescens's positions. In the context (2.3 and 2.11.2) Crescens is explicitly named as the opponent, together with "such who are equally irrational as he." This phrase explains the use of the plural in 9.1. In Justin's original manuscript, 2.3 came to stand directly before chapter 9, i.e., in the immediate context.

72. Since Hellenism, philosophy was understood as *ars vitae*, as a system of moral rules, which were supported by knowledge of nature and skill in argumentation and which were confirmed in the lifestyle of the philosophers. An illustration for Rome is the Platonist Nigrinus, whose lectures Lucian heard several times on the occasion of his visit to Rome, just at the time of Justin. Nigrinus purely taught morality (Lucian, *Nigr*). Further, cf., e.g., Lucian, *Menippus* 3f.: Lucian expected from his philosophical teachers that they direct him to a reliable *way of behavior* (cf. Justin, *Dial.* 8.1f.). Further material in R. L. Wilken, "Towards a Social Interpretation," 444f.; P. Rabbow, *Seelenführung*, 260ff., passim.; L. Friedländer, *Sittengeschichte* 3.266ff. (philosophy as moral guide, primacy of ethics).

attempted not only through his writings but also in the social relations
of his daily life to do justice to his claim of being a philosopher, a teacher
of *ars vitae*. The philosophical opponents, for their part, appeared to
accept him as such; they engaged with him in ethical disputes.[73]

b. That Justin was accepted by the world about him as a Christian philosopher, but quite certainly as philosopher (cf. above, Galen
in regard to the Christians in general), is seen further in the essentially reliable *Acta Iustini*. The Roman city praefect Rusticus—the same
Q. Iunius Rusticus, who, as a Stoic, decisively influenced[74] Marcus Aurelius — addresses Justin as scholar (ποίους λόγους μεταχειρίζῃ: "with
what intellectual direction do you busy yourself?"; 2.3; rec. A and B).
He appeals to Justin as to a λεγόμενος λόγιος.[75] And he engages Justin in
an exchange of words that has nothing directly to do with the charges
laid in the trial. The exchange deals with the philosophical question
of the soul's immortality, concerning which the Stoic Rusticus questions Justin because of his interest in the subject; even the Stoic term
ἐκπύρωσις occurs (5.2; rec. A and B). The praefect finally calls himself
to order (5.4; rec. B): "Let us come to the matter at hand...," namely,
to the defendant's refusal to offer sacrifice.

The social environment appears to have hesitantly acknowledged Justin's philosophical role, which was carried out wearing the philosopher's
mantle, even though his contemporaries might have been inclined to
shake their heads over the content of the new Christian "philosophical
school" (if they took the time to look more seriously at its teachings).
Not even Crescens had taken the trouble to do this (2.3.3ff.).

Justin's School

a. Justin's school belongs to the philosopher's role. In Rome, listeners
and students gathered around Justin. In *Acta Iust.* 3.2f., the praefect
interrogates Justin: "Tell me, where do you gather, in what place do you
assemble your disciples?"[76] Justin responds, "I live above the baths of
Myrtinus...I know of no other place of assembly, only that one, and

---

73. That *one* of the disputation partners, Crescens, was only a dirty Cynic from the
street (cf. Martial, 4.53) does not oppose this observation.

74. Cf. *Hist. Aug. Vit. Marci.* 1.7; 3.3; Cassius Dio, 71.35.1. Rusticus was *consul suffectus* in the year 133, *consul ordinarius* in 162 C.E., praefect of the city between the years
163 and 168.

75. *Acta Iust.* 5.1; only in rec. B. The relationship of text rec. A (Paris, graec. 1470,
from the year 890) to rec. B (Cambridge, Cant. Add. 4489, eighth century) needs further
text-critical studies. B represents the older manuscript, but it is longer than A. Therefore, G. Lazzati (*Gli sviluppi della letteratura sui martiri nei primi quattro secoli* [Turin,
1956]) gives preference to A. Both text editions are edited by H. Musurillo, *The Acts of
the Christian Martyrs* (Oxford, 1972).

76. δοῦλος καίσαρος, *Acta Iust.* 4.3, rec. B.

when anyone wished to come to me, I was accustomed to share with him words of truth."[77]

At least two students of Justin are known to us by name: Tatian, the most prominent (see below), and Euelpistus, an imperial slave.[78] (Ἰουστίνου ἡδέως ἤκουον τῶν λόγων, *Acta Iust.* 4.7; rec. A and B). It is noteworthy that both disciples, as their teacher, come from the east: Tatian from Assyria (Tatian, *Or.* 42.1) and Euelpistus from Cappadocia, where his parents still live (*Acta Iust.* 4.7; rec. A and B).

According to the *Acta*, Justin and Euelpistus, together with five other Christians, were arrested and led before the praefect of the city, Iunius Rusticus, on charges of refusing to offer sacrifice.[79] The other five Christians were a woman named Charito[80] and four men, Chariton, Hierax, Paion, and Liberianus.[81] At least one of them was eastern: Hierax came from Phrygia (4.8; rec. A and B). That these five Christians belonged to Justin's circle of students is not explicitly stated. Several things, however, speak in favor of this: In 4.5 (rec. A and B) the praefect asks the defendants whether Justin has made them Christians.[82] The praefect's question is repeated for each of the accused[83] and betrays his point of view. To him Justin appears to be the head of the group. The praefect addresses him alone as a scholar. He interrogates him first and most extensively (chaps. 2–3) and, after a brief interrogation of the others,[84] returns again to Justin (chap. 5) in order to engage in a new altercation with him. Therefore, nothing stands in the way of identifying the entire group which was arrested with Justin and Euelpistus as Justin's circle

77. 3.2 in Rec. B. In Rec. A, ἀθροίζεις τοὺς μαθητάς σου is missing. The meaning is the same.

78. In regard to the relationship between Justin's school and the rest of Roman Christianity see in detail chap 38. Justin's school is in fellowship with the rest of Roman Christianity but organized free and independent from it. Therefore Justin can play the role of a free philosopher to the "world."

79. Cf. 1.1, as well as 5.6 in rec. A or 5.8 in rec. B.

80. Cf. 4.2 Rec. A and B.

81. In the middle of the second century, social status can no longer be determined by the names; see above the chapter on Rom 16. Therefore, one cannot say very much concerning the social status of the five people. (a) Nevertheless, from the fact that the *Acta* explicitly identify only Euelpistus as an imperial slave, we may conclude that the others were not. (b) The educational level of the six appears to have been below that of Justin since Justin was clearly the spokesperson for the accused group. (c) Hierax may have been a common slave. He states that he came to Rome when he was "torn away" (ἀποσπασθείς) from his homeland Phrygia (4.8 rec. B; rec. A ἀπεσπάσθην). Apparently he did not come of his own free will.

82. Euelpistus and Paion answer that they already had Christian parents: 4.6f. rec A and B. Hierax answers that he has been a Christian for a long time (ἔκπαλαι) (4.5 rec. A; similar in rec. B); accordingly, the praefect also tries to ascertain information about his parents (4.8 rec. A and B).

83. Rec. A of 4.5, 6: Ἰουστῖνος ὑμᾶς ἐποίησε Χριστιανούς; — τίς σε ἐδίδαξεν; (rec. B similarly).

84. Chapter 4 contains only a short inquiry concerning their confession; there is no dialogue, as between Rusticus and Justin.

of students. It also follows from the hearing that only Justin's lodgings "above the baths of Myrtinus" were known to the authorities as
the group's assembly place. It must have been there, in the dwelling of
the teacher, that the group had been surprised and apprehended as a
suspicious assembly.[85]

Along with Tatian, there are seven known students of Justin:

- 1 woman — 6 men

- at least 3 easterners. One of them, the Cappadocian Euelpistus,
  is an imperial slave; the Phrygian Hierax is perhaps also a slave
  (n. 79).

- at least 2 have been brought up as Christians by their parents: Euelpistus and Paion. Also Hierax says of himself that he has been a
  Christian "for a long time."

b. Did Justin accept money in payment for instruction in his Christian philosophy? Some statements indicate that Justin did not make a
living from his teaching:

Dial. 58.1 emphasizes that Justin instructed Trypho "gratis" (ἀμισ-
θωτί). "Free of charge...I ask all to be my companions in enjoyment (of
the correct understanding of scripture). I do not wish to be condemned
on the day of judgment for neglect of this obligation." The same idea
is found in *Dial.* 82.3. 82.4 states: "If we strive to speak according to
scripture, we do so out of fear, not out of avarice...; no one can accuse
us of such a thing. We do not wish to do the same as the leaders of your
(Jewish) people whom God criticizes with the words, 'Your leaders are
companions of thieves; they love gifts and strive after payment.' If you
find among us men of such disposition [they exist! in Hermas, *Mand.*
11.12, some Christian prophets take money], then you may not because of them immediately revile Christ." Justin's student Tatian writes
(*Or.* 32.2): "Among us, not only the rich "philosophize" (φιλοσοφοῦσι),
but also the poor enjoy instruction gratis, for what comes from God
surpasses the recompense of earthly gifts." *Dial.* 2.3 criticizes the peripatetic teacher who demands money from his students. According to

---

85. Cf. the piercing questions of the praefect to discover places of assembly (3.1f. rec.
A and B: Where was the place of assembly? Whether Justin knew of still other assembly places? Whether the accused first found their way to Christianity through Justin or
through other persons? Where can these other persons be found?) The praefect probes to
discover the extent of the "conspiracy." The refusal of the accused to render sacrifice (5.6
rec. A; 5.8 rec. B; 2.1 rec. B) is tantamount to disloyalty in the eyes of the praefect. Tertullian in *Apol.* 10 (*maiestatis rei;* cf. further 28 and 35 with 2) shows that being a Christian
could be seen as related to high treason. In the eyes of some pagan contemporaries, Christians are politically suspect (Justin, *Apol.* 1.11). Hippolytus, *Dan.* 20.3, offers a parallel
to Justin's arrest: Christians are dragged from the place of assembly and ordered, "Have
community with us and *adore our gods.*" If they refuse, they are reported as people "who
disobey the order of the emperor." Their trial ends in execution.

Justin, his desire for money makes it questionable whether he really is a philosopher.

The question remains, where did Justin obtain his support? Did he receive it from his own private means? From occasional free gifts from his students? From revenue obtained by occasional manual labor? The question remains open.

c. If one seeks a pagan analogy for the school of the Christian philosopher Justin, one encounters those Greek philosophical schools that, in the form of religious associations, cultivate common meals and discussions.[86] It is possible that in Rome by the Porta Maggiore one such neo-Pythagorean school has been excavated, with an underground assembly basilica and a vestibule.[87] In any case Justin, with his religiously oriented school, was by no means unfaithful to his role as "philosopher."

The Role of the Philosopher in Second-Century Society

Justin laid claim to the role of a philosopher in an environment that was partly predisposed to the claim. The extent of his education corresponded to this claim. Justin was equal to Middle Platonic philosophers. What we know of the social relations in which Justin lived corresponded to his claim as well. What social status did a man one encountered on the street dressed in the mantle of a philosopher have? Let us for the moment disregard the Cynics on the street. Martial (4.53) caricatures the Cynic in this manner: "His ash-grey hair is repulsive; a dirty beard falls upon his chest, and a yellowed mantle is wrapped around him, fitting to the miserable bed...." Anti-intellectual and socially little respected, the Cynics could not be ranked on the same social level as the Platonists.

---

86. Cf., e.g., a community of philosophers in Alexandria, in Strabo, 17.1.8. See further, R. W. Wilken, "Towards a Social Interpretation," 455; U. v. Wilamowitz-Moellendorff, "Die Philosophenschulen und die Politik," and "Die rechtliche Stellung der Philosophenschulen," in *Antigonos von Karystos*, 263ff., 178ff. Philosophical schools as well as cultic associations could be described by the same term: "Thiasos." Cf. C. Colpe, "Genossenschaft," *RAC* 10:90. For the fact that in Justin's circle not only did instruction take place but also worship services and the Eucharist were celebrated, see below Part 5.

87. J. Carcopino, *La Basilique Pythagoricienne de la Porte Majeure*, 10th ed. (Paris, 1944). The walls of the building were inexpensively built, but the builders provided rich decoration, colorful paintings, stucco, and a mosaic floor. The complex dates from the early imperial period and appears to have been used for only a short time. Of course, "cultic place for neo-Pythagoreans" is only one possible interpretation of this archaeological discovery. It can likewise be considered as a place of burial (cf. F. Coarelli, *Rom*, 214–17).

How would one describe the social position of a non-Cynic philosopher in the second century?[88]

a. The role of the philosopher had three variants. There was the philosopher as:

* educator and adviser of individuals

* teacher of ethics in schools open to the public

* missionary and popular preacher.[89]

If we wish to categorize Justin, the first and third variants come into question. Justin's disciples belong in the first category. "Whenever someone wanted to come to me, I took care to impart to him the words of truth" (*Acta Iust.* 3.3). Justin taught in individual discussion or in small circles, as is also indicated by the number of only six defendants apprehended with him. On the other hand, we see Justin as popular preacher when he publicly disputed about ethical questions.

b. One has to distinguish between the social origin of a philosopher (Justin is a freeborn)[90] and the status that a philosopher as philosopher possessed in the society. A famous example: The former slave Epictetus was numbered among the highly honored personalities of his time; Hadrian is said to have courted his friendship (*Hist. Aug. Hadr.* 16.10). In other words, (1) social advancement *could* result from becoming a philosopher in the second century. (2) In the second century the activity of a philosopher stands open to any class, from slave to senator.[91] Also C. Tutilius Hostilianus, a Stoic philosopher in Rome at the time of Vespasian, originated neither from the equestrian nor the senatorial class but from the lower strata of society (*CIL* 6:9785; Cassius Dio, 65.13.2).

c. The question remains: What "recognition" does one enjoy who walks about the streets of Rome dressed in the mantle of a philosopher and who, as teacher, can be asked about the questions of life and morals? This is the question of the social standing of "education" in general in second century Rome. We observe a shift since the republic: In imperial times the various fields of education became increasingly

---

88. Selected literature: J. Christes, *Bildung und Gesellschaft*, 228ff.; L. Friedländer, *Sittengeschichte*, especially 3.243ff.; J. Gagé, *Les classes*, for literature; H. Bardon, *La notion*, 101ff.; W. Jaeger, *Paideia*, 1–3; F. Kühnert, *Allgemeinbildung*; H. Fuchs, "Enkyklios Paideia," *RAC* 5:365–98; A. Gwynn, *Roman Education*; H.-J. Marrou, *Geschichte der Erziehung*.

89. Dio Chrysostomus (*Or. to the Alexandrians*, no. 32) names also those who most privately busy themselves with philosophy without teaching. Cf. material in L. Friedländer, *Sittengeschichte*, 3:280ff.; J. Christes, *Bildung und Gesellschaft*, 238, 242; M. Rostovtzeff, *Kaiserreich*, 1:97f.; and above, chap. 4, n. 12, for literature.

90. Because the filiation is named. What the father, Priscus (*Apol.* 1.1.1) did professionally in Flavia Neapolis is unknown.

91. Cf. material in L. Friedländer, *Sittengeschichte*, 3:280ff.; J. Christes, *Bildung und Gesellschaft*, 238, 242.

esteemed socially.[92] Caesar had already granted Roman citizenship to teachers of philosophy and promised it to other scholars if they settled in the city of Rome (Suetonius, *Caes.* 42). Augustus, who wished to drive the foreign elements out of Rome, explicitly exempted primarily professors (Suetonius, *Oct.* 42). Tax reduction was granted to teachers of the *artes liberales;* the state sometimes took over the payment of their salary.[93] Public instruction and public libraries prospered in the second century.[94] A nice archaeological example of this is Celsus's library in Ephesus, which was established by the son of the governor. The motto reads, *honor studiis* (cf. Pliny, *Ep.* 4.16). Education was in demand; it had become a social factor that had an influence on social status. Only professions and activities related to education were respected by the materially independent upper class.[95] (Stoic) philosophy had made its way into the ranks of the senate.[96] Since the death of Domitian who still persecuted philosophers, we observe a positive change in the imperial attitude toward the philosophers. From the time of Nerva they increasingly were respected as bearers of ethical education.[97] The imperial sponsorship of philosophers goes so far in the second century that Tatian makes a joke about certain philosophers who were paid 600 ducats yearly from the treasury, "so that they do not have to wash their wavy beards for nothing."[98] In the second century the philosopher's beard became fashionable, as we can see from the busts since Hadrian. The closely shaven officer's face becomes passé. With Marcus Aurelius the philosopher himself ascends the throne and the synthesis between power and philosophy becomes perfect. Justin bears witness to the latter when he appeals to the philosophical self-understanding of the emperor (see above on *Apol.* 1.2f.).

The social ascent of the intellectual professions distinguishes them from manual labor. Already Seneca was of the opinion: "The place of philosophy is higher (than that of the artisan's skill); philosophy does

---

92. Cf. J. Christes, *Bildung und Gesellschaft,* 233ff.; further literature on p. 239.

93. J. Christes, *Bildung und Gesellschaft,* 240; M. Rostovtzeff, *Kaiserreich,* 1:108. Vespasian established in Rome schools of rhetoric open to the public, with teaching positions financed by the state. Quintilian was the first to occupy one of the new positions (Suetonius, *Vesp.* 18).

94. For literature, cf. M. Rostovtzeff, *Kaiserreich,* 1, chap. 4, n. 32.

95. J. Christes, *Bildung und Gesellschaft,* 236.

96. E.g., Seneca, also Paetus Thrasea and Helvidius Priscus: Tacitus, *Ann.* 16.21ff. Cf. also the opposition in the senate influenced by Stoicism in the early period of imperial Rome.

97. M. Friedländer, *Sittengeschichte,* 3:252ff.

98. Tatian, *Or.* 19.1; cf. *Hist. Aug. Anton. Pius* 11; ibid., *Marc. Aurel.* 23. The social recognition of philosophy is also indicated in Tatian, *Or.* 25.1: Whoever as a philosopher does not draw a state income lets himself be fed by the rich. And 32.1 testifies that pagan philosophy was practiced especially by the rich themselves (φιλοσοφοῦσιν οἱ πλουτοῦντες).

not train the hands but is mistress of our intellect."[99] Justin bears witness to the place of the intellectual profession above manual labor by formulating: "Not only (οὐ μόνον) φιλόσοφοι and φιλόλογοι but also (ἀλλὰ καί) χειροτέχναι and παντελῶς ἰδιῶται" may be encountered among the Christians (2.10.8).[100]

Where did the increased esteem of the intellectual professions, particularly of philosophy, come from? Since the end of the first century, a hunger had grown for philosophy, especially in the upper classes of Rome. Demand for ethical orientation allowed philosophers to become influential counselors, even beyond the period of school instruction.[101] In this regard, Christes (241, 169ff.) refers to the principle of utilitarianism: In the imperial culture, it is not the intellectual character *in itself* that bestows social status upon an activity. Intelligence was esteemed where it was useful, for example, in ethical questions (cf. also Quintilian, 7.1.38).

d. One point must be cleared up separately in regard to Justin, namely, the income of a philosopher. Whether or not a teacher is paid for his efforts depends on his social origin.[102] If he is born of a senatorial family, he naturally does not demand an honorarium. A member of the senatorial class is forbidden to engage in gainful employment. He draws an income from his property and is economically independent.[103] A different kind of mentality in regard to livelihood dominates the other classes. Remuneration is accepted for educational instruction.

In regard to payment for scholarly teachers, Ulpian's *Dig.* 50.13 is informative:[104] It was forbidden for philosophers and legal scholars, in contrast to rhetoricians, grammarians, and teachers of geometry, to take action to enforce demands for honoraria (1.4f.). The regulation reflects the fact that jurisprudence and philosophy are the most esteemed sciences, which are also taught by members of the senatorial upper class. Ulpian is therefore concerned to adapt both disciplines to the norms of the senatorial class (without, however, advocating a principle of the gratis character of these disciplines; it is not the honorarium itself that is prohibited but the legal action to enforce demands for honoraria).

---

99. Seneca, *Ep.* 90.26; cf., e.g., also 24f.; Galen, *Protrep.* 14.38f.; Cicero, *Off.* 1.42.150f.; Cassius Dio, 46.4.2; further, Lucian, *Nigrim.* 24.

100. See also, *Dial.* 2.1; further 3.3; 4.3: The philosopher is exalted above the crowd. *Dial.* 88.8 shows that for Justin the artisans are on one level with the common people: Jesus' renunciation of rank, his coming "without glory," is also expressed in his profession as carpenter.

101. L. Friedländer, *Sittengeschichte Roms,* 3:266ff., 272ff., and see above on the primacy of ethics in the philosophy of that time.

102. Cf. L. Friedländer, *Sittengeschichtes Roms,* 3:260ff.; J. Christes, *Bildung und Gesellschaft,* 230, 232, 239.

103. Cf. Th. Mommsen, *Römisches Staatrecht,* 3:898f.

104. In this regard see J. Christes, *Bildung und Gesellschaft,* 243–45; W. Kunkel, *Herkunft und soziale Stellung,* 343.

Ulpian's (ibid.) reasoning is formed by the senatorial ethos: it is suitable for philosophers to disdain paid labor.[105] Teachers of grammar and geometry, on the other hand, never belong to the senatorial order. They need to earn their livelihood, and their right of legally enforcing demands for honoraria is therefore never questioned.

Let us compare Justin's renunciation of a honorarium (see above). No one will conclude that Justin originally belonged to the "ordo senatorius" — even if Justin's *Dial.* 2.3 (desire for money makes it questionable that someone is actually a philosopher) echoes completely Ulpian's understanding. This reference in the *Dialogue* shows that Justin's renunciation of payment helps to support his claim as a Christian to be also considered a genuine philosopher. Besides this, eschatological reasons play a role: " . . . I exhort all to partake in my teaching gratis; I will not be condemned on the day of judgment for neglecting this obligation" (*Dial.* 58.1; cf. 82.2ff.). Justin is driven by eschatological fear (δέος).[106] An otherwise exclusively social-historically determined behavior (renunciation of an honorarium as a result of membership in a certain social class) is here influenced by Christian eschatological doctrines.

Our thesis is that Justin also as a Christian played the role of scholar, of philosopher, and that he consequently at least partly shared in the general social recognition of scholars in the second century, as all the others who wore the philosopher's mantle. Formerly pagan philosophers, like Justin, contributed to the development that Christianity was increasingly respected as "education" and as a "philosophical school."[107] Their work had two sides:

1. From the point of view of the history of theology, it led to stronger infiltration of philosophical thinking into Christian doctrine. The penetration of Christian teaching by pagan philosophical presuppositions encountered in the apologists is sufficiently known and is treated at length in the various histories of theology (cf. also the table in Appendix 2). Here we are more interested in the interrelations between social background and teaching. Because Christianity began to encroach on the social world of pagan philosophical education and to win over philosophers within it, it opened itself to new ways of thinking. In other words, whoever, as Justin, had had the benefit of a pagan philosophical education, had studied with a Platonist, traveled about as a Platonic philosopher, and also, as a Christian, continued to play the role of a philosopher inevitably examined Christian *topoi* of belief in Platonic light

---

105. Cf. also, e.g., Lucian, *Nigrin.* 25: οἱ ἐπὶ μισθῷ φιλοσοφοῦντες are judged to be contemptible.

106. *Dial.* 82.4. Cf. Tatian (32.2), whose theological argument is similar: What comes from God surpasses fundamentally any remuneration through earthly donation; therefore Christian doctrines are transmitted gratis.

107. Cf. Tertullian, *De pallio* 6.

wherever it was possible. If someone as a Christian embraced the educational profession of philosophy — to which in the second century eclecticism and the knowledge of competing systems of learning belonged — then influences of these teachings could not fail to appear in the inherited system of Christian doctrine.

2. The work of the Christian philosophers had, moreover, a social-historical effect. It made Christianity more socially acceptable, so that — as we saw and will be observable in individual cases later — the higher social strata increasingly were represented in Christianity, particularly beginning with the second half of the second century. For example, in the second half of the second century in Rome, the distinguished Apollonius was attracted by a Christianity colored by Platonism (cf. chap. 29).

The importance of these double catalytic functions of the Apologists can hardly be overestimated.

Chapter 26

Tatian and Rhodon

Directly or indirectly, Tatian and Rhodon are dependent upon Justin's school.

1. Tatian is a student of Justin's.[1] His unconventionality, which would later scandalize the church (encratism, etc.), does not yet appear during his sojourn in Rome but first comes to light in the east. How can we know this? Tatian's Roman student Rhodon,[2] securely rooted within the community of the traditional church, worked fervently in Rome against heretics so that his teacher, Tatian, could not have taken any positions in Rome that would have deviated far from the views of his teacher, Justin.[3]

In Rome Tatian heard the lectures of Justin, could claim at least one student as his own, Rhodon, and was involved, together with Justin, in the dispute with Crescens (*Or.* 19.1). From the point of view of social history, Tatian's pagan classical education is of interest to us. There is nothing extant from Tatian's (pre-Christian?) philosophical productivity — not even from his book "On Animals" (*Or.* 15.2). We must rely upon information from Tatian's *Discourse to the Greeks*. M. Elze, contrary to the older interpreters who reconstruct Tatian's thought primarily within an oriental, "Syrian" or "Gnostic" scenario, wished to discover Tatian's philosophical background in Middle Platonism. Tatian agrees in several ways with the Middle Platonic direction represented by Albinos.

---

1. Justin's student: Tatian, *Or.* 18.2 quotes from a lecture of "Justin, who is most worthy of admiration." 19.1: Tatian was involved in Justin's conflict with Crescens. The description of conversion in *Or.* 29 shows the greatest similarity to Justin's (cf. N. Hyldahl, *Philosophie und Christentum*, 237, 239–55; he also notes other influences from Justin). Further see Irenaeus, 1.28.1; Eusebius, *Hist. Eccl.* 4.29; Hippolytus, *Ref.* 8.16.

2. See Rhodon himself in *Ecc. Hist.* 5.13.1, 8.

3. Similarly, Irenaeus, 1.28.1: As long as Tatian "was with Justin, he represented nothing of that sort (heretical encratism). Only after the latter's martyrdom did he distance himself from the church ... and advance his peculiar doctrine." Did his "apostasy" occur while he was still in Rome or in the east, where he returned (Epiphanius, *Haer.* 46.1)? It is highly questionable whether this alleged apostasy *actually* took place. Cf. M. Elze, *Tatian and his Theology*, 113. Tatian did not apostatize, at least not in Rome. After Justin's death, he left Rome for the east. But he himself did not want to break away from the church.

Not only in the understanding of truth[4] or of time[5] does Tatian derive his thought from Middle Platonic presuppositions but also in his doctrine of God he employs Platonic terminology,[6] just as he constructs his doctrine of principles according to the Platonic example.[7] His style reproduces at times typically Platonic expressions[8] and terms.[9]

If we consider these elements of philosophy, they rank below Justin's philosophical education, both quantitatively and qualitatively. They remain on the level of some eclectically assimilated *topoi*[10] and do not indicate a thorough philosophical knowledge. Totally superficial are the gossipy stories about individual philosophers (*Or.* 2f.; cf. Appendix 3). And when Tatian (*Or.* 7–10) in Platonic style maintains the freedom of the created person against Stoic determinism, he is not directly dependent on an education in a pagan Platonic school but rather on his teacher, Justin (*Apol.* 1.43). The same also appears to be true in *Or.* 20.1, where he betrays a knowledge of Plato's *Phaedrus* 248B. Justin also employed this passage from Plato (*Dial.* 2.6).[11] Did Tatian first come into closer contact with individual philosophical *topoi* through his Christian teacher, Justin? A separate study of Tatian's dependence upon Justin might prove extremely fruitful.

On the other hand, when Tatian is not being specifically philosophical, he offers disproportionately more elements of *literary* education than Justin does (see the most essential material in Appendix 3). He

---

4. M. Elze, *Tatian und seine Theologie,* 128f.; 14.

5. *Or.* 26.1. In regard to this see M. Elze, *Tatian und seine Theologie,* 103–5: particularly Albinos as a parallel.

6. M. Elze, *Tatian und seine Theologie,* 64f.

7. Ibid., 75; 114.

8. *Or.* 21 end; cf. M. Elze, *Tatian und seine theologie,* 61. On *Or.* 20.1, cf. Plato, *Phaedr.* 248B, further, M. Elze, *Tatian und seine Theologie,* 30, 94.

9. Examples in M. Elze, *Tatian und seine Theologie,* 90, 94. For further elements of the Platonic school see M. Elze, ibid., 30f., 91, n. 2; 66f.; 71; 73–78; 80–85; 38. On the remaining philosophical elements of education see below, Appendix 3.

10. Cf. similarly L. W. Barnard, "Apologeten," *TRE* 3 (1974): 379f.: only a few superficial similarities with teachings of the philosophical schools.

11. Further philosophical *topoi* used by both Tatian and his teacher are:

- 25.2 (cf. 4) rages in Platonic style against Stoic materialism: God is ἀσώματος — Justin, see App. 2.

- 25.2 the world is immortal — Justin, see App. 2.

- 25.2 Immortality of the soul — Justin, see App. 2.

- 25.2; 6.1 Stoic *ekpyrosis* — Justin, see App. 2.

- On 13.2, cf. the "seminal forces" — Justin, see App. 2.

- 5.1 the logos as greatest power — Justin, see App. 2, as well as *Apol.* 1.32.10; 23.2; *Dial.* 105.1.

claims a knowledge of all kinds of poems, plays, and authors, a virtual array of material, but it is unclear whether Tatian has actually read any of it. A list of authors such as that found in *Or.* 41 makes one strongly suspect that the list is assembled from handbooks. One may also pose the same question regarding *Or.* 31 and 36ff., which offer an "overview of the research" concerning the study of Homer at that time and cite an abundance of historiographic books (cf. Appendix 3). They seem to deal with a superficial knowledge gleaned from handbooks rather than the fruit gathered from the study of primary literature.

The language: The Christian Tatian takes a fancy to the simple style of the Old Testament prophets (29), detests the extravagancies of Greek rhetoric (1.3; 16.1), ridicules[12] the Atticizing movement of his day, and desires his speech to be "easily understood" (30.2). On the other hand, he can often not hide that he was once trained in literary style. Unlike Justin, Tatian clearly was educated in high literary classicism.[13]

If we arrange the total findings (cf. Appendix 3), we find in Tatian someone who has undergone the rhetorical education of his time but, unlike Justin, not the philosophical. Tatian best fits into the picture we have of the rhetoric of the first and second centuries, the picture of an ostentatious eloquence that marshals an impressive array of educational elements but remains superficial. "You speak loud and pompous with many gestures about the battle of Cannae and the wars of Mithridates and about the Punic's cunning rage and about all kinds of people called Marius, Mucius, or Sulla. Speak, Postumus, about the three goats.... My lawsuit is solely about three goats" (Martial, 6.19). Building upon the grammar schools, the teachers of rhetoric, in the choice of their material, continue to trot within the circle of ideas and views which the grammarians have already walked up and down. Apart from present reality, events from the ancient past are passionately treated, as well as legends from nebulous early days, things comical, obscure, exotic, fantastic and exaggerated, the more absurd the better (Aulus Gellius, 17.12). The "controversies" (*controversiae*) of the elder Seneca give us an insight.[14] Tatian's predilection for anecdote, obscurities, and mythical elements (cf. Appendix 3) corresponds to the picture of the rhetorician of that time. The same is true of exotic oddities, such as the "better worlds" and their mild climate (Tatian, *Or.* 20). The same is also true of Tatian's condemnation of the theater and the gladiators' games (*Or.* 23). Here — and not only here (cf. Appendix) — Tatian is influenced by

---

12. 1.2; 26.3f.; 30.2; 27.3; cf. the usual polemic, e.g., Plutarch, *De auditu.* 9.

13. See C. Fabricius, "Der sprachliche Klassizismus," 187ff., 195f.; A. Wifstrand, *Die alte Kirche,* 28ff.

14. Cf. further, e.g., Suetonius, *Rhet.* I; Tacitus, *Dial. de Or.* 35.4f.; Juvenal, 7.150ff. or the Pseudo-Quintilian *Declamationes* (first/second century). "The teacher miserably dies of the nonsense that he repeated so many times" (Juvenal, 7.154).

the great orator Dio of Prusa and shows himself to be in the tradition of contemporary rhetorical instruction. The rhetoricians' predilection for historical material explains Tatian's knowledge of so many historiographic book titles (Appendix). Also his educated classicistic language fits well into this picture.[15]

If we add to our indirect evidence the direct testimony by Tatian himself, the picture becomes more complete. (a) Born in the Syrian east (42.1), he testifies, "I have traveled a large portion of the earth ... until I took up residence in the city of Rome" (35.1). (b) When Tatian tells his addressees they have no better origin than he (γένεσις; 26.2), we may at least conclude that he was not born a slave. (c) 29.1 announces that he let himself be initiated into several pagan mysteries. This was not rare as, for example, his contemporary Apuleius (e.g., *Met.* 3.15.2) or some inscriptions in Rome, *CIL* 6:500; 504; 507, indicate. (d) Above all, and this confirms our thesis concerning Tatian's educational background, he passed through a Greek course of studies (42.1: παιδευθεὶς δὲ πρῶτον μὲν τὰ ὑμέτερα), taught as a pagan rhetorician (35.1: σοφιστεύσας τὰ ὑμέτερα), encountered "many" arts and sciences (τέχναις δαὶ ἐπινοίαις ἐγκυρήσας πολλαῖς, ibid.) and looked behind the scenes of pagan scholars, particularly of grammarians and stylists (26). 1.3f. states that some Christians were held in high regard because of their Greek education before they converted to Christianity; the statement is formulated in such a way that the reader is supposed to count Tatian among them.[16]

As one coming not from philosophy but from rhetoric, Tatian represents a different type of higher Greek education than Justin. Common to both, however, is the purely pagan educational past, and in this both are different from teachers such as Irenaeus, who as children went to a pagan school (cf. Tertullian, *De idol*; see also below, chap. 35, no. 5) but at the same time were brought up from childhood as Christians (Irenaeus, 3.3.4; *Ep.* in Eusebius, *Hist. Ecc.* 5.20.5) and had correspondingly less interest in philosophical thinking. They could not call Aristotle anything but "hair-splitting" and "small-minded" (Irenaeus,

---

15. J. Geffcken (*Apologeten*, 105ff.) thought that Tatian's variegated layout of material was philistine, but this is not completely correct, as the above discussion of the problematic structure in Justin's works attempted to show. Even though repetitions occur and digressions flourish (e.g., 15.2; 26.3bf.; 30.2; 40.1bf.), the longest excursion (31.4– chap. 35) still follows Quintilian's rule (4.3.14) that a digression has to be logically connected to the subordinate theme. At the same time this digression brings variation (cf. Quintilian, ibid., 1f.), because it interrupts in an entertaining way the sober proof of the validity of the Judeo-Christian tradition because of its age. In 35.2, Tatian shows that he is aware of his digression; he justifies it as "necessary" (τὸ κατεπεῖγον). On the problem of the arrangement of material, see already R. C. Kukula, *Tatian*, 180ff., especially 187f., where he tries to save Tatian's reputation as a rhetorician.

16. Eusebius (*Hist. Ecc.* 4.16.7) knows to add that Tatian at first gave instruction in the treasures of Greek education and that he "reaped no small honor from this, leaving behind numerous scholarly monuments."

2.14.5). They perceived many-sided knowledge as dangerous (2.26.1), and accordingly could hardly do justice to a man such as Tatian (Irenaeus, 3.23.8; 1.28.1; cf. M. Elze, *Tatian und seine Theologie,* 108). Here a gap is apparent between those who were already brought up from childhood in the Christian tradition and those new converts from paganism who had experienced a pagan education: a social-historical problem within the early church, which should perhaps be considered more thoroughly in future treatments of the heresy / orthodoxy subject.

Like his teacher, Justin, Tatian claims that the Christian teaching is a philosophy. Christianity may not be Greek, but it is still a "paideia" and a "philosophia" (12.5; 35.1f.; 31.1; 32.1, 3; 33.2).[17] In the final chapters of his *Oratio* Tatian outstrips pagan philosophies: the Christian philosophy is superior in dignity to Greek education because of the greater age of its authorities. Moses, as Tatian tries to demonstrate in a scholarly manner, is older than Homer. Tatian calls himself κῆρυξ of truth (17.1), as the Cynic philosophers do.[18] Tatian calls himself ὁ κατὰ βαρβάρους φιλοσοφῶν (42.1). κατὰ βαρβάρους serves as a title of honor, which is supposed to vouch for the truth of Tatian's φιλοσοφία. Tatian here echoes a Greek notion that has been current since the third century B.C.E. According to this notion, philosophy demonstrates its truth when it agrees with the exotic wisdom of the barbarians. Megasthenes was of the opinion that all cosmological insights of Greek philosophy were already expressed by the sages of India. The exotic teaching of the Brahmans, Magi, and Druids was considered as originating from the primeval knowledge of primitive humankind.[19] In this context stands Tatian's argumentation that seeks to prove that the Judeo-Christian traditon is older and therefore more true and less spoiled than Greek culture.

If the only true and primeval philosophy has been rediscovered in Christianity, as Tatian and his teacher assert, then Tatian's biting criticism of Greek education and culture becomes understandable. Tatian has bid farewell "to the bragging of the Romans and the chilly prattle of

17. Also the report of the conversion in *Or.* 29 demonstrates that Tatian considers Christianity as philosophy. Christianity deals with the same themes as Hellenistic philosophy (in regard to this passage see M. Elze, *Tatian und seine Philosophie,* 23f.; N. Hyldahl, *Philosophie und Christentum,* 239).

18. Epictetus, 3.22.69. Cf. P. Wendland, *Kultur,* 82, 93. Characteristically, the section in *Or.* 17 is delivered totally in diatribe style (cf. M. Elze, *Tatian und seine Philosophie,* 33, for literature).

19. For popular philosophical sources of Tatian's positive concept of the barbarians (unspoiled nature of the barbarian people, high regard for them) cf. M. Elze, *Tatian und seine Philosophie,* 25f., for literature; N. Hyldahl, *Philosophie und Christentum,* 244f. Hyldahl mentions here the possible influence of Numenios and his understanding of barbarian wisdom. Other authors also talk positively about the barbarians: Lucian, *Fugit.* (6–8); Strabo 16.2.37, 39; Philostratus, *Apollonius* 3.16, 25 end; 2.26; Aelius, *Var. hist.* 2.31; Origen, *Contra Cel.* 1.25; see further below, App. 3.

the Athenians" (τῇ Ῥωμαίων μεγαλαυχίᾳ καὶ τῇ Ἀθηναίων ψυχρολογίᾳ, 35). Of course, the irony is that many aspects of Tatian's criticism were already given to him by the Greek culture itself, which he reviled and which had developed niches of self-criticism. Thus Tatian's own pagan rhetorical training hands him the ammunition when he, just as the great orator Dio of Prusa, criticizes the fighting games (cf. App. 3) or when he, as Seneca,[20] rages against the γραμματικοί or when he ridicules the multi-colored variety of hypotheses (δογμάτων ποικιλίαι; 32.1), using the contradictions and ruptures between the doctrines of the Greek philosophers as an argument against them (3.3; 25.2; 25.1): this argument was already rooted in post-Aristotelian philosophy.[21] Tatian's polemic against culture is not original but is cultivated by the Greek literary educational system itself.[22] One should therefore hesitate to interpret Tatian within the horizon of oriental presuppositions (here I agree with M. Elze) or to connect Tatian with the Greek / Oriental conflict, that is, with the anti-Hellenizing renaissance of indigenous cultures during the second century. Tatian composed the original text of the Diatessaron in Greek and not in Syriac. Also Tatian's positive concept of the barbarians does not result from his Syrian nationality (see above n. 19). The extent to which Tatian participated in this renaissance must be decided by further studies. This question is not within the limits of a work concerning Roman Christianity, because the more one is prepared to let Tatian participate in this renaissance, the more one will be inclined to locate the place Tatian wrote the *Oratio* in the east and not in Rome anymore. The localization of the *Oratio* remains an entirely open question.

2. We observed dependencies between Justin and Tatian, particularly regarding philosophical *topoi*. Similar dependencies also surface between the teacher Tatian and his student Rhodon. Also here there are indications that originally pagan educational elements were transmitted through the Christian teacher. Does Christianity again (cf. *1 Clem.*) turn out to be the transmitter of initially pagan classical material? Admittedly, the extent of the source material remains modest. Of Rhodon, who in Rome wrote as an immigrant from Asia Minor[23] and disputed mainly during the reign of Commodus, we know only the quotes found in Eusebius's *Hist. Ecc.* 5.13. Nevertheless, even in this small section

---

20. *Ep.* 88.39; similarly, e.g., Sextus Empiricus, *Adv. gramm.* 97.

21. Cf. O. Gigon, "Die Erneuerung," 35f. See also Lucian, *Menipp.* 4.

22. Cf., e.g., also the sophist Philostratos who, as Tatian, not only speaks positively of the barbarians (see above n. 19) but also caricatures things Greek (*Apoll.* 3.25; 6.2).

23. Eusebius, *Hist. Ecc.* 5.13: A writing against the syllogisms of Apelles or against Marcion's heresy in general; a commentary on the biblical story of creation. He also planned to write an answer to Tatian's προβλήματα.

we observe agreements with his teacher Tatian that are rooted in pagan education:

a. Similar to Tatian (*Or.* 19.4; cf. 13.1; 3.3), Rhodon emphasizes in an intellectual way that faith needs to be "proven" and that it therefore is connected with research and understanding (Eusebius, *Hist. Ecc.* 5.13.6f.). In the educated pagan world there are analogies for such an emphasis. The Roman contemporary Galen, for example, wrote fifteen volumes "Concerning scientific proof." Certainly, in Tatian and Rhodon one does not find Galen's sympathy for Aristotelian logic. Nevertheless, they share with pagan educated people such as Galen the intellectualistic concern that separates them from other Christians such as Apelles. Apelles, Rhodon's Marcionite opponent in disputation, in spite of the rational and logical vigor with which he criticizes the contradictions within the Old Testament, refuses "proof" as soon as metaphysical questions come into the debate (cf. below, App. 1). He depends upon the revelations of the prophetess Philoumena.

b. In the doctrine of the ἀρχαί (Rhodon, like his teacher Tatian, holds for one single principle), Rhodon comments on the position of his opponents with the sentence: μὴ εὑρίσκοντες τὴν διαίρεσιν τῶν πραγμάτων (5.13.4). This sentence reflects Tatian's procedure: Tatian, on the basis of Platonic presuppositions, expressed by means of "distinction" (διαίρεσις) "the dialectic in the Being of God as the first and only principle and thus could deduce plurality without encroachment on the unity [of God]." One "could hardly express Tatian's method in a shorter formula than that used here by Rhodon."[24]

---

24. M. Elze, *Tatian und seine Theologie*, 114, cf. 75ff., for the Middle Platonic concept of "diairesis."

Chapter 27

Valentinians

Introduction

The "sociological location" of Gnosticism for a long time depended less upon evidence than on the ingenious intuitions of Max Weber. Weber[1] saw the motivator for a belief in redemption such as that of the gnostics in the de-politicizing of an intellectual class: intellectuals who are politically incapacitated and robbed of political influence have a tendency to flee from the world into religious redemption. "Usually, socially privileged classes of a people develop a religiosity of redemption most effectively when they are demilitarized and excluded from the possibility of or interest in political activity." According to Weber, Gnosticism is a religion of intellectuals.

H. G. Kippenberg[2] has deductively drawn out this hypothetical line of thought for ancient Gnosticism. According to Kippenberg, the cosmological speculations of the gnostics concerning the relation of the demiurge to humankind (the power of the demiurge is evil, holding human beings in dependence and constraint) are a reference to how the

---

1. *Wirtschaft und Gesellschaft*, 306f.
2. "Versuch einer soziologischen Verortung des antiken Gnostizismus," *Numen* 17 (1970): 211–31. Cf. P. Munz, "The Problem of 'Die soziologischen Verortung des antiken Gnostizismus,'" *Numen* 19 (1972): 41–51; K. Rudolph, "Das Problem einer Soziologie und 'sozialen Verortung' der Gnosis," *Kairos* (1977): 35–44. For other approaches, cf. E. M. Mendelson, "Some Notes on a Sociological Approach to Gnosticism," *Le Origini dello Gnosticismo*, Numen Suppl. 12; ed. U. Banchi (Leiden, 1967), 668–76; also in the same volume, Th. P. v. Baaren, "Towards a Definition of Gnosticism," 174–80. Further, P. Pokorny, "Der soziale Hintergrund der Gnosis," *Gnosis und NT*, ed. K.-W. Tröger (Berlin, 1973), 77–87, especially 86f. P. Pokorny, "Die gnostische Soteriologie in theologischer und soziologischer Sicht," *Religionstheorie und Politische Theologie, 2: Gnosis und Politik*, ed. J. Taubes (Munich and Paderborn, 1984), 154–62; H. Cancik, "Gnostiker in Rom," *Gnosis und Politik*, 163–84; K. Rudolph, "Randerscheinungen des Judentums und das Problem der Entstehung des Gnostizismus," in idem, *Gnosis und Gnostizismus* (Darmstadt, 1975), 776ff.; H. A. Green, "Suggested Sociological Themes in the Study of Gnosticism," *VC* 31 (1977): 169–80; H. Kippenberg, "Intellektualismus und antike Gnosis," *Sozialphilosophie zur Ideolgie und Wissenschaft, Soziologische Texte 10*, 2d ed. (Neuwied, 1966), 261–96; E. Fromm, *Das Christusdogma und andere Essays* (Munich, 1965), 71–76. Finally, H. A. Green, *The Economic and Social Origins of Gnosticism*, SBL Diss. 77 (Atlanta, 1985).

gnostics experienced the empirical power structure and system of rule of the Roman Empire. They experienced it as constraint from which they sought to flee through religious redemption. Gnostic teaching, according to this view, is an expression of the rejection of the authoritarian, bureaucratic, and militaristic Roman state in which the gnostics are excluded from political participation and experience themselves as objects in the hands of unreasonable powers. Precisely this experience of the world is projected onto the gnostic model of cosmology.

Preliminary Methodological Remarks

Can metaphysics be interpreted as transparent for the empirical world? Before we can focus on this problem, the two hypotheses need to be tested, that (a) the gnostics were intellectuals and (b) belonged to socially privileged classes. In this regard, Kippenberg worked deductively from Weber's intuition. The time has come to approach these two presuppositions inductively by confronting them with source material. In regard to (a), there have been affirmative voices since the church fathers (n. 3). For (b), on the other hand, hardly any inductive material has been collected, although specifically for Rome newer (epigraphic) material exists.

Only when we have dealt inductively with both social-historical aspects can we return to ask whether the social background of the gnostics has a connection with their theology. Only then will it be legitimate to explore the correlations between "social circumstances" and "metaphysical doctrines." In other words, it is hardly methodologically correct to extrapolate the social background of the gnostics simply from the structure of their theological thinking — because one has certain already preconceived (Weberian) ideas of correlations between "social circumstances" and "metaphysical doctrines." The procedure is to be reversed.

The Roman Valentinians
as "Intellectuals"?

F. C. Baur and A. Harnack[3] already maintained that the gnostics were intellectuals with a primarily "Platonic foundation." Their intellectual existence reveals itself prima facie in that they were more productive

---

3. F. C. Baur, *Die christliche Gnosis*, 141–45; A. Harnack, *Mission und Ausbreitung* 2:32: There were "among the so-called gnostics first-class scholars and thinkers. No

literarily than the established church. Irenaeus (1.20.1)[4] also observed:
"They produce a countless number of...writings, which they themselves have devised." Much earlier than the representatives of the
established church, the Valentinians busily wrote interpretations of New
Testament texts.[5] The confusing diversity in the Valentinian doctrines
(cf. Irenaeus, 4.35.4; 1.5.3) is witness to an industrious and continuous
investigation of the biblical scriptures.[6]

It is sufficient in the following to highlight some aspects of the Roman
Valentinians. *Valentinus* came to Rome during the tenure of Hyginus
(ca. 136–40 C.E.), "grew in influence under Pius, and remained until
Anicetus" (ca. 155–66 C.E.; Irenaeus, 3.4.3).[7] He then left Rome probably to continue his teaching activity on Cyprus (Epiphanius, *Pan. Haer.*
31).[8] Consequently, Valentinus lived in Rome at least fifteen years. Before Rome, Valentinus sojourned in Alexandria, where he gained his
Greek education (τῶν Ἑλλήνων παιδείαν; oral tradition in Epiphanius,
ibid., 31.2.3).

Concerning Valentinus's literary activity few fragments are preserved.[9]
But what has survived gives evidence of (a) a beautiful and poetic language.
In all the fragments Valentinus attaches great importance to the rhythm
of the language. In form and content he uses antithetical points. In short,
a philologist like E. Norden who credits Valentinus with stylized literary
prose (*Kunstprosa*), enthusiastically praises him as an example of "fusion
of Christianity with the Hellenic."[10] Even the opponents of Valentinus
concede to him, in spite of the polemic venom which they spurt forth,
a "brilliant mind" (Jerome, *In Hos.* 2.10), "*ingenium*" and "*eloquium*"

---

one can read the extant fragments of Valentinus without feeling touched by the acute intellect and fine education of the man. The same may be said for his students Ptolemy
and Heracleon." Cf. also, e.g., H. Langerbeck, *Aufsätze:* "The philosophical and rhetorical education of the heretics has hardly ever been doubted" (p. 172); "the great gnostics
(Basilides and Valentinus) are Platonists, precisely because and insofar as they are Christians" (p. 82). Cf. further, e.g., W. Theiler, "Gott und Seele," 104–23; A. J. Festugière, *La
Révélation,* 92–140. Cf. how, for example, NHC 6:5 (pp. 48, 16–51, 23) deals with Plato
Rep. 588B–589B and the Naassene sermon (Hippolytus, *Ref.* 5.7.29–5.8.4) with Homer,
Od. 24. For voices of the church fathers (polemically) counting the gnostics among in-
tellectuals who were influenced by pagan philosphy and education, cf., e.g., Irenaeus
1.10.2–3 (cf. 2.26); Justin *Dial.* 35.6; Origen, *Contra Cels.* 3.12; Hippolytus, *Ref.* 7.36;
Tertullian, *Praescr.* 7.

4. Cf. also 3.11.9; Origen, *John Comm.* 5.8; *Test Ver.* (NHC 9:3) 56.18–20; 44.8;
68.28f.; on this K. Koschorke, *Die Polemik,* 154.

5. Cf. in particular the material in K. Koschorke, *Die Polemik,* 213–15.

6. In regard to this see ibid., 216.

7. Cf. Eusebius, *Ecc. Hist.,* 4.10; Tertullian, *Praescr.* 30; Clement, *Strom.* 7.17.106f.

8. Was he driven from Rome by the great plague of 166 C.E.? Galen also fled from it
to Pergamon. Valentinus was never excommunicated by the Roman Christians (see below,
Part 5).

9. In Clement, *Strom.* 2.36.2–4; 114.3–6; 3.59.3; 4.89.1–3, 6–90.2; 6.52.3f.; Hippolytus, *Ref.* 6.42.2; 6.37.6–8; cf. also Anthimus, *De sancta ecclesia* 9.

10. *Die antike Kunstprosa,* 545–47, here 547.

(Tertullian, *Adv. Val.* 4). Tertullian (*De carne* 17) writes that Valentinus also composed psalms and hymns. A linguistically exquisite metrical hymn fragment from the pen of Valentinus is preserved by Hippolytus (*Ref.* 6.37.6–8). Thus, at least in regard to form, Valentinus stands parallel to Plato. Plato also composed hymns, to the universe, the creator, and to Eros (e.g., *Phaedr.* 237–41; 244Aff.; *Timaeos*).

b. Also from the point of view of content, Valentinus follows the example of Plato. For example, the fragment of Valentinus preserved in Clement, *Strom* 4.89.6–90.2, resounds with Platonic tones. It contrasts the spiritual world of Ideas, the eternal immutable Being, with the changeable empirical world, subject to time and variability, the imperfect reflection of the spiritual world (cf., e.g., Plato, *Tim.* 37C ff.). G. C. Stead[11] has collected the possible parallels between Plato and Valentinus. Valentinus's Platonizing is unquestionable; Tertullian was already of this opinion.[12] It is more difficult to determine the degree of his philosophical education. The concepts and terms borrowed from Platonism — particularly from the generally known central section of *Timaeos*[13] — show that Valentinus is at least[14] one of the intellectuals of his time who possessed a general philosophical education. These intellectuals relied upon knowledge from anthologies and, at least in the handbooks, sometimes also familiarized themselves with original sections of philosophical works. Valentinus knows the passage from Plato's letter *Ep.* 2.312E and interprets it in the style of Middle Platonic exegesis;[15] this means that he at least takes up contemporary reports *about* Plato. Whether he, as

---

11. "In Search of Valentinus," *The Rediscovery of Gnosticism* I, ed. B. Layton (Leiden, 1980), 75–102; cf. 112f.; 115f. Also cf. H. Bloom, "Lying against Time: Gnosis, Poetry, Criticism," *The Rediscovery of Gnosticism,* 1:58, 65f. (in regard to the dependence on *Timaeos*); 57ff.; 60ff. (in regard to Valentinus's poetic ability); J. Dillon, "The Descent of the Soul in Middle Platonic and Gnostic Theory," *The Rediscovery of Gnosticism,* 1:357ff., particularly 363f.; important is H. J. Krämer, *Der Ursprung der Geistmetaphysik* (Amsterdam, 1967), 223ff.; 229f.; 238–64; particularly 248; 251 (Pythagorean-Platonic influences); H. Langerbeck, *Aufsätze zur Gnosis,* 65f.; further 67–73; 80f.; 51f. Against Langerbeck's interpretation of the Valentinian doctrine of nature in terms of philosophical categories see, however, E. H. Pagels, "The Valentinian Claim to Esoteric Exegesis of Romans as Basis for Anthropological Theory," *VC* 26 (1972): 241–58, esp. 256. See further H. Leisegang, *Die Gnosis,* 294, in regard to Platonic-Pythagorean number speculations in the teaching about aeons; and K. Koschorke, *Hippolyt's Ketzerbekämpfung,* 14ff. In regard to Stoic motifs cf., e.g., E. Norden, *Kunstprosa,* 546, or F. Sagnard, *Clément,* 215 (App. B). On the parallel between the 30 pairs of Valentinian aeons and the 30 gods paired with each other in Hesiod's *Theogony,* cf. already Epiphanius, *Pan. Haer.* 31.2f.

12. Tertullian, *Carn.* 20; *Praescr.* 30 ("Platonicae sectator"); 7.7; 6; similarly, Hippolytus, *Ref.* 6.37 and 6.29f. Tertullian, *De Anima* 23.3–6: Plato's *Phaidon* and *Timaeos* have become the "grocery store" especially for Valentinians and their doctrine of the soul ("condimentarium").

13. In comparison to Valentinus, see *Timaeos* 41A–C; 42DE; cf. G. C. Stead, "In Search of Valentinus," 81.

14. Cf. similarly, G. C. Stead, ibid., 84, 98, 96.

15. Hippolytus, *Ref.* 6.37.5; on this H. J. Krämer, *Der Ursprung,* 251.

Philo and Plotinus, read the original works of Plato cannot be determined on the basis of the extant fragments. Had he enjoyed a rather
intensive philosophical schooling as Justin had? Was he only a superficial Platonist, as most of the intellectuals of the second century were
Platonists in some respect?[16] The alternative must remain open.

Valentinus's students Ptolemy and Heracleon became known in the
second century as leaders of the Italian branch of the Valentinian
school.[17] Therefore, we probably find them in Rome, at least for a substantial period of time, since their teacher was influential there for more
than a decade. Both men founded their own schools.[18]

Ptolemy's letter to Flora has been (a) linguistically researched especially by E. Norden,[19] who came to the exuberant conclusion: "This
letter is masterful in its development of ideas which are saturated
with Platonic writings as well as in its style"; literarily and stylistically
"plainly exemplary." A beautiful and clearly rhythmic prose is revealed.
The structure seduces one with its clarity.[20] (b) To this is added pedagogical sensitivity. Flora does not yet belong to the circle of gnostic
initiates. Therefore, Ptolemy does not overwhelm her with gnostic doctrine and its special terminology (e.g., the Valentinian *terminus technicus*
ψυχικός appears nowhere). Rather, a first exoteric introduction is cautiously given, which has been aptly tailored (4.4ff.) to Flora's personal
problem (questions of divorce; cf. on this chap. 23, above). Ptolemy
takes up the terminology of the established church[21] in order to encircle
his teaching with the aura of innocence. At the end he entices his reader
to let herself eventually be introduced more closely into the esoteric
gnostic teaching. Tertullian (*Adv. Val.* 1) saw clearly the pedagogical
method of the Valentinians: Even to their disciples they entrusted their

---

16. Cf. J. Whittaker's discussion with G. C. Stead, in G. C. Stead, "In Search of
Valentinus," 96. What was said about the Platonic elements also holds true for the Stoic
notion of an all-permeating spirit and cosmic bond that Valentinus expresses in his hymn
preserved in Hippolytus, *Ref.* 6.37.7. This notion does not have to be directly derived
from Stoic sources. It was widely known. A close parallel wording can be found in the
Corpus Hermeticum (3.2), for example.

17. Hippolytus, *Ref.* 6.35.

18. Cf., e.g., Irenaeus, 1.12; Hipp., 6.38; Photius, *Ep.* 134 (οἱ παῖδες Ἡρακλέωνος).

19. *Kunstprosa*, 920–22; 547, n. 2. One can agree with Norden's observations, except
that Ptolemy in 4.13 and 5.7 altered the Old Testament quotations (Isa 29:13; Lev 20:9)
in order to correct them stylistically: Ptolemy quotes both Old Testament passages from
Matt 15. Furthermore, Norden's *clausula heroica* of 6.6 (ἔδειξε Παῦλος) is text-critically
too poorly attested: see G. Quispel, *Ptolémée*, 99.

20. 3.8 = propositio; 4.1–6.6 = Part 1; 7 = Part 2. These parts are then finely subdivided.

21. E.g., 7.9: ἀξιουμένη τῆς ἀποστολικῆς παραδόσεως. 5.1ff. appears consciously to
take up Justin's categories (cf. *Dial.* 44). Further cf. 5.8ff. with, e.g., Tertullian, *Adv. Iud.*
3–5; Clement, *Ec. Proph.* 14.1; or 5.13 with Hermas, *Sim.* 5.1.4; Clement, *Strom.* 6.102;
Origen, *In Levit. hom.* 10; as well as 5.15 with 1 Cor 5:7. See also the many quotations
of Jesus' words.

doctrine only after when they had totally won them over. "They have a method which does not lack skill; they convince before they teach."[22] (c) Like his teacher, Valentinus, Ptolemy takes up the Platonic εἰκών category (7.7). In 3.2 (πατέρα κτλ.) he echoes the passage *Timaeos* 28E, which was widely circulated in the second century. He takes up Stoic vocabulary in 5.3 (the dialogue serves εἴς τε ἀπαγόρευσιν [or ἀναίρεσιν] τῶν ἀφεκτέων καὶ εἰς πρόσταξιν τῶν ποιητέων).[23] The idea in 3.6 that God's providence is knowable is originally Stoic.[24] As is apparent in this sketchy overview, Ptolemy undoubtedly belongs to the educated circles of the second century.

Heracleon is called by Clement the "most regarded of the Valentinian school (δοκιμώτατος τῆς Οὐαλεντίνου σχολῆς).[25] Fragments of his commentary on John are preserved in Origen. (a) H. Langerbeck has carefully examined the language of his fragments in Origen's commentary and concluded (*Aufsätze,* 171f.), as did Norden in regard to Valentinus and Ptolemy, that the parts incontestably originating not from Origen but from Heracleon are "without exception rhythmic." (b) Origen, who often cites his exegetical opponent venomously, still acknowledges in one place[26] that Heracleon's argument is "fairly powerful" (ἁδρός — ἁδρότερον): ἁδρός, as a concept from rhetoric, means high eloquence, the grand genre that passionately sweeps one along.[27] (c) Like his teacher, Heracleon is influenced by the Platonic φύσις concept;[28] he also knows the Platonic concept of will, which excludes θέλειν τὰ κακά.[29]

The findings about these three Valentinian teachers converge. The three belonged to the educated circles of the second century, even if finding specific information regarding their early pagan education remains

---

22. That the Ptolemean-Valentinian school had something like a "psychology" also becomes clear in the metaphysical speculations concerning the Aeons, *Ennoia* and *Thelema:* for example without Thelema (will), Ennoia (the thought) is powerless (Irenaeus, 1.12.1). Irenaeus (2.15.3; 2.13.10) shows that here and there metaphysics is a projection of psychology. The entities of the pleroma, as archetypes, are reflected in the "hominum affectiones et motiones mentis et generationes intentionum."

23. Cf., e.g, *Stobaei Eclogae* 2.96.10 (ed. Wachsmuth); further Clement, *Strom.* 3.84.1 as well as the reminiscence of Stoic natural ethics in Irenaeus, 4.15.1; 4.16.4. On this see G. Quispel, *Ptolémée,* 91f.

24. Then also, e.g., Apuleius, *De mundo* 24; Minucius Felix, *Oct.* 17.3; cf. Cicero, *De nat. deor.* 2.147.

25. *Strom.* 4.71. Student of Valentinus: Origen, *Joh. Comm.* 2.14.

26. *Joh. Comm.* 6.39 — on the sandals in John 1:27.

27. Quintilian, 12.10.58–63.

28. Cf. H. Langerbeck, *Aufsätze,* 64, 71–75; cf. also E. Mühlenberg, "Erlösungen," 171, 177.

29. Cf. Heracleon in Origen, *John. Comm.* XX 23, 24, 28. Cf. H. Langerbeck, *Aufsätze,* 67ff., 80f., on the Platonic background of these Heracleon texts; cf. especially Plato, *Theaetet.* 176E.

impossible (higher education with one or more philosophers? or with a rhetorician? or both?).

The result of our exploration does not exclude the possibility that the Valentinian followers of these teachers could have been half-educated or even uneducated. In Gaul, Irenaeus knows that the Valentinians find their following in the "crowd" of "simpliciores" and "rudes."[30] How valid is this for Rome? The Roman Valentinian Florinus (see below) with his writings from Rome captivated the πολλοί among the orthodox Christians in Gaul:[31] In the capital city itself he hardly did otherwise. Thus, the generalization that Valentinianism was a Gnosticism mainly of "educated" circles (e.g., Harnack, *Lehrbuch*, 1:252f.) is not valid. It is valid for the "inventors" of this Gnosticism, for the outstanding teachers whose crowd of followers was nevertheless not uniformly "intellectual" but rather stratified.

Members of "Socially Privileged Classes"?

At the Via Latina a marble inscription was found. Its fragments are preserved in the Capitoline Museum.

)τρα δ'ἐμοὶ παστῶν δᾳδουχοῦσιν συν(

)απίνας πεινοῦσιν ἐν ἡμετέρο(

)γοῦντες γενέτην καὶ υἱέα δοξάζον(

)γῆς ἔνθα μόνης καὶ ἀληθείης ῥύ(.[32]

I will try to fill in the blanks and to translate the text:

---

30. In the *multitudo* of the *simpliciores,* and in the great number of the *communes ecclesiastici:* see Irenaeus, 3.15.2; cf. also 1 *praef.* They seduce "many": 1.8.1. Tertullian, *Scorp.* 1; *Resurr.* 2: *multi rudes, simplices plures.* Further comparable references in K. Koschorke, *Die Polemik,* 223, n. 8, 230. H. Langerbeck, *Aufsätze,* 176, characterizes the disciples of Ptolemy, against whom Irenaeus battles, as second-class intellects who enjoy "mythological abracadabra."

31. Irenaeus, *Fragm. syr.* 28 (Harvey, 2:457).

32. Cf. L. Moretti, "Iscrizioni greche inedite di Roma," *Bullettino comunale* 75 (1953–55) 83–86; M. Raoss, "Iscrizione cristiana-greca di Roma anteriore al terzo secolo?" *Aevum* 37 (1963): 11–30; A. Coppo, "Contributo all'interpretazione di un'epigrafe greca cristiana dei Musei Capitolini," *RivArCr* 46 (1970): 97–138; M. Guarducci, "Valentiniani a Roma," *Mitt. d. Dt. Archäol. Inst. Röm. Abt.* 80 (1973): 169–89; Guarducci, "Ancora sui Valentiniani a Roma," ibid., 81 (1974): 341–43; Guarducci, "Iscrizione cristiana del II secolo nei Musei Capitolini," *Bullettino comunale* 79 (1963–64): 117–34. P. Lampe, "An Early Christian Inscription in the Musei Capitolini," *Studia Theologica* 49 (1995): 79–92. Manlio Simonetti (orally) was the first to suspect a Valentinian origin of the inscription, followed by M. Guarducci.

Co(brothers [συνάδελφοι]) of the bridal chambers, celebrate with torches the (ba)ths (λουτρά) for me;[33]

They hunger for (ban)quets (εἰλαπίνας) in ou(r rooms [ἡμετέροισι δόμοισι]),[34]
(La)uding the Father,[35] and praisin(g [δοξάζοντες]) the Son;
Oh, may there be flow(ing [ῥύσις εἴη]) of the only (sp)ring (πηγῆς)[36] and of the truth in that very place (or: then).

The length of the reconstructions of the text at the left and right margins fits well. I have even cross-checked them by means of a computer-assisted photo montage, using letters from within the inscription itself to fill in the blanks.[37]

The reconstructions fit well also metrically. The four epigraphic lines represent hexameters:

λουτρὰ δ'ἐ|μοὶ πασ|τῶν δα|δουχοῦ|σιν συνά|δελφοι
εἰλαπίν|ας πει|νοῦσιν ἐν|ἡμετέ|ροισι δό|μοισι
ὑμνοῦν|τες γενέ|την καὶ|υἱέα|δοξά|ζοντες
πηγῆς|ἔνθα μό|νης καὶ ἀλ|ηθεί|ης ῥύσις|εἴη.[38]

Paleographically, the inscription most likely dates to the second century, during the time of the Antonines, as M. Guarducci has shown by

33. With an accusative, δᾳδουχέω ("to carry a torch, to illuminate") means "to celebrate" (e.g., "to celebrate mysteries," Them. *Or.* 5.71a). Instead of συνάδελφοι an analogous term could be read, too, e.g., σύντεκνοι, "co-children," "foster siblings" (*Corpus fabularum Aesopicarum*, ed. A. Hausrath and H. Hunger, 147.2.9; Ancient Greek Inscriptions in the British Museum 1010). Metrically, this reading would create a spondaic hexameter.

34. This is the epic meaning of δόμος; cf., e.g., H. G. Liddell and R. Scott, *A Greek-English Lexicon*, 9th ed. (Oxford, 1982), s.v. The meter requires a plural form. Another possibility would be: "in our dining rooms" (ἡμετέροις ἀναγαίοις), cf. Mark 14:15. ἡμετέροισι δόμοισι, however, fits better in its length, having one less letter.

35. Possible parallel terms to δοξάζοντες are ὑμνοῦντες, αἰνοῦντες, or σεμνοῦντες.

36. Other possibilities would be: "of the only light" (αὐγῆς), or even the Valentinian technical term σιγῆς ("of the only silence"). L. Moretti (*Iscrizioni*, 83) proposed στοργῆς. But (a) if we filled in four missing letters at the beginning of the line, this line would be too long, starting farther to the left than the previous lines. (b) Moretti's translation of υἱέα δοξάζοντες στοργῆς as "compiacendosi col figlio per l'amore" is hardly convincing. (c) "Spring" better matches the metaphor of "flowing." Moretti (83) also pondered μονῆς ("abiding") instead of μόνης. But how does line 4 make sense this way? By translating μονῆς...ῥῦ[σίς μοι] (sic) as "è per me la difesa della tranquillità," Moretti only provokes questions. If there is the possibility of another, smoother reading, we definitely should choose it! ἔνθα denotes either place or time (Liddell and Scott, s.v.).

37. Photos, however, cannot help to decide about the reading of individual letters, as C. Scholten assumes ("Gibt es Quellen zur Sozialgeschichte der Valentinianer Roms?" *ZNW* 79 [1988]: 244–61, esp. 246 and 249, n. 21). For the deficiencies of this method, see, e.g., E. Meyer, *Einführung in die lateinische Epigraphik* (Darmstadt, 1983), 103.

38. For καί as short sound, cf., e.g., Homer *Il.* 5.300. Guarducci (1973), 170, following Coppo, completes with ῥύσις ἐστίν at the end. ἐστίν, however, would make line 4 too long in comparison with the other lines.

comparing several hundred texts.[39] If the inscription is Christian, it represents one of the earliest epigraphic Christian documents. A detailed discussion of the epigraph, therefore, is justified.

C. Scholten has questioned the Valentinian interpretation proposed by M. Simonetti, M. Guarducci, and me (notes 32 and 37). Scholten denies a Christian (M. Raoss) or religious reading. Instead, the epigraph is supposed to represent a pagan wedding inscription, as one learns from scattered hints in his article (pp. 253, 250, 247). Scholten does not inform us which secular wedding inscriptions could be seen in parallel to our epigraph. He does not try to show how the praising of father and son (line 3) and the flowing of truth (line 4) could be interpreted in the framework of a secular nuptial inscription. In fact, Scholten does not even make an effort to fill in the missing letters in order to obtain a text that makes sense. His alternative is untenable, as long as he does not take the trouble to spell out a complete reading and translation on his own and to find parallels that could make his version plausible. Any attempt to disprove other readings runs aground as long as no solid alternative is offered.

As Scholten did not do it himself, we must test a pagan secular reading on our own.

a. In the first line one clearly can read "of the bridal chambers" and "they celebrate with torches for me." How do both fit into a sentence that makes sense?

At a pagan wedding the bride's way from her parental house to the groom's house — i.e., to the nuptial chamber — was indeed illuminated with torches at nightfall; torch-bearers led the procession.[40] In Plautus, *Cas.* 1.1.30, this custom is called *lucere novae nuptae facem.* Thus, in a pagan interpretation the "for me" in our inscription would have to be spoken by a bride.[41] At the beginning of the line we would have to read λέκ)τρα,[42] if the line were to make sense: They "carry torches to the beds of the bridal chambers for me." δε in this case would be the enclitic particle -δε, which is added to an accusative in order to denote motion towards something (e.g., Homer, *Od.* 8.292 λέκτρονδε = "to bed").

Very quickly, however, difficulties arise for a pagan reading of this line.

---

39. M. Guarducci, "Valentiniani," 169–70, and "Iscrizione," 127–32. She makes passé older attempts to assign it to the first or second centuries C.E. (L. Moretti, "Iscrizioni," 83) or to the third century. C.E. or later (J. and L. Robert, reviewing Moretti in *REG* 71 [1958]: 359–60; M. Raoss, *Iscrizione* [1963], 30).

40. Cf., e.g., the materials in J. Marquardt, *Das Privatleben der Römer,* I, 2d ed. (Leipzig, 1886; Darmstadt, 1975), 53–56.

41. Not by the groom, as L. Moretti ("Iscrizioni," 84) assumed. If the groom were referred to in our epigraph, this would be in line 3 in the third person — if at all.

42. Or φίλ)τρα ("love")? Moretti's ("Iscrizioni," 83) reading, στοιβάδ᾽ ἐμοὶ (στοιβάς "bed"), is impossible: Moretti falsely reads an iota, where there clearly was a Γ, T, E, or Σ.

- The plurals of "beds" and "bridal chambers" would be awkward, since only one bride ("for me") is guided to her nuptial bed.

- Wedding songs used to be sung by friends and not by the bride herself.[43]

- In pagan nuptial processions young boys carried the torches for the bride,[44] not any "co-(...)." In which way could the torch-bearers be labelled "co-" in relation to the bride in a pagan nuptial setting?

- In a pagan setting, the festive banquet used to take place before the procession with torches, not after, as our epigraphical lines 1 and 2 would suggest.[45]

On the whole, a pagan reading of line 1 does not seem plausible. Our Christian reading "baths" at the beginning of the line, on the other hand, does not create problems. βάπτισμα and λουτρόν are interchangeable in both Valentinian and other Christian texts (cf., e.g., Justin, *Apol.* 1.61.3; Clement of Alexandria, *Exc. ex Theod.* 4.78). According to Justin (*Apol.* 1.65), Christian baptism used to take place *before* the congregation celebrated the eucharist, which matches the sequence of baptisms (line 1) and "banquets" (line 2) in our inscription.

After a Christian provenance of line 1 has been conceded, the question of the particularly Valentinian character has to be raised. With παστοί ("bridal chambers"), a Valentinian keynote is hit. Not only is the nuptial theme a predominant subject in Valentinianism, the Valentinian motif of the "bridal chamber" stands for the eschatological union of the pneumatics (the "images") with their angels in the *pleroma*. In this world this union is anticipated in sacramental rituals.[46]

---

43. Cf., e.g., Catullus, *Carm.* 62; 61.36–40; J. Marquardt, *Das Privatleben*, 54. Already Moretti (84–85) admitted that our poem does not match well with Greco-Roman wedding customs.

44. "Tollite, o pueri, faces": Catullus, *Carm.* 61.114. See the materials in J. Marquardt, *Das Privatleben*, 55–56.

45. See, e.g., Catullus, *Carm.* 62.3 and J. Marquardt, *Das Privatleben*, 52–53. The next meal for the guests was not served before the next day at the after-celebration called *repotia* (cf. J. Marquardt, *Das Privatleben*, 57). But line 2 cannot refer to the *repotia*, since both lines 1 and 3 focus on the wedding day itself (procession, wedding songs). The texts quoted by Moretti ("Iscrizoni," 85), which talk about a dinner given by the groom (Cicero, *Ad Quint.* fr. 2.3.7; Juvenal, 6.202), were put in the right light by Marquardt (*Das Privatleben*, 53, n. 1). According to the usual custom, first the banquet in the bride's paternal house took place and afterwards the bride's procession from there to the groom's house.

46. E.g., Irenaeus, 1.21.3–4; 1.13.3, 6; 1.7.1, 5; Clement, *Exc. ex Theod.* 63.2; 64; 65.1; 36.2; Heracleon in Origen, *Joh. Comm.* 13.11; 10.19; *Phil. Evg.* from Nag Hammadi (NHC 2:3) logia 68; 76; 87; 102; 122; 124; 126–27; 60–61; 66–67; 73; 79; 80; 82; 95; cf. also *Trac. Trip.*, NHC 1:5 (122, 12ff.); Clement, *Strom.* 3.1.1; Tertullian, *Adv. Val.* 30–32. J.-M. Sevrin ("Les Noces Spirituelles Dans L'Evangile Selon Philippe," *Le Muséon* 87 [1974]: 143–93) correctly observed that the sacramental anticipation of the

The expression "co-brothers/co-children of the bridal chambers" (see note 33) corresponds well to the Valentinian self-description as "children of the bridal chamber" in *Phil. Evg.* logia 87; 102; 127.

If probability points in the Christian-Valentinian direction, we have to cross-check whether the rest of the line can be understood in a Valentinian light. δαδουχῶ ("to illuminate with torches," "to celebrate with torches") denotes the celebration of the Eleusinian mysteries in Clement Alex., *Protrep.* 2.12; Themistius, *Or.* 5.71a, and other texts. And Tertullian, indeed, reproaches the Valentinians for Eleusinian influence (*Adv. Val.* 1).

Baptisms (λουτρά, "baths") are celebrated by the Valentinians[47] as one form of anticipation of the eschatological "bridal chamber."[48] The torches fit this well. They are not only a traditional Roman nuptial symbol; for the Valentinians the "bridal chamber" is also particularly characterized by light and the receiving of light,[49] so that the torches could have a double symbolic value.

The plural in "bridal chambers" is a problem for *any* reading of the inscription, but in the Valentinian frame of reference it seems to create the smallest problem. In the *pleroma* the pneumatics unite themselves with their angels (plurals), which might have inspired the unprecedented plural in our epigraph.

b. Line 2 by itself is neutral when it comes to deciding between a Christian and pagan reading. Festive dinners were of course celebrated both in pagan and Christian contexts. In a Christian framework εἰλαπίνη might allude to the eucharistic meal, as it parallels λουτρόν/ baptism in line 1. Christian εἰλαπίναι are mentioned in Justin, *Dial.* 10.1: Justin quotes the pagan defamation that "after the banquet" (μετὰ τὴν εἰλαπίνην) the Christians extinguish the lights and practice improper sex. True, the epic-poetic εἰλαπίνη would be only a periphrastic term for the eucharist; there is no certain evidence for a technical eucharistic usage of εἰλαπίνη before the seventh century (see Raoss [1963], 28, note 53). But this does not rule out a possible eucharistic reading of our line. In a poetic text like ours, nobody with some sense for the genre would require a technical term for the eucharist.

---

eschatological "bridal chamber" probably did not take place in a separate "bridal chamber" sacrament, as many scholars have thought (this possibility, however, is not totally ruled out by Sevrin, 192), but rather in the rituals of anointing, baptizing, eucharist, and liturgical kiss.

47. Cf., e.g., *Phil. Evg.* logia 68; 76; Irenaeus, 1.21.3; Clement Alex., *Exc. ex Theod.* 78.2.

48. See Sevrin in note 46.

49. *Phil. Evg.* Logia 127; 122; for further references see J.-M. Sevrin, "Les Noces Spirituelles," 169–71. For the torch as Roman nuptial symbol, see J. Marquardt, *Das Privatleben,* 55. For those who want to maintain the hypothesis of a separate Valentinian "bridal chamber" sacrament, it also would be possible to read λέκτρα ("couches," "bridal beds") in line 1 as a direct reference to this sacrament.

In itself line 2 is open to both pagan and Christian interpretations. Because of line 1, however, we have to cross-check whether line 2 can be understood in a Valentinian light. This creates no problem. Eucharistic celebrations by the Valentinians are evidenced in, e.g., Irenaeus, 1.13.2; *Phil. Evg.* logion 68; Clement Alex., *Exc. ex Theod.* 82.1. Like the baptism, the eucharist anticipates the eschatological "bridal chamber" for the Valentinians (see note 46).

c. The praising of Father and Son in line 3 is easily understood in a Christian frame of reference. C. Scholten ("Quellen," 246–47) claims that γενέτης does not denote God in Christian texts before Gregory of Nazianzus. This is not true. Jews in Egypt and Christians sang of God as γενέτης much earlier. In Egypt in the second century C.E.,[50] the Jewish Sibyl (3.604; cf. also 3.550) called God the γενέτης of all human beings. Between 80 and 130 C.E. in Egypt,[51] the Jewish Sibyl prayed to God as "begetter of all" (παγγενέτωρ; 5.328). The hymn to Christ in Sibyll. 6 starts out: "I speak from my heart of the great famous son (υἱόν) of the Immortal, to whom the Most High, his begetter (γενέτης), gave a throne to possess":

> Ἀθανάτου μέγαν υἱὸν ἀοίδιμον ἐκ φρενὸς αὐδῶ,
> ᾧ θρόνον ὕψιστος γενέτης παρέδωκε λαβέσθαι.

These are hexameters, as in our inscription. The hymn sings about Christ's life, his baptism in the Jordan River, and his cross. Lactantius (*Div. Inst.* 4.15.3, 25; 4.13.21; 4.18.20) quotes this song; it therefore was composed some time *before* ca. 300 C.E. As the metric quality is better than in most texts of the third century, we might want to date it to the second century C.E. — without certainty, however. The geographical provenance is unknown.

As Scholten did not even try to spell out a pagan reading of line 3, we have to test this alternative on our own. Anyone would have a hard time finding pagan nuptial inscriptions in which the bride's father-in-law was praised[52] or in which the groom was revered as "son." I see, however, the possibility of interpreting "son" as Hymen(aeus), the god of marriage, who could be sung of at weddings (e.g., Catull., *Carm.* 61–62) and who was called son of the Muses (Schol. Pindar, *Pythia* 4.313) or "Urania's offspring" ("Uraniae genus," Catull., *Carm.*, 61.2). The γενέτης would be Hymen's father (Apollo or Dionysus). However, even this reading has serious problems. Why is there only mention of

---

50. For place and date, see J. J. Collins, "Sibylline Oracles," in J. H. Charlesworth, ed., *The Old Testament Pseudepigrapha* I (New York, 1983), 354–55.

51. For place and date, see Collins (1983), 390–91.

52. If at all, the bride's father could be honored (Claudianus, *Fescennina* 13). The bride's father, however, is not mentioned by our inscription. Line 3 talks about a son and not about a daughter.

the father and not of the mother? It would also be strange for Hymen to be referred to only by his sonship, and not by his name or any other title. Metrically it would have been possible to say Ὑμένα (accusative of Ὑμήν) instead of υἱέα. As Hymen's name was a frequent refrain in wedding songs (e.g., Catull., *Carm.* 61–62), it would have been unusual to paraphrase this god's identity without mention of his name. Not even the father's name is given. The absolute "Father" and "Son" are much more easily understood in a Christian reading of line 3 than in a pagan one.

The last step will be again to cross-check whether the line remains plausible in a Valentinian framework. The combination Father — Son — Bridal Chamber, indeed, occurs again in, e.g., *Phil. Evg.*, logion 82. And in Clement's *Excerpta ex Theodoto* (1.6–7) the Valentinians refer to the son (υἱός) as Μονογενής of the father (πατήρ), which at least comes close to the terminology of our epigraphical line. "Father," "Son," and "Monogenes" are also dealt with in the *Valentinian Exposition*, Nag Hamm. 11.2.22–25, 28, 36–37. Moreover, in the liturgical fragments of a Valentinian celebration of baptism and the eucharist (Nag Hamm. 11.2.40, 43) glory is sung "to thee, the Father in the Son." "Jesus Christ" is referred to as "the Monogenes," and the Valentinian celebrants of the eucharist sing "O Father ... [Glory] be to thee through thy Son [and] thy offspring (ⲘⲓⲤⲉ, γεννητός) Jesus Christ." It is true, the specific term γενέτης itself does not occur in the few *Greek* Valentinian texts that we have. In Valentinus's Egyptian homeland, however, the Jews had been calling God γενέτης for a long time, and Christian hymnic hexameters picked up this term, as we saw above.

d. In line 4 the pendulum swings again into the Christian direction. So far we have no single pagan wedding text in which the "flowing of truth" plays a role. A Christian reading of line 4, on the other hand, runs smoothly. The "flowing of the only spring" is a common Christian motif derived from Judaism. The Septuagint calls God πηγὴν ὕδατος ζωῆς (Jer 2:13; cf. also, e.g., Barn 11:2; Ezek 47; Isa 55:1). Justin quotes Jer 2:13 and interprets Christ as πηγὴν ζῶσαν (*Dial.* 19.2).[53] According to 1 Cor 10:4, Israel "drank from" Christ. But we do not even have to interpret the spring narrowly as Christ. John 4:14 leaves the identity of "spring" and Christ unsettled. According to Rev 21:6 (cf. 7:17), "he who sat upon the throne ... will give from the fountain (πηγή) of the water of life." This spring is the site of abundance from which the life

---

53. In Justin's version of the OT text God talks about the "living spring" in the third person; αὐτόν, therefore, only can denote Christ. In the previous sentence Justin talks about τὸ βάπτισμα τὸ τῆς ζωῆς (19.2), which is also called λουτρόν in 13.1; 14.1. Justin's combination of βάπτισμα / λουτρόν and Christ-πηγή parallels our inscription.

prepared by Christ flows. μόνης is easily understood in this light. And μόνη πηγή is paralleled by several Christian and Jewish texts, even in connection with ἀλήθεια (truth), as in our epigraphical line.[54]

We have to use our Valentinian cross-check question again. Like line 3, line 4 represents common Christian motifs and therefore is possible also as a Valentinian verse if line 1 suggests a Valentinian reading of the whole poem. It was characteristic of the Valentinians to use common Christian language ("similia enim loquentes fidelibus," Irenaeus, 3.17.4; "communem fidem adfirmant" Tertullian, *Adv. Val.* 1).

Again, the poetic metric form fits well with Valentinus's style. Even Ionic dialect (ἀληθείη) is echoed,[55] just as in Valentinus's only pre-served poetic fragment (Hippolytus, *Ref.* 6.37. 6–8), where an Ionic form (αἴθρης) can be found.

For the Valentinians, ἀλήθεια "existed since the beginning" (*Phil. Evg.* logion 16). It is nutrition for eternal life given by Jesus (93). It can be interpreted christologically (47), and the "bridal chamber" is for those who have the ἀλήθεια (110; 73; 127; 123–25). More than six motifs of our poem, ἀλήθεια, "co(children) of the bridal chambers," water ("baths," "spring," "flowing"), fire and light ("to illuminate with torches"), "Father," and "Son," reoccur in logia 66–67 ("It is from water and fire and light that the child of the bridal chamber [came into being].... Truth did not come into the world naked.... The bridal cham-ber and the image must enter through the image into the truth: this is the restoration. Not only must those who produce the name of the Father and the Son and the Holy Spirit do so...").

To sum up the Christian reading of the marble epigraph: In the first person a host (line 1), opening his or her rooms (line 2) for Christian rituals, speaks.[56] At the host's residence, the congregation regularly cel-ebrates baptisms (line 1) and looks forward to the eucharistic meals afterwards (line 2), singing praise to the Father and the Son (line 3). When and where the rituals are celebrated, there is "flowing of the only

---

54. Epiphanius, *Haer.* GCS 25, p. 157, 22–23: ἥτις μόνη ἐστὶ πηγὴ σωτηρίας καὶ πίστις ἀληθείας. Athanasius, *Epistula ad Afros episcopos* MPG 26: 1033.12–13: καταλείψαντες τὴν μόνην πηγὴν τοῦ ζῶντος ὕδατος. Cf. also Philo, *Vit.Mos.* 1.48.8 (ed. Cohn): λόγον, ὃς μόνος ἐστὶν ἀρετῶν ἀρχή τε καὶ πηγή; Athanasius, *Contra Sabellianos* MPG 28.97.30ff.; Ps.-Origen, *Fragmenta in Psalmos* 58. 17, 18 (ed. Pitra).
55. Cf. M. Guarducci, "Valentiniani," 181; ἀληθείη as in Homer.
56. The dative ἐμοί in line 1 can be interpreted as "for me," "in my interest," "to my delight" (*dativus commodi*) or as *dativus ethicus*. The latter denotes that a speaker is men-tally and emotionally involved in the action, i.e., the baptisms that he or she talks about. (Cf., e.g., R. Kühner and B. Gerth, *Ausführliche Grammatik der griechischen Sprache: Satzlehre*, I, 4th ed. (Hannover, 1955), 423, with numerous examples where μοι is used in this way). ἐμοί hardly indicates that the speaker talks about his or her own baptism. The end of line 2 strongly advocates that a host is speaking. ἡμέτερος can stand for ἐμός from Homer's time to the third cent. C.E. (Liddell and Scott, s.v.).

spring and of the truth" (line 4), the speaker hopes. The image of flowing at the end fits well with the baptismal baths at the beginning of
the poem.

The most logical conclusion is that the epigraph was displayed in the
room where the baptisms took place. The eucharists were celebrated in
this room and/or in adjacent accommodations of the same house, with
line 2b using the plural. The inscription fits Justin's description (*Apol.*
1.61; 65), according to which Christian eucharists were celebrated *after*
the baptismal rituals and often in *different* accommodations, since the
baptisms required a locality with a water supply.

The Valentinian character is suggested by verse 1, and the following
lines can be easily understood in a Valentinian frame of reference. Valentinians celebrated the sacraments as anticipations of the eschatological
unions ("bridal chamber") of the pneumatics with their angels.

The δέ in line 1 does not suggest that the four verses once were part of
a larger poem. The *delta* was inserted for poetic reasons to avoid hiatus
between the two vowels *alpha* and *epsilon*. Also epigrams by Pittacus
and Timon, e.g., start out with an unexpected δέ without reference to a
previous context (Μεγαρεῖς δὲ φεῦγε πάντας· εἰσὶ γὰρ πικροί: *Anthologia
Graeca*, ed. H. Beckby, 11:440; 11:296). Likewise in Homer, *Od.* 4.400,
a story is begun with δέ.

On our marble slab clearly neither a previous nor a subsequent text
was inscribed. Except for occasional abrasions, the slab's upper edge
runs parallel to the first row of letters. More importantly, the free space
between the upper edge and this first row equals the height of two epigraphical lines, i.e., the height of two rows of letters plus the free space
between these two rows. We thus observe the result of a stone-mason's
calculations, and the preserved upper edge of the slab is more or less
identical with the upper edge that the stone-mason had in his hands. No
previous text has broken off.

The same is true about the end of the epigraph. The margin below
the last row of letters is more than 25 percent higher than the said
upper margin. This layout makes it highly improbable that our four
verses were followed by more text. Taking the extant epigraphical evidence into account, usually big spaces were not left between paragraphs.
Space was expensive, especially on marble slabs that had to be imported
to Rome. In Rome, therefore, marble was used much less often for
inscriptions than at other places, such as Greece.[57]

Scholten's speculations, after all, are unfounded. He objected (*Quellen*, 253, n. 43) that our epigraph could be "the rest of a bigger
inscription" and that this larger text could have been not only a pagan

---

57. Cf., e.g., E. Meyer, *Einführung*, 17, 84. Already L. Moretti, "Iscrizioni," 83,
observed correctly that parts of the slab's original *lower* edge are also preserved.

nuptial but alternatively also a funereal epigraph (without specify-
ing the details of this other reading). No, our inscription represents
a rounded-off unit, without conventional grave inscription formulas,
without names, without dates.

In spite of the handicap that no internal clue hints at a funereal
interpretation, let us hypothesize for a moment that external evidence
pointed to this direction, i.e., that the epigraph was attached to a mausoleum and not to a suburban house at the Via Latina, as we concluded
above. How could the epigraph be understood on the basis of this assumption? The implied author of the inscription would be a deceased
person speaking about his or her own funeral: "Co(brothers) carry
torches to beds of bridal chambers for me." True, torches are not only
a symbol of the wedding, but of the funeral as well.[58] But an explicit
nuptial motif (here παστῶν) usually is absent in burial contexts. Only
in one text (Herodas, 4.56) is there *question* whether or not the term
παστός could mean "shrine." In which second-century frame of reference would it be possible to state that death gave access to "beds
of bridal chambers?" On the basis of a funereal hypothesis, again the
Valentinian perspective would give possible meaning to this line — if
at all.

What would ἔνθα mean in line 4? Where and when is there "flowing
of the only spring and of the truth" in a funereal context? ἔνθα could
refer back to the "beds of bridal chambers" in line 1, and then again
only a Valentinian reading of verse 4 would be plausible to some extent,
with a specific funereal aspect, however, missing in this line.

The "banquets" in line 2 could be interpreted as the funeral repast
and the annual meals at the grave. The tomb would be referred to as
"our rooms."[59] But why would anybody "*hunger*" for these repasts, as
line 2 states? A hunger for nonfunereal, eucharistic meals in a suburban
house ("in our rooms") makes much more sense.

At the pagan funeral the *deceased* was praised,[60] not the "Father"
and the "Son." Whoever wants to maintain a funereal hypothesis probably has to admit that a Christian reading of line 3 remains the most
probable one, and that a specific funereal aspect is absent in this verse.

In conclusion, the epigraph was a Valentinian inscription at the Via
Latina. Rather than at a burial site, it was displayed in a suburban house
where Valentinians celebrated sacramental rituals. Only this latter interpretation allows a coherent understanding of all lines, running into the
least number of difficulties compared to the other alternatives.

---

58. Cf., e.g., J. Marquardt, *Das Privatlaeben*, 55, 343–45.
59. Cf., e.g., J. Marquardt, *Das Privatleben*, 378–85, 369. For the tomb as "domus"
cf., e.g., CIL 3:2165; 3171; 5:2255; 8:7541; 8751; 9949.
60. Cf., e.g., J. Marquardt, *Das Privatleben*, 352, 357–60.

What the inscription reveals from the point of view of social history will occupy our attention. First, however, we should glance at another find. In the nineteenth century, L. Fortunati[61] discovered the marble gravestone of Flavia Sophe[62] during the excavation at the third mile marker on the Via Latina. It contains two epigraphs in hexameter that date from the end of the second or the first half of the third century.[63]

I

φῶς πατρικὸν ποθέουσα / σύναιμε σύνευνε Σόφι μου /
λουτροῖς χρεισαμένι Χ(ριστο)ῦ / μύρον ἄφθιτον ἁγνόν /
Αἰώνων ἔσπευσας ἀθρῖ / σαι θεῖα πρόσωπα /
βουλῆς τῆς μεγάλης μέγαν / Ἄγγελον, Υἱὸν ἀληθῆ /
( )ς νυμφῶνα μολοῦσα καὶ εἰς / (-)ους ἀνοροῦσα /
(-)πατρικοὺς κα(- -

II

οὐκ ἔσχεν κοινὸν βιότου τέ / λος ἥδε θανοῦσα· /
κάτθανε καὶ ζώει καὶ ὁρᾷ / φάος ἄφθιτον ὄντως. /
ζώει μὲν ζωοῖσι, θάνεν δὲ / θανοῦσιν ἀληθῶς. /
γαῖα, τί θαυμάζεις νέκυος / γένος; ἦ πεφόβησαι;

I

Longing for the fatherly light, O sister bride, my Sophe,
In the ablutions of Ch(rist) anointed with imperishable holy
     balsam
You have hastened to gaze upon the divine countenances of the
     Aeons,
upon the great angel of the great counsel, the true Son,
You have gone (to) the bridal chamber and ascended to
     the ... ... fatherly an(d) ...

II

This deceased did not have a usual ending of life:
She died away and lives and sees a truly imperishable light.
She lives to the delight of the living, is really dead to the dead.
O earth, why are you astonished about this type of corpse?
Are you terrified?

Text I of the stele offers the acrostic ΦΛΑΒ, which is to be completed as Φλαβία: "Flavia Sophe" is the name of the deceased. A Valentinian

61. *Relazione generale degli scavi e scoperte fatte lungo la via Latina* (Rome, 1859), 43ff., n. 41.
62. *CIG* 4:9595a. Cf., among others, C. Cecchelli, *Monumenti*, 149–53; M. Guarducci, "Valentiniani," 182ff.
63. M. Guarducci, "Valentiniani," 183; A. Ferrua, "Questioni," 165ff.; here 178–93.

character of the inscription is possible, if not probable: (a) After death, Sophe goes into the "bridal chamber" (νυμφών)[64] in order to look upon the eternal "fatherly light."[65] (b) She sees personified divine "aeons." This motif can hardly be explained without some gnostic background. (c) "Christ," the "true Son," is given the title "Angel of the great counsel," as in *Exc. ex Theodoto.*[66] (d) Line 1.2 alludes to the Valentinian sacraments, one of which was the "anointing."[67] With the words λουτροῖς χρεισαμένι Χ(ριστο)ῦ, the inscription appears to presuppose that the two rituals of "baptism" and "anointing" were drawn together into one single sacramental act. Irenaeus (1.14.3–4) testifies to precisely this practice of Valentinians. And Hippolytus (*Ref.* 6.41.2–42.2) specifies Irenaeus's account in regard to the Roman Marcosian Valentinians who practiced two "baptisms," using the plural in the same way as our inscription. The second one, called "redemption," could be practiced as a death-bed ritual.[68] (e) The final line: The sphere of influence of the demiurge, γαῖα is "terrified" about the successful ascension to the Light. It is true that for some of these individual motifs non-Valentinian parallels can also be found, even for the bridal chamber (Matt 9:15). What makes this epitaph most probably Valentinian is the *combination* of these motifs.

What are the social-historical implications of this investigation? While the inscription of Flavia Sophe is a burial monument, the first inscription comes from a house. The marble slab is 0.375 x 0.6 m. in size and was originally attached to the wall of a dwelling. The precise place of discovery along the Via Latina is no longer known. A notation, preserved with the inscription, states, "probabilmente Tor Fiscale," which refers to the area around a medieval tower. Nevertheless, we do gain valuable information. The place of discovery was an undetermined location along the Via Latina, outside the city, where, in a quiet area, the rows of graves along the arterial road have been here and there broken by a suburban villa. Near the "Tor Fiscale" in the location "Vignacce," there are, as an example, the ruins of a large villa from the Hadrian period.[69]

---

64. Also σύνευνε might allude to this. The alternative is that the stele was erected by her husband, who calls his Sophe σύνευνε = "bed companion."

65. Cf., e.g., *Exc. ex Theod.* 64: εἰς τὸν Νυμφῶνα ἐντὸς τοῦ Ὅρου εἰσίασι, καὶ πρὸς τὴν τοῦ Πατρὸς ὄψιν ἔρχονται: "they go into the bride chamber, which lies within the Horos, and come to see the father...."

66. The Saviour = ὁ τῆς βουλῆς Ἄγγελος, *Exc. ex Theod.* 43.2. Cf., however, also, e.g., Justin, *Dial.* 126.1; *Apol.* 1.6.1f.; LXX Isa 9:5.

67. *Phil. Evg.* log. 68; Irenaeus, 1.14–3; *Exc. ex Theod.* 82.1, and other places.

68. Dunderberg now plausibly argues in favor of a Marcosian-Valentinian provenance of the inscription (SBL paper given in Rome in 2001).

69. In regard to these ruins, cf. M. Guarducci in *Bullettino Comunale di Roma* 79 (1963–64): 133ff., n. 63.

This inscription probably hung in the suburban villa of a wealthy Valentinian man or woman. Its donor chose marble as material and in a cultivated manner commissioned a metrical poetic text to be inscribed in the slab. Then he had it fastened in the house where what was spoken of in the text apparently took place, namely, the sacramental assemblies and rites of the co-consecrated. The "I" (ἐμοί) of the inscription explicitly names these co-brothers. The suburban villa on the Via Latina is open to them ("the co-brothers celebrate for me...")

In the seclusion of the suburban retreat ("silence" is even a technical term in Valentinian theology),[70] poetry allows them to celebrate Ionic dialect, mysticism, and anticipation of the "bride chamber." The atmosphere of such a place can be sensed from Pliny's letters: "Charming suburban retreat, the colonnade, continuously springlike, the shading plane trees..., the bath, pure sunshine streaming inside and out, the dining rooms for great festivities, for intimate social gatherings; the living rooms and bedrooms..." (*Ep.* 1.3). "...I hear nothing and say nothing, which I could later regret...I converse with myself alone and with my books....Oh you sweet idleness" (*Ep.* 1.9). "...I have visited Cornelius Rufus at the time of Domitian, as he reposed in his suburban retreat; the slaves left the room, which he was accustomed to reserve for the visit of particularly trusted friends..." (1.12). "...when the philosophers had been expelled from the city (by Domitian), I visited (the philosopher Artemidor) in his suburban villa..." (3.11). "Your library of fine noble estate from where the reader has a view of the neighboring city..." (Martial, 7.17).[71]

It is not known who the "co-brothers" were who gathered here beyond the city in the suburban villa of the "socially privileged" Valentinian host. The possibility of a socially stratified Valentinian group remains open. That even slaves could find the free time for such a gathering when their master was understanding or like-minded is seen in the example of Epictetus, who as a slave attended the lectures of Musonius Rufus with the permission of his master, Epaphroditos.

The grave stele of Flavia Sophe from the end of the second or the first half of the third century presents itself even a little more poetic in its hexameters: The reader may let the marked poetic forms ring (σύνευνε, μολοῦσα, βίοτος, γαῖα, νέκυς), may note the plural λουτρά (with possibly singular meaning) or εἰς (instead of πρός). These elements testify

---

70. A quality that is reflected at the top of the Pleroma: Irenaeus, 1.1.1, among others. Cf. also the ἀνάπαυσις in Heracleon in Origen, *Joh. Comm.* 1.10.19. *Phil. Evg.* log. 86: "The works of man...are his children, who arose from silence." Irenaeus, 1.2.1: "...the σιγή wished to lead all to reflection and to the desire to find their original father."

71. Cf. the dining rooms (*triclinia*) of the suburban villa in Pliny, *Ep.* 1.3, with the plural in line 2 of the Valentinian inscription: ἐν ἡμετέρο(ισ) ἀναγαίοις,"they hunger for banquets in our rooms."

not to an *exceptional* education: verses in Homeric Greek could often be fabricated at this time. The general level of education, which can be gleaned from the written language, had risen continuously in the second century C.E. Nevertheless, in the context of two other indications, the elements of education indicate a social milieu that is comparable to the Valentinian suburban villa: The stele was likewise created from marble. And the deceased bore a famous *gentilicium,* probably as descendant of a freed person of a Flavian emperor.[72]

Both discoveries refer to the *Via Latina,* while in no other part of Rome up to now have traces of the Valentinians come to light.

This convergence is supported by two further findings. (a) The Greek marble grave inscription of a Christian, Iulia Evaresta,[73] was discovered in the same area as the previous grave stele, at the third milestone of the Via Latina. It is to be dated[74] in the third century and probably was not orthodox but influenced by gnosticism: "flesh (σάρξ) of Iulia Evaresta, most beloved by God, rests here; but the Psyche, renewed through the P(neum)a of Ch(rist) and attired with the body of an angel (ἀγγελεικὸν σῶμα λαβοῦσα), has been taken up into the heavenly kingdom of Ch(rist) together with the saints."

(b) Farther outside Rome along the Via Latina on the right-hand side of the road, at about the fifth milestone from the city itself, there lies the small catacomb of "Cava della Rossa," which contains a pictorial representation[75] of the eucharist[76] from the fourth century. This picture reminds one of the Valentinian form of the eucharist.[77]

Both finds show that still in the third and fourth centuries gnostic Valentinian tradition is alive on the Via Latina, while the rest of Roman archaeology remains silent concerning the Valentinians.

What does this accumulation on the Via Latina mean? Where did Flavia Sophe, Iulia Evaresta as well as the users of the small private catacomb "Cava della Rossa" live? Who usually buried their dead along

---

72. Cf. finally the objects found together with the stele: a sarcophagus fragment and an engraved gold ring with an emerald. Of course, these findings tell us little since it is not certain that the stele was discovered *in situ.*

73. *ICUR* I, p. cxvi.

74. Cf. M. Guarducci, "Valentiniani," 186.

75. G. Wilpert, *Le pitture,* tab. 265–67; R. Kanzler, "Di un nuovo cimitero," 173–86; C. Cecchelli, *Monumenti,* 154–56, tab. 45; M. Guarducci, "Valentiniani," 187f.

76. Noteworthy: Four eucharistic vessels, each with two handles, are displayed symmetrically; a fifth *larger* vessel is separately placed; 12 companions are pictured around the table. In orthodox representations of the eucharistic meal, only seven figures customarily appear (most prominent example in the Capella Greca of the catacomb of Priscilla). In heavenly banquets the number varies, but 12 never appear.

77. Irenaeus, 1.13.2, testifies to vessels in different sizes used during the Valentinian Marcosian eucharist. Also for the Valentinians, not only is the number "four" sacred but also the number "twelve." Cf. Irenaeus, 1.15.1; 1.18.4.

the Via Latina? For the inhabitants of the Caelius hill the next largest main roads leading out of the city were the Via Labicana and the Via Latina. The Caelius hill, which stretches between the two streets, was a quarter where wealthy and well-to-do people lived. It was occupied by the dwellings of honorable families. In the villa of Domitia Lucilla Minor, Marcus Aurelius was born. It is possible that our heretics buried along the Via Latina lived on the Caelius hill and were well-to-do. This would agree with the above results, as would the fact that the users of the "Cava della Rossa" catacomb were able to afford a private burial complex instead of being buried in a communal cemetery.

Let us leave the evidence gleaned from the monuments and turn our attention again to the literature. Here again individual pieces of the puzzle fall together that point in the direction of "socially privileged persons" in Weber's sense:

If the Christian teacher Ptolemaeus in Justin's *Apol.* 2.2 is identical with the Valentinian teacher of the same name (see above, chap. 23), then we meet in the distinguished lady in Justin's *Apol.* 2.2 a person sympathetic to Valentinianism. Also if the identity should not be valid, it remains that the addressee of the Valentinian, Flora, belongs to an educated public (see above, ibid.)

To illustrate: one may read what Irenaeus (1.13.3) writes about the Valentinian Marcus: "He mostly dedicates himself to women and indeed to those who wear fine dresses, are clothed in purple, and are very rich." Marcus allegedly became enormously rich through these woman.[78]

Heracleon (in Origen, *Joh. Comm.* 13.15) describes the Samaritan woman at Jacob's well as a prototype of a pneumatic woman who before her conversion "had neglected everything that was necessary for her life out of ignorance of God and of duties corresponding to God, while otherwise the things in life were always available to her" (. . . καὶ ἄλλως ἀεὶ τῶν ἐν τῷ βίῳ τυγχάνουσαν). Heracleon seems also to include material "things" in this.

Those who are initiated must allegedly bring money with them: "They appear to me not to wish to teach all people publicly but only those who could pay high honoraria for this type of secrets (= the Valentinian doctrine of aeons)" ... "the secrets are entrusted only for substantial payment ... who would not surrender his entire fortune to hear (the Valentinian cosmology)!" (Irenaeus, 1.4.3). Irenaeus pokes fun and shakes his head that one could spend money for this "cabbage and

---

78. The distinctly Marcosian direction of the Valentinian gnosis is attested in Asia Minor and in the Rhone valley, but Hippolytus (*Ref.* 6.41f., see above) and the above-depicted eucharistic scene in the private catacomb Cava della Rossa show Marcosian influence most likely also in Rome.

turnip doctrine" (Irenaeus, 1.11). Of course, φιλαργυρία appears stereo-typically in the polemic against heretics,[79] so that Irenaeus's note is to be taken with caution.

Unfortunately, also *Phil. Evg.* (logion 73, cf. 87) can hardly be uti-lized for social history. According to this text, "slaves" are excluded from the Valentinian "bridal chamber." This does not say anything about the social structure of Valentinian communities. In the wider con-text, "slave" and "free" are used as metaphorical terms, denoting, e.g., a person's relationship to sin and fleshly desire (logia 110; 123; 125 [end]; 62).

At the end of the century in Rome the presbyter Florinus[80] repre-sents a doctrine of gnostic Valentinian character. Excluded from the priesthood by Victor, he teaches in the circles of his students and busies himself with writing.[81] In regard to his origin, Irenaeus communicates to him in a letter (in Eusebius, *Ecc. Hist.* 5.20.5): "When I was still a boy, I saw you in lower Asia with Polycarp; you had a splendid posi-tion in the imperial court (εἶδόν σε λαμπρῶς πράσσοντα ἐν τῇ βασιλικῇ αὐλῇ) and sought to win the favor of Polycarp." Ambrosius, the sponsor of Origen, had a similar position (τῶν διαφανῶν ἐν αὐλαῖς βασιλικαῖς, Epiphanius, *Haer.* 64.3). Although little can be concretely grasped, a position like that was at least connected with affluence: Ambrosius financed for Origen a complete scriptorium with more than seven per-sons who could write rapidly; "there were also no small number of calligraphers next to the girls skilled in ornate calligraphy. Ambro-sius generously bears the expenses for this entire personnel" (Eusebius, *Ecc. Hist.* 6.23.2).[82] Florinus is most likely to be numbered among the imperial freedmen.

These tangible pieces of the puzzle in favor of Weber's thesis of the "socially privileged" may not, of course, lead us to draw premature con-clusions. I recall the references (see above, n. 30) that point to a socially *stratified* circle of Valentinian followers. The *rudes* and *simplices* among the Valentinians, however, were less noteworthy for our sources.

---

79. Cf., e.g., Koschorke, *Die Polemik,* 117.

80. See Agapios's *Kitab al-Unvan* (Patrologia Orientalis 7, fasc. 516f.) as well as Irenaeus, *Fragm. syr.* no. 29 (Harvey, 2:457); also Eusebius (*Ecc. Hist.* 5.20.1), who trans-mits the titles of the writings of Irenaeus against Florinus: "To Florinus concerning the sole reign of God or that God is not the creator of evil" and "Concerning the number eight" (cf. the Valentinian ogdoad of aeons). Cf. further, A. Baumstark, "Die Lehre," 306–19.

81. Agapios, ibid.; Irenaeus, *Fragm. syr.,* ibid.; Eusebius, *Ecc. Hist.* 5.15.

82. Not uninteresting: Also the wealthy Ambrosius was a Valentinian before he found his way "to the true doctrine of the church" through Origen (Eusebius, *Ecc. Hist.* 6.18.1).

Interrelations between Valentinian Metaphysics and Social Background?

If we return to the hypothetical trail of Weber and Kippenberg and ex-
perimentally follow it further, then all that follows is valid only for the
"inventors," the "promoters" of Valentinian Gnosticism who actually
belonged to an intellectual, socially elevated milieu. The masses who followed these promoters remain excluded. These people might have had
completely other motives for choosing Valentinian redemptive religiosity than the "de-politicization of socially privileged." The motives of the
followers remain hidden in the sources.

One motive of the ordinary people might have been this: "Gnosticism" might have given them the feeling of belonging to the "educated."
Other contemporaries from the upper classes first reached this feeling
after years of higher study in philosophy and rhetoric. "Gnosticism" had
without doubt an emancipatory function for the common person.

What was the motive of the "socially privileged" promoters? How
much had they been moved in the formulation of an escapist redemptive
religiosity by what Weber and Kippenberg designate as "de-politicization
of socially privileged intellectuals"? Was it the *loss of shared political responsibility and possibility of influence* that led them to their metaphysics?
On the basis of a Platonically influenced concept of reality, they interpreted
the empirical world as nothing, as intoxication, as an unreal nightmare
(e.g., *Evg. Ver.* NHC 1:22, 15ff.; 29f.; *Phil. Evg.* log. 97). They sought true
reality in a hidden Pleroma to which one establishes contact (anticipation
of the "bridal chamber") by becoming self-absorbed in private life, in one's
spirit and innermost being — in the silent gardens of an idyllic suburban
villa, in the splendid colonnades, under the shade of plane trees. . . .

That the "socially privileged intellectuals" of the second century
would have *generally* been robbed of potential political influence appears to me not to be sufficiently supported by the evidence. The loss of
the autonomy of the *polis* had been a problem centuries ago. Force and
arbitrary action in the Hellenistic monarchies, which lacked a strong
system of laws, had been replaced by a more progressive Roman Empire.
In the second century the exercise of political influence *was* possible. We
see Florinus in the second century in his younger years as a λαμπρῶς
πράσσοντα ἐν τῇ βασιλκῇ αὐλῇ. It is true that the political influence of
imperial slaves and freedmen had diminished since Hadrian. They no
longer occupied the highest offices in court nor enjoyed the extensive
power with which they had been entrusted under Caligula, Claudius,
Nero, and Domitian.[83] Nevertheless, imperial liberti exercised political

---

83. Cf., e.g., G. Alföldy, *Sozialgeschichte*, 96, 112. The politically influential positions
now were occupied by equestrians.

influence also in the second century, for example, in the function of high chamberlain (see below in regard to Prosenes and Hyacinth). Besides this, a "socially privileged intellectual" possessed potential political influence if he belonged to the three highest orders, to the senatorial order, the equestrian order, or the municipal decurion order. For him it was then nothing unusual in the early and middle periods of life to hold offices (*magistratus*) and to dedicate himself to *"res publica"* (Pliny, *Ep.* 4.23). Whoever as a freeborn raised the minimum amount of wealth to attain the decurion level (it varied from city to city; in Como it was 100,000 Sesteres [Pliny, *Ep.* 1.19.2]) was capable of taking over municipal magistrate positions and to be accepted into the decurion order.[84]

That *public offices were an economic burden*, so that one might wisely not aim at taking over political responsibility, may be correct for Egypt, the home of Valentinus and other gnostics;[85] already the decurions of Antonius's period started to sense this, in Egypt and in other places.[86] But it revealed itself as a serious problem only after Marcus Aurelius.[87] Only from Septimius Severus on were the decurions openly forced into services and deprived of initiative of their own (cf., e.g., *Dig.* 50.4.1ff.), that is, in the third century, when the wave of Gnosticism had already abated.

In other words, the material hardly allows us to speak of a "political incapacitation" of wealthy intellectuals as early as the first half of the second century, especially when they had emigrated out of Egypt, as Valentinus had.

---

84. It is true that freed slaves, with few exceptions, were excluded from the decurion order, but were frequently endowed with the *ornamenta decurionalia* in recognition of their contributions to the public without becoming members in the order. (Cf., e.g., M. Reinhold, *Usurpation*, 287f.; G. Alföldy, *Sozialgeschichte*, 116, 113.) These wealthy freedmen influenced municipal life in their own way by financing expensive building projects and contributing to the provisioning of the inhabitants (e.g., *ILS* 7812). That means that, even without public office, they were in a position to shape political life by the power of their financial resources.

85. In Egypt already in the first half of the second century, because of surviving Ptolemaic traditions, almost all official positions were burdensome forced services. Those who held these positions were not paid. They were also responsible for the success of the office, so that, for example, a financial officer was personally responsible for losses. (Cf. M. Rostovtzeff, *Kaiserreich*, 2:94.) In Alexandria and the district capitals of Egypt, city councils, in which one might have been politically active, were absent in the second century. (Cf. e.g., M. Reinhold, "Usurpation," 291f., 295.) For the Egyptian Valentinus Kippenberg's explanation this is true. But at the same time it becomes obvious how limited this explanation is. For non-Egyptian Valentinians it fails, and for Valentinus it grasps only part of it. Valentinus turned his back on Egypt. In the cities outside of Egypt also foreigners had the chance of being active as decurions (examples in G. Alföldy, *Sozialgeschichte*, 113f.).

86. City dwellers repeatedly submitted applications for immunity from paying city expenses. Cf. G. Alföldy, *Sozialgeschichte*, 116.

87. Cf. ibid., 116, 142f., 149f.

Why do the Valentinians despise the world to an extent far beyond what we find among the contemporary intellectuals of Middle Platonism.[88] In my opinion, the thesis concerning the loss of political influence must be modified. The intellectual gnostic becomes a despiser of the world not because he belongs to the allegedly politically discouraged stratum of intellectuals and well-to-do people of the second century but because he can be no longer *as a Christian* be politically active in public office. For most[89] Christians, neither administrative activity, which is connected with participation in pagan sacrifices, nor official posts, in which they would have to participate in death sentences or torture and have to organize games, are an option.[90] In addition, the mere fact of being Christian, if denounced to a court, evoked immediate condemnation (see above, chap. 25), so that public political activity had also been from this point of view more or less impossible. A public official who of necessity comes into contact with pagan religious activities can hardly keep his *nomen christianum* a secret, and whoever wishes him evil accuses him at once of his Christianity. The Roman Christian Apollonius, who probably belonged to the senate (chap. 29), was executed. It was dangerous to let anything of one's faith be glimpsed by the governing "powers," ἐπὶ τῶν ἐξουσιῶν (so Heracleon himself in Clement, *Strom.* 4.71f.). Public office and being a Christian were incompatible in the situation at that time (Tertullian, *Apol.* 21.24).[91] Christians did not sit on the councils of the cities (Aelius Aristides, *Or.* 46.2.404, Dindorf).

A wealthy intellectual, however, brings with him the ability and energy for political activity. Only his being Christian prevents him from exercising this energy, and it is precisely this that leads to its introversion.[92] In other words, it is not a general political incapacitation of the intellectual class of the second century that leads to the Valentinians' escapism from the world, but much more a combination of intellectual

---

88. While for the Valentinians the *Nous* belongs to the higher world of the spirit and is widely separated from the chaotic world, Middle Platonists see the *Nous* as the ordering and forming principle *in* the world and *present* in the state. Cf. the material in H. G. Kippenberg, "Versuch," 227f.

89. Not all: Tertullian, *De idol.* 17, presupposes a few Christians in Carthage who seem to consider public offices to be compatible with Christianity. Tertullian attacks them.

90. Cf. above *Traditio Apostolica* 16; further Tertullian, *De idol.*; Minucius Felix 31.6; 8.4; Origen, *Exhort. ad mart.* 45. Celsus (Origen, *Contra Cel.* 8.75) laments the Christians' reluctance to take public office at the level of the city (on this, see above, part 3). Cf. on the whole question the literature in W. Eck, "Der Einfluss," 579, with references; further A. Bigelmair, *Die Beteiligung,* 125ff.

91. Cf. 38.3, *De pallio* 5. Origen, *Contra Cel.* 8.75, does not refer to Christian equestrians and senators in administrative offices of the empire; see above, part 3.

92. The situation of Christianity in the Roman state during the second century leads to this blockage; it is not an a priori inherent apolitical character of Christianity.

existence / affluence and Christianity that de facto incapacitated them politically and encapsulated their political energy.[93]

We tried to identify one motive, certainly among others, for the Valentinian escapism. What in the sources supports this? It strikes me that in the sources it is continuously assumed that someone is first a "normal" Christian and only later evolved into a Valentinian gnostic. Florinus, in his youth, seeks the (orthodox) circle of Polycarp. The educated Flora, whom Ptolemaeus would like to recruit for the Valentinianism, is already a Christian. The entire Valentinian propaganda is directed exclusively toward Christians and not toward pagan circles.[94] Here in orthodox Christianity lay the fertile ground on which the Valentinian seed was sown. The Valentinian propagandists did not at all turn to "socially privileged intellectuals" among the pagans. The gnostic, according to Valentinian self-understanding, first needed the same upbringing through faith and works as the "psychic" orthodox Christian. According to Valentinian understanding, only in the orthodox church and nowhere else could the future gnostic be prepared.[95] This "mechanism" (from orthodox Christian to Valentinian) is striking. It fits precisely with the structure that we found when trying to explain Valentinian escapism.

Valentinus himself gives a second indication. The wording of a Valentinian quotation appears to indicate that Valentinus's religiosity indeed compensated for the lack of political influence. Valentinus writes: "When you (as the initiated) dissolve the world and are not dissolved yourselves, you are *lords of all creation* and of all that is perishable" (in Clement, *Strom.* 4.89.3). Clearly Valentinus uses the concept of power and dominion: κυριεύετε. What is denied the Valentinian in public life (the empirical world is a "shackle")[96] he wins back through gnostic consciousness, the feeling of a κυριεύειν, the consciousness of superiority

93. Florinus does not prove the contrary. (a) It is completely open whether, at the time he composed Valentinian writings in Rome, he still occupied a splendid office in court as he once did in the east (Irenaeus, in Eusebius, *Ecc. Hist.* 5.20.5). Irenaeus's text speaks against this: He does not say: "I saw you in lower Asia when you had, already at that time, a splendid position in the court," but he says, "I saw you in lower Asia when you had a splendid position...." (b) Florinus in the east temporarily combined being an orthodox Christian (closeness to Polycarp) and the possibility of influence in a court office. This perhaps confirms the rule. Did he have to give up his splendid office at court because it was not compatible anymore with his being a Christian? Did he therefore become a Valentinian? We would gladly know more.

94. Tertullian, *Praescr.* 42.1–3 ("non ethnicos, sed nostros"); Irenaeus, *Fragm. syr.* 28 (Harvey, 2:457) in regard to Florinus ("non tantum asseclis...sed et nostris"); also *Phil. Evg.* NHC 2:3, logion 4. On this with further material (e.g., Heracleon, fragm. 27) K. Koschorke, *Die Polemik*, 222–24, 229, 168, 176f.

95. K. Koschorke, *Die Polemik*, 228, 220f., 180 (with important reference to Origen, *Comm. Prv.* 2.16); 183.

96. For example, *Evg. Ver.* NHC 1:31.20ff.

over what surrounds him.[97] The self-esteem of the Christian intellectual and affluent reconstitutes itself. The gnostic religion of redemption gives a person the consciousness to be "from above,"[98] to be immortal by nature and "from the very beginning,"[99] to carry the characteristics of divinity in oneself.[100] The gnostic mysteries imbue the person with the satisfaction of possessing something that others do not have; they imbue with the satisfaction of being elevated. The initiated reconstitute themselves as an elite, but on a level apart from political life—in the shade of plane trees and in the silence of a splendid suburban villa. This is a mechanism of strengthening one's identity that doubtlessly can evoke for the initiated the same "feeling of fulfillment" as in one who enjoys political influence.

97. Analogously cf. the Carpocratians: "They exercise the black arts, saying they have the power to rule over the sovereigns and creator of this world and beyond this over all creatures in the world" (Irenaeus, 1.25.3). Magic here is a transformed political protest (see on this the next chapter), a substitute.

98. For example, *Evg. Ver.* NHC 1:22.1ff.

99. Valentinus, in Clement, *Strom.* 4.89.1–3.

100. Valentinus, in Clement, *Strom.* 2.36.2–4.

Chapter 28

Carpocratians

From the social-historical point of view, little can be said of the remaining gnostic groups in Rome. I mention, however, the Carpocratians.

1. Their engagement would have been eminently political, if they had directed it externally. The Carpocratian group in Rome was founded by a woman named Marcellina during the period of Anicetus (c. 155–66 C.E.).[1] As the foundation of their doctrine, the Carpocratians brought with them an explosive writing, entitled περὶ δικαιοσύνης (partly quoted in Clement, *Strom.* 3.5ff.), which deduced from arguments of natural law and the Platonic concept of δικαιοσύνη the equality of all humans. God "makes no distinction between rich and poor, folk and ruler, stupid and smart, woman and man,[2] free and slave...," "so that no one has more or can take something away from the neighbor..." (Clement, *Strom.* 3.6.2), "...the concepts of mine and yours were first introduced into the world through the laws, so that one no longer makes use of the earth and property communally — and also not of marriage" (ibid., 7.3).

As far as we know, the explosive force of this idea had no effect outside of the Carpocratian community. Within the congregation, however, the principles appear to have been practiced. At least the demand for equality between man and woman was not simply theory within the Roman group: a woman, Marcellina, stood as teacher and leader at the head of the group.[3] Within the gnostic circle, there was created a microcosm of people who rejected society and expressed their disdain for the *archontes* by disregarding in their small circle the laws of the *archontes*, especially their property laws and other social conventions (Irenaeus, 1.25, cf. also above, chap 27, n. 95).

---

1. Irenaeus, 1.25.6: "multos exterminavit"! Cf. Origen, *Contra Cel.* 5.62; Epiphanius, *Haer.* 27.6.1.

2. See also Clement, *Strom.* 3.8.1.

3. Also Origen, *Contra Cel.* 5.62, emphasizes the role of the women as official leaders within the Carpocratian cult. Analogously, women play an active role in the liturgy of Valentinian-Marcosian Gnosticism (Irenaeus, 1.13.2f., 7; 1.6.3). In regard to women's receptiveness for gnostic ideas, see also Epiphanius, *Haer.* 33.9.1. See above on Flora and in chap. 27 the two burial inscriptions on the Via Latina. For general information concerning the essential role of women in the gnostic assemblies, see Tertullian, *Praescr.* 41; further H. Kraft, *Gnostisches Gemeinschaftsleben,* 145ff.

2. Concerning the level of education of the Roman Carpocratians one can say little. The work περὶ δικαιοσύνης was not written in Rome. Its conception of a state follows neo-Pythagorean thought, as well as Stoic and Cynic ideas. Also Plato was used. Clement is not wrong when he mentions that its author "is schooled in a general education and in Platonic philosophy" (ibid., 5.3). The language of the writing reveals skill; it is even strongly rhythmic in part.[4] But this says little concerning the Roman Carpocratians.

The fact that besides the image of Christ, the images of Plato, Aristotle, Pythagoras, and other philosophers were honored by them (Irenaeus, 1.25.6) points less to a particular education than to syncretism. Irenaeus comments on this: "In such customs, they distinguish themselves little from the pagans" (ibid.).

3. The syncretism apparent in the Carpocratian cultic images (Irenaeus, 1.25.6; cf. also Epiphanius, *Haer.* 27.6) could be of interest to us from another aspect. What does "syncretism" mean sociologically? It shows that someone puts himself or herself in a position from which he or she can *communicate*. Does the syncretist have the desire to remain open to communication with pagan circles, perhaps with the intention of converting contemporaries to his or her own doctrine?[5]

---

4. E. Norden, *Kunstprosa,* 464, 547, n. 2.

5. Epiphanius pretends finally to know something concerning the affluence of the group: The images they honored were made of gold and silver (ibid., 27.6.9); also the initiated wallowed in debauchery (ἀσωτία) and sensuous pleasure (εὐπάθεια σωμάτων; 27.4.1). But how does he know this? In 27.6.9 he appears merely to have expanded Irenaeus's tradition; 27.4.1 (cf. already Irenaeus, 1.25.3) is an anti-heretical commonplace.

Chapter 29

The Martyr Apollonius

1. Eusebius (*Hist. Ecc.* 5.21.2–5) had access to written acts of the martyrs, from which he extracted the following information. (a) In the 80s of the second century[1] there was martyred "in the city of Rome a man named Apollonius, who was regarded highly by the faithful of his time because of his education and erudition." As a result of a denunciation, Apollonius had been ordered to appear before the praefect Perennis. He had delivered "a very ingenious speech in defense of the faith that he confessed" and "was beheaded."

(b) In 5.21.1, Eusebius mentions Roman Christians who in the time of Commodus "enjoyed highest regard as a result of wealth and birth." In 2–5 he names Apollonius as one representative of these aristocratic Christians.

Can we check these two social-historical statements? What is Eusebius's source? At the end of the nineteenth century, the Acts of Apollonius's martyrdom was rediscovered in two textual versions, an Armenian (A) and a Greek (G), which, despite divergences, represent an identical primary text. Was this Eusebius's source?[2] The older research tended toward the opinion that the discovered Acts was even rooted in the authentic transcript of the hearing, the *acta praefectoria*.

According to Harnack and particularly Klette, 1b–10; 11b–45a contain a copy of the official transcript of the court stenographer.[3] As evidence for this, one can point to the fact that the transcript of direct speech abruptly ends after 45a (G, A). The wording of the judge's sentence is missing. That means that the Acts stops where a court

---

1. The trial took place under the "praefectus praetorio Perennis" (*Ecc. Hist.* 5.21.3), that is, between 183 and 185 C.E. For the dating with respect to Galen (Migne, 111:989f.); Cassius Dio 72.9 and Lamprid. *vit. Comm.* 4; 14, see C. Erbes, "Das Todesjahr," 269f.

2. For the older literature see E. Th. Klette, *Process*, 1f. More recent literature in H. Musurillo, *The Acts*, LXV, n. 19; H. Paulsen, "Erwägungen," 117f., n. 1 and 4; B. Altaner and A. Stuiber, *Patrologie*, 560; further, 90, 92; W. Eck, "Das Eindringen," 393, n. 61.

3. For the possibility of looking at such records from the imperial archives, cf. Eusebius, *Hist. Ecc.* 5.18.9; 7.11.6ff.; Tertullian, *Ad. Scap.* 4; Cyprian, *Ep.* 68; *Acta Tarachi prooem.* in E. Th. Kette, *Der Process*, 18, n. 3.

stenographer laid down his pen, since the sentence would have been formulated by the judge himself and recorded on a *tabella* (πινακίς).[4] Later,
this "court transcript" was, of course, revised by editors, as Klette himself (47f.) noted, especially in the framework where the two versions (A
and G) diverge most[5] and in a passage of the "transcript" itself, 35b (G),
where Klette admits secondary redaction.[6]

In more recent literature, skepticism prevails. Secondary redaction
not only in the framework but also in the speech sections sometimes
is considered so great that nothing authentic seems to remain for the
historical Apollonius.

Musurillo, for example (*The Acts*, 24f.), misses Roman color particularly in the section against the gods (*Acts*, 14ff.). According to him, it
might have been eliminated in favor of the discussion concerning Athe-
nian, Cretan, Egyptian, and Syrian deities. Still in the fifth and sixth
centuries, possible changes to the text might have been made; Eusebius's
copy might perhaps have already been corrupted. It even appears possible to view the entire *Acts* as a fiction of the second or third century,[7] or
to locate it, along with Paulsen ("Erwägungen," 125f.) in Alexandria
in the circle of Clement of Alexandria. According to Paulsen, well-
established Christian apologetic *topoi* might have been woven into a
tradition about some martyr by some writer.

However one might decide the question (which I believe to be still
open) concerning the historical value of the extant *Acts*, we nevertheless can pin down some valuable information. Eusebius had access to
some Acts of Apollonius, which he incorporated into his collection of
Acts of Martyrs before writing his history of the early church (*Hist. Ecc.*
5.21.5). Eusebius's Acts of Apollonius thus originated at least from the
third century, and for Eusebius it documented the erudition and aristocratic descent of this martyr from the end of the second century. We can

---

4. E. Th. Kette, *Der Process*, 41f.; 47; 18, n. 2f.; cf. Tertullian, *Apol.* 2; *Ad nat.* 1.15;
Pliny, *Ep.* 10.58.

5. G, over against A and Eusebius, distorts or invents the name, the epithet, and
the geographical origin of the martyr as well as the historical office title of the praefect
Perennis (1a). In 45b, G offers a piece of fantasy for the type of execution (on this see
below, n. 26; correct are A and Eusebius). A, over against G and Eusebius, distorts the
name of Perennis (1). It is clear that the book was at least in part not edited in Rome: G at
the end designates both the Roman and the Asiatic month and in the introduction places
the martyrdom — as opposed to A and Eusebius — in the province of Asia. Klette comes
to the conclusion (31ff.) that in regard to the framework, A may be given preference over
G, whereas in the actual "court transcript" G may be more faithful.

6. According to him, a wordplay with *Logos tou theou* cannot be credited to the
praefect: ὁ λογώσας κτλ., may be secondary.

7. Cf. R. Freudenberger, "Die Überlieferung," 111. Freudenberger himself (128f.)
doubts the authenticity of the *speech* sections (*Acts* 43f., for example, might be redactional); on the other hand, the material in *Acts* might be trustworthy in regard to the legal
process.

do nothing else but check these two social-historical observations by Eusebius against the *Acts* available to us today. If they can be confirmed in our *Acts*, then Eusebius's social-historical information retains the value it had prior to the discovery of our *Acts*. If they are not confirmed, then Eusebius would not be refuted, but his witness would have to be used more cautiously.

2. What social-historical information is contained in the *Acts?* Apollonius claims, as Justin, to be a Christian "philosopher." He compares the persecution of Christians (38 G, A) with that of the philosophers, particularly with that of Socrates.[8] According to his opinion, the uneducated take offense at Christianity (38, G). Apollonius values education and disdains ἀπαιδευσία (17, G).

That the Christian Apollonius not only claimed the role of philosopher but also played it is evident from several passages in the *Acts* that portray interaction. (a) Interested philosophers participated in the public[9] trial of Apollonius (σοφοὶ μεγάλοι; 11, G). (b) One of the philosophers heckled the trial, which led to a short altercation between him and Apollonius (33f.; G, A). Both passages make it clear that Apollonius stands within the philosophical scene and argues with philosophers, so that they even make an effort to attend his trial and one of them cannot restrain himself from entering a dispute. (c) The praefect Perennis comments upon Apollonius's speech with the remark that he has digressed into philosophizing (10 and 23, A). (d) Also in 35 (G), Perennis comments on the presentation of the defendant by citing the Stoic Logos idea and confirming a fundamental Stoic consensus between himself and Apollonius.[10]

Apollonius's philosophical claim corresponds to that of Justin,[11] the author of the letter to Diognetus, and other apologists in that Apollonius emphasizes ethics (G and A: 26–30; 36–38; 42; 44): Christianity is a doctrine of virtue. Christology has its *skopos* in ethics (G and A: 36–42; 5), Christ brings the true ἀρετή (36, G; 38, G; 42, G, A). Adoration of God expresses itself in ethics (44, G, A). All of this corresponds to the primacy of ethics in contemporary philosophy.

Individual elements of education. (a) In Apollonius's ethics the concept of φιλανθρωπία plays a particular role (36 and 44, G).[12] (b) Also

8. 41 (G, A). Cf., for example, Justin, *Apol.* 1.5; Tatian, *Or.* 31; Tertullian, *Apol.* 14.
9. Cf. public trials of Christians also in Justin, *Apol.* 2.2; Hippolytus, *in Dan* 1.25.2; Eusebius, *Ecc. Hist.* 5.1.49.
10. Cf. on 35 (G) Stoic physics and the hymn of Cleanthes to Zeus.
11. Cf., for example, *Apol.* 1.6 or *Dial.* 11: Christianity as "new law."
12. Completely worthy of a philosopher: cf. for example, Plato, *Leg.* 4 (713D); *Symp.* 189D; Plutarch, *Mor.* 402A; Philo, *Dec.* 110; *Spec. Leg.* 2.141; *Cher.* 99; the educated apologist of the letter to Diognetus (8.7; 9.2); as an element of education also in Acts 27:3.

the concept of σχῆμα — οὐσία.[13] (c) And the concepts of ἕξις — φύσις — αἴσθησις — λόγος (G: 16b; 20; 21; 22), which take up the originally Stoic philosophical division of the world into inorganic, organic, animal, and rational things.[14] At the same time, Apollonius aptly uses the four terms as the structuring elements for his speech. (d) Apollonius, as Justin, has a Logos doctrine (5, G; cf. 26, G; 32, G, A; 36, A; on 35, G see above, n. 10). 32 (G)[15] is in essence Stoic.[16] (e) There are Platonic-Aristotelian echoes in 36 (G): Christ taught "what the final end of virtue was for the life of an honorable *Politeia*": τί τέλος ἀρετῆς ἐπὶ σεμνὴν πολιτείαν. That is said completely in the sense of Plato and Aristotle, according to whom the moral excellence of a person can find its fulfillment only in community life; indeed, perfect morality does not exist outside the *politeia*.[17] (f) The critique of the belief in gods is philosophical (14–22, G, A). Similar remarks can be read in the other Christian philosophers.[18]

(g) The following elements of literary education come to light:

- *17 G:* the Egyptians worship a foot-bathtub formed into an idol by the Egyptian king Amasis, as one can read in many authors (παρὰ πολλοῖς καλουμένην). See, for example, Herodotus, 2.172; on the Christian side (later?) Minucius Felix, *Oct.* 23.12, and others.

- *18 G, A:* (1) the bull's head worshiped by the Athenians: cf. Pausanias, 1.24.2; Lucilius, *Sat. Frag.* 339. (2) the τύχη Ἀθηναίων: cf. Philostratus, *Vit. Soph.* 2.1.5. Apollonius, however, incorrectly identifies her with the βοῦς ἐν πόλει.

- *19 G, A:* Socrates swears by the plane-tree (G, A) and by the dog (A), a tradition that is also found in Philostratus's *Vita Apoll.* 6.19, Lucian's *Vitarum auctio* 16 and *Icaromenip.* 9, Tertullian's *Apol.* 14.7 and *Ad nat.* 1.10, and Theophilus's *Ad Aut.* 3.2.

---

13. In a humorous variation on the Aristotelian categories of form and matter (by virtue of the form εἶδος, μορφή — the essence — οὐσία — becomes manifest in matter — ὕλη), Apollonius ridicules the idols made of clay, which have hands but don't grasp and have feet but don't walk: "The form (hands, feet...) does *not* change the essence," they remain inanimate gods: τὸ γὰρ σχῆμα τὴν οὐσίαν οὐχ ὑπαλλάττει (19, G; cf. A).

14. Cf. for example, Chrysippus: *StVFr* 2.205.16ff. (19ff.; 144ff.; 302.17ff.). See also H. Paulsen, "Erwägungen," 119ff. (literature in nn. 13ff.), for example, Philo and Sallustius.

15. The same is offered by A, but shorter.

16. See Stoic epistemology; cf. Sextus Empiricus, *Adv. Mathem.* 7.93.

17. Cf. in regard to this *topos* W. Windelband and H. Heimsoeth, *Lehrbuch*, 130.

18. For example, Justin, *Apol.* 1.9; *Letter to Diognetus* 2. On the pagan side, cf. the ἄθεοι, e.g., already Euhemerus with his utopian state concept ἱερὰ ἀναγραφή, which traces the belief in gods back to ancestor worship and hero worship; or Democritus, Critias, and Epicurus.

- *21 G, A; 17 A:* Onion and garlic as gods of the Pelusians (G; A: the Egyptians). Cf. Juvenal, 15.9; Pliny, *Nat. hist.* 19.101; Aristides, *Apol.* 12; Minucius Felix, *Oct.* 28.9f.

- *21 G, A:* Animals are revered in Egypt (dog, baboon, crocodile, ox, poisonous snake, wolf) and in Syria (fish and pigeon). G correctly differentiates between Egyptian and western Asian gods. Cf. Juvenal, 15; Lucian, *De sacrif.* 14; Aristides 12; Minucius Felix, *Oct.* 28.8; Theophilus, 1.10.

- *22 G:* Knowledge of pagan myths (ὡς ἐξελέγχουσιν οἱ παρ' αὐτοῖς μῦθοι). Examples are named: Hercules tied to the stake, the rending of Dionysus, Zeus's grave in Crete. See similarly Diodorus Siculus, *Biblioth.* 3.62.7; 4.38.4; 3.61.2; cf. Lactantius, *Inst. div.* 1.11; Aristides, 10; Justin, *Apol.* 1.21; Tatian, *Or.* 21.27; Minucius Felix, *Oct.* 21f.; Tertullian, *Apol.* 14f., 25; Theophilus, 1.9f. etc.

- In regard to readiness to die (27f., G, A; 37, G, A) cf. not only Rom 8:18ff. but also, for example, Plato *Apol.* 40C; Marcus Aurelius εἰς ἑαυτόν 11.3; Justin, *Apol.* 1.57; Tatian, *Or.* 19; Minucius Felix, *Oct.* 8. It is a philosophical school question. On *Acts* 30 (G, A); 42 (G) cf. the Stoic equanimity toward life and death.

- *37 G, A:* Stoic λύπας ἐκκόπτειν.

- *37 G, A; 42 G:* ψυχὴν ἀθάνατον: cf. Plato, for example, *Phaedr.* 245C; in the apologists, for example, Justin, *Apol.* 1.44.

- Last but not least: *40 (G, A)* takes up a passage of Plato with marginal inaccuracies in the quotation (Plato, *Rep.* 2.361E). This type of quotation corresponds well to an oral speech.

The spectrum up until Plato's quotation is somewhat respectable; also occasional *loci communes* do not change this impression. The structure of the speech has been well thought out.[19] Specific structural compo-

---

19. See already above on the structural pattern of ἕξις — φύσις — αἴσθησις — λόγος, in which the material was aptly integrated. A further structural factor is found in 8a, where Apollonius summarizes the previously handled *topoi*. In regard to the disposition:

1. *Main section of the speech:* Rejection of the pagan belief in gods 14–22:
    - 14–16a general
    - 16b–22 detailed presentation (here the clear subdivisions according to ἕξις κτλ., see above)

2. *Main section of speech:*
    - 24 Introduction: unjust killing of Christians
    - 25 Eschatology, especially judgment/death for all
    - 26 Christian ethics: to die to the world and its lusts
    - 27–30 the Christian attitude to death, life, and eternal life

nents assist the reader.[20] Apollonius's apologetic speech is refreshingly short and clear — according to the motto, "Use the scissors when it appears necessary to you." So the experienced defense orator Pliny implores a friend who corrects a speech for him (*Ep.* 2.5.4).

First conclusion: Education, erudition, intelligent speech are to be credited to Apollonius, not only on the basis of Eusebius's source but also in the light of our *Acts*.

3. According to Eusebius's second datum, Apollonius belongs to Rome's most distinguished families — in regard to "wealth and descent." This datum concurs with five indications in our *Acts*.

a. In *Acts* 11 (G) one reads that Apollonius defended himself before an audience of councillors (βουλευτικοί) and learned men (σοφοὶ μεγάλοι) *and* a great number of senators (πλῆθος συγκλητικῶν). This interesting note may be interpreted in two ways: (1) The senators function in the imperial court of Perennis as official assessors.[21] Then it is probable that Apollonius was of senatorial rank. As a rule, senators were present as assessors at an imperial court, when the proceedings were against a member of their own class.[22] Jerome consequently has the tradition that Apollonius was "Romanae urbis senator" (*Ep.* 70.4; *De vir. ill.* 42). (2) Even if the senators were not present *ex officio* (cf. n. 21), their appearance points to Apollonius's noble origins. That senators would show private interest in an imperial trial under the chairmanship of an equestrian lets one suspect that they made the effort to attend because of friendship with or interest in the defendant. It was hardly the theoretical problem of trials against Christians that attracted them to court — unless someone from their own social circle was directly involved.

b. In *Acts* 28 (A), Apollonius speaks of his wealth, which in the event of his execution would fall to the state treasury.[23]

---

3. *Main section of the speech concerning Christology and its ethical scopus:*

- 36 Christological exposition
- 37 Christian ethics
- 38–42a Parallels between Christ as teacher of virtue and the philosophers and prophets
- 42b Legitimation of Christ as a teacher of virtue by means of predictions of the prophets
- 42c Conclusion (Christianity as a teaching of virtue)

20. δεύτερον 21a (G, A); τρίτον 21b (G); τέταρτον 22 (G). πρῶτον in 16b is absent, which is understandable in an oral speech. The redactor of A introduced, incorrectly from the point of view of content, "first" in 20.

21. In *Acts* 11 (G), the senators stand parallel to the imperial councillors of the court (βουλευτικοί). The only snag in this interpretation lies in the fact that *Acts* 11 (G) first mentions the senators' presence at the second trial date.

22. Th. Mommsen, *Staatsrecht*, 2:951, n. 2; Cf. Hist. Aug. *Vita Marci.* 10.6.

23. A realistic assessment: cf. *Dig.* 48.20, 1f.

If Apollonius belongs to the senatorial order, this wealth, according to the census since Augustus, amounts to at least 1 million sesterces. For comparison, the equestrian census, since the Republican period, amounts to 400,000 sesterces. Pliny writes to a friend (*Ep.* 1.19.2) "that you have a census of 100,000 is clear, because you are a councilman (*decurio*) in our town."

c. During the hearing, the praetorian praefect not only treated Apollonius respectfully (e.g., 10) but also set him free, without *custodia*, during the period between the proceedings[24] — a possibility that would especially be conceded to a person of rank.[25]

d. A further social-historical fact enlarges the picture. Apollonius was a master of slaves. We obtain this information from the section of Eusebius's *Acts* that report the pre-hearing.[26] In the pre-hearing, the validity of the accuser was customarily investigated. Eusebius (5.21) reports that the praefect Perennis punished the accuser with the penalty of *crurifragium*, the breaking of his legs. This was a typical punishment for slaves.[27] The question why the denouncer was so severely punished leaves practically only one possibility open: the accusing slave was a slave of Apollonius. Only thus is the condemnation of the accuser understandable, for it was strictly forbidden for slaves to accuse their own masters.

(1) Numerous documents verify this, for example, *Dig.* 48.2.8 §6; 48.10.7; 1.12.1 §8; 49.14.2 §6; Cassius Dio, 68.1.2; Hist. Aug. *Vita Pertin.* 9.10; *Cod. Theod.* 9.5.1; *Cod. Iust.* 10.11.7; 8.1f.

(2) Crurifragium and crucifixion were considered to be on the same level (Firmicus Maternus, *Math.* 8.6; further material in Th. Klette, *Der Process*, 60, n. 7; cf. also John 19:31; *Gos. Pet.* 13f.). For slaves

---

24. 11 (G): κληθῆναι = summons of the accused, who is free to move about, by means of the *praeco*, of a judicial herald. Cf. on this possibility *Dig.* 48.3.1; Cassius Dio, 71.28.2; Eusebius, *Ecc. Hist.* 7.15.3–5. Acts 10 (A) ("he ordered that he be led into prison") goes against 11 (G) and is a secondary lectio facilior: it increases the reader's admiration for the edifying suffering of the martyred hero.

25. Cf., for example, Cassius Dio and Eusebius in the preceding note.

26. In the extant versions of the *Acts* the pre-hearing is missing, because it was apparently not edifying enough for reading at the liturgy (cf. 47, G, which is redactional). The redactor of G only retained one element of the pre-hearing: the punishment of the accuser (having his legs broken: Eusebius, 5.21) is said by the redactor of 45 (G) to have happened to Apollonius (the more gruesome the martyrdom, the more edifying it becomes), although a contradiction to 45a (G) arises. 45a (G): Perennis desires to prescribe a milder death penalty, which can only be beheading, as is reported correctly by Eusebius (ibid.) and Acts 45 (A).

27. Galen, *De dogm. Hippocr. et Plat.* 4; Plautus, *Poen.* 4.2.64; Seneca, *De ira* 3.32; Suetonius, *Aug.* 67 and *Tib.* 44. Further material in Th. Klette, *Der Process*, 60, n. 2; 4–7; Th. Mommsen, "Der Process," 503, n. 6. Eusebius appears to have found the same information in his source: he calls the accuser a διάκονος of the devil. (διάκονος = "slave," e.g., *Pap. Flor.* 121.3) The metaphysical coloring ("of the devil") originates with Eusebius, διάκονος apparently from the source. Also Jerome (*De vir. ill.* 42) describes the accuser of Apollonius as a slave.

who denounce their own master, the punishment of crucifixion is often witnessed (Hist. Aug. *Vita Pertin.* 9.10; Herodian 5.2.2; Appian, *Bell. Civ.* 4.29; *Schol. Juv. Sat.* 8.266ff.; *Cod. Theod.* 9.5.1; cf. Cassius Dio, 54.3.7; Cicero, *Pro Milone* 59f.; further material in Th. Klette, *Der Process,* 61, n.1)

(3) That Eusebius does not explicitly mention these aspects of the case (denunciation of one's own master) is due to his tendency. By concealing these aspects he is able to suggest to his readers that the legs of the accuser were broken because he had denounced a *Christian* (5.21.3). This "friendliness of the authorities towards Christians" fits Eusebius's tendency — but not the situation of the second century. Apollonius was beheaded in an unfriendly way, as Eusebius cannot avoid admitting.

(4) If the slave was condemned for denouncing his own master, then there is nothing contradictory about the actions of Perennis, who condemned both the accuser and the accused. Why the slave was condemned is clear. And that the accused — in spite of the condemnation of the accuser — was not acquitted is also plausible. (a) From a juridical point of view, the condemnation of the accuser does not automatically lead to the acquittal of the accused. That the prerequisite for a legally effective charge is absent — as in this case — does not halt the legal proceedings against the accused. The charge can again be raised by a new accuser.[28] (b) If Christians "are charged (with being Christian) and convicted, they are to be punished. Nevertheless, whoever recants being a Christian...obtains pardon" (Trajan in Pliny, *Ep.* 10.97). This principle of suspicion in regard to the *nomen christianum,* sanctioned by an emperor, still shaped the legal sphere.[29] Also Justin testifies to this when in his *Apology* he urged that there should no longer be condemnation simply on the grounds of the *nomen christianum.* It is true that the denunciation of the slave was not legally effective, but the officially recommended suspicion authorized the praefect to uphold, from the side of the state, the accusation and to initiate an official trial.

e. The different manner in which the accuser and the accused were handled — the former received gruesome "crurifragium," the latter "only" beheading — illustrates once more the elevated rank of Apollonius.[30]

4. Result: In light of the extant versions of the *Acts,* also Eusebius's second social-historical datum stands firm.

---

28. Cf. Papinian, *Dig.* 48.16.10 pr.; Paulus, *Dig.* 48.2.3 §1.4; W. Waldstein, *Untersuchungen,* 155f., 212, 127f.

29. Eusebius's "old law" (*Ecc. Hist.* 5.21.4b) is Trajan's legal decree: "according to an old law, Christians, once they were ordered to court, were not allowed to be acquitted unless they changed their faith." Whatever the senate's decision in *Acts* 13f. (G, A), Eusebius 5.21, and the decree of Commodus in *Acts* 45 (G) might have stated, they changed nothing with respect to this legal situation: cf. *Acts* 13 (G, A) with Pliny, *Ep.* 10.97!

30. Cf. above in chap. 23 how differently the lady and her teacher were treated.

In Apollonius we encounter that second-century type of man (since the time of Hadrian always represented with a beard in sculpture) who effortlessly combined noble origin and erudition, a combination that is otherwise absent in our difficult material. Either we encountered an educated person like Justin, of whose social origin we are more or less ignorant, or we met the senatorial lady Flavia Domitilla, about whose education we have nothing explicit.

Chapter 30

Marcus Aurelius Prosenes and Other Members of Caesar's *Familia*

Marcus Aurelius Prosenes

Besides Apollonius, did Marcus Aurelius Prosenes belong to the rich and highly esteemed Christians who according to Eusebius (*Ecc. Hist.* 5.21.1) had increased since Commodus in Roman Christianity?

Prosenes's sarcophagus with two inscriptions (*CIL* 6:8498)[1] dates from the year 217 C.E.

A

> M. Aurelio Augg.lib.Proseneti a cubiculo Aug. proc. thesauro-rum proc. patrimoni proc. munerum proc. vinorum ordinato a divo Commodo in kastrense patrono piissimo liberti benemerenti sarcophagum de suo adornaverunt.

B

> Prosenes receptus ad deum V non...s Sa...nia Praesente et Ex-tricato II regrediens in urbe ab expiditionibus. scripsit Ampelius lib.

What do we observe? M. Aurelius Prosenes is an imperial freedman, Augustorum libertus, who was freed by Marcus Aurelius and his brother Verus (still before Verus's death in 169 C.E.) or, more likely, by Marcus Aurelius and the co-regent Commodus (that is, between 176 and 180 C.E.).

In any case, under Commodus (180–92 C.E.) Prosenes begins a re-spectable career administering a series of court offices (supervising the transport of wine from Italy to Rome, particularly for the table of the emperor [*mensa Augusti*]; director of the imperial gladiator games; stew-ard of the imperial assets; administrator of the treasure chamber) and

---

1. Literature in W. Wischmeyer, *Griechische und lateinische Inschriften*, 32f.

advances to the most influential position of an imperial chief chamberlain under Caracella ("a cubiculo Augusti"). Especially in the office of chief chamberlain, imperial freedmen could still exercise power after freedmen had been denied access to all higher positions in the administration, particularly since the time of Hadrian. Numerous personnel stood at the chamberlains' command. Their political influence was considerable — particularly since Commodus. In the court of Commodus, they held the reins of government as more or less unofficial representatives of the emperor (Saoterus, Cleander, Eclectus). Chief chamberlain M. Aurelius Cleander appointed consuls and the praefect of the guard.[2] About Prosenes nothing similarly spectacular is known. His rank, however, is the highest that he as an imperial freedman could wish to possess.

Prosenes possessed a *familia* with his own freed persons, who commissioned the sarcophagus. One of Prosenes's freedmen was called Ampelius.

What Prosenes's freed persons did after the death of their patron is in many ways unusual.

Ampelius commissioned the second inscription that is peculiar. It is engraved on the top rim of the right small side of the sarcophagus over a figure of a griffin, that is, in an unusual place not intended for an inscription.

In Ampelius's inscription, Prosenes is designated as "taken back unto God" (*receptus ad deum*). This is not a proof but one of the indications that Ampelius and Prosenes were Christians. *"Receptus ad deum"* was never used by pagans; but similar expressions are found in Christian inscriptions of a later period (fourth and fifth centuries).[3] Granted, the latter comparison is anachronistic, but it must remain, because there is hardly any comparable Christian material for comparison in this early period. In the area of recognizably Christian epigraphy, Christians are still newcomers.

Prosenes was buried in a *sarcophagus* and not placed in an urn. Burial, not cremation, was cherished by the Christians (for example, Minucius Felix, *Oct.* 34.10) with their hopes for resurrection and was also preferred in the second century in pagan circles; it is, however, unusual for Prosenes. Prosenes did not die in Rome, where the freedmen buried him, but somewhere in the east. The name of the location is unfortunately garbled (possibly, "Same in Cephallenia"). As chief chamberlain he had accompanied Emperor Caracalla on the Parthian campaign and died during the return journey to Rome ("regrediens

---

2. Cf. Friedländer, *Sittengeschichte*, 39, esp. 56–58.

3. Cf. *ILCV* 3, indices pp. 580 and 382. "Receptus in pace" (for example, *ILCV* no. 2922; often); "iit ad Deum" (*ILCV* 90: 359 c.e.); "ad deum in pace" *ILCV* 3337). Cf., however, the pre-Christian "dei Manes receperunt" (*CIL* 2:2255: 19 b.c.e.).

in urbe ab expiditionibus"). Instead of cremating the body of Prosenes and sending the "more transportable" urn to Rome, the freedmen
did not spare the expense of transporting the body all the way to
Rome. Not even the body of Caracalla himself was handled in this
way when he was murdered during the Parthian campaign on April 8,
217, and his ashes sent to Rome. What was the motive for this expense
on the part of Prosenes's freedmen? The desire for a Christian burial
explains everything.

Conspicuous in inscription A is that the official titles are partly
imprecise and shortened. According to the concordance, in the entire
CIL 6 a manager of the imperial gladiator games is never again called
"procurator munerum."[4] To be complete, one must speak of "munus
gladiatorium" or something similar.[5] Were Prosenes's freedmen not very
interested in the worldly titles of their patron? Were they interested in
avoiding the word "gladiatorium"?

If Prosenes died a Christian, one may ascertain a date for his entrance into the Christian catechumenate. He would have been "manager
of the imperial gladiator games" — this was the chronologically second
administrative office of his career — before his entrance into the catechumenate. The *Traditio Apostolica* c. 15 (see above) — contemporaneous
with Prosenes — held explicitly that a person officially engaged in gladiatorial activity ("publicus qui est in re gladiatoria") was unacceptable
for the catechumenate. One might almost suspect that this paragraph of
the *Traditio* was kindled by the case of Prosenes.

If Prosenes and a number of his freedmen were Christians, the unusual place of inscription B would be understandable. They venture to
speak cautiously of the Christianity of the deceased on the upper rim of
the right small side of the sarcophagus, a place not visible at first sight.
One still does not dare publicly to display one's Christianity engraved in
stone (cf. above, chap. 15). One still hesitates — and for the rest of the
decoration follows the examples of the pagan milieu. Inscription A on
the front side, which a person first observes, is completely neutral, and
so are the pictures of dolphins, cupids, and cornucopias.[6] According to

---

4. The same is true of "proc.vinorum" and "proc.thesaurorum." However, *CIL*
6:37764 possibly needs to be completed as "proc.? t)hensauro(rum." *ILS* 1518 offers a
more complete version: "p)roc.ration.thesaurorum."

5. Cf. K. E. Georges, *Handwörterbuch*, 2:1058; for example, Apuleius, *Met.* 10.18.8.
A "procurator a muneribus" only in *CIL* 11:3612; "tabularius a muneribus" *CIL*
6:33981; 10162.

6. Prosenes's freedmen may have purchased second-hand the marble box with its neutral, not particularly Christian pictures (dolphins, cupids, cornucopias with fruit, quivers
and bows, torches, griffins, bundles of scrolls, winged genies). The area of the inscription
appears to have been abraded before the chiseling of the present epigraph (cf. Bovini and
Brandenburg, *Repertorium*, no. 929). The freedmen looked for a sarcophagus decorated
as neutrally as possible. A sarcophagus of the second third of the third century, clearly
Christian as indicated by its inscription (*Repertorium*, no. 123), exhibits similar neutral

pagan custom, there even appears on the front side the usual[7] epigraphic "divus Commodus."

The adoption of pagan elements — particularly in the funereal area — is not completely uncommon among the general church folk (cf. above, chaps. 12, 22) We saw how on the Vatican a libation canal was built into the Christian grave γ; how Hermas drew into the face of his figure of mother church characteristics of the Sibyl of Cumae and unabashedly took up material from pagan novels. The former slave Hermas displayed here as little inhibition as Prosenes's freedmen. (These also appear to stand not too distant from Hermas in regard to education: the lettering of the sarcophagus exhibits linguistic and orthographic irregularities: "regrediens in urbe [!] ab expiditionibus [!]") Among church folk, the mixing of Christian and pagan was not perceived as a problem. As Hermas picks up the pagan motif of the "divine beloved" (see above, *Vis.* 1.1.7), so also Prosenes's freedmen use the usual epigraphical expression "divus Commodus." They of course refrain from such other pagan religious formulas as "dis manibus."

Both indications that speak for a non-Christian interpretation of Prosenes's sarcophagus (the title "divus Commodus" and the past official function in the gladiator games) carry less weight than the fourfold evidence *for* Christianity. Both "pagan elements" are interpretable on the basis of a Christian provenance of the sarcophagus. The opposite is not the case. In a pagan interpretation of the sarcophagus, the elements that speak for Christianity would be unintelligible exceptions; particularly their accumulation makes a pagan interpretation of the sarcophagus difficult.

The almost hidden Christian confession of faith on the small side of the sarcophagus requires further interpretation. The fact that it is "almost hidden" is not surprising, after what we discovered in the sections about the martyrs Apollonius and Ptolemaeus and about the motives for the Valentinian escapism. The legal situation was such that, once an ill-willed person denounced a Christian, this Christian was condemned merely on the grounds of the *nomen christianum.* What is more astonishing to us is that Prosenes managed to combine high official positions in the imperial court with his Christian faith without being bothered by denunciation. Does this refute what we have said concerning the factually existing "political incapacitation of socially and intellectually privileged Christians" (chap. 27)? Here are some answers:

First, from everything we know, Prosenes did not use his office of chief chamberlain in the same political manner as his predecessors had

---

decoration: dolphins as well as a horse, a lion, a goat, and a panther, each with a fish tail. Also winged genies were chosen by Christians, as sarcophagus no. 976 demonstrates (middle of the third century; Christian inscription).

7. For example, *CIL* 6:1259; 31229; 36930; 1031.

done. He fulfilled his duty (in this he accompanied the emperor on the Parthian campaign — with all the organizational duties connected with the task) but did not apparently exploit the office by exercising political influence. Was he afraid of being exposed as a Christian? Did he wish to offer no area for attack, to create no enemies who might have used the first best political conflict to get rid of him by denouncing him for his Christianity?

Second, as the front side of Prosenes's sarcophagus does not reveal his Christianity to the observer, so Prosenes, during his life-time at the imperial court, may have cultivated a facade that did not immediately betray his Christianity. Prosenes seems to have offered little opportunity to be charged as a Christian.

A third observation affords, I think, the most important possible answer. The circle of people of Christian faith who advanced at least into the proximity of political influence and nevertheless were spared from persecution and martyrdom was a specific, very limited group. The martyrs Apollonius, Ptolemaeus, Justin, and Valentinus did not belong to it. What group do I mean? That of Caesar's *familia*. The Christian members of the "familia Caesaris" (list of names in chap. 35, n. 1) remained, as a rule, unmolested in spite of their Christianity,[8] while others were treated in accordance with the usual legal practice and martyred. H. U. Instinsky[9] has, in my opinion, correctly indicated that Christian imperial slaves and freedmen enjoyed a privileged protection from legal denunciation because of their personal relationship of patronage to the emperor. This led to the paradox that an emperor, under whom Christians were legally condemned because of their faith, tolerated Christians in his own household and granted them within this household protection that they were not able to find anyplace else.[10] Nobody had an interest in denouncing imperial slaves or freedmen. As far as possible, one avoided legal conflict with this group of people; Martial clearly formulates this.[11]

The remaining, not yet mentioned Christians of the imperial household in Rome at the end of the second century (since the time of Commodus) were the following:

---

8. Exception: Justin's student Euelpistus, who was arrested together with a group of Christians (see above, chap. 25). Alexamenos was only mocked (see below). Whether Florinus was forced to resign his "illustrious position" because of his Christianity remains uncertain (chap 27, n. 91).

9. *Marcus Aurelius Prosenes: Freigelassener und Christ am Kaiserhof*, 113ff., here 127.

10. Tertullian reflects the same paradoxical situation, when he plays off the emperor's tolerance in regard to Christians in his own household against the severity of the governor in the practice of law (*Ad scap.* 4).

11. 2.32: "Often my neighbor Patrobas ignores our boundary. However, he is an imperial freedman! Therefore I have no chance."

Karpophorus

Karpophorus "from the household of the emperor" (ἐκ τῆς Καίσαρος οἰκίας, Hippolytus, *Ref.* 9.12) had at his disposal, during the decade of the 180s, a considerable sum of money (χρῆμα οὐκ ὀλίγον) and at least one slave of his own. With that sum of money, he commissioned this slave, Callistus, who was likewise a Christian, to operate a bank (τράπεζα) on the east side of the Aventine in the twelfth region. Christians entrusted deposits (παραθήκη) to the bank, and many Jews also were among its clientele.[12]

Whether Karpophorus was an imperial slave or freedman must remain open.[13] Among Christians, Karpophorus enjoyed respect (πρόσχημα). As someone "from the house of the emperor" he remained unassailed as a Christian — even though his slave Callistus was involved in a trial through which the slave's Christianity became public.

That Karpophorus had other slaves at his disposal can only be surmised because, after the bankruptcy of the τράπεζα, he placed Callistus under guard (φρουρεῖσθαι). Karpophorus had staff at his disposal.

Did Karpophorus own as a business the πίστρινον, the grinding mill, in which he retained Callistus? Incarceration in private prisons was legally prohibited from the time of Hadrian (Hist. Aug. *Hadr.* 18.10; cf. Pliny, *Nat. hist.* 18.36; Seneca, *De ira* 3.36). Perhaps, in regard to the πίστρινον motif, we have before us Hippolytus's literary elaboration.

---

12. Cf. above on Hippolytus, *Ref.* 9.12. On details (as well as their historical credibility): H. Gülzow, "Kallist von Rom," 102–21; H. Gülzow, *Christentum und Sklaverei,* 149ff.; R. Bogaert, "Changeurs," 239–70; here 252–55, 269.

13. H. Gülzow, "Kallist von Rom," 105, addresses Karpophorus as an imperial slave without any further explanation. That might be possible: Callistus then belongs as a vicarious slave (as *servus vicarius*) to the "peculium" of the *servus ordinarius* Karpophorus (on this possibility, for example, Horace, *Sat.* 2.7.79; *Mart.* 2.18.7; further in E. Weiss, "Sklaven," Pauly/Wissowa 5/2: 553; M. Kaser, "Das römische Privatrecht," 287; P. Huttunen, "Social Strata," 89, on CIL 6:1884: the *vicarius* of an imperial slave). Moreover, the fact that Callistus, after his trial before the city praefect Fuscianus (c. 188 C.E.), is automatically transferred into the hands of the state (he works as *servus poenae* in the Sardinian mines) and after his pardon returns to Rome as a freedman, without Karpophorus being reimbursed, could point in this direction: The *servus vicarius* of an imperial slave belongs, strictly speaking, to the property of the emperor. The legal situation, however, is not totally clear. Whether a slave released from prison had to be given back to his former master or what legal status he had after his imprisonment, was a legally *disputed* problem at that time (...non esse eum in potestatem domini postea reddendum, Ulpianus, *Dig.* 48.19.8.12; on this see H. Gülzow, *Christentum und Sklaverei,* 112). That Karpophorus was not reimbursed for the loss of his slave, therefore, does not allow any conclusion about his having a slave status. If Karpophorus possessed the status of a freed person, he could be identical with M. Aurelius Augg.lib. Carpophorus of CIL 6:13040, who also was master of slaves and gave them their freedom. This burial inscription, of course, contains no Christian evidence.

Hyacinth

Under Bishop Victor (c. 189–99 C.E.), the Roman presbyter (πρεσβύτε-ρος) Hyacinth (Hippolytus, *Ref.* 9.12) was an imperial slave or freedman and a eunuch (σπάδων), who had brought up (θρέψας) Commodus's concubine Marcia.[14]

With a decree from Commodus, he was sent by Marcia on a trip to Sardinia in order to organize the release of Roman Christians who were condemned to the local mines. By pointing out his position at the imperial court (θρέψας εἶναι Μαρκίας) he managed also to free Callistus in Sardinia, although Callistus's name was not mentioned in the decree.

What happened before this amnesty? Marcia had summoned Bishop Victor (προσκαλεσαμένη!) to discuss the release of the Sardinian martyrs. What prompted Marcia to summon Victor and to listen to his appeal for release? Even if Hippolytus does not explicitly note it, it appears to me that the meeting between Victor and Marcia was arranged by Hyacinth. As Victor's presbyter and Marcia's tutor, Hyacinth is the sole explainable "bridge" for the social contact between them. Also, that Victor's appeal for release of the Christians in the Sardinian mines was benevolently entertained by Marcia and that she actually used her influence with Commodus on behalf of these Roman Christians appears to be essentially attributable to Hyacinth's influence upon Marcia, since Marcia herself was not a Christian.[15] Third, that Marcia entrusted to Hyacinth (and not to Victor) the execution of the decree for the release of the Christians which she procured from Commodus points to Hyacinth as the actual key figure in the Sardinian amnesty.

Victor–Hyacinth–Marcia–Commodus or, better, Bishop–presbyter / tutor of imperial slaves–former pupil / bed partner–emperor, so appears the chain of relationships through which the amnesty was procured for the Christians.

We see in Hyacinth a Christian of the imperial household who not only remained unmolested as a Christian but actually exercised a certain amount of influence there, even carried on "diplomacy" for the Roman Christians in order to secure the release of their prisoners.

---

14. On imperial eunuchs, see, for example: W. L. Westermann, *The Slave System*, 111.

15. Hippolytus calls her φιλόθεος (9.12.10f.), but this distinguishes her from the point of view of vocabulary from the Christians whom he designates in the same chapter as πιστός (Callistus and Karpophorus) or as ἀδελφοί. The first to assert that Marcia had been a Christian was the Byzantine Xiphilinos in the text of Cassius Dio, 73.4.7 (Loeb edition). Later, the same Marcia was a party to planning the murder of Commodus in December 192 (Herodian, 1.16.4–17.11; Cassius Dio, 72.22.4).

Caracalla's Wet-nurse

A Christian woman slave was the wet-nurse for the oldest son of Septimius Severus, the later emperor Caracalla (born 186 C.E. in Lyon).[16] The little Caracalla came very soon to Rome — even before his education (Cassius Dio, 77.11.2–4). His younger brother, Geta, was born in Rome in the year 189 (Hist. Aug. *Sev.* 4.2; against *Geta* 3.1). Everything thus indicates that the Christian wet-nurse also sojourned in Rome. After 193, the year of the imperial proclamation of Septimius Severus, she probably numbered among the imperial family.

Proculus

A Christian named Proculus Torpacion (Tertullian, *Ad scap.* 4) had once healed Septimius Severus from a sickness by using oil (per oleum aliquando curaverat). Why he would be doing this is not known. Later, Proculus managed the assets of a certain woman named Euhodia (Euhodiae procurator). Administrators of private citizens, who managed the household, slaves, and finances, were, as a rule, at least freedmen, since both slaves and freedmen worked under them.[17] However, if Euhodia's household was more modest, Proculus could also have been a slave. A third stage in the life of Proculus is transmitted to us. Septimius Severus remembered Proculus's previous service and summoned him to stay at the palace until his death (requisivit et in palatio suo habuit usque ad mortem eius). Is there hidden behind this terse sentence that Septimius Severus purchased Proculus from Euhodia for the imperial household? We could wish for more information. We do know, however, that Proculus, while at the court of Septimius Severus (193–211 C.E.), became well known to the young Caracalla (optime noverat). Thus Caracalla had a personal relationship with at least three Christians (with his wet-nurse, with his subsequent chief chamberlain, Prosenes, and with Proculus). We see in Proculus another Christian at the imperial court who remains unmolested and even enjoys favor.

It would be alluring to identify the Proculus of the imperial court with the leader (προϊστάμενος) and advocate (ὑπερμαχῶν) of Montanism

---

16. Tertullian, *Ad Scap.* 4: "lacte Christiano educatus." Cf. on this, Hist. Aug. *Car.* 1: The little Caracalla played with a Jewish boy. Jews and Christians could still be confused by pagans (see above, chapter 20, near note 6). Therefore the "Jewish boy" could have been the Christian son of the wet-nurse.

17. On this P. Huttunen, *Social Strata,* 110. Cf. such procurators in *CIL* 6:9830; 9835.

named Proclus, who also lived in Rome and debated with Gaius.[18] Tertullian, in *Adv. Val.* 5.1, ascribes literary ability to Proculus, the Montanist. He calls him a shining example of Christian "eloquentia."

Alexamenos

The graffito from a room (room III) of the *imperial pages* on the edge of the Palatine (today in the antiquarium of the Palatine) is dated about 200 (at the latest, from the first half of the third century).[19] A pagan teases a Christian colleague by scratching on the wall the image of a believer who adores a crucified man with the head of a donkey. The scoffer writes a caption to the picture, "Alexamenos prays to God." Minucius Felix, for example (*Oct.* 9.3, similarly 28.7; Tertullian, *Apol.* 16.12), also knows of this reproach: "One hears that they (the Christians) adore the head of an... ass."

The discovery shows how even in the imperial court — in spite of the above-mentioned rule — a Christian had "problems" because of his faith. It was only a harmless raillery, however, reflecting contempt, and it did not cost Alexamenos his life. For the amusement of his fellow pages the mocker takes up a well-known slander.

Vitalinis

A female slave named Vitalinis, born in the imperial household, died a "virgin" ("virgo") at the age of sixteen (AE 1948, 91 no. 176). The formulaic "dd. nn. vern." (dominorum nostrorum verna) dates this Roman burial inscription from the beginning of the third century.[20] Vitalinis's parents, imperial slaves, noted on the inscription the date of her death, which identifies them as Christians.[21]

---

18. Cf. Gaius's literary dialogue with Proclus in Eusebius, *Hist. Ecc.* 2.25.5ff.; cf. 6.20.3; 3.31; 3.28. That Proclus sojourned in Rome is revealed by such formulations as "You (= Proclus) might like to go up to the Vatican or along the road to Ostia..." (ibid., 2.25.7). His birthplace is Asia Minor. In contrast to Gaius, he represents Asia Minor traditions (ibid., 3.31).

19. History of the research in E. Dinkler, *Signum Crucis*, 150–53 (literature).

20. Cf. H. Chantraine, *Freigelassene*, 271f., 257, for parallels.

21. Cf. the congress discussions in *ACIAC* 9 (1978): 631ff. Also the word "virgo" was interpreted as an indication of Christianity in the sense of "virgo sacra" or "virgo Dei" (H. U. Instinsky, *Marcus Aurelius Prosenes*, 121; cf. *ICUR* 1:1702; 1399 and other places). However, it is to be understood here, in regard to a sixteen-year-old, in the secular sense as "unmarried" (parallels in *SICV* 2, pp. 204ff.).

Aurelius Primus and Alexander

The following Roman inscriptions represent only possibilities of naming Christians from the imperial family at the turn of the second and third centuries:

The burial inscription *CIL* 6:9057 from the Via Salaria Vetus names a certain "Aurelius Primus Aug.lib.," who wishes his deceased daughter, Aurelia Procope, "Peace be with you" (pax tecum). This wish is a hapax legomenon in *CIL* 6; pagans did not use it. "Pax tecum" and "pax tibi" are encountered on clearly Christian inscriptions (*ILCV* 2256ff.). Dating is difficult. Emperors from Antoninus Pius (before his adoption in 138 C.E.) through Marcus Aurelius, Commodus, Caracalla, Elagabal, and Alexander Severus until Diocletian and Maxentius (307–12 C.E.) used the *gentilicium* "Aurelius." The inscription was discovered in the catacomb Bassillae, which existed at least from 234 C.E. (*ILCV* 2807). Our Aurelius Primus was a *tabularius* (scribe, bookkeeper, and archivist); he belonged to the lowest ranks of the imperial officials (see above, chap. 17).

Inscription *CIL* 6:8987 also comes from the Via Salaria Vetus and is equally difficult to date. *"Alexander, Augg.Ser."* erects a gravestone for his son, Marcus, a tailor, and requests, "peto a bobis, fratres boni, per unum deum, ne quis (h)un(c) titelo(m) moles(tet) pos(t) mort(em meam)." "Unus deus" is almost unique in *CIL* 6. Only *CIL* 6:18080 (not before Constantine) formulates "in paci qui in unu deu crededit in pace" and identifies itself clearly as Christian through the CHI-RHO monogram.[22]

---

22. "Augg.Ser." (Augustorum Servus) betrays at least that the inscription was carved after 161 C.E., the beginning of the common reigns of several rulers (cf. H. Chantrine, *Freigelassene,* 253, 259). Diehl (*ILCV* 3872) points out that emperors were also called "Alexander" and "Marcus" (e.g., Severus Alexander, 222–35 C.E.; M. Antonius Gordianus, 238–44 C.E.). This, however, offers little for the dating. Both names were widespread and only seldom were imperial slaves named according to the cognomen or even the praenomen of the emperor (cf. H. Chantraine, *Freigelassene,* 129). Three further examples (among them is *CIL* 14:1877 from Ostia with an Aug.lib., the assistant to the administrator of the imperial theater and stage) in H. U. Instinsky, *Marcus Aurelius Prosenes,* 121. Their Christian provenance, however, is most uncertain. In *IGR* 4.530, a Christian imperial slave of the third century can be found. The Roman inscription *CIL* 6:9077 ("Aug. n. vern.") is, with the words "somno aeternali," more likely pagan than Christian. 1 Thess 4:13ff.; 1 Cor 15:18–20, 51f.; Matt 27:52; John 11:11 (cf. further, Acts 7:60; 1 Cor 7:39; 11:30; 15:6; 2 Pet 3:4; Eph 5:14) call death "sleeping" but understand it not as "eternal"; it is merely the preliminary stage to the resurrection. As the closest New Testament parallel, perhaps, Acts 13:36 comes to mind (David "fell asleep" and "underwent decay"). Much closer is, nevertheless, Vergil's *Aeneid* 10.746; 12.310: "Death as iron sleep . . . in the eternal night" (ferreus urget *somnus,* in *aeternam* clauduntur lumina noctem).

Chapter 31

Two Wives of Governors
Women of Senatorial Rank

Hippolytus (*in Dan.* 4.18) narrates in about 204 C.E. that "not long ago" the Christian wife of a governor of Syria[1] intervened with her husband to prevent the persecution of Syrian Christians. She belonged to the senatorial class. Perhaps she originated — as did Flavia Domitilla — from Roman nobility. But even if she and her husband were provincial folk, they were still obliged to maintain a domicile in Rome, besides their residence in the province (cf., above, chap. 13, on *Dig.* 1.9.11; Pliny, *Ep.* 6.19; Hist. Aug. *Vita Marci* 11.8). The same needs to be stated about the Christian wife of "Claudius Lucius Herminianus," the governor of Cappadocia in about 200 C.E. (Tertullian, *Scap.* 3.4).[2] Both women increase the number of distinguished Christian ladies in Rome.

---

1. Of Syria Coele or Syria Phoenice? Or of the province of Syria before the division in 194 C.E.?
2. Overlooked by D. Magie, *Roman Rule in Asia Minor* (Princeton, 1950), 2:1954.

Chapter 32

Representatives of
Western Latin Education

Apart from persons belonging to the senatorial class and to the imperial court, there are other social-historically relevant names to be mentioned from the turn of the century.

Zephyrinus

In chap. 3, we considered Zephyrinus's property on the Via Appia and his wealth. When Hippolytus in *Ref.* 9.6f., 11 reproaches Zephyrinus for his lack of learnedness, he only uses a stereotyped polemic that he carries on also against others (*Ref.* 5.28; 7.29.1; 9.13).

Representatives of
Western Latin Education

Concerning the Roman bishop Victor, who was possibly from North Africa,[1] Jerome claims that he had written in Latin[2] and that he produced only "mediocria volumina."[3] Only with Tertullian and Minucius Felix did outstanding Latin authors appear on the scene. Tertullian lived in Rome for a period during the second half of the second century (Tertullian, *De cultu fem.* 1.7), but whether as a Christian is highly questionable.[4] His Christian literary activity began in Africa.

---

1. So the *Liber Pontificalis,* s.v.
2. *De vir. ill.* 53.
3. *Chron. Pertinax* I (to the year 193, ed. Helm, 210); *De vir. ill.* 34.
4. Jerome's dubious comment (*De vir. ill.* 53) that the *Roman* clergy drove Tertullian out into Montanism (invidia postea et contumeliis clericorum Romanae eccelesiae ad Montani dogma delapsus), has hardly anything to do with this sojourn in Rome, which is to be dated *before* the orthodox period of Tertullian's life in North Africa.

We may also look at Minucius Felix, who lived in Rome.[5] He wrote his dialogue, *Octavius,* after the turn of the century,[6] but even before this he belonged to the Christian community of Rome.[7]

Minucius's education was splendid: His use of sources evidences immense reading, especially Cicero[8] and Seneca.[9] Latin and Greek historians like Nepos, Cassius, Thallus, Diodorus, Josephus, and Antonius Iulianus are known, and there are echoes of Lucretius, Horace, Tibullus, Ovid, Juvenal, Martial, Vergil, Sallust, Florus, Tacitus, Suetonius, Gellius, Apuleius, and others. On the Greek side, he is above all familiar with Homer and Plato. Jerome (*Ep.* 70.5) says with praise: quid gentilium scripturarum dimisit intactum? Also, the work excels formally. The arrangement of the mass of material is clear and follows an antilogistical scheme that also characterizes some of Cicero's dialogues. The style is capable of astonishing variations, and he draws on varied categories of rhetoric.[10] "With unique aptitude Minucius understood, on the basis of Cicero's philosophy and Seneca's diction, to recommend the new religion to educated pagans in an elegant style sufficient for the most demanding standards. He knew to apply with charm the most elegant figures of the modern sophistic style, which ... is gained through study...."[11]

Marcus Minucius Felix is a *jurist,*[12] whom the younger dialogue partner Caecilius joined in order to receive an education as an attorney (*Oct.* 3.1). At the time of Minucius Felix the profitable occupation of lawyer was more and more exercised[13] also by men below the senatorial and

---

5. *Oct.* 2.1. Cf. Jerome, *De vir. ill.* 58; *Ep.* 70.5. The description of the scenery in Ostia (*Oct.* 2–4) has occasionally awakened doubt whether the author ever saw Ostia. But this skepticism is not warranted; see H. von Geisau, "Minucius Felix," Pauly/Wissowa Suppl. 11:956–58.

6. Regarding the dating and the question of the priority of Tertullian's *Apology,* see, e.g., B. Kytzler, *M. Minucius Felix,* 20ff., 25f.; or Pauly/Wissowa Suppl. 11:996.

7. 2.1ff.: Already many years before writing the work (cf. 1.3 with 2.1f.), Minucius Felix lived as a Christian in Rome. Although the dialogue itself may be fictitious, this information was verifiable for every Roman reader. Were it created from the imagination, it would be more injurious than helpful for the dialogue.

8. Particularly Cicero's *De nat. deor.* Especially *Oct.* 5; 17–19 go back to this dialogue of Cicero. On *Oct.* 7.4; 12.7; 13.5; 23.4; 24.6; 26.4.6f.; 36.2, see Cicero's *De divinatione.* There are also echoes of Cicero's other writings scattered throughout the entire *Dialogue.*

9. Particularly in *Oct.* 36f. For the use of sources, see the comprehensive overview in H. v. Greisau, "Minucius Felix," Pauly/Wissowa 983ff., with literature; cf. also the list of philosophical, especially Stoic, elements of education, 970ff.

10. Details in H. v. Geisau, ibid., 979ff.

11. E. Norden, *Kunstprosa,* 605f.; 943.

12. *Oct.* 2.3; cf. Jerome, *Vir. ill.* 58; *Ep.* 70.5; Lactantius, *Inst.* 5.1.22 ("causidicus"). Occasionally, he lapses into juridical terminology: *Oct.* 16.6; 30.1; 38.1, 5; 40.3.

13. Cf. W. Kunkel, *Herkunft,* 271ff., 290ff.; L. Friedländer, *Sittengeschichte Roms,* 1:185; J. Christes, *Bildung,* 232f.

equestrian ranks. In the first of the two classes, it was favored because it opened career opportunities in the imperial service.[14]

In the second century the legal profession was divided into a number of ranks. The highest position was occupied by the *iuris periti,* followed by the *causidici,* the advocates, and, finally, the less respected *pragmatici.* Lactantius and Jerome (n. 12) identify Minucius Felix as *causidicus.* The *causidisi* were masters at the art of speaking (for questions of law they relied for help upon the *pragmatici* and the legal assistants called *assessores*).[15] During their pre-professional training, the rhetorical school, which followed the grammar school, prepared them for public speaking and imparted the considerable literary education that we see in Munucius Felix.

Three coinciding factors are noticeable. The first Christian representatives of *Latin education* are *jurists* of *African* origin.

Jurists: Minucius Felix and Tertullian appear to be not the only Christian jurists of the period. The *Dialogue of Octavius* (40) mentions the conversion to Christianity of the Roman jurist Caecilius. Even if Caecilius were a fictitious literary figure, this nevertheless indicates what the author of the *Dialogue* considered readily possible. Also the author of the Roman Muratorian Canon betrays what he at the end of the second century in Rome considered possible: he characterizes the author of Luke / Acts as *iuris studiosum!*

The *North African origin* is apparently valid not only for Victor (n. 1), for Tertullian, for the Caecilius of the *Dialogue,*[16] who is practicing in Rome, but probably also for Minucius Felix.[17] At this time in Rome the African element already has a profile regarding the level of education (Fronto) as well as politics (Septimius Severus). Roman Christianity thus does not stand alone when it exhibits in its ranks Latin North Africans who distinguish themselves through engagement in church politics (Victor) and excellent education (Minucius Felix).

---

14. J. Christes, *Bildung,* 231f., 242; W. Kunkel, *Herkunft,* 301f.

15. W. Kunkel, *Herkunft,* 63ff.; J. Christes, *Bildung,* 232.

16. Provided that he represents a historical figure. Caecilius comes from Cirta: *Oct.* 9.6; 31.2. On the inscriptions *CIL* 8:6996; 7094–98 cf. members of the Caecilii family in Cirta as possible relatives.

17. (a) He knows the Numidian deities well (22.6; 24.1; 25.9; 30.3). (b) His ridicule of Roman history (25) suggests the view of a provincial. (c) The name "Minucius Felix" is only in North Africa epigraphically evidenced more frequently: *CIL* 8:1964; 12449; 19600; 25584.

Chapter 33

The Theodotians

Several social-historical elements can be gleaned in regard to the Roman Theodotians.

1. Having come from Byzantium, Theodotus worked in Rome during the time of the Bishop Victor (c. 189–99 C.E.). He was "the originator and father of the movement" that taught a dynamistic adoptionism in Christology. Theodotus was a σκυτεύς, leather worker, shoemaker.[1] What we observed in chap. 6 in regard to Aquila is, from the social-historical point of view, essentially valid also for him as a craftsman. The *collegia* (clubs) of the shoemakers are among the oldest (Plutarch, *Num.* 17). They are often freeborn men.[2] As a rule, they work in stalls, *tabernae*.[3] Only in exceptional cases does their economic wealth reach exceptional proportion; Martial (3.59) is aware of one rich shoemaker who sponsors performances. The "comparator mercis sutoriae" of *CIL* 5:5927 has at his disposal *liberti* and *libertae*.[4] In order to categorize Theodotus more accurately, we would need more concrete information.

2. At the time of Zephyrinus (c. 199–217 C.E.) two of the students of Theodotus are prominent, a certain Asclepiodotus and another also named Theodotus, whose occupation is τραπεζίτης, moneychanger, banker.[5] The occupation of banker is an important branch of economic life.[6] Public and private banks (τράπεζαι) exist in the entire empire, and Rome is the world center for finance and banking. The τράπεζαι transfer payments, accept deposits, and, to some extent, pay interest on deposits.[7] They also buy and sell foreign currencies (money changing) or

---

1. See the anonymous work against Artemon in Eusebius, *Hist. Ecc.* 5.28, which was composed in Rome in the first half of the third century (5.28.7f.). Also cf. Hippolytus, *Ref.* 7.35; Hippolytus, *Syntagma* (in Ps.-Tertullian, *Adv. haer.* 8; Filastr., *Haer.* 50.1; Epiphanius, *Haer.* 54).

2. Cf. *Dig.* 9.2.5 §3; *CIL* 6:9897; J. Marquardt, *Privatleben*, 596; P. Huttunen, *Social Strata*, 123.

3. For example, Seneca, *De benef.* 7.21.

4. Further, see O. Lau, *Schuster und Schusterhandwerk* (Diss. Bonn, 1967).

5. See the anonymns in Eusebius, *Hist. Ecc.* 5.28.9; Hippolytus, *Ref.* 7.36.

6. On the whole question, for example, M. Rostovtzeff, *Kaiserreich*, 1:148ff.; n. 45 for literature on banking in Rome and Italy.

7. So-called "open" deposits (as opposed to "closed") were left to the banker for free use; they therefore gained interest for the depositor.

act as houses of credit.[8] The business is not considered very honorable. There are complaints of "usurers of the day" (ἡμεροδανεισταί), "interest diggers" (τοκογλύφοι), "money retailers" (ἀργυροκάπηλος).[9] But the business is lucrative; free citizens such as the grandfather of Augustus, C. Octavius, did not shrink from it.[10] In the second century, Apuleius characterizes the typical money changer "Chryseros": Possessing an extensive fortune, he is one of the richest men of the city (*Met.* 4.9ff.). At the time of our Theodotus, an archaeological monument in Rome reflects the economic situation of the τραπεζῖται: On the Forum Boarium in the year 204 c.e., the money changers and merchants of that place commission an arch to be erected in honor of Septimius Severus: the "arcus argentariorum." That they decided to erect this monument reflects, on the one hand, their prosperity. They render thanks to the emperor, since, after ten years of reign, Septimius Severus succeeded in stabilizing the state after initial chaos. In the same year (204 c.e.), he even was able to revive with splendor the tradition of the games, the symbol of Roman prosperity. On the other hand, the monument warns against overestimating the present prosperity of the bankers. The donors did not go to excessive expenses. In view of comparable structures, the arch, measuring 6.8 x 5.86 m., is modest. The workshop that was entrusted with the reliefs is apparently accustomed to simpler commissions. It is skilled only in ornamental work; with relief figures it is almost overwhelmed. The figures are mediocre and executed completely in the same style as the ornaments. If the bankers had anticipated how catastrophically the currency crisis would develop from about the year 220,[11] they would hardly have rallied to erect a monument honoring the imperial household. Already by the end of the reign of Septimius Severus we hear about the difficulties of the bankers in Mylasa who, as holders of the

---

8. The business of credit, however, lies mostly in the hands of private investors (*feneratores*), and less in those of the *argentarii* / τραπεζῖται (Laum, "Banken," Pauly / Wissowa Suppl. 4:76). Prototype of a private *fenerator* is Petronius's freedman Trimalchio: He pleasurably spends the waning years of his life with the revenue of his property and the interest from his loans.

9. See R. Herzog, "Nummularius," Pauly / Wissowa 17/2,1452; particularly, Laum, "Banken," Pauly / Wissowa Suppl 4:82; cf. also Cicero, *Off.* 1.42.150.

10. Cf. Suetonius, *Aug.* 2.2; 4.2. In the imperial period the *nummularii* come from all social strata; cf. the charts in R. Herzog, Pauly / Wissowa, "Nummularius," 1451–53; 1443f.; 1448.

11. The rate of interest sank sharply in the period between Caracalla and Alexander Severus (G. Billeter, *Geschichte des Zinsfusses,* 211ff.). The reign of Caracalla marked a turning-point in the gradual devaluation of the silver currency and in the disappearance of gold coins. From that point on the buying power sank more and more. In the middle of the third century, the denarius had sunk to a thirtieth of its worth in the second century. (Cf. M. Rostovtzeff, *Kaiserreich,* 2:177; Hultsch, "Denarius," Pauly / Wissowa 5:211; K. Regling, "Münzwesen," Pauly / Wissowa 16/1:482. In regard to the inflation between 225–300 c.e. cf. R. Duncan-Jones, *Economy,* 9ff.)

exchange monopoly, suffered loss through wild, secret currency speculation. At the head of the crisis was the accelerating increase in prices, the increasing devaluation of the currency.[12]

3. Asclepiodot and the banker Theodotus persuade a certain Natalius to separate from the greater ecclesiastical community led by Zephyrinus and to let himself be named "president" (πρωτοκαθεδρία, ἐπίσκοπος) of their Christian adoptionist community for the "monthly sum of 150 denarii" (Eusebius, *Ecc. Hist.* 5.28.10ff.) How is this monthly σαλάριον (= 1,800 denarii = 7,200 sesterces per year) to be evaluated? It is a considerable sum, although not extravagant. In the second century the yearly income of a minor military officer amounted to 3,800 denarii,[13] more than twice as much. Top positions in the imperial administration were endowed with more than 50,000 denarii per year,[14] a staggering sum considered from the point of view of Natalius. In the second century, Natalius would have been able to buy ten donkeys for his monthly income,[15] or 25 empty barrels.[16] At the beginning of the third century, the 150 denarii bought him less because of the price inflation effective especially since the turn of the century. In first-century Pompeii, Natalius could have acquired with his salary 40 loaves of bread every day.[17] One hundred thirty years later, at the beginning of the third century, he could scarcely buy 20 loaves of bread per day for the same amount.[18]

4. The *level of education* of the Theodotians is interesting. Theodotus, the shoemaker, was extolled as "very learned," πολυμαθής.[19] The anonymous writing against Artemon supplies details (in Eusebius, *Ecc. Hist.* 5.28.13–15): The Theodotians "labor zealously to find *logical conclusions* as a base for their godlessness. If someone holds up to them a passage from divine scripture, they investigate it to see whether it is allowed to apply the *conjunctive* or the *disjunctive* conclusion."[20] Consequently, "they admire Aristotle and Theophrastus." "They busy themselves with *geometry*, studying diligently the *geometry of Euclid.*"

---

12. On the difficulties of the bankers in Mylasa ca. 210 C.E., cf. *OGIS* 515; M. Rostovtzeff, *Kaiserreich*, 2:178f. The speculators probably hoarded good silver currency.

13. H. Pleticha and O. Schönberger, *Römer*, 169.

14. See above, the comparative material in chap 24.

15. In the second century, Apuleius let his donkey change hands on the open market for 11, for 12.5, for 17, and for 18.75 denarii (*Met.* 10.13.1; 9.31.4; 8.25.5; 9.10.5) — an average of 15 denarii. The poor gardener who bought the donkey for 12.5 denarii found this, nevertheless, to be expensive.

16. Apuleius, *Met.* 9.6.2 and 9.7.4: an empty barrel changed hands for 5 to 7 denarii.

17. See above, the prices of bread in chap. 18.

18. In the 100 years between the beginning of the second century and the beginning of the third century the price of bread approximately doubled; cf. R. Duncan-Jones, *Economy*, 10.

19. Mentioned three times in Epiphanius, *Haer.* 54.1 (probably based upon Hippolytus's *Syntagma*). Cf. also ἐν παιδείᾳ Ἑλληνικῇ ἄκρος.

20. πότερον συνημμένον ἢ διεζευγμένον δύναται ποιῆσαι σχῆμα συλλογισμοῦ.

"Galen perhaps was even worshiped (προσκυνεῖται) by some." They "use the *sciences of the unbelievers* (ταῖς τῶν ἀπίστων τέχναις),...and they distort the childlike faith of divine scriptures with the cunning of the godless." They audaciously practice text criticism on the divine scriptures (ibid., 15–18).

The Theodotians in their scholarly assiduity study and adore Galen, and Galen himself indicates several times that he has heard of Christianity (above, chap. 25, n. 64). It is therefore not remote to assume contact between the Roman doctor and the Roman Christian group around Theodotus (students of Galen?). The doctor philosopher was called back to Rome as the personal physician for Marcus Aurelius and Verus, after having already lived there from 161 to 166 C.E. He remained in the city until his death in 199 C.E. At least a passing personal contact between him and the Theodotian circle is neither chronologically nor geographically out of the question. On the contrary, the parallels between Galen and the Theodotians are startling.

a. The Theodotians base their logic on Aristotle and Theophrastus;[21] Galen also bases his logic on both. Galen even writes commentaries on some passages from both.[22] At least it appears possible that the Theodotians gained their Aristotelian-Theophrastic knowledge of logic from Galen's lectures or from his fifteen-volume work on scholarly proof (περὶ ἀποδείξεως). Galen insists upon mathematical and logical training, on ἀπόδειξις as logical demonstration. When the Theodotians set out to explain the Christian faith in the terminology of post-Aristotelian Hellenistic logic (in Eusebius, *Ecc. Hist.* 5.28), they are attempting to apply precisely Galen's program of logic to their theology.

b. The Theodotians apply text criticism to sacred scriptures (in Eusebius, *Ecc. Hist.* 5.28.15–18); they do not even shrink from μεταγράφειν (ibid., 18). In this they are doing nothing other than what pagan philologists do to the texts of Homer, Hippocrates, and Aristotle in order to obtain a trustworthy text. Text criticism was applied especially to Hippocratic writings—also by Galen. Likewise, Galen criticizes the text of Plato's *Timaeos* (77).[23] Another formal methodological parallel is thus opened between Galen and the Theodotians.

c. Finally, when the Theodotians are accused of contradicting themselves in their works and that one and the same author even comes to contradictory conclusions in different manuscripts (Eusebius, *Ecc. Hist.*

21. See above, Eusebius, *Ecc. Hist.* 5.28. Cf. also Theodotus's exegesis of Deut 18:15 and Luke 1:35 in Hippolytus, *Syntagma* (Epiphanius, *Haer.* 54.3; cf. Hippolytus, *Ref.* 7.35): It shows a sober syllogistic thinking, totally devoid of allegory.
22. Cf. Galen, *De libr. propr.* 2; further references in R. Walzer, *Galen,* 40; 78f.
23. Galen, *In Platonis Timaeum commentarii Fragmenta,* 13.3–7 (ed. Schroeder); on this cf. R. Walzer, *Galen,* 80–83.

5.28.16f.), this corresponds exactly to Galen's program of a constant re-examination of knowledge, which means continuous μεταδιδάσκεσθαι.[24]

5. I mentioned (in chap. 25) how in the second century members of all social strata can be familiar with scholarly education; indeed even a slave can develop himself into a sought-after philosopher. In the ranks of the Theodotians we find further confirmation of this when we see education coupled with vocations such as σκυτεύς or τραπεζίτης.

Similarly, the Stoic Cleanthes grinds grain in a mill in order to earn his livelihood. Plutarch commends him as an example (*De vit. aere al.* 830CD). Instead of accumulating debt, the intellectual should work as a seaman or guard (ibid., AB; similarly Epictetus, *Diss.* 3.26.7), as fisherman or longshoreman (Lucian, *Tox.* 18; 31). Also Paul may be mentioned in regard to combining education and manual labor. Moreover, our shoemaker Theodotus reminds us of the cobbler Simon, to whom Socrates came in order to discuss learned topics (Diogenes Laertius, 2.122).

---

24. Cf., e.g., *Scr. min.* 2.77.17ff.; 81.19ff.; 82.20ff. (ed. Mueller).

Chapter 34

Praxeas, Gaius, and the Problem of "Hippolytus"

For other theological teachers in Rome at the end of the second century there are only fragments of relevant social-historical material.

1. Tertulian in *Adv. Prax.* 1 calls the modalist Praxeas, who appears in Rome from Asia about 190 C.E., "doctor." But how far Praxeas, with Stoic resources, already refined modalism into a systematic doctrine can hardly be determined. This refinement might have been first carried out by Sabellius, Cleomenes, and Epigonus in Rome in the third century.[1] In *Adv. Prax.*, Tertullian is not actually fighting against Praxeas but his North African successors who were influenced by Stoic thought (ibid., 1.7).[2] It is perhaps significant that not Praxeas but Epigonos and Kleomenes in the third century first founded a regular διδασκαλεῖον in Rome (Hippolytus, *Ref.* 9.6–11; 10.27).

Modalistic ideas were especially in vogue in the naive, uneducated belief of the common folk.[3] Therefore, the representatives of the established Christianity in Rome, Victor, Zephyrinus, and Callistus, sympathized for some time with modalistic monarchianism.[4] The church-goers whom they represented apparently cherished such modalistic ideas.

---

1. With nominalistic logic, also Stoic metaphysics, cf. the details in Harnack, *Dogmengeschichte*, 4th ed., 1:737f., n. 1.

2. With these successors, Stoic influence is evident at least in "compassus est pater filio" (*Adv. Prax.* 29); also see the reflections about the nature of the Logos (ibid., 5–7). See further Harnack, ibid.

3. (a) The fictitious acts of the apostles, a typical *popular* entertaining and edifying literature, represent a Christology tinged with a modalistic monarchianism. (Cf. E. Hennecke and W. Schneemelcher, *Ntl. Aprokryphen,* 2:187.) (b) Tertullian, *Adv. Prax.* 1: precisely those attracted to the "simplicitas doctrinae" go to Praxeas and fall into the trap of his modalistic theology. (c) Tertullian, *Adv. Prax.* 3: "*Simplices* quique, ne dixerim imprudentes et idiotae, quae maior semper credentium pars est, quoniam et ipsa regula fidei a pluribus diis saeculi ad unicum et verum deum transfert, non intellegentes unicum quidem, sed cum sua οἰκονομία esse credendum, expavescunt ad οἰκονομίαν ... Itaque duos et tres iam iactitant a nobis praedicari, se vero unius dei cultores praesumunt ... monarchiam inquiunt tenemus." (d) Similarly, Origen, *Joh. Comm.* 2:3: "the great masses who are considered believers" know nothing other than the crucified Jesus Christ and hold this incarnate Logos for the totality of the divinity.

4. Hippolytus, *Ref.* 9.7, 11f.; Ps.-Tertullian, *Adv. haer.* 8 (Victor allowed Praxeas to gain strength: "corroborare curavit").

Praxeas may have here found his followers. In any case, Tertullian (*Adv. Prax.* 1) readily testifies that Praxeas exercised influence on the representative of established Christianity in Rome, the "episcopum Romanum" (he probably meant Victor).

2. We know little of *Gaius*,[5] who worked in Rome at the end of the second and the beginning of the third century and who, under Zephyrinus, wrote the Greek *Dialogue against Proclus* (Eusebius, *Hist. Ecc.* 6.20.3; 2.25.6). Eusebius calls him "highly learned" (λογιώτατος). Because of the few source fragments, this can scarcely be verified. It might be significant that he clothes his polemic in the favored dialogue form of the educated world. Gaius reveals himself as meticulous scribe when he deals in his critique of the Apocalypse of John "chapter by chapter," juxtaposing passages in order to prove that the Apocalypse of John contradicts the sacred scriptures.[6]

3. We place in quotation marks the problem "Hippolytus." The literarily prolific personality (or are there more than one?), who hides himself behind this name, is without doubt rich in philosophical education.[7] He circulates in the best of circles, even among the household of the emperor (Eusebius, *Hist. Ecc.* 6.21). His followers erected for him the famous marble sculpture in the Vatican Museums that depicts a scholar upon a professional chair. Hippolytus's activity in Rome hardly began already under Victor (about 189–199 C.E.); it falls into the third century. Hippolytus makes no mention of Praxeas in his polemic against the modalists, as if he has not personally known Praxeas, who lived in Rome during the 190s. Also Hippolytus apparently knows only secondhand the eventful life of Callistus as a slave (*Ref.* 9.12). As a great representative of the Greek-eastern education in Rome, he apparently did not immigrate from the east to Rome before the beginning of the third century.[8]

---

5. On Gaius: G. Maier, *Johannesoffenbarung*, 69–85.

6. Cf. Dionysius in Eusebius, *Hist. Ecc.* 7.25. Also the fragments from Hippolytus's *Capita adversus Caium*; on these see G. Maier, *Johannesoffenbarung*, 70, n. 266; 75.

7. Cf., for example, in Hippolytus, *Ref.*, the philosophical digressions that try to prove that the heretics suck up their nourishment from pagan philosophical roots. Rhetorical education is visible, e.g., in the homily against the Noetians. Cf. E. Norden, *Kunstprosa*, 547f.

8. Cf. also Hippolytus, *In Dan.* 4.8.7; 4.9.2f.; 4.13.2f.; 4.58.2, which are written more from the perspective of a provincial.

Chapter 35

Summary

On what points do the two diachronic sections, Parts 3 and 4, agree?

1. Most impressive is the convergence with respect to the Christian members of the *familia Caesaris*. In the first as well as in the second section they increasingly appear from Commodus on.[1] The agreement between both sections is indeed interesting because the general information of the first section originates from sources other than the prosopographic examples of the second section. The material of the second section confirms that of the first. I could formulate it thus: In the second section our task was not to generalize from individual cases (what method would one use for this?) but to illuminate concretely the generalizations that the sources themselves made in the first section.

2. If we leave Pomponia Graecina and especially Acilius Glabrio aside, we encounter Christians of *senatorial rank* in the second section, under Domitian (Flavia Domitilla), very probably under Commodus during the time of peace with the church (Apollonius) and certainly under Septimius Severus (the two wives of governors). In the first section they appear from the time of Septimius Severus and on.

3. The imposing high portion of immigrants to Rome under the prosopographic examples (Part 4) illustrates the predominant Greek-speaking character of Roman Christianity (Part 3, chap. 15).

Beyond this, the high portion of Christian foreigners (*peregrini*) in the second section corresponds to the number of Christians without citizenship in the first section (self-imposed slavery, crucifixions, etc.). Christian Roman citizens in the second section are not only the aristocrats just mentioned in point 2 above and, most probably, the woman in Justin's *Apology* 2.2, but also especially Christian freed persons of Rome.[2] If we

---

1. Christian members of the *familia Caesaris* in the second section since Commodus: Prosenes, Carpophorus, Hyacinth, Florinus, a wet-nurse, the page Alexamenos, Vitalinis with parents; possibly: Proculus, Aurelius Primus, Alexander. At the time of Justin: Euelpistus. Already in the first century: Claudius Ephebus and only possibly: Iulia, Herodion [Iunia(nu)s].

2. (a) Christian imperial freed persons: Claudius Ephebus, Prosenes; only possible: Iulia and Aurelius Primus. It is uncertain whether the others in n. 1 had been freed. (b) The freedman of Prosenes, Ampelius. (c) The (descendants of) freed persons with names of famous *gentes*, who probably also attained from their patrons Roman citizenship together

add up the persons who come into question as Roman citizens, there are fewer than 20 from the more than 80 Christians in the second section.

The high portion of immigrants among the Roman Christians reflects the situation in Rome in general. The city of Rome itself swarmed with non-Roman elements ("una cunctarum gentium in toto orbe patria" (Pliny, *Nat. hist.* 3.6), especially people from the east (Juvenal, 3.60ff.). Seneca mentions that the "major part" of the population was not born here (*Helv.* 6). Accordingly, one finds in Hermas the emphasis upon "living in a foreign land" (*Sim.* 1.1; cf. 1 Pet 1:17) and the corresponding theological motif of the "heavenly city" (ibid., 1ff.). An experience from everyday life is turned into a theological principle.

4. Like the first section, the second section[3] also reveals that among the social elite the portion of women is great, although not greater than that of the male examples. Only in the senatorial class do the examples of women predominate.

Women active in church life (first section, chap. 15) are found as prosopographic examples in Rom 16 (chap. 16; there the relationship to the first section is discussed) as well as in Hermas (cf. Grapte), and in connection with Marcion (cf. chap. 24), Apelles (cf. Philumene) and the Carpocratians under Marcellina. A woman among the students of Justin (cf. Chariton) as well as Flora, to whom Ptolemaeus's letter is addressed, are interested in theology or even theologically educated.

Although especially from the end of the first century on, women were deprived from actively participating in the shaping of Christian teaching and communal life (first section, chap. 6), one must ask whether at least the great number of socially distinguished women exercised an *indirect* influence. Christian life and doctrine had to be so constructed that women of the upper social strata were not alienated. Ptolemaeus sought by all means to please Flora with his presentation of doctrine. The Acts of Peter, from the end of the second century, emphasizes, as do other acts of the apostles, sexual asceticism (*Act. Verc.* 22; 33ff., et al.), which Christian women married to pagans often received with approval (cf. the Christian woman in Justin's *Apology* 2.2). At least one must reckon in this way with the indirect influence of women.

---

with the famous names: Valerius Biton, the already-mentioned Iulia, Iunia (probably to be read thus), and Maria (most likely a *gentilicium,* see above). However, as we have seen in chap. 7, manumission by a Roman with full citizenship does not automatically bring with it full citizenship since the "lex Aelia Sentia" from 4 C.E. and the "lex Iunia" from about 19 C.E.) (d) In regard to the lawyers Marcus Minucius Felix and Caecilius Natalis (chap. 32), born in Africa, Roman citizenship is possible but unprovable. Were they born free? Set free? Children of veterans? They obtained citizenship at the latest in 212 C.E. under the "Constitutio Antoniniana."

3. See the examples of Pomponia Graecina (?), Flavia Domitilla, the woman in Justin's *Apology* 2.2, and/or Flora, Flavia Sophe, other distinguished women of gnostic sympathy, and the two wives of governors.

5. In regard to the relationship of Christians to the *pagan milieu*, I again take up only a few points. We observed at several points that Christians hesitated to let their Christianity become visible to those outside (see chap. 15.3 and the chapters on Prosenes and Pomponia Graecina).

Mixing pagan and Christian elements was no great problem for ordinary Christians. This phenomenon is found in the archaeological sources (chapters on Prosenes, and on tombs under S. Sebastiano and on the Vatican hill) as well as in literary documents (Hermas, chap. 22).

On higher levels the same problem appears when those versed in more sophisticated pagan education (Justin, Theodotians, and others) rethink the Christian tradition from the point of view of pagan philosophical presuppositions (chaps. 26, end; 33, end; 25; et passim).

In the first section we already saw for the first century the handing down of non-Christian educational elements within a chain of Christian teachers (chaps. 5, end; 6, end). In the prosopographic examples the same phenomenon is best seen in the chain of teaching from Justin to Tatian to Rhodon (chap. 26).

That Christians acquire individual pagan educational elements from Christians does not mean that early Christianity attempted to replace the pagan elementary, grammar, and rhetorical schools with Christian ones. Christians continued to send their children to pagan schools (Tertullian, *De idol.*). A moving example is found in the school notebook of a Christian child (fourth century; in H.-J. Marrou, *Geschichte der Erziehung*, 592). In a pagan class the child notes mythological names and moral and obscene anecdotes; yet each time before he begins a new page, he draws a cross with a monogram of Christ.

6. *Inner-Christian process of education.* The relationships between teachers and students in the second section correspond to the inner-Christian process of passing on a genuine Jewish-Christian education as observed in the first section (chap. 5, especially Clement). *Beside* the pagan education and school operation in which the Christian children and youth participated, there developed an independent activity of Christian teaching whose contents were the Christian doctrines of faith and rules of life. Christianity with its statements of doctrine became a proper culture and cultural heritage, which was transmitted within the church communities. *First Clement* 21:8 calls this teaching "Paideia in Christ."[4]

Inner-Christian educational activity took place on three levels. At home, the parents instructed their children in Christianity (*1 Clem.* 21:6,

---

4. In regard to this cf. G. Ruhbach, "Bildung in der Alten Kirche," *Kirchengeschichte als Missionsgeschichte*, 1:294ff., with literature.

8; Eph 6:4; cf. Heb 12:7–10; Col 3:21).[5] What happens when the parents die? In Rome we have the good fortune to know a regulation for such a case. In the first half of the second century, the Christians of Rome had entrusted a woman named Grapte with the Christian instruction of the orphans (Hermas, *Vis.* 2.4.3).[6] At the same time, Grapte was commissioned to teach the widows. Why? Had the deceased husbands been responsible for the Christian instruction of these women? As with the children, did Grapte take the place of the deceased husbands? *1 Clem.* 21:6f. indeed points in this direction. We men, writes Clement in the sense of 1 Cor 14:35, "wish to correct our women." At least the Roman Christians with Grapte appointed a *woman* for the Christian instruction of orphans and widows. She did have a preaching mission, although it was "only" for women and children.

On a second level, there is instruction of catechumens. The *Traditio Apostolica* (15ff., ed. Botte) regulates who may be admitted to this instruction. The instruction is given by the presbyters who also instruct the members of the community.[7]

On the third level, there are the lectures of independent teachers and philosophers like Justin and Valentinus who gathered circles of students and worked apart from the ecclesiastical officials.

7. The relationship of *education* to *social status* is multileveled. Even though a higher social origin generally raises[8] the educational opportunities of the individual, education can be linked with every social provenance. A shoemaker can also pursue Aristotelian logic and a slave attend philosophical lectures. In the second section, therefore, it was impossible to infer a person's social status from his or her classical pagan education.

In the prosopographic presentations I have nevertheless drawn attention to the degree of a person's education. Although it was impossible to infer social status from education, it was interesting to observe how, in the case of Hermas, Marcion, the Valentinians, Apollonius, Minucius Felix, (Flora and Proculus), and the Theodotians, a certain degree of education was connected with a certain social background that was revealed from other source material. What can be known of Hermas's

---

5. Cf. P. Lampe, "Zur gesellschaftlichen und kirchlichen Funktion," 535ff.

6. Therefore, Hermas gave to her his small book so that she might preach his prophecies to the widows and the orphans of the city. Grapte is a nice early example of ecclesiastically organized instruction of children.

7. Cf. 1 Tim 5:17. From Hermas (see below in detail, esp. *Vis.* 2.4.2) one may conclude that the Roman presbyters, after Hermas had explained his prophecy to them, were to preach this prophecy to the Roman Christians in the individual house churches: The presbyters were responsible for the instruction of the ecclesiastical communities. The "teachers" whom Hermas names in *Sim.* 9.25.2; 9.16.5 were itinerant missionaries of the apostolic period, whom Hermas looks back upon as past phenomena.

8. Cf., e.g., above, chap. 22, n. 56.

educational niveau "fits" that of a freedman engaged in business. That of Minucius Felix fits the lawyer trained in the rhetorical school. The elements of education among the Valentinians are what one would expect of persons living in a suburban villa, where poetry and Ionian dialect were cultivated, etc. In the case of Hermas, we also observed how his modest education coincided with a lack of theological depth.

With Tatian and especially with Justin, it became clear what social consequences education can have. Their pagan classical education helped Justin and Tatian to build a foundation for their claim that Christianity represented a philosophy. Tacitus, Suetonius, and Pliny had categorized Christian doctrine as "superstition" (*Ann.* 15.44; Seutonius, *Claud.* 25.3; *Nero* 16.2; Pliny, *Ep.* 10.96.8), but Lucian and Galen already called it "wisdom" and "philosophy" (chap. 25; Galen in Rome placed Christianity, although in his opinion it was dogmatically encrusted, on the same level as the contemporary philosophical schools). In the period *between* these pagan statements, the activity of the Christian philosophers and apologists like Justin took place. It is thanks to these philosophically educated teachers that Christianity hesitantly was acknowledged by the contemporary world as a cultural entity. It became slowly more attractive as a depository of learning for the more educated pagans, as the increasing influx of socially distinguished pagans to Christianity in the second half of the second century illustrates.

8. In regard to our material, it only rarely was possible to infer from writings with educational elements (literary or philosophical allusions, etc.) the education level of Christian *readers* in Rome. The intended readers were either pagan (Justin's *Apology*; Tatian, *Or. ad Graecos*; Minucius Felix, *Oct.*; Apollonius's *Speech*) or did not dwell in Rome (*1 Clem.*). Only in Hermas, who directs his writings to the Christians in the city of Rome (*Vis.* 2.4.2), did we discern that he was representative of a wide circle of the Christian community (chap. 22, end). We may assume that, with his educational elements (e.g., material from entertaining popular fictional literature), he appealed to the taste of wider circles of Roman Christianity. They must have been as semi-educated as he was (see also the analogous statements on the readers of the Acts of the Apostles in chap. 13). The same may be said of Marcion's readers. The scarcity of philosophical elements in Marcion allows one to conclude that not many of his hearers were philosophically demanding. Apelles (Appendix 1) appears to have been the most demanding. What social function the educational elements in Valentinian texts could have had for the Valentinian followers we have sketched out in chap. 27. Concerning the primary intended audience of Justin's *Dialogue* (Jews? Christians? his own students? Christian heretics?) the final word does not seem to have been spoken.

Part 5

THE FRACTIONATION OF
ROMAN CHRISTIANITY

After the prosopographic investigation, I turn once again to the totality of Roman Christianity. The phenomenon of fractionation, to be considered in Part 5, will correspond to the findings of Part 2, where we observed Roman Christianity as being spread over different parts of the city. Also Part 4, which focused on different Christian groups and small groupings in the city, will be consistent with this.

Chapter 36

The Evidence of Fractionation

The Letter to the Romans

The *entirety* of Roman Christianity is never designated in any passage of Romans as ἐκκλησία, not even in Rom 1:7 where, according to the standard of other Pauline letters, it would be expected.

In Rom 16:5, not the totality but only a part of the city's Christians is addressed as ἐκκλησία: ἡ κατ᾽ οἶκον αὐτῶν ἐκκλησία, the house community assembled around Aquila and Prisca.[1]

The same chapter indicates that there were in Rome several such concentrations:

- the believers who are gathered with Asyncritus, Phlegon, Hermes, Patrobas, and Hermas (v. 14: οἱ σὺν αὐτοῖς ἀδελφοί)

- the saints who congregate around Philologus, Julia, Nereus, his sister, and Olympas (v. 15: οἱ σὺν αὐτοῖς πάντες ἅγιοι)

- the slaves or freed persons belonging to the household of a certain Aristobulus (v. 10: οἱ ἐκ τῶν Ἀριστοβούλου)

- the slaves or those manumitted belonging to the household of a certain Narcissus (v. 11: οἱ ἐκ τῶν Ναρκίσσου οἱ ὄντες ἐν κυρίῳ)

Thus, in the capital city of Rome, we count five different Christian islands. If we assume that the other fourteen people of Romans 16 do not belong to any of these five crystallization points and that they hardly could all have belonged to only one other additional circle, then this results in at least seven separate islands of Christianity.

At least an eighth may be added to this when Paul sojourned in Rome and gathered Christians in his rented accommodation (see above, on Acts 28:30f.). There is nowhere any indication of a central location for

---

1. Apparently, it reached relative independence, since Paul at other places only designates a city-wide church as ἐκκλησία (in the same chapter, Rom 16:1, 23; further 1 Cor 1:2; 11:18; 14:23; 2 Cor 1:1; 1 Thess 1:1, and other places). Only in Ephesus and in the Lycus Valley is once again a house community called ἐκκλησία: 1 Cor 16:19 (cf. possibly also 1 Cor 14:34; plural); Phlm 2; Col 4:15. On M. Gielen, "Zur Interpretation," *ZNW* 77 (1986): 109–25, cf. chap. 18, n. 26.

the different groups scattered over the city. Each circle of Christians may
have conducted worship services by itself in a house or apartment, so
that it can be referred to as a house community.

The Origins of Titular Churches

We encounter the same phenomenon of local fragmentation if we proceed chronologically from the opposite direction and ask concerning the
origins of the Roman titular churches (*tituli*).[2]

The Roman *tituli* of late antiquity are relatively independent parishes
within the city ("quasi diocesis"),[3] with their own place of assembly,
their own clergy, cult, baptistery, and burial place. We know the number and the names of the *tituli* from the signature lists of the Roman
synods.[4] Some 25 titular parishes can be gleaned from the lists.[5]

Tituli

Aemilianae = SS. Quatuor Coronatorum
Anastasiae
Byzantis = Pammachii, SS. Johannis et Pauli
Caeciliae
Callisti = Iulii, S. Mariae trans Tiberim
Chrysogoni
Clementis
Crescentianae = S. Sixti via Appia (?)
Cyriaci
Equitii = S. Silvestri, S. Martino ai Monti
Fasciolae = SS. Nerei et Achillei
Gai = S. Susannae

2. Selected literature: Chr. Huelsen, *Le Chiese di Roma:* see especially the introduction on the ancient titular churches, pp. lxvi–lxviii; J. P. Kirsch, *Die römischen Titelkirchen
im Altertum* and *Die christlichen Cultusgebäude in Alterthum;* R. Krautheimer, *Corpus
Basilicarum Christianarum Romae* and *Early Christian and Byzantine Architecture,* especially 1–15; J. L. Laurin, "Le lieu du culte," 39ff.; P. Testini, *Archeologia Cristiana,*
547–58; R. Vieilliard, *Recherches sur les origines,* especially 31–49; 142f.; "Les titres romains," 89ff. Further cf. L. Voelkl, in *RivArCr,* 29 (1953): 49ff.; 30 (1954): 99ff. J. M.
Petersen, "House-Churches," 264–72; F. V. Filson, "The Significance," 105–12; F. X.
Kraus, "Basilika," 109ff.; H. J. Klauck, *Hausgemeinde.*
3. *Liber Pontificalis* 1.74, ed. Duchesne.
4. Esp. the Roman synods of 499 and 595. The material is in J. P. Kirsch,
Titelkirchen, 6ff.
5. Cf. J. P. Kirsch, *Titelkirchen,* 7ff.; 127–29; Chr. Huelsen, *Chiese,* pp. lxvii ff. The
titular church of S. Matthaei is not considered here, since we hardly know anything about
it. This church was located up till the eighteenth century close to SS. Marcellini et Petri.
Also not included are the numerous cemeterial churches outside the city, which led Op-
tatus of Mileve (*De schism. Donat.* 2.4) ca. 312 C.E. to register more than 40 churches
in Rome.

Lucinae = S. Laurentii in Lucina
Marcelli (= Romani)
Nicomedis = SS. Petri et Marcellini (?)
Praxedis
Priscae
Pudentis = S. Pudentianae
Sabinae
Tigridae = S. Balbinae (?)

Apostolorum = Eudoxiae, S. Petri ad vincula
Damasi = S. Laurentii in Damaso
Eusebii
Marci
Vestinae = S. Vitalis, SS. Gervasi et Protasi

This was the situation in the fifth and sixth centuries. If we inquire into the pre-Constantine roots of these churches, at least five Constantinian and post-Constantinian titular churches may be eliminated, namely, the last five. They are all together literarily or epigraphically attested as foundations of the fourth or the beginning of the fifth century.[6]

We possess no certain references concerning the founding of the rest of the twenty tituli other than legendary local traditions. J. P. Kirsch (*Tirelkirchen*, 129) and Chr. Huelsen (*Chiese*, lxvii) consider that the majority of the twenty titular churches existed before Constantine. The reasons are the following.

a. Reliable sources of Constantinian and post-Constantinian times, which willingly and reliably give information about five titular foundations from that period (n. 5), are silent concerning other foundations.

b. In the middle of the third century, Cornelius (in Eusebius, *Hist. Ecc.* 6.43.11) records 46 presbyters in Rome. If we calculate that in the third century 2–3 presbyters worked at one titulus (this relationship is at least attested by the signature lists of the Roman synods of late antiquity), we arrive at 15–23 titular parishes in the middle of the third century. This number corresponds to the above ca. 20 assumed pre-Constantinian tituli. Besides this, Cornelius counts 52 "lectors, exorcists, and doorkeepers." If we take one-third of that number, we come

---

6. For evidence concerning *Vestinae, Damasi,* and *Marci* see p. 363. For reference to the titular church Apostolorum, see J. P. Kirsch, *Titelkirchen*, 41ff.; 45ff.; 127. Further cf. Chr. Huelsen, *Chiese*, lxvii ff.; R. Vielliard, *Origines*, 30. For evidence concerning the titular church *Eusebii*, see J. P. Kirsch, *Titelkirchen*, 58ff. As sixth case the titular church *Equitii* could be mentioned. The *Liber Pontificalis* places its origin in the first half of the fourth century, in the time of Sylvester, which, however, does not necessarily have to go back to a historical source (cf. J. P. Kirsch, *Titelkirchen*, 41ff.). Archaeology (see below) opens the slight possibility of dating the Titulus to the third century.

to about 17 doorkeepers, which corresponds to the number of worship places and again agrees best with our picture of the situation.

c. Already in the fifth and sixth centuries, the Roman Christians were convinced that the titular churches dated from the pre-Constantinian period. Besides the legendary material from the fifth and sixth centuries (cf. chap. 3) the *Liber Pontificalis* (1.126) offers evidence for this. According to this source, Bishop Evaristus (c. 100 C.E.) allegedly distributed the titular churches among the pastors of Rome ("titulos in urbe Roma dividit presbiteris").[7] Even though such statements are legendary in detail, their common denominator is to set the date of the tituli early.

d. The Christian usage of the term *tituli* is often seen to originate in the pre-Constantine period when Christian communities assembled in private homes. A *titulus* would have been the inscription of the name of the host. This inscription would have been located above the entrance of the house or apartment and visible to everyone who entered the assembly on Sunday.[8]

Even if we understood the term "titulus" connected with a name of a person (e.g., "titulus Sabinae") as a purely juridical term,[9] it would refer back to the pre-Constantine period when the communities were dependent upon the private property of individuals; "titulus" was a concept of property rights and indicated the legal basis for the ownership of material goods.

c. It fits this understanding of the term that the original names of the tituli were names not of saints but of private persons who had founded these title churches.

The evidence for this is as follows:

- "Tigrida," "Byzas/Bizantius," and "Equitius" were not names of Roman saints or martyrs.[10] The names point to private persons in Rome, concerning whom nothing other than their name is passed down in tradition. Later, therefore, their unknown names were exchanged for the names of saints. In the sixth century, the titular church "Byzantis" was renamed after Saints John and Paul.[11]

7. Cf. also the reference concerning Dionysius (259–68 C.E.): "Hic presbiteris ecclesias dedit et cymiteria et parrocias diocesis constituit" (*Liber Pont.* 1:157). Also cf. *Liber Pont.* 1:122, in regard to Cletus, and 164; 73–75 in regard to Marcellus.

8. So, e.g., J. Martin, *Atlas* 19ˣ. Naming the place after the host corresponded to practical needs. (In present-day community life community circles that regularly meet in the same home often call themselves by the name of the host, for example, "Meier's sowing circle.")

9. Cf., e.g., R. Vielliard, *Origines,* 28; R. Krautheimer, *Corpus,* 8. Skeptical is Ch. Pietri, *ACIAC* 9 (1978): 566.

10. While "Tigrida" and "Byzas/Bizantius" are not names of saints at all, there is a sixth-century saint named Equitius from outside of Rome (cf. E. Stadler and J. N. Ginal, *Heiligen-Lexikon,* 2:76); at that time the Roman title "Equitii" had long been established and attested, e.g., in the synod list of 499.

11. Material in J. M. Petersen, *House-churches,* 268ff.

Since the sixth century, the titular church "Equitii" was named after St. Pope Silvester,[12] and the titular church "Tigridae" after St. Balbina.[13]

- At the Roman synod of 499 the Roman presbyters still signed their names with "tituli Caeciliae," "tituli Clementis," etc.; only at the synod of 595 did they sign with "tituli *sanctae* Caeciliae," "tituli *sancti* Clementis,"etc.[14] In the sixth century the names of the anonymous founders thus were identified with names of known saints, or those title churches were renamed for which no matching saints' names could be found (as with "Tigrida," "Byzas," "Equitius").

- In the fourth and fifth centuries the old tradition of naming a title church after its founder was still fostered when a new titular church was erected. I cite four examples. The *Liber Pontificalis,* which for the fourth and fifth century as a rule utilizes reliable and partly official documents, gives a creditable report concerning the founding of the tituli Vestinae, Damasi, and Marci. According to this source, at the beginning of the fifth century, the matron Vestina donated the real estate for the youngest titular church of Rome. Although the church was consecrated in the name of the holy martyrs Gervasius and Protasius, nevertheless, it received the name of the donor, Vestina.[15] Also the titular churches Damasi and Marci were named after their donors, the fourth-century popes Damasus and Marcus.[16] Finally, the titulus "Eusebius" was called after the founder of this titular church; in all versions the *Martyrologium Hieronymianum* notes on the 14 of August, "Eusebi tituli *conditoris*" ("of the title of Eusebius, the founder") (ed. De Rossi-Duchesne 106).[17]

---

12. Cf. J. P. Kirsch, *Titelkirchen,* 41ff.

13. Ibid., 94ff. Cf. further the renaming of the titular church "Gai" to "St. Susannae" in the sixth century (ibid., 70ff.).

14. See the signature lists in J. P. Kirsch, *Titelkirchen,* 7f.

15. *Liber Pont.* 1:220. At the synod of 499, three presbyters of this titular church still signed with the words, "tituli Vestinae." The donor's name still appeared on an epitaph from about 700 c.e.: *ICUR* 1:1185.

16. On the titular church *Damasi,* cf. *Liber Pont.* 1:212 and the Damasus inscriptions in the titular church (in J. P. Kirsch, *Titelkirchen,* 85f.) as well as Gregory the Great's *Dialog.* 4.31: The church still carried the name of the donor in the sixth century, although it was consecrated to a martyr, Laurentius. On the title church *Marci,* cf. *Liber Pont.* 1:202. Further, cf. the title *Apostolorum,* which at times carried the name of Empress Eudoxia, because she had financed the construction work under Sixtus III: *Liber Pont.* 1:508, 512; 2:3, 11, 24.

17. The high portion of women in the list of the 20 pre-Constantine tituli founders is striking: 9 women as compared to 10 men ("Fasciola" is not a woman's name but a topographical designation). Valerian, in his persecution of Christians, expressly ordered that socially distinguished matrons be exiled and stripped of their fortune (Cyprian, *Ep.*

Conclusion: The 15 to 20 pre-Constantinian titular house churches (most likely from the third century; cf. Cornelius in the middle of third century) are indebted to private individuals who put space at the disposal of house communities. We arrive at the same result as in point 1: In the pre-Constantine period, the Christians of the city of Rome assembled in premises that were provided by private persons and that were scattered across the city (fractionation). In principle, there exists, therefore, a continuity between the structure presupposed in Rom 16 and the later net of titular churches in Rome. A small linguistic observation already points to this continuity. The tituli of the city of Rome are not the earliest proof that Christian community groups in the city were named after private persons who provided the facilities. The New Testament formula[18] ἡ κατ᾽ οἶκον τινὸς ἐκκλησία indicates that this was already the case in the first century C.E.[19]

The Christian fractionation stands against the background of *a Jewish community in the city of Rome that was broken up into a number of independent synagogue communities* (see in detail, Appendix 4). The parallelism is amazing, whether one wishes to consider the Jewish structure as a direct model for the Christians or not.

I have already offered further evidence for house-church communities scattered across the city:

a. In chap. 27, the Valentinian community in the *suburban villa on the Via Latina.*

b. In the legendary material (from chaps. 3, 13) the fractionated structure of house-church communities was presupposed throughout. Also to be mentioned are the acts of Nereus and Achilles (22: καὶ γέγονεν ὁ οἶκος...καθάπερ ἐκκλησία); *Act. Verc.* 13–15; 19f.; 29; Ps.-Clement, *Epit.* 2.144, and other places.

c. Justin's circle met in a rented lodging "above the bath of Myrtinus" (see above, on *Act. Just.* 3). In the same work, Justin attests that there are other house churches in Rome besides his. To the question, "Where do you assemble?" he answers, "There, where each one will and can." "Or do you mean that we all are accustomed to assemble in

80). On private persons who donated a synagogue for a Jewish community, see Hengel, "Stobi," 162–64.

18. Rom 16:5; 1 Cor 16:19; Phlm 2; Col 4:15.

19. The described structural continuity does not mean that somewhere there would be any continuity between an individual house church of the first century and an individual titular church of the third century. It is also improbable that the 15 to 20 gathering-places of the third century were in the same locations on which the titular basilicas from the fourth and the following centuries were erected. J. P. Kirsch interprets too categorically the Roman dwellings beneath the titular basilicas as house churches, without possessing sufficient archaeological proof (cf. below). His view of a continuity between titular house churches and later titular basilicas *in the same locations* has long been abandoned (cf. the congress acts ACIAC 9 [1978], 569, or the conference discussions RivArCr 61 (1985): 350–56).

the same place? It is by no means so." Justin claims that he does not even know the other assembly places (ibid.).

d. Justin, *Dial.* 47.2 testifies that the Christians met in private dwellings (κοινωνεῖν ἑστίας).

e. One can conclude from this evidence of fractionation an interpretation of *Apol.* 1.67. In this text Justin reports of a Sunday liturgy "in one place" (ἐπὶ τὸ αὐτό, 67.3); but a central assembly of Christianity in the city of Rome is by no means envisioned.[20] Justin here formulates much more generally, describing the Sunday worship of Christians, not only in Rome but in the entire world, in "cities and villages" (67.3). They gather "in one place" and together they all hold an assembly (κοινῇ πάντες τὴν συνέλευσιν ποιούμεθα, 67.7). *Apol.* 1.67 is analogous to *Act. Just.* 3, where Justin speaks of the assemblies in his rented lodging with the same term, συνέλευσις. *Apol.* 1.67 describes a *typical* liturgy in a house-church community as a pattern that takes place everywhere in the world on Sundays. To identify the "presider" (προεστώς) of the liturgy, who appears in *Apol.* 1.65.3, 5; 67.4f., with a monarchical Roman bishop who conducts a central liturgy for the Romans would be to read into the passage things that are not there. (For the history of the monarchical episcopacy in Rome, see below, chap. 41). The liturgy described in *Apol.* 1.67 was celebrated on Sundays in numerous places at the same time.

---

20. This sentence was already written when H. J. Klauck, *Hausgemeinde*, appeared. I am pleased that Klauck (70) independently comes to the same conclusion.

Chapter 37

Private Property Utilized
by the Church Community

What did the places of assembly provided by private persons look like? Second, did they remain the property of the private people who provided them, so that these persons can be called "hosts?" Or did these private individuals donate the premises, which, honored with the name of the donor, became the collective property of the community? Or were both legal forms valid for different periods?

Archaeological and Literary Findings

Only from the third century does archaeology first bring to light dwellings in which rooms were exclusively reserved for worship. These rooms were separated from the everyday household activity that surrounded them. The classic archaeological example of such house-churches of the third century is in Dura Europos.[1] This type of assembly rooms for worship in dwellings of the third century can only be hypothetically ascertained for Rome. I cite three examples.

a. Under the titular basilica of SS. *Giovanni e Paolo* (beginning of fifth century), an extensive living complex has been excavated,[2] which passed through several building phases and goes back to the Flavian period. It is located on the ancient Clivus Scauri, the present day Via SS. Giovanni e Paolo, on the west slope of the Caelius. On the Clivus side, the dwelling complex in the middle of the third century received a new facade with portico, above which were two rows of windows.

---

1. E. Dinkler, "Dura Europos III," *RGG*[3] 2:290ff. A house church in *Aquileia* dates from the time before Diocletian. On this see H. Kähler, *Kirche*, 65, 68f.; G. Synder, *Ante Pacem*, 73–75. For pagan cults in dwelling houses, cf., e.g., Delos (*IG* 11.4.1299). Synagoges in dwelling houses: Delos (first century B.C.E.), Dura Europos (third century), Stobi (third century), Hammam Lif in Tunisia, Priene, Aegina, and others. Cf. M. Hengel, "Stobi," *ZNW* 57 (1966): 161, 162, n. 57f.

2. Cf. A. Prandi, *SS. Giovanni e Paolo*; C. Cecchelli, *Monumenti*. Useful ground plan in F. Coarelli, *Archeologica*, 184. At the end of the second century, part of the complex, a *nymphaion*, was painted with a pagan fresco.

R. Krautheimer[3] concludes from the grouping and intervals of the windows, from the monumental steps, and from the reinforcement of the bottom floor walls (third century) that a great assembly room, extending through two stories of the edifice, was located in the second and third floors of the complex. The visitor entered the hallway on the ground floor and from there ascended to the assembly room, which was subdivided into two long sections by a line of pillars. There exists the *possibility* that this hall was designated for Christian assembly.[4] In any case, we find at the beginning of the fourth century,[5] only a half century later, Christian frescoes on the ground floor (among them a woman praying and an apostle-philosopher).[6] Later, in the fourth century, a so-called *confessio* was established under the assembly hall, which may be considered as a forerunner of the crypts in later basilicas. In the latter part of the fourth century, it was painted with Christian frescoes.[7]

　　b. In the immediate vicinity of *S. Martino ai Monti,* on the Mons Oppius, the remains of a two-story house were excavated. In its center there lay a hall, which, similar to that in SS. Giovanni e Paolo, is divided by two pillars. Smaller rooms are laterally joined to it.[8] One *can* ascribe a cultic function to this establishment and interpret it as a house church of the third century, as the titulus Equitii.

　　c. A brick complex from the second half of the third century belonging to the buildings under *S. Clemente* does not have intermediate walls. Therefore it could have been a great hall subdivided by pillars, which

---

　　3. *Architecture,* 8f.; *Corpus,* 1:267ff.

　　4. Besides R. Krautheimer, also, e.g., P. Testini, *Archeologia,* 552f.; J. P. Kirsch, *Titelkirchen,* 120ff. On the construction of an assembly hall in the middle of the third century, cf. Eusebius, *Ecc. Hist.* 8.1.5, where Eusebius confirms that new churches were built in the third century.

　　5. J. P. Kirsch, *Titelkirchen,* 123, even assumes the end of the third century, i.e., the long period of peace before Diocletian's persecution. M. T. Cecchelli, *Osservazioni,* 560, even proposes the middle of the third century.

　　6. Illustrations can be found in J. Wilpert, *Mosaiken,* 2:632, 635, 637f.; chart, 127f.; 129, 2. In the storage room cf. also the jugs decorated with a monogram of Christ and an Alpha/Omega (De Rossi, *Bullettino* [1890] 29ff.).

　　7. Illustrations in J. Wilpert, *Mosaiken,* chart 131.

　　8. Cf. R. Vielliard, *Origines;* P. Testini, *Archeologia,* 551f.; J. P. Petersen, *House-Churches,* 270f.; J. P. Kirsch, *Titlekirchen,* 119. Literary parallels may be cited for a worship assembly hall with diverse adjoining rooms: (a) In Cirta, before Diocletian's persecution, there existed next to a room used for cultic worship a dining room (*triclinium*), an archive, and an office for the poor with storage rooms for clothing and food (*Gesta apud Zenophilium,* Migne, *PL* 8:731f.). Considering that Cornelius counts 1,500 recipients of ecclesiastical relief and 155 clerics in Rome in the middle of the third century (Eusebius, *Ecc. Hist.* 6.43), one can vividly envision corresponding rooms for helping the poor as well as living quarters for clerics connected with liturgical assembly halls. (b) In Antioch during the second half of the third century, the house church, the τῆς ἐκκλησίας οἶκος, was connected with the bishop's quarters (Eusebius, *Ecc. Hist.* 7.30.19. (c) Synagogues with adjoining rooms can be found in Stobi, Ostia, and other places. Cf. M. Hengel, "Stobi," 164f.; 171, n. 92.

had wide entrances on the sides. These entrances opened into adjoining rooms, courtyards, or porticoes. In any case, they did not open into the street; the street was not close enough to the building. Also here one *can* imagine a titulus (cf. n. 7). The strongest argument, however, is that in the fourth century the area was remodeled by Christians into the present-day lower church of the basilica.[9]

There are analogous hypotheses for the Roman buildings under S. Prisca on the Aventine, S. Anastasia at the Circus Maximus, S. Caecilia in Trastevere, etc.[10] For us the negative evidence is important: such archaeological possibilities for liturgical assembly halls are nowhere evident for the first and second centuries. The literary evidence corresponds to this archaeological finding: terms such as "domus ecclesiae," "domus Dei," or "sacraria" are not yet attested for the first two centuries.[11] The term "basilica" used for a church is only first attested at the beginning of the fourth century.[12] Also the ecclesiastical office of doorkeeper (*ostiarius*), which indicates ecclesiastically administered localities, is not evident before the middle of the third century (Cornelius, in Eusebius, *Ecc. Hist.* 6.43.11).

In view of the concurrence of archaeological and literary evidence, we may conclude that, in the first two centuries, there were no "house churches" in the sense of specific rooms permanently set side for worship in secular houses.[13] Positively speaking, the Christians of the first and second centuries celebrated their liturgy in rooms that were used in everyday life. This means that the rooms used for Sunday worship had no special immoveable cultic equipment.[14] This explains the absence of

9. In regard to the complicated excavation findings under S. Clemente, see F. Guidobaldi, *S. Clemente,* and the review of this book by A. Nestori in *RivArCr* 56 (1980): 187–90 (Christian evidence at the earliest in the second half of the third century).

10. The new insula excavation in the area of San Lorenzo in Lucina on the Mars Field offers the latest possibility for building hypotheses. In regard to the results of the excavation, cf. F. Rakob, *Die Urbanisierung des nördlichen Marsfelds: Neue Forschungen im Areal des Horologium Augusti,* in: "L'Urbs, espace urbain et histoire (I siècle av. J. Chr–III. siècle ap. J. Chr), *Actes du colloque international organisé par le Centre national de la recherche scientifique et l'Ecole française de Rome (Rome 8–12 mai 1985)* (Rome, 1987), 687–712, here 704–5. In regard to Christian presence in the insula, of course only hypothetically on the basis of local tradition, see C. P. Thiede, "Rom: Archäologie, Frühchristliche Zeit," *Grosses Bibellexikon* 3 (1989).

11. Cf. further J. P. Petersen, *House-Churches,* 265f. On "Sacraria" see below, Minucius Felix.

12. J. P. Kirsch, *Cultusgebäude,* 16: the first time in the records of the African confiscation.

13. So also J. P. Petersen, *House-Churches,* 265f.; P. Testini, *Archeologia,* 112ff., 551, 555; R. Krautheimer, *Architecture,* 5f.; J. P. Kirsch, *Titelkirchen,* 126. The "house churches" as rooms permanently set aside for worship cannot be dated before 230 (Dura Europos) and not after 400 C.E. Cf. further P. Lampe, "Funktion," 533ff.

14. This is similarly valid for synagogues until 70: "the sacramental holiness of material things first found its way into the synagogues after the destruction of the Temple": M. Hengel, "Synagoge," 166.

any archaeological evidence for Christian assembly rooms in the city of Rome for the first two centuries. Christian circles met someplace in the basilica privata[15] of a wealthy Christian or on the third floor of an insula (cf. Acts 20:7ff.), in a rented lodging "over the bath of Myrtinus" (Justin, *Acta* 3), or in a suburban villa on the Via Latina (chap. 27). Justin witnesses that the gatherings of Christians in Rome took place where one preferred it or where it was possible.[16] One was not limited to special cultic rooms.[17]

Still at the beginning of the third century, Minucius Felix (*Oct.* 10.2–4) lets the pagan Caecilius Natalis complain on the beach at Ostia about the Christians: "Why do they take pains to hide the object of their worship.... Why have they no altars, no known sanctuaries? Why do they never speak publicly, never meet openly?... The deplorable Jewish people also worship one God, but nevertheless in public." The Christians have no "delubra et aras" (*Oct.* 32.1); they are "a social gathering shunning the light, silent in public, loquacious in a corner" (lucifugax natio, in publicum muta, in angulis garrula, *Oct.* 8.4).[18]

This may be valid until the third century. Minucius Felix, nevertheless, indicates in another passage the difference between the second and third centuries. He is the first to document the use of the term "sacraria" (9.1) for the Christian places of assembly, i.e., "cultic places," rooms that are apparently set apart for one specific function.

Private Property–Community Property?

For us the question of the legal background is relevant. One must assume — first heuristically — that, in the first two centuries, there was no real estate which was owned collectively and centrally administered by the church community. On the contrary, all property used by the church was de jure individual private property (owned or rented), that one fraternally placed at the disposal of the community according to the motto: "We have no hesitation to let one another partake of our property. With us everything belongs to everyone — with the exception of

15. Cf. Vitruvius, *De architectura* 6.5f. and 3.8; Pliny, *Nat. hist.* 36.4f.

16. "eo unumquemque convenire quo vellet ac posset" (*Acta Just.* 3). Justin, *Dial.* 41.3: the eucharist is offered ἐν παντὶ τόπῃ.

17. Cf. possibly also Hippolytus, *In Dan.* 1.17.6f.: "The church is not called a place or a house of stone or clay.... What is then the church? The holy assembly of those living in righteousness." In Justin, *Apol.* 1.65.1, it becomes obvious that the assembly rooms were not equipped for a baptismal immersion. After the baptism in any location where there is water (ἔνθα ὕδωρ ἐστί, 61.3), which could be a fountain in the courtyard, a bath, etc., the newly baptized was led into the place where the believers were assembled (ἄγομεν ἔνθα συνηγμένοι εἰσί): the two locations were not the same.

18. Minucius admits: "We know one God... and do not speak of him openly — unless a judicial hearing compels us to do so" (19.15).

the women."[19] The heuristic assumption is based on an observation of
the legal situation. In the Roman law governing organizations, the community treasury (arca communis) was also not considered property of a
corporation (corpus) but as the undistributed property of the individual
members. Correspondingly, a corporation could not be appointed heir;
it was not a legal person.[20]

Going outside the gates of the city to the catacombs, we find the confirmation that corporate community property, centrally administered,
was established *at the earliest* in the third century. Parallel to the "spe-
cialization" of rooms in private dwellings into "house churches" of the
third century, an interesting analogous development took place in the
necropolis. In the middle of the third century, as can be shown from
the literary and archaeological evidence,[21] extensive renovations were
undertaken in the catacombs, which were aimed at opening and extending the tombs of private families for a Christian general public. Within
the city, at the same time, around the middle of the third century, the
house on the Clivus Scauri was remodeled (see above, SS. Giovanni e
Paolo). The renovation, consisting of a new facade with a portico and a
great hall, presumably marked the end of the private use of a section of
the building in order to devote it exclusively to cultic function.

One can hardly help seeing behind these events of the third century
a legal transformation. Apparently, private property was turned over to
a now existing corporate ownership of the church community and was
centrally administered by the church.[22]

A further indication for the new arrangement in the third century
may be added. The division of the city into seven ecclesiastical regions
most probably originated with the same Pope Fabian (236–50 C.E.),
who remodeled the catacombs (n. 21). The *Catalogus Liberianus* reports
that Fabian divided Augustus's fourteen regions of the city among the
deacons (cf. *Liber Pont.* 1:4–5; 148; 124, n. 6; ed. Duchesne). Fabian's
successor, Cornelius, records in his letter the existence of seven deacons together with seven subdeacons (Eusebius, *Ecc. Hist.* 6.43). The

---

19. Tertullian, *Apol.* 39.10f.; cf. Gal 6:6; Phil 4:15; *Did.* 4:8; *Barn.* 19:8; Acts 2:42–
47; 4:32–37; 12:12.

20. In regard to this, cf. further C. Colpe, "Genossenshaft," *RAC* 10 (1978): 114.

21. *Liber. Pont.* 1:148; 157 (ed. Duchesne) on the pontificates of Dionysius and
Fabian. The *Catalogus Liberianus* (ibid., 1.4) already reads: Fabian (c. 236–50 C.E.) "mul-
tas fabricas per cimiteria fieri iussit." Cf. also C. Kirch, *Enchiridion,* 334, 547. On the
archaeological evidence, e.g., F. de Visscher, *Le Droit,* 275ff.; U. M. Fasola and P. Testini, "Cimiteri," 139 (from the middle of the third century onward). Archaeological and
literary findings coincide.

22. Cf. similarly, e.g., P. Styger, *Katakomben,* 129f., who dates the change of legal possession in the first half of the third century. Further, e.g., P. Testini, *Archeologia,* 112ff.;
120–22; J. P. Kirsch, *Cultusgebäude,* 5; 8: corporate, ecclesiastically administered property first from the beginning of the third century onward through gifts, bequests, and
purchases.

establishment of the seven ecclesiastical administrative districts would actually be most understandable if a corporate possession of real estate had arisen which was in need of administration.

I am not certain that already by the time of Zephyrinus (c. 199–217 C.E.) the cemetery on the Via Appia, supervised by Callistus, was *community* property (see chap. 3 for the reasons), as is continually asserted (e.g., H. Gülzow, "Kallist," 104; cf. *Christentum*, 166). The cemetery may be first referred to as community property when one began to bury bishops here around 235 C.E. Fabian here buried his predecessors, Anteros and Pontianus (see chap. 3). It appears to me that the legal change is most probable under his episcopate.

I will name further possible evidence for corporate ownership of real estate; all the examples date, at the earliest, from the third century:

a. At the beginning of the fourth century, the private property of individuals still appears to play a prominent role in community life. The edict circulated by Constantine and Licinius explicitly distinguishes the corporate property of the community from Christian private estates: ad ius corporis eorum id est ecclesiarum, non hominum singulorum, pertinenta. That is one side. On the other, this "Edict of Milan" testifies to the existence of corporate ecclesiastical property already before Diocletian's persecution; as corporate property, assembly places, and cemeteries were restored (Lactantius, *De mort. persec.* 48; Eusebius, *Ecc. Hist.* 10.5; cf. Augustine, *Breviarium collationis cum Donatistis,* 3.34, 36).

b. Lampridius (*Hist. Aug. Sev. Alex.* 49.6) narrates a (legendary?) episode from the years 222–35 C.E. Christians in Rome occupied a site that was contested by owners of hot food stands and taverns. The trial was decided by Alexander Severus: The place should belong to the Christians, because it is better that God be worshiped there — no matter in which way — than that the smells of food from a kitchen rise to heaven: "cum christiani quemdam locum, qui publicus fuerat, occupassent, contra propinarii dicerent sibi eum deberi, rescripsit (the emperor) melius esse ut quemadmodumcumque illic Deus colatur quam propinariis dedatur." Are Christians collective property holders here?

c. In Africa, Tertullian writes (*Ad Scap.* 3) that there are Christian cemeteries (areae Christianorum), which are known to the pagans as Christian property. This suggests community property administered by the church, because Tertullian (*Apol.* 39.5f.) asserts that the community takes care of the burial of the needy.

d. Further possible examples in Eusebius, *Ecc. Hist.* 7.30.19; 7.13; 8.1.5.

e. Under which legal title did the pre-Constantinian church communities of the third century possess corporate property? This is a difficult problem that, fortunately, is not mine to deal with but rather that of historiographers of the third century. De Rossi advocated the thesis that the communities appeared in the legal dress of burial societies and as such were capable of owning property. This thesis was repeated frequently, but it is not based on sufficient evidence. Only a few individual phenomena allow comparison with the *collegia tenuiorum*, such as the community treasury or the office of "presider" (e.g., Justin, *Apol.* 1.67.6; Hermas, *Vis.* 2.4.2f.; 2.6; 3.1.8). Others, like Marucchi, completely deny pre-Constantinian corporate Christian possessions; according to them, at least de jure, also in the third century everything was private property of individuals.[23]

To sum up: there was no community-owned real estate in the first two centuries. The real estate used by Christians lay divided in different private hands. The earliest cores of catacombs were scattered private tombs. The worship took place in private dwellings, in the homes of Christians who had room to assemble a house community.

If we combine chapters 36 and 37, we realize a connection between a social-economic factor (divided real estate possessions in different private hands) and a community structure (different house-church communities scattered over the city with no central location).

A second connection arises from a theoretical consideration. A house-church community consists only of as many members as there is room for in a private home.[24] This means that the lower the social level of the Christians, the smaller the dwellings and the smaller the house-church communities, and the greater the number of house-church communities that are necessary. And the greater the number is, the more fractionated is the entire Christianity in the city. Or, conversely, the more house communities (subfractions) are established in a city, the lower the social status of the Christians in this city. If, however, the number of Christians in the city increases while the number of the subfractions decreases, remains the same, or increases little in comparison (compare *at least* eight demonstrable house communities in the first century — probable many more — with *at most* twenty *tituli* in the third century; the number of Christians during this time rose by more than a factor of 2.5), then it is a sign that the social status of Christians has risen. There are more socially elevated among them than previously. This agrees completely with the results of Parts 3 and 4.

---

23. Literature: G. B. De Rossi, *Roma sotterranea*, 1:101ff.; 209f.; 2:8ff.; 258; 370ff.; 3:473; 507ff.; *Bullettino* (1864): 57f.; (1865): 90; R. L. Wilken, "Social Interpretation," *Church History* 39 (1970): 437–58; O. Marucchi, *Manuale*, 94ff.; G. Krüger, *Die Rechtsstellung*; G. Bovini, *La proprietá*; J. P. Waltzing, *Etude*, passim; P. Testini, *Archeologia*, 112–22 (overview of the research); F. De Visscher, *Le Droit*, particularly, 261ff.

24. For a Jewish worship community, a group of ten adult men is sufficient (*Meg.* 4:3 = T. Meg 4:14. If these bring along their wives, there are twenty. Matt 18:20 ("two or three" = "a few") presupposes still smaller house communities.

Chapter 38

The External Image of
Christian House-Church Congregations

What image did the house-church communities that gathered in private homes during the first two centuries project to those outside? Was it that of a guild or club (*collegium*,[1] *thiasos*)? Here is not the place to trace the *internal* organization of the house communities (the diverse offices). It concerns much more the question how the Christian house communities presented themselves *outwardly* to the pagan milieu and how they were understood by this environment.

I can only sketch a question[2] which in modern research has not been satisfactorily answered and which suggests points for further study. This study would have to operate not only, as here, on a local-historical basis but empire-wide. The question, connected with legal problems, is complex. Seeking in the sources terms that designate a Christian community group (διδασκαλεῖον, σχολή, collegium, curia, ἐκκλησία . . .), we must be aware that these terms were used on four levels of communication:

a. as a self-designation of Christians vis-à-vis themselves (e.g., ἐκκλησία, λαός; usage *within the community*)

b. as self-designation of Christians vis-à-vis the *pagans* (e.g., in the Apologies, as Tertullian, *Apol.* 39.21: "curia")

c. as a pagan designation of Christians (e.g., "conventiculum," in Galerius's edict of tolerance, Lactantius, *Mort. pers.* 34.4)

d. as a polemical designation by *Christians* for *heretical Christians* (e.g., διδασκαλεῖον, Hippolytus, *Ref.* 9.12).

These are four subjective levels of expression. What do we do, for example, if on the level of (d), Hippolytus reviles the Roman church

---

1. The second-century inscription from Rome that reads, "*collegium* quod est in *domo* Sergiae L.f.Paullinae," must be excluded (*CIL* 6:9148f.; 10260–64). This was suggested to be Christian by M. Sordi and M. L. Cavigiolo ("Chiesa domestica," 369–74). Detailed refutation in M. Bonfioli and P. Panciera, "Della cristianità," 185–201; "In Domo," 133–38.

2. Cf., e.g., C. Colpe, "Genossenschaft," *RAC* 10 (1978): 83ff., especially 142ff.; R. L. Wilken, "Kollegien," *Zur Soziologie*, ed. W. Meeks, 165ff.

community under Callistus as a simple "school," διδασκαλεῖον (*Ref.* 9.12)? For the characterization of the Roman Christians led by Callistus, this says nothing. We may obtain a "more objective" (i.e., "more intersubjective") picture of the appearance of Christian communities in the pagan society if a term of level (c) is encountered at the same time on level (a) or (b). Only then can we assert: yes, this was the "role" that the Christian community played in their milieu, a role that corresponded not only to the self-understanding of the players but also to the understanding of the observers. But such concepts are rare. De Rossi (chap. 37, n. 23) thought he had found one such concept when he postulated that Christian groups had organized themselves as legal *collegia tenuiorum* or *collegia funeraticia* and had been acknowledged as such. This hypothesis has long been abandoned for lack of evidence. That the Christian groups were not *legalized* as *corpora* or *collegia* is one of the certain statements we can make. The government at best considered the Christian groups as *prohibited* societies (Pliny, *Ep.* 10.96.7: as prohibited *hetaeria;* cf. Tertullian, *Apol.* 38.1). In the geographical and chronological boundaries established here (Tertullian and Cyprian, e.g., would contribute some essential information),[3] I do not see myself in the position to do justice to the problem. I can only inductively collect fragments from the Roman material and with these stimulate further research. This makes more sense than deductively applying results from later sources that originate from outside of Rome to the Roman house-church communities of the first and second centuries.

1. The first and, in my opinion, still the most fitting concept we have to adhere to, although this may sound banal, is that of the οἶκος (Rom 16:5; Hermas, *Sim.* 8.10.3; 9.27.2).[4] The community life of the Christians formed itself in many respects according to the *oikos* model; 1 Tim 3:4f. formulates this clearly.[5] What does that mean for the house communities that assemble in private homes? In the categories of *oikos*-structure these assemblies are neither social gatherings of *collegiums* nor meetings of a philosophical *thiasos,* but simply the *private invitation of a host* to the fellow Christians in his district of the city.

Before I cite material that shows this type of appearance of the Roman Christian assemblies, I would like to illustrate the custom of

---

3. Cf. some information in C. Colpe, "Genossenshaft," *RAC* 10 (1978): 142ff.

4. The Christians were delighted to take fellow Christians into their homes: ἡδέως εἰς τοὺς οἴκους αὐτῶν ὑπεδέξαντο τοὺς δούλους τοῦ θεοῦ. In my opinion, what is reflected here is not only hospitality for travelling strangers but also the form of socialization that we call "house-church community." Cf. also *Mand.* 8.10.

5. Cf. further, P. Lampe, "Funktion der Familie," 539. Cf. also D. Lührmann, "Haustafeln," 83–97, especially 93; 85ff., on the Greek authors "concerning management of a household" since Xenophon, which is parallel to the New Testament household codes.

apophoreta with the aid of Petronius's *Sat. 56*. A pagan host was accustomed to present his guests with small souvenirs, which they took home with them from the table. One received a side of bacon, another salted pretzels, a third raisins and Attic honey. We readily find evidence of this custom in Roman Christian assemblies. *Traditio Apostolica* 28 (ed. Botte) reads: "si communiter vero omnibus oblatum fuerit quod dicitur graece *apoforetum* accipite ab eo."[6] In the context, in *Trad. Apost.* 25–30, different types of gatherings for a meal are dealt with (eucharist, agape, feeding of widows); the *apophoreta* of 28 are given at the agape banquets. Occasionally these agapes, as with pagan banquets, were marked by excessive convivial drinking: *Trad. Apost.* 28 found it necessary to warn explicitly against drunkenness, noise, and quarreling (non ad ebrietatem! inquietudo, dissolutio, contentio). Otherwise he who had invited you ("qui vocat/vocavit vos") would be upset.

> "et non ut...tristetur, qui vocat vos, in vestra inquietudine, sed oret ut dignus efficiatur ut ingrediantur sancti ad eum": "and that he who invites you be not grieved by your disturbance; he should pray to be proved worthy, that the saints enter into his home."

Here the private host is explicitly mentioned.[7] A few lines further, the host of the banquet sends the leftovers from the banquet to the people who could not be present ("qui vocavit vos, mittat... "). And in a chapter before this, in 27, each participant in the banquet is reminded to be grateful to the one who invited him or her, since it is for this reason that the latter invited the guests under his roof ("memor sit...eius qui illum vocavit; propterea enim depraecatus est ut ingrediatur sub tecto eius").

The oikos-situation characterized by the relation between host and guests defines the external appearance of many Christian assemblies, at least of meetings where the agape was celebrated. But, in my opinion, not only there: it is improbable that a pagan neighbor could distinguish whether the Christians who arrived in the neighboring house assembled for an agape or for a eucharist. The gathering for eucharistic worship would also have appeared to the pagan neighbor looking out of his window to be a private party of an owner of a dwelling — although *inside* during the eucharistic celebration the host did not play as much of a role as during an agape, but rather church officials, presbyters, did. The question here is how the house communities assembled for worship

---

6. In view of the technical term ἀποφόρητον (cf. also Athenaeus, 6.229C), it is highly unlikely that this involves any particles of the communion host. At best, this understanding may be valid for later editors of the text (v. 1: "si dantur vobis partes omnibus simul, accipies partem tuam tantum"): cf. E. Peterson, "ΜΕΡΙΣ," 3–12.

7. Although the next sentence reads, "Vos enim, *inquit,* estis sal terrae" (Matt 5:13), here Christ is not spoken of as the actual host: "oret...etc." excludes such an interpretation. That the word "inquit" is unexpectedly inserted without a mark of change in the subject is understandable in connection with a well-known Jesus logion.

appeared to the external world. It is noteworthy that the house communities were named by the Christians after their private hosts: "the church in the home of Prisca and Aquila," "the titulus of Sabina," etc. (see above). The hosts continuously played a prominent role for the house communities even though their position within the house communities might have been surpassed by the presbyters and deacons.

2. Justin's circle represents another type of house community, with a different emphasis. The private character remains common with the previous type. The Christian philosopher Justin taught individual students or groups of students in his home as a private teacher (see above, chap. 25). "I (Justin) live above the bath of Myrtinus...I do not know any other place of assembly, only the one there. Whenever anyone wished to come to me, I shared with him the words of truth" (*Acta Just.* 3). Justin also functions as private host, but, at the same time and above all, his house circle is centered in his person as *teacher*. As we saw, Justin presents himself and his students consciously as a *philosophical school*. From the pagan point of view, his Roman contemporary Galen (see above) can actually later place Christianity on the same plane as the philosophical schools. That means that here a consensus is achieved between some pagans and some Christians concerning how a portion of the Christian groups are to be designated. We have before us the unusual case that the three levels of understanding, *a* to *c* above, coincide.

On the relation of Justin's philosophical circle to the other house-church communities of the city there is, unfortunately, little source material extant:

a. Justin feels himself closely bound to the rest of Christianity in the city; he defends it in his *Apology*. But that does not mean that all of his theological views, for example, his predilection for a thousand-year reign, were shared by the other Christians of Rome. In *Dial.* 80.2–5 it becomes apparent that not only heretics like Marcion but also orthodox believers can think differently from him: among the orthodox believers, Justin says, there are those who "in all points" possess the correct view and those who only in general share the "authentic view." Justin's theology of the Logos was not shared either by the common folk among the orthodox believers but was viewed with suspicion.[8]

b. The (only relative) theological proximity of Justin to the other orthodox house-church communities of the city does not mean that he cultivated intense social contact with them. In the hearing before the praefect, Justin testifies (in the above quote) that he is cognizant only of the assembly place "above the bath of Myrtinus." Justin and his followers do not go on Sundays to another location and to another house community for the worship. Since Justin in his *Apol.* 2.4.4 (and 2.10)

---

8. See below, chap. 39 with n. 9.

emphasizes the Christian's obligation during a judicial hearing "to tell the truth in everything," we cannot easily dismiss the statements of his own hearing as false testimony given to protect fellow Christians. We have to consider that Justin's circle existed very autonomously, as a free school, an organization independent from the rest of the house-church communities of the city.

c. After all is said, we must conclude that Justin's group, meeting "above the bath of Myrtinus," conducts its own worship services, in which a "presider" (προεστώς), a "lector," and "deacons" function, as described in *Apol.* 1.67. This text neither describes a central worship service for all the Christians of Rome nor offers an "eyewitness report" of the Sunday liturgy in Justin's dwelling but rather describes the *type* of worship that takes place *everywhere* in the city, the land and the world (πάντων κατὰ πόλεις ἢ ἀγροὺς μενόντων); we saw this at the end of chap. 36. Justin's circle would have celebrated according to this type. Schools with religious rituals and common meals are also not uncommon in paganism (chap. 25, n. 84). From the sources I do not see what stands in the way of the thesis that *each* Christian group that gathered as a house community in a private dwelling in Rome had its *own* liturgical officers, a "presider," a "lector," and "deacons," who assisted the "presider" (see further chap. 41).

Roman Christian groups that crystallized around a teacher as their center are found similarly gathered around Tatian,[9] Cerdo,[10] or Marcion's disciples Apelles[11] (Syneros[12] and Lucanus[13]). Also the Valentinians in their esoteric gatherings have the character of an individual school. They designate themselves as μαθηταὶ Χριστοῦ and with this they adapt themselves to the terminology of the philosophical schools; the orthodox "Great Church" of that time had reserved the title μαθητής for the martyrs and the historical disciples of Jesus.[14] Terms designating a school structure are frequent in regard to the Valentinians: διδασκαλεῖον, σχολή, διδάσκαλος ἐπιφανής or δόκιμος, μανθάνων, μαθητής, ἀκροατής.[15]

---

9. See above; at least one Roman student, Rhodon.

10. Cf. Epiphanius, *Haer.* 41.

11. Rhodon in Eusebius, *Ecc. Hist.* 5.13.7: διδάσκαλος. E.g., Tertullian, *De carne* 8; Epiphanius, *Haer.* 44.1: σχολή.

12. Rhodon in Eusebius, *Ecc. Hist.* 5.13: he has his own school.

13. Origen, *Contra Cel.* 2.27: τοὺς ἀπὸ Λουκάνου.

14. E.g. Ignatius, *Eph.* 1.2; Ignatius, *Trall.* 5.2; Ignatius, *Rom* 5.3; Ignatius, *Pol.* 7.1; *Mart. Pol.* 17.3.

15. See H. Kraft, *Gnostisches Gemeinschaftsleben* (Diss. Heidelberg, 1950), 107f., 177f., 154. On the school structure cf. also *Evg. Ver.* NHC 1:19.15ff. as well as the diatribe style of the Rheginus letter, which is perhaps Valentinian (NHC 1:43.25–50.18). Ptolemaeus's letter to Flora is a skillful pedagogical instruction concerning the Old Testament (see above, chap. 19).

3. Other characteristics of the Valentinians remind one of a *mystery cult*. The circle of initiated, the pneumatics, are held together by a "secret tradition."[16] We saw how the Valentinians celebrated their sacramental rites with torches.[17] In these rites the singing of Valentinian hymns (e.g., in Hippolytus, *Ref.* 6.37) had their *Sitz im Leben*. Also the Carpocratians with their cultic pictures and their idiosyncratic community life, in which neither social origin nor individual possessions nor sex played a role (see above), are most readily to be compared to a mystery cult.[18]

On the whole we find in the texts of the gnostics little direct information concerning their worldly community life; for them this topic was not sufficiently important. "When the Valentinian texts speak of the ἐκκλησία of the pneumatics, this term does not designate *the manner in which the pneumatics exist in the world or even their organization* but solely an ἀντίτυπος τῆς ἄνω ἐκκλησίας."[19] Tertullian, *Praescr.* 41,7f. confirms that the gnostics are indifferent to ecclesiastical community structures in the world, especially to the church community's offices ("alius hodie episcopus, cras alius; hodie diaconus, qui cras lector; hodie presbyter, qui cras laicus; nam et laicis sacerdotalia munera iniungunt"). The Valentinian community regulation NHC 11:1[20] reinforces this impression. It does not deal with "official positions" but with manifold "gifts of the spirit." Community is a dynamic spiritual organism.

Minucius Felix (9.5) attests that pagans can actually compare the Christian community organizations with mystery cults. Some pagans spread rumors concerning alleged initiation rites of the Christians ("de initiandis tirunculis") and imaginatively depicted mysterious things that allegedly took place during the initiations ("sacris inbuatur").

4. A fourth form of a Christian house-church community that was understandable for pagans may be sketched. According to Rom 16:10f., Christian slaves or freedpersons of the pagan master Aristobulus congregate in a house-church community of their own; so do the Christian slaves of freedpersons of the pagan master Narcissus.[21] The same phenomenon can be seen in four cases regarding the Roman Jews: Slaves or freedpersons of the same household come together to form a synagogue of their own: the συναγωγὴ Ἀγριππησίων, the synagogue τῶν Αὐγουστησίων, and the synagogues of the Volumnenses and of the

---

16. Secret tradition: cf., e.g., the end of the letter of Ptolemaeus to Flora; Irenaeus, 1.4.3; 1.15.6; Clement, *Strom.* 7.106.

17. Cf., e.g., the enumeration of sacramental rites in *Phil. Evg.* logion 68 or Tertullian, *Adv. Val.* 30; Irenaeus, 1.21; 1.13.

18. So also C. Colpe, "Genossenschaft," *RAC* 10 (1978): 150.

19. H.-G. Gaffron, *Philippusevangelium*, 91 (emphasis mine).

20. In K. Koschorke, *Die Polemik*, 69–71; also his article "Gemeindeordnung," 30–60.

21. Treated more extensively under two different aspects above, chaps. 36 and 16.

Herodians (see Appendix 4). That the domestics of a house form an independent cultic entity was also common in paganism. In pagan households and estates associations of slaves took care of the cult of the Lares or of the cult of the master's genius. The slaves themselves exercised the honorary functions in these cultic communities, including priesthood.[22]

5. Summary. What did Christian communities look like to pagan contemporaries? Some looked like an assembly of guests in the dwelling of a hosting houseowner, others like a philosophical school, others like a mystery cult, others like a cultic unity within the servant population of one household. These four categories offer the pagan contemporary possibilities of classifying the Christian communities. All Christian communities that can be associated with one of the four types can be designated by us as "house-church communities," as worship communities, if we consider their internal activity:

a. Groups with the character of a school, such as the Valentinians, nevertheless celebrate liturgical sacraments. This applies, in my opinion, also to Justin's school.

b. Groups reminiscent of the mystery cults, such as the Carpocratians, understand themselves as Christian communities (Irenaeus, 1.25.3) that congregate for common worship. In the case of the Carpocratians, cultic pictures were involved in this worship.

c. Christian slaves of the same household or

d. Christian guests of a house owner congregate on Sundays for worship.

The term "house-church community" (= "worship group in a house") is adequate for all of these groups, as long as we do not also define "house-church community" as a group that exhibits a certain order of offices (with presbyters and deacons). The New Testament worship assemblies of the first generation show that this latter definition would be impossible. The way offices and functions were organized cannot determine whether the term "house-church community" can be attributed to a community or not. We also do not come any further in the discussion if we keep reserving the term "house-church community" for orthodox congregations and designate the heretical groups as "conventicles." The heretical congregation was also a "house-church community," and the orthodox groups, which met in private dwellings, also "conventicles."

I am aware that I have merely opened a can of worms surrounding these problems. The root of the difficulty in the material lies probably

---

22. Cf. E. M. Staerman, "Der Klassenkampf," 324f. Cf. also the households of Christian masters in which pagan slaves worshiped idols (*Can.* 41 Elvira) or Roman households in which the domestic servants fostered an eastern religiosity that was foreign to the master (Tacitus, *Ann.* 14.44.3).

in the fact that no one in the ancient world really knew how the Christian community organizations were to be described as phenomena in the pagan society. The apologists groped for analogies from pagan organizations and cults. The pagan Caecilius called the Christians simply "an obscure society," inscrutable (Minucius Felix, 8.4; 10.2ff.). Therefore, the suspicion of many pagans was aroused, *suspicio*. Apparently, Christians did not succeed in making themselves so "transparent" in the pagan milieu that accusations and prejudices would have been reduced. Prejudices, accusations, legal uncertainty, and fear of denunciation hindered Christians from venturing into the public light and from making themselves "transparent" — a vicious circle. There was a communication deficit between the two sides. Misunderstanding dominated broad areas — just as it had been for Jesus of Nazareth, who was erroneously executed by the Romans as a political messianic pretender. This deficit in communication between Christians and the pagan milieu, which at least the apologists sensed, would be the theme for a separate monograph.

Chapter 39

Fractionation and
Theological Pluralism

Does the phenomenon of fractionation have any consequences for *theology*?

1. Does the fractionation into house communities that were scattered throughout the metropolis favor the development of theological pluralism? In Rome of the second century we find evidence of breathtaking theological diversity. Besides the representatives of orthodox Christianity,[1] we saw in their own circles Marcionites with their independently (Apelles!) developed school sections, Valentinians, Carpocratians, dynamistic monarchians (= Theodotians), modalistic monarchians under Praxeas, Montanists (even in two theologically distinctly marked groups),[2] Quartodecimans,[3] Jewish Christians with Torah observance,[4]

---

1. They outnumber the others. Celsus pictures orthodox Christianity over against the heretics as the "Great Church" (Origen, *Contra Cel.* 5.59; cf. 5.61). On the other hand, one must note that in the third century Hippolytus (*Ref.* 9.12) can still get away with polemically giving the title of διδασκαλεῖον to the "Great Church" gathered around Callistus without risking being laughed at by his listeners. Hippolytus distances himself from the Christians under Callistus as from other heretical groups by calling them "school group."

2. At the latest by the last quarter of the second century a group of Montanists from Phrygia in Asia Minor lived in Rome: Eusebius, *Ecc. Hist* 5.3.4; cf. Tertullian, *Adv. Prax.* 1. About 200 C.E. there are *two* groups, one more influenced by modalism under a certain Aeschines (Ps.-Tertullian, *Adv. haer.* 7f.; cf. Hippolytus, *Ref.* 8.19; 10.26; Jerome, *Ep. ad Marcellam* XLI) and a group tending towards Logos theology (Ps.-Tertullian, ibid.) under Proclus (see above, chap. 30, n. 18).

3. Since the first half of the second century, they foster their eastern fasting and Easter praxis in Rome: Irenaeus in Eusebius, *Ecc. Hist.* 5.24.14f. At the end of the century, Blastus is one of their leaders (Eusebius, *Ecc. Hist.* 5.15 and 5.20.1; Ps.-Tertullian, *Adv. haer.* 8.1).

4. Justin, *Dial.* 47.3, gives evidence of a group of Jewish Christians who keep the Torah, force it upon other fellow Christians, and withdraw from every association with them when fellow Christians are unwilling to comply with the Torah. The Roman situation, among others, is likely to be reflected here (see above, chap. 11, n. 10). It appears to me questionable, however, that the (Jewish) Christians mentioned in *Dial.* 47.1, 2, who keep the Torah but neither force others to do so nor refrain from associating with those who don't, actually existed in Rome (so C. Osiek, *Poor and Rich,* 117). Justin is constructing here in the *Dialogue* a theoretical, hypothetical case. Correspondingly, G. H. Williams's assertion about the "still quite Jewish and Jewish-Christian milieu of the community of faith out of which Justin writes" appears to be quite exaggerated (see above, chap. 5, end) ("Baptismal Theology and Practice in Rome as Reflected in Justin Martyr, in

Cerdo with his Gnosis.... [5] Hermas is annoyed at the "false" teachers
(διδαχὰς ἑτέρας εἰσφέροντες *Sim.* 8.6.5 passim). The anonymous author in Hippolytus, *Ref.* 8.10.8ff., observes a multiplicity of Christian
αἱρέσεις.[6]

I observe the simultaneous appearance of topographical fractionation
and theological multiplicity. It makes sense therefore to presume that the
one promoted the other, even if not in a causal genetic sense. Most of
the theological tendencies represented in Rome did not *originate* there
but were imported into the capital city. With the word "promoted" is
meant that the fractionation made possible for a long period of time the
survival of the theological multiplicity that inundated Rome.

2. A further social-historical factor stands in correlation with the
theological pluralism. Some Roman circles of Christians are aligned according to their country of origin — at least the Montanists, who came
from Asia Minor (n. 2), and the Quartodecimans, who continued to
foster in Rome their Asia Minor fasting and Easter practices (n. 3).
The Quartodecimans were more attached to their native bishops in Asia
Minor than to Bishop Victor in Rome.[7]

It is evident that a cohesiveness in national groups encouraged theological particularism: in circles of people from the same geographical
region, peculiar native traditions could continue to be fostered. However, this correlation can also be viewed from the opposite direction:

A. Blane and T. Bird, eds., *The Ecumenical World of Orthodox Civilization: Russia and Orthodoxy,* Festschrift for G. Florovsky [The Hague, 1974], 11).

5. Cf. a list of Roman heretics already in C. P. Caspari, *Quellen,* 309ff. The Elkasaite Alkibiades (Hippolytus, *Ref.* 9.13) first appeared in Rome in the third century. The modalist Noetus (Hippolytus, *Ref.* 9.7ff.; 10.27; Epiphanius, *Haer.* 57) hardly taught himself in Rome; only his student Epigonus and the latter's student Cleomenes worked there at the beginning of the third century (Hippolytus, *Ref.* 9.7; see above, chap. 24).

6. In this he perhaps had the Roman scene in view; thus K. Koschorke, *Die Polemik,* 190. In his *Hippolyt's Ketzerbekämpfung,* 100f., Koschorke presumes that behind Hippolytus's bundle of sources there stands a Roman group from the end of the second century, a group of gnostic provenance. The author in 8.10.8ff. would consequently be a gnostic. Celsus offers the same picture of multiplicity (in Origen, *Contra Cel.* 5.61–65): in Christianity a multiplicity of ideas, voices, and traditions mingled without resolution. W. Bauer (*Rechtgläubigkeit,* 219, n. 1), who otherwise praises Rome as a refuge of orthodoxy (231ff.), presumes that Celsus had acquired his picture of Christianity in Rome, among other places.

7. This is to be deduced from Victor's "two-front battle" during the Easter controversy (Eusebius, *Ecc. Hist.* 24.8ff.; 23.3) against the *Roman* Quartodecimans under Blastus (Eusebius, *Ecc. Hist.* 5.15; 5.20.1) as well as against the Quartodeciman bishops in *Asia Minor.* This double front, in my opinion, makes Victor's harshness in the Easter controversy more understandable. Because the problems with Blastus's faction in his own city were urgent (and indeed so that Blastus successfully gained followers from Victor [ibid., 5.15]), Victor was unforgivingly harsh in the empire-wide Easter controversy against the mother communities of the Quartodecimans, in Asia Minor. His attitude moved many contemporaries to misgiving and to attempts at appeasement (ibid., 24.10ff.) It appears to me that Victor's harshness in the foreign politics of the Easter controversy was in good part motivated by internal political reasons.

because one holds on to native traditions, one unites with fellow countrymen in a foreign country. It appears important to me that we do not exploit these kinds of correlations in a one-way causal manner. It is a matter of more complicated, reciprocal interaction.

The phenomenon of national grouping is, as expected, not confined to Christians in the metropolis of Rome. In the fractionated Jewish population of Rome (see Appendix 4), several synagogues are aligned according to geographical origin. The natives of Tripoli (*CIJ* 1:390), the people from Arca/Lebanon (*CIJ* 1:501), those from Skina/North Africa (*CIJ* 1:7), and those from Elaea (*CIJ* 1:281; 509)[8] — all have their own synagogues. Also the pagan immigrants show the same tendency. Athenaeus (*Deipnosophistes* 1.20b) confirms many colonies of immigrants living independently in Rome in a relatively isolated way (κατ᾽ ἰδίαν δὲ τὰς πολλάς), so that Rome actually consists of many cities.

3. Finally, not only are there the fractionated external topographical reality and the grouping by geographical origin, but also, third, the social educational differences that run parallel to the theological pluralism. All four factors correlate with each other. In Part 4 we observed the most diverse educational backgrounds and saw how these combined with the most diverse theological ways of thinking. Here were the Theodotians arising from Aristotelian Galenic logic (chap. 33), there the Valentinians tinged with, for instance, Plato (chap. 12). The uneducated folk tended toward modalistic notions (chap. 34). Justin's Platonically influenced school advocated a Logos theology, which was viewed with suspicion by the uneducated Christian folk.[9] We see how theological differences most naturally correlate with social-educational differences.

4. That "orthodoxy" was finally victorious over the many other tendencies has, in my opinion, *also* social-historical reasons.

a. Behind "orthodoxy" stands the mass of uneducated Christian folk. The orthodox Christian does not need a perfect secular education to grasp the truths of his or her faith, as is often attested (Lactantius, *Inst. div.* 6.21; Clement, *Strom.* 1.99.1; Tertullian, *Praescr.* 7.9–13; Origen, *Contra Cel.* 3.44). "Any Christian manual laborer can find God!" (Tertullian, *Apol.* 46.9). The victory of orthodoxy was thus also a "majority decision": the followers of the heretics were numerically outnumbered; orthodoxy, easily comprehended by the masses, constituted the "Great Church" (Origen, *Contra Cel.* 5.59: μεγάλη ἐκκλησία; the

---

8. Different cities named "Elaea" in H. J. Leon, *The Jews of Ancient Rome*, 146f.

9. For the mass of Christian folk, for the "simplices," the "economic" (οἰκονομία) Trinity and the christological usage of the Logos concept were suspect; modalistic ideas were favored by them (Tertullian, *Adv. Prax.* 3: "simplices...maior semper credentium pars...exapavescunt ad oikonomian"; cf. chap. 34, n. 3). Correspondingly, representatives of the "Great Church" Christian community like Zephyrinus and Callistus did not take up the Logos theology. Hippolytus could not find firm footing with it in the "Great Church" orthodox Christian community of Rome.

term was coined by Celsus). Whoever has this "Great Church" behind him succeeds. It is a simple law of gravity.

b. When one compares H. Gülzow's works on Callistus and Hippolytus (e.g., "Soziale Gegebenheiten," 223f.; *Christentum*, 162ff.), a further aspect emerges besides the social-educational one. Callistus commended himself to the masses of common people through a comprehensive charity program with which Hippolytus did not compete in any comparable way. It is not by chance that our sources concerning early Christian assistance to the poor are, not exclusively but mostly, orthodox sources. Also in this regard, orthodox Christianity was more attractive to the masses, and it succeeded.

Chapter 40

Fractionation and Tolerance of People with Other Theological Opinions

A further correlation between the fractionation and the theology cultivated in the city is to be considered. Did the fractionation into topographically separate house communities favor not only a theological pluralism but also a tolerant attitude toward people with other theological opinions? We encounter this type of patience and tolerance in the Roman material at several places (see below). Had it something to do with the fractionation? As a model for connecting the two, we can reflect that the less closely one lives with persons of different thinking the less necessary it becomes to argue and to distinguish oneself from them. The further one lives apart, the fewer the points of contention.

I anticipate the conclusion: Before the end of the second century, specifically before the episcopacy of Victor (c. 189–99 C.E.), hardly any Roman Christian group excluded another group in the city from the communion of the faithful — apart from a few significant exceptions (see below). But how was ecclesiastical communion between topographically separate house communities made manifest? To illustrate, I name one means of attesting unity — there were others, which will be treated in the final chapter. In order to ensure fellowship and spiritual communion between themselves, the topographically separate congregations in the city sent pieces of the eucharistic elements to each other through messengers.

The evidence:

- Irenaeus in Eusebius, *Ecc. Hist.* 5.24.15: In Rome "people were never excluded because of this conduct [what is meant is the Easter and fasting practice of Asia Minor]; on the contrary, the presbyters who were in office before you [= Victor], who themselves did not follow (this specific practice) were accustomed to send the eucharist to those from other congregations who did observe

385

this practice" (οὐδέποτε διὰ τὸ εἶδος τοῦτο ἀπεβλήθησάν τινες, ἀλλ᾽ αὐτοὶ μὴ τηροῦντες οἱ πρὸ σοῦ πρεσβύτεροι τοῖς ἀπὸ τῶν παροικιῶν τηροῦσιν ἔπεμπον εὐχαριστίαν). Two things are clear: (a) The "presbyters before Victor" celebrated their eucharists in Rome topographically separated from the circles adhering to the Asia Minor practice of faith. Here the fractionation within the city is clearly presupposed. There were numerous separate liturgical gatherings, between which something could be sent back and forth. (b) Community and fellowship with each other were assured by sending the Eucharist.

• This sending became an established custom in Roman Christianity. Still later, at the time of the titular churches of late antiquity, the eucharistic gifts were sent out from the bishop's mass to the different titular churches in order to testify to the unity between the bishop and the titular priests. (*Liber Pont.* 1:169 and 216, Duchesne; De *fermento* vero, quod . . . per titulos mittimus . . . ut se a nostra communione . . . non iudicent separatos," so Innocent, *Ep. ad Decentium*, c. 5). In my opinion, the following texts may also be interpreted in this light.

• Justin, *Apol.* 1.67.5; 65.5 documents: The eucharist was sent by a messenger to those who were not physically present, and with whom communion should be maintained: τοῖς οὐ παροῦσι πέμπεται / ἀποφέρουσι. Must we think here only of sick or incapacitated members of one's *own* house-church community? The text does not compel such a limited interpretation. It is conceivable also that with the words "those who do not attend" members of *other* house-church communities in the city are meant.

• Also *Trad. Apost.* 28 testifies how important it was to send portions of a community meal to others who were absent. Chapter 28 is concerned with the sending of the remains of an agape meal. Those present should satisfy themselves but still leave some remaining in order that the host (qui vocavit te/vos), who gave the meal, can send the remains to others (mittat). As in Justin's text the note is open to both interpretations: those to whom the remains are sent need not be only absent members of one's *own* community circle. The host sends "to whomever he wishes" (quibuscumque voluerit/ad eos quos vult).

Let us investigate the connecting threads between the Christian groups. At which points were the ties of spiritual communion and fellowship severed ("excommunication")?[1]

---

1. On the problem, see the article by G. Lüdemann, "Zur Geschichte," 86–114 (investigates the relationship of Roman orthodox Christianity to Marcion, Valentinus,

1. In regard to the Quartodecimans, so we just learned from Irenaeus, in Eusebius, *Ecc. Hist.* 5.24.14f., no one severed ties prior to Bishop Victor. Victor and the community around Blastus were the first to break off having spiritual communion with each other (Eusebius, *Ecc. Hist.* 5.15; 5.20.1; 5.24.9).[2]

2. In the first half of the second century, Hermas knows several teachers whom he thinks are false. *Sim.* 9.22.1f.; 5.7.2; 8.6.5 bring into relief such "gnostics" (θέλοντες πάντα γινώσκειν).[3] But nowhere in all the polemic is there any word that they would have been separated from the community. *Sim.* 9.22.4 even talks mildly about them (οὐκ ἐγένοντο γὰρ πονηροί, μᾶλλον δὲ μωροὶ καὶ ἀσύνετοι); the second repentance announced to all Christians also is available to them (cf. also 9.19.2f.; 8.6.6). Within the framework of the numerous classifications that Hermas introduced for Christians, there is no distinction between teachers still remaining within the ecclesiastical community and those excommunicated.

3. The attitude of the Valentinians towards the remaining ("psychic") Christians has been worked out especially by K. Koschorke[4] and is here briefly sketched.

In the Valentinian model of ecclesiology, the church as a spiritual organism consists of two concentric bodies; the inner represents the Valentinian "pneumatics," the outer, the "psychics." As different levels of perfection, they constitute one organism. Not two exclusive, but two concentric spheres characterize the ecclesiological model.[5]

On the level of praxis this theoretical model means that the Valentinian explicitly seeks community with psychic Christians. He meets not only with the initiated in Valentinian house communities — for example, on the Via Latina — but beyond this he also goes out to house communities in which "psychic" Christians meet. There he is not to be distinguished from them in his expressions of faith (Irenaeus, 3.15.2). He formulates there the same expressions of faith as the "psychic"

Ptolemaeus; redactional and tradition-historical analysis of the most important texts). His conclusion is not totally new; cf. G. Bardy, "Les écoles romaines," 501–32, here 520f., 531; G. La Piana, "The Roman Church," 201–77, here 214; H. Langerbeck, *Aufsätze,* 173ff. (Valentinus "till the end as member of the Roman [orthodox] community").

2. On οἱ πρὸ Σωτῆρος in Irenaeus/Eusebius, *Ecc. Hist.* 5.24.14., cf. H. v. Campenhausen ("Ostertermin," 114–38, especially 121, 138): From *Soter* on, the pre-Easter fasting became customary also in Rome. That *Soter* cut the ties of communion (N. Brox, "Tendenzen," 291–324, here 304f.) is not stated in this text; Irenaeus's argument against Victor (Victor should emulate his peace-loving predecessors!) otherwise would collapse.

3. It is difficult to identify the content of their teaching. They apparently hold that libertinism does no harm, because all flesh is perishable.

4. "Gemeindeordnung," 30–60; so also *Die Polemik,* passim (9f., 2f., 7, 67f., 71, 79, 84, 89, 162f., 167f., 173, 176–91, 204, 207, 220–23, 228–30, 245–48).

5. E.g., *Exc. ex Theod.* 58.1. On this see K. Koschorke, *Die Polemik,* 220f.; cf. 191f.

Christians do in order to document his community with them.[6] But
he silently interprets the statements of faith differently. The "psychic"
understanding, in his eyes, is not false but a superficial and preliminary
stage of understanding, which is surpassed by the gnostic understanding.[7] Therefore the Valentinian lovingly labors with his "psychic" fellow
Christians[8] with the objective of leading those among them who are capable to the beginning of a higher, gnostic insight of faith, which will
finally be revealed in the house community of the initiated on the Via
Latina.[9]

Ptolemaeus's letter to Flora offers an example: A Valentinian in Rome
attempts to cautiously recruit his woman reader for a later initiation into
esoteric gnostic teaching.[10] At the same time the letter shows clearly
the author's effort to cultivate spiritual communion with the "psychic" Christians: Ptolemaeus avoids condemning the faith of the psychic
Christians who unreflectedly accept the whole Old Testament as given
"from the God and Father" (33.3.2–4). But he shows that one must
build upon this naive acceptance of the Old Testament; one must interpret the Old Testament and learn to differentiate. In this way he comes
to his complicated classification of the Old Testament laws in 2 x 3
parts. He clearly attempts to preserve the Old Testament for Christian
use in the face of wholesale Marcionite rejection. Ptolemaeus's model,
with its positive attitude toward the Old Testament, has the capacity to
be communicable to the representatives of "psychic" Christianity, and

---

6. References: Irenaeus 3.17.4 ("similia enim loquentes fidelibus"; cf. Tertullian, *Resurr.* 19; *Anima* 50). Irenaeus, *5.26.2; 4.33.3;* 1 praef.; 2.14.8; 2.28.4; 3.15.2; 3.16.6, 8;
4.32.1; 5.31.1; 5.18.1; 5.8.3. Tertullian, *Adv. Val.* 1 (*"communem* fidem adfirmant").
Therefore, they complain that Irenaeus desires to exclude them from the communion of
saints (Irenaeus, 3.15.2; "similia nobiscum sentire"). They understand themselves as Christians (*Phil. Evg.* NHC 2:3, log. 6, 49, 67, 95, 97; Justin, *Dial.* 35.2, 4, 6; Tertullian,
Adv. Val. 4.1) and protest against names such as "Valentinians" (Tertullian, *Adv. Val.* 4:
"scimus, cur Valentinianos appellemus, licet non esse videantur"). Tertullian, *Praescr.* 41.3
(*"pacem* quoque passim cum omnibus miscent"). Cf. also Tertullian, *Praescr.* 42.6 as well
as the perhaps gnostic author in Hippolytus, *Ref.* 8.10.8ff. (Jesus belongs to *all* αἱρέσεις;
in spite of all varieties, there is the desire for community).
7. References: Irenaeus, 3.17.4; 5.26.2; 3.12.12; 4.33.3; Tertullian, *Praescr.* 38; *Carne*
1; Ptolemaeus to Flora in Epiphanius, *Haer.* 33.5.9.
8. *Phil. Evg.* (NHC 2:3) log. 110f., 118, 45; Interpretatio (NHC 11:1) in
K. Koschorke, *Die Polemik,* 71, 168 (ibid., cf. also Heracleon, *Frag.* 17 and 27!).
Then Tertullian, *Praescr.* 42.5: they comport themselves as "humiles et blandi et sub-
missi"; Origen, *Hom.* 8.3 on Ezekiel: "gentle," no trace of nursing conflict. In regard
to the missionary impulse towards the psychic orthodox Christians cf. also *Ev. Ver.*
(NHC 1:3) 32.35ff.; Irenaeus, *Fragm. syr.* 28, Harvey, 2:457; Clement, *Strom.* 4.89.2;
91.3.
9. Cf. Tertullian, *Adv. Val.* 1, pointedly: First they convince them, then they teach
them. The latter occurs esoterically and most privately (Irenaeus, 3.15.2).
10. Only at a later point in time should Flora be instructed in esoteric doctrines:
33.7.8–10. Ptolemaeus recommends himself as teacher to her.

that means to keep its author in community with them. A connection between theological doctrine and irenic attempts at socialization becomes visible here.

Community also is emphasized when Ptolemaeus consciously uses common Christian terminology, for example, that of the "Apostolic Tradition" (33.7.9); he himself, Ptolemaeus affirms, stands in it. Again and again he quotes from the Gospels and Paul in order to document his agreement with the common Christian doctrines (33.3.5f.; 33.4.4, 11ff.; 33.5.7, 15; etc.). He emphasizes that his argumentation is exclusively based on the (Synoptic) "words of our Redeemer" (e.g., 33.3.8; 33.4.1, 3f.; especially 33.7.9).

The Valentinian Florinus extols his community with the "psychic" Christians of Rome (se unum esse e vobis: Irenaeus, *Fragm. syr.* 28, Harvey, 2:457). He flatters himself in the fact that he labors as a presbyter in union with Bishop Victor.[11]

The attitude of the Valentinians towards the other Christians is one side of the picture. What was the attitude of the rest of Christianity towards the Valentinians? In regard to Florinus, we just saw that Victor accepted him as a presbyter. Unhampered, Florinus circulated his Valentinian writings (Irenaeus, *Fragm. syr.* 28). In his letter to Florinus, also Irenaeus presupposes that the Christians under Victor are cultivating community with Florinus.[12]

It was quite a long time before Victor took offense at Florinus. Significant is the manner in which that occurred. First an *outsider*, Irenaeus from Gaul, incited Victor to intervene against Florinus and to suppress his writings, which had circulated as far as Gaul (Irenaeus, *Fragm. syr.* 28, Harvey, 2:457). Victor "obeyed": Florinus had to lay down his priestly office; the separation was made (Eusebius, *Ecc. Hist.* 5.15).

Of further interest is that Irenaeus insinuated that Victor had not read Florinus's Valentinian writings yet. Can Victor's behavior (tolerance until externally incited; ignorance) be comprehended in the face of the fractionation of the Roman scene? Victor accepted Florinus as a presbyter who served faithfully among the orthodox Christians in the sense of "similia loquens fidelibus" (n. 5). In the community of the "psychics," the Valentinian did not speak differently from them. Florinus's specifically Valentinian existence was spent elsewhere, for example, in

---

11. Irenaeus, in Eusebius, *Ecc. Hist.* 5.20.4; cf. 5.15. On heretical office holders in the "Great Church" who seek community with the orthodox Christians, see also Irenaeus, 4.26.3f.; cf. Tertullian, *Praescr.* 3.

12. In Eusebius, *Ecc. Hist.* 5.20.4: "These doctrines of yours, Florinus, . . . are at variance with the church; they plunge those who confess them into the greatest godlessness. The heretics who stand outside the church (as the Marcionites) have never dared to propose such doctrines." Florinus does not stand "outside" the church yet.

the esoteric house community on the Via Latina outside the city. Therefore it either escaped Victor's knowledge or was silently tolerated by him
because, there outside the city, it "harmed" hardly anything. Whether ignorance or silent tolerance, both possibilities lead to the same result: the
fractionation made it easy for Victor to continue to consider Florinus as
a brother.[13] It is first Irenaeus who comes between them. He is the first
successfully to draw clear boundaries:

a. Irenaeus (*Haer.* 4; *Praef.* 2) attests that the anti-Valentinian authors before him[14] had little success with their polemic (non...satis
potuerunt contradicere his, qui sunt a Valentino). He judges the reason
they had little success was that they were ignorant regarding the esoteric
doctrines of the Valentinians (quia ignorabant regulam ipsorum). That
corresponds to Victor's ignorance.

b. In Justin's *Apology* (1 and 2) the Valentinians are not mentioned
as heretics. *Apol.* 1.26 names only Simon, Menander, and Marcion. If
the teacher Ptolemaeus in *Apol.* 2.2 and the Valentinian Ptolemaeus are
identical (see above), Justin even praises him: he was a lover of truth
(2.2.10) and represented the doctrines of Christianity (2.9, 14) — in the
awareness of goodness διὰ τὴν ἀπὸ τοῦ Χριστοῦ διδαχήν (2.13).

About one decade later the scenario has changed. In the *Dialogue*
(35.6) Justin now also attacks the Valentinians: the name "Christian,"
which they claim for themselves, they do not deserve. "We have communion with none of them" (35.5: ὧν οὐδενὶ κοινωνοῦμεν). Behind the
"we" stands first of all the circle around Justin, which exists very independently in itself (see chap. 38) and whose views (chiliasm and Logos
theology) are not completely shared by all orthodox believers of the city
(*Dial.* 80.2–5, and see above, chap. 39, n. 9). The question is whether
Justin could convince other house-church communities in Rome of his
later anti-Valentinian position in the *Dialogue*. In view of the foregoing
note from Irenaeus (*non satis* potuerunt contradicere!) but also especially, in view of the tolerant attitude of Victor in the early years of

---

13. A further motive for Victor's tolerance could have been a high position that Florinus might have held in the imperial court, something advantageous for the Christians.
(Florinus held an imperial office in his younger years in the east: Eusebius, *Ecc. Hist.*
5.20.5. That he still held this office in Rome is not directly verifiable. There are even
reasons against this possibility mentioned above, chap. 27, n. 91). Two juxtaposed possibilities of explanation cannot be "either-or." A plant grows because it is watered *and*
because it is planted in the ground. Even if consideration of Florinus's imperial position
had contributed to Victor's tolerance, he could not have so fully realized his tolerance
without the fractionated structure of Christianity in the city.

14. Cf. as "fighters" against the Valentinians in the second century — but not in
Rome — an Asia Minor presbyter (Irenaeus, 1.15.6) as well as the rhetorician Miltiades
from Asia Minor (Tertullian, *Adv. Val.* 5; cf. Eusebius, *Ecc. Hist.* 5.28.4). Also Hegesippus
(in Eusebius, *Ecc. Hist.* 4.22.5) imparts a short polemical remark about the Valentinians.
On Justin see below.

his episcopacy, this is not probable.[15] Three further indications can be added to these two:

c. Traditions such as Irenaeus, 3.4.3 (Οὐαλεντῖνος μὲν γὰρ ἦλθεν εἰς Ῥώμην ἐπὶ Ὑγίνου· ἤκμασε δὲ ἐπὶ Πίου καὶ παρέμεινεν ἕως Ἀνικήτου) and Epiphanius's comment in *Haer.* 31 (in Egypt and Rome Valentinus still was considered to possess "some piety and orthodox faith"),[16] attest that Valentinus's teaching was unchallenged in Rome.

d. The anti-Valentinian writers of the second century (n. 13) find themselves disproportionately in the minority in relation to the anti-Marcionite authors of the same period. Communion with the Valentinians generally continued longer than that with the Marcionites.

e. Irenaeus (3.15.2) attests that as late as the 180s Valentinians often held lectures before orthodox Christians — and then were shocked when Irenaeus urged withdrawal from their fellowship.

Conclusion: Not only did the Valentinians seek fellowship with the other Christians but it also was offered to them in Rome well into the time of Victor. The circle gathered around Justin constituted the sole exception to this — and this was only in the later phase of Justin's group.[17]

---

15. The representatives of Logos theology (Justin, Irenaeus) and not the representatives of the Roman "Great Church" such as Victor, Eleutherus, Soter, and Anicet were the first to work towards the excommunication of the Valentinians. (See also M. Elze, "Häresie und Einheit," 389ff.). It took some time until the Logos theologians succeeded with this initiative in the "Great Church" community.

16. Cf. also Epiphanius, *Haer.* 30.7: in Cyprus Valentinus first broke with the orthodox church.

17. Further texts concerning the relationship between the Valentinians and the rest of the Christian community are historically unusable (see thus also G. Lüdemann, "Zur Geschichte," 89–94:

a. According to Tertullian, *Praescr.* 30, Valentinus — at first a follower of the "catholica doctrina" of the "ecclesia Romanensis" — was excommunicated for good just like Marcion ("novissime in perpetuum discidium relegati") after having been temporarily excluded before ("semel et iterum eiecti"). This is an old tradition exclusively concerning Marcion. The extension of the tradition to include Valentinus clearly goes back to Tertullian's redaction. The words "semel et iterum eiecti" are followed by a tradition that only concerns Marcion (the gift of money was returned). The same applies to the information contained in the words "in perpetuum discidium relegati": it follows a story that relates only to Marcion (his failed attempt at repentance). For Tertullian, Marcion, and Valentinus already belonged so tightly together (Irenaeus had set the example before him) that he unhesitatingly expanded traditions about Marcion to Valentinus.

b. Tertullian, *Adv. Val.* 4.1, reproduces a *commonplace* polemic against heretics (cf. K. Beyschlag, "Kallist und Hippolyt," 103ff.; K. Koschorke, *Die Polemik,* 68), which for Valentinus is no good evidence. According to this polemic, Valentinus had separated himself from orthodox Christianity ("de ecclesia authenticae regulae abrupit) because of injured ambition (without success he strove for the "episcopacy" in Rome). Tertullian himself admits that what he here reports about Valentinus might be a *general* customary revengeful reaction of ambitious people ("ut *solent* animi pro prioratu exciti praesumptione ultionis accendi"; cf. *Bapt.* 17. 2: "episcopatus aemulatio scismatum mater est"). Furthermore, Tertullian contradicts his other version in *De Praescr.* 30: here he writes "abrupit," there, "eiectus."

4. How the rest of the Roman Christians related to the Carpocratians in the 150s and 160s is hardly discernible. Irenaeus, 1.25.3: "Satan had sent forth these people (the Carpocratians) to blaspheme the holy name of the church, so that the (pagan) people turn their ears from the preaching of truth when they hear their different way of teaching and think we Christians are all like them. Indeed, when they see their religiosity, they dishonour us all." "They misuse the (Christian) name as a mask." All this means at least:

a. The Carpocratians, as the Valentinians, included themselves with the other Christians under the same name.

b. At least for the outsiders, the Carpocratian circle appeared to be connected to the rest of Christianity.

Irenaeus, who seeks to draw clear lines of demarcation, asserts in the 180s in Gaul that "we have no fellowship with them either in doctrine or in morals or in our daily social life" (ibid.). But that says little about the Roman situation in the 150s/160s of the second century when Marcellina and her Carpocratian group lived in Rome (ibid., 1.25.6).

We must leave open whether in Rome the representatives of the orthodox "Great Church" let the Carpocratians silently and without closer knowledge about them go their own way as they met in a house community in a private home somewhere in the city to venerate particular images (Irenaeus, 1.25.6) or whether they actively announced an excommunication of them.

5. A significant exception to the tolerance between different groups in the city was the case of the Marcionites. When Marcion appeared in Rome, he enjoyed fellowship at first.[18] There followed an interval when Marcion disturbed the Roman believers.[19] He appears to have

---

c. Irenaeus 3.3.4, sentence 1: "His (Polycarp's) authority is certainly greater and his testimony more reliable than that of Valentinus and Marcion and of the rest of the fools." Sentence 2: Polycarp, during his visit to Rome under Anicetus, had caused "many of the previously named heretics to return to the church" (πολλοὺς ἀπὸ τῶν προειρημένων αἱρετικῶν ἐπέστρεψεν εἰς τὴν ἐκκλησίαν τοῦ θεοῦ). The text appears at first glance to presuppose a division between the Valentinians and the rest of the Christians. Let us look closer. Clearly, the mention of the Marcionites and the Valentinians in sentence 1 as a value judgment of Irenaeus is attributable to the redaction. The tradition concerning Polycarp's leading "heretics" back to the church (sentence 2 — one thinks first of the Marcionites) thus is first connected with the Valentinians by secondary redaction. For Irenaeus, the redactor, the Valentinians and the Marcionites are to be named in one breath.

d. That Valentinus went from Rome to Cyprus (Epiphanius, *Haer.* 31) by no means indicates that he had been excommunicated or had feared such. The great plague of 166 also forced Galen to leave Rome for Pergamon. In other words, we know nothing concerning Valentinus's reasons for leaving Rome.

18. See above, chap. 24, in regard to the gift of money. In a letter (in Tertullian, *De Carne* 2, cf. *Adv. Marc.* 1.1; 4.4) Marcion himself testifies that he at first had fellowship with the other Roman Christians. Also Tertullian, *Praescr.* 30: Marcion "in catholicam primo doctrinam credidisse apud ecclesiam Romanensem."

19. Tertullian, *Praescr.* 30: "inquieta semper curiositas, qua fratres vitiabat."

been more than once expelled from fellowship for a short time and then again reinstated.[20]

What happened in the summer of 144? Epiphanius (*Haer.* 42.1f.) preserves an old tradition.[21] On Marcion's *own* initiative he met with the "presbyters and teachers" of the city in order to dispute with them concerning Luke 5:36f.[22] These discussions led to the separation; from then on there was no fellowship between the Marcionites and the rest of the Christians in the city.[23]

Who finally drew the line of division is not completely clear. Statements such as "eiectus" and "relegatus" (Tertullian, *Praescr.* 30) attribute the initiative for this final step to the "presbyters and teachers." Having been put under pressure by Marcion's attempt at reform, they would not have been able to do anything else than to distance themselves from Marcion's Christianity, which was devoid of the Old Testament. On the other hand, it is also correct that Marcion himself had provoked this reaction with his enthusiasm for reform. What would have happened if Marcion had been satisfied in his house community with only teaching his own followers? If he had not had the missionary impulse of a reformer of Christianity who sought to force decisions on other congregations by means of a synod? As the previous and following examples show, Marcion in all probability would have been able to remain in eucharistic fellowship with the other house communities of the city.[24]

---

20. Ibid.: "semel et iterum eiectus...novissime in perpetuum discidium relegatus."

21. See the history of tradition analysis of Epiphanius's text in G. Lüdemann, "Zur Geschichte," 96, n. 28. For the parallel texts of Filastrius and Pseudo-Tertullian see A. Harnack, *Marcion* 24[x]–28[x]. The age of the tradition is indicated particularly by the archaic situation mirrored in the formula "presbyters and teachers": a presbyterial constitution and governance is presupposed; there is no mention yet of a bishop with teaching authority (on this see below chap. 41).

22. So Epiphanius. See *Ps.-Tertullian:* concerning Luke 6:43, i.e., concerning the doctrine of God, for with this passage Marcion proved the existence of two gods (cf. Tertullian, *Adv. Marc.* 1.2). Filastrius: concerning both passages. At least the statement underlying these versions is historical, i.e., that Marcion sought to introduce reform with exegetical arguments.

23. Cf. subsequently also Justin's severe polemic against the Marcionites: *Apol.* 1.26; 1.58; *Dial.* 35.5; 80.4; also his lost *Syntagma* (mentioned in 1.26.8; Irenaeus, 4.6.2; Eusebius, *Ecc. Hist.* 4.18.9).

24. Cf. also Epiphanius 42.2, end: "*This Marcion caused the division*...he said: 'I will split off your church [the church of the Roman presbyters].'" This appears to be tradition, since it contradicts Epiphanius's context. Epiphanius's redaction idealizes the faithfulness and orthodoxy of the Roman presbyters. According to him, the presbyters never even accepted Marcion in their fellowship when he arrived in Rome, because of their loyalty to Marcion's father, who had rejected his son. For the redactor the division had already existed since Marcion's arrival, so that a tension arises in the text in regard to the previous quote.

6. Cerdo in the 130s constitutes the second exception. Irenaeus, 3.4.3, describes how Cerdo was at first integrated into the Christianity of the city; then the relationship grew slowly worse, until after a longer period of ups and downs a division took place: "...He came into the church (of Rome) and confessed (the faith). Soon he was teaching in secret, then he confessed again, but then he was put to shame by some for false teaching and withdrew from fellowship with the pious." (...ποτὲ μὲν λαθροδιδασκαλῶν, ποτὲ δὲ πάλιν ἐξομολογούμενος, ποτὲ δὲ ὑπό τινων ἐλεγχόμενος ἐφ' οἷς ἐδίδασκε κακῶς καὶ ἀφιστάμενος τῆς τῶν θεοσεβῶν συνοδίας).

Two aspects are interesting.

a. Already before the end of his fellowship with the church, Cerdo taught "in secret" (λαθροδιδασκαλῶν). We may conclude from this remark that there was a circle of followers of Cerdo who met separately somewhere in a house in the city. This house group listened to Cerdo as a teacher and also conducted worship, at least after his withdrawal from fellowship with the church.

b. The end of fellowship with the church was caused by Cerdo himself. Cerdo withdrew (ἀφιστάμενος) from fellowship with the rest of the city's congregations. There is no mention of an excommunication on the part of the others.

7. The same is true of the Jewish-Christian circle (see above, Justin, *Dial.* 47.3), who followed the Mosaic Law and refused fellowship with all Christians who were not faithful to the Torah. The group isolated *itself* from every contact with others for the sake of its own purity.

8. In regard to the *Montanists* we observe something similar to what we saw with the Valentinians. A third person, coming from the outside, first incites Bishop Victor (c. 189–99 C.E.) to withdraw fellowship from the Montanists. The bond between them was previously not severed.

Victor's predecessor, Eleutherus (c. 175–89 C.E.), planned to dissociate[25] from them. The martyrs of Gaul, however, sent to Rome through Irenaeus an irenic letter, in which Eleutherus was called upon to exercise clemency and peace (Eusebius, *Ecc. Hist.* 5.3.4–5.4.2). The appeal was successful. For Victor still acknowledged the Montanists at first ("agnitio") and even dispatched letters of peace to their mother congregations in Asia and Phrygia (Tertullian, *Adv. Prax.* 1).[26]

---

25. The most plausible interpretation of the succinct note in Eusebius, *Ecc. Hist.* 5.3.4, that the martyrs of Gaul "wrote to Eleutherus...in the interest of ecclesiastical peace," is that Eleutherus's attitude endangered peace. In Rome an old prejudice was harbored against the tradition of Asia Minor and the Johannine writings (cf. W. Bauer, *Rechtgläubigkeit,* 208–10). Eleutherus's attitude is apparently influenced by this background.

26. The most probable solution is to identify the "episcopus Romanus" with Victor; cf. in this regard, e.g., G. La Piana, "The Roman Church," 245.

How did the break occur? The modalist Praxeas (chap. 34) immigrated from Asia to Rome and successfully urged ("coegit") Victor to withdraw acknowledgment and fellowship from the Montanists (Tertullian, ibid.). Praxeas thus "imported" from Asia Minor an antagonism toward the Montanists. On his initiative the Paraclete was driven from Rome, Tertullian complains (ibid.: "negotia diaboli Praxeas Romae procuravit: prophetiam expulit . . . paracletum fugavit").

As a result an anti-Montanistic work also was written in Rome now. Gaius composed his dialogue against Proclus about 200 C.E. (cf. above, Eusebius, *Ecc. Hist.* 6.20.3; 3.28.2).[27]

9. The *modalists* themselves enjoyed fellowship in Rome well into the third century (cf. chap. 34). They first experienced opposition in Rome when a burning controversy broke out between Hippolytus's school and the modalists Epigonus, Cleomenes, and Sabellius. Zephyrinus and Callistus still endeavored to formulate a compromise, but the break between Callistus and Sabellius could now no longer be prevented (Hippolytus, *Ref.* 9.11).

10. Finally, with the *Theodotians* it is again Victor who withdraws fellowship from Theodotus, the shoemaker, and his followers (ἀπεκή-ρυξε τῆς κοινωνίας, anonymous, from the first half of the third century, in Eusebius, *Ecc. Hist.* 5.28.6, 9).

11. Conclusion: Well into the time of Victor, we observe the concurrence of fractionation, on the one hand, and extensive tolerance,[28] on the other. That between both juxtaposed elements a causal connection exists is suggested by the thrust of the above model of connection (see above, chap. 40, introduction).

The concentration on Victor in the previous material is striking. Partly from outside influences, partly from personal initiative, Victor withdrew fellowship from several Christian groups in the city at the

---

27. Praxeas tried to convince Victor by claiming that already Victor's predecessors made anti-Montanist statements (Tertullian, ibid.: "praecessorum eius auctoritates defendendo"), probably alluding to Eleutherus's plans. It is unlikely, however, that already Soter (c. 166–75 C.E. had an anti-Montanist attitude, as the plural in the quoted text suggests (Praedestinatus, 26, even infers from this text that Soter wrote against the Montanists). There was no break under Soter, otherwise Eleutherus would not have had any reason to plan a withdrawal of fellowship. Tertullian emphasizes that Praxeas's argumentation was not sound ("falsa adseverando"). Therefore not much may be inferred from "praecessorum eius auctoritates defendendo."

28. Important: "Tolerance" is here equated with letting alone those who teach other doctrines; no consequences for the mutual spiritual fellowship result from theological divergences. Conceptions of an active enduring are only to be associated in a limited way. Not in all cases were the theological divergences consciously perceived. Each taught in his or her own place in the city. A discussion like that between Marcion and the "presbyters and teachers" was an exception that promptly led to the edge of excommunication.

end of the second century. Previously there prevailed a period of extensive tolerance (with only few exceptions — Marcion, Cerdo, a circle of Jewish Christians faithful to the Torah and, at most, possibly the Carpocratians).[29]

---

29. W. Bauer (*Rechtgläubigkeit,* 231ff.) praised Rome as the refuge of orthodoxy in the ancient world. What is to be said of this? (a) Bauer, *Rechtgläubigkeit,* 132: The spiritual life of the Roman Christians "remained spared from difficult disturbances well into the second century." 124: The danger of heresy was "first experienced comparatively late in Rome." These impressions, in my opinion, are correct. Bauer interprets them, however, in the direction that there had been in Rome for a long time no heretics or they had remained by far in the minority (195, 197, 231), so that in Rome grew "the only church of reliable orthodoxy" (132). I acknowledge gladly that the "orthodox" house communities were in the majority in Rome (see above, n. 1). I hold it to be false, however, that the capital city of the world, into which "all abominations flowed" (Tacitus, *Ann.* 15.44.3), should have been less infiltrated by heresies than other cities. If we gain with Bauer the impression that "well into the second century" the faith life of the Romans remained "spared from difficult disturbances" and that the danger of heretics "was first experienced later," this was so not because of a scarcity of "heretics" but because of the fractionated structure of Christianity in the city. Scattered throughout the city, different groups could exist next to each other and let each other go their own way without it immediately coming to an "explosion" between them. This is the reason why we hear little about "difficult disturbances" for such a long period, indeed well into the time of Victor. In the capital city, where everything disperses, the potential for friction was smaller from the start. In smaller cities, on the other hand, Christian groups of disparate thinking could more easily collide with one another (Ignatius, *Phil.* 7–8; Eusebius, *Ecc. Hist.* 4.24; 5.16.2ff.). (b) Bauer himself (177) observes (in view of Ptolemaeus's letter to Flora) that "even in Italy near the end of the second century, Gnostics and 'orthodox' oriented Christians still stood in close personal relations." Therefore, Rome could hardly have been such an antiheretical stronghold. (c) On page 135 Bauer asserts that at the beginning of the second century excommunications did not yet exist in the churches of the Roman Empire; "everyone who was baptized remained at least externally connected in unity." During the entire second century it was not yet "the rule that the heretic found himself excluded" (ibid.). This statement is valid also for Rome, the alleged protector of orthodoxy. (d) Polycarp and others do not represent an orthodoxy dependent on Rome but an independent orthodoxy in Asia Minor. To infer from *1 Clement* a claim of Rome to doctrinal authority or to a decisive anti-heretical position is mistaken (see the review of Bauer in the supplement to the second edition, 288ff.).

Chapter 41

Fractionation, Monarchical Episcopacy, and Presbyterial Governance

Thesis: The fractionation in Rome favored a collegial presbyterial system of governance and prevented for a long time, until the second half of the second century, the development of a monarchical episcopacy in the city. Victor (c. 189–99) was the first who, after faint-hearted attempts by Eleutherus (c. 175–89), Soter (c. 166–75), and Anicetus (c. 155–66), energetically stepped forward as monarchical bishop and (at times, only because he was incited from the outside) attempted to place the different groups in the city under his supervision or, where that was not possible, to draw a line by means of excommunication. Before the second half of the second century there was in Rome no monarchical episcopacy for the circles mutually bound in fellowship.

It would be presumptuous here to wish to write again a history of the ecclesiastical offices that are mentioned especially in *1 Clement* and Hermas. My concern is to describe the correlation between fractionation and one factor of ecclesiastical order, the monarchical episcopate. This bridge should be illuminated. What happens across the bridge in the field of the history of ecclesiastical offices can only be here briefly sketched[1] — and perhaps motivate one to further investigation.[2]

1. Fractionation into house congregations does not exclude that the Christian islands scattered around the capital city were aware of being

---

1. Important works, among others: H. Lietzmann, "Zur altchristlichen Verfassungsgeschichte," *Das kirchliche Amt,* ed. K. Kertelge, 93–143, especially 125ff.; J. Rohde, *Urchristentum,* contains literature on the topic. Already Harnack reckoned with a late development of the monarchical office of bishop in Rome (e.g., Marcion 19^x, n. 2; 4^x, n. 4, and other places): Telesphorus and Hyginus in the first half of the second century, according to him, were *simultaneously* office holders in Rome.

2. A further introductory remark is necessary. The above thesis does not seek to answer the question how the presbyterial governance originated (model of Judaism or the result, e.g., of Pauline ecclesiology, which hardly corresponds to a monarchical episcopacy). The above thesis wants to explain why a presbyterial governance could *last* for such a long period in Rome. The cause of its origin and the reasons for its continuance are to be distinguished. The same held true for the interrelation between fractionation and theological pluralism in Rome (see above, chap. 39, beginning).

in spiritual fellowship with each other, of perceiving themselves as cells of one church, and of being united by common bonds.

Paul writes to several house communities in Rome (Rom 16; see above, chap. 36) and presupposes that these send his letter, with the greetings, from one to another (cf. similarly Col 4:16). The continually repeated ἀσπάσασθε receives meaning if there were messengers between the various, topographically separate groups. In other words, not only were eucharistic gifts sent to and fro (see above, chap. 40) but also letters and greetings from outside the city were exchanged.

That means that people writing from outside of Rome could address the Roman Christians as a unity. Not only Paul but also Ignatius and Dionysius of Corinth did this. Conversely, the Roman Christians as an entirety could send letters to those outside: *1 Clement* and a further letter to Corinth around 170 c.e. (Eusebius, *Ecc. Hist.* 4.23.11). The totality of Roman Christianity undertook shipments of aid to those outside (see above on Dionysius, in Eusebius, *Ecc. Hist.* 4.23.10). People from the outside consequently spoke of *the* Roman church (e.g., Ignatius, *Rom. praescr.*).

It was useful to assign to someone in Rome the work connected with external communication. Hermas knows such a person by the name of Clement.[3] In *Vis.* 2.4.3, Hermas prepares two copies of his small book and sends (πέμπω, within the city) one of them to Clement, who forwards it "to the cities outside, for he is entrusted with that task" (πέμψει Κλήμης εἰς τὰς ἔξω πόλεις, ἐκείνῳ γὰρ ἐπιτέτραπται).

It is important to note that Hermas's "minister of external affairs" is not a monarchical bishop. In the second next sentence, Hermas describes how he circulates his little book within the city. He makes it known "to this city together with the presbyters who preside over the church" (εἰς ταύτην τὴν πόλιν μετὰ τῶν πρεσβυτέρων τῶν προϊσταμένων τῆς ἐκκλησίας). A plurality of presbyters leads Roman Christianity. This Christianity, conscious of spiritual fellowship within the city, is summed up under the concept "ecclesia," but that changes nothing in regard to the plurality of those presiding over it. In *Vis.* 3.9.7, Hermas also calls them προηγούμενοι or πρωτοκαθεδρίται.

Hermas knows to report the human side of the presiders: they quarrel (διχοστασίαι) about status and honor (περὶ πρωτείων καὶ περὶ δόξης; *Vis.* 3.9.7–10; *Sim.* 8.7.4–6). What are πρωτεῖα? Are the presbyters "wrangling" for first place within their own ranks, for the place of *primus inter pares*? Whatever the answer may be, Hermas — in the first half of the second century — never mentions the success of such efforts, the actual existence of a single leader. Instead, he speaks of

---

3. Whether he is identical with the author of *1 Clement* or not is not relevant to the topic, cf. chap. 21, n. 1.

προϊστάμενοι,[4] προηγούμενοι, πρωτοκαθεδρίται, πρεσβύτεροι, all in the *plural* (*Vis.* 2.4.2f.; 2.2.6; 3.1.8).

Correspondingly, we find in Paul's and Ignatius's letters to the Romans nothing of a Roman monarchical leader, even though Ignatius knew of a monarchical bishop's office from his experience in the east.[5] In the year 144 Marcion, at the Roman synod meeting that he initiated (see above, chap. 40), also saw himself facing "presbyters and teachers" and not a monarchical bishop.

First Clement presupposes the same presbyterial governance: ἡγούμενοι (1:3); προηγούμενοι (21:6); πρεσβύτεροι (44:5; 47:6; 54:2; 57:1); ἐπίσκοποι (42:4f. = Isa 60:17; LXX). As in Hermas (*Vis.* 3.5.1; *Sim.* 9.27.1; cf. 9.31.5f.), the word "bishop" is in the plural. And *First Clement* 44:5 clarifies who exercises ἐπισκοπή (44:1, 4): the πρεσβύτεροι! A *number of them* (ἐνίους), who *simultaneously* had ἐπισκοπή in Corinth, were dismissed by the Corinthians (44:4, 6; cf. also 54:2). In 47:6; 57:1 the dismissed men are called πρεσβύτεροι.[6] In short, by πρεσβύτεροι and ἐπίσκοποι 1 *Clem.* designates the same persons.[7] The two terms are interchangeable, as in Hermas (*Vis.* 3.5.1).

"Bishops" are presbyters with a special function. With what function are they entrusted? Hermas in *Mand.* 8.10; *Vis.* 3.9.2; *Sim.* 1.8 uses the verb ἐπισκέπτεσθαι not in relation to an office but referring to all Christians in the sense of "to care for the needy, to visit them." *Sim.* 9.27.2f. portrays the official "bishops" correspondingly as those who care for (διακονία) the needy (ὑστερημένους) and the widows (χήρας). In this work they are supported by the deacons (*Sim.* 9.26.2). Our comparison of ἐπισκέπτεσθαι and ἐπίσκοποι shows that Hermas with the functional term "episkopos" still clearly associates ἐπισκέπτεσθαι and its social-diaconal content. The wordplay ἐπίσκοποι — ἐσκέπασαν in *Sim.* 9.27.2 demonstrates the same.

---

4. The same term is found in Rom 12:8. There, according to the context (ὁ μεταδιδούς, ὁ ἐλεῶν), προϊστάμενος does not designate one concrete figure but refers to a general case: "whoever takes the lead...." That can also be in a house community.

5. Whether the monarchical episcopacy was established everywhere in the east is, however, questionable. Ignatius, *Phil.* 7–8 (cf. *Magn.* 6–8) presupposes Christians who do not wish to be under a bishop. In Ancyra around 190 C.E. there was still no bishop presiding but only a group of presbyters; anonymous, in Eusebius, *Ecc. Hist.* 5.16.5.

6. Cf. also 42:4 with 54:2: the appointed bishops in 42:4 are, according to 54:2, the appointed πρεσβύτεροι. The same verb is encountered in both places (καθίστανον — καθεσταμένοι).

7. According to 42:4; 44:2 they were — just like the deacons — already instituted by the apostles as their rightful successors. As such, they are the legitimate carriers of the tradition who pass down the correct *doctrine* of faith (42:1, 3f.: εὐηγγελίσθησαν, εὐαγγελιζόμενοι, κηρύσσοντες). In *this* regard, thus, they stand in the succession of the apostles, according to 1 *Clement*. There is nothing that attests to the apostolic succession of a monarchical bishop.

On the relation between "presbyters" and "bishops" I see two possibilities. Model 1 is two concentric circles. The bishops belong to the group of presbyters; they are one *part* of it, but not all presbyters care for the poor. Model 2 is two congruent circles. *All* presbyters are at the same time "bishops," and the latter designation specifies one of their special duties.

Evidence for model 2 is that in Justin's *Apol.* 1.67.6 the worship leader always is at the same time also in charge of taking care of the poorer members in his liturgical assembly. *Each* presbyter in Rome apparently leads a worship assembly in a house community and therefore also takes care of needy fellow Christians there.[8]

I summarize my view of the sources. Individual presbyters preside over the different house communities in the city, leading the worship and, as bishops, directing the care of the poor in their own house congregation. Each individual congregation therefore also has its own treasury, administered by the individual "episcopus" (*Apol.* 1.67). Still at the end of our period of time, the group of Theodotians from whom fellowship was withdrawn designates its "presider" Natalius as ἐπίσκοπος who holds the πρωτοκαθεδρία of the Theodotian community (cf. chap. 33). At the same time, Proclus as προϊστάμενος presides over the Montanist community in the city (cf. chap. 30). Both examples from the end of the century illustrate what was customary at least until the middle of the century for each group in the city: each individual group was presided over by its own presbyter-bishop.

2. How and whether the presbyters of the different Roman communities that acknowledged spiritual fellowship with each other assembled for occasional *conventions* remains obscure in the sources. We must presuppose such conventions if we wish to understand several phenomena.

The totality of Roman congregations delegated to a "minister of external affairs" the tasks that arose through communication with Christian communities of other cities (Hermas, *Vis.* 2.4.3). Roman Christianity was capable of acting as a unity to carry out external affairs.

The letters that were sent outside and were composed always in the name of the Romans and not in the name of an individual[9] pre-

---

8. We saw at the end of chap. 36 that *Apol.* 1.67 does not reflect a central mass of a monarchical Roman bishop. For a house community in the second century one has to reckon most probably with only one presbyter. Two or three presbyters for a single house-church community can only be established at the earliest for the third century (see above, chap. 37). In the third century the total number of Christians in Rome had increased in comparison to the first and second centuries, without the number of individual congregations correspondingly increasing (see above, chap. 37, end). From this we need to conclude that the individual congregations encompassed more members in the third century than in the second and that they correspondingly needed also more clerics.

9. *1 Clem;* the letter written under the direction of Soter and sent to Corinth (Dionysius in Eusebius, *Ecc. Hist.* 4.23.11); even still the writing concerning the date of Easter

suppose previous coordination of the individual congregations and the establishment of common opinion.

Grapte, who had to instruct the widows and orphans, was entrusted with this work by all the communities of Rome (Hermas, *Vis.* 2.4.3).[10]

All this is only intelligible if on a level *above* the individual house communities occasional conventions of presbyters took place. Hermas appears to have in mind such an assembly of presbyters when he writes, "You will say to the presiders of the church..." (*Vis.* 2.2.6; cf. 4.2f.; 3.9.7; 3.1.8). The text shows that Hermas made his small prophetic book known to Roman Christianity in an indirect way. He presented it to the presiders of the church; these should then in turn proclaim it to their individual communities. We see in this passage the presbyters assembled as an audience. At the same time, we observe the awareness of Roman Christianity as a whole as "ecclesia." It is a consciousness that Ignatius, who views Rome from the outside, already expressed in the prescript to his letter to the Romans.

Finally Marcion attempted to succeed with his reform before a forum of "presbyters and teachers," which led to the end of fellowship with him (see above). Separation from him was binding not only for some but for all non-Marcion communities in the city. All this points to conventions at which the presbyters of the city's individual communities, which acknowledged spiritual fellowship with each other, gathered together.[11]

All in all, we unfortunately know little of this convention level above the individual house communities. The same applies to internal church communications in general. Had the members of two individual house communities, who were not presbyters, the possibility to speak with each other? As far as we can see, such encounters were institutionally not planned. They remain the initiative of the individual, like the debate between Rhodon and the Marcionite Apelles (Rhodon in Eusebius, *Ecc. Hist.* 5.13.5–7; on disputations between theologically quarreling parties see also Tertullian, *Praescr.* 15–19; Irenaeus, *Haer.* 2.15.3; Hippolytus, *Ref.* 9.11; Eusebius, *Ecc. Hist.* 4.24; 5.16.2, 4, 10, 17; possibly Ignatius, *Phil.* 6–8). Often communication between the individual house

---

that was composed under the direction of Victor (Eusebius, *Ecc. Hist.* 5.23.3: τῶν ἐπὶ Ῥώμης).

10. She is named together with her work parallel to Clement's "office of external affairs." Whether she went from house community to house community in order to instruct the widows and orphans we do not know. In regard to her work, see the more detailed description in chap. 21.

11. V. Saxer (in his review of my book in *Rivista di storia della chiesa in Italia* 42 [1988]: 207) points out that outside of Roman Christianity *presbyteroi* always preside as a group and never as individual figures. This is correct, but the group that Saxer *per analogiam* is looking for in Rome is hardly a presbyter-committee on the level of the individual house communities but rather the convention on the level of the city in the second century.

communities of the city appears to have been carried out not in personal encounter (see above on Justin, chap. 38) but in writing and through courier: Hermas did not "give" his small book to his fellow Roman Christians Clement and Grapte; he "sent" it to them (*Vis.* 2.4.3).

3. How did a monarchical episcopacy develop in the second half of the second century? In the first half of the second century a "minister of external affairs" was responsible for the correspondence with other cities (ἐκείνῳ γὰρ ἐπιτέτραπται, Hermas, *Vis.* 2.4.3). The shipments of aid to congregations in other cities probably also passed through his hands.

The shipments of aid to outsiders presuppose in my opinion that there must have been in Rome a central collection place for offerings to such shipments: a central fund — *apart* from the cash funds of the individual communities administered by the "bishops" of these congregations and used to care for the needy *in* the city.[12]

The following observation is interesting: The first presbyters whom we can address as harbingers of and transitional figures toward a monarchical episcopacy in the second half of the second century appear in the few contemporary notes that are extant concerning them always in this role of a "minister of external affairs":

a. *Soter.* Dionysius of Corinth (in Eusebius, *Ecc. Hist.* 4.23.10) writes to Rome: "From the beginning you had the custom ... of sending support to many communities in all cities ... Soter did not only retain this custom; he even expanded it." Besides this, Dionysius (ibid.) describes Soter as fatherly host for pilgrims in Rome. Apparently under his leadership the letter of the Romans to Dionysius and the Corinthians also was composed (ibid., 11), although this is not explicitly stated.[13]

b. Before Soter, *Anicetus* is identifiable (after the middle of the second century). The little we know about him is that he took care of foreign guests in Rome: Polycarp of Smyrna (Irenaeus in Eusebius, *Ecc. Hist* 5.24.16) and Hegesippus (see below on Hegesippus in Eusebius, *Ecc. Hist.* 4.22.3).

c. The care of foreign guests is recorded again for Soter's successor, *Eleutherus.* The martyrs of Gaul sent a letter to him (in Eusebius, *Ecc. Hist.* 5.4.2) and asked him to take care most graciously of the bearer of the letter.

The following is the most plausible reconstruction:

---

12. Did Marcion's great donation (see above) also flow into this central fund?

13. ὑμῶν before τὴν ἐπιστολήν means the Romans, who are addressed in the writing of Dionysius (ibid., 10) in the second person plural; Soter is spoken of in the third person. Thus Soter is neither the explicit sender of the letter of the Romans to Corinth nor the addressee of Dionysius's letter to Rome, although such is always asserted in the secondary literature (e.g., by W. Bauer, *Rechtgläubigkeit,* 108, n. 1; even by Eusebius, ibid., 9).

a. A presbyterial governance still prevails in the first half of the second century. The presbyters quarrel occasionally concerning the superiority of one over the other (Hermas, *Vis.* 3.9.7ff.; *Sim.* 8.7.4–6), so that an incipient tendency towards the establishment of a *monarchos* is to be recognized; none of them, however, actually succeeded in breaking through the plural of προϊστάμενοι. Even the one among them who is entrusted with the external affairs is still by no means a "primus" among these "pares."

b. First from the middle of the second century this presbyter entrusted with external affairs gains ever more "prominence," until at the latest with *Victor* (c. 189–99) a powerful *monarchos* has developed. Before him, *Eleutherus* (c. 175–89), with his attempt to intervene against the Montanists (see above, chap. 40), shows a notable self-confidence. Beyond this Irenaeus's (*Haer.* 3.3.3; cf. below 4.) famous "catalogue of Roman bishops" originates from Eleutherus's time. It shows that around 180, Eleutherus sees himself already as *the* Roman guardian of apostolic tradition, not as one among others but as the authoritative bearer of the tradition who has risen above the others of his generation. Before Eleutherus, *Soter* (c. 166–75) is referred to by Dionysius (Eusebius, *Ecc. Hist.* 4.23.10) as μακάριος ἐπίσκοπος. But, if one approaches the text impartially, it remains open whether a monarchical bishop or one ἐπίσκοπος among others is meant.[14] More instructive for Soter's self-confidence instead is that he on his own increases (ηὔξηκεν, ibid.) the Roman shipments of aid to those outside. Not only Eleutherus, but already *Anicetus* before Soter could self-confidently present himself to the foreign guest Hegesippus around 160 C.E. as the authoritative caretaker of the apostolic tradition in Rome (see below, on Hegesippus in Eusebius, *Ecc. Hist.* 4.22.3).

The four named persons from the second half of the second century are to be acknowledged not only as Roman "ministers of external affairs" but also as harbingers of and transitional figures toward the monarchical episcopacy in Rome. Why could the overseer for external relations, who is clearly attested for the first half of the second century, develop in the second half of the century into a powerful *monarchos*? What tasks originally fell to him? He was to send letters *from* Rome (Hermas, *Vis.* 2.4.3; *1 Clement* as a letter from the entire Roman Christianity). Somebody had to organize the circulation of letters addressed *to* Rome within the city and to make sure that the greetings connected with them were conveyed: ἀσπάσασθε, ἀσπάσασθε . . . Rom 16. Somebody was to organize the shipments of aid from Rome to other cities, an old tradition of Roman Christians long before Soter (Dionysius in

---

14. For W. Bauer (*Rechtgläubigkeit,* 118), who praises Rome as the refuge of orthodox belief, Soter is the *first* monarchical bishop of Rome.

Eusebius, *Ecc. Hist.* 4.23.10). It is important that in all these tasks the "minister of external affairs" represented the *totality* of Roman house communities to the outside world, and within the city he had to coordinate the congregations in order to be able to fulfill the external tasks. In this way his authority increased also internally. In addition he concentrated a piece of economic power in his own hands. He administered the central treasury for the shipments of aid to the outside. All in all, the role of "external minister" was predestined to flow into a monarchical episcopacy in the second half of the second century[15]

4. What is the significance of Irenaeus's (in the 180s) and Hegesippus's (c. 160 C.E.) so-called "lists of Roman bishops"?"[16]

Hegesippus, in Eusebius, *Ecc. Hist.* 4.22.1–3, writes: "During my visit to Rome I made a succession list/διαδοχή up to Anicetus, whose deacon was Eleutherus. Soter followed Anicetus and then followed Eleutherus" (γενόμενος δὲ ἐν Ῥώμῃ διαδοχὴν ἐποιησάμην μέχρις Ἀνικήτου). Hegesippus visited Rome around 160 C.E. at the time of Anicetus and recorded his memoirs about the visit around 180 C.E. at the time of Eleutherus. In spite of all the difficulties the text presents to the researcher (Harnack and Zahn even conjectured διατρίβην: "I took up residence in Rome until Anicetus"), a consensus may be formed. Hegesippus's interest lay in the *pure doctrine* (4.22.2) as it allegedly was passed down uninterruptedly from the apostles until the present. During his trip, Hegesippus tried to convince himself that this passing down had indeed occurred in the different cities of the world. Also in Rome he investigated to his satisfaction that it had been so. In other words, it by no means concerned him to prove a succession of monarchical bishops from the apostles until the present. What he pictured in his mind were chains of bearers of correct belief, and he was of the opinion that he could recognize such a chain also in Rome. More than this is not in the text.

Irenaeus, *Haer.* 3.3.3, provides for the first time a long catalogue of twelve names from the apostles to Eleutherus. The interest of the list is to anchor the present doctrine with a successive chain of authorities back to the apostles.

---

15. After it had once *originated*, the Roman monarchical episcopacy developed very rapidly into a powerful position in the empire (already in the Easter dispute). The bishop of Rome gained special importance as the bishop of the capital of the world. If at first the huge size of the city had favored the fractionation of Roman Christianity that delayed the establishment of a monarchical episcopacy, nevertheless the monarchical episcopacy, once established, gained prominence on the basis of Rome's role as capital of the world. This prominence led to primacy. The size of the city and its importance as capital are two distinct factors, which exerted influence in different ways.

16. For literature cf. Th. Klauser, "Bischofsliste," *Gesammelte Arbeiten*, ed. E. Dassmann (Münster, 1974), 121–37; H. Kemler, "Hegesipps römische Bischofsliste," *VC* 25 (1971): 182–96.

In my opinion we can reliably estimate the age of the list. Irenaeus did not himself put the catalogue together but in *Haer.* 3.3.3 uses a previously prepared list.[17] This does not mean that the list is old:

a. Eleutherus constitutes its last, twelfth member. The list explicitly emphasizes δωδεκάτῳ τόπῳ. The "apostolic" number twelve lends beauty to the list: the apostles are followed by twelve guardians of tradition from Linus to Eleutherus, inclusively. The number twelve is not accidental but deliberate. One could have begun with Peter instead of Linus and then would have had thirteen members. Also, that with Sextus the "half-way mark" is noted ("as sixth, Sextus is appointed") shows the framework of twelve members to be intentional, already in the composition of the list before Irenaeus.[18] This means that the twelfth, Eleutherus, is absolutely essential for the catalogue. Thus, the provenance of the catalogue cannot be proved to be earlier than Eleutherus (c. 175–89).

b. About 180, when Hegesippus records his memoirs, he mentions by name only three members of the Roman διαδοχή: Anicetus, Soter, Eleutherus. All three belong to the second half of the second century. Hegesippus is of the opinion that for the time before the middle of the second century, the continuity of tradition back to the apostles can also be asserted; interestingly, however, he gives no names but is satisfied with the general statement. The catalogue preserved in Irenaeus, *Haer.* 3.3.3, which identifies nine persons by name for the time before 150, in contrast to Hegesippus's list, gives a more elaborate and therefore a younger impression.

About 160, during his visit to Rome, Hegesippus simply acknowledged that Anicetus stood in the succession of correct doctrine. A chain of monarchical guardians of tradition, as Hegesippus happily presents them for the time *after* his visit to Rome in the succession of Anicetus — Soter — Eleutherus, did not occur to him in those days of his visit to Rome. The reason is simple. In those days there did not as yet exist a chain of monarchical bearers of tradition. Before the middle of the second century in Rome, at no time did one single prominent person pass on the tradition; this was done by a plurality of presbyters.

What is the result? At the time that Rome experiences the development of a monarchical episcopacy, a twelve-member list of names going back to the apostles is constructed. Analogously to the present situation of Eleutherus one now also presumes about the past single prominent

---

17. He interrupts a bare catalogue of names in the present tense (διαδέχεται / succedit, etc.) with historical and literary comments in the imperfect. Therefore the tradition and the redaction are relatively easily separated. Cf. Th. Klauser, "Bischofsliste," 136.

18. The succinct note about Sextus is formulated in the present tense and is a constituent component of the list prior to Irenaeus.

bearers of tradition, passing on the tradition one by one. The presence of a monarchical bearer of tradition is projected back into the past. This model of history abstracts from the actual course of history; one would have had to present a "bundle" of chains before the middle of the second century in order correctly to portray the historical plurality of presbyters as Roman bearers of tradition. But this type of unpopular complex representation was badly suited for a handy model of history by which the integrity of Eleutherus's doctrine was suppsed to be proved.

Result: The list of Irenaeus (*Haer.* 3.3.3) is with highest probability a historical construction from the 180s, when the monarchical episcopacy developed in Rome. Above all, the framework of "apostolic" twelve members (from Linus to Eleutherus) points in the direction of a fictive construction. The names that were woven into the construction were certainly not freely invented but were borrowed from the tradition of the city of Rome (for example, "Clement" or the brother of Hermas, "Pius"). They had belonged to presbyters of Roman church history. These persons, however, would never have understood themselves as monarchical leaders — especially Pius at the time of Hermas.[19]

5. The *Traditio Apostolica* is worth a final glance.[20] Here the monarchical episcopacy is fully developed. For example, the bishop appoints persons to the other offices (διδόναι κλήρους / *dare sortes;* 3, cf. 8 and 26).

It is interesting for us that:

a. There is still not a central place where the monarchical bishop "resides." Every day the bishop calls together deacons and presbyters "at a place which he designates to them" (in locum quem episcopus praecipiet eis, 39). Apparently this place can vary.

Also 28 presupposes that the bishop abides at one time in one house community, at another time in another community. Different situations for a Christian house meeting are allowed for:

- at one time the bishop is there

- at another time he is not, but only a presbyter is present (si autem non est episcopus ibi ...)

- a third time there is only a deacon present

---

19. On the plurality of presbyters/bishops at the time of Hermas, see above. L. Hertling (*Namen und Herkunft*) tries to identify some of these names as names of freed persons. It is to be observed methodologically, however, that already in the second century the names are so completely equalized that conclusions concerning the social origin of the person become impossible (see above, chap. 16).

20. Cf., e.g., J. E. Stam, *Episcopacy in the Apostolic Tradition of Hippolyt* (Basel, 1969).

- a fourth time no clerics are there (laici autem qui sunt simul sine clerico); then the laypersons should nevertheless conduct themselves respectably, so admonishes the *Traditio* (comedant cum disciplina).

b. The diaconal-social duty, which once nonmonarchical *episcopoi* looked after, are now fulfilled by the monarchical bishop; his personal helpers are entrusted especially with the care of the poor (8). The social duty becomes likewise evident in 23: the bishop accepts the donations of food for the agape meals. Because he himself must taste from the donations, he alone among the clergy need not observe any particular fast days.

In the hands of the now *one* bishop the administration for the poor is centralized. One must picture it thus: There was a great mass of the poor ("*plerique* pauperes," Minucius Felix, 36.3) and a correspondingly overwhelming duty of the bishop, but also considerable economic power was centered in his hands in order to feed more than one thousand persons needing support (Cornelius, in Eusebius, *Ecc. Hist.* 6.43.11). In other words, the social-historical factor ("plerique pauperes") stabilized the now existing monarchical office. Not only the mass of poor, who were dependent on the bishop as their bread-winner and who at the same time stood behind him as his power base, but also the necessary finances in the treasury of the bishop for the poor helped to consolidate permanently the position of the bishop. In order not to be misunderstood: that the masses of poor were to be taken care of did not lead to the development of the monarchical episcopacy. It is possible to take care of more than one thousand poor more easily in a decentralized system. My thesis is that the care of many poor stabilized the office of monarchical bishop after it had developed on other grounds. The causes of its origin and the causes of its continuance are again to be distinguished.

Summary. There is apparently a complicated wickerwork of interrelations:

1. For a hundred years fractionation favored a presbyterial governance in the city. Only after the middle of the second century did a monarchical bishop become visible for the "Great Church" communities of the city.

2. The development towards the monarchical episcopacy was promoted also by social-historical factors: The shipments of aid to other cities by the "minister of external affairs" and a central treasury at his disposal for this task contributed to the gradual strengthening of his position. Because he had to coordinate the individual house congregations of the city for the sending of letters and the shipments of aid to places outside the city, his authority grew. From the presbyter with external duties there arose the monarchical bishop.

3. A social-historical factor, *plerique pauperes*, appears likely to have contributed to the stabilizing of the by then developed monarchical office.

4. Conversely, the structure of the ecclesiastical offices affected the economy. The transition observed in the third century of real estate moving out of private hands into a centrally administrated church patrimony (see above, chap. 37) would hardly have been conceivable without the monarchical episcopacy. But that the administrator of the then centralized care for the poor, who was endowed with economic potential from donations, finally also took real estate into his own hands was no more than logical.

The *reciprocal* interplay among the factors means that a static model (like substructure and superstructure) is not suitable. What is here "sub" is there "super" — and the reverse.

Part 6

FINAL REMARKS

To work inductively on the level of local history means to move from the level of the empire down to the individual cities — *and* later to compile data from the individual cities, to compare them and thus to advance to more general statements. Rome as the capital city might receive a prominent role; it might be more representative for the entire empire than other cities. For Tacitus the history of the empire is portrayed to a great extent as history of the city of Rome. *How* representative the social history of Christianity in the city of Rome was for ancient Christianity as a whole, however, will first become apparent when more studies from other parts of the empire are produced. The question cannot be answered a priori. It involves detailed understanding of the largest possible amount of material from sources gleaned from the most diverse regions and only *then* the establishing of more general propositions on the widest possible basis.

The following considerations and questions, bequeathed to future research, warn against premature generalizations of the results gleaned from the city of Rome.

a. In Rome there was no class of decurion senators who played a great role in the provinces and who to some extent were Christianized (see above, e.g., on Pliny's "omnis ordinis" in *Ep.* 10.96).

b. We must remain open to the possibility that in the second and third quarters of the first century fewer socially elevated people were numbered among the Christians of Rome than in eastern cities such as Corinth. In the time indicated, numerous freeborn people in Rome sold themselves into slavery in order to provide the Christian community to which they belonged funds for *diaconal* works (see above on *1 Clem.* 55:2). This shows that there were not enough other resources, particularly financial donations, at the disposal of the Roman congregations for the care of the numerous poor. In the second century at the latest, the picture changes. Now the Roman Christians send shipments of aid to needy churches to a greater extent than do other Christians anywhere else. More money stands at their disposal than at the disposal of communities in other cities. Taken together, both observations could mean that Roman Christianity after the third quarter of the first century experienced a steeper social ascent than Christianity in the eastern cities.[1] The absence or presence of the decurion class could be *one* explanation for this.

c. The quantitative relationship of indigenous to immigrants in the Christianity of Rome might essentially differ from that in other cities. Apparently more immigrants are numbered among the Christians of Rome than among the Christians of eastern cities. Even if the nonindigenous Roman Christians originated mostly from the east, this does not mean that they were "representative" of Christianity in the east. People who travel often are different kinds of people from those who remain "at home."

d. The diversity of nationalities of the immigrating population is greater in Rome than in other cities. Rome experiences immigration from the entire empire.

e. Rome is by far the largest city in the empire (probably about one million; Antioch in Syria and Alexandria, a few hundred thousand; most of the more than one thousand cities of the empire hardly more than ten to fifteen thousand). The fractionation of Roman Christianity (cf. Part 5) is related to this size of the city; and a greater theological pluralism is, in turn, connected with this fractionation. The abundance of Christian groups teaching diverse doctrines is apparently greater than in other cities. Also the delayed development of a monarchical episcopacy in Rome is connected with the fractionation. Later than in the eastern cities, the monarchical office of bishop succeeded in establishing itself in Rome. On the other hand, as soon as it was possible, it reached a position of primacy as the episcopate of the capital of the world (cf. Part 5).

f. My thesis regarding the leading Valentinians cannot even be generalized for the Valentinians themselves. We saw that the socially lower and uneducated multitude of Valentinian disciples had other motives to embrace gnostic doctrine than the educated and socially elevated leaders of the movement had. The motives of most of the extant gnostic authors outside of Rome were probably rather in line with those of the multitude of Valentinian disciples that we briefly sketched. It appears to me important that we set aside the question of a generally valid sociologically oriented theory for *the* Gnosis and turn our attention in a more subtly differentiated way to individual gnostic groups.

---

1. Above, we actually did not observe any particularly "wealthy" Christians or any senatorial Christians in Rome before the 90s of the first century. The number of recognizable Roman members of the emperor's *familia* (freed persons, etc.) in the first century amounted to only four, at the *maximum*.

To come to know the men and women of Christian belief in Rome of the first two centuries in their everyday life and in their social reality was one of my interests. To search them out in their *situation* was a research objective in itself. Besides this, the interrelations between situation and matters of religious faith were of interest (cf., among others, Part 3 and 4, *Hermas;* Part 4, Marcion, Valentinians, also Justin, Praxeas, the Carpocratians; Part 5, fractionation, especially chaps. 39 and 40). With none of the observed interrelations we tried to reduce the "kingdom of the spirit," of theology, to social history. Even where we, as in the chapter about Marcion, observed a correspondence in structure between individual theological statements and the experience of social reality, we could not claim that a theologumenon was "deduced" from the experience of social reality: the theological tenets corresponding to the experience of reality were not simply "projections" of social reality but always at the same time theologically founded, which means inner-theologically deducible. The latter, however, should not lure us to inner-theological monocausalisms. My approach involves abolishing the false alternative between interpreting texts either on the basis of theology and history of tradition, on the one hand, or on the basis of sociological categories, on the other. Each approach should be connected with the other, like the height and width of a room. I have called this "three dimensional" text interpretation (*Die Apokalyptiker,* 88). What moved an author like Marcion to take advantage of inner-theological possibilities of derivation, to reach back into tradition, in order to support a theological tenet? It *also* was the experience of social reality that let the theological tenet appear plausible to him. The situation influences the way one relates to tradition.

It was fruitful to observe the social tasks that religious phenomena can fulfill. Marcion and the leading Valentinians used particular metaphysical elements in order to be able to cope with certain experiences of social reality. Hermas's prophecy of repentance had a social task in view of the care of the needy in the church (Part 3). I have suggested a cybernetic circle (*Regelkreis*) as a model for connecting Hermas's belief system with social-economic factors. Not a static (as superstructure/substructure) but only more complex dynamic models will, in my opinion, help us to discover the *reciprocal* relations between theology and social reality.

When we explored the social tasks of religious phenomena, it was important to pay attention to the frames of reference. The social task of Hermas's prophecy was considered within the frame of Christian communities (Part 3). The compensating task of some religious doctrines in Marcion and Valentinus was considered within the prosopographic frame of reference (Part 4); it was related to the "personal systems" of Marcion and some of the leading Valentinians. The entire society as a frame of reference came into view where we observed the integrating power of Christianity. Christianity promoted not only cohesion within the lower strata (see above, e.g., the giving of oneself over to slavery for diaconal purposes in *1 Clem.* 55:2) but also between representatives of different social classes (see above, e.g., in Hermas) and, third, between representatives of various ethnic groups (see above, e.g., in Justin, *Apol.* 1.14.3). At these points Christianity contributed to the integration of the whole society. Also where there was talk of the social task of a Christian philosophy, as with Justin, the entire society was the frame of reference: Christianity became more attractive as an educational entity, so that it increasingly drew followers from higher classes.

For the completely open question of how the relationship between purpose and usefulness ("task"), on the one hand, and causality, on the other, is to be determined, models have now been offered not only from sociology and philosophy but much more from biologists. Is the purpose of a thing to be integrated into the concept of causality? And if yes, who tells us that this would be valid also for socioreligious correlations? It was interesting that in all places where we thought we might speak of a "causality" (influence of a social-historical factor on another phenomenon, e.g., chaps. 39 and 41), a causal *genetic* linking could not be meant but rather factors that made possible the survival and *continuation* of something.

"Non potui magis in rem praesentem te perducere. dices: 'non fuit tanti; quid enim mihi cum tam longa epistula?' nolito ergo identidem quaerere quid *Romae* geratur!" (I could not introduce you more into this matter. You may want to say: "It was not that much. Why do you convey it to me with such a long letter?" Then don't always ask what happens at *Rome*). (Pliny, *Ep.* 3.9.26f.).

APPENDIXES

Appendix 1

Students of Marcion

I

Apelles[1] taught in Rome after a lengthy stay in Alexandria.

a. He produced three types of literary works. He continued the text-critical work of Marcion; he edited the Φανερώσεις of the prophetess Philumene, who was associated with him; and in his at least 38-volume work "Syllogisms," he "unmasked" the Old Testament as contradictory and logically impossible in many aspects.

b. In the fragments preserved in Origen (available, e.g., in Harnack, *Marcion*, Appendix 412ˣff.), the rational and logical rigor of Apelles's work is visible. His criticism of the Old Testament corresponds to that of educated Greeks (judgments concerning the Old Testament by educated Greeks can be found in Harnack, *Mission und Ausbreitung*, 1:361) and differs essentially from that of Marcion: Marcion did not consider the Old Testament as a book of contradictory fables but as truthful in every word. He rejected it not on rational and logical grounds but solely on theological grounds.

It is interesting to note that Apelles begins his own teaching at the points where Marcion's expositions were logically weak (cf. Harnack, *Marcion*, 188ff.).

Do we have here the first indication that Apelles possesses a higher pagan education than Marcion? There are seven other pieces of evidence that point in this direction. It appears that Apelles was better philosophically trained than his teacher, Marcion (on Marcion's philosophical education, see above in the text). Harnack (*Mission*, 178) was of the opinion that one can call Apelles "highly educated."

c. Unlike his master, Marcion, Apelles teaches that, in the imperfect world, human souls are of heavenly origin and originate from the μία ἀρχή (e.g., Tertullian, *De anima* 23; cf. Harnack, *Marcion*, 189).

---

1. Cf. Rhodon in Eusebius, *Hist. Ecc.* 5.13; Tertullian, *Praescr.*, 30; 33; 6; *Adv. Marc.* 4.17; 3.11; *De Carne*, 1; 6ff.; Hippolytus, *Ref.* 7.11f., 38; 10.20; Hippolytus, *Syntagma* (Pseudo-Tertullian, *Adv. haer.*, 6; Filastr., 47; Epiphanus, *Haer.* 44.1f.); Origen, *Contra Cel.* 5.54; the same in Ambrosius, *De paradiso*, 5.28; Jerome, *Ep.* 133.4.

This reflects Platonic influence. Evidently, Apelles attempts to integrate Marcion's dualism with Platonic philosophy (cf. also Rhodon, in Eusebius, *Hist. Ecc.* 5.13, in regard to Apelles's insistence on *a single* world principle).

d. Expressions such as τὸ πρᾶγμα τὸ περὶ θεοῦ πάντων ἀσαφέστατον (cf. Rhodon, in Eusebius, *Hist. Ecc.* 5.13) correspond to the Platonic understanding that knowledge about the Most High basically is ἄρρητον, so that all the teaching that refers to it is merely hinting, drawing near, or circling that which is actually hidden.

e. Conceptually, Apelles (cf. Rhodon, in Eusebius, *Hist. Ecc.* 5.13) distinguishes sharply between three levels: rational knowledge of the world (with whose help God cannot be known); an internal spiritual state of being moved (κινεῖσθαι), which can lead to metaphysical statements that are rationally unverifiable; and the ἠλπικέναι ἐπὶ τὸν ἐσταυρωμένον, which is based on history and which alone is necessary for salvation. The κινεῖσθαι in this context is a Stoic idea (cf. E. Norden, *Agnostos Theos,* 19ff.; Harnack, *Marcion,* 184; M. Pohlenz, "Paulus und die Stoa," *ZNW* 42 (1949): 69–104; also H. Hommel, *ZNW* 48 (1957): 193–200; *TWNT* 3:717–19; P. Colaclides, *VC* 27 (1973): 161–64).

f. Apelles has in common with philosophy that he formulates the primacy of ethics before metaphysics (cf. Rhodon, in Eusebius, *Hist. Ecc.* 5.13.2 and 5).

g. Apelles speaks philosophically about the εἷς ἀγένητος θεός (cf. Eusebius, *Hist. Ecc.* 5.13.7), as, among the apologists, the philosophical Athenagoras often does. On the philosophical background of the concept see J. Lebreton, "Ἀγέννητος dans la tradition phiosoph. et dans la litter. chrét. du 2ᵉ siècle," *RSR* 16 (1926): 431–43.

h. Apelles portrays the God of the Old Testament as a fiery demigod or angel (e.g., Tertullian, *Praescr.* 34; *De carne* 8; *De resurr.* 5; *De anima* 23; Hippolytus, *Ref.* 7.38; 10.20). At least Tertullian is of the opinion that this idea is influenced by Heraclitus's fire philosophy (cf. *Praescr.* 7). Apocalyptic influence, however, is also conceivable (Dan 7).

i. Hippolytus (*Ref.* 7.12) attests, of course polemically, that Apelles is influenced by the philosophers who studied nature: ἐκ φυσικῶν δογμάτων κινηθείς. Hippolytus, in 7.38, however, does not give any evidence of this.

II

In Rome, Rhodon (in Eusebius, *Hist. Ecc.* 5.13) waged a polemic against Marcion's students Syneros, Potitus, and Basilikus, saying that they taught ψιλῶς καὶ ἀναποδείκτως. That says little about their actual education. It is very doubtful that Marcion's Assyrian student, Prepon (Hippolytus, *Ref.* 7.31.1), also lived in Rome.

III

Lucanus (cf. Hippolytus, *Ref.* 7.11 and 37; Epiphanius, *Haer.* 43f.; Tertullian, *De resurr.* 2; Origen, *Contra Cel.* 2.27; Pseudo-Tertullian, *Adv. haer.* 6.3) produced a text critical work on the Gospels and at least three theological works, which are no longer extant (concerning the soul; concerning marriage and asceticism; concerning the Old Testament God, the creator). Two small, but well-matched, details point to a philosophical education:

a. Viderit unus aliqui Lucanus, nec huic quidem substantiae (of the soul) parcens, quam secundum *Aristotelem* dissolvens aliud quid pro ea subicit, tertium quiddam resurrecturus, neque anima neque caro, i.e., non homo, sed ursus forsitan, qua Lucanus (Tertullian, *De resurr.* 2).

Tertullian wishes to show, in a polemical way, that Lucanus studied Aristotle and relied upon him for his doctrine of the soul: Lucanus analyzed the soul as Aristotle did. According to Lucanus, there is a third, higher element in the human being (cf. the Aristotelian νοῦς), and only this element will rise from the dead. Lucanus's doctrine, Tertullian asserts, is unique among heretics, since almost all the others believe in the salvation and preservation of the soul (animae salutem, quoque modo volunt, non negant).

b. Epiphanus (*Haer.* 43) quotes a sentence from Lucanus: ἀφ' οὗ γάμος, εὐθηνία διὰ τῆς παιδοποΐας ἐν κόσμῳ τῷ δημιουργῷ γίνεται. The term εὐθηνία goes back to Aristotle (Aristotle, *Rhetor.* 1360^b 16 et al.; cf. Pauly/Wissowa, s.v.). However, it is also found, for example, in the LXX Gen 41:29.

Appendix 2

Justin

Educational Components

D = *Dialogue*, 1/2 = *Apology* 1 or 2
To be compared with each other are

A

1.18.5	Homer, *Od.* 11.93ff.
1.62.1	e.g., *Iliad* 1.449
D 1.3	*Iliad* 6.123; 15.247; 24.387
D 3.1	*Iliad* 6.202: a passage seldom cited at that time (cf. references in N. Hyldahl, *Philosophie,* 56)
1.59.6	e.g., Hesiod, *Theog.* v. 123.
1.39.4	Euripides, *Hippol.* 612.
2.3(8).7	Reference to the Cynic doctrine of ἀδιαφορία. The technical term is used.
2.11.2	Implicit knowledge that the Cynics had chosen Heracles as their protector (cf. Lucian, *Cynicus* 13; *Convivium* 16). Justin refutes his Cynic opponent, Creszens, with the help of the latter's own star witness, Heracles. For further Cynic elements in D 2.3–6 (e.g., the Cynic συντόμως motif); 7.1; 2.3(8).1f., cf. N. Hyldahl, *Philosophie,* 247.
1.43.6; 28.3f.	Allusion to the Epicurean doctrine according to which ethical concepts possess only hypothetical character (material in C. Andresen, "Justin," 157–95, here 186). Justin's critique of Epicureanism corresponds to what was customary in school Platonism (see above, chap 25, n. 24). School Platonism had for its part taken over the polemic from Stoicism (evidence in C. Andresen, "Justin," 186f.).

418

1.18.3–5 (the soul is conscious even after death)

> Refers correctly to Pythagoras (cf., e.g., the ridicule by Xenophanes B 7; further Porphyry, *Vita* 19; Diogenes Laertius, 8.28; Aetios, *Plac.* 4.7.1) and to Empedocles, who indeed taught Orphic-Pythagorean reincarnation and punishment for previous failings when one is reborn (cf., e.g., Empedocles' term καθαρμοί, Frg. B 115, 117).

1.20.1
> Reference to a Sibylline prophecy, as it is contained in 4 *Sibyll.* 172ff. (but possibly a Jewish-Christian tradition)

D 102.4 (καθολικαὶ καὶ μερικαὶ κρίσεις)
> Aristotelian dialectic, yet also picked up by Platonic school philosophy: e.g., Albinos, *Didask.* 5f.; Apuleius, *De interpret.* 5.

D127
> The Aristotelian idea of God as unmoved mover, yet also picked up by Platonic school philosophy (on this cf. L. W. Barnard, *Justin Martyr,* 30f., 15f., with reference particularly to Albinos).

On the possibility of knowledge of the existence of God in D 4.7 cf. Aristotle, *Fr.* 10f. (28.12f./29.6–12, Rose) but also Plato, *Leg.* 12.966CD.

On the Aristotelian arguments in D 5, which probably are taken from a general doxography, cf. R. M. Grant, "Aristotle," 246–48.

On Aristotelian material in D 6.1f. that is transmitted via Stoicism, cf. N. Hyldahl, *Philosophie,* 222–27.

B. Platonic Traditions

1.8.4
> Plato, *Gorg.* 523E, 524A, *Rep.* 10.615A, *Phaedr.* 249A.

2.3(8).6
> Plato, *Rep.* 10.595C.

2.10.6
> cf. Plato, *Rep.* 10.595AB (expulsion of the poets from the ideal state: probably general doxographic knowledge).

1.44.8
> Plato, *Rep.* 10.617E, is presented from a Middle Platonic perspective (references in C. Andresen, "Justin," 188).

1.3.3
> Plato, *Rep.* 5.473DE; also a maxim of Marcus Aurelius (on this cf. H. H. Holfelder, "EUSEBEIA," 57, n. 36, with literature). Justin addresses his apology to Marcus Aurelius!

1.12.3
> Plato, *Rep.* 2.365CD.

D 3.7–4.1f.
> Plato, *Phaedo* 65E–66A; *Rep.* 6.509B (7.533D); *Philebus* 30D; *Phaedr.* 247C; *Ep.* 7.341CD; further cf. *Sympos.* 210E–212A and, in school Platonism, e.g., Maximus Tyrius, *Or.* 11. The Platonic idea of συγγένεια (Stoic

analogy: Aratos in Acts 17:28) can be found also in Justin, 2.13.3 (on this, Plato, *Rep.* 10.611E; *Leg.* 10.892A; *Ep.* 2.312E).

D 4.4 Behind this stands *Phaedo* 72E–73A; 76C; 66B; further 66E–67A; 67E–68A.

1.2.3f.; 3.1; cf. 17.4 Echo of Socrates: Plato, *Apol.* 30C; cf. Plutarch, *De tranquill. anim.* 17 (475E).

2.10.5f.; 1.5.3f. Reference to the demythologizing of Homeric demons by Socrates, cf., e.g., Plato, *Apol.* 24BC and Xenophon, *Men.* 1.1.1.

1.68.2 Plato, *Criton* 43D.

D 3.1f. For the role of the old man cf. perhaps Plato, *Parm.* 127B (or also Lucian, *Herm.* 24; other parallels in N. Hyldahl, *Philosophie,* 163ff.; direct literary dependence cannot be proved).

1.18.1 Plato, *Phaedo* 107C; cf. Plutarch, *Quomodo non posse* 10 (1093A); 29 (1106B) and Atticos in Eusebius, *Pr. Ev.* 15.5.4f.

1.6.2 ἐξομοιουμένων (likeness to God)
E.g., Plato, *Theae.* 176AB; further cf. *Phaedr.* 246E; Middle Platonic references in C. Andresen, "Justin," 162, n. 20.

D 3.6f.; 4.1 Plato, *Phaedr.* 247C; the passage, originally understood in an ontological sense, is interpreted theologically not only by Justin but also in Middle Platonism, e.g., Albinos, *Didask.* 10; Celsus, *Fr.* 6.64 (Bader); further, Plutarch, *De Iside* 76 (382B).

D 4.5 Plato, *Phaedr.* 249DE.

1.18.5; cf. D 5.1; 4.2 Reference to the divine immortality of the soul in Plato. Cf. particularly in *Phaedo* (76ff.) and *Phaedrus* (e.g., 246A); Middle Platonic references for this topos in C. Andresen, "Justin," 162, n. 18.

D 1.5; 4.4ff. Reference to the Platonic teaching of metempsychosis (Plato, *Rep.* 614; *Tim.* 42BD; Middle Platonic references Andresen, 162, n. 18). D 4.7 has the technical term μεταμείβουσιν (*Tim.* 92C and Albinos, *Didask.* 25: of course, as διαμ.).

D 4.5 (μέμνηται)
Together with the doctrine of the transmigration of the soul, *anamnesis* constitutes a doctrinal topos in Middle Platonism: Albinos, *Didask.* 25; Atticos, in Eusebius, *Pr.*

Ev. 15.9.5. *Anamnesis* in Plato: e.g., *Menon,* passim, *Phaedo* 74AB, 91E, *Phaedr.* 249C.

D 4.2–4   Reference to the Pythagorean-Platonic conception of animals as rational beings? (cf., e.g., Plutarch's *Dialogues,* "The animals possess reason," and "Are land animals or water creatures the smartest?").

2.10.6   Plato, *Tim.* 28C, in a wording that is not in fact taken from the original text of Plato but from the Middle Platonic tradition; cf., e.g, Albinos, *Didask.* 27 (further references in C. Andresen, "Justin," 167, n. 42). Justin interprets the passage in a Middle Platonic manner: cf., e.g., Apuleius, *De Plat.* 1.5 (further references in C. Andresen, "Justin," 167, nn. 41, 40).

1.60.1, 5–7   Plato, *Tim.* 34AB, 36BC. Justin understands these two combined passages in the light of Middle Platonic presuppositions (cf. especially Atticos): C. Andresen, "Justin," 188–90, references. The same is valid for:

D 5.4   Plato, *Tim.* 41AB, is interpreted out of context. Cf. the interpretation of this passage from Plato by Atticos et al. (Eusebius, *Pr. Ev.* 15.6.3ff.; further material in C. Andresen, "Justin," 163f.)

1.10.2 (cf. 16.7) Plato, *Tim.* 29AE (the benevolent Creator of the world); Middle Platonic references in C. Andresen, "Justin," 164, n. 26;

on this cf. also 1.59; 20.4a

Reference to Plato's cosmogony.

especially 1.10.2; 59.1f.

Plato, *Tim.* 50D (51A, 29E); further *Tim.* 30A; Middle Platonic references in C. Andresen, "Justin," 164f., nn. 27f.

1.59.5 (ἐκ τῶν ὑποκειμένων κτλ.)

A concept of the Platonic school, e.g., Albinos, *Didask.* 8; other Middle Platonic references in Andresen, 165, n. 29.

D 5.1f.   Justin here knows the position taken by, e.g., Albinos (*Didask.* 14; cf. 5) and Apuleius (*De Plat.* 1.8) in the Platonic school argument, that the world never had an origin (and therefore is everlasting); cf. further the older representatives of the academy, Xenocrates and Eudoros, in Plutarch, *De an. procreat.* 3.

D 2.6; cf. 2.7(6). 8 (ἀσώματα)

Reference to Plato's doctrine of ideas; in school Platonism, cf., e.g., Attikos in Eusebius, *Pr. Ev.* 15.13.5, 1f.; Albinos, *Didask.* 9–11; Diogenes Laertius, 3.64. On ἀνεπτέρου in D 2.6 cf. Plato, *Phaedr.* 246AB. On the τέλος of seeing God in D 2.6 cf. Plato's myth of the soul in *Phaedr.* (248AB), further *Theaet.* 176B.

2.7(6).8   The ἀσώματα (the ideas) are separately mentioned alongside of the three principles (God, ideas, and matter, cf., e.g., Apuleius, *De Plat.* 1.5; Albinos, *Didask.* 8–10). This corresponds to the cosmological interpretation of Plato's doctrine of ideas in Middle Platonism (see, e.g., Albinos, *Disask.* 8–11). According to Albinos (11) an extra chapter concerning the noncorporeity of the attributes belongs to the doctrine of ideas (on this see C. Andresen, "Justin," 168f.).

2.8.1 (ὁ ἠθικὸς λόγος)

cf. ὁ ἠθικὸς τόπος in Attikos (Eusebius, *Pr. Ev.* 11.2.1) and Celsus, *Fr.* 1.4 (Bader); cf. the school Platonic threefold division of philosophy into ethics, physics, and dialectics (references in C. Andresen, "Justin," 178).

D 2.6   religious objective of Middle Platonism: Attikos, in Eusebius, *Pr. Ev.* 15.13; Albinos, *Didask.* 27; Celsus, *Fr.* 7.45; 8.63B (Bader).

D 3.5 the definition of being

Attikos, in Eusebius, *Pr. Ev.* 15.13.5.

1.60.6f.   Pseudo Plato, *Ep.* 2.312E (modified quotation).

D 8.1 (cognition as dialogue of the soul with itself)

Cf. Albinos, *Didask.* 4; behind this stands again Plato, *Soph.* 263E.

2.11.6 (τὰ δοκοῦντα)

Cf. τὰ λεγόμενα ἀγαθά in Albinos, *Didask.* 27.

D 1.4; 8.2; 142.3; 2.11.6 (εὐδαιμονία)

Middle Platonic topos; references in C. Andresen, "Justin," 179f., nn. 89, 88, 94. Stoic and Aristotelian parallels to D 1.4 in J. C. M. v. Winden (*An Early Christian Philosopher: Justin Martyr's Dialogue with Trypho* [Leiden, 1971], ad rem). Closer are nevertheless the Cyrenean parallels to D 1.4 in J. Pépin ("Prière et providence au 2ᵉ siècle," in *Images of Man in Ancient and Medieval Thought* [Louvain 1976], 119ff.). Apparently this was a widely circulated topos.

1.43.6; 57.1 et al. (μετατίθεσθαι)

A concept of philosophical anthropology, particularly in the Platonic tradition: Plato, *Gorg.* 493CD; cf. 523–27; Plutarch, *Mor.* 120E (further material in H. H. Holfelder, "EUSEBEIA," 62f.). In 1.61 Justin correspondingly develops the understanding of baptism in the light of the philosophical changing of ways. See Holfelder (64f.) and the philosophical terminology in 1.61.10.

1.14.1; 6.2   Plutarch, *De recta ratione aud.* I (37D): θεῷ ἕπεσθαι! Cf. for this originally Pythagorean topos also the Platonists Apuleius, *De Plat.* 2.23, and Albinos, *Didask.* 28.

2.11 (Heracles at the crossroads)

Xenophon, *Mem.* 2.1.21ff. Frequent theme in popular philosophy, also in Middle Platonism (references in C. Andresen, "Justin," 180, nn. 90, 94). When Justin parallels Heracles with the Christians who are prepared for martyrdom (2.11.1), he is close to Attikos's remarks about Heracles (Andresen, 180f.).

The transcendental concept of God in 1.9.3; 10.1; 61.11; 63.1; 2.6(5).1f.; 10.8; 11.4; 13.4; D 126.2; 127.2–4; 4.1 ("unnameable" and "indefinable," etc.; on 2.10.6 see above); cf. further the descriptions of God in 1.8.22; 13.1; 26.5; 45.1; 58.1; D 7.3; 16.4; 34.8; 48.2; 50.1; 55.1; 66.4; 3.5 (the philosophical concept of God in the ontological sense)

Cf., for example, Apuleius, *De Plat.* 1.5: "indictum," "innominabilem"; Albinos, *Didask.* 10 and 28; further Middle Platonic parallels in C. Andresen, "Justin," 167, n. 39.

Justin's doctrine of the Logos (especially in 1.60 and 55)

influences of Middle Platonism: C. Andresen, "Justin," 188–94.

The *Dialogue* in the beginning chapters is not only loaded with philosophical themes and problems (see the references above), it is also in the same chapters loosely imitating especially Plato's *Protagoras*. Cf., e.g., for the introduction D 1.1f. (9.3): Plato, *Prot.* 317DE; 314E; 315B; 316BC; 318A; *Phaedr.* 227A; 228E; 229AB; 230AE; *Leg.* 1.625BC. For D 8.3: *Prot.* 334C (319C), but also *Euthyd.* 276BD. (On the whole, see, e.g., W. Schmid, "Die Textüberlieferung," *ZNW* 40 [1941]: 137, n. 45ff.; P. Keseling, "Justins 'Dialog gegen Trypho' (c. 1–10) und Platons 'Protagoras,'" *Rhein. Mus. f. Philolog.* NF 75 [1926]: 223–30. N. Hyldahl, *Philosophie,* 88ff.; 232f., is more skeptical: for him there are mostly only allusions and no explicit literary dependence; he concedes the latter only for D 9.2: *Prot.* 335CD).

C. Stoic Elements

2.7(6), 8   Reference to the antithesis between the Middle Platonic and Stoic doctrine of principles (περὶ ἀρχῶν). In opposition to the Middle Platonic teaching of ἀσώματα (see above), the Stoics teach the corporality of the attributes

(*Stoicorum Veterum Fr.*, ed. von Arnim, 2:380–86; 389). Like Albinos (*Didask.* 11) Justin turns here against the Stoic doctrine of the principles; unlike Albinos, he even explicitly names his opponents. Justin correctly formulates the difference between Stoic teaching and school Platonism (ἀσώματα).

2.5.2; cf. 1.13.2

Allusion to the Stoic proof for the existence of God from the seasons; cf., e.g., Cicero, *Tusc.* 1.68f.

D 2.3

Reference to the concept of God in Stoicism; Justin claims that his Stoic teacher did not advance his knowledge of God. The passage refers to the Stoic monistic concept of God, which must have appeared horrible to a Platonic spiritualist; cf., e.g., Plutarch, *De Stoic. repugn.* 31ff.; *De comm. notit.* 31f.; *De defectu.* 19, 24. Justin's critique of his Stoic teacher is determined by his Platonically tinted glasses. The same is true for his position, stated in, e.g., D 2, in regard to other philosophical tendencies: Peripatetics (cf. Attikos, in Eusebius, *Pr. Ev.* 15.5.6f.), Epicureans (cf. above, chap. 25, n. 24), and Pythagoreans (cf. C. Andresen, "Justin," 160ff.)

1.20.2; 2.7(6).9

Likewise, reference to Stoic monism, e.g., on the Stoic theology and cosmology: God-Logos is identical with the world substance (cf. STVFr. 1.85, 160, 162, 557; 2.1027); the world always generates itself anew in repeated conflagrations of the entire world (cf. Zeno of Citium; knowledge of Stoic cycles also in D 1.5); consequently, God is changeable. Justin's polemic against the Stoics is at this point again a Middle Platonic topos (references in C. Andresen, "Justin," 170, n. 54).

2.7(6).3; 1.20.2, 4; cf. 57.1; 60.8–10

Reference to the Stoic doctrine of the conflagration of the world.

2.8(7).1; 7(6).8

Reference to Stoic ethics. The praise of Stoic ethics is parallel to that of school Platonism (Middle Platonic references in C. Andresen, "Justin," 178, particularly Apuleius, *De Plat.* 2.20–23).

D2.1f.

Behind the idea that the history of philosophy can be described as a splitting up of philosophy into different tendencies and behind the protreptic praise of philosophy as well as behind other individual motifs of D

2.1f. stands Posidonius's *Protreptikos* (in Diogenes Laertius, 7.91, 129; Seneca, *Ep.* 90; further Lucian, *Fug.* 5, 9–11; on this, cf. N. Hyldahl, *Philosophie,* 120–40); behind Posidonius himself is, among others, Plato, *Tim.* 47AB, *Phileb.* 16C. On D 2.2 πολύκρανος cf. perhaps Plato, *Rep.* 9.588C. Whether Justin himself had read Posidonius can hardly be ascertained. N. Hyldahl (*Philosophie,* 139) holds that there was a general circulation of Posidonius's ideas (Seneca, *Ep.* 90, and Lucian, *Fug.* 5ff., indicate this), or that Justin was informed indirectly through a source that cannot be more closely determined. The latter is also true for:

D 5f. The idea that the ζωτικὸν πνεῦμα of the mortal soul escapes had probably been introduced by Posidonius; cf. K. Reinhardt, "Poseidonios," Pauly / Wissowa 22/1: 780f.

D 3.4 (εὐδαιμονία through philosophy alone)

Cf. STVFr. 1.187; 3.49–67. The Stoic idea was taken up by, among others, Middle Platonism (e.g., Attikos in Eusebius, *Pr. Ev.* 15.4.1f.; further material in C. Andresen, "Justin," 179f., n. 88; M. Pohlenz, *Die Stoa* 1:120f.).

D. 5.5f. The next parallel is STVFr. 1.529 (the originally Aristotelian proof for the existence of God *ex gradibus*); but there also are Middle Platonic parallels: Albinos, *Didask.* 10, cf. 5; Celsus, in Origen, *Contra Cel.* 7.42; Maximus Tyrius, *Or.* 11.8.

1.29.1 Cf. the Stoic Musonius, *Fr.* 13.

Stoic concepts and ideas are known:

- Stoic composure and calm: ἀπάθεια, ἀπαθής, 1.57.2; 58.3; 2.1.2; cf. D 45.4; 46.7; 124.4; 1.5; 1.25.2; 10.2; ἀτάραχοι, 1.46.4

- The natural law: ὁ τῆς φύσεως νόμος, 2.2.4. Cf. STVFr. 1. 179; 3.4–9; 149; 264

- Stoic epistemology in D 3.6 (αἱ μὲν ... αἱ δὲ): STVFr. 2.83

- The natural notions: αἱ φυσικαί or κοιναὶ ἔννοιαι D 93.1; cf. 47.2; 2.14.2; 6.3. Cf., e.g., STVFr. 2.83.53ff. But Justin's a priori understanding resembles the Middle Platonic understanding, e.g., Albinos, *Didask.* 4 (further references in C. Andresen, "Justin," 177f.): Stoic conceptions are again seen through Middle Platonic lenses.

- The διαφθορά of the natural notions, D 93.1: cf. the Stoic doctrine of the distortion of the original reason (STVFr. 3.228–36; Musonius, *Fr.* 6 διαφθορά). Also this Stoic doctrine had been taken up eclectically by school Platonism: Albinos, *Didask.* 32.

- The λόγος ὀρθός, 2.2.2; 7.7; 9.4; D 3.3; 141.1. On Justin's Middle Platonic interpretation of this Stoic concept, see C. Andresen, "Justin," 178f., especially the references in n. 83. In D 3.3 cf. also the Stoic principle, to live ὁμολογουμένως (i.e., κατὰ τὸν λόγον).

- Reference to the Stoic "unalterable" (ἀπαράβατος) εἱμαρμένη, 1.43.1–8 (43.7 ἀπαράβατος); 44.11; 2.7(6).3f., 8f.: cf., e.g., STVFr. 2.266, 293. Justin's critique of the Stoic teaching of εἱμαρμέρη corresponds to that of Middle Platonism (C. Andresen, "Justin," 184–87, with reference to Albinos, Apuleius, and Plutarch, among others).

- The definition of "philosophy" as "knowledge of divine and natural things" D 3.5: cf. STVFr. 2.35f.; 1017; further M. Pohlenz, *Die Stoa*, 2.53. It is certainly known also in Middle Platonism (Albinos, *Didask.* 1, further references in C. Andresen, "Justin," 162, n. 20); cf. already Plato, *Symp.* 186B as well as the peripatetic Aristoxenos, *Fr.* 53 (Wehrli 2).

- 2.7(6).8f.; 8(7).1, 3 refer to the Stoic Logos doctrine. As in 2.13.3, the technical term λόγος σπερματικός is used. (Cf. also the terminology in 2.13.5f.: λόγος, σπορᾶς, σπέρμα; further D 13.6; 14.6; 44.1; 55.3; 123.5; 135.6; 1.19.4, 1f.; 44.9f.; 51.3; 53.7; 61.10, etc.).

The Stoic term *Logos spermatikos* is important for Justin's doctrine of the Logos; it has, of course, been modified by him. In the Stoa it is found in a cosmological and materialistic-pantheistic sense, in Justin in the sense of a spiritual and ethical principle. Justin's interpretation is based on philosophical presuppositions that have their roots in Antiochus of Ascalon (in Cicero, *De. fin.* 4f.). The line of tradition of a spiritual ethical interpretation of the "seminal forces" begins with Antiochus and extends through Areios Didymos into Middle Platonism (especially Albinos and Apuleius; on this see C. Andresen, "Justin," 170–74).

Possibly not only the spiritual-ethical but also the cosmological aspect of Justin's *Logos Spermatikos* is based on Middle Platonic presuppositions; on this see C. Andresen, "Justin," 174–78, with reference to Plutarch: the *Logos spermatikos* is the Logos of the Platonic world-soul. In this way the Stoic concept regains its original cosmological aspect, no longer in a Stoic monistic manner but in a Platonic dualist way.

Appendix 3

Tatian

Educational Components

Tatian's comprehensive critique of culture is directed toward

Chaps. 1–3 (esp. 1.3f.; 2.1)	rhetoric, poetry, and philosophy
8	mythology
9f.	astrology with its fatalism
17 et al.	superstitious practices
18 (same as 20.1)	medicine
19.2ff. (same as 12.5)	mantic practices
22 and 24	theaters
23	gladiatorial games
25 (same as 26.2ff.)	the pagan philosophers, expressly Cynics, Platonists, Epicureans, followers of Aristotle, Democritus, Pythagoras. According to Tatian, the philosophical schools are evidence for the dismemberment of truth, as it takes place in Greek culture
26.2	the grammarians
27.3	astronomy, geometry; the methods of conclusion in philosophy
28	the lack of uniformity in legislation
29 and 33	the cults
31.2ff.	historiography
33–35	the fine arts

This polemic regarding culture represents at the same time an imposing assembly of educational elements. The critique of the *fine arts* (33–35), for example, offers an extensive catalogue of artists and works that Tatian has collected especially from sophist sources (on this cf.

M. Elze, *Tatian*, 17; A. Kalkmann, *Tatians Nachrichten*, 520f.). The critique of pagan *mythology* represents a veritable fireworks of mythological knowledge from, for example, Chrysaor to Hephaistos, who works in Homeric fashion with bracelets and ear clips (*Or.* 8.3, cf. Homer, *Il.* 18.401; *Or.* 8.2f., cf. Hesiod, *Theog.* 278ff., 979ff.; see the whole chapter *Or.* 8; in 9 the second half; *Or.* 10; 21; also 6.1; 17.1; 20.1; 25.2f.; 32.2f.; 33f.). When Tatian carries on an argument against the *cults* (29 and 33), he shows how much especially the knowledge of the scenery of the city of Rome had impressed him. Like his teacher, Justin (*Apol.* 2.12.5), Tatian in 29.1, for example, condemns the sacrificial practices for Zeus Latiaris in the Alban mountains (blood from executed criminals was offered to him) or the cult for Artemis in the Alban mountains (probably Diana Nemorensis in Aricia). The passage 33.1 possibly alludes to a sacrilege in the temple of Isis in Rome: Josephus, *Ant.* 18.65ff.; cf. Tacitus, *Ann.* 2.85; Suetonius, *Tib.* 36.

For the pagan literary education compare:

8.1	Homer, *Il.* 1.599; *Od.* 8.326
8.3	*Il.* 18.401, 393
10.2	*Od.* 11.298ff.; 15.133
19.3	*Il.* 2.372
21.1f.	*Il.* 22.226f.; 21.448; 20.39; 2.3ff.
27.2	*Il.* 1.225 ("doe"); 2.212 (Thersites)
32.2	*Il.* 8.87ff.
32.3	*Il.* 2.212 and 219
36.1	*Il.* 20.215ff.
34.2	reference to Aesop and his fables
35.2	to Solon, *Fragm.* 22 (Diehl)
33.2	to Sappho's songs
33.1	to the poetess Praxilla
1.2	to a cultural-historical comment by Hellonikos (*Fragm. hist. Graec.*, ed. C. Müller, Fragm. 163a, b)
27.1	to the lyrical poet Diagoras ὁ ἄθεος of Melos (cf., e.g., Cicero, *Nat.* 1.2; 3.89)
34.2	to Sophron and his mimes
24.1	to the plays of Euripides, Hegesippus (cj.), Menander
10.3; 33.4; 3.1	to Euripides, esp. Euripides, *Orestes* (1294; 1301), and Euripides's lost tragedy Μελανίππη ἡ σοφή
1.3; cf. 15.1	to Aristophanes' *Frogs* 92f.; comically Tatian changes Aristophanes' swallows into crows
8.4f.	*Trag. Fragm. adesp.* 471; 565

27.2	to Herodoros's famous comments on the story of Heracles, *Fragm.* 9 (*Fragm. hist. Gr.*, ed. Müller, 2:27ff.)
27.1	to Callimachus's *Hymn. in Jov.* 8f.
8.4	*Orphic Fragm.* 4.1 (ed. Abel, p. 144)
27.1	to Leon of Pella (cf. *Fragm. d. gr. Histor.*, ed. F. Jacoby, 659)
34.3	to the obscene literature that circulates under the names of Philainis and Elephantis (see also above Justin, *Apol.* 2.15)
41	offers a complete list of authors, e.g., Aristeas of Prokonnesos with his Ἀριμάσπεια ἔπη (cf., e.g., Aeschyl. *Prom.* 803ff.)

For the listing of cultural achievements of the barbarians in *Or.* 1, cf., e.g., Straton of Lampsakos, in Clement, *Strom.* 1.16.77.

"Philosophical" Components of Education:
   The gossip stories about philosophers in *Or.* 2f. are on the level of the caricature Γοήτων φώρα of Oinomaos of Gadara (on this cf. M. Elze, *Tatian*, 26, n. 2). In a polemical manner, Tatian refers to *Heraclitus* (*Or.* 3.1ff.; modified quotation from Heraclitus; cf. *Fragm.* 80; Diogenes Laertius, 9.5; Plutarch, *Adv. Colot.* 1118C; on *Or.* 3.1 cf. Diogenes Laertius 9.6); on *Pythagoras* and *Pherecydes* (*Or.* 3.2f.; 25.2); on *Empedocles* (3.2); *Democritus* and his teacher, *Ostanes* (17.1; 25.2; cf. Pliny, *Nat. hist.* 30.8f.); on *Aristippos* (*Or.* 2.1); *Plato* (e.g., 25.1; 2.1 anecdote about Dionysius, cf. Tertullian, *Apol.* 46.15; allusion to the doctrine of the transmigration of the soul in *Or.* 3.3, cf. 25.2); on *Aristotle* and his student *Alexander* (2.1f.; 25.2); in 2.2 and 27.3 reference to the *Nicomachean Ethics* (N.E. 1178b.33–1179a.5; 1146b.29f.). *Or.* 24 refers to Aristotle's student *Aristoxenos* of Tarent with his book περὶ αὐλητῶν, whose interest in the famous flute player Antigenides (fourth c. B.C.E.) is reported. There is reference to *Anaxarchos* (19.2); *Diogenes* (2.1, cf. on this Lucian, *Vit. auct.* 10; Plutarch, *De es. carn.* 995D); to his student, the Cynic *Crates* (*Or.* 3.3; cf. on this Lactantius, 3.15; Clement, *Strom.* 4.19.121f.); *Epicurus* and his proverbial contempt for God (*Or.* 25.1f.; 27.2); to the book on Homer by Epicurus's friend *Metrodoros of Lampsacos* (cf. Diogenes Laertius, 2.11), from which material is reported (*Or.* 21.3). The text 21.2 makes reference generally to the widely circulated allegorical interpretation of Homer (cf., e.g., in the Stoics). Reference is made to *Zeno* the Stoic and his doctrine on the conflagration of the world (3.1f.; 6.1; 25.2). For the knowledge of other individual Stoic (particularly in pneumatology) and peripatetic characteristics, cf.

M. Elze, *Tatian*, 30f. (n. 5); 127, 68f., 84f., 87f., 96; N. Hyldahl, *Philosophie*, 250–52. *Or.* 25.1 refers to the contemporary Cynic *Peregrinus Proteus* (cf. Lucian's work περὶ τῆς Περεγρίνου τελευτῆς). On the individual Cynic motifs in *Or.* 29.2 and other places, see N. Hyldahl, *Philosophie*, 245–47. *Or.* 25.2 also treats other philosophical topoi, such as the immortality or mortality of the soul (philosophical parallels in M. Elze, *Tatian*, 89ff.; cf. 121) and the indestructibility of the world (on this see above Justin). Philosophical themes also in *Or.* 8–11; 7.1f. (εἱμαρμένη — free will); 4.1f. (material concept of God). For the common philosophical negative descriptions of God, see, e.g., *Or.* 4.

On *Or.* 23, cf. the older contemporary *Dio of Prusa* with his critique of the gladiatorial games (in the Rhodes' speech and the speech to the Nicomedians: 31 §121; 38 §17). On *Or.* 28 and 30.1 see likewise Dio of Prusa, Euboicos (7 §134 and 137) *Or.* 9.1 is comparable to Dio of Prusa's "Concerning the Demon" (25 §1). Tatian's distinction between the false *paideia* of the Greeks and the genuine *paideia* of the Christians corresponds to Dio's (4 §29–31) double *paideia*. That Dio Chrysostom, the famous speaker and philosopher who was banished from Rome under Domitian, influenced Tatian's work is no surprise in view of the impressive history of Dio's influence (cf., e.g., the praise in Philostratus, *Vit. Soph.* 1.7; *Vit. Apoll.* 5.37).

20.2	knowledge of *the geographers*. Cf. Strabo, 15 p. 697C (the south burned out); ibid., 1 p. 63C; Pliny, *Nat. hist.* 4.13.27; Dionysius, *Perieg.* 32 (the north frozen); further references in M. Elze, *Tatian*, 84, n. 1.
31	reference to the *historiographers*. Here is offered a critical "history of the research" on Homer at that time. Beginning with Theagenes of Rhegium, Tatian enumerates a total of sixteen names of authors. Emphasis is placed upon the contradictions in the chronology of Homer found in *Crates, Eratosthenes, Aristarchos, Philochoros* (cf. *Fragm.* 52: *Fragm. hist. Gr.* 1:392), and *Apollodoros*. With the short summary of so much "education," Tatian wishes consciously to impress his readers; he writes for such educated persons "who are in the position to research (what is said) in detail" (τοῖς ἐπ' ἀκριβὲς ἐξετάζειν δυναμένοις, 7). Cf. further on historiography *Or.* 36ff., where an imposing collection of educational material is offered. For example:
36.1f.	reference to *Berosus's* three books concerning Babylon (cf. *Fragm.* 14a: *Fragm. hist.Gr.* 2:508) and to *Jubas's* Assyrian history (cf. *Fragm.* 21: *Fragm. hist.Gr.* 3:472).
37.1	reference to Greek translations of Phoenician historiographers as well as to *Menander* of Pergamon or Ephesus

	(cf. *Fragm.* 3: *Fragm. hist.Gr.* 4:445–48; Josephus, *Contra Apion*, 1.18); further to *Laetus* (*Fragm. hist.Gr.* 4:437).
38	reference to *Ptolemaius's* Egyptian history (Ptolemaius of Mendes; cf. *Fragm.* 1: *Fragm. hist.Gr.* 4:485; Tertullian, *Apol.* 19; Clement, *Strom.* 1.21). Tatian knows of it perhaps only through Apion: *Or.* 38.1.
38.1; 27.1	reference to *Apion's* work concerning Egypt (cf. *Fragm.* 2: *Fragm. hist.Gr.* 3:506–16; further, e.g., Pliny, *Nat. hist.* praef. 25; Josephus, *Contra Apion*).
39–41	reference to an abundance of well-known topoi in ancient historiography: e.g., to Cadmus, the founder of Cadmea in Boeotia and the bringer of the alphabet to Greece, etc.

As further educational elements cf. besides the cultural historical notes in 1.1–2; 28, e.g., the allusion to an anecdote about Thales (26.1; cf. Diogenes Laertius, 1.34); the proverbial cask of the Danaids (26.1; since Pseudo-Plato, *Axioch.* 371E); the accusers of Socrates, Anytos and Meletos (3.2). On the cosmology referred to in 27.2 cf. Anaxagoras in Diogenes Laertius, 2.8; on 3.2, Diogenes Laertius, 8.69, 75; on 1.1, Lucian, *Fugit* 6–8; on 2.1f., e.g., Plutarch, *Alex.* 51f.; Seneca, *De ira* 3.17; on 12.5 Plutarch, *Sol.* 5; Herodotus, 4.76; on 18.2, Pliny, *Nat. hist.* 25, especially 91ff.; Aelian. *h. var.* 1.9; on 3.2 (Busiris), Apollod. *bibl.* 2.117; on 21.1, e.g., Apollod. 2.65f.; Diodorus Siculus, 4.38; on 8.4f., Ovid, *Met.* 1.452ff.; 10.174ff.; on 19.2, Cicero, *Tusc.* 2.52; *De deor. nat.* 3.82; on 26.1 (argumentation with nautical imagery), e.g., Poseidonios in Aetios's *Placita* 3.5.1; Lucretius, 4.384ff.; Sextus Empiricus, *Adv. mathem.* 7.414. Such elements are typical of the colorfulness of sophisticated eloquence.

Appendix 4

Fractionation of Roman Jewry

Philo already knew of a number of προσευχαί in Rome.[1]

The inscriptions verify a maximum[2] of fourteen different individual congregations:

- a συναγωγὴ Ἀγριππησίων[3]

- a συναγωγὴ τῶν Αὐγουστησίων[4]

- one of the Volumnenses or βολουμνησίων[5]

- one of the (He)rodians[6]

- a synagogue on the Mars Field[7]

- one in the *Subura* quarter[8] (Σιβουρήσιοι)

- a συναγωγὴ Αἰβρέων/Ἐβρέων[9]

- a συναγωγὴ Ἐλαίας[10]

- a "proseucha" near the republican wall between the Porta Esquilina and the Porta Collina[11]

---

1. *Leg. ad Gaium* 155f.: ἠπίστατο οὖν καὶ προσευχὰς ἔχοντας καὶ συνιόντας εἰς αὐτὰς, καὶ μάλιστα ταῖς ἱεραῖς ἑβδόμαις κτλ. Cf. similarly Alexandria (Philo, ibid., 132ff.: πολλαί), Damascus (Acts 9:20), Salamis (Acts 13:5), Jerusalem (Acts 6:9), etc. That new communities of worship were established in a city next to already existing communities was not unusual for Jewish circumstances. A group of ten men capable of worship were enough to form a new community (*Meg.* 4.3 = *t.Meg.* 4.14).

2. See n. 11. We cannot completely exclude the possibility that one community might have had two names or that one was renamed.

3. CIG 9907; CIJ 1:503; 425; 365.

4. CIL 6:29757; CIG 9902f.; CIJ 1:284; 301; 338; 368; 416; 496.

5. CIL 6:29756; CIJ 1:343; 402; 417; 523. "Volumnius" was a Roman *nomen gentile*. One bearer of the name was legate in Syria in 8 B.C.E. and a friend of Herod's (Josephus, *Bell.* 1.535; 538; *Ant.* 16.277ff.; 332; 354).

6. CIJ 173:...ΡΟΔΙΩΝ. H. J. Leon, *Jews of Ancient Rome*, 159ff., denies the existence of this synagogue.

7. CIL 6:29756; CIG 9905; CIJ 1:88; 319; 523.

8. CIG 6447; CIJ 1:18; 22; 67; 140; 380.

9. CIG 9909; CIJ 1:510; 291; 317; 535.

10. CIG 9904; CIJ 1:281; 509.

11. CIJ 1:531. A fruit dealer had his shop nearby. Since "proseucha" denotes a synagogue building while the other names in the list denote synagogue *communities,* we

- a synagogue of the *Calcarenses*[12]
- of the Tripolitans[13]
- Ἀρκ[ης Λι]βάνου[14]
- of the Σεκηνῶν[15]
- of the *Vernaculi*[16]

These are individual communities, independently organized, each with its own place of assembly, its own council of elders (γερουσία), and its own community officials.[17] These communities were only loosely associated with each other. Throughout the entire imperial period there is no evidence of a union of Roman Jewish communities under one single council of elders (γερουσία),[18] a finding that is a contrast to Alexandria, where the diverse synagogues formed one big political corporation.[19] At least five of the communities listed above existed already in the first century C.E.[20]

The background of a fractionated Roman Jewry serves as a foil to the fractionation of Roman Christianity.

---

cannot exclude the possibility that one of the synagogue communities named in the list was housed in this building next to the republican wall.

12. *CIJ* 1:304; 316; 384; 504; 537; possibly 433.

13. *CIJ* 1:390; 408; Τριπολειτῶν.

14. *CIJ* 1:501. What is meant is the place of birth of Alexander Severus: Arca/Lebanon, from whence the founders of the synagogue came. H. J. Leon, *Jews of Ancient Rome*, 163ff. denies the existence of this synagogue — without reason.

15. *CIJ* 1:7.

16. *CIJ* 1:318; 383; 398; 494.

17. Cf. among others the γερουσιάρχης συναγωγῆς Αὐγοστησίων *CIG* 9902; the ἄρχων Σιβουρησίων *CIG* 6447; the official of the Αὐγουστησίων synagogue *CIG* 9903; the official of the Ἀγριππησίων synagogue *CIG* 9907; the μελλάρχων ἐκ τῶν Αὐγουστησίων *CIL* 6.29757; the πατὴρ συναγωγῆς Ἐλαίας *CIG* 9904. Further material in R. Penna, "Les Juifs à Rome," 329f.

18. Cf. R. Penna, ibid., 327ff. (particularly nn. 55, 30); H. Solin, "Juden und Syrer," 696f. The newly discovered and previously not documented term ἀρχιγερουσιάρχης (cf. U. M. Fasola, "Le due catacombe ebraiche," 36, fig. 15; fourth century), found in the catacomb of the Villa Torlonia on the Via Nomentana, is probably a pleonastic rendering of γερουσιάρχης. See the analogous term "archigerusiastes" in Hellenistic civic administration (in an inscription from Prusias ad Hypium: F. K. Dörner, "Bericht," no. 7; other analogous material in H. Solin, ibid.).

19. Cf., e.g., E. Schürer, *History*, 3:92ff.

20. Cf. R. Penna, ibid., 328 (that of the Hebrews, of the *Vernaculi*, the *Augustenses*, the *Agrippenses*, and of the *Volumnenses*). Also the *proseucha* near the republican wall belongs to the first century C.E.

Abbreviations

ACIAC	*Actes du congrès international d'archéologie chrétienne*
AHR	*American Historical Review*
AJA	*American Journal of Archaeology*
AJP	*American Journal of Philology*
AKG	Arbeiten zur Kirchengeschichte
ANRW	*Aufstieg und Niedergang der römischen Welt*
AuC	Antike und Christentum
B	J. Baumgart, "Die Lehre des römischen Slavennamen," diss. Breslau, 1936.
B.C.E.	Before the Common Era
BiLi	*Bibel und Liturgie*
BKV	Bibliothek der Kirchenväter
Bl-D-R	F. Blass, A. Debrunner, and F. Rehkopf, *Grammatik der neutestamentlichen Griechisch* (Cf. F. Blass, A. Debrunner, and R. W. Funk, *A Greek Grammar of the New Testament*)
BU	Biblische Untersuchungen
Bullet(tino)	*Bullettino di Archeologia Cristiana* (Rome, 1983–94); continued in *Nuovo Bullettino de Archeologia Cristiana* (Rome, 1895–1922); continued in *Revista de Archeologia Cristiana* (Rome, 1924–)
Bullettino communale	*Bullettino della Commissione archeologica communale de Roma* (1872–)
BZ	*Biblische Zeitschrift*
CBQ	*Catholic Biblical Quarterly*
C.E.	Common Era
ChronEg	*Chronique d'Égypte*
CIG	*Corpus Inscriptionum Graecarum*, vols. 1–4 (Berlin, 1828–77)
CIJ	*Corpus Inscriptionum Judaicarum*, vols. 1–2 (Vatican, 1936, 1952)
CIL	*Corpus Inscriptionum Latinarum* (Leipzig and Berlin, 1893–)
CMind	*Catholic Mind*

CP	*Classical Philology*
CPJ	*Corpus Papyrorum Judaicorum*, 3 vols. (Cambridge, 1957–64)
CQ	*Classical Quarterly*
CSRB	*Council on the Study of Religion: Bulletin*
CthMi	*Currents in Theology and Mission*
DÖAW	Denkschriften, Österreichische Akademie der Wissenschaften
ÉgT	*Église et theologie*
EKK	Evangelisch-Katholischer Kommentar zum Neuen Testament
EPRO	Études préliminaires aux religions orientales dans l'empire romain
EvTh	*Evangelische Theologie*
EWNT	*Evangelische Wörterbuch zum Neuen Testament*
ExpT	*Expository Times*
FRLANT	Forschungen zur Religion und Literatur des Alten und Neuen Testaments
FS	Festschrift
GTA	Göttinger Theologische Arbeiten
HAW	Handbuch der Altertumswissenschaft
HDG	Handbuch der Dogmengeschichte
HNT	Handbuch zum Neuen Testament
HTR	*Harvard Theological Review*
HZ	*Historische Zeitschrift*
ICUR	*Inscriptiones Christianae Urbis Romae*, ed. G. B. De Rossi, J. Gatti, A. Silvagni, and A. Ferrua (Rome, 1857–)
IG	*Inscriptiones Graecae*, 1 (Berlin, 1873)
IGR	*Inscriptiones Graecae ad Res Romanas Pertinentes* (Paris, 1906–27)
ILCV	*Inscriptiones Latinae Christianae Veteres*, ed. E. Diehl; 3 vols. (Berlin, 1925–31; 2d ed., 1961); 4 Suppl., ed. J. Moreau and H. I. Marrou (Dublin, 1967)
ILS	*Inscriptiones Latinae Selectae*, ed. H. Dessau (Berlin, 1892–1916; repr. 1974)
JAC	*Jahrbuch für Antike und Christentum*
JAC Erg.	*JAC,* Supplements
JBL	*Journal of Biblical Literature*
JRH	*Journal of Religious History*
JRS	*Journal of Roman Studies*

JSJ	*Journal of the Study of Judaism in the Persian, Hellenistic, and Roman Periods*
JTS	*Journal of Theological Studies*
KEK	Kritisch-exegetischer Kommentar über das Neue Testament
KlPauly	*Der Kleine Pauly,* ed. K. Ziegler and W. Sontheimer (Stuttgart, 1964)
LP	Liber Pontificalis
LWQF	Liturgiewissenschaftliche Quellen und Forschungen
MBPF	Münchener Beiträge zur Papyrusforschung and antiken Rechtsgeschichte
NHS	Nag Hammadi Studies
NovT	*Novum Testamentum*
NTD	Das Neue Testament Deutsch
NTS	New Testament Studies
OGIS	*Orientis Graeci Inscriptiones Selectae,* ed. W. Dittenberger (Leipzig, 1903–5)
Pauly/ Wissowa	*Real-Encyclopädie der classischen Altertumswissenschaft* (Stuttgart, 1839–; supplements, 1903–1956; 11 vols.; 2d series, 1914–18)
RAC	*Reallexikon für Antike und Christentum*
RB	*Revue biblique*
RdQ	*Revue de Qumran*
RE	*Realencyklopädie für protestantische Theologie und Kirche*
REA	*Revue des études anciennes*
RevSR	*Revue des sciences religieuses*
RivArCr	*Rivista di Archeologia Cristiana*
Röm. Mitt.	*Römische Mitteilungen*
RQ	*Römische Quartalschrift für christliche Altertumskunde und Kirchengeschichte*
RSLR	*Revista di storia e letteratura religiosa*
RSR	*Recherches de science religieuse*
SBL	Society of Biblical Literature
SBS	Stuttgarter Bibelstudien
SICV	*Sylloge inscriptionum christianarum veterum musei vaticani,* ed. H. Zilliacus; Acta institute romani finlandiae 1/1–2 (Helsinki, 1963)
SIG	*Sylloge inscriptionum graecarum,* ed. W. Dittenberger, 3d ed. (Leipzig, 1915–24)

SJLA	*Studies in Judaism in Late Antiquity*
StNT	*Studien zum Neuen Testament*
Str-B	Hermann Strack and Paul Billerbeck, *Kommentar zum Neuen Testament aus Talmud und Midrasch*
StTh	*Studia Theologica*
STVFr	*Stoicoram veterim fragmenta,* ed. H. v. Arnim (Leipzig, 1903– 24)
SUNT	Studien zur Umwelt des Neuen Testaments
TB	Theologische Bücherei
ThGl	*Theologie und Glaube*
ThR	*Theologische Rundschau*
ThRv	*Theologische Revue*
ThZ	*Theologische Zeitschrift*
TLZ	*Theologische Literaturzeitung*
TRE	*Theologische Realenzyklopädie*
TS	*Theological Studies*
TU	Texte und Untersuchungen zur Geschichte der altchristlichen Literatur
TWNT	*Theologisches Wörterbuch zum Neuen Testament,* ed. G. Kittel and G. Friedrich (Stuttgart, 1933–79). English translation: *Theological Dictionary of the New Testament* (Grand Rapids: Eerdmans, 1964–76)
TZ	*Theologische Zeitschrift*
UB	Urban-Bücher
VC	*Vigilae Christianae*
VCaro	*Verbum caro*
WF	Wege der Forschung
WUNT	Wissenschaftliche Untersuchungen zum Neuen Testament
ZÄS	*Zeitschrift für ägyptische Sprache und Altertumskunde*
ZAW	*Zeitschrift für die alttestamentliche Wissenschaft*
ZEE	*Zeitschrift für evangelische Ethik*
ZKG	*Zeitschrift für Kirchengeschichte*
ZKT	*Zeitschrift für katholische Theologie*
ZNW	*Zeitschrift für die neutestamentliche Wissenschaft*
ZTK	*Zeitschrift für Theologie und Kirche*

Bibliography

Abbott, F. *The Common People of Ancient Rome: Studies of Roman Life and Literature.* New York, 1965 (1911).

Achelis, H., ed. *Acta SS. Nerei et Achilei.* TU XII, 2. Leipzig, 1893.

———. "Altchristliche Kunst." *ZNW* 12 (1911): 296–320; 13 (1912): 21–46; 14 (1913): 324–48; 16 (1915): 1–23.

Acta Sanctorum. Ed. J. Bolland and G. Henschen. Antwerp, 1643ff.; 2d ed., Venice, 1734–70; 3d ed., Paris, 1863–1870; Brussels, 1894, ed. J. B. De Rossi and L. Duchesne.

Aland, K. "Methodische Bemerkungen zum Corpus Paulinum bei den Kirchenvätern des 2. Jh." In *Kerygma und Logos,* ed. A. M. Ritter, 29–48. Göttingen, 1979.

———. "Der Schluss und die ursprüngliche Gestalt des Römerbriefes." In K. Aland, *Neutestamentliche Entwürfe,* 284–301. TB 63. Munich, 1979.

———. "Das Verhätnis von Kirche und Staat nach dem Neuen Testament und den Aussagendes 2. Jh." In ibid., 26–123 (lit.).

Alfaric, P. *Origines sociales du christianisme.* Paris: Publications de l'Union nationaliste, 1959 = *Die sozialen Ursprünge des Christentums.* Darmstadt, 1963.

Alföldy, G. "Die römische Gesellschaft: Struktur und Eigenart." *Gymnasium* 83 (1976): 1–25.

———. *Konsulat und Senatorenstand unter den Antoninen.* Bonn, 1977.

———. *Römische Sozialgeschichte.* 2d ed. Wiesbaden, 1979; 3d ed., 1984. ET: *The Social History of Rome.* Trans. D. Braund and F. Pollack. Totowa, N.J., 1985

———. *Die Rolle des Einzelnen in der Gesellschaft des Römischen Kaiserreiches.* Sitzber. Heidelbg. Ak. Wiss., Phil-hist. Kl. Heidelberg, 1980.

———. "Die Freilassung von Sklaven und die Struktur der Sklaverei der römischen Kaiserzeit." In *Sozial- und Wirtschaftsgeschichte der römischen kaiserzeit,* ed. H. Schneider, 336–71. WF 552. Darmstadt, 1981.

———. "Soziale Konflikte im römischen Kaiserreich." In ibid., 372–95.

Allard, P. *Les esclaves chrétiens depuis les premiers temps de l'église jusqu'à la fin de la domination romaine en occident.* 2d ed. Paris, 1876; 5th ed., 1914.

Altaner, B., and A. Stuiber. *Patrologie.* 8th ed. Freiburg, 1978.

Andresen, C. "Justin und der mittlere Platonismus." *ZNW* 44 (1952f): 157–95.

———. *Logos und Nomos.* AKG 30. Berlin, 1955.

———. *Die Kirche in ihrer Geschichte: Einführung in die christliche Archäologie.* Göttingen, 1971.

Apollonij Ghetti, B. M., A. Ferrua, E. Josi, E. Kirsehbaum, and L. Kaas. *Esplorazioni sotto la confessione di S. Pietro in Vaticano, Eseguite negli anni 1940–1949*. Vatican, 1951.

Apollonij Ghetti, B. M. "Le chiese titolari di S. Silvestro e S. Martino ai Monti." *RivArCr* 37 (1961): 271–302.

———. "Problemi relativi alle origini dell'architettura paleocristiana." *ACIAC* 9 (1978): 491– 511.

Applebaum, S. "The Social and Economic Status of the Jews in the Diaspora." In *The Jewish People in the First Century*, ed. S. Safrai and M. Stern, 2:701–27. Assen and Philadelphia, 1976.

d'Arcais, F., P. Brezzi, J. Ruysschaert, S. Garofalo, and E. Cattaveo. *Pietro à Roma*. Rome, 1967.

Arnim, H. v. *Stoicorum veterum fragmenta*. Leipzig, 1903–24.

Baaren, Th. P. v. "Towards a Definition of Gnosticism." In *Le Origini dello Gnosticismo*, ed. U. Bianchi, ed. *Numen* Supp. 12 (1967): 174–80.

Baker, D., ed. *Church, Society and Politics*. Oxford, 1975.

Baldi, A. *La Pompei giudaico-cristiana*. Cava dei Tirreni, 1964.

———. *L'anatema e la croce: Ebrei e Cristiana in Pompei Antica*. Cava dei Tirreni, 1983.

Balsdon, J. P. V. D. "Woman in Imperial Rome." *History Today* 10 (1960): 24–31.

Bang, M. "Die Herkunft der römischen Sklaven." *Röm. Mitt.* 25 (1910): 223–51; 27 (1912): 189–221.

Banks, R. *Paul's Idea of Community: The Early House Churches in Their Historical Setting*. Grand Rapids, 1980.

Bannert, H., ed. "Der antike Roman." Manuscript.

Barbieri, G. *L'Albo Senatorio da Settimio Severo a Carino*. Rome, 1952.

Bardon, H. "La notion d'intellectuel à Rome." *Studi Classice* 13 (1971): 95–107.

Bardy, G. "Le Pasteur d'Hermas et les livres hermétiques." *RB* 8 (1911): 391–407.

———. "Expressions stoïciennes dans la 1ª Clementis." *RSR* 12 (1922): 73–85.

———. "L'Eglise romaine sous le pontificat de saint Anicet." *RSR* 17 (1927): 489ff.

———. "Les écoles romaines au second siècle." *Revue d'histore ecclésiastique* 28 (1932): 501–32.

———. *La question des langues dans l'église ancienne*, 1. Paris, 1948, esp. 81ff.

———. " 'Philosophico' et 'philosophe' dans le vocabulaire chrétien des premiers sièles." *Rev. d'Ascetique et de Mystique* 25 (1949): 97–108.

Barnard, L. W. "Clement of Rome and the Persecution of Domitian." *NTS* 10 (1963–64): 251–60.

———. "Hermas and Judaism." *Studia Patristica* 8 (1966): 3–9.

———. *Justin Martyr: His Life and Thought*. Cambridge, 1967.

———. "Apologeten." In *TRE* 3:379f.

Barnes, A. S. *Christianity at Rome in the Apostolic Age*. London, 1938. Reprint, Westport, Conn., 1971.

Bartelink, G. J. M. "Umdeutung heidnischer Termini im christlichen Sprachgebrauch." In Frohnes (below), *Kirchengeschichte als Missionsgeschichte*, 397ff.

Bauer, W. *Griechisch-deutsches Wörterbuch zu den Schriften des NT und der übrigen urchristlichen Literatur.* 5th ed. Berlin, 1971.

———. *Rechtgläubigkeit und Ketzerei im ältesten Christentum.* 2d ed. Tübingen, 1963. Engl. trans.: *Orthodoxy and Heresy in Earliest Christianity.* Philadelphia, 1971.

Bauman, R. A. *Impietas in principem: A Study of Treason against the Roman Emperor with Special Reference to the First Century* A.D. Munich, 1974.

Baumgart, J. "Die römischen Sklavennamen." Diss. phil. Breslau, 1936.

Baumstark, A. "Die Lehre des römischen Presbyters Florinus." *ZNW* 13 (1912): 306–19.

Baur, F. C. *Christliche Gnosis.* Tübingen, 1835.

Becher, L. "Der Isiskult in Rom, ein Kult der Halbwelt?" *ZÄS* 96 (1970): 81–90.

Bechtel, F. *Die Attischen Frauennamen.* Göttingen, 1902.

Belo, F. *Lecture matérialiste de l'évangile de Marc.* Paris, 1974.

Benko, S. "The Edict of Claudius of A.D. 49 and the Instigator Chrestus." *ThZ* 25 (1969): 406–18.

———. *Pagan Rome and the Early Christians.* London, 1985.

Benko, S., and J. J. O'Rourke, eds. *The Catacombs and the Colosseum: The Roman Empire as the Setting of Primitive Christianity.* Valley Forge, Pa., 1971.

———, ed. *Early Church History.* London, 1972.

Benveniste, E. "Le nom de l'esclave à Rome." *Rev. des Etud. lat.* (Paris) 10 (1932): 429–40.

Berchem, D. v. *Les distributions de blé et d'argent à la plèbe romaine sous l'Empire.* Geneva, 1939.

Berger, K. "Wissenssoziologie und Exegese des Neuen Testaments." *Kairos* 19 (1977): 124–33.

Berwig, D. "Mark Aurel und die Christen." Phil. Diss. Munich, 1970.

Besnier, M. *L'île Tibérine dans l'antiquité.* Paris, 1901.

———. *Eglises chrétiennes et collèges funéraires: Mélanges A. Dufourcq.* Paris, 1932, 9–19.

Betz, H. D. *Lukian von Samosata und das NT.* Berlin, 1961.

Beyschlag, K. "Kallist und Hippolyt." *TZ* 20 (1964): 103–24.

———. *Clemens Romanus und der Frühkatholizismus.* Tübingen, 1966.

———. "Zur ΕΙΡΗΝΗ ΒΑΘΕΙΑ (1 Clem 2,2)." *VC* 26 (1972): 18–23.

Bibliotheca hagiographica Latina antiquae et mediae aetatis. Ed. Socii Bollandiani, Brussels, 1898–1901; 2d ed., 1911.

Bibliotheca hagiographica Graeca. Ed. F. Halkin. Brussels, 1957.

Bibliotheca sanctorum. Istituto Giovanni XXIII nella pontificia università Lateranense. Rome, 1962ff.

Bigelmair, A. *Die Beteiligung der Christen am öffentlichen Leben in vorconstantinischer Zeit.* Veröfftl. aus dem Kirchenhist. Sem. München 8. Munich, 1902.

———. "Zur Frage des Sozialismus und Kommunismus im Chrt. der ersten 3 Jh." In *Beitr. z. Gesch. d. chr. Altertums u.d. byz. Lit.*, ed. A. M. Königer, 73–93. FS A. Ehrhard. Bonn, 1922.

Billeter, G. *Geschichte des Zinsfusses im gr.rom. Altertum bis auf Justinian.* Leipzig, 1989.

Bisi, A. M. "Su una base con dedica a Dusares nell'Antiquariurn di Pozzuoli." *Annali Istituto Orientale di Napoli,* NS 22 (1972): 381–87.

Blanck, H. *Einführung in das Privatleben der Griechen und Römer.* Darmstadt, 1976 (lit.).

Blass, F. "XPHCTIANOI–XPICTIANOI." *Hermes* 30 (1895): 465–70.

Blass, F., A. Debrunner, F. Rehkopf. *Grammatik des ntl. Griechisch.* 14th ed. Göttingen, 1976.

Bleicken, J. *Verfassungs- und Sozialgeschichte des römischen Kaiserreiches.* 2 vols. 2d ed. Paderborn, 1981.

Bloom, H. "Lying against Time: Gnosis, Poetry, Criticism." In *The Rediscovery of Gnosticism,* ed. B. Layton, 1:57–72. Leiden, 1980.

Boelcke, W. A. *Wirtschafts- und Sozialgeschichte: Einführung, Bibliographie, Methoden, Problemfelder.* Darmstadt, 1987.

Bogaert, R. "Changeurs et banquiers chez les pères de l'Eglise." *Ancient Society* 4 (1973): 239–70.

Boissieu, A. de. *Inscriptions antiques de Lyon.* Lyon, 1846–54.

Bolkestein, H. *Wohltätigkeit und Armenpflege im vorchristlichen Altertum.* Utrecht, 1939; Groningen, 1967.

Bömer, F. *Untersuchungen über die Religion, der Sklaven in Griechenland und Rom.* 4 vols. Ak. Wiss. u. Lit. Mainz, Geistes- u. Sozwiss. Kl., 1957–63. 2d ed. Wiesbaden, 1981.

Bonfioli, M., and S. Panciera. "Della Cristianità del collegium, quod est in domo Sergiae Paullinae." *Rendiconti della Pont. Accad. Rom. d'Arch.* 44 (1971–72): 185–201.

———. "In Domo Sergiae Paullinae." In *Rendiconti della Pont. Accad. Rom. d'Arch.,* 45 (1972–73): 133–38.

Bonhoeffer, D. *Das jüdische Element im I. Clemensbrief.* In ibid., *Ges. Schriften,* ed. E. Bethge, 5:17–63. Munich, 1972. Engl. trans.: "The Jewish Element in First Clement." In Dietrich Bonhoeffer Works 9: *The Young Bonhoeffer 1918–1927,* 216–56. Minneapolis: Fortress, 2003.

Bonner, S. F. *Education in Ancient Rome: From the Elder Cato to the Younger Pliny.* Berkeley, Calif., 1977.

Boren, H. C. *Roman Society: A Social, Economic and Cultural History.* Lexington, Mass., and Toronto, 1977.

Borg, M. "A New Context for Romans XIII." *NTS* 19 (1972–73): 205–18.

Botte, B. *La Tradition Apostolique de Saint Hippolyte: Essai de reconstitution.* Liturgiewiss. Quellen u. Forsch. 39. 4th ed. Münster, 1972.

Boudreaux, P., ed. *Catalogus Codicum Astrologorum Graecorum.* 8/3. Brussels, 1912.

Boulvert, G. *Esclaves et affranchis impériaux sous le haut-empire romain: Rôle politique et administratif.* Naples, 1970.

———. *Domestique et fonctionnaire sous le haut-empire romain: La condition de l'affranchi et de l'esclave du prince.* Paris, 1974.

Boulvert, G., and M. Morabito, "Le droit de l'esclavage sous le Haut-Empire." In *ANRW II* 14 (1982): 98–182.

Bousset, W. *Jüdisch-Christlicher Schulbetrieb in Alexandrien und Rom.* Göttingen (1915), Reprint, 1975.

Bovini, G. *La proprietà ecclesiastica e la condizione giuridica della chiesa in età precostantiniana.* Milan, 1948.

———. *Gli studi di archeologia cristiana.* Bologna, 1968.

———, and H. Brandenburg. *Repertorium der christlich-antiken Sarkophage.* Vol. 1: *Rom und Ostia.* Ed. F. W. Deichmann. 2 vols. Wiesbaden, 1967.

Bowersock, G. W. *Greek Sophists in the Roman Empire.* Oxford, 1969.

Boyancé, P. "Les deux démons personnels dans l'Antiquité grecque et latine." *Rev. de Philol.* 9 (1935): 189–202.

Brandenburg, H. "Überlegungen zum Ursprung der frühchristlichen Bildkunst." *ACIAC* 9 (1978): 331–60.

———. "Das Grab des Papstes Cornelius und die Lucinaregion der Calixtus-katakombe." *JAC* 11/12 (1968–69): 42–54.

Brewster, E. H. *Roman Craftsmen and Tradesmen of the Early Roman Empire.* Philadelphia, 1917.

Brezzi, P., P. Ciprotti, S. Garofalo, and P. Testini. *Studi Paolini.* Rome, 1969.

Brockmeyer, N. *Sozialgeschichte der Antike.* UB 153. 2d ed. Stuttgart, 1974.

———. *Antike Sklaverei.* EdF. 116. Darmstadt, 1979.

Brödner, E. *Untersuchungen an den Caracallathermen.* Berlin, 1951.

Brooten, B. "Junia... Outstanding among the Apostles (Romans 16:7)." In *Women Priests,* ed. L. Swidler and A. Swidler, 141–44. New York, 1977.

Brown, P. R. L. "Aspects of the Christianisation of the Roman Aristocracy." *Journal of Roman Studies* 51 (1961): 1–11.

Brown, R. E. "Episkope and Episkopos: The New Testament Evidence." *TS* 41 (1980): 322–38.

———, and J. P. Meier. *Antioch and Rome: New Testament Cradles of Catholic Christianity.* New York, 1983.

Brox, N. *Der Hirt des Hermas.* Göttingen, 1991.

———. "Tendenzen und Parteilichkeiten im Osterfeststreit des 2. Jh." *ZKG* 83 (1972): 291–324.

Bruce, F. F. "Some Roman Slave-Names." *Proceedings of the Leeds Philos. and Liter. Societ., Hist. Sect. V,* 1 (1938): 44–60.

Bruyne. *See* De Bruyne.

Burford, A. *Craftsmen in Greek and Roman Society.* New York, 1972.

Buzzetti, B. "Nota sulla Topografia dell'Ager Vaticanus." *Quaderni dell'Istituto di Topografia Antica* 5 (1968): 105ff.

Cadoux, C. J. *The Early Church and the World.* Edinburgh, 1925.

Cagnat, R. "Le commerce et la propagation des religions dans le monde romain." *Conférences faites au Musée Guimet* 31 (1909): 131ff. (on Puteoli and Rome).

Calabi Limentani, I. *Studi sulla societè romana: Il lavoro artistico.* Milan, 1958.

Calvino, R. "Cristiani a Puteoli nell'anno 61." *RivArCr* 56 (1980): 323–30.

Calza, G. "La statistica delle abitazioni e il calcolo della popolazione in Roma imperiale." *Rend. Acc. Linc.* 5/26 (1917): 60ff.

———, and G. Lugh. "La popolazione di Roma antica." *Bull. Comunale* 69 (1941): 142ff.

Campbell, I. A. "Noble Christian Families in Rome under the Pagan Emperors." *The Dublin Review* 126 (1900): 356ff.

Campenhausen, H. v. "Ostertermin oder Osterfasten?" *VC* 28 (1974): 114–38.

———. "Glaube und Bildung im NT." In *Tradition und Leben,* 17–47. Tübingen, 1960.

Cancik, H. "Gnostiker in Rom: Zur Religionsgeschichte der Stadt Rom im 2. Jh. n. Chr." In *Religionstheorie und Politische Theologie,* Vol. 2: *Gnosis und Politik,* ed. J. Taubes, 163–84. Munich and Paderborn, 1984.

Capocci, V. "Gli scavi del Vaticano alla ricerca del sepolcro di S. Pietro e alcune note di diritto funerario romano." *Studia et documenta historiae et iuris* 18 (1952): 204–7.

Carcopino, J. *La vie quotidienne à Rome à l'apogée de l'Empire.* Paris, 1939. Page numbers cited from the German edition: *Rom. Leben und Kultur in der Kaiserzeit.* Stuttgart, 1977.

———. "Nuovi appunti statistici sulla popolazione di Roma antica." *Atti V. Conv. Naz. Studi Romani* 11 (1940): 298ff.

———. *La Basilique Pythagoricienne de la Porte Majeure.* 10th ed. Paris, 1944.

Carettoni, G., A. M. Colini, L. Cozza, and G. Gatti. *La Pianta marmorea di Roma antica–Forma Urbis Romae.* 2 vols. Rome, 1960.

Carta archeologica di Roma. Florence, 1962–64.

Caspar, E. "Die älteste römische Bischofsliste." In FS P. Kehr, *Papsttum und Kaisertum,* ed. A. Brackmann. Munich, 1926.

———. *Die älteste römische Bischofsliste.* Schr. der Königsberger Gelehrten Gesellsch., Geistesw. Kl. 2,4. Berlin, 1926.

———. *Geschichte des Papsttums.* Vol. 1. Tübingen, 1930.

Caspari, C. P. *Quellen zur Geschichte des Taufsymbols und der Glaubensregel.* Vol. 3. Oslo and Brussels (1875), 1964, 267ff., 309ff.

Casson, L. *Travel in the Ancient World.* London, 1974.

Castagnoli, F. "Il Campo Marzio nell'antichità." *Memorie Accademia Lincei* 8, 1 (1946): 93–193.

———. "Roma nei versi di Marziale." *Athenaeum* 28 (1950): 67ff.

———. *Roma antica: Topografia e urbanistica di Roma.* Bologna, 1958.

———. *Topografia e urbanistica di Roma antica.* Istituto di Studi Romani. Bologna, 1969.

———. *Roma antica, profilo urbanistico.* Rome, 1978.

Castritius, H. "Die Gesellschaftsordnung der römischen Kaiserzeit und das Problem der sozialen Mobilität." *Mitt. d. TU Braunschweig* 8 (1973): 38ff.

Cecchelli, C. *Monumenti cristiano-eretici di Roma.* Rome, 1944.

———. "Archeologia ed arte cristiana dell'antichità e dell'alto medio evo." *Doxa* 3 (1950): 97–160; 4 (1951): 1–75 (bibl. from 1940 to 1950).

Cecchelli, M. Trinci. "Osservazioni sul complesso della 'domuso' celimontana dei SS. Giovanni e Paolo." *ACIAC* 9 (1978): 551–62.

Chadwick, H. *Early Christian Thought and the Classical Tradition.* Oxford, 1966.

Chantraine, H. *Freigelassene und Sklaven im Dienst der römischen Kaiser: Studien zu ihrer Nomenklatur.* Wiesbaden, 1967.

Charles-Picard, G., and J. Rougé. *Textes et documents relatifs à la vie économique et sociale dans l'Empire romain.* Regards sur l'Histoire 6. Paris, 1969.

Chastagnol, A. "Le sénateur Volusien." *REA* 58 (1956): 241–53.

———. "La problème du domicile legal des sénateurs romains à l'époque impériale." In *Mélanges offerts à L. Sédar Senghor.* Dakar, 1977.

———. "Les femmes dans l'ordre sénatorial." *Revue Historique* 262 (1979): 3–28.

Christ, K. *Römische Geschichte: Eine Bibliographie.* Darmstadt, 1976. P. 25, additional bibl. on ancient economic history and social history.

Christes, J. *Bildung und Gesellschaft.* EdF 37. Darmstadt, 1975.

———. *Sklaven und Freigelassene als Grammatiker und Philologen im antiken Rom.* Forschungen zur antiken Sklaverei 10. Wiesbaden, 1979.

Christophe, P. *L'usage chrétien du droit de propriété dans l'Ecriture et la Tradition Patristique.* Paris, 1963.

Clarke, M. L. *Die Rhetorik bei den Römern.* Göttingen, 1968.

Clementi, F. *Roma imperiale nelle XIV regioni augustee.* Rome, 1935.

Clévenot, M. *So kennen wir die Bibel nicht.* Munich, 1978.

———. *Les hommes de la Fraternité.* 2 vols. Paris, 1981.

Coarelli, F. "Navalia, Tarentum e la Topografia del Campo Marzio meridionale." *Quaderni dell' Istituto di Topografia* 5 (1968): 27ff.

———. *Rome: I grandi monumenti.* Verona, 1971.

———. "Il complesso pompeiano del Campo Marzio e la sua decorazione scultorea." *Rendiconti della Pontificia Accademia Romana di Archeologia* 44 (1971–72): 99–122.

———. *Guida Archeologica di Roma.* Mailand, 1974. Page numbers cited from the German trans.: *Rom. Ein archäologischer Führer.* Freiburg im B., 1975.

Coccia, E. "Il 'titolo' di Equizio e la basilica dei SS. Silvestro e Martino ai Monti." *RivArCr* 39 (1963): 235–45.

Cochrane, C. N. *Christianity and Classical Culture.* 5th ed. New York, 1966.

Codex Theodosianus. Ed. Th. Mommsen, P. Kröger, and P. Meyer. Zurich, 1970–71.

Coleman-Norton, P. R. "The Apostle Paul and the Roman Law of Slavery." In *Studies in Roman Economic and Social History in Honor of A. C. Johnson,* 155–77. Princeton, 1951.

Colini, A. M. "La scoperta del santuario di Giove Dolicheno." *Bullettino Comunale* 63 (1935): 145ff.

———. "Storia e topografia del Celio nell'antichitá." *Atti della Pont. Accadem. Rom. di Archeol., Memorie* 8 (1955): 137ff.

Colini, A. M., F. Castagnoli, and G. Macchia. *Via Appia.* Rome, 1973.

Collon, S. "Remarques sur les quartiers juifs de la Rome antique." *Mél. Ec. Franc.* (1940): 72ff.

Colpe C. et al., "Genossenschaft." *RAC* 10 (1978): 83–155.

Colson, J. *L'Episcopat catholique: Collégialité et primauté dans les trois premiers siècles.* Paris, 1961.

Condorelli, S. *Aspetti della vita quotidiana a Roma e tendenze letterarie nella Historia Augusta.* Biblioteca di Helikon, Testi e Studi 6. Messina, 1968.

Conzelmann, H. "Miszelle zu Apk 18,17." *ZNW* 66 (1975): 288–90.

Copalle, S. "De servorum graecorum nominibus capitas duo." Diss. Marburg, 1908.

Coppo, A. "Contributo all'interpretazione di un'epigrafe greca cristiana dei Musei Capitolini." *RivArCr* 46 (1970): 97–138.

Corcoran, G. "Slavery in the New Testament." *Milltown Studies* 5 (1980): 1–40; 6 (1980): 62–83.

Corpus Juris Civilis. Vol. 1: *Institutiones et Digesta;* vol. 2: *Codex Justinianus;* vol. 3: *Novellae.* Ed. Th. Mommsen, P. Krüger, R. Schoell, and G. Kroll. Zurich, 1970–1973.

Countryman, L. W. *The Rich Christian in the Church of the Early Empire: Contradictions and Accommodations.* New York, 1980.

Coyle, J. K. "Empire and Eschaton: The Early Church and the Question of Domestic Relationships." *ÉgT* (O) 12 (1981): 35–94.

Cozza, L. "Pianta marmorea severiana: Nuove ricomposizioni di frammenti." *Quaderni dell' Istituto di Topografia* 5 (1968): 9ff.

Cracco Ruggini, L. "Nuclei immigrati e forze indigene in tre grande centri commerciali dell'impero." *Memoirs of the American Academy in Rome* 36 (1980): 55–76.

Cressedi, G. "I porti fluviali in Roma antica." *Rend. Pont. Acc.* 25–26 (1949–51): 53–65.

Cullmann, O. "Das Urchristentum und die Kultur." In *Vorträge und Aufsätze (1925–1962),* 485–501. Tübingen, 1966.

Cumont, F. *Les religions orientales dans le paganisme romain.* Paris 1929. German trans.: *Die orientalischen Religionen im römischen Heidentum.* 7th ed. Darmstadt, 1975.

Curtius, L., and A. Naivrath. *Das antike Rom.* 5th ed. Vienna, 1970.

Daniélou, J. *Les origines du christianisme latin.* Histoire des doctrines chrétiennes avant Nicée 3. Paris, 1978.

Darsy, F. M. D. *Recherches archéologiques à Saint-Sabine sur l'Aventin.* Vatican City, 1968.

Davies, S. L. *The Revolt of the Widows: The Social World of the Apocryphal Acts.* Carbondale, Ill., 1980.

Davis, J. G. *Daily Life in the Early Church.* London, 1952.

De Bruyne, L. "L'importanza degli scavi lateranensi per la cronologia delle prime pitture." *RivArCr* 44 (1968f.): 82–113.

———. "La 'capella greca' di Priscilla." *RivArCr* 46 (1970): 291–330.

Decroix, J., and J. Daoust. "Des chrétiens vivaient-ils à Pompéi et à Herculanum?" *Bible et Terre sainte* 126 (1970): 15ff.

Deichmann, F. W. *Einführung in die Christliche Archäologie.* Darmstadt, 1983.

Deissmann, A. *Das Urchristentum und die unteren Schichten.* 2d ed. Göttingen, 1908.

———. *Licht vom Osten.* 4th ed. Tübingen, 1923. Engl. trans.: *Light from the Ancient East.* New York, 1927.

de Labriolle, P. *La réaction païenne: Etude sur la polémique antichrétienne du Ier au VIe siècle.* 10th ed. Paris, 1934, 1948.

Delehaye, H. *Les légendes hagiographiques.* Brussels, 1905.

———. *Commentarius perpetuus in Martyrologium Hieronymianum ad recensionem Henrici Quentin.* Brussels, 1931.

———. *Les origines du culte des Martyrs.* 10th ed. Brussels, 1933.

Delling, G. "Zur Taufe von 'Häusern' im Urchristentum." *NovT* 7 (1965): 285–311.

De Robertis, F. M. *Storia delle corporazioni e del regime associativo nel mondo romano.* 2 vols. Bari, 1973.

———. *Lavoro e lavoratori nel mondo romano.* Bari, 1963.

De Rossi, G. B. *La Roma sotterranea cristiana.* 3 vols. Rome, 1864–77.

———. See also *Bullettino di Archeologia Cristiana,* ed. De Rossi.

De Visscher, F. "L'affranchissement des esclaves et son effet acquisitif du droit de cité." *L'Antiquité classique* 14 (1945): 139ff.

———. "Le régime juridique des plus anciens cimetières chrétiens à Rome." *Analecta Bollandiana* 69 (1951): 39–55.

———. *Le droit des Tombeaux Romains.* Milan, 1963.

De Waal, "I. Clemens." In *Kraus' Real-Encyklopädie der christlichen Alterthümer,* p. 301. Freiburg/B., 1882–86.

Dibelius, M. "Der Offenbarungsträger im 'Hirten' des Hermas." In Harnack-Ehrung, *Beiträge zur Kirchengeschichte,* 105–18. Leipzig, 1921.

———. *Der Hirt des Hermas.* Die Apostolischen Väter IV, HNT, suppl. vol. Tübingen, 1923.

———. *Urchristentum und Kultur.* Heidelb. Unireden 2. Heidelberg, 1928; on 1 Clem esp. pp. 15, 27.

———. *Botschaft und Geschichte.* Vol. 2. Tübingen, 1956, 160ff; 177–228 (= "Rom und die Christen im ersten Jahrhundert").

Dictionnaire d'Archéologie chrétienne et de Liturgie. Ed. F. Cabrol, H. Leclercq, and H. Marrou. 15 vols. Paris, 1903–53.

Dihle, A. *Die griechische und lateinische Literatur der Kaiserzeit.* Munich, 1989.

Dill, S. *Roman Society from Nero to Marcus Aurelius.* 2d ed. London, 1905.

Dillon, E. *Living in Imperial Rome.* London, 1974.

Dillon, J. "The Descent of the Soul in Middle Platonic and Gnostic Theory." In *The Rediscovery of Gnosticism,* vol. 1, 357ff., ed. B. Layton. Leiden, 1980.

Dinkler, E. "Die Petrus-Rom-Frage." *ThR* 25 (1959): 189–230; 289–335; 27 (1961): 33–64.

———. *Signum Crucis.* Tübingen, 1967, esp. 134ff.

Dobschütz, E. v. "Der Roman in der altchristlichen Literatur." *Deutsche Rundschau* 3 (1901–2): 61ff.

———. *Die urchristlichen Gemeinden: Sittengeschichtliche Bilder.* Leipzig, 1902. Engl. trans.: *Christian Life in the Primitive Church.* New York, 1904.

Doelger, F. J. *Antike und Christentum.* 6 vols. Münster, 1929–50.

———. " 'Kirche' als Name für den christlichen Kultbau." *AuC* 6 (1950): 161–95.

Doer, B. *Die römische Namengebung.* Stuttgart, 1937; Hildesheim and New York, 1974.

Dörner, F. K. "Bericht über eine Reise in Bithynien." *DÖAW* 75/1 (1952): no. 7.

Dörrie, H. Review of A.-J. Festugière, *La Révélation d'Hermes Trismégiste. Göttingische Gelehrte Anzeigen* 209 (1955): 230ff.

———. Review of C. Andresen, *Logos und Nomos. Gnomon* 29 (1957): 185–96.

———. *Platonica Minora.* Stud. et Testim. ant. 8. Munich, 1976.

Drexhage, H. J. "Wirtschaft und Handel in den frühchristlichen Gemeinden (1–3. Jh. n. Chr.)." *RQ* 76 (1981): 1–72.

Duchesne, L. *Scripta minora, Etudes de topographie romaine et de géographie ecclésiastique.* Rome, 1973.

———, ed. *Le Liber Pontificalis* 1. Paris, 1886.

Dudley, D. R. *Urbs Roma: A Source Book of Classical Texts on the City and Its Monuments.* London and Aberdeen, 1967.

Duff, A. M. *Freedmen in the Early Roman Empire.* 2d ed. Cambridge, 1958.

Dufourcq, A. *Etudes sur les Gesta Martyrum romains.* Paris, 1900, esp. 101ff.

Duncan-Jones, R. *The Economy of the Roman Empire: Quantitative Studies.* Cambridge, 1974.

———. "Abrundung von Altersangaben: Analphabetentum und soziale Differenzierung im Imperium Romanum." In *Sozial- und Wirtschaftsgeschichte der römischen Kaiserzeit,* ed. H. Schneider, 396–429. Darmstadt, 1981.

Durry, M. *Les cohortes prétoriennes.* Paris, 1938, 348ff.

———. "Le christianisme dans les cohortes prétoriennes." In *Hommages à J. Bidez et F. Cumonte,* 85–90. Coll. Latom. 2. Brussels, 1949.

Eck, W. "Das Eindringen des Christentums in den Senatorenstand bis zu Konstantin d. Gr." *Chiron* 1 (1971): 381–406.

———. "Der Einfluss der Konstantinischen Wende auf die Auswahl der Bischöfe im 4. und 5. Jh." *Chiron* 8 (1978): 561–85.

———. "Christen im höheren Reichsdienst im 2. und 3. Jh.?" *Chiron* 9 (1979): 449–64 (lit.).

———, H. Galsterer, and H. Wolff, ed. *Studien zur antiken Sozialgeschichte.* Cologne, 1980.

Edmundson, G. *The Church of Rome in the First Century.* London, 1913.

Eggenberger, Chr. *Die Quellen der politischen Ethik des 1.Klemensbriefes.* Zurich, 1951.

Ehrhardt, A. "Soziale Fragen in der Alten Kirche." In *Existenz und Ordnung,* 155–82. Frankfurt, 1962.

———. "Social Problems in the Early Church." In *The Framework of the New Testament Stories,* 275–312. Cambridge, 1964.

Eisenhut, W. *Einführun in die antike Rhetorik und ihre Geschichte.* Altertumswissenschaft. Darmstadt, 1982.

Elliott, J. H. *A Home for the Homeless: A Sociological Exegesis of 1 Peter, Its Situation and Strategy.* Philadelphia, 1982.

———, ed. *What Is Social-Scientific Criticism?* Minneapolis, 1993.

Elliott-Binns, L. E. *The Beginnings of Western Christendom.* London, 1948.

Elze, M. *Tatian und seine Theologie.* Göttingen, 1960.

———. "Häresie und Einheit der Kirche im 2. Jh." *ZTK* 71 (1974): 389–409.

Erbes, C. "Das Todesjahr des römischen Märtyrers Apollonius." *ZNW* 13 (1912): 269f.

Erbse, H. "Über Aristarchs Iliasausgaben." *Hermes* 87 (1959): 275–303.

Ermini, L. Pani. "L'ipogeo detto dei Flavi in Domitilla, 1: Osservazioni sulla sua origine e sul carattere della decorazione." *RivArCr* 45 (1969): 119–73.

———. "2: Gli ambienti esterni." *RivArCr* 48 (1972): 235–69.

Esplorazioni. See Apollonij Ghetti.

Fabre, G. *Libertus: Recherches sur les rapports Patron: Affranchi à la fin de la république romaine.* Rome, 1981.

Fabrega, V. "War Junia[s], der hervorragende Apostle (Rom. 16,7), eine Frau? *JAC* 27/28 (1984–85): 47–64.

Fabricius, C. "Der sprachliche Klassizismus der griechischen Kirchenväter." *JAC* 10 (1967): 187ff.

Falanga, L. *La "croce" di Ercolano: Cronistoria di una scoperta.* Naples, 1981.

Fallon, F. T. "The Law in Philo and Ptolemy: A Note on the Letter to Flora." *VC* 30 (1976): 41–45.

Fasola, U. M. *Karte der Katakomben Roms.* Pontificio Istituto di Archeologia Cristiana. Rome, 1976.

———. "Le due catacombe ebraiche di Villa Torlonia." *RivArCr* 52 (1976): 7–62.

———. *Peter und Paul in Rom.* Rome, 1980.

———. *The Catacomb of Domitilla.* Rome, n.d.

———, and P. Testini. "I cimiteri cristiani." *ACIAC* 9 (1978): 103–39.

Felletti Maj, B. M. "Il santuario della triade eliopolitana e dei misteri al Gianicolo." *Bullettino Comunale* 75 (1953–55): 137–62.

Ferrua, A. "Questioni di epigrafia eretica romana." *RivArCr* 21 (1944–45): 165ff.

———. "Due mausolei da pagani cristiani." *RivArCr* 28 (1952): 13–41.

———. *S. Sebastiano e la sua catacomba.* 3d ed. Rome, 1968.

———. "L'epigrafia cristiana prima di Costantino." *ACIAC* 9 (1978): 583–613.

———. "Lavori a Callisto." *RivArCr* 51 (1975): 213–40.

———. "Ultime scoperte a Callisto." *RivArCr* 52 (1976): 201–19.

Festugière, A.-J. *La Révélation d'Hermes Trismégiste.* Vol. 4: *Le Dieu Inconnu et la Gnose.* Paris, 1954.

Février, P.-A. "Études sur les catacombes romaines." *Cahiers archéologiques* 10 (1959): 1–26; 11 (1960): 1–14.

Filson, F. V. "The Significance of the Early House Churches." *JBL* 58 (1939): 105–12.

Finley, M. I. *Atlas der klassischen Archäologie.* Munich, 1979. Engl. orig.: *Atlas of Classical Archeology.* New York, 1977.

———. *Die antike Wirtschaft.* 2d ed. Munich, 1980. Engl. orig. *the Ancient Economy.* Berkeley, 1973.

———. *Die Sklaverei in der Antike: Geschichte und Probleme.* Munich, 1981. Engl. orig.: *Ancient Slavery and Modern Ideology.* New York, 1980.

———, ed. *Studies in Ancient Society.* Boston, 1974.

———, ed. *Studies in Roman Property.* Cambridge, 1976.

Fischer, J. A. *Die Apostolischen Väter.* 7th ed. Darmstadt, 1976.

Floriani Squarciapino, M. "Ebrei a Roma e ad Ostia." *Studi Romani* 11 (1963): 127–41.

Flory, M. B. "Family and 'Familia': A Study of Social Relations in Slavery." Diss. Yale, 1975.

Fortunati, L. *Relazione Generale degli Scavi e Scoperte fatte lungo la via Latina.* Rome, 1859.

Fraenkel, E. "Namenwesen." Pauly/Wissowa, 2d ed., 16:1611–70.

Frank, T. "Race Mixture in the Roman Empire." *AHR* 21 (1915–16): 689–708.

———. *An Economic History of Rome.* 2d ed. Baltimore, 1927.

———, ed. *An Economic Survey of Ancient Rome.* 4 vols. Baltimore, 1933–40.

Frend, W. H. C. *Martyrdom and Persecution in the Early Church.* Oxford, 1965.

———. "Town and Countryside in Early Christianity." In *The Church in Town and Countryside,* ed. D. Baker, 25–42. Oxford, 1979.

Freudenberger, R. "Die Acta Justini als historisches Dokument." In *Humanitas–Christianitas,* FS W. v. Loewenich, ed. K. Beyschlag, G. Maron, and E. Wölfel, 24–31. Witten, 1968.

———. "Die Überlieferung vom Martyrium des römischen Christen Apollonius." *ZNW* 60 (1969): 111–30.

———. *Das Verhalten der römischen Behörden gegen die Christen im 2. Jh.* MBPF 52. 2d ed. Munich, 1969.

Frey, J. B. "Les communautés juives à Rome aux premiers temps de l'Eglise." *RSR* 20 (1930): 269–97; 21 (1931): 129–68.

Friedländer, L. *Darstellungen aus der Sittengeschichte Roms in der Zeit von Augustus bis zum Ausgang der Antonine.* 10th ed. Leipzig, 1921–23. Reprint, Aalen, 1964; Stuttgart, 1980.

Frier, B. W. *Landlords and Tenants in Imperial Rome.* Princeton, 1980.

Frohnes, H., and U. W. Knorr, eds. *Kirchengeschichte als Missionsgeschichte.* Vol. 1: *Die Alte Kirche.* Munich, 1974.

Fromm, E. *Das Christusdogma und andere Essays.* Munich, 1965.

Frutaz, A. P. *Le piante di Roma.* Rome, 1962 (maps).

———. "Titolo di Pudente." *RivArCr* 40 (1964): 53–72.

Fuchs, H. "Die frühe christliche Kirche und die antike Bildung." In Klein (below), WF 267. 33ff.

———. "Tacitus über die Christen." *VC* 4 (1950): 5–93.

Gaffron, H.-G. "Studien zum koptischen Philippusevangelium unter besonderer Berücksichtigung der Sakramente." Diss. Bonn, 1969.

Gagé, J. *Les classes sociales dans l'Empire Romain.* 2d ed. Paris, 1971.

Gager, G. "Marcion and Philosophy." *VC* 26 (1972): 53–59.

Gager, J. G. *Kingdom and Community: The Social World of Early Christianity.* Englewood Cliffs, N.J., 1975.

Gallinari, L. *Cristianesimo primitivo ed educazione.* Cassino, 1970.

Gamber, K. *Domus Ecclesiae.* Regensburg, 1968.

Gamble, Jr., H. *The Textual History of the Letter to the Romans.* StD 42. Grand Rapids, 1977.

Garcia Merino, C. *Análisis sobre el estudio de la demografía de la antiguedad y un nuevo método para la época romana.* Studia archaeologica 26. Valladolid, 1974.

Garnsey, P. *Social Status and Legal Privilege in the Roman Empire.* Oxford, 1970.

Garnsey, P., and R. Saller. *The Roman Empire: Economy, Society and Culture.* Berkeley, 1987.

Garofalo, S., M. Maccarone, J. Ruyssehaert, and P. Testini. *Studi Petriani.* Rome, 1968.

Gatti, G. "Saepta Ilulia e Porticus Aemilia nella Forma Severiana." *Bullettino Comunale* 62 (1934): 123–50.

———. "L'arginatura del Tevere a Marmorata." *Bullettino Comunale* 64 (1936): 55ff.

———. "Topografia dell' Iseo Campense." *Rend. Pont. Acc.* 20 (1943–44): 117–63.

————. "Caratteristiche edilizie di un quartiere di Roma del II. secolo d. C." *Quademi dell' Istituto di Storia dell' Architettura* 31–48 (1961): 49–66 (on the Via Lata).

Gauckler, P. *Le sanctuaire syrien du Janicule.* Paris, 1912.

Gayer, R. *Die Stellung des Sklaven in den paulinischen Gemeinden und bei Paulus.* Europ. Hochschulschr. XXIII 78. Bern and Frankfurt, 1976.

Geffeken, J. *Zwei griechische Apologeten.* Leipzig, 1907.

Geisau, H. v. "Minucius Felix." Pauly / Wissowa Suppl. 9: 956–58.

Gerard, J. *Juvénal et la réalité contemporaine.* Paris, 1976.

Gerkan, A. v. "Die Einwohnerzahl Roms in der Kaiserzeit." *Röm. Mitt.* 55 (1940): 149ff.; 58 (1943): 213ff.

————. "Zur Hauskirche von Dura-Europos." In Mullus, FS T. Klauser, 143–49. *JAC* Erg. Münster, 1964.

————. "Kritische Studien zu den Ausgrabungen unter der Peterskirche in Rom." *Trierer Zs* 22 (1954): 26–55.

————. "Petrus in Vaticano et in Catacumbas." *JAC* 5 (1962): 23–32, cf. 39–42.

Gerke, F. *Die christlichen Sarkophage der vorkonstantinischen Zeit.* Berlin, 1940.

Gewalt, D. "Ntl. Exegese und Soziologie." *EvTh* 31 (1971): 87–99.

Giannelli, G., and U. E. Paoli, eds. *Rom und seine grosse Zeit.* 3d ed. Würzburg, 1972.

Gielen, M. "Zur Interpretation der pln. Formel *he kat' oikon ekklesia.*" *ZNW* 77 (1986): 100–25.

Giet, S. *Hermas et les pasteurs.* Paris, 1963.

————. "Un courant judéo-chrétien à Rome au milieu du Ile siècle." In *Aspects du judéochristianisme,* Colloque de Strasbourg, 95–112. Paris, 1965.

Gigon, O. "Die Erneuerung der Philosophie in der Zeit Ciceros." *Entretiens sur l'antiquité classique* 3 (1957): 25–61.

————. *Die antike Kultur und das Christentum.* Gütersloh, 1966.

Gilbert, O. *Geschichte und Topographie der Stadt Rom im Altertum.* 3 vols. Leipzig, 1883–90.

Gilbert, R. *Die Beziehungen zwischen Princeps und stadtrömischer Plebs im frühen Prinzipat.* Bochum, 1976.

Giordano, C., and J. Kahn. *Gli Ebrei a Pompei, Ercolano, Stabia e nelle città della Campania felix.* Naples, 1979.

Goodhue, N. *The Lucus Furrinae and the Syrian Sanctuary on the Janiculum.* New York, 1975.

Goodspeed, E. *Die ältesten Apologeten.* Göttingen, 1914.

Gordon, M. L. "The Nationality of Slaves under the Early Roman Empire." *JRS* 14 (1924): 93–105.

Gough, M. R. E. *The Origins of Christian Art.* London, 1973.

Grabar, A. *Le premier art chrétien.* Paris, 1966.

————. *Christian Iconography: A Study of Its Origins.* London, 1969.

Graber, R. *Die Familie als häusliches Heiligtum.* Munich and Zurich, 1980.

Graeve, V. v. "Tempel und Kult der syrischen Götter am Janiculum." *Jb. des Deutsch. Archäol. Inst.* 87 (1972): 314–47.

Grant, R. M. "Pliny and the Christians." *HTR* 41 (1948): 273–74.

————. "Aristotle and the Conversion of Justin." *JTS NS* 7 (1956): 79ff., 246ff.

————. *Early Christianity and Society.* San Francisco, 1977. German trans.: *Christen als Bürger im römischen Reich.* Göttingen, 1981.

————. "The Social Setting of Second-Century Christianity." In *Jewish and Christian Self-Definition,* ed. E. P. Sanders, 1:16–29. Philadelphia, 1980.

Green, H. A. "Suggested Sociological Themes in the Study of Gnosticism." *VC* 31 (1977): 169–80.

————. *The Economic and Social Origins of Gnosticism.* SBL Diss. 77. Atlanta, 1985.

Greeven, H. *Das Hauptproblem der Sozialethik in der neueren Stoa und im Urchristentum.* Gütersloh, 1935.

————. *Evangelium und Gesellschaft in urchristlicher Zeit.* FS Eröffhung Univ. Bochum, 105–21. Bochum, 1965.

Griffe, H. "La persécution contre les chrétiens de l'an 64." *Bull. de Littérat. ecclés.* 65 (1964): 3–16.

Grimal, P. *Les jardins romains à la fin de la République et aux deux premiers siècles de l'Empire.* 2d ed. Paris, 1969.

Grimm, B. *Untersuchungen zur sozialen Stellung der frühen Christen in der römischen Gesellschaft.* Bamberg, 1975.

Groag, E., and A. Stein. *Prosopographia Imperii Romani, saec. I–III.* Berlin, 1933ff.

Guarducci, M. "Documenti del primo secolo nella necropoli vaticana." *Rendiconti della Pont. Accad. Rom. di Archeol.* 29 (1956f.): 111–37.

————. *I Graffiti sotto la confessione di San Pietro.* 3 vols. Rome, 1958.

————. "Die Ausgrabungen unter St. Peter." In *Das frühe Christentum im römischen Staat,* ed. R. Klein, 364–414. Darmstadt, 1971.

————. "L'isola Tiberina e la sua tradizione ospitaliera." *Rendiconti morali dell'Accademia dei Lincei* 26 (1971): 267–81.

————. "Valentiniani a Roma." *Mitt. d. Dt. Archäol. Inst. Röm.* 80 (1973): 169–89.

————. "Ancora sui Valentiniani a Roma." *Mitt. d. Dt. Archäol. Inst. Röm.* 81 (1974): 341–43.

————. *Petrus, sein Tod, sein Grab.* Regensburg, 1975.

Guidobaldi, F. *Il complesso archeologico di S. Clemente: Risultato degli Scavi più recenti e riesame dei resti architettonici.* Rome, 1978.

Gülzow, H. "Kallist von Rom." *ZNW* 58 (1967): 102–21.

————. *Christentum und Sklaverei in den ersten drei Jahrhunderten.* Bonn, 1969.

————. "Soziale Gegebenheiten der altkirchlichen Mission." In H. Frohnes and U. W. Knorr (above), 189–226.

Gurnmerus, H. *Cognomen und Beruf, Commentationes phil. I. A. Heikel.* Helsinki, 1926, 48–74.

Gutmann, J. "Was There Biblical Art at Pompeii?" *Antike Kunst* 15 (1972): 122–24.

Gwynn, A. *Roman Education: From Cicero to Quintilian.* Oxford, 1926.

Hadot, H. *Seneca und die griechisch-römische Tradition der Seelenleitung.* Quellen und Studien z. Gesch. d. Philos. 13. Berlin, 1969.

Hahn, I. "Freie Arbeit und Sklavenarbeit." In *Sozial- und Wirtschaftsgeschichte der römischen Kaiserzeit,* ed. H. Schneider, 128–54. Darmstadt, 1981.

Hainz, J. "Die Anfänge des Bischofs- und Diakonenamtes." In *Kirche im Werden: Studien zum Thema Amt und Gemeinde-Ordnung,* idem, ed., 91–107. BU 9. Regensburg, 1972.

Halfmann, H. *Die Senatoren aus dem östlichen Teil des Imperium Romanum bis zum Ende des 2. Jh. n. Chr.* Hypomnemata 58. Göttingen, 1979.

Halkin, E. *Légendes grecques de "martyres romaines."* Brussels, 1973.

Hammon, A. *Vie liturgique et vie sociale.* Paris and Tournai, 1968.

———. *La vie quotidienne des premiers chrétiens (95–197).* Paris, 1971.

Hands, A. R. *Charities and Social Aid in Greece and Rome.* New York, 1968.

Harnack, A. "Christianity and Christians at the Court of the Roman Emperors before the Time of Constantine." *Princeton Review* (July 1878): 262ff.

———. "Die ältesten christlichen Datierungen und die Anfänge einer bischöflichen Chronographie in Rom." *Sitzber. Ak. Wiss.* Berlin, Phil.-hist. Kl. 1892, 617–58.

———. "Der Prozess des Christen Apollonius." *Sitzber. Ak. Wiss.* Berlin, 1893, 721–46.

———. *Geschichte der altchristlichen Literatur bis auf Eusebius.* 3 vols. Leipzig, 1897; 2d ed., 1958.

———. "Über die Herkunft der 47 ersten Päpste." *Sitzber. Ak. Wiss.* Berlin, 1904, 1044–62.

———. *Analecta zur ältesten Geschichte des Christentums im alten Rom.* TU NF 13,2. Leipzig, 1905.

———. *Militia Christi: Die christliche Religion und der Soldatenstand in den ersten drei Jahrhunderten.* Berlin, 1905; repr. 1963. Engl. trans.: *Militia Christi.* Philadelphia, 1981.

———. *Der Vorwurf des Atheismus in den drei ersten Jh.* TU NF 13,4a. Leipzig, 1905.

———. *Lehrbuch der Dogmengeschichte.* 3 vols. 4th ed. Tübingen, 1909; 5th ed., 1931f.

———. "Die älteste uns im Wortlaut bekannte dogmatische Erklärung eines römischen Bischofs, Zephyrin bei Hipp. ref. IX 11." *Sitzber. Ak. Wiss. Berlin,* Phil.-hist. Kl. 1923, 51ff.

———. *Marcion.* 2d ed. Leipzig, 1924. Engl. trans.: *Marcion: The Gospel of the Alien God.* Durham, N.C., 1990.

———. *Die Mission und Ausbreitung des Christentums in den ersten drei Jahrhunderten.* 4th ed. Leipzig, 1924. Engl. trans.: *The Mission and Expansion of Christianity....* 2 vols. New York, 1908.

———. *Dogmengeschichte.* 7th ed. Tübingen, 1931. Engl. trans.: *History of Dogma.* 7 vols. London, 1894–99.

Harrington, D. J. "Sociological Concepts and the Early Church: A Decade of Research." *TS* 41 (1980): 181–90.

Harvey, R. A. *A Commentary on Persius.* Mnemosyne Suppl. 64. Leiden, 1981, 176ff. (Persius on the Jews of Rome).

Hasenclever, A. "Christliche Proselyten der höheren Stände im I. Jh." *JPTh* 8 (1882): 34–78, 230–71.

Hauck, F. *Die Stellung des Urchristentums zu Arbeit und Geld.* Gütersloh, 1921.

Hauschild, W.-D. "Christentum und Eigentum: Zum Problem eines altkirchlichen 'Sozialismus.'" *ZEE* 16 (1972): 34–49.

Heiler, C. L. *De Tatiani Apologetae dicendi genere*. Marburg, 1909.

Helfritz, H. "1 Clem. 20:1." *VC* 21–22 (1967–68): 1–7.

Helgeland, J. "Christians in the Roman Army." *ANRW* II 23,1 (1979): 724ff.

Heller, E., ed. *P. C. Tacitus, Annalen*. Darmstadt, 1982.

Hellholm, D. *Das Visionenbuch des Hermas als Apokalypse: Formgeschichtliche und texttheoretische Studien zu einer literarischen Gattung*. Lund, 1980.

Helm, R. *Der antike Roman*. 2d ed. Göttingen, 1956.

Hempel, H. L. "Synagogenfund in Ostia Antica." *ZAW* 74 (1962): 72f.

Hengel, M. "Die Synagogeninschrift von Stobi." *ZNW* 57 (1966): 145–83.

———. *Gewalt und Gewaltlosigkeit: Zur "politischen Theologie" in ntl. Zeit*. Stuttgart, 1971.

———. "Proseuche und Synagoge: Jüdische Gemeinde, Gotteshaus und Gottesdienst in der Diaspora und in Palästina." In *Tradition und Glaube*, FS K. G. Kuhn, ed. G. Jeremias et al., 157–84. Göttingen, 1971.

———. *Eigentum und Reichtum in der frühen Kirche*. Stuttgart, 1973. Engl. trans.: *Property and Riches in the Early Church*. Philadelphia, 1974.

———. "Mors Turpissima Crucis." In *Rechtfertigung*, FS E. Käsemann, ed. J. Friedrich, W. Pöhlmann, and P. Stuhlmacher, 125–84. Tübingen, 1976.

———. "Entstehungszeit und Situation des Markusevangeliums." In *Markus-Philologie*, ed. H. Cancik, 1–45. WUNT 33. Tübingen, 1984.

Hennecke, E., and D. Schneemelcher. *Ntl. Apokryphen*. Tübingen, vol. 1, 4th ed., 1968; vol. 2, 4th ed., 1971. Engl. trans.: *New Testament Apocrypha*. 2 vols. Philadelphia, 1963–64.

Hermansen, G. "The Population of Imperial Rome: The Regionaries." *Historia* 27 (1978): 129–68.

Herter, H. "Die Soziologie der antiken Prostitution im Lichte des heidnischen und christlichen Schrifttums." *JAC* 3 (1960): 70–111.

Hertling, L. *Namen und Herkunft der römischen Bischöfe der ersten Jahrhunderte*. Miscellanea Historiae Pontificae edita a Facultate Historiae Ecclesiasticae in Pontificia Universitate Gregoriana 21. Rome, 1959, 1–16.

Herzog, R. *Aus der Geschichte des Bankwesens im Altertum: Tesserae Nummulariae*. Giessen, 1919, 38–40.

Hilhorst, A. *Sémitismes et latinismes dans le Pasteur d'Hermas*. Nijmegen, 1976.

Hock, R. F. "Paul's Tentmaking and the Problem of His Social Class." *JBL* 97 (1978): 555–74.

———. "The Workshop as a Social Setting for Paul's Missionary Preaching." *CBQ* 41 (1979): 438–50.

———. *The Social Context of Paul's Ministry: Tentmaking and Apostleship*. Philadelphia, 1980.

Hodge, P. *Roman Family Life*. Aspects of Roman Life. London, 1974.

Hofmann, "Tertullians Aussage über die Christen in Pompeji." *Wiener Studien* 87 (1974): 160–72.

Holfelder, H. H. "EUSEBEIA KAI PHILOSOPHIA: Literarische Einheit und politischer Kontext von Justins Apologie." *ZNW* 68 (1977): 48–66, 231–51.

Holl, K. "Kultursprache und Volkssprache in der altchristlichen Mission." In Frohnes (above), 389ff.

Holte, R. "Logos Spermatikos: Christianity and Ancient Philosophy according to St. Justin's Apologies." *Studia Theol.* 12 (1958): 109–68.

Holzberg, N. *Der antike Roman: Eine Einführung.* 2d ed. Düsseldorf and Zurich, 2001.

Hommel, H. "Platonisches bei Lukas." *ZNW* 48 (1957): 193–200.

Homo, L. *Rome impériale et l'urbanisme dans l'Antiquité.* Paris, 1951; 2d ed., 1971 (lit.).

Hopkins, C. *The Discovery of Dura-Europos.* Ed. B. Goldman. New Haven, 1979.

Horsley, G. H. R. *New Documents Illustrating Early Christianity: A Review of the Greek Inscriptions and Papyri Published since 1976.* North Ryde, 1981.

Hubik, K. *Die Apologien des Hl. Justinus des Philosophen und Märtyrers: Literarhistorische Untersuchungen.* Theol. Studien der Leo-Gesellschaft 19. Vienna, 1912.

Huelsen, Chr. *Le Chiese di Roma nel Medio Evo: Cataloghi ed Appunti.* Florence, 1927 (introduction on the ancient tituli).

Hüntemann, U. "Zur Kompositionstechnik Justins: Analyse seiner ersten Apologie." *ThGl* 25 (1933): 410–28.

Huttunen, P. *The Social Strata in the Imperial City of Rome: A Quantitative Study of the Social Representation in the Epitaphs Published in CIL 6.* Oulu, 1974.

Hyldahl, N. *Philosophie und Christentum: Eine Interpretation der Einleitung zum Dialog Justins.* Copenhagen, 1966.

———. *Udenfor og indenfor: Sociale og oekonomiske aspekter i den aeldste Kristendom.* Tekst og Tolkning 5. Copenhagen, 1974.

Imbert, J. "Réflexions sur le christianisme et l'esclavage en droit romain." *Rev. intern. des droits de l'antiquité* 2 (1949): 445–76.

Instinsky, H. U. "Marcus Aurelius Prosenes: Freigelassener und Christ am Kaiserhof." *Akad. d. Wiss. u. d. Lit. Mainz, Abh. d. Geistes- u. Sozwiss. Kl.* Wiesbaden, 1964, 113–29 (on this H. Brandenburg in *JAC* 7 [1964]: 155ff.).

Jaeger, W. "Echo eines unerkannten Tragikerfragments in Clemens' Brief an die Korinther." *Rhein. Museum f. Philol.* 102 (1959): 330–40.

———. *Paideia.* 3 vols. 4th ed. Berlin, 1959.

———. *Das frühe Christentum und die griechische Bildung.* Berlin, 1963.

Jaubert, A. "Thèmes lévitiques dans la prima Clementis." *VC* 18 (1964): 193–203.

———. "Les sources de la conception militaire de l'Eglise en 1.Clem 37." *VC* 18 (1964): 74–84.

Jeffers, J. "The Influence of the Roman Family and Social Structures on Early Christianity at Rome." In *SBL 1988 Seminar Papers,* ed. D. J. Lull, 370–84. Atlanta, 1988.

———. "Social Foundations of Early Christianity at Rome: The Congregations behind 1 Clement and the Shepherd of Hermas." Diss., University of California, Irvine, 1988.

———. *Conflict at Rome: Social Order and Hierarchy in Early Christianity.* Minneapolis, 1991.

Jerovsek, A. "Die antike heidnische Sklaverei und das Christentum." *Jahresber. Staatl. Oberrealschule.* Marburg, 1902–3.

Jervell, J. *Der Brief nach Jerusalem: Über Veranlassung und Adresse des Römerbriefs.* StTh 25. Lund, 1971.

Johann, H.-Th., ed. *Erziehung und Bildung in der heidnischen und christlichen Antike.* WF 377. Darmstadt, 1976.

Joly, R. *Le Tableau de Cébès et la philosophie religieuse.* Coll. Latomus 61. Brussels, 1963, esp. 81ff., 46ff.

————. *Hermas le Pasteur.* Sources Chrétiennes 53. 2d ed. Paris, 1968 (lit.).

————. *Christianisme et philosophie: Etudes sur Justin et les apologistes grecs du 2ᵉ siècle.* Brussels, 1973.

Jones, A. H. M. *Were Ancient Heresies Disguised Social Movements?* Philadelphia, 1966; cf. *JTS* 10 (1959): 280–98.

————. "Der soziale Hintergrund des Kampfes zwischen Heidentum und Christentum." In Klein (below), WF 267, 337ff.

————. *The Roman Economy: Studies in Ancient Economic and Administrative History.* Oxford, 1974.

————. "Das Wirtschaftsleben in den Städten des römischen Kaiserreichs." In *Sozial- und Wirtschaftsgeschichte der römischen Kaiserzeit,* ed. H. Schneider, 48–80. Darmstadt, 1981.

Jonkers, J. "Das Verhalten der Alten Kirche hinsichtlich der Ernennung von Sklaven, Freigelassenen und Curiales zum Priester." *Mnemosyne* 10 (1942): 286–302.

Jordan, H. *Forma Urbis Romae regionum XIV.* Berlin, 1874.

————, and Chr. Huelsen. *Topographie der Stadt Rom im Altertum,* I, 1–3 and II. Berlin, 1871–1907. Reprint, Rome, 1970.

Josi, E. *Il Cimitero di Callisto.* Rome, 1933.

————. "Note sul Cimitero di Pretestato: Iscrizioni relative alla gerarchia ecclesiastica e all' aristocrazia romana." *RivArCr* 13 (1936): 18–24.

————, and L. v. Matt. *Frühchristliches Rom.* Würzburg and Zurich, 1961.

Judge, E. A. *Christliche Gruppen in nichtchristlicher Gesellschaft.* Neue Studienreihe 4. Wuppertal, 1964. Engl. ed.: *The Social Pattern of the Christian Groups in the First Century.* London, 1960.

————. and G. S. R. Thomas. "The Origins of the Church at Rome: A New Solution?" *Reformed Theological Review* (Hawthorn, Austral.) 25 (1966): 81–94.

————, "The Social Identity of the First Christians: A Question of Method in Religious History." *JRH* 11 (1980): 201–17.

Kähler, H. *Die frühe Kirche: Kult und Kultraum.* Frankfurt, Berlin, and Vienna, 1982.

————. "Christliche Kreuze aus Pompeji and Herculaneum." *Bolletino dell' associazione internazionale degli amici di Pompei* 1 (1983): 279–308.

Kajanto, I. "Onomastic Studies in the Early Christian Inscriptions of Rome and Carthage." *Acta Instituti Romani Finlandiae* 2/1. Helsinki, 1963, 6ff.

————. *The Latin Cognomina.* Helsinki, 1965, 132–34 (on social-specific names).

Kalkmann, A. "Tatians Nachrichten über Kunstwerke." *Rhein. Mus. f. Phil.* 42 (1887): 489–524.

Kanzler, R. "Di un nuovo cimitero anonimo sulla via Latina." *Nuovo Bull. di Archcol. Cr.* 9 (1903): 173–86.

Käsemann, E. *Das wandernde Gottesvolk.* FRLANT 55. Göttingen, 1939. Engl. trans.: *The Wandering People of God.* Minneapolis, 1984.

———. *An die Römer.* HNT 8a. 3d ed. Tübingen, 1974. Engl. trans.: *Commentary on Romans.* Grand Rapids, 1980.

Kaser, M. "Die Geschichte der Patronatsgewalt über Freigelassene." *Zs. d. Savigny-Stiftg. f. Rechtsgesch., Roman.* 58 (1938): 88ff.

———. *Das römische Privatrecht.* HB d. Altertumswiss. 3,3, 1. 2d ed. Munich, 1971.

———. *Römische Rechtsgeschichte.* 2d ed. Göttingen, 1978.

Kaufmann, C. M. *Handbuch der altchristlichen Epigraphik.* Freiburg im B., 1917.

Kautsky, K. v. *Der Ursprung des Christentums.* Stuttgart, 1908.

Keck, L. E. "The Poor among the Saints in the NT." *ZNW* 56 (1965): 100–129.

Kee, H. C. *Das frühe Christentum in soziologischer Sicht.* UTB 1219. Göttingen, 1982. Engl. ed.: *Christian Origins in Sociological Perspective.* Philadelphia, 1980.

Kehl, A. "Antike Volksfrömigkeit und das Christentum." In Frohnes (above), 313ff.

Kehnscherper, G. *Die Stellung der Bibel und der alten christlichen Kirche zur Sklaverei.* Halle, 1957.

Keil, B. *Die solonische Verfassung in Aristoteles' Verfassungsgeschichte Athens.* Berlin, 1892 (p. 179).

Kellenbenz, H., ed. *Handbuch der europäischen Wirtschafts- und Sozial-geschichte.* Vol. 1: *Römische Kaiserzeit.* See Vittinghoff.

Kemler, H. "Hegesipps römische Bischofsliste." *VC* 25 (1971): 182–96.

Kennedy, G. *The Art of Rhetoric in the Roman World.* Princeton, 1972.

Keresztes, R. "The Jews, the Christians, and Emperor Domitian." *VC* 27 (1973): 1–28.

———. "The Imperial Roman Government and the Christian Church, 1. From Nero to the Severi." In *ANRW II* 23,1 (1979): 247–315.

Kiepert, H., and Chr. Huelsen. *Formae Urbis Romae Antiquae.* 2d ed. Berlin, 1912.

Kippenberg, H. G. "Versuch einer soziologischen Verortung des antiken Gnos-tizismus." *Numen* 17 (1970): 211–31.

———, ed. *Seminar: Die Entstehung der antiken Klassengesellschaft.* Frankfurt, 1977.

———. "Intellektualismus und antike Gnosis." In *Max Webers Studie über das antike Judentum,* ed. W. Schluchter, 201–18. Frankfurt, 1981.

Kirch, C. *Enchiridion fontium historiae ecclesiasticae antiquae.* 9th ed. Barcelona, 1965.

Kirsch, J. P. *Die christlichen Cultusgebäude im Alterthum.* Cologne, 1893.

———. *Die hl. Cäcilia in der römischen Kirche des Altertums.* Paderborn, 1910.

———. *Die römischen Titelkirchen im Altertum.* Paderborn, 1918.

————. "Die vorkonstantinischen christlichen Kultusgebäude im Lichte der neuesten Entdeckungen im Osten." *RQ* 41 (1933): 15–28.

————. "Origine e carattere degli antichi titoli cristiani di Roma." *Atti III. Congr. Naz. Studi Romani,* 1. Bologna, 1934, 46ff.

Kirschbaum, E. *Die Gräber der Apostelfürsten.* 3d ed. Frankfurt, 1974.

Klauck, H.-J. *Hausgemeinde und Hauskirche im frühen Christentum.* SBS 103. Stuttgart, 1981 (lit.).

————. "Die Hausgemeinde als Lebensform im Urchristentum." *MThZ* 32 (1981): 1–15.

————. "Gütergemeinschaft in der klassischen Antike, in Qumran und im NT." *RdQ* 41 (1982): 47–79.

Klauser, Th. "Die Anfänge der römischen Bischofsliste." *Bonner Zs. f. Theol.* 8 (1931): 193–213. Published also in:

————. "Der Übergang der römischen Kirche von der griechischen zur lateinischen Liturgiesprache." In *Misc. G. Mercati,* 467–82. Rome, 1946.

————. *Die römische Petrustradition im Lichte der neuen Ausgrabungen unter der Peterskirche.* AG f. Forsch. des Landes NRW 24. Cologne and Opladen, 1956.

————. "Studien zur Entstehungsgeschichte der christlichen Kunst." *JAC* 2 (1959): 116–45; 3 (1960): 112–33.

————. "Die Deutung der Ausgrabungsbefunde unter S. Sebastiano und am Vatikan." *JAC* 5 (1962): 33–38.

————. "Erwägungen zur Entstehung der christlichen Kunst." *ZKG* 76 (1965): 1–11.

————. "Christen seit Mark Aurel in höheren Posten in Heer und Verwaltung?" *JAC* 16 (1973): 60–66.

————. *Gesammelte Arbeiten zur Liturgiegeschichte, Kirchengeschichte und christlichen Archäologie.* Ed. E. Dassmann. *JAC* Erg. 3. Münster, 1974.

Klein, R., ed. *Das frühe Christentum im römischen Staat.* WF 267. Darmstadt, 1971.

————. *Die Romrede des Aelius Aristides.* Darmstadt, 1983.

Klette, Th. *Der Process und die Acta S. Apollonii.* TU 15,2. Leipzig, 1897.

Kloft, H. *Die Wirtschaft der griechisch-römischen Welt: Eine Einführung.* Darmstadt, 1992.

Knoche, U. "Betrachtungen über Horazens Kunst der satirischen Gesprächsführung." *Philologus* 90 (1935): 372ff., 469ff. Reprinted in D. Korzeniewski, *Die römische Satire.* Darmstadt, 1970, 285ff.

Knopf, R. "Über die soziale Zusammensetzung der ältesten heidenchristlichen Gemeinden." *ZTK* 10 (1900): 325–47.

————. *Der 1. Clemensbrief.* TU NF 5/1. Leipzig, 1901.

————. *Der erste Clemensbrief.* In W. Bauer, M. Dibelius, et al., Die Apostolischen Väter I. HNT suppl. vol. Tübingen, 1920.

Koestermann, E. "Ein folgenschwerer Irrtum des Tacitus (*Ann.* 15.44.2ff.)?" *Historia* 16 (1967): 456–69.

Kolb, F. "Zur Statussymbolik im antiken Rom." *Chiron* 7 (1977): 239–59.

Koschorke, K. *Hippolyt's Ketzerbekämpfung und Polemik gegen die Gnostiker.* Wiesbaden, 1975.

———. *Die Polemik der Gnostiker gegen das kirchliche Christentum.* NHS 12. Leiden, 1978.

———. "Eine neugefundene gnostische Gemeindeordnung." *ZTK* 76 (1979): 30–60.

Kraabel, A. T. "The Disappearance of the 'God-Fearers.'" *Numen* 28 (1981): 113–26.

———. "Social Systems of Six Diaspora Synagogues." In *Ancient Synagogues: The State of Research,* ed. J. Gutmann, 79–121. Chico, Calif., 1981.

Kraft, H. "Gnostisches Gemeinschaftsleben." Diss. theol. Heidelberg, 1950, manuscript.

———. *Clavis Patrum Apostolicorum.* Darmstadt, 1963.

Kramer, H. J. *Der Ursprung der Geistmetaphysik.* Amsterdam, 1967.

Kraus, F. X. *Real-Encyklopädie der christlichen Alterthümer.* Freiburg im B. 1, 1882–86.

Krautheimer R., et al. *Corpus Basilicarum Christianarurn Romae.* Vatican, 1937–77.

———. *Early Christian and Byzantine Architecture.* Baltimore, 1965.

———. *Rome.* Princeton, 1980.

Krenkel, W. "Währungen, Preise und Löhne in Rom." *Altertum* 7 (1961): 167–78.

———. *Römische Satiren.* Darmstadt, 1976.

Kreissig, H. "Zur sozialen Zusammensetzung der frühchristlichen Gemeinden im ersten Jahrhundert u. Z." *Eirene* 6 (1967): 91–100.

———. "Das Frühchristentum in der Sozialgeschichte des Altertums." In *Das Korpus der griechischen christlichen Schriftsteller,* ed. J. Irmscher and K. Treu, 15–19. TU 120. Berlin, 1977.

Kroll, W. "Hermes Trismegistus." In Pauly/Wissowa 8:822.

Krüiger, G. *Die Rechtsstellung der vorkonstantinischen Kirchen.* Stuttgart, 1935.

Kuch, H., et al. *Der antike Roman: Untersuchungen zur literarischen Kommunikation und Galtungsgeschichte.* Berlin, 1989.

Kügler, U.-R. *Die Paränese an die Sklaven als Modell urchristlicher Sozialethik.* Erlangen, 1977.

Kühnert, F. *Allgemeinbildung und Fachbildung in der Antike.* Dt. Akad. d. Wiss. Berlin, Sektion Altertumswiss. 30. Berlin, 1961.

Kukula, R. C. *Tatian des Assyrers Rede an die Bekenner des Griechentums.* BKV Frühchr. Apologeten I. Kempten and Munich, 1913.

Kunkel, W. *Herkunft und soziale Stellung der römischen Juristen.* 2d ed. Graz, Vienna, and Cologne, 1967.

Kyrtatas, D. J. *The Social Structure of the Early Christian Communities.* London, 1987.

Kytzler, B. M. *Minucius Felix, Octavius.* Munich, 1965.

Lake, K. "The Shepherd of Hermas and Christian Life in Rome in the Second Century." *HTR* 4 (1911): 25–46.

Lambert, J. *Les operae liberti: Contribution à l'histoire des droits de patronat.* Paris, 1934.

Lambertz, M. *Die griechischen Sklavennamen.* 57 and 58 Jahresbericht des k.k. Staatsgymnasiums im VIII. Bezirke Wiens. Vienna, 1907–8.

Lampe, P. "Das Spiel mit dem Petrusnamen." *NTS* 25 (1978–79): 227–45, here 229.

———. *"hina,"* in *EWNT* II (1981): 460–66; *"me,"* ibid., 1038–40; *"mepote,"* ibid., 1044–45 (on the various social levels of New Testament authors).

———. "Die Apokalyptiker: Ihre Situation und ihr Handeln." In *Eschatologie und Friedenshandeln,* ed. U. Luz et al., 59–114. SBS 101. 2d ed. Stuttgart, 1982.

———. "Zur gesellschaftlichen und kirchlichen Funktion der 'Familie' in ntl. Zeit." *Reformatio* 31 (1982): 533ff.

———. " 'Fremdsein' als urchristlicher Lebensaspekt." *Reformatio* 34 (1985): 58ff.

———. "Iunia/Iunias: Sklavenherkunft im Kreise der vorpaulinischen Apostel (Röm 16,7)." *ZNW* 76 (1985): 132ff.

———. "Keine 'Sklavenflucht' des Onesimus." *ZNW* 76 (1985): 135ff.

———. "Zur Textgeschichte des Römerbriefes." *NovT* 27 (1985): 273–77.

———. "Paulus–Zeltmacher." *BZ* 31 (1987): 256–61.

———, and U. Luz. "Nachpaulinisches Christentum und pagane Gesellschaft." In *Die Anfänge des Christentums,* ed. J. Becker et al., 185–216. Stuttgart, 1987.

Lanata, G. *Gli atti dei martiri come documenti processuali.* Milan, 1973.

Lanciani, R. *The Ruins and Excavations of Ancient Rome.* London, 1897; New York, 1979.

———. *Storia degli scavi di Roma.* Rome, 1902–12.

———. *L'antica Roma.* Reprint, Rome, 1970.

Langen, J. *Geschichte der römischen Kirche bis zum Pontifikate Leo's I.* Bonn, 1881.

Langerbeck, H. *Aufsätze zur Gnosis.* Ed. H. Dörries. Göttingen, 1967.

Lanne, D. E. "L'Eglise de Rome 'a gloriosissimis duobus apostolis Petro et Paulo Romae fundatae et constitutae ecclesiae' (*Adv. haer.* 111.3.2)." *Irénikon* 49 (1976): 275–322.

Lanzoni, F. "I titoli presbiteriali di Roma antica nella storia e nella legenda." *RivArCr* 2 (1925): 195ff.

La Piana, G. "The Roman Church at the End of the Second Century." *HTR* 18 (1925): 201–77 (on p. 203, n. 3, his older studies of the church at Rome).

———. "Foreign Groups in Rome during the First Centuries of the Empire." *HTR* 20 (1927): 183–403.

Lappas, J. "Paulus und die Sklavenfrage." Diss. Vienna, 1954.

Latte, K. *Römische Religionsgeschichte.* HAW V, 4. Munich, 1960.

Lau, O. "Schuster und Schusterhandwerk." Diss. Bonn, 1967.

Laub, F. *Die Begegnung des frühen Christentums mit der antiken Sklaverei.* SBS 107. Stuttgart, 1982.

Lauffer, S. "Sklaverei in der greichisch-römischen Welt." *Gynmasium* 68 (1961): 370–95.

———. *Einführung in die antike Wirtschaftsgeschichte.* See Kloft (above).

Laurin, J. L. "Le lieu du culte chrétien d'après les documents littéraires primitifs." *Atti del Congr. Intern. tenuto nella Pont. Univ. Gregoriana in occasione del centenario delta sua fondazione.* Rome, 1954, 39ff.

Layton, B., ed. *The Rediscovery of Gnosticism.* Vol. 1: *The School of Valentinus.* Leiden, 1980.

Lazzati, G. *Gli sviluppi della letteratura sui martiri nei primi quattro secoli.* Turin, 1956.

Lechler, G. V. *Sklaverei und Christentum.* 3 vols. Leipzig, 1877f.

Le Gall, J. *Recherches sur le culte du Tibre.* Paris, 1953.

Leipoldt, J. *Der soziale Gedanke in der altchristlichen Kirche.* Leipzig, 1950; repr. 1972.

Leisegang, H. *Die Gnosis.* Leipzig, 1924.

Leon, H. J. *The Jews of Ancient Rome.* Philadelphia, 1960.

Lepelley, C. *L'empire romain et le christianisme.* Paris, 1969.

Leutzsch, M. *Die Wahrnehmung sozialer Wirklichkeit im "Hirten des Hermas."* Göttingen, 1989.

Licordari, A. "Considerazioni sull' Onomastica Ostiense." In *L'Onomastique Latine: Paris 13–15 Octobre 1975.* Colloques internationaux du centre national de la recherche scientifique, no. 564. Paris, 1977.

Liebenam, W. *Zur Geschichte und Organisation des römischen Vereinswesens.* Leipzig, 1890. Reprint, Aalen, 1964.

Lieberg, G. *Puella divina: Die Gestalt der Göttlichen Geliebten bei Catull im Zusammenhang der antiken Dichtung.* Amsterdam, 1962.

Lietzmann, H. *Die Briefe des Apostels Paulus.* HNT 3. Tübingen, 1913; 5th ed., 1971.

———. "Zur altchristlichen Verfassungsgeschichte" (1914). In *Das kirchliche Amt im NT,* ed. K. Kertelge, 93–143. WF 439. Darmstadt, 1977.

———. *Geschichte der alten Kirche,* 1. Berlin, 1932. Engl. trans.: *A History of the Early Church.* New York, 1937, 1950.

———. *Petrus und Paulus in Rom.* 2d ed. Berlin, 1927.

Lightfoot, J. B. *The Apostolic Fathers 1: S. Clement of Rome 1.2.* London, 1890, 394ff.

Lipsius, R. A., and M. Bonnet, eds. *Acta Apostolorum Apocrypha.* Leipzig, 1891.

Liversidge, J. *Everyday Life in the Roman Empire.* London, 1976.

Loane, H. J. *Industry and Commerce of the City of Rome 50 B.C.–200 A.D.* Baltimore, 1938.

Lohmeyer, E. *Soziale Fragen im Urchristentum.* Leipzig, 1921.

Lohse, E. "Die Entstehung des Bischofamtes in der frühen Christenheit." *ZNW* 71 (1980): 58–73.

Lösch, M. S. *Epistula Claudiana.* Rottenburg, 1930.

———. *Der Brief des Clemens Romanus.* FS P. Ubaldi. Pubblicazioni della Università cattolica del Sacro Cuore, sér. V 16. Milan, 1937, 177ff.

Lüdemann, G. "Zur Geschichte des ältesten Christentums in Rom." *ZNW* 70 (1979): 86–114.

———. *Paulus der Heidenapostel,* 1. FRLANT 123. Göttingen, 1980. Engl. trans.: *Paul, Apostle to the Gentiles.* Philadelphia, 1984.

Lugli, G. *I monumenti antichi di Roma e suburbio.* 3 vols. Suppl. Rome, 1930–40.

———. "Aspetti urbanistici di Roma antica." *Rend. Pont. Acc.* 13 (1937): 73–98.

———. "Il valore topografico e giuridico dell'insula in Roma antica." *Rend. Pont. Acc.* 18 (1941–42): 191ff.

———. *Roma antica: Il centro monumentale.* Rome, 1946. Reprint, 1968.

———. "Il Vaticano nell'età classica." In G. Fallarini and M. Escobar. Vatican and Florence, 1946, 1ff.

———. *Fontes ad topographiam veteris Urbis Romae pertinentes.* 7 vols. Rome, 1952–69.

———. "La Roma di Domiziano nei versi di Marziale e di Stazio." *Studi romani* 9 (1961): 1–17.

———. *Itinerario di Roma antica.* Milan, 1967; Rome, 1975.

Lührmann, L. "Ntl. Haustafeln und antike Ökonomie." *NTS* 27 (1980–81): 83–97.

Maccarrone, M. "La cathedra Petri e lo sviluppo dell'idea del primato papale dal II al III sec." In *Misc. Piolanti,* 37–56. Rome, 1964.

———. "L'Episcopato nel II sec. e la cathedra episcopale." In *Problema di Storia della Chiesa,* 85–206. Milan, 1970.

MacMullen, R. *Enemies of the Roman Order: Treason, Unrest and Alienation in the Roman Empire.* Harvard, 1966.

———. *Roman Social Relations 50 B.C. to A.D. 284.* New Haven and London, 1974; 2d ed., 1976.

———. "Women in Public in the Roman Empire." *Historia* 29 (1980): 208–18.

Maddoli, G. "Speisen und Getränke." In *Rom und seine grosse Zeit: Leben und Kultur im antiken Rom,* ed. G. Giannelli and U. E. Paoli, 45–54. Würzburg, 1978.

Maeder, M. *La liberté et l'esclavage dans l'Eglise primitive.* Paris, 1951.

Magie, D. *Roman Rule in Asia Minor.* Princeton, 1950.

Mahon, J. R. "Liberation from Slavery in Early Christian Experience." Diss. Ann Arbor, 1974 (microfilm).

Maier, F. G. "Römische Bevölkerungsgeschichte und Inschriftenstatistik." *Historia* 2 (1953f.): 318–51.

Maier, G. *Die Johannesoffenbarung und die Kirche.* Tübingen, 1981, 69ff. (on Gaius).

Malherbe, A. J. *Social Aspects of Early Christianity.* 2d ed. Philadelphia, 1983.

———. *Paul and the Thessalonians.* Philadelphia, 1987.

Malina, B. J. "Limited Good and the Social World of Early Christianity." *Biblical Theology Bulletin* 8 (1978): 162–76.

———. "The Social World Implied in the Letters of the Christian Bishop-Martyr (named Ignatius of Antioch)." In *SBL Seminar Papers* II, ed. P. Achtemeier, 71–119. Missoula, Mont., 1978.

———. "The Individual and the Community: Personality in the Social World of Early Christianity." *Biblical Theology Bulletin* 9 (1979): 126–38.

———. *The New Testament World: Insights from Cultural Anthropology.* Atlanta, 1981; 3d ed. 2001.

———. *Christian Origins and Cultural Anthropology.* Atlanta, 1986.

Mancinelli, F. *Katakomben und Basiliken: Die ersten Christen in Rom.* Florence, 1981.

Marchetti-Longhi, G. "Il quartiere greco-orientale di Roma nell'antichità e nel Medioevo." *Atti IV Congr. Naz. St. Romani,* I. Rome, 1938, 169ff.

Marco, A. de. *The Tomb of Saint Peter: A Representative and Annotated Bibliography of the Excavations.* Leiden, 1964.

Marek, H. G. "Die soziale Stellung des Schauspielers im alten Rom." *Altertum 5* (1959): 101–11.

Marichal, R. "La date des graffiti de la Basilique de Saint Sébastien à Rome." *La Nouvelle Clio 5* (1953): 119–20.

———. "La date des graffiti de la Triclia de Saint-Sebastien et leur place dans l'histoire de l'écriture latine." *RevSR 36* (1962): 111–54.

Marquardt, J. *Das Privatleben der Römer.* 2d ed., 1886. Reprint, Darmstadt, 1975.

Marrou, H.-J. "Sur les origines du titre romain de Sainte-Sabine." *Archivium Fratrum Praedic.*, 2:316–25. Paris and Rome, 1932.

———. *Geschichte der Erziehung im klassischen Altertum.* Ed. R. Harder. Freiburg and Munich, 1957. Reprint, 1977.

Martin, J. *Antike Rhetorik.* Munich, 1974.

Martin, J., et al. *Atlas zur Kirchengeschichte.* Freiburg, 1970.

Martin, R. "Plinius d. J. und die wirtschaftlichen Probleme seiner Zeit." In *Sozial- und Wirtschaftsgeschichte der römischen Kaiserzeit,* ed. H. Schneider, 196–233. Darmstadt, 1981.

Martino, F. de. *Wirtschaftsgeschichte des Alten Roms.* Munich, 1985.

Marucchi, O. "Nota sulle memorie cristiane esplorate nello scavo di S. Sebastiano." *Notizie degli Scavi* 20 (1923): 80–103.

———. *Manuale di Archeologia Cristiana.* 4th ed. Rome, 1933.

———. *Le Catacombe romane.* Rome, 1934.

Maxey, M. *Occupations of the Lower Classes in Roman Society.* Chicago, 1938.

Mazzoleni, D. "Le catacombe ebraiche di Roma." *Studi Romani* 23 (1975): 289–302.

McDonald, J. I. H. "Was Romans XVI a Separate Letter?" *NTS* 16 (1970): 369–72.

McKay, A. G. *Houses, Villas and Palaces in the Roman World.* London, 1975 (lit.).

Meeks, W. A. "The Social World of Early Christianity." *CSRB* 6 (1975): 1–2.

———. "Jews and Christians in Antioch in the First Four Centuries." In *SBL Seminar Papers,* ed. G. MacRae, 33–35. Missoula, Mont., 1976.

———. *The First Urban Christians: The Social World of the Apostle Paul.* New Haven, 1983.

———, and R. L. Wilken. *Jews and Christians in Antioch in the First Four Centuries of the Common Era.* SBL Sources for Biblical Study 13. Missoula, Mont., 1978.

———, ed. *Zur Soziologie des Urchristentums.* TB 62. Munich, 1979 (lit.).

Mendelson, E. M. "Some Notes on a Sociological Approach to Gnosticism." In *Le Origini dello Gnosticismo,* ed. U. Bianchi, 668–76. Numen Suppl. 12. Leiden, 1967.

Merlin, A. *L'Aventin dans l'antiquité.* Paris, 1906.

Meslin, M. *Le christianisme dans l'Empire romain.* Paris, 1970.

Meyer, E. *Einführung in die lateinische Epigraphik.* Darmstadt, 1983.

Michelini, R. *Schiavitù, religioni antiche e cristianesimo primitivo.* Manduria, Bari, and Perugia, 1963.

Milano, A. *Storia degli Ebrei in Italia.* Torino, 1963.

Milburn, R. *Early Christian Art and Architecture.* Berkeley and Los Angeles, 1988.

Minnerath, R. *Les chrétiens et le monde (Ier et IIe siècles).* Paris, 1981.

Moeller, W. O. *The Mithraic Origin and Meaning of the ROTAS–SATOR Square.* Leiden, 1973.

Mohrmann, Chr. "Les origines de la latinité chrétienne à Rome." *VC* 3 (1949): 67–106, 163–83.

———. *Etudes sur le latin des chrétiens.* 3 vols. Rome, 1958–65.

Moisdon, R. *Sociologie humano-chrétienne des Actes des Apôtres.* Montsur, 1975.

Molthagen, J. *Der römische Staat und die Christen im 2. und 3. Jh.* 2d ed. Hypomnemata 28. Göttingen, 1975.

Mommsen, Th. "Grabschrift aus Rom." *Hermes* 2 (1867): 156–59.

———. "Die ital. Bodentheilung." *Hermes* 19 (1884): 393–416.

———. *Römisches Staatsrecht,* I–III (5 vols.). 3d ed. Leipzig, 1887f. Reprint, 1971.

———. "Der Prozess des Christen Apollonius unter Kommodus." *Sitzber. kgl. Pr. Ak. Wiss. Berlin.* 27 (1894): 497–503.

———. *Römisches Strafrecht.* Leipzig, 1899. Reprint, 1961.

———. *Die Katakomben Roms, in Reden und Aufsätze.* Berlin, 1905.

———. "Bürgerlicher und peregrinischer Freiheitsschutz im römischen Staat." In *Ges. Schriften* III, 1ff. Berlin, 1907.

———, ed. *Liber Pontificalis = Monumenta Germaniae Historica, Gesta Pontificum* 1,1. Berlin, 1898.

Moreau, J. *Die Christenverfolgung im römischen Reich.* 2d ed. Berlin, 1971.

Moretti, L. "Iscrizioni greche inedite di Roma." *Bulletino communale* 75 (1953–55): 83–86.

Mossé, C. *Le travail en Grèce et à Rome.* 2d ed. Paris, 1971.

Mrozek, S. *Prix et rémunération dans l'occident romain* (31 av.n.è.–250 de n.è.). Danzig, 1975.

———. "Wirtschaftliche Grundlagen des Aufstiegs der Freigelassenen im römischen Reich." *Chiron* 5 (1975): 311–17.

Mühlenberg, E. "Wieviel Erlösungen kennt der Gnostiker Herakleon?" *ZNW* 66 (1975): 170–93.

Munz, P. "The Problem of 'Die soziologische Verortung des antiken Gnostizismuso.'" *Numen* 19 (1972): 41–51.

Murphy-O'Connor, J. *St. Paul's Corinth: Texts and Archaeology.* Wilmington, Del., 1983.

Musurillo, H. "Early Christian Economy." *ChronEg* 31 (1956): 124–34.

———. *The Acts of the Christian Martyrs.* Oxford, 1972.

Nadelli, M. *La chiesa di Roma nel I sècolo.* La chiesa di Roma nell'antichità e nel alto medioevo. Brescia, 1967.

Nash, E. *A Pictorial Dictionary of Ancient Rome.* 2 vols. 2d ed. London, 1968 (lit.).

Nestle, E. "War der Verfasser des 1. Clemensbriefes semitischer Abstammung?" *ZNW* 1 (1900): 178–80.

Nestori, A. "La Catacomba di Catepodio al III miglio dell'Aurelia vetus e i sepolcri dei papi Callisto I e Giulio I." *RivArCr* 47 (1971): 169–278; cf. ibid., 48 (1972): 193–233; ibid., 51 (1975): 135ff.; ibid., 44 (1968): 161–72.

——. *Repertorio topografico delle pitture delle catacombe romane.* Vatican, 1975.

Neumann, K. J. *Der römische Staat und die allgemeine Kirche bis auf Diocletian,* 1. Leipzig, 1890.

Newbold, R. F. "Social Tension at Rome in the Early Years of Tiberius' Reign." *Athenaeum Pavia* 52 (1974): 110–43.

——. "Some Social and Economic Consequences of the A.D. 64 Fire at Rome." *Latomus* 33 (1974): 858–69.

Nicolai, K. "Feiertage und Werktage im römischen Leben, bes. in der Zeit der ausgehenden Republik und in der frühen Kaiserzeit." *Saeculum* 14 (1963): 194–220.

Nilsson, M. P. "Roman and Greek Domestic Cults." In *Opuscula Selecta* 3:271–85. Lund, 1960.

Norden, A. "Libellus de regionibus Urbis." *Acta Instituti Romani Regni Sueciae* 3 (1949): 1ff.

Norden, E. *Agnostos Theos.* Leiden, 1913.

——. *Die antike Kunstprosa vom VI. Jh. v. Chr. bis in die Zeit der Renaissance.* 2 vols. 9th ed. Stuttgart, 1983.

Norris, F. W. "The Social Status of Early Christianity." *Gospel in Context* 2 (1979): 4–14.

North, A. *Prolegomena till den Romerska Regionskatalogen.* Lund, 1937.

Oates, W. J. "The Population of Rome." *CP* 29 (1934): 101ff.

O'Connor, D. W. M. *Peter in Rome: The Literary, Liturgical and Archeological Evidence.* New York, 1969 (lit.).

Ollrog, W.-H. *Paulus und seine Mitarbeiter.* WMANT 50. Neukirchen, 1979.

——. "Die Abfassungsverhätnisse von Röm 16." In *Kirche,* FS G. Bornkamm, ed. D. Lührmann and G. Strecker, 221–44. Tübingen, 1980.

L'Onomastique Latine. Paris 13–15 octobre 1975. Colloques internationaux du centre national de la recherche scientifique Nr. 564. Paris, 1977.

Orr, D. G. "Roman Domestic Religion: The Evidence of the Household Shrines." *ANRW* II/16,2 (1978): 1557–91.

Osborn, E. S. *Justin-Martyr.* Tübingen, 1973.

——. *The Beginning of Christian Philosophy.* Cambridge, 1981.

Osiek, C. *Rich and Poor in the Shepherd of Hermas.* Washington, D.C., 1983.

——. *The Shepherd of Hermas.* Hermeneia. Minneapolis, 1999.

Overbeck, F. "Über das Verhältnis der alten Kirche zur Sklaverei im römischen Reiche." In *Studien zur Geschichte der alten Kirche,* 158–230. Schloss Chemnitz, 1875.

Packer, J. E. "Housing and Population in Imperial Ostia and Rome." *JRS* 57 (1967): 80–95.

Pagels, E. H. "The Valentinian Claim to Esoteric Exegesis of Romans as Basis for Anthropological Theory." *VC* 26 (1972): 241–58.

Pani Ermini: see Ermini.

Paulsen, H. "Erwägungen zu Acta Apollonii 14–22." *ZNW* 66 (1975): 117ff.

Pekáry, Th. *Die Wirtschaft der griechisch-römischen Antike.* 2d ed. Wiesbaden, 1979.

Pellegrino, M. *Il cristianesimo del 2.sec. di fronte alla cultura classica.* Torino, 1954.

Pelletier, A. *Les oeuvres de Philon d'Alexandrie, XXXII. Legatio ad Gaium.* Paris, 1972, 40ff. (on the Jews at Rome).

Penna, R. "Les Juifs à Rome au temps de l'Apôtre Paul." *NTS* 28 (1982): 321–47.

Pépin, J. *Mythe et allégorie: Les origines grecques et les contestations judéo-chrétiennes.* Paris, 1958.

Pergola, Ph. "La région dite du Bon Pasteur dans le cimetière de Domitilla sur l'Ardeatina: Etude topographique de son origine." *RivArCr* 51 (1975): 65–96.

———. "La condamnation des Flaviens 'chrétiens' sous Domitien, persécution religieuse ou répression à caractère politique?" *MEFRA* 90 (1978): 407–23.

———. "Il Praedium Domitillae sulla via Ardeatina. Anàlisi storico-topografica delle testimonianze pagane fino alla metà del III sec.D.C." *RivArCr* 55 (1979): 313–35.

Perry, B. E. *The Ancient Romances: A Literary-Historical Account of Their Origins.* Berkeley and Los Angeles, 1967.

———. "Chariton and His Romance from a Literary-Historical Point of View." *AJP* 51 (1930): 93–134.

Pervo, R. *Profit with Delight: The Literary Genre of the Acts of the Apostles.* Philadelphia, 1987.

Petersen, J. M. "House-Churches in Rome." *VC* 23 (1969): 264–72.

Peterson, E. "MEPIC, Hostien-Partikel und Opferanteil." *Ephemerides liturgicae* 61 (1947): 3–12.

———. *Frühkirche, Judentum und Gnosis.* Freiburg, Vienna, and Rome, 1959.

Pfeffer, M. E. *Einrichtungen der sozialen Sicherung in der griechischen und römischen Antike unter bes. Berücksichtigung der Sicherung bei Krankheit.* Berlin, 1969.

Pfeiffer, R. *Geschichte der Klassischen Philologie.* 2d ed. Munich, 1978.

Pietri, Ch. *Roma Christiana: Recherches sur l'Eglise de Rome, son organisation, sa politique, son idéologie de Miltiade à Sixte III (311–440).* 2 vols. Rome, 1976.

Pitigfiani, L. "A Rare Look at the Jewish Catacombs of Rome." *Bibl. Arch. Rev.* 6 (1980): 32–43.

Platner, S., and T. Ashby. *A Topographical Dictionary of Ancient Rome.* Oxford, 1929. Reprint, Rome, 1965.

Plümacher, E. *Lukas als hellenistischer Schriftsteller.* SUNT 9. Göttingen, 1972.

———. *Identitätsverlust und Identitätsgewinn.* Neukirchen, 1987.

Pohlenz, M. "Paulus und die Stoa." *ZNW* 42 (1949): 64–104.

———. *Die Stoa.* 2 vols. 5th ed. Göttingen, 1978–80.

Pöhnann, R. v. *Geschichte der sozialen Frage und des Sozialismus in der antiken Welt.* 2 vols. 3d ed. Munich, 1925.

Pokorný, P. "Der soziale Hintergrund der Gnosis." In *Gnosis und Neues Testament*, ed. K.-W. Tröger, 77–87. Berlin, 1973.

———. "Die gnostische Soteriologie in theologischer und soziologischer Sicht." In *Religionstheorie und Politische Theologie*, vol. 2: *Gnosis und Politik*, ed. J. Taubes, 154–62. Munich and Paderborn, 1984.

Poland, F. *Geschichte des griechischen Vereinswesens*. Leipzig, 1909.

———. "*Technitai.*" *RE* 2:2474–2558.

Pomeroy, S. B. *Goddesses, Whores, Wives, and Slaves: Women in Classical Antiquity*. New York, 1975.

Poschmann, B. *Busse und letzte Ölung*. HDG 4/3. Freiburg, 1951.

Prandi, A. *Il complesso monumentale della basilica celimontana dei SS. Giovanni e Paolo*. Vatican, 1953.

———. *La zona archeologica della confessione vaticana: I monumenti del II. sec.* Vatican, 1957.

Preysing, K. "Der Leserkreis der Philosophumena Hippolyts." *ZKT* 38 (1914): 421–45.

Prigent, R. *Justin et l'Ancient Testament*. Paris, 1964.

Puech, A. *Recherches sur le Discours aux Grecs de Tatien*. Paris, 1903.

Puzicha, M. *Christus peregrinus: Die Fremdenaufnahme (Mt 25,35) als Werk der privaten Wohltätigkeit im Urteil der alten Kirche*. Munich, 1980.

Quacquarelli, A. "Note sugli edifici di culto prima di Costantino." *VetChr* 14 (1977): 239–51.

Quispel, G. *La lettre à Flora par Ptolémée*. Sources chrétiennes 24. 2d ed. Paris, 1966.

Rabbow, P. *Seelenführung, Methodik der Exerzitien in der Antike*. Munich, 1954.

Raepsaet-Charlier, M.-T. "Tertullien et la législation des mariages inégaux." *Rev. intern. des droits de l'antiquité* 29 (1982): 253–63.

Raffeiner, H. *Sklaven und Freigelassene: Eine soziologische Studie auf der Grundlage des griechischen Grabepigramms*. Commentationes Aenipontanae XXIII, Book 2, Phil. u. Epigr. Innsbruck, 1977.

Rahner, H. *Griechische Mythen in christlicher Deutung*. Zurich, 1945, 361–413. Engl. trans.: *Greek Myths and Christian Mystery*. London, 1963.

Rakob, F. "Die Urbanisierung des nördlichen Marsfeldes: Neue Forschungen im Areal des Horologium Augusti." In *L'Urbs, espace urbain et histoire (I.siècle av. J. Chr.–III. Siècle ap. J. Chr.)*. Actes du colloque international organisé par le Centre national de la recherche scientifique et l'Ecole français de Rome, 687–712. Rome, 1987.

Raos, M. "Iscrizione cristiana-greca di Roma anteriore al terzo secola?" *Aevum* 37 (1963): 11–30.

Rawson, B. "Family Life among the Lower Classes at Rome in the First Two Centuries of the Empire." *CP* 61 (1966): 71–83.

Reekmans, L. "Le développement topographique de la région du Vatican." In *Mélanges Lavalleye*, 43–78. Louvain, 1972.

———. *La tombe du Pape Corneille et sa région cémétériale*. Roma Sotterranea Cristiana IV. Vatican, 1964.

Reekmans, T. "Juvenal's Views on Social Change." *Ancient Society* 2 (1971): 117–61.

Regling, K. "Munzwesen." Pauly / Wissowa 16/1:482.

Reichmuth, J. "Die lateinischen Gentilicia." Diss. Zurich, 1956.

Reinhold, M. "Usurpation of Status and Status Symbols." *Historia* 20 (1971): 275–302.

Reitzenstein, R. *Poimandres: Studien zur gr.-ägypt. und frühchristlichen Literatur.* Leipzig, 1904, 11ff., 32ff.

———. *Die hellenistischen Mysterienreligionen nach ihren Grundgedanken und Wirkungen.* 3d ed. Leipzig, 1927; Darmstadt, 1977.

Reville, J. *La valeur du témoignage historique du Pasteur d'Hermas.* Paris, 1900.

Robertis, F. de. See above, De Robertis.

Robertson, E. H. "The House Church." In *Basileia.* FS W. Freytag, 366–71. Wuppertal, 1959.

Rodriguez, Almeida, E. *Novedades de epigrafia anforaria del Monte Testaccio.* In P. Baldacci et al., *Recherches sur les amphores romaines.* Rome, 1972.

Roebuck, C., ed. *The Muses at Work: Arts, Crafts and Professions in Ancient Greece and Rome.* Cambridge, Mass., 1969.

Rogers, H. L., and T. R. Harley. *Roman Home Life and Religion.* Oxford, 1923.

Rohde, J. *Urchristentum und frühkatholische Ämter.* Theol. Arbeiten 33. Berlin, 1976.

Rordorf, W. "Was wissen wir über die christlichen Gottesdiensträume der vorkonstantinischen Zeit?" *ZNW* 55 (1964): 110–28.

———. "Was heisst: Petrus und Paulus haben die Kirche in Rom 'gegründet'?" In *Unterwegs zur Einheit,* FS H. Stirnimann, ed. J. Brantschen and P. Selvatico, 609–16. Freiburg, Switz., and Vienna, 1980.

———. "Die Neronische Christenverfolgung im Spiegel der Apokryphen Paulus-akten." *NTS* 28 (1981): 365–74.

Rose, H. J. "The Religion of a Greek Household." *Euphrosyne* 1 (1957): 95–116.

Rossi. See De Rossi.

Rostovtzeff, M. *Gesellschaft und Wirtschaft im römischen Kaiserreich.* 2 vols. Leipzig, 1929; 2d ed., 1957.

———. *Gesellschafts- und Wirtschaftsgeschichte der hellenistischen Welt.* Stuttgart, 1955–56.

Rouland, M. *Pouvoir politique et dépendance personnelle dans l'Antiquité romaine: Genése et rôle des rapports de clientèle.* Coll. Latomus 166. Brussels, 1979.

Rudolph, K. "Randerscheinungen des Judentums und das Problem der Entstehung des Gnostizismus." In *Gnosis und Gnostizismus,* 776ff. Darmstadt, 1975.

Ruhbach, G. "Bildung in der Alten Kirche." In Frohnes (above), 293ff.

———. "Das Problem einer Soziologie und 'sozialen Verortung' der Gnosis." *Kairos* 19 (1977): 35–44.

Ruysschaert, J. "Nouvelles recherches concernant la tombe de Pierre au Vatican." *Rev. Hist. Eccl.* 60 (1965): 822–32; cf. ibid., 48 (1953): 574–631; 49 (1954): 5–58; 52 (1957): 791–831.

———. "Les premiers siècles de la tombe de Pierre: Une discussion dégagée d'une hypothése." *Rev. des Archéologues et Historiens d'Art de Louvain* 8 (1975): 7–47.

Rydbeck, L. *Fachprosa, vermeintliche Volkssprache und NT.* Uppsala, 1967.

Rykwert, J. *The Idea of a Town: The Anthropology of Urban Form in Rome, Italy and the Ancient World.* Princeton, 1977.

Sagnard, F. *Clément d'Alexandrie, Extraits de Théodote.* Paris, 1970.

Salmon, P. *Population et dépopulation dans l'Empire romain.* Coll. Latomus 137. Brussels, 1974.

Sanders, E. P., ed. *Jewish and Christian Self-Definition.* Vol. 1: *The Shaping of Christianity in the Second and Third Centuries.* Philadelphia, 1980.

Sanders, L. *L'hellénisme de Saint Clément de Rome et le Paulinisme.* Louvain, 1943.

Sauser, E. *Frühchristliche Kunst.* Innsbruck, 1966.

Savage, S. M. "The Cults of Ancient Trastevere." *Memoires of the American Academy in Rome* 17 (1940): 26ff.

Saxer, V. "Martyrium Apollonii Romani." *Rend. Pont. Accad. Rom. Di Archeol.* 55/56 (1982–84): 265–98.

———. "L'Apologie au Sénat du martyr romain Apollonius." *Mélanges de l'Ecole français de Rome Antiquité* 96 (1984): 1017–38.

Schade, H.-H. *Apokalyptische Christologie bei Paulus.* GTA 18. Göttingen, 1981.

Schäfer, P. "Rabbi Aqiba and Bar Kohkba." In *Approaches to Ancient Judaism* 2: 113–330. Brown Judaic Studies 9. Ann Arbor, 1980.

Schaller, H. "Das Christentum in den antiken Grossstädten." *Altertum* 8/1 (1962): 26–39.

Scheele, J. "Zur Rolle der Unfreien in den römischen Christenverfolgungen." Diss. Tübingen, Bochum, 1970.

Schenke, L. "Zur sog. Oikosformel im NT." *Kairos* 13 (1971): 226–43.

Schermann, Th. *Griechische Zauberpapyri und das Gemeinde- und Dankgebet im I. Klemensbrief.* Leipzig, 1909.

Schilling, O. *Reichtum und Eigentum in der altkirchlichen Literatur.* Freiburg, 1908; Frankfurt, 1985.

———. "Der Kollektivismus der Kirchenväter." *Theol. Quartalsschr.* 114 (1933): 481–92.

Schmid, W. "Die Textüberlieferung der Apologie des Justin." *ZNW* 40 (1941): 137.

———. "Frühe Apologetik und Platonismus." In Ἑρμενεία, 163–82. FS O. Regenbogen. Heidelberg, 1952.

Schmithals, W. *Der Römerbrief als historisches Problem.* StNT 9. Gütersloh, 1975.

Schneider, A. M. *Die ältesten Denkmäler der römischen Kirche: FS 200-jähr. Bestehen der Akad. Wiss. Göttingen,* II, Phil.-hist. Kl. Berlin, Göttingen, and Heidelberg, 1951, 166–98.

Schneider, C. *Geistesgeschichte des antiken Christentums.* 2 vols. Munich, 1954.

Schneider, H., ed. *Sozial- und Wirtschaftsgeschichte der römischen Kaiserzeit.* WF 552. Darmstadt, 1981.

Schoedel, W., and R. L. Wilken, eds. *Early Christian Literature and the Classical Intellectual Tradition.* FS R. M. Grant. Théologie historique 53. Paris, 1979.

Schöllgen, G. *Ecclesia sordida? Zur Frage der sozialen Schichtung frühchristlicher Gemeinden am Beispiel Karthagos zur Zeit Tertullians.* JAC Erg. 12. Münster, 1984.

———. Review of Plümacher, *Identitätsverlust.* *ThRv* 84 (1988): 298–300.

————. "Was wissen wir über die Sozialstruktur der paulinischen Gemeinden? *NTS* 34 (1988): 71–82.

Scholten, C. "Gibt es Quellen zur Sozialgeschichte der Valentinianer Roms?" *ZNW* 79 (1988): 245–61.

Schottroff, W., and W. Stegemann, *Der Gott der kleinen Leute: Sozialgeschichtliche Auslegungen.* 2 vols. Munich and Geinhausen, 1979.

Schrage, W. *Die Christen und der Staat nach dem Neuen Testament.* Gütersloh, 1971.

Schreiber, A. *Die Gemeinde von Korinth: Versuch einer gruppendynamischen Betrachtung der Entwicklung der Gemeinde von Korinth auf der Basis des ersten Korintherbriefes.* NTA NF 12. Münster, 1977.

Schulz, H. "Spuren heidnischer Vorlagen im Hirten des Hermas." Diss. Rostock, 1913.

Schulz-Falkenthal, H. "Gegenseitigkeitshilfe und Unterstützungstätigkeit in den römischen Handwerkergenossenschaften." *WissZHalle* 20 (1971): 59–78.

Schulze, W. *Zur Geschichte der lateinischen Eigennamen.* Berlin, 1904.

Schumacher, R. *Die soziale Lage der Christen im apostolischen Zeitalter.* Paderborn, 1924.

Schürer, E. *Die Gemeindeverfassung der Juden in Rom in der Kaiserzeit.* Leipzig, 1879.

————. *Geschichte des Jüdischen Volkes im Zeitalter Jesu Christi.* 3 vols. 4th ed. Leipzig, 1901–9. Engl. trans.: *The History of the Jewish People in the Age of Jesus Christ.* Edinburgh, 1973ff.

Schwartz, J. "Survivances littéraires païennes dans le Pasteur d'Hermas." *RB* 72 (1965): 240–47.

Scivoletto, N. "Pietro e Paolo nel quartiere ebraico dell'Appia." *Giornale italiano di filologia* 13 (1960): 1–24.

Scroggs, R. "The Earliest Christian Communities as Sectarian Movement." In *Christianity, Judaism and other Greco-Roman Cults,* ed. J. Neusner, 2:1–23. FS Morton Smith. Leiden, 1975.

————. "The Sociological Interpretation of the New Testament: The Present State of Research." *NTS* 26 (1980): 164–79.

Seipel, J. *Die wirtschaftsethischen Lehren der Kirchenväter.* Theol. St. d. Leo-Gesellsch. 18. Vienna, 1907.

Sevrin, J.-M. "Les Noces Spirituelles dans l'Evangile selon Philippe." *Le Muséon* 87 (1974): 143–93.

Sherwin-White, A. N. *Roman Society and Roman Law in the NT.* Oxford, 1963.

————. *Racial Prejudice in Imperial Rome.* Cambridge, 1967.

Shurden, R. M. "The Christian Response to Poverty in the New Testament Era." Diss. Ann Arbor, 1970 (microfilm).

Siegert, F. "Gottesfürchtige und Sympathisante." *JSJ* 4 (1973): 109–64.

Simon, M. "Les Juifs de Rome au début de l'ère chrétienne." *Bible et Terre Sainte* 94 (1967): 9–15.

————. *La civilisation de l'Antiquité et le christianisme.* Paris, 1972.

————. "Les Juifs d'Rome à 1er siècle." *Le Monde de la Bible* 18 (1981): 33f.

Simonetti, M. "Eracleone e Origene." *Vetera Christianorum* 3 (1966): 133ff.

Smallwood, E. M. *The Jews under Roman Rule: From Pompey to Diocletian.* SJLA 20. Leiden, 1976.

Smith, J. Z. "The Social Description of Early Christianity." *Religious Studies Review* 1 (1975): 19–25.

Smith, R. H. "Were the Early Christians Middle-Class? A Sociological Analysis of the New Testament." *CThMi* 7 (1980): 260–76.

Snyder, G. *The Shepherd of Hermas.* Camden, N.J., 1968.

————. *Ante Pacem: Archeological Evidence of Church Life before Constantine.* Macon, Ga., 1985.

Söder, L. *Die apokryphen Apostelgeschichten und die romanhafte Literatur der Antike.* Stuttgart, 1932. Reprint, 1969.

Solin, H. "Probleme der römischen Namenforschung: Die griechischen Personennamen in Rom." *Beiträge zur Namenforschung,* Heidelberg NF 5 (1970): 276–300.

————. *Beiträge zur Kenntnis der griechischen Personennamen in Rom,* vol. 1. Helsinki, 1971.

————. *Die griechischen Personennamen in Rom: Ein Namenbuch.* 3 vols. Berlin, 1982.

————. "Juden und Syrer im westlichen Teil der römischen Welt." *ANRW* II 29/2 (1983): 587–789.

————. *Die stadtrömischen Sklavennamen.* 3 vols. Forschungen zur antiken Sklaverei, Beiheft 2. Stuttgart, 1996.

Sontheimer, W. *Tacitus Annalen XI–XVI.* Stuttgart, 1967.

Sordi, M., and M. L. Cavigiolo. "Un'antica 'chiesa domestica' di Roma?" *Rivista di storia della Chiesa in Italia* 25 (1971): 369–74.

Spanneut, M. *Le stoïcisme des pères de l'Eglise de Clément de Rome à Clément d'Alexandrie.* Paris, 1958.

Speigl, J. *Der römische Staat und die Christen: Staat und Kirche von Domitian bis Commodus.* Amsterdam, 1970.

Spence-Jones, H. D. M. *The Early Christians in Rome.* London, 1910.

————. *The Foundation of the Church in Rome, the Influence of St. Peter, the Early Christians in Rome.* New York, 1911.

Staats, R. "Die martyrologische Begründung des Romprimates bei Ignatius von Antiochien." *ZTK* 73 (1976): 461–70.

————. "Deposita pietatis: Die Alte Kirche und ihr Geld." *ZTK* 76 (1979): 1–29.

Stadler, E., and J. N. Ginal, *Vollständiges Heiligen-Lexikon.* Augsburg, 1882; Hildesheim and New York, 1975.

Staerman, E. M. and M. K.Trofimova, *La schiavitù nell'Italia imperiale, I–III sec.* Rome, 1975.

————. "Der Klassenkampf der Sklaven zur Zeit des römischen Kaiserreiches." In *Sozial- und Wirtschaftsgeschichte der römischen Kaiserzeit,* ed. H. Schneider, 307–35. Darmstadt, 1981.

Stam, J. E. "Episcopacy in the Apostolic Tradition of Hippolyt." Diss. Basel, 1969.

Stambaugh, J. E., and D. L. Balch. *The New Testament in Its Social Environment.* Philadelphia, 1986.

St. Barnes, A. *Christianity at Rome in the Apostolic Age.* London, 1938; reprint, Westport, Conn., 1971.

Stead, G. C. "In Search of Valentinus." In *The Rediscovery of Gnosticism,* ed. B. Layton, 1:75–102. Leiden, 1980.

de Ste. Croix, G. E. M. "Early Christian Attitudes to Property and Slavery." In *Church, Society, and Politics,* ed. D. Baker, 1–38. Oxford, 1975.

Steinmann, A. *Sklavenlos und Alte Kirche: Eine historische exegetische Studie über die soziale Frage im Urchristentum.* Apologet. Tagesfragen 3. 4th ed. Munich-Gladbach, 1922.

Stern, M. *Greek and Latin Authors on Jews and Judaism.* 2 vols. Jerusalem, 1976–80.

Stevenson, E. "Some Insights from the Sociology of Religion into the Origin and Development of the Early Christian Church." *ExpT* 90 (1979): 300–305.

Stevenson, J. *Im Schattenreich der Katakomben.* Bergisch Gladbach, 1980.

Stockmeier, P. "Der Begriff Paideia bei Klemens von Rom." In *Studia Patristica* 7, 401ff. TU 92. Berlin, 1966.

———. "Glaube und Paideia: Zur Begegnung von Christentum und Antike." *Theol. Quartalschr.* 147 (1967): 432ff.

Stöger, A. "Das Finanzwesen der Urkirche." *BiLi* 50 (1977): 96–103.

Strasburger, H. *Zum antiken Gesellschaftsideal.* Abh. d. Heidelb. Akad. Wiss., Phil.-hist. Kl. 4. Heidelberg, 1976.

Strobel, A. "Der Begriff des 'Hauses' im griechischen und römischen Privatrecht." *ZNW* 56 (1965): 91–100.

Strong, D., and D. Brown, eds. *Roman Crafts.* London, 1976.

Stuiber, A. "Clemens romanus I." *RAC* 3:195.

Stuhlmacher, P. *Der Brief an Philemon.* EKK. Neukirchen and Zurich, 1975, 70–75.

———. "Der Abfassungszweck des Römerbriefes." *ZNW* 77 (1986): 180–193.

Styger, P. *Die römischen Katakomben.* Berlin, 1933.

———. *Juden und Christen im alten Rom.* Berlin, 1934.

———. *Die römischen Märtyrergrüfte.* Berlin, 1935.

Suolahti, J. "Position sociale des personnes mentionnées dans les inscriptions." In *Sylloge Inscriptionum Christianarum Musei Vaticani,* 167–84. Acta Instituti Romani Finnlandiae 2. Rome, 1963.

Tailliez, F. "Un vulgarisme du Clemens latinus (inpinguis = pinguis!) et la langue vulgaire de Rome." *Neophilologus* 35 (1951): 46–50.

Tateo, R. *Tradizione apostolica.* Turin, 1972.

Taylor, L. Ross. "Freedmen and Freeborn in the Epitaphs of Imperial Rome." *AJP* 82 (1961): 113–32.

Teichmüller, E. *Der Einfluss des Christentums auf die Sklaverei im griechisch-römischen Altertum.* Dessau, 1894.

Testini, P. *Le catacombe e gli antichi cimiteri cristiani in Roma.* Bologna, 1966.

———. *Archeologia Cristiana.* 2d ed. Rome, 1958; Bari, 1980.

Theiler, W. "Gott und Seele im kaiserzeitlichen Denken." In *Forschungen zum Neuplatonismus.* Quellen und Studien z. Gesch. d. Philos. 10, 104–23. Berlin, 1966.

Theissen, G. *Untersuchungen zum Hebräerbrief.* StNT 2. Gütersloh, 1969.

———. *Studien zur Soziologie des Urchristentums.* WUNT 19. Tübingen, 1979; 2d ed., 1983 (331–48, extensive bibliog.); in which see esp.:

————. "Soziale Schichtung in der korinthischen Gemeinde." *ZNW* 65 (1974): 232–72. Engl. trans.: *Social Reality and the Early Christians.* Minneapolis, 1992.

————. *Soziologie der Jesusbewegung.* Munich, 1977. Engl. trans.: *Sociology of Early Palestinian Christianity.* Philadelphia, 1978.

Thiede, C. P. "Rom: Archäologie, Frühchr. Zeit." In *Grosses bibellexikon* 3. 1989.

Thierry, J. J. "Note sur TA ELACHISTA TON ZOON au chapitre XX de la I Clementis." *VC* 14 (1960): 235–44.

Thümmel, H. G. "Soziologische Aspekte des frühen christlichen Inschriftenformulars." In *Die Rolle der Plebs im spätrömischen Reich,* ed. V. Besevliev and W. Seyfarth, 71ff. Dt. Akad. Wiss. Berlin, Schrift. Sekt. Altertumswiss. 55,2. Berlin, 1969.

Thyen, H. *Der Stil der jüdisch-hellenistischen Homilie.* Göttingen, 1955.

Thylander, H. *Etude sur l'épigraphie latine.* Lund, 1952.

Timothy, H. B. *The Early Christian Apologists and Greek Philosophy.* Assen, 1972.

Tolotti, F. "L'area recinta ove ebbe origine il cimitero di Priscilla." *RivArCr* 42–43 (1966–67): 261–314.

————. *Il cimitero di Priscilla: Studio di topografia e architettura.* Vatican, 1970.

————. "Ricerca dei luoghi venerati della spelunca magna di Pretestato." *RivArCr* 53 (1977): 7–102.

————. "Influenza delle opere idrauliche sull'origine delle catacombe." *RivArCr* 56 (1980): 7–48.

Topitsch, E. "Marxismus und Gnosis." In *Sozialphilosophie zur Ideologie und Wissenschaft,* 261–96. Soziol. Texte 10. 2d ed. Neuwied, 1966.

Tran Tam Tinh, V. "Le culte des divinités orientales en Campanie en dehors de Pompei, de Stabies et d'Herculaneum." *EPRO* 27 (1972): 141–58.

Troeltsch, E. *Die Soziallehren der christlichen Kirchen und Gruppen.* Ges. Schriften 1, 1912. Reprint, Aalen, 1961.

Tuker, M. A. R., and H. Malleson. *Handbook to Christian and Ecclesiastical Rome.* London, 1900.

Uhlhorn, G. *Die christliche Liebestätigkeit.* 2d ed. Stuttgart, 1895; Neukirchen and Darmstadt, 1959.

Unnik, W. C. v. "Is 1 Clement 20 Purely Stoic?" *VC* 4 (1949–50): 181–89.

————. "1 Clement 34 and the 'Sanctus.'" *VC* 5 (1951): 204–48.

————. "'Tiefer Friede' (1 Klemens 2,2)." *VC* 24 (1970): 261–79.

————. "Noch einmal 'Tiefer Friede.'" *VC* 26 (1972): 24–28.

Urlichs, C. L. *Codex urbis Romae topographicus.* Würzburg, 1871.

Valentini, R., and G. Zucchetti. *Codice topografico della Città di Roma.* 4 vols. Rome, 1940–53.

Varone, A. "Giudei e cristiani nell'area vesuviana." In *Pompei 79,* Suppl. to *Antiqua* 15 (1979): 131–46.

————. *Presenze giudaiche e cristiane a Pompei.* Naples, 1979.

Vermaseren, M. J. *De Mithrasdienst in Rome.* Nijmegen, 1951.

————, ed. *Die orientalischen Religionen im Römerreich.* Leiden, 1981.

Vermaseren, M. J., and C. C. van Essen. *The Excavations in the Mithraeum of the Church of Santa Prisca in Rome.* Leiden, 1965.

Verner, D. C. *The Household of God: The Social World of the Pastoral Epistles.* Baltimore, 1983.

Vielhauer, Ph. *Geschichte der urchristlichen Literatur.* Berlin, 1975.

Vielliard, R. "Les titres romains et les deux éditions du Liber Pontificalis." *RivArCr* 5 (1928): 89ff.

———. *Les origines du titre de Saint-Martin aux Monts à Rome.* Studi di Antichità Cristiana IV. Vatican, 1931.

———. *Recherches sur les origines de la Rome chrétienne.* Mâcon, 1941; Rome, 1959.

Visscher: see De Visscher.

Vittinghoff, F. "Soziale Struktur und politisches System der hohen römischen Kaiserzeit." *HZ* 230 (1980): 31–56.

———, ed. *Europäische Wirtschafts- und Sozialgeschichte in der römischen Kaiserzeit.* Handbuch der Europäischen Wirtschafts- und Sozialgeschichte. Stuttgart, 1990.

Voelkl, L. "Apophoretum, Eulogie und Fermentum." In *Misc. G. Belvederi,* 391–414. Rome, 1954.

Vogelstein, H., and P. Rieger. *Geschichte der Juden in Rom.* 2 vols. Berlin, 1895f.

Vogler, W. "Die Bedeutung der urchristlichen Hausgemeinden für die Ausbreitung des Evangeliums." *TLZ* 107 (1982): 785–94.

Vogliano, A. "La grande Iscrizione Bacchica del Metropolitan Museum." *AJA* 37 (1933): 215ff.

Vogt, J. "Alphabet für Freie und Sklaven: Zum sozialen Aspekt des antiken Elementarunterrichts." *Rhein. Mus.* 116 (1973): 129–42.

———. "Der Vorwurf der sozialen Niedrigkeit des frühen Christentums." *Gymnasium* 82 (1975): 401–11.

———. "Die Sklaven und die unteren Schichten im frühen Christentum: Stand der Forscbung." *Gymnasium* 87 (1980): 436–46.

———, and N. Brockmeyer. *Bibliographie zur antiken Sklaverei.* Bochum, 1971.

Vouaux, L. *Les Actes de Paul et ses lettres apocryphes.* Paris, 1913.

de Waal, A. "Zu Wilpert's Domus Petri." *Röm. Quartalschr.* 26 (1912): 123–32.

Wachsmuth, D. "Aspekte des antiken mediterranen Hauskults." *Numen* 27 (1980): 34–75.

Waldstein, W. *Untersuchungen zum römischen Begnadigungsrecht.* Innsbruck, 1964.

Walsh, J. E. *The Bones of Saint Peter.* New York, 1982.

Walton, C. S. "Oriental Senators in the Service of Rome." *JRS* 19 (1929): 38ff.

Waltzing, J.-P. *Etude historique sur les corporations professionnelles chez les Romains.* Leuven, 1895–1900; New York, 1979.

Walzer, R. *Galen on Jews and Christians.* London, 1949.

Waszink, J. H. "Der Platonismus und die altchristliche Gedankenwelt." *Entretiens sur l'Antiquité classique* 3 (1955): 139–79.

———. "Bemerkungen zu Justins Lehre vom Logos Spermatikos." In *Mullus,* 380–90. FS Th. Klauser. *JAC* Erg. 1. Münster, 1964.

———. "Bemerkungen zum Einfluss des Platonismus im frühen Christentum." *VC* 19 (1965): 129–62.

Watson, J. K. "Les premiers chrétiens de Rome." *Bull. du Cercle Ernest Renan* 22 (1974): 5ff.

———. "Tacite et les chrétiens (*Ann.* 15.44)." Ibid., 23 (1975): 28ff.

Weaver, P. R. C. "Nomina ingenua." *CQ* 58 (1964): 311–15.

———. "Irregular Nomina of Imperial Freedmen." *CQ* 59 (1965): 323–26.

———. *Familia Caesaris: A Social Study of the Emperor's Freedmen and Slaves.* Cambridge, 1972.

———. "Social Mobility in the Early Roman Empire: The Evidence of the Imperial Freedmen and Slaves." In *Studies in Ancient Society,* ed. M. I. Finley, 121–40. London, 1974.

Weber, M. *Wirtschaft und Gesellschaft: Studienausgabe hg. v. J. Winckelmann.* Cologne and Berlin, 1964; 5th ed., Tübingen, 1980.

Wehofer, Th. *Die Apologie Justins des Philosophen und Märtyrers in literarhistorischer Beziehung zum erstenmal untersucht.* Röm. Quartalschrift Suppl. 6. Freiburg im B., 1897.

Weismann, W. *Kirche und Schauspiele: Die Schauspiele im Urteil der lateinischen Kirchenväter unter bes. Berücksichtigung von Augustin.* Warzburg, 1972.

Wendland, H. D. "Die sozialethische Bedeutung der ntl. Haustafeln." In *Die Leibhaftigkeit des Wortes,* 34–46. FS Köberle. Hamburg, 1958.

Wendland, P. *Die hellenistisch-römische Kultur in ihren Beziehungen zum Judentum und Christentum.* HNT 1/2f. Tübingen, 1907; 2d ed., 1912; 4th ed., 1972.

Westermann, W. L. *The Slave Systems of Greek and Roman Antiquity.* Philadelphia, 1955.

White, L. M. "Domus Ecclesiae–Domus Dei." Diss. Yale, 1982.

Whittaker, M., ed. *Tatianus, Oratio ad Graecos and Fragments.* Oxford and New York, 1982.

Wiedemann, Th. *Greek and Roman Slavery.* London, 1981.

Wiefel, W. "Die jüdische Gemeinschaft im antiken Rom und die Anfänge des römischen Christentums." *Judaica* 26 (1970): 65–88.

———. "Erwägungen zur soziologischen Hermeneutik urchristlicher Gottesdienstformen." *Kairos* 14 (1972): 36–51.

Wifstrand, A. *Die alte Kirche und die griechische Bildung.* Bern, 1967.

Wilamowitz-Moellendorff, U. v. *Antigonos von Karystos.* Philolog. Untersuchungen IV. Berlin, 1881, 178ff., 263ff.

Wilckens, U. *Der Brief an die Römer.* EKK 6/1–3. Zurich and Neukirchen, 1978–82.

Wilde, J. "A Social Description of the Community Reflected in the Gospel of Mark." Diss. Ann Arbor, 1977 (microfilm).

Wilder, A. N. "Social Factors in Early Christian Eschatology." In *Early Christian Origins,* 67–76. FS H. R. Willoughby. Chicago, 1961.

Wilken, R. L. "Towards a Social Interpretation of Early Christian Apologetics." *Church History* 39 (1970): 437–58.

———. "Kollegien, Philosophenschulen und Theologie." In Meeks, ed. (above), 1979, 165–93.

———. *The Christians as the Romans Saw Them.* New Haven, 1984.

Wilpert, G. *Le pitture delle catacombe romane.* Rome, 1903.

————. *Papstgräber und die Cäciliengruft in der Katakombe des Hl. Kallistus.* Freiburg, 1909.

————. *Die römischen Mosaiken und Malereien.* 4 vols. Freiburg im B., 1916.

Wilson, W. J. "The Career of the Prophet Hermas." *HTR* 20 (1927): 21–62.

Windelband, W., and H. Heimsoeth. *Lehrbuch der Geschichte der Philosophie.* 15th ed. Tübingen, 1957.

Winden, J. C. M. v. *An Early Christian Philosopher.* Leiden, 1971.

————. "Le portrait de la philosophie grecque dans Justin, *Dialogue* 1 4–5." *VC* 31 (1977): 181–90.

Wirth, F. *Die römischen Wandmalereien.* Berlin, 1934.

Wischmeyer W., ed. *Griechische und lateinische Inschriften zur Sozialgeschichte der Alten Kirche.* Texte z. Kirchen- und Theol. gesch. 28. Gütersloh, 1982.

————. *Rom und die Christen: Zur Auseinandersetzung zwischen Christen und römischem Staat.* Stuttgart, 1970.

————. "Die Rechtsgrundlagen der Christenverfolgungen der ersten zwei Jahrhunderte." In Klein (above), WF 267, 275ff.

Wlosok, A. "Christliche Apologetik gegenüber kaiserlicher Politik bis zu Konstantin." In Frohnes (above), 147ff.

Woltmann, J. "Der geschichtliche Hintergrund der Lehre Markions vom 'Fremden Gott.' " In *Wegzeichen,* ed. E. Chr. Suttner and C. Patock, 15–42. FS H. M. Biedermann. Würzburg, 1971.

Wong, D. W. F. "Natural and Divine Order in I Clem." *VC* 31 (1977): 31–87.

Wotschitzky, A. *Das antike Rom.* Innsbruck, 1950.

————. *Hochhäuser im antiken Rom, Natalicium C. Jax,* I. Innsbrucker Beitr. z. Kulturwiss. 3, 1955, 151ff.

Wrede, W. *Untersuchungen zum Ersten Klemensbriefe.* Göttingen, 1891.

Zahn, Th. *Der Hirt des Hermas.* Gotha, 1868.

————. *Sklaverei und Christentum in der alten Welt.* Erlangen, 1879.

————. "Die soziale Frage und die innere Mission nach dem Brief des Jakobus." In *Skizzen aus dem Leben der Alten Kirche,* 93–115. 3d ed. Leipzig, 1908.

Zeegers-van der Vorst, N. *Les citations des poétes grecs chez les apologistes chrétiens du 2e siècle.* Louvain, 1972.

Ziebarth, E. *Das griechische Vereinswesen.* Leipzig, 1896. Reprint, Wiesbaden, 1969.

Zimmermann, F. "Aus der Welt des griechischen Romans." *Die Antike* 11 (1935): 293ff.

Zintzen, C., ed. *Der Mittelplatonismus.* WF 70. Darmstadt, 1981.

Maps, Diagrams, and Figures

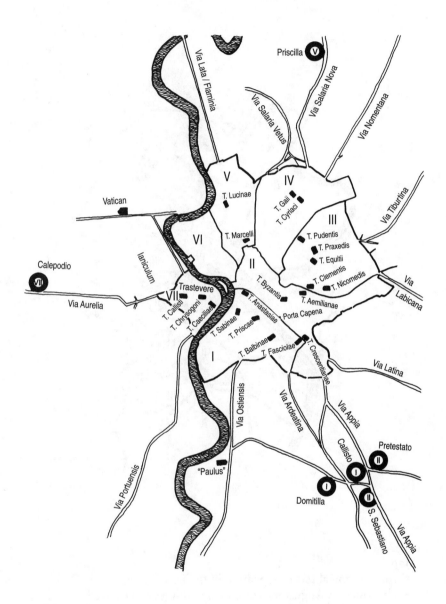

Map 1.
- The seven ecclesiastical regions
- Early burial places outside the city (Roman numerals indicate the ecclesiastical region to which each belongs)
- *Tituli* in the city

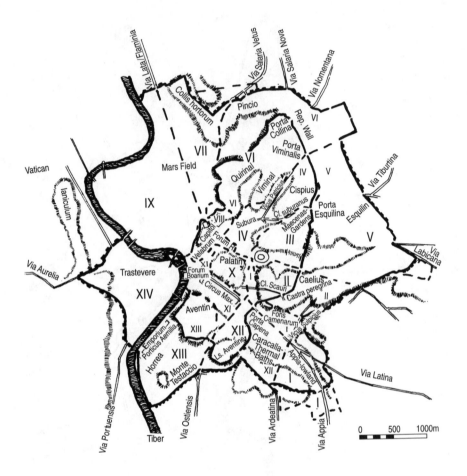

Map 2.
- Topographical terms appearing in the text
- The fourteen Augustan regions (dotted lines or city walls; Roman numerals)
- The hills of the city

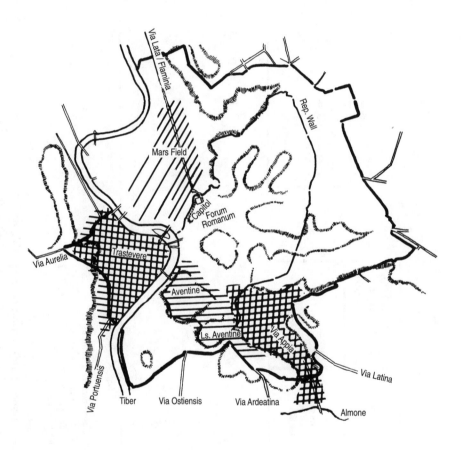

Map 3. Concentrations of Christian population

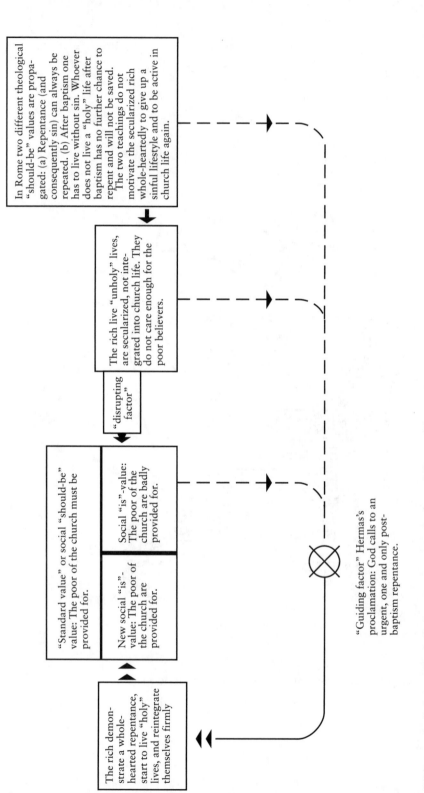

In Rome two different theological "should-be" values are propagated: (a) Repentance (and consequently sin) can always be repeated. (b) After baptism one has to live without sin. Whoever does not live a "holy" life after baptism has no further chance to repent and will not be saved.

The two teachings do not motivate the secularized rich whole-heartedly to give up a sinful lifestyle and to be active in church life again.

The rich live "unholy" lives, are secularized, not integrated into church life. They do not care enough for the poor believers.

"disrupting factor"

"Standard value" or social "should-be" value: The poor of the church must be provided for.

Social "is"-value: The poor of the church are badly provided for.

New social "is"-value: The poor of the church are provided for.

The rich demonstrate a whole-hearted repentance, start to live "holy" lives, and reintegrate themselves firmly

"Guiding factor" Hermas's proclamation: God calls to an urgent, one and only post-baptism repentance.

Diagram 4. Cybernetic circle I: momentary solution of the problem

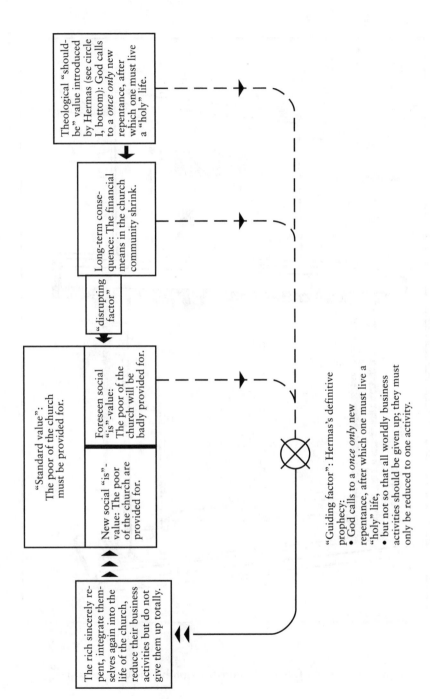

Standard value":
The poor of the church must be provided for.

New social "is"-value: The poor of the church are provided for.

Foreseen social "is"-value: The poor of the church will be badly provided for.

"disrupting factor"

Long-term consequence: The financial means in the church community shrink.

Theological "should-be" value introduced by Hermas (see circle I, bottom): God calls to a *once only* new repentance, after which one must live a "holy" life.

The rich sincerely repent, integrate themselves again into the life of the church, reduce their business activities but do not give them up totally.

"Guiding factor": Hermas's definitive prophecy:
• God calls to a *once only* new repentance, after which one must live a "holy" life,
• but not so that all worldly business activities should be given up; they must only be reduced to one activity.

Diagram 5. Cybernetic circle II: permanent solution of the problem

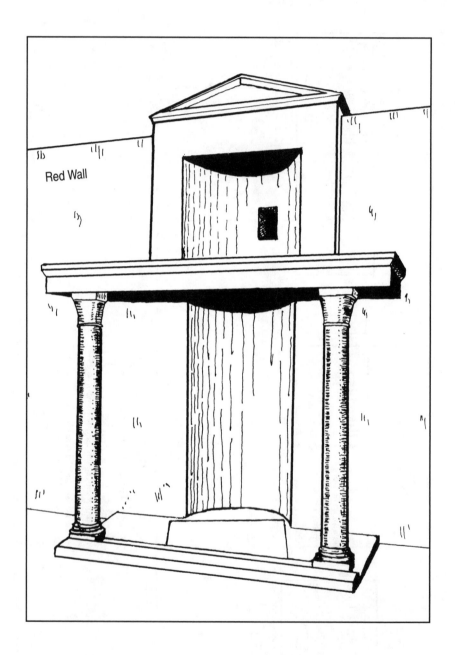

Red Wall

Figure 6. The Vatican Edicula (reconstruction by the excavators)

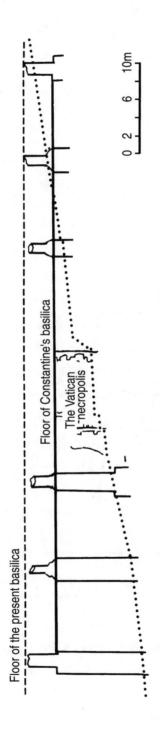

Floor of the present basilica

Floor of Constantine's basilica

The Vatican
necropolis

0 2   6   10m

Figure 7. Cross-section of the foundation of Constantine's basilica (according to Klauser, Plate 17)

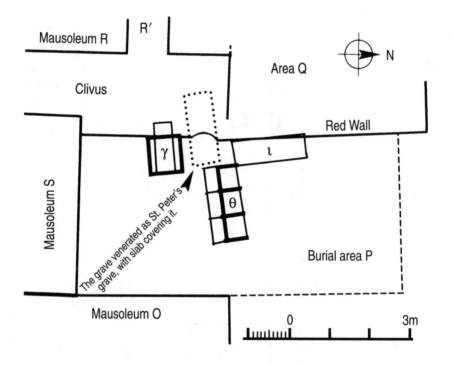

Figure 8. Burial area P in the Vatican (cf. Klauser, 56)

Mausoleum R

R′

Area Q

N

Clivus

Red Wall

γ

ι

Mausoleum S

The grave venerated as St. Peter's grave, with slab covering it.

θ

Burial area P

Mausoleum O

0

3m

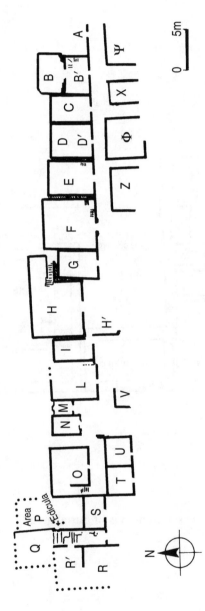

Figure 9. The necropolis under St. Peter's basilica

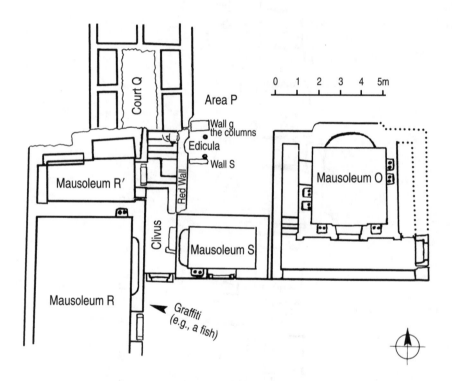

Figure 10. The immediate surroundings of burial area P

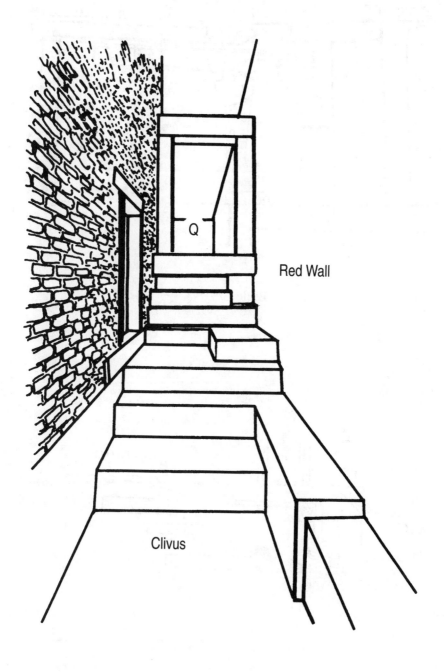

Figure 11. Reconstruction of the Clivus (according to Esplor. 68)

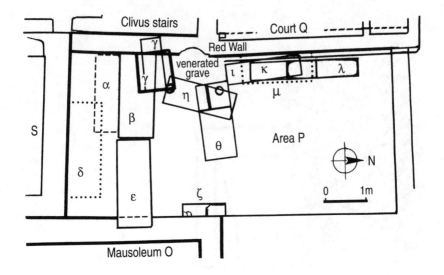

Figure 12. Burial area P (cf. Esplor. 79)

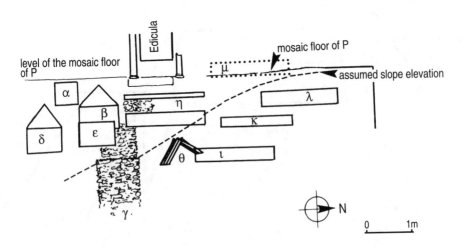

Figure 13. Longitudinal section in burial area P (cf. Esplor. 81)

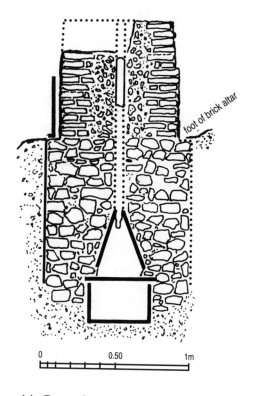

Figure 14. Grave Gamma (according to Esplor. 80)

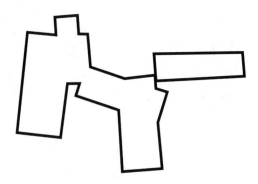

Figure. 15. The sepulchers surrounding the venerated grave

Index

1. SELECTED ANCIENT TEXTS

Not every specific reference to ancient literature can be listed here. In many instances the name of the author or a specific document (or an individual book or chapter) refers the reader to the pages on which the specific references can be found. In addition, the numerous references on the following pages do not recur here: 79, n. 51; 206–17; 229–34; 261; and 370. Index entries do not indicate whether a reference occurs once or more than once on a given page.

C. ANCIENT AUTHORS AND WRITINGS

2. CHRISTIAN PERSONS IN THE CITY OF ROME IN THE FIRST TWO CENTURIES

Summary:

A. Historically probable: 100, of which 23 are women
B. Uncertain: 21, of which 4 are women
C. Legendary: 42, of which 19 are women
D. Visitors: 6+

Only those persons who are mentioned in this book are listed. The above numbers show that, in our sources, women are represented as frequently as men only when we are dealing with legendary sources. It is interesting to observe that the Christian sources not only mention socially elevated persons but also leave ample room for slaves and members of the underclass.

3. OTHER NAMES AND SUBJECTS

514

Ateius Praetextatus, 179
Athenagoras, 415
Atrium, 8, 63, 189
Attorneys (*see also* Jurisprudence), 59
Augustenses, 83, 367–68
Augustine (*see also* [1] above), 112
Augustus, Augustan, 9, 38, 43, 49, 62,
 64, 83, 187, 281
Aurelia Procope, 339
Aurelia Tatia, 118
Aurelian, 43, 55
Aurelii/-ius, 32, 339
Autarkeia, 222, 231
Autochthon, 167–70
Aventine (*see also* Lesser Aventine), 20–
 23, 34, 38, 41–46, 56, 58–61,
 66, 335
Awnings, 187–88
Axia Aeliana, 120

Bacchus, 55, 98
Bakeries, 54, 58, 63
Balbinus, 29
Balbus, 63
Banishment (*see also* Claudius, edict
 of), 11–15, 38–39, 47, 69, 84,
 157, 198–204
Banks, bankers, 42, 45, 94–97, 174,
 335, 344–45, 348
Baptism, 11, 26, 95, 131, 251, 302–6,
 309, 360, 369, 421
Barbarians, conceptions of, 289–90
Barracks (*see also* Military), 56, 135
Basilicas, 55, 104, 109, 367–68
Basilides, 241, 249, 250, 294
Baths, 57, 59, 62, 218–19, 225, 259,
 276, 301–2, 310, 364, 369, 376
Baths, thermal: *see* Baths
Benevento, 136, 248
Berosus, 429
Biblical style, 216
Birth control, 119–21
Bishops, 22, 25–28, 31, 34, 89, 101,
 115, 144, 224, 234, 244, 251,
 336, 341, 365, 367, 371, 377,
 382, 385, esp. 397–408, 410
Bithynia, 117, 224
Body, motif of members of, 213
Bolani, 53
Bona Dea Subsaxana, 58
Bordello: *see* Prostitution
Boundary stone, 43
Bread, 31, 61, 194, 347
Brickwork, tilework, 25, 28, 31, 35,
 113, 50, 64, 106, 108–10, 113,
 130
Bridal chamber, 298–314, 378
Bruttius, 199–203

Bucolic motifs, 30, 32, 222, 227
Burial area P, 34, 38, 105–16, 141,
 332–33
Burial places (memorials) (*see also*
 Catacombs), 19–38, 44, 52,
 55–57, 98, 104–16, 122, 130,
 140–44, 149–50, 187–90, 309–
 11, 331–32, 339, 360, 362,
 370–71
Business, commerce, 7, 9–10, 50–51,
 56, 60–61, 65, 80, 91, 95–97,
 101–2, 140, 146, 148, 158, 174,
 179, 188, 190–91, 193, 218,
 222–26, 234, 241, 354
Byzantium, 195, 344

Cabinet maker, 50
Caecilius, 343
Caelius, 21, 34, 39, 44–47, 56, 59,
 149, 312, 366
Caesar, 49, 56, 136, 188, 281
Caligula, 49, 52, 187
Callistus, 1
Camenae, 39
Campania, 7–10, 175
Campus Agrippae, 63
Campus Lanatarius, 56
Capella Graeca, 25, 36, 311
Cappadocia, 125, 277, 340
Capua, 10
Caracalla, 25, 118, 331, 337–38, 345
Caracalla, baths of, 41, 57
Care of the poor, 20, 27, 80, 84–87,
 90–102, 115–16, 123–28, 139,
 143, 146, 225, 367, 372, 384,
 398, 399–400, 401–4, 407–9,
 411
Carpenter, 189
Carpocratians, 319–20, 352, 378–79,
 381, 392, 396, 411
Carthage, 118, 316
Cassia Faretria, 119
Cassius Agrippa, 117
Cassius Dio (*see also* [1] above), 201
Castra Peregrina, 134
Catacombs/Cemeteries (*see also* Burial
 places), 22–38, 50, 141, 144,
 236, 311, 370–72, 432
Anonymous, on the Via Latina, 150
Balbina, 23
Bassilla, 36
Calepodio, 35, 38, 44
Callistus, 22, 23–28, 31, 44, 120,
 130, 143
Cava della Rossa, 311
Domitilla, 23, 32–34, 44
Giordani, 24, 37
Jewish, 39, 432

Hagiography: *see* Legends
"Hatred of the human race," 35, 84
Hegesippus, 390, 402–5
Heliopolis, 55
Helios, 30
Helvidius Priscus, 281
Heraclitus, 273, 415
Herculaneum, 7–10, 194
Hercules (Heracles), 55, 58, 150, 211,
    325, 417, 422, 428
Heretics (*see also* Gnostics; Mar-
    cionites), 37, 147, 160, 241,
    249–51, 260, 285, 289–320,
    350, 355, 373, 376, 379–80,
    385–96
Herma, 173, 180
Hermes (god), 228
Herod, Herodians, 165, 169, 177–78,
    379, 431
Herodian, 169, 177–78
Hetaeria, 374
Hexameter, 299, 303
Hierapolis, 115
High chamberlain, 315, 331, 333
Hills, 46–54
Hippocrates, 347
Historiography, 180, 199–200, 287–
    88, 426–27, 429–30
Homer, 209, 289, 311, 342, 347, et
    passim
Hospitality, 81, 100, 125, 128, 130,
    158, 183, 191–92, 362–63,
    366–80, 386, 402
Hostilianus, 280
House church, 366–69
House community (*see also* Commu-
    nity; Assembly; Titulus), 41, 75,
    100–102, 158, 191–93, 354,
    359–80, 385, 398–99, 400–401,
    406–7
House, possession of (*see also* Villa;
    Insula), 20–23, 47, 53, 57–61,
    64–65, 91, 98–99, 125, 130,
    183, 191–93, 221, 222, 237–38,
    245, 309–10, 353, 359, 362,
    366–69, 370–71, 374–76, 379
Household (Lares), 379
Humiliores (*see also* Widows; Orphans;
    Slaves; Freedpersons; People),
    27–29, 35, 39, 46, 50–57, 59–
    65, 71, 80–102, 108, 112–17,
    119–48, 170, 171–72, 190–92,
    222, 230, 233–34, 246, 280–82,
    298, 313, 319, 349, 372, 407–12,
    et passim
Hydria Tertulla, 118
Hystaspes, 268

Iconia, 12
Ignatius (*see also* [1] above), 88–89,
    186, 224, 398
Illiteracy, 100–101, 130, 234
Imperial court, 89, 117, 121, 123, 125,
    185, 247–48, 313, 316, 330–39,
    390
Imperial cult, 200–201, 202
Imperial freedpersons, 89, 123, 126,
    173–82, 183–89, 311, 313–14,
    330–39, 351, 390, 409
Imperial slaves, 89, 123, 126, 173–82,
    183–89, 277, 314, 330–39, 351,
    409
India, 289
Inflation, 194–95, 345–46, et passim
Inheritance, 27, 33, 90
Innocentiores, 29
Inscriptions (*see also* [1] above),
    140–43, 148, 190, 298–312
Insula: *see* Residence
Integration, 80, 86–87, 92–99, 102–3,
    411–12, et passim
Intellectuals (*see also* Education),
    292–98, 314–18
Interest (on loans), 344–45
Ionian, 310, 355
Irenaeus (*see also* [1 and 2] above),
    288, 389–92, 394
Isis, 43, 55, 61, 427
Isola Sacra, 108, 110, 112
Italy, Italians, 7, 9–10, 77, 118, 157,
    172, 194–95
Itineraries, 26
Iulia daughter of Drusus, 164
Iulia Evaresta, 311

Jason, 74
Jerome, 59
Jerusalem, 12, 159
Jeweler, 190
Jewish Christians, 11–12, 15, 69–79,
    83, 146, 176–77, 211, 229
Jewish quarters, 19, 38–40
Jewish schools, 77–78
Jews, Hellenistic, 208, 210–14, 216–
    17, 230
Jews, Jewish, 8–16, 30, 38–40, 42–44,
    47, 55–57, 69–79, 83, 90, 103,
    115, 132, 141–44, 146, 158,
    161, 169, 175, 184, 197–205,
    209, 210–11, 219, 229, 248–49,
    255, 335, 337, 364–66, 368–69,
    372, 378, 383, 431–32
Josephus (*see also* [1] above), 14
Joshua b. Hananiah, 78, 158
Juba, 429
Judge, 245

Melito of Sardis, 250
Memorial, grave, 25–26
Messalina, 184, 196
Messengers, 385–86, 398, 401–2
Messengers, delegated, 101, 385–86,
    398, 400–408
Military (see also Centurion), 57, 84,
    117, 124–25, 134, 173, 182,
    189, 207, 214, 242, 247–48, 346
Miller, 50, 193
Miltiades, 390
Minerva, 60
Minicianus, 1
Minister of External Affairs, 398,
    400–404, 407
Minucia, 62
Mithras, Mithraic, 9, 48, 57, 61
Mixed marriages, 103, 118–22, 147,
    150, 196–97, 237–40
Modalists, 349–50, 381–84, 395
Modestus, 250
Monarchians, 344–48, 381
Money (see also Possessions; Bank;
    Prices), 193–95
Money Exchange, 344–45
Monism, 423, 425
Monselice, 108
Montanists, 337–38, 341, 381, 395,
    400, 403
Monte Testaccio, 59, 60
Mosaics, 30–31, 49, 57, 59, 64, 107,
    115, 140, 142, 279
Musonius Rufus (see also [1] above),
    310
Mutatorium Caesaris, 57
Myra, 7
Myrtinus, 259, 276, 364, 369, 376
Mysteries, 55, 61, 102, 132, 266–67,
    288, 310, 312, 318, 378, 388
Mysticism (see also God, direct
    contemplation of), 310
Mythology, 209, 265, 325, 427

Nabateans, 10
Names, 141–42, 157, 165, 167–83,
    405–6
Naples, 236
Narcissus (person), 124, 164, 165, 183,
    359, 378
Nature: see Cosmos
Naukleros, 241–56
Naumachia, 49
Navicularius, 241–56
Necropolis (see also Burial places),
    107–16
Nero, 10, 13, 16, 47, 49, 62, 82–84,
    89, 123, 125, 146, 165, 188, 201,
    211, 227, 242

Nerva, 204, 281
Nestorianus, C. Julius, 118
Networking, "connections," 89, 336
Nicea, 117
Nicomedia, 117
Nigrinus, 275
Ninos, 126
Noetus, Noetians, 350, 382
Novatian, 144, 252
Numenios, 289
Nummularius, 174
Nymphaeum, 39, 41, 59, 366

Oaths, 134, 202
Octavia, 63
Octavius, 345
Odium: see "Hatred of the human
    race"
Office holders, state, 133, 339, 351
Office, office holder (see also Bishop;
    Elder; Deacon; Clergy), 117–18,
    130, 139, 251, 315–17, 330–34,
    342, 346, 376–80, 389, 397–98,
    432
Officials, 20, 133, 138, 186–87, 207,
    245, 314–17
Oikos: see House
Old Testament (see also [1] above),
    240, 249, 255, 272, 388, 393,
    414–16
Olive o, il, 10, 74, 223, 243
Onesiphorus, 193
Opus mistum, 58
Oracles, 92, 267
Origen (see also [1] above), 313
Orosius (see also [1] above), 14
Orphans, 90, 93, 100, 125, 148, 354,
    401
Orphic, 215, 418, 428
Osiris, 43, 55
Ostia, 10, 30, 46, 63, 65, 104, 108,
    175, 244, 338–42, 367

Paccia, 107
Paetus Thrasea, 281
Pagan and Christian, mixing of (see
    also Syncretism), 29–31, 112,
    226, 333, 352
Pagan world, contacts with, 73 et
    passim
Page, 180, 337
Paideia (see also Education), 289, 353,
    429
Painting, painters (see also Frescoes),
    136, 141, 179, 191
Palaistra, 57
Palatine, 51–52, 59
Palestine, 118, 202, 258